THE GOSPEL OF LUKE

This volume offers a comprehensive overview of one of the four New Testament gospels and brings a unique approach to the genre of Bible commentary. Featuring distinct Jewish and Christian voices in respectful conversation, Amy-Jill Levine and Ben Witherington methodologically break new ground in exploring why scholars disagree on questions of history (what actually happened, what is authorial invention, how do we address different versions of the same account), literature (what does this story tell us about Jesus and Peter, Mary Magdalene and Judas, among other characters), and theology (what can we say about resurrection and divine justice, or about Jesus as the Messiah). They show how Luke has been used to create both tragedy and hope, as well as to promote sexism, anti-Semitism, and religious intolerance, thereby raising important questions regarding ethically responsible interpretation. It will be essential reading for theologians, clergy, and anyone interested in biblical studies and Jewish/Christian dialogue.

Amy-Jill Levine is University Professor of New Testament and Jewish Studies and Mary Jane Werthan Professor of Jewish Studies at Vanderbilt, Affiliated Professor, Centre for the Study of Jewish-Christian Relations, Cambridge, UK, and an elected member of the prestigious Studiorum Novi Testimenti Societas (SNTS). Her numerous publications include the prize-winning volumes *The Misunderstood Jew: The Church and the Scandal of the Jewish Jesus*; *Short Stories by Jesus: The Enigmatic Parables of a Controversial Rabbi*; the edited thirteen-volume *Feminist Companions to the New Testament and Early Christian Writings*; and the coedited *Jewish Annotated New Testament*.

Ben Witherington is Amos Professor of New Testament for Doctoral Studies at Asbury Theological Seminary and on the doctoral faculty at St. Andrews University in Scotland. Considered one of the leading evangelical scholars in the world, he is an elected member of the prestigious Studiorum Novi Testimenti Societas (SNTS), a society dedicated to New Testament studies. Witherington has written more than fifty books, including *The Jesus Quest* and *The Paul Quest*, both of which were selected as top biblical studies works by *Christianity Today*. He also writes for many church and scholarly publications, and is a frequent contributor to the Patheos website.

NEW CAMBRIDGE BIBLE COMMENTARY

The New Cambridge Bible Commentary (NCBC) aims to elucidate the Old Testament/Hebrew Bible and New Testament for a wide range of intellectually curious individuals. While building on the work and reputation of the *Cambridge Bible Commentary* popular in the 1960s and 1970s, the NCBC takes advantage of many of the rewards provided by scholarly research over the last four decades. Volumes utilize recent gains in rhetorical criticism, social scientific study of the Scriptures, narrative criticism, and other developing disciplines to exploit the growing advances in biblical studies. Accessible jargon-free commentary, an annotated "Suggested Readings" list, and the entire New Revised Standard Version (NRSV) text under discussion are the hallmarks of all volumes in the series.

PUBLISHED VOLUMES IN THE SERIES
Genesis, Bill T. Arnold
Exodus, Carol Meyers
Judges and Ruth, Victor H. Matthews
Psalms, Walter Brueggemann and William H. Bellinger, Jr.
Matthew, Craig A. Evans
Mark, Darrell Bock
The Gospel of John, Jerome H. Neyrey
1–2 Corinthians, Craig S. Keener
Galatians, Craig Keener
James and Jude, William F. Brosend II
Revelation, Ben Witherington III

The Gospel of Luke

Amy-Jill Levine
Vanderbilt University

Ben Witherington III
Asbury Theological Seminary

CAMBRIDGE
UNIVERSITY PRESS

University Printing House, Cambridge CB2 8BS, United Kingdom

One Liberty Plaza, 20th Floor, New York, NY 10006, USA

477 Williamstown Road, Port Melbourne, VIC 3207, Australia

314–321, 3rd Floor, Plot 3, Splendor Forum, Jasola District Centre,
New Delhi – 110025, India

79 Anson Road, #06-04/06, Singapore 079906

Cambridge University Press is part of the University of Cambridge.

It furthers the University's mission by disseminating knowledge in the pursuit of
education, learning, and research at the highest international levels of excellence.

www.cambridge.org
Information on this title: www.cambridge.org/9780521859509
DOI: 10.1017/9781139029353

First published 2018

Printed in the United States of America by Sheridan Books, Inc.

A catalogue record for this publication is available from the British Library.

ISBN 978-0-521-85950-9 Hardback
ISBN 978-0-521-67681-6 Paperback

For Jews and Christians in hopes that they love the Bible like we do, and in hopes that this commentary may show how the Bible can be used as a bridge to build better Jewish-Christian relationships

Contents

Introduction

Many years ago, we, Ben and Amy-Jill, agreed to write a commentary on the Gospel of Luke for the New Cambridge Bible Commentary series. At the time, we did not realize we were attempting something unprecedented – a Jew and a Christian writing an exegetical and theological commentary together on a Gospel. This project has been many years in the gestation stage, and this is probably a good thing, because we have both become better New Testament scholars, more seasoned and experienced, than we were a decade ago. We had already been friends for many years. Many deeply invested in the Bible can agree, and also disagree, without being disagreeable.

We knew from the outset that there would be some strong disagreements along the way. Ben is a Methodist evangelical New Testament scholar; Amy-Jill is a Jewish feminist agnostic New Testament scholar. But there were also many things we agreed on as well. There was some serendipity and several nice surprises in writing this commentary and letting it age slowly like a good wine. One could say that we learned the lesson Jesus taught: you don't put new wine into old wineskins, or the converse (Amy-Jill proposes that this point was not original to Jesus; Jews already knew something about wine-making). Both the wine and wineskins needed to be aged properly. In writing this commentary, we've aged, but we've aged well. In fact, we can both say that we've been stretched in differing ways by the exercise of writing this commentary together, and not merely each of us contributing our separate chapter portions.

From the first century to the twenty-first, Luke's Gospel has informed, instructed, and inspired readers. It has also prompted a never-ending set of questions: Who is "Luke": Jew or gentile, man or woman, slave or free? How and why does Luke's portrait of Jesus differ from those painted by Mark, Matthew, and John? What sources did Luke use, and where is Luke's own voice to be found? Where did Luke write, and is the Gospel addressed to any specific community? What is Luke's view of the Roman state, the social roles of men and women, economics and politics, physical ability and demonic possession, Christology, Scripture, the Jerusalem Temple, and the Church?

The authors of this volume have no delusions about being able to answer *definitively* all – or perhaps even any – of the questions Luke's Gospel poses to historians, literary critics, theologians, and people who read the Bible for spiritual direction and inspiration. Indeed, definitive answers elude us, and they always will. We simply do not have the information we require. Further, as scholars approach Luke's Gospel with different questions and through different methodological lenses, they will see different things and find different meanings. Readers in their late teens will see the text with different eyes than when they reread it in their late sixties. Even if we could answer these questions today, they would only lead us to more questions tomorrow. With Gospel studies, there is no closure of meaning. If there were, pastors and priests could pack up their sermon notes, and biblical studies professors would need to find new jobs.

Unlike most commentaries, this one does not seek the "one right reading"; nor are we looking only to exegesis "in front of the text" to determine what the Gospel means to each of us as individuals. We are looking rather for a conversation, one between history and literature, the past and the present, a Christian and a Jew. We seek to show how studies of Roman and Jewish history, rhetoric, and hermeneutics inform our understanding of the Third Gospel.

Next, our goal is to show how and why we as students of the Bible come to disagree over questions of history and interpretation and how our own experiences impinge on our exegetical work. For example, Ben finds Luke to be advocate for women; Amy-Jill finds Luke to be an advocate for women's *ancillary* roles.[1] When the text calls for commentary on such matters, there *in situ* we'll offer the discussion. The style is the inelegant "Ben argues" or "Amy-Jill suggests." We realize that speaking of ourselves in the third person is awkward, but it is also more efficient that "I (Ben) suggest" or "I (Amy-Jill) argue." When we agree, we'll just say "we ..." In

---

[1]   See Ben Witherington III, *Women in the Ministry of Jesus* (SNTSMS 51; Cambridge: Cambridge University Press, 1984), *Women in the Earliest Churches* (SNTSMS 59; Cambridge: Cambridge University Press. 1988); *Women and the Genesis of Christianity* (Cambridge: Cambridge University Press, 1990), and Amy-Jill Levine with Marianne Blickenstaff (eds.), *A Feminist Companion to Luke* (FCNTECW 3; Sheffield: Sheffield University Press/New York: Continuum, 2002).

this process, our approach is one based on friendship and commitment to mutual respect. Biblical studies should not be a contact sport, with its own sections of cheerleaders; nor should it be parochial, with the "liberal camp" (however defined) reading works by Amy-Jill and the conservative camp (again, however defined) reading only books and blogs by Ben. Such selective approaches create an infinite feedback loop, where readers primarily have their presuppositions confirmed rather than challenged.

We are committed to both academic integrity and personal friendship. We have been invited to do numerous public talks, ranging from "The Bible and Homosexuality" to "The Resurrection of Jesus" to "The Jesus of History and the Christ of Faith." The intent of the organizers has been often a point/counterpoint agenda, where we two will spar on stage and then the audience, which is usually a partisan group, remains convinced of the truths they had when they walked in the door. We are reminded, each time, of the old *Saturday Night Live* Weekend Update sketch, where Dan Akroyd would turn to Jane Curtain and say, "Jane, you ignorant slut ..." We are not going there. We also realize that half the readers of this volume are too young to remember the sketch.

We find old and tired the debate format when it comes to theology. In every case, we have refused the format of point/counterpoint. Instead, we have had conversations addressing the deeper issues: why do you say that, and, more important, what import does your claim have on the way you live your life? At times, we have surprised each other. At times, we have surprised the audiences. Knowing a person's theological starting point does not necessarily mean we know how a person reads a particular text.

Third, we seek to show our appreciation for this text: why it fascinates and inspires us, and how this ancient Gospel, so long a source of tension between Jews and Christians, can be approached in a critical as well as sensitive way by scholars from very different backgrounds: a woman who belongs to an Orthodox synagogue and a man who worships in a Methodist church. Each chapter has a "Bridging the Horizons" section that looks at how the text speak to the present-day context. Here we sometimes choose to tell personal stories. Several chapters also contain "A Closer Look," where we explore historical and redactional questions.

Despite our profound differences in theological as well as exegetical views, we do agree, in almost all cases, that these subjects bear discussing and that conflicting views need to be surfaced rather than suppressed. Were we only to introduce in the classroom what we, personally, think to be the case, then we would be providing a disservice to our students. Our role as teachers is to help our students understand the discipline of biblical studies as well as the various reading strategies and major hypotheses that help us in the act of interpretation. Once students have both the critical tools and examples of their application, they can then do their own assessment of theories offered as well as make their own contributions.

Despite the impossibility of surety in matters exegetical, we do think we have something to say today about both what the text meant in its own time period and what it might mean to our readers. We'll mark throughout where we disagree on matters of historicity, the meaning of a saying or parable, and the more productive ways of analyzing a passage. We shall not, however, repeat all the arguments and conclusions that can be found in any major commentary on Luke or any decent Study Bible's introductory paragraphs: the manuscript tradition and text-critical problems; the various arguments about date, authorship, and so on. The conclusions usually do not make much difference for assessing individual passages.

We shall keep footnotes to a minimum; there are plenty of other commentaries devoted to the Greek text, to Luke's reception history, and to Luke's theology to which readers can turn. Readers wanting more of Ben's views on the details on Luke the author and on the relationship of the Gospel to Acts can look at his commentary on Acts;[2] for Amy-Jill's views, see her notes and annotations to Luke in the *Jewish Annotation New Testament*.[3] Rather, we shall concentrate, idiosyncratically, on the material will think will be useful for readers – academic, church-based, anyone curious about the Gospel – of this commentary. We shall also include what we, as authors, find of interest.

Here's how we proceeded. In the first place, we divided up the book equally, with Ben doing the even number chapters and Amy-Jill doing the odd numbered ones. To prevent this process from leading to an uneven commentary, we also commented extensively on each other's chapters. At times, we make clear where there is a strong disagreement on matters historical, exegetical, social, literary, and so on. Underlying the willingness to proceed in this way is a willingness to be open and honest enough to say, "I could be wrong on this; what is your take on the matter?" Sometimes, commentators in their zeal to defend this truth or that truth cannot recognize that they may well be wrong.

---

[2]   Ben Witherington III, *The Acts of the Apostles: A Socio-Rhetorical Commentary* (Grand Rapids: Eerdmans, 1997), which has a 102-page introduction.

[3]   Amy-Jill Levine, "The Gospel of Luke," in Amy-Jill Levine and Marc Z. Brettler (eds.), *The Jewish Annotated New Testament*, 2d ed. (New York: Oxford University Press, 2017), 107–67.

As Ben puts it, "We tried in this commentary to avoid putting the 'dog' back in 'dogma.'" Ben's mentor C. K. Barrett once said,

> When people are troubled, there is always hope. I will tell you how I have seen that happen. I have seen people begin their theological studies in a severe self-confidence, a far greater confidence that they have settled the problems of theology than I dare admit. And I have no hope of their learning any-thing worth learning until they begin to be troubled, to see that the ocean of truth is a bigger thing than the parish pool they thought of. Bishop Westcott was once asked why there is in the Prayer Book no prayer for theological students. "Oh, but," he said, "there is." "Which is it then?" "Why the one headed 'for those at sea.'" Well, let me have the person that is at sea, rather than the one who is roped up to his homeport, and has never ventured out. Whenever a person is troubled in mind, in spirit, or in conscience, there is hope.[4]

Amy-Jill, whose family was in the scallop business and therefore who knows something about seafaring and fishing, finds the comparison apt. She also notes the traditional Jewish communal blessing for the student of Torah, the *Kaddish d'rabbanan*:

> Exalted and hallowed be His great Name. *(Congregation responds: "Amen.")*
> Throughout the world which He has created according to His will. May He establish His kingship, bring forth His redemption and hasten the coming of His Meshiach [Messiah]. *(Cong: "Amen.")*
> In your lifetime and in your days and in the lifetime of the entire House of Israel, sword, famine and death shall cease from us and from the entire Jewish nation, speedily and soon, and say, Amen. *(Cong: "Amen. May His great Name be blessed forever and to all eternity, blessed.")*
> May His great Name be blessed forever and to all eternity. Blessed and praised, glorified, exalted and extolled, honored, adored and lauded be the Name of the Holy One, blessed be He. *(Cong: "Amen.")*
> Beyond all the blessings, hymns, praises and consolations that are uttered in the world; and say, Amen. *(Cong: "Amen.")*
> Upon Israel, and upon our sages, and upon their disciples, and upon all the disciples of their disciples, and upon all those who occupy themselves with the Torah, here or in any other place, upon them and upon you, may there be abundant peace, grace, kindness, compassion, long life, ample sustenance and deliverance, from their Father in heaven; and say, Amen. *(Cong: "Amen.")*

---

4   This quote is taken from one of C. K. Barrett's sermons that Ben is transcribing for pub-lication with Wipf and Stock Publishers in *Luminescence Vol. One* (2017), 48–50.

May there be abundant peace from heaven, and a good life for us and for all Israel; and say, Amen. *(Cong: "Amen.")*

He Who makes peace *(Between Rosh Hashana and Yom Kippur substitute:* "the peace") in His heavens, may He make peace for us and for all Israel; and say, Amen. *(Cong: "Amen.")*

Peace-making marks our commentary. One of the more fascinating aspects of the process was that even when we agreed on a particular exegetical point, we sometimes disagreed on the applicability, or the way to apply the material today, to this or that faith community. The "Bridging the Horizons" section of each chapter includes applications from both of us. We wanted this commentary to be as fair and as balanced as we could produce; neither of us pulled punches, and neither of us compromised our convictions. As Amy-Jill wrote years ago, "there is no reason for Jews and Christians to sacrifice their particular beliefs on the altar of inter-faith sensitivity."[5] Ours is not a debating commentary; ours is a "come let us reason together and talk" commentary. The rabbis teach, "Any dispute which is for the sake of Heaven will in the end yield results, and any which is not for the sake of Heaven will in the end not yield results. What is a dispute for the sake of Heaven? This is the sort of dispute between Hillel and Shammai. And what is one which is not for the sake of Heaven? It is the dispute of Korach and all his party" *(Pirke Avot* 5.17). Our arguments, we believe, are for the sake of seeing the meanings in the text; they are designed to show how the same text can lead to different readings and, more, why those readings matter. Our commentary is not just an academic exercise, although it is that. It is also a pastoral one. We believe that anyone writing about sacred Scripture must have respect both for the text and for the people who consider it holy.

We also agree that scholarship should be written for the sake of clarity. We have written this commentary in order to be read and not simply consulted. We go verse by verse to point out what we find to be of interest; where we disagree, we disagree in the context of that conversation with Luke.

Here's where we are on the basics. Regarding authorship, Ben finds no reason to question and every reason to accept that the author is Luke, the sometime companion of Paul (cf. Col 4.14; Phlm 24; 2 Tim 4.11). Here he is consistent with ancient sources, as Ben delineated in his commentary on

---

[5]   Amy-Jill Levine, *The Misunderstood Jew: The Church and the Scandal of the Jewish Jesus* (New York: HarperOne, 2007), 6.

Acts.[6] As to whether Luke was a physician, Ben thinks "yes" and Amy-Jill remains unconvinced. H. J. Cadbury (yes, of the chocolate family) showed that the various medical terms in Luke/Acts appeared in the works of non-medical writers such as Plutarch, Lucian, and others.[7] For the sake of convenience, and because Lucan authorship is by no means impossible, we refer to the author as "Luke." However, we will not refer to the author as "he," because we do not know, for certainty, the author's identity, and because we recognize that women sometimes wrote under pseudonyms. We agree, following the distinction in the prologue (1.1–4) between the author and the "eyewitnesses and ministers," that Luke is writing in the second or perhaps third generation of the followers of Jesus.

The preface, and indeed the Greek in the two volumes, suggests a native speaker of Greek who knows the conventions of Greco-Roman rhetoric and historiography. The author may have read other Greek historians such as Polybius, Thucydides, or Ephorus. The Gospel's stress on the relation of history to the plan or providential counsel of God may also suggest a familiarity with the work of Diodorus Siculus.[8] In regard to the prefaces of Luke and Acts, Loveday Alexander proposes that the author was familiar with the conventions for prefaces found in scientific writings.[9]

Luke does not, however, appear to know either Hebrew or Aramaic, save the term *amen*, which was surely common in Christian and Jewish assemblies throughout the Empire. Although the author shows little familiarity with the geography of the land of Israel, the text does indicate extensive familiarity with the LXX, the Greek version of the Hebrew Scriptures. Thus, Luke could be a Diaspora Jew, or perhaps a non-Jew who had been a synagogue adherent (i.e., a "God-fearer") before becoming a Christian. Nevertheless, we agree that Luke depicts an increasing distance between the followers of Jesus and other Jews.

In terms of the author's own social location, given the time required and leisure to write a two-volume work, Luke was either a person of independent means or, more likely, a retainer of a well-to-do person. "It surely is informative that the inscribed author of Luke-Acts has used the same

---

6   Witherington, *Acts*, 56–57.

7   H. J. Cadbury, *Style and Literary Method of Luke*, Part I (Cambridge: Harvard University Press, 1920). The older argument for Luke's medical knowledge appears in W. K. Hobart, *The Medical Language of St. Luke* (London: Longmans Green, 1882).

8   See J. T. Squires, *The Plan of God in Luke-Acts* (Cambridge: Cambridge University Press, 1993), 15ff.

9   Loveday Alexander, *The Preface to Luke's Gospel* (Cambridge: Cambridge University Press, 1993).

address in the prologues that subordinates use of their Roman superiors in the stories of Acts [cf. Acts 23.26; 24.2; 24.24]. These data suggest that our inscribed author addresses Theophilus in a mode associated with a person who is willingly or unwillingly in a subordinate position to a person of rank in Roman society."[10] This subject position may account for Luke's extensive interest in, and critique of, people with wealth and resources. The favorable attitude Luke displays toward artisans (e.g., textile workers) is not typical of the Roman (gentile) elite, but it is typical of how artisans and retainers viewed themselves. It is also the case that Jewish sources, especially rabbinic ones, have a positive view of artisans. As David Fiensy documents, "rabbinic sources extol both manual labor ... and teaching one's son a craft ... Artisans often receive special recognition."[11] At least in terms of class issues, Luke is closer to Jewish than to Roman gentile sources.

Ben finds convincing the argument by J. Nolland that Theophilus had been a synagogue adherent and therefore required instruction on why so many Jews had rejected claims made for Jesus and why "the Way" should be seen as the true expression of God's people, Jews and gentiles both.[12] He further suggests that Luke's emphasis on a continual return to the synagogue and to Jews, despite rejection, would have encouraged Theophilus not to sever all social ties he may have had with Jews. Amy-Jill finds this an extremely generous reading. She sees the major thrust of Luke-Acts to show that synagogues are places to be avoided and Jews are people who generally will not listen to Christian teaching. Here we have a major disagreement. Ben, like most commentators, sees an openness to Jews and Judaism in the Gospel; Amy-Jill is much less optimistic. We do agree that Luke had had great love for many of the traditions of Judaism, especially the Scriptures. However, love of a particular history does not necessary translate into love for rival guardians of that tradition.

We agree that the intended or ideal audience of the Gospel and Acts is represented by Theophilus, the man to whom both the Third Gospel and Acts are dedicated. Ben regards Theophilus as a real person, and perhaps the patron who paid Luke to prepare the two volumes. Amy-Jill thinks it plausible that Luke has invented this ideal reader, whose name means

[10] Vernon K. Robbins, "The Social Location of the Implied Author of Luke-Acts," in J. H. Neyrey (ed.), *The Social World of Luke-Acts* (Peabody: Hendrickson, 1991), 305–32 (321–22).
[11] David A. Fiensy, *Christian Origins and the Ancient Economy* (Eugene: Cascade, 2014), 19, citing *Pirke Avot* 1.10; *Abot deRabbi Natan B.* XXI, 23a; *m. Bik.* 3.3; *b. Qidd.* 33a, etc.
[12] J. L. Nolland, *Luke's Reader's: A Study of Luke 4.22–28; Acts 13.46; 18.6; 28.28 and Luke 21.5–36* (D.Phil. dissertation; Cambridge: Cambridge University Press, 1977).

"lover of God." In either case, the ideal audience is what Theophilus would represent to any contemporary reader of the Gospel. Theophilus is an "insider,"[13] someone who already knows something about Jesus and his followers. He is positioned as an upper-class gentile with some familiarity with Jewish Scripture and practice as well as a person with some sympathy for the Roman system with its military presence. We agree that the name does not move us to construct a Lucan community; a text is not a "community."

Ben dates the Gospel to the 70s or early 80s, during the earlier part of the reigns of the Flavian emperors (69–96, including Vespasian, Titus, and Domitian), when books were burned (Tacitus reminds us concerning the victims of Nero and the Flavians that "cruel punishment fell not only on the authors but even on their books. The public executioners had the task of burning in the Forum those tributes to our noblest philosophers" [*Agricola* 2]). Therefore, Ben sees Luke as writing at the time when books claiming some human being *other* than the Emperor to be Lord, God, or the like would be designed for the flames. Perhaps, Ben suggests, Luke is so cautious in presenting Roman authorities in both of the volumes because of the dangers that Tacitus recounts. Ben's relatively early dating also makes it more likely that the author of the "we" passages in Acts was Luke, the companion of Paul. Amy-Jill thinks the Gospel dates to the end of the first century, and she notes that until the Decian campaign in 250, persecution of Jesus' followers was both sporadic and localized. She also finds it unlikely that Romans are reading Gospels (indeed, most are unlikely to be literate). The opening of the Gospel starting in 1.5, with its stress on the Jewish context, would be of little interest to Rome. She also grants that nothing prohibits an earlier dating.[14] As far as our exegesis is concerned, the date does not matter much.

As for the question of "history" – put in crass terms, "did it happen?" – we have some strong disagreements. As demonstrated through this commentary, Ben is more likely to regard Luke as recording "what happened" and "what Jesus said" (there is nothing he finds that could not have happened or that he could not have said; it's very hard to prove a negative), whereas

---

13 David Peterson, "The Motif of Fulfilment and the Purpose of Luke-Acts," in Bruce W. Winter and Andrew D. Clarke (eds.), *The Book of Acts in Its First Century Setting, Vol. 1, The Book of Acts in Its Ancient Literary Setting* (Grand Rapids: Eerdmans/ Carlisle: Paternoster, 1993), 83–104, esp. 103.

14 See Luke Timothy Johnson, *The Gospel of Luke* (Sacra Pagina; Collegeville: Liturgical Press, 1991), 2.

Amy-Jill remains skeptical of the historicity of certain accounts. Ben accepts as historical the account of a Sanhedrin trial of sorts that binds Jesus over to Pilate for execution. Amy-Jill finds the idea that the entire Jerusalem political infrastructure would meet, on the first night of Passover, to address a Galilean teacher, only to send him to Pilate, strains the imagination. Instead, she finds the Johannine account, which depicts only a hearing before Annas, the high priest's father-in-law and former high priest, to have a higher degree of credibility. Of greater import, Ben the Christian accepts the literal incarnation of the God of Israel and the literal resurrection of the body of Jesus. Such theological claims have no hold on Amy-Jill, although she is very interested in how belief in divine action influences people's behavior. Here we agree that the "so what" question matters: if one believes in the Gospel's supernatural claims, what difference do those beliefs make in one's attitude and action?

On the matter of Luke's agenda, we recognize that the Gospel and Acts provide Christianity what it needed toward the end of the first century. It needed theological coherence, since various groups of Jesus followers had different Christologies, ecclesiologies, and understanding of their relationship to the Scriptures of Israel in their various forms and languages as well as varying relations to Jews who did not accept their claims. It needed a secure tradition: the story to be told, and those who had the authority to tell it. Luke's Gospel answers these needs. Therefore, Luke, like all authors, has an agenda. Having an agenda or a bias *does not mean* that the material one produces did not happen; nevertheless, knowledge of this agenda helps us to determine why and how certain stories are told.

To produce the Gospel, Luke had sources, as the prologue indicates ("having investigated everything carefully from the very first" [1.3] the materials presented by the eyewitnesses). Yet the historicity of the sources themselves cannot be securely confirmed. Luke may have taken received tradition as historical, although that is no guarantee that the events "really happened." For example, Luke may even have been familiar with the writings of Josephus. But citing Josephus just pushes the question of history back one step: Luke may think that Josephus records, accurately and in order, with objectivity and neutrality, what happened, but what Josephus records and what actually happened are not necessarily the same.

We agree that Luke is not an historian in the modern sense of the term, for the Gospel is neither comprehensive nor objective. The Gospel's focus is on providing guidelines for the nascent, Greek-speaking Church, sometime in the late first century. Luke takes received information and edits and augments it in a manner designed to instruct and inspire. Here again we have critical problems, for we cannot be certain what material is tradition (i.e., what Luke heard or read) and what material is redactional (i.e., what Luke created). Whereas we both follow the scholarly consensus in regarding Mark's Gospel as a source for Luke, we do not know if any of the versions of Mark that survive today was the version Luke had. Did Luke omit the account of the Canaanite/Syrophoenician woman (Matt 15.21–28//Mark 7.24–30), or was Luke's copy of Mark's Gospel defective? (we think Luke omitted the material, but certainty again eludes us).

The same question applies to the story of the woman who anoints Jesus' head for his burial, whose story will be told "in memory of her" (Matt 26.6–13//Mark 3–9): did Luke change this story into an account of a "sinful woman" who anoints Jesus' feet (7.36–50), or did Luke receive a different version of the account of a woman who anoints Jesus? Luke lacks the material in Matt 15.1–20//Mark 7.1–23 about purity concerns regarding eating, only to see a variant on the subject come to light in Acts 10 with Peter. Luke's Passion Narrative lacks the charge about Jesus attacking the Temple found in Mark 14.58, a charge that nevertheless surfaces in Acts 6.14 in the accusations against Stephen. Luke may be a good and careful editor who does not wish to tread the same path, unless there is some special point of emphasis, as with the three tellings of Saul's conversion in Acts. Or, Luke's sources may have lacked these accounts, or Luke may not have agreed with them. Amy-Jill suspects that Luke omitted the Syro-Phoenician woman because she gets the better of Jesus in a discussion about those who were to benefit from his powers of exorcism; she also thinks that Luke intentionally turned the story of the woman who anoints Jesus' head into the story of a "sinner" who anoints Jesus' feet. Ben disagrees, thinking these are two different stories with some obvious similarities, and Luke chooses the one instead of the other. Determining why something is *not* in a text is no easy task.

The majority of biblical scholars accept the idea that Luke and Matthew, but not Mark or John, had access to a source, comprised primarily of Jesus' sayings. The source, labeled "Q" (from the German for *Quelle*, "source") provides such memorable materials as the beatitudes ("Blessed are …") and the "Our Father" prayer. Ben is mostly convinced of the existence of Q; Amy-Jill has increasing doubts, and she finds credible the idea that Luke had copies of both Mark and Matthew. Whether John had access to the Synoptics – Ben thinks "probably not" and Amy-Jill thinks "probably" – also impacts our assessments. However, when it comes to determining what Luke's Gospel is saying, the source-critical materials are less important than they may seem at first. Luke the author had freedom to include or omit, edit or create. Therefore, we concentrate in this commentary on the text of the Gospel and not on the hypothetical sources behind it or on the parallel configurations of a story in Matthew and/or Mark.

Whether Luke intended the Third Gospel to replace these earlier sources remains debatable. Ben follows Joel Green, who stresses that the major question here is not validation but signification: how has the past been represented, what is its significance?[15] Therefore, "Luke's purpose is hermeneutical. He is not hoping to prove *that* something happened, but rather to communicate *what these events signify*."[16] By referring to fulfillment, Luke is suggesting that one can only understand these things in the larger framework he provides. Amy-Jill agrees with the signification, but she sees no reason why defining the significance of particular accounts should be mutually exclusive with correcting or even replacing the earlier ones. In either case, were Luke's agenda to replace Mark (and perhaps Matthew and Q), then Luke did not succeed.

Complementing the difficulties of source criticism are the difficulties of genre criticism. In order to assess a text accurately, we must know what it is designed to do. Here genre enters: a cook book has a different function than a physics textbook, even though both have formulae, comments about mass and density, and information on how shapes change based on heat and pressure. A history book has a different function than a novel, although both can be set in the same time period and draw upon the same events. Thus, a number of biblical scholars seek to determine what the genre of Luke's Gospel is: history or biography.

Standard commentaries on Luke's Gospel invest a great deal of time and space to determining the genre. Most readers scan these discussions quickly to get to what Luke actually says. Ben finds this subject fascinating (and so we shall delineate the discussion in the following paragraphs); Amy-Jill finds it usually tedious, because at the end of the discussion, we find ourselves with labels about what Luke may have wanted to say as an author, but we are no closer to determining either what actually happened or how ancient audiences received the texts.

---

[15]   See Joel B. Green, "Internal Repetition in Luke-Acts, Contemporary Narratology and Lukan Historiography," in Ben Witherington (ed.), *History, Literature, and Society* (Cambridge: Cambridge University Press), 283–99.

[16]   Ibid., 288; emphasis in the original.

Discussions of genre rarely detail why the determination matters, and in the end, it might not (save to help academics get tenure or promotion). Generally, the discussions have as a subtext the question of how much "history" the author is recording. Plutarch, like Nepos before him, distinguishes between biography and historiography: biography is concerned with virtues and characterization for ethical ends, and historiography is concerned with deeds or actions that caused historical change and their significance. Ancient biography focused on character and characterization, usually for some didactic purpose, as is the case with Plutarch's *Lives*; events and speeches were related, or imagined, insofar as they served to reveal the person's character. Ancient historiography, by comparison, focused on events *more* than on persons or personalities, and it sought not only to record significant happenings but to probe and if possible explain their causes.

However, rigid genre distinctions are unnecessary. The Gospel presents itself as a work of both historiography and biography. Biographically, the narrative reveals Jesus' character; historiographically, the concern for causation permeates Luke as well as Acts, which depict the theme of God's plan or counsel. Both narratives stress the fulfillment of Scripture to explain why things turned out as they did, including such potentially problematic things as Jesus' death and the rejection of his message by the majority of Jews.

Various ancient historians, including especially the more serious ones like Tacitus, frequently protest that they were writing *sine ira et studio* (*Annals* 1.1.3), without malice, preconception, favoritism, or what we would call bias. Lucian insists that the historian is "in his books a stranger and a man without a country, independent, subject to no sovereign, not reckoning what this or that man will think, but stating the facts" (41.1). Such remarks were meant to indicate that the author had not been unduly influenced by a patron or other socially and politically important figures who were alive and figured in the narrative. Ben is inclined to trust Luke's prologue as well as the rest of the Gospel as "stating the facts"; Amy-Jill is far less sanguine.

Lack of bias did *not* mean that the author was claiming to be a neutral observer. Josephus sought both to present a positive image of Jews to the Roman Empire and to explain to Jews how God granted Rome authority. Luke seeks to show how Jesus of Nazareth is the world's preeminent teacher, healer, and savior who should be heeded, imitated, and finally worshiped.

Historiographers will also note why their reconstruction of events is more accurate than what others have written. In *War* 1.1–2, the Jewish historian

Josephus, likely a slightly older contemporary of Luke, writes concerning reporting on the First Jewish Revolt against Rome (66–70):

> [W]hile some men who were not concerned in the affairs themselves, have gotten together vain and contradictory stories by hearsay, and have written them down after a sophistical manner; and while those that were there present have given false accounts of things, and this either out of a humor of flattery to the Romans, or of hatred towards the Jews; and while their writings contain sometimes accusations, and sometimes encomiums, but nowhere, the accurate truth of the facts, I have proposed to myself, for the sake of such as live under the government of the Romans, to translate those books into the Greek tongue, which I formerly composed in the language of our country ... I Joseph, the son of Matthias, by birth a Hebrew, a priest also, and one who at first fought against the Romans myself, and was forced to be present at what was done afterwards, [am the author of this work]" (*War* 1.1–3).

How much of what Josephus himself recounts is historical is open to much discussion. That he contradicts himself in his other writings, *Antiquities of the Jews* and his autobiographical *Life*, offers some nuance to his objectivist, universalizing claims.

Ben and Amy-Jill both dismiss the old argument that the ancients were unable to distinguish fact from fiction. Thucydides, Polybius, and Tacitus display critical scrutiny. Even Lucian, while never attempting to write history in the manner in which he discussed it, nevertheless knew very well the high standards true historians should set for their narrative. His treatise on "How History Ought to be Written" insists, "History cannot admit a lie, even a tiny one ..." (9) for "the historian's sole task is to tell the tale as it happened ..." (42). Lucian stresses that the good historian must investigate rather than simply rely on documents or on what others recount (38): "As to the facts themselves, he should not assemble them at random, but only after much laborious and painstaking investigation. He should ... be an eyewitness, but, if not, listen to those who tell the more impartial story, those whom one would suppose least likely to subtract from the facts or add to them out of favor or malice ..." (50). Such standards were not always observed. To do so would be impossible. Luke may have interviewed others, but Luke had no mechanism for determining if the reports received were themselves credible. If Luke's primary or only sources are "eyewitnesses and ministers of the word," then Luke is not dealing with impartial sources. Indeed, Luke's own Gospel demonstrates how accounts can develop. According to 24.4, "two men" appear to the women at the tomb. In Cleopas's retelling on the road to Emmaus, the two men become "a vision of angels" (24.23). Similarly, Acts has Paul report his visionary experience on the Road to Damascus in three different ways. This is how writing *chreia* functioned in Roman rhetoric – take a story and develop it, or recast it for new situations – and this is what Luke does.

Ben finds an important distinction bearing on our evaluation of Luke-Acts to be the differences between historiography in the Greek tradition of Thucydides and Polybius prior to the first century CE and the history writing that developed in the Roman Empire, beginning with Fabius Pictor and continuing through the series of annalists leading up to and including Tacitus. Greek historians accentuated personal observation (Greek: *autopsy*) and participation in events, travel, inquiry, and the consultation of eyewitnesses. Roman historians such as Livy were often satisfied to stay at home and consult documents and records. In this matter, Ben finds Luke to be, at least by his expressed goals, nearer to Greek historiography. Comparable is Josephus, who places weight on being a leading participant in the events that he chronicles, both as a military figure and as a statesman and advocate on the behalf of the Jews. Amy-Jill is not convinced by this distinction, at least as it relates to the Gospel, in which Luke does not put in a personal appearance. Luke's consultation with the eyewitnesses and ministers need not mean that Luke spoke to people present at the events. It can mean that Luke consulted works by them, or people whom they knew. Further, eyewitness testimony even today is flawed, and some things we think we have seen did not actually happen.

Greek historians strove for a certain objectivity and even neutrality and so did not hesitate to criticize their own nation to a degree not usually characteristic of Roman historiography. In Greek historiography, "individuals were not necessarily good or bad because of the side they represented or because they were Greeks or barbarians. Even in a work intended for the winning side, there was no room for caricature of an opponent simply because he was an opponent ..."[17] The question of whether the Gospel caricatures Jesus' opponents or, more benignly put, those who choose not to follow Jesus, remains, as we shall see, unsettled. Whereas Ben sees Luke as writing in the Greek tradition and so not like a Livy or for that matter like Dionysius of Halicarnassus – both of whom would have history subsumed under a large rhetorical umbrella, leading to distortion – Amy-Jill sees Luke as subsuming history under the large rhetorical umbrella of Christian apologetic. Thus, she views Luke's description of Jesus' opponents – Pharisees,

---

[17]   Charles W. Fornara, *The Nature of History in Ancient Greece and Rome* (Berkeley: University of California Press, 1983), 62.

the people in the Nazareth synagogue, the chief priests and scribes, the population of Jerusalem, and finally the Jewish people as a whole – as partisan rhetoric rather than accurate depiction. Whether Luke has composed a supersessionist polemic remains an open question. Ben is convinced that Luke is not supersessionist; Amy-Jill believes the text *can* be interpreted as such, although it *need not* be. Ben thinks that Amy-Jill's apologetic for the early Jewish reaction to Jesus himself both underplays Jesus' critique of his own Jewish traditions and at the same time underestimates the degree of actual opposition Jesus faced from some of the leaders of his own people.

Just as scholars debate the genre of Luke, so they debate the forms of rhetoric Luke employs. Here is another subject that Ben finds fascinating and Amy-Jill usually finds tedious. Ben finds distinctions in rhetorical forms helpful for understanding an author's purpose; Amy-Jill finds that often labeling functions only for the sake of labeling, or it tells us something we already know (e.g., Luke is trying to persuade readers). We both grant that ancient historical works were meant to be heard, and this meant that considerable attention had to be given to aural impression. Because the primary audiences for such works were typically a well-educated group who would have had some rhetorical education, they would expect rhetorical flourishes. Wishing for Theophilus to give ear to the Gospel, Luke would have attended to the Gospel's rhetorical potentialities.

The art of persuasion, otherwise known as rhetoric, was essential in history writing. Serious historians utilized deliberative rhetoric, which had to do with giving advice and counsel, and perhaps also forensic rhetoric, which had to do with defending the past. Ben sees Luke, like these other ancient historians, as largely staying away from epideictic rhetoric, the rhetoric of free invention, and of mere display and declamation. Amy-Jill sees Luke using such rhetoric frequently, from the infancy accounts that mimic the style of the Septuagint to the speeches in Acts, which serve apologetic purposes rather than history. We agree, however, that Luke follows the advice of the rhetoricians to vary style in order to appeal to a literate audience. Luke 1–2 and Acts 1–12 court listeners who appreciated the cadences of the Septuagint, the Greek translation of the Hebrew Scriptures. This Semitizing or Septuagintalizing was also a form of deliberate archaizing not unlike those who Atticized their historical narrative in the latter part of the first century CE. Archaizing further served to stress a link with the past, which is one of Luke's purposes. For Luke, Christianity is not to be seen as a purely new tradition, but rather the only appropriate continuity and fulfillment of a very old one. Ben here emphasizes Luke's universalizing of the earlier material; Amy-Jill sees Luke as foreclosing all interpretations of that material save (literally) the one through Jesus and thus a narrowing of the tradition.

This topic of how Luke addresses history, especially Jewish history, leads inevitably to the question of Jewish–Christian relations. Ben sees openings and generosity; Amy-Jill sees closing out and coopting. Ben sees the challenges to the Pharisees as based on what "some Pharisees" are like and not intended to be generalized excoriations; Amy-Jill finds a cumulative impression that all Jewish groups, indeed all Jews who do not follow Jesus, are condemned. Yet we both recognize that readers choose how to read. In working with Ben, Amy-Jill has found Luke a bit more sympathetic; in working with Amy-Jill, Ben has recognized how comments from Luke, and from Luke's other readers, can be understood as presenting an ugly image of Judaism. Both agree that Jesus had no such purely negative view of his fellow Jews.

This brief introduction already reveals several differences: Ben sees Luke as enhancing women's roles and as encouraging positive Jewish/Christian relations; Amy-Jill sees Luke as restricting women's roles and as shutting down Synagogue/Church connections. Ben sees an author interested in history and historical accuracy; Amy-Jill sees an author reconstructing a particular history for both Jesus and the Church, adapting sources in some cases and inventing material in others. We both agree, however, that Luke is a splendid writer and that the Gospel opens to multiple interpretations.

At this point, we fear that our readers are ready to take sides, as if there's a "team-Ben" and a "team-Amy-Jill," and the reading exercise is to award points. This is not what we want. We want our readers to see the same text through different lenses: Jewish and Christian (of particular sorts), historical and literary, behind the text and in front of the text as well as in the text. We want our readers to read Luke, and then read our comments, and then to join us in the conversation.

Luke 1 Prologue, Preparations, and Poems

[1] Since many have undertaken to set down an orderly account of the events that have been fulfilled among us, [2] just as they were handed on to us by those who from the beginning were eyewitnesses and servants of the word, [3] I too decided, after investigating everything carefully from the very first, to write an orderly account for you, most excellent Theophilus, [4] so that you may know the truth concerning the things about which you have been instructed.

ZECHARIAH AND ELIZABETH

[5] In the days of King Herod of Judea, there was a priest named Zechariah, who belonged to the priestly order of Abijah. His wife was a descendant of Aaron, and her name was Elizabeth. [6] Both of them were righteous before God, living blamelessly according to all the commandments and regulations of the Lord. [7] But they had no children, because Elizabeth was barren, and both were getting on in years.
[8] Once when he was serving as priest before God and his section was on duty, [9] he was chosen by lot, according to the custom of the priesthood, to enter the sanctuary of the Lord and offer incense. [10] Now at the time of the incense offering, the whole assembly of the people was praying outside.
[11] Then there appeared to him an angel of the Lord, standing at the right side of the altar of incense. [12] When Zechariah saw him, he was terrified; and fear overwhelmed him.
[13] But the angel said to him, "Do not be afraid, Zechariah, for your prayer has been heard. Your wife Elizabeth will bear you a son, and you will name him John. [14] You will have joy and gladness, and many will rejoice

at his birth, [15] for he will be great in the sight of the Lord. He must never drink wine or strong drink; even before his birth he will be filled with the Holy Spirit. [16] He will turn many of the people of Israel to the Lord their God. [17] With the spirit and power of Elijah he will go before him, to turn the hearts of parents to their children, and the disobedient to the wisdom of the righteous, to make ready a people prepared for the Lord."

[18] Zechariah said to the angel, "How will I know that this is so? For I am an old man, and my wife is getting on in years." [19] The angel replied, "I am Gabriel. I stand in the presence of God, and I have been sent to speak to you and to bring you this good news. [20] But now, because you did not believe my words, which will be fulfilled in their time, you will become mute, unable to speak, until the day these things occur."

[21] Meanwhile the people were waiting for Zechariah, and wondered at his delay in the sanctuary. [22] When he did come out, he could not speak to them, and they realized that he had seen a vision in the sanctuary. He kept motioning to them and remained unable to speak. [23] When his time of service was ended, he went to his home.

[24] After those days his wife Elizabeth conceived, and for five months she remained in seclusion. She said, [25] "This is what the Lord has done for me when he looked favorably on me and took away the disgrace I have endured among my people."

THE ANNUNCIATION TO MARY

[26] In the sixth month the angel Gabriel was sent by God to a town in Galilee called Nazareth, [27] to a virgin engaged to a man whose name was Joseph, of the house of David. The virgin's name was Mary. [28] And he came to her and said, "Greetings, favored one! The Lord is with you." [29] But she was much perplexed by his words and pondered what sort of greeting this might be.

[30] The angel said to her, "Do not be afraid, Mary, for you have found favor with God. [31] And now, you will conceive in your womb and bear a son, and you will name him Jesus. [32] He will be great, and will be called the Son of the Most High, and the Lord God will give to him the throne of his ancestor David. [33] He will reign over the house of Jacob forever, and of his kingdom there will be no end."

[34] Mary said to the angel, "How can this be, since I am a virgin?" [35] The angel said to her, "The Holy Spirit will come upon you, and the power of the

Most High will overshadow you; therefore the child to be born will be holy; he will be called Son of God. [36] And now, your relative Elizabeth in her old age has also conceived a son; and this is the sixth month for her who was said to be barren. [37] For nothing will be impossible with God." [38] Then Mary said, "Here am I, the servant of the Lord; let it be with me according to your word." Then the angel departed from her.

THE VISITATION

[39] In those days Mary set out and went with haste to a Judean town in the hill country, [40] where she entered the house of Zechariah and greeted Elizabeth. [41] When Elizabeth heard Mary's greeting, the child leaped in her womb. And Elizabeth was filled with the Holy Spirit [42] and exclaimed with a loud cry, "Blessed are you among women, and blessed is the fruit of your womb. [43] And why has this happened to me, that the mother of my Lord comes to me? [44] For as soon as I heard the sound of your greeting, the child in my womb leaped for joy. [45] And blessed is she who believed that there would be a fulfillment of what was spoken to her by the Lord."

[46] And Mary said,

"My soul magnifies the Lord,
[47] and my spirit rejoices in God my Savior,
[48] for he has looked with favor on the lowliness of his servant.
Surely, from now on all generations will call me blessed;
[49] for the Mighty One has done great things for me,
and holy is his name.
[50] His mercy is for those who fear him
from generation to generation.
[51] He has shown strength with his arm;
he has scattered the proud in the thoughts of their hearts.
[52] He has brought down the powerful from their thrones,
and lifted up the lowly;
[53] he has filled the hungry with good things,
and sent the rich away empty.
[54] He has helped his servant Israel,
in remembrance of his mercy,
[55] according to the promise he made to our ancestors,
to Abraham and to his descendants forever."

[56] And Mary remained with her about three months and then returned to her home.

THE BIRTH AND NAMING OF JOHN

⁵⁷ Now the time came for Elizabeth to give birth, and she bore a son. ⁵⁸ Her neighbors and relatives heard that the Lord had shown his great mercy to her, and they rejoiced with her.

⁵⁹ On the eighth day they came to circumcise the child, and they were going to name him Zechariah after his father. ⁶⁰ But his mother said, "No; he is to be called John." ⁶¹ They said to her, "None of your relatives has this name." ⁶² Then they began motioning to his father to find out what name he wanted to give him. ⁶³ He asked for a writing tablet and wrote, "His name is John." And all of them were amazed. ⁶⁴ Immediately his mouth was opened and his tongue freed, and he began to speak, praising God. ⁶⁵ Fear came over all their neighbors, and all these things were talked about throughout the entire hill country of Judea. ⁶⁶ All who heard them pondered them and said, "What then will this child become?" For, indeed, the hand of the Lord was with him.

⁶⁷ Then his father Zechariah was filled with the Holy Spirit and spoke this prophecy:

⁶⁸ "Blessed be the Lord God of Israel,
    for he has looked favorably on his people and redeemed them.
⁶⁹ He has raised up a mighty savior for us
    in the house of his servant David,
⁷⁰ as he spoke through the mouth of his holy prophets from of old,
⁷¹ that we would be saved from our enemies and from the hand of all who hate us.
⁷² Thus he has shown the mercy promised to our ancestors,
    and has remembered his holy covenant,
⁷³ the oath that he swore to our ancestor Abraham,
    to grant us
⁷⁴ that we, being rescued from the hands of our enemies,
    might serve him without fear,
⁷⁵ in holiness and righteousness
    before him all our days.
⁷⁶ And you, child, will be called the prophet of the Most High;
    for you will go before the Lord to prepare his ways,
⁷⁷ to give knowledge of salvation to his people
    by the forgiveness of their sins.
⁷⁸ By the tender mercy of our God,
    the dawn from on high will break upon us,

⁷⁹ to give light to those who sit in darkness and in the shadow of death,
to guide our feet into the way of peace."

⁸⁰ The child grew and became strong in spirit, and he was in the wilderness until the day he appeared publicly to Israel.

PROLOGUE

Luke's Prologue (**vss. 1–4**), a single sentence in Greek, shows the author's literary abilities, even as it locates the reader, and all readers, as "Theophilus" (**vs. 3**), a relatively common Greek name that means "one who loves God." In ancient Greek literature, authors had patrons: some paid for the volume to be copied; other times the author dedicated the volume to the patron either in gratitude for previous aid or in hopes of new support. It appears in the first instance that this volume was written to a specific individual, though without question it was shared thereafter with other followers of Jesus. For our author Luke, all readers are to be lovers of God, and such lovers require instruction in the object of their devotion.

The instruction also serves as a corrective. Luke knows of other accounts of the life of Jesus, accounts that most likely included the Gospel of Mark and perhaps included the Gospel of Matthew and/or a hypothetical collection of Jesus' sayings known as Q. If among the earlier accounts are our canonical Gospels, a question necessarily arises regarding Luke's view of Scripture. Did Luke think Mark was, as a Gospel, somehow insufficient or even inaccurate? Was Luke's goal to supplement Mark, or even to replace it? Perhaps Luke's interest in events "from the beginning" (**vs. 2**) suggests that a Gospel must begin with the Nativity account rather than the Baptism (so Mark 1).

That one canonical writer would disagree with another should not surprise; the both Testaments already display multiple views of the same issue, whether the subject is kingship (a bad idea, since it reflects the people's rejection of the kinship of God [1 Sam 8.7], or a good idea, since without a king in Israel, the people did what was "right in their own eyes" [Judg 21.25], which included rape and slaughter), the building of a Temple (absolutely, so 1 Chron 22; not needed, so Acts 7.48–49), or even the question of how to understand Jesus (given four separate Gospel portraits). Or, perhaps Luke simply found Mark incomplete and in need of amplification through the use of other sources. Following in the creative steps of the people who collected the Scriptures of Israel, the people who put the New Testament together allowed different voices to be heard. No one text can completely display the history of Israel or the life of Jesus.

In speaking of the "things which have been accomplished," or, literally, "have been fulfilled" (**vs. 1**), Luke suggests more than a detailing of the life of Jesus. The language of fulfillment implies also the response to prophecy. Luke thus locates his history in the context of Israel and of the divine word. Coupled with this appeal to the prophets, Luke also cites "eye witnesses" and "servants" (**vs. 2**). Luke does not list "apostles" or "disciples," although people holding these titles may well be included. Rather, Luke's focus is more broad: not only people who hold ecclesial office, but all who have memories, or memories of memories. Because Luke's infancy materials focus on Mary (Matthew's first two chapters focus on Joseph), some readers include Mary among these eyewitnesses; a few suggest that Mary herself was the author, but she chose to write under a pseudonym to disguise her gender, much as did Mary Anne Evans (George Eliot), Amantine Lucile Aurore Dupin (George Sand), and Karen Blixen (Isak Dinesen). Ben finds Mary to be a plausible source; Amy-Jill has doubts.

The memories of these eyewitnesses and ministers are of the "word"; the Greek term *logos* has, in the Gospel of John (1.1) and likely here as well given its use in Acts (8.4; 10.36; 11.19; and 14.25), a technical sense: the word is both Jesus and the story about him. Luke will recount what has been "handed on," as did other historians, but Luke will also add materials. Historians are never totally constrained by their sources: they necessarily contextualize received material to tell a new story; they omit and add and subtract, and they present what they believe their readers should hear.

Missing in this introduction is the subject of the volume. Luke's Prologue mentions neither Jesus nor the Church. Theophilus thereby becomes positioned as someone already within the Christian orbit, and so Luke's ideal reader is someone who already knows the story.

"Most excellent" (**vs. 3**) does not necessarily indicate someone rich or politically well positioned, but the term gives the impression that Theophilus is a patron, and so someone who would reward, or pay, Luke for the written text. Here the term is more than a compliment: anyone who loves God and wants more details about the object of this love – who wants to be "instructed" (**vs. 4**; the Greek is *katēkhéō*, as in "catechism") is already, for Luke, "most excellent." All readers become invited to hear the Gospel again, this time from Luke's perspective. Nor will Luke's version be the only one they encounter, for it will be followed by John's, and then Paul's, and so on through the centuries.

A CLOSER LOOK: THE RELATION OF LUKE 1–2 TO THE REST OF
THE GOSPEL

With the remainder of chapters 1 and 2, Luke shifts from the formal introduction at home in Greek history and scientific treatises to language that
echoes the Septuagint, the Greek translation of Israel's Scriptures. The
mood entirely changes, as readers are immersed in stories that resonate
with earlier texts even as, with all retellings, they make their own, distinct
contributions. The material that follows is distinct to Luke. Although its
themes – the Holy Spirit, the fulfillment of prophecy, setting Jesus on the
world stage – are also sounded throughout the rest of the Gospel and
in Acts, there are also substantial differences. For example, the infancy
materials have very positive views of the Temple whereas the adult
Jesus treats the Temple as, at best, a "cave of thieves" (19.46); the first
two chapters treat Jewish communal practice (pilgrimage, circumcision,
purity observance) positively while the rest of the Gospel regards similar
practices (synagogue settings, Sabbath observance) as a problem rather
than as a blessing; the infancy materials give women voice, whereas the
rest of the Gospel either depicts silent women or has men correcting
women's commentary.

Such differences can lead to the conclusion that chapters 1 and 2 are later
additions to the text and that they serve a particular purpose: resonances
of what the Church would come to call the "Old Testament," the exceptionally positive views of Jewish piety, and the stress on Jesus' physicality,
from his pregnant mother to his birth to his circumcision, all run counter
to the views associated with an early second-century figure, Marcion.
That teacher insisted that God of the Old Testament was distinct from
the God of Jesus and the Church; therefore, the Torah, the Law, was the
product of a secondary divinity and should be rejected. Marcion also
promoted a negative view of the human body and especially of sexuality
and childbearing; the first two chapters of Luke refute such claims. Luke
1–2 can therefore be read as anti-Marcionite additions to Luke's original
Gospel, which may have started not with the birth of John the Baptist,
but, as in the Gospel of Mark, with John's mission (3.1). Amy-Jill finds
this view an intriguing possibility, and one that explains why the first
two chapters would so celebrate Jewish people and traditions, and so
promote women's voices, but why the rest of the Gospel does not. Ben
finds the idea implausible since Luke likely wrote before Marcion's time.

> Ben also thinks that there isn't a *consistent* agenda in Luke 3–24 to silence women, or portray synagogues and Jewish leaders negatively. Rather, the presentation is mixed.

ZECHARIAH AND ELIZABETH

The echoes of the earlier Scriptures begin with **vs. 5**, where Luke sets up the context for the story to come. King Herod of Judea is typically regarded as Herod the Great, the one who rebuilt the Jerusalem Temple, and the one who, according to Matthew's Gospel, massacred the children in Bethlehem in order to kill the newborn "King of the Jews" (Matt 2.1–15). Herod died in 4 BCE, and as Luke 2.2 indicates, the birth of Jesus took place at the time of the census undertaken by Quirinius, which occurred 6/7 CE. The easiest means of resolving this discrepancy is to take Luke's Herod not as Herod the Great (37–34 BCE), but as his son, Archelaus, who ruled over Judea from his father's death until he was deposed in 6 CE.[1] The census took place following this deposition, at which point Rome gained direct rule over Judea and replaced Herodian descendants with prefects, including Pontius Pilate. This alternative reading has the additional advantage of creating a stronger comparison of John the Baptist to Jesus. John's conception takes place not on the world stage of Caesar Augustus, nor even on the broad stage of international politics suggested by Herod, which would include Galilee, Iturea, Trachonites, Abilene, and Tiberius, all mentioned in 3.1; rather, John's birth is localized to Judea, as in 3.1.

Ben points out that the Greek of the relevant phrase (2.2) can refer to the census "before" the famous Quirinius census, but Amy-Jill finds that to be a strained reading. In Ben's reading, Luke's chronology is pushed back some years and can be integrated with Matthew's version, where Herod the Great is on the throne. Amy-Jill finds the entire census episode much more likely to be Lucan apologetic than historical reporting. But we shall follow Luke's lead and wait to chapter 2 for this discussion.

---

[1] Mark D. Smith, "Of Jesus and Quirinius," *CBQ* 62.2 (2000): 278–93. Smith proposes that it is Matthew who invents the account of Herod's Slaughter of the Innocents in order to complete the midrashic associations of Jesus with Moses. Ben notes, however, that the presentation of Herod the Great in Josephus (and in Matthew) as paranoid about usurpers, even to the point of killing members of his own family, suggests there is no reason to doubt an historical basis for the Slaughter of the Innocents, especially since Bethlehem was a small village and few children would be involved, not enough even to warrant mention by Josephus when there were so many other bloody deeds by Herod.

While Herod the king designates the time period, Luke's focus is on Zechariah the priest. Priesthood in Judaism is not a vocation, as it is in Christian contexts, but an inherited role. One is a priest if one's father is a priest; Jewish priests trace their ancestry to Aaron, Moses' brother. To this day, Judaism recognizes those in the priestly line (priests are called in Hebrew *kohanim*, from *kohen*, the term for "priest"), as it does the Levitical line, which is also based on paternal descent. Amy-Jill is a Levite because her father was a Levite; her children are not, because their father is not. The twenty-four priestly divisions, which become lost to history formally after the destruction of the Jerusalem Temple in 70 CE, are demarcated in 1 Chron 24.10.

Zechariah, whose name derives from the Hebrew for "remember," is an ordinary village priest; he is not based in Jerusalem, and he is not among the "high priests" to whom Luke ascribes the plot to kill Jesus. He might be compared to the equally ordinary priest who, in the Parable of the Good Samaritan, passes by the injured man (10.31). And indeed, like the priest in the parable, Zechariah will mistake his role. As the priest in Luke 10 fails to follow Torah in loving the neighbor, so Zechariah will fail to trust the divine word.

Zechariah's wife Elizabeth shares her name (in Hebrew, *Elisheva*) with Aaron's wife, appropriate given her own priestly lineage. The mention of this couple, both "righteous" and "living blamelessly according to all the commandments and regulations of the Lord" (**vs. 6**), indicates that for Luke, as for Paul (Phil 3.6), faithful following of Torah is possible. The Torah was not an impossible burden, and following it was, for the vast majority of Jews, a delight. Therefore, Elizabeth and Zechariah are, to use the Protestant term, "justified" in relation to the divine; they are in a "right relationship" with God. Ben is reminded of Paul's claim to be "blameless when it comes to a righteousness that comes from the Mosaic Law" (Phil 3.6); therefore "blameless" here in Luke means someone who lives in full fidelity to Torah. What blameless does not mean is perfect; it simply means someone who keeps Torah.

Luke's reference to the commandments and regulations not only reflects back on the Torah, it projects forward to the importance of the Torah for Jesus and then for the Church. The "Law" is explicitly mentioned again in 2.22, 23, and 27, such that the births of John and Jesus take place within lives lived under Torah. Blamelessness is a category already known in Judaism, as we see in its numerous uses in Israel's Scriptures, such as with Abraham (Gen 17.1), Daniel (6.22), and the Psalms (e.g., 37.37; 119.1). We make these points about the Law explicit given that a number of Christian readers are convinced that the Torah creates an impossible burden and that Jesus came to free "us" from the "burden" of the Law. These are false views of the Torah and mischaracterizations of Jewish practice. Gentiles were never under the distinct commands of Torah such as circumcision, Sabbath observance, the dietary regulations, wearing fringes to remind them of the commandments, and so on, since these laws functioned to separate Jews from the broader gentile world. One cannot be "freed" from something to which one is not bound. Nor was Torah observance a "burden" but a delight, as practicing Jews to this day attest.

This blamelessness means that Elizabeth's inability to conceive a child (**vs. 7**) was not a punishment. Nor would most Jews, as far as we can tell, regard infertility as the result of sin, any more than they would regard conception as requiring righteousness on the part of the parents.[2] Israel's Scriptures make it very clear that it is God who opens the womb. Luke's righteous couple who are unable to have children immediately recollect major figures in those Scriptures: Sarah and Abraham (Genesis 18), Rebekah and Isaac (Genesis 25), Rachel and Jacob (Genesis 30), Manoah and his (unnamed) wife (Judges 13), Hannah and Elkanah (1 Samuel 1), and the (unnamed) "Great Woman" of Shunem and her (unnamed) husband (2 Kings 4). All these couples experience, in various ways, the direct intervention of the divine in their lives. John the Baptist will take his place as the last canonical figure to be born from parents presumed to be infertile; the tradition will continue in the patristic period with accounts of the birth of the Virgin Mary to an elderly and righteous Jewish couple (*Protevangelium of James*).

Of all these ancestors, John will bear the closest connection to Samuel, the child of Hannah and Elkanah, and Samuel's story in turn provides one of the base notes to Luke's first two chapters. As Samuel will anoint King David, so John will prepare the way for David's son, Jesus.

The plot begins when Zechariah was on duty in the Temple (**vs. 8**) and was "chosen by lot" (**vs. 9**) to make the incense offering. Because there were too many priests for all to serve fulltime and too few rituals for all the priests on duty to perform, the lot became the means by which the priests would determine who did what (*m. Tamid* 5.2–6.3 provides details on both drawing lots and the activities surrounding the incense offering). It also foreshadows the choosing, by lot, of Matthias to replace Judas among the apostles (Acts 2). That

[2] See Candida R. Moss and Joel S. Baden, *Reconceiving Infertility: Biblical Perspectives on Procreation and Childlessness* (Princeton: Princeton University Press, 2015).

the divine hand was involved in both choices would be an appropriate inference. What may appear to one person to be luck may be providence to another.

The assembly outside prays at the "time of the incense offering" (**vs. 10**), likely in the early evening (Exod 30.7–8); the cost was part of the Temple tax paid by all Jewish males. Luke does not provide the contents of these communal prayers. Some may have been offering thanksgiving or praise to God; others may have repented of sin; still other may have made personal petitions, for health, or a successful crop, or even for children. Their presence not only demonstrates the people's view of the sanctity of the site, it provides the comedic audience for what happens next. The frequent comments in Christian sources that the Temple was a flawed institution that "served to perpetuate distinctions between Jews and non-Jews, priests and non-priests, men and women, and so on,"[3] ignores the biblical notion of both holiness and creation as involving separation – light and darkness, heaven and earth, humanity and animals, Israel and the nations. It also ignores the same separation in Christian sources (saved and not saved; insider and outsiders) as well as traditional Christian practice (those who can participate in Eucharist; those who cannot). Whereas Luke will engage in criticism of the Temple's leadership, condemning this Jewish institution for its infidelity to biblical tradition is, at best, unnecessary. Had Jesus himself found the system abhorrent, that his followers continued to worship there makes no sense. Further, Paul connects the Temple to Israel's adoption, glory, covenants, giving of the Law, and the promises (Rom 9.4, where "worship" [Greek: *latreia*] refers to the Temple service). These facts make such negative comments unwarranted.[4]

As the crowd prays, the priest experiences an angelophany. Josephus reports that the Hasmonean King John Hyrcanus (175–104 BCE), while he was serving as the high priest and offering incense (*Ant.* 13.282), heard a heavenly voice announcing that his sons had just won a battle. Hyrcanus then "openly declared before all the multitude on his coming out of the Temple; and it accordingly proved true." Were Luke familiar with Josephus's writing, this possible allusion sets up a nice irony: Zechariah's son, John, will confront Herod Antipas, whose Herodian family replaced the Hasmoneans, who were serving as both monarchs and high priests.

3   Joel Green, *The Gospel of Luke* (NICNT; Grand Rapids: Eerdmans, 1997), 4–5.
4   See Mark Nanos, "Romans," in Amy-Jill Levine and Marc Z. Brettler (eds.), *Jewish Annotated New Testament*, 2d ed. (New York: Oxford University Press, 2017), 285–320 (304); Paula Fredriksen, review of N. T. Wright, *The Faithfulness of God*, CBQ 77 (2015): 387–91 (388).

The traditional biblical reaction to an appearance of an angel is fright, and Zechariah is, appropriately, "terrified" (**vs. 12**); the same Greek term, *tarassō*, will appear in 24.38 to describe the disciples' reaction to seeing the resurrected Jesus, and a cognate will describe Mary's own reaction to seeing Gabriel (1.29). Angels then, typically, tell the surprised person not to be afraid (**vs. 13a**). This angel comes with good news, just as did the angels who visited Abraham and Sarah (Gen 18): Zechariah's prayer has been heard, and his wife Elizabeth will bear him a son (**vs. 13b**). Zechariah's prayer itself goes unrecorded. It may have indeed been for a son, but Luke leaves open the possibility of a prayer beyond that of children. Zechariah may have been praying for the messianic age, for peace on earth, for the healing of the nations.

For the first time in an annunciation story, the angel identifies the child: "You will name him John" (**vs. 13c**). The name, derived from the Hebrew meaning "God is gracious," will become a point of contestation, since it is not a name within the families of Zechariah or Elizabeth. Luke intimates a break from family tradition, and more. Luke also quickly alerts Theophilus, the ideal reader who may only be familiar with the Gospel of Mark and thus lacking any Nativity account, that the birth being predicted is that of John (the Baptizer), not Jesus.

The next line moves the angel's message from the personal observation that Zechariah will experience joy to the more general claim that many will rejoice at the child's birth (**vs. 14**). The first claim is obvious; the second is unclear unless one already knows the story. Many can rejoice that an infertile couple who wanted a child are now to have one; Luke, however, is intimating something more. The public rejoicing is not simply in regard to the birth of the child, it concerns the child himself. The announcement of conception thus becomes an announcement of good news for the people of Israel.

John will be great in the sight of the Lord (**vs. 15a**); he is not, however, the greater. Luke is using a rhetorical device known today as "step parallelism"[5]: John's greatness anticipates Jesus' even greater role. John's mother was infertile; Jesus' mother will be a virgin at the time of his conception. John will be filled by the Spirit; Jesus is conceived by the Spirit. Zechariah and Mary both encounter an angel, but Zechariah expresses doubt and will be struck mute whereas Mary expresses confidence and then sings

5   Richard J. Dillon, "The Benedictus in Micro- and Macrocontext," *CBQ* 68.3 (2006): 457–80 (462).

the Magnificat. Luke knew that John the Baptizer had disciples and that these disciples continued to follow their master even after his beheading. The message to Theophilus is, therefore, follow the tradition that proclaims Jesus and not the tradition that proclaims John, no matter how splendid a teacher John was.

The two men, Jesus and John, are also distinct, as the angel's prenatal instructions begin to delineate. The instruction to avoid alcohol (**vs. 15b**) reflects the regulations for priests in the Temple (Lev 10.9) and the Nazirite tradition (Num 6.3); John will be set apart for holiness, as he will spend his entire life serving the divine. Like Samuel and Samson, two others sons of previously infertile mothers and two other men associated with the Nazirite tradition, John will be, in today's parlance, *intoxicated* not by wine but *by the Spirit* (**vs. 15c**). Conversely, in Luke's Gospel, Jesus eats and drinks, quite a lot and at banquets, such that he is accused of being a "glutton and a drunkard" (7.34); John not only eschews wine and strong drink, he will frequently fast (see 5.33–34).

It is through the power of the Spirit that John will "turn" many in Israel to their God (**vs. 16**). "Turning" has a technical sense in Jewish thought. The Hebrew term *shuv*, meaning both "turn" and "return," has the connotation of repenting, of turning from sin and toward righteousness, of turning off the crooked path and on to the right one. It also evokes Malachi's prediction about the return of Elijah the prophet, who will be sent back to "prepare the way" (Mal 3.1; the verse also speaks of the "Lord whom you will see suddenly come to his Temple") before the great and terrible day of the Lord comes in order to "*turn* the hearts of parents to their children and the hearts of children to their parents" (Mal 4.5–6; versification in the Masoretic Text [MT] is 3.23–24). John is, symbolically, the new Elijah, but his role in Luke's Gospel is not to announce the messianic age as Malachi predicts; it is to announce the Messiah. Luke has thus changed Elijah's job description. For the Christian reader, the "Lord" Malachi mentions is Jesus. This double reference reflects "Luke's literary strategy to associate yet differentiate God the Father and Jesus."[6]

Zechariah, thinking practically rather than theologically or eschatologically, queries the angel: "I am old," he states bluntly, and then a little more discretely notes that Elizabeth is "getting on in years" (**vs. 18**). Questioning a divine revelation is almost as common as displaying fear at an angelic appearance. In Gen 15.8, Abraham, having "believed the Lord" and so determined to be righteous, asks about the promise of land, "How am I to know

---

6   Richard Vinson, "The God of Luke-Acts," *Interpretation* 68.4 (2014): 376–88 (378).

that I shall possess it?" Zechariah's question resembles Sarah's query upon overhearing from the divine visitor that she will conceive: "So Sarah laughed to herself, saying, 'After I have grown old, and my husband is old, shall I have pleasure?'" (Gen 18.12 MT; the LXX does not mention her "pleasure").

Like Abraham's visitor, who responds to Sarah's incredulity by asking, "Is anything too wonderful for the Lord?" (Gen 18.14), the angel responds to Zechariah with a theological lesson. He begins, likely in a somewhat huffy tone, by identifying himself: "I am Gabriel," and, "I stand in the presence of God" (**vs. 19**). Gabriel means "Man of God"; he is the messenger who, according to Dan 9.20–25, will announce the messianic age. In particular, he brings "good news" (vs. 19); the Greek is *euangelisasthai*, from the prefix *eu*, meaning "good," as in euphemism or eulogy, and *angelos*, meaning "message," as in the derivative "angel" or "messenger." The term *eu-angelos* comes into Old English as "godspell," then in Middle English as "go(d) spel," and finally as Gospel – literally, "good news." In the Septuagint, the Greek terms translate the Hebrew *mebaseret*, where it refers to the good news of God's redemption of the people from Babylonian captivity as well as of God's rule in general.[7] For example, Isa 52.7 proclaims, "How beautiful upon the mountains are the feet of the messenger who announces peace, who brings good news, who announces salvation, who says to Zion, 'Your God reigns.'" In the Roman world, *euangelion* referred to the beneficence of the emperor, such as the granting of a tax holiday. Luke offers a distinct view of the contents of the good news, but the reader must continue in the Gospel to learn the details.

Ironically, Zechariah will not, at least not directly, be able to proclaim any good news. His punishment for not believing Gabriel's words is that he "will become mute, unable to speak," until, Gabriel states, vaguely, "these things occur" (**vs. 20**). The situation is, at best, awkward, for Zechariah is expected to bless the people at the conclusion of the incense offering. Plus, he's running late (**vs. 21**).

Finally, he emerges, although he is not able to fulfill his priestly duties. The blessing the people are to receive, Luke intimates, will come from another source. Luke remarks that the people "realized he had seen a vision" (**vs. 22**), although no explanation to account for that realization is given. At most, we are told that "he kept motioning to them." Given that narratives about Jesus were, initially, not read silently by individuals but performed to a group, the comedic possibilities of this scene are extensive. We can imagine hand

---

[7]   Isa 40.9; 52.7; 60.6; Psa 40.9; 68.11; 96.2; etc.

motions to indicate an angelic appearance; we can also imagine, but we shall not, what motions served to indicate that Zechariah and Elizabeth would conceive a child.

Luke's message also has less humorous aspects. Given that the author knows the Temple was destroyed in 70, the silencing of the priest can foreshadow the end of serving in the Temple, and so the Temple service. Ben thinks this is a stretch; Amy-Jill hopes that it is.

Zechariah returns home (**vs. 23**), and after explaining, perhaps in writing, what had occurred in the Temple, he and Elizabeth conceive a child (**vs. 24a**). The pregnant Elizabeth then remains in seclusion for the first five months (**vs. 24b**); according to Luke, she recognizes both the divine favor showed upon her and the removal "the disgrace" she had endured (**vs. 25**), apparently for being infertile. Her comment brings her close to the matriarch Leah, who emphasizes her disgrace in the eyes of her husband Jacob (see, e.g., Gen 29.32: "Leah conceived and bore a son, and she named him Reuben; for she said, 'Because the Lord has looked on my affliction; surely now my husband will love me' "). Elizabeth also finds a connection to Rachel, who at the birth of her son Joseph states, "God has taken away my reproach" (Gen 30.23). Leah and Rachel are rival mothers in the same household and both speak of disgrace; Elizabeth and Mary will prove to be rival mothers as well, but in their case the elder cedes precedence to the younger, and there is no strife. Nor, in the case of Mary, is there any explicit notice of shame or disgrace.

Whereas a previously infertile mother might want to announce the pregnancy immediately, Elizabeth's reaction rings true in at least two practical ways. First, the pregnancy would not be obvious to everyone until around the sixth month, so her announcement will come with the proof shown by her body. Second, by the sixth month, she will have passed the time of the likelihood of miscarriage. Luke's phrasing also indicates that women normally were not in seclusion: Elizabeth's remaining hidden is her own choice, not one imposed upon her. In terms of the plot, the seclusion has a third motivation: Mary will be the first person explicitly to recognize her cousin's pregnancy just as Elizabeth will be the first to remark upon Mary's own pregnancy.

THE ANNUNCIATION TO MARY

The scene shifts "in the sixth month" of Elizabeth's pregnancy (**vs. 26**). No longer is time marked by the year of the ruling authority; it is marked by the months of pregnancy.[8] How we understand time – the calendar year, with its Western dating from the birth of Jesus; the year on the Jewish calendar; the academic year; the fiscal year; the year since graduation, and so on – speaks to our values and to how we locate ourselves in time. Gabriel goes to Nazareth, a Galilean town so insignificant that outside the Gospels, no contemporary source mentions it.[9] Luke's term here translated "town" is *polis*, or "city." Luke is being generous.

Whereas Luke provides details about Zechariah and Elizabeth's lineage and righteousness, the description of the angel's new interlocutor concentrates, in order, on her virginity; her engagement to a fellow named Joseph from the Davidic house; and finally, after repeating the point about her virginity, her name (**vs. 27**). The first mentioned attribute, virginity, does not suggest that she is somehow more "pure" than women who have had sexual intercourse. Luke has already noted that Elizabeth is blameless, but there is no reason to think that she and Zechariah had not tried to have children. In Luke's narrative, Mary's virginity serves as indication of the miraculous conception to follow. The one miracle greater than that of a postmenopausal woman conceiving is that of a virgin conceiving. What Mary will experience in Luke's account is not, contrary to the common expression, a "virgin birth"; rather, Luke speaks of a virginal conception. The idea that Mary remained a virgin not only prepartum but also in partu, and postpartum appears in the second-century *Protevangelium of James*. Luke, like the other evangelists, presumes that Mary and Joseph had other children (e.g., 8.19–20).

Joseph, the fiancé, shares his name with that earlier Joseph, son of Rachel, but unlike Matthew, Luke does not exploit this connection. In Matthew's Gospel, Joseph the son of Jacob (Matt 1.16) replays the roles of that earlier

---

[8] Brigitte Kahl, "Reading Luke Against Luke: Non-Uniformity of Text, Hermeneutics of Conspiracy and the 'Scriptural Principle' in Luke 1," in Amy-Jill Levine with Marianne Blickenstaff (eds.), *A Feminist Companion to Luke*, 70–88 (esp. 79–80, "Time-Break: Mothers' and Children's Time [Lk. 1.24–57]").

[9] Ben notes that this is not entirely correct. There is a famous prohibition against grave robbing in Nazareth written in Greek, from the Emperor no less, which according to the epigraphers dates to the first half of the first century CE. See https://en.wikipedia.org/wiki/Nazareth_Inscription. Amy-Jill notes that the text never mentions "Nazareth"; it is called the "Nazareth Inscription" because it was shipped from Nazareth to the Louvre. See discussion by David E. Graves at http://biblicalarchaeologygraves.blogspot.com/2014/12/bonus-107-nazareth-inscription.html. The marble tablet may have originally come from the Decapolis; see B. M. Metzger, "The Nazareth Inscription Once Again," *New Testament Studies: Philological, Versional, and Patristic* (New Testament Tools and Studies [NTTS] 10; Leiden: Brill, 1980), 75–92; and J. Spencer Kennard Jr., "The Burial of Jesus," *JBL* 74.4 (1955): 227–38.

Joseph son of Jacob, who dreams dreams, goes to Egypt, and saves his family. The Lukan Joseph functions here primarily to represent "the house of David"; his import is not righteousness, but lineage (see 2 Sam 7).

The name "Mary" is, here in Luke's text, actually *Mariam.* Just as English translations typically translate the Greek "Iakob" as "James" when dealing with New Testament figures, so the Aramaic/Hebrew "Miriam" becomes the Christianized "Mary." The translation "Mary" misses the echoes of Moses' sister Miriam, the leader of the women, who rejoices by singing praises at the salvation of Israel at the Red Sea. The LXX uses "Mariam," the same spelling Luke has here in 1.27. In 2.19 and following, however, Luke spells the name as "Maria." Echoes, perhaps fainter, might be heard of Herod Archelaus' stepmother and Herod the Great's Hasmonean wife, Mariamme, whose family represented independent Jewish rule in the Jewish homeland before the Romans gained control in 63 BCE. Jesus' mother is associated, by name, with two other women who represented self-determination and freedom from oppression.

Mary herself receives no familial description, save that she is a relative of Elizabeth (vs. 36) and so has priestly connections. We do not know her age, although Jewish women in the late Second Temple period married in their late teens or early twenties, with their husbands being about ten years older.[10] We do not know whether Mary is rich or poor; Luke says nothing about her parents or any siblings; we do not know what she looks like. Nor do we know what Jesus looked like.

The angel adds to Mary's description something more important than class or family or appearance: he says "Greetings, favored one" (**vs. 28**). The Greek is a pun: "Greetings" is the Greek *chaire,* or "rejoice, hail" (hence the popular version, "Hail Mary"); the noun form is "charis" or "grace." "Favored" is from the same root, *charis*; thus, literally it means "to be gracious, to be favored." The Vulgate's translation is *gratia plena,* or "full of grace."

Although the NRSV describes Mary as "perplexed" (**vs. 29**), the Greek *diatarassō,* related to Zechariah's reaction to the angel (1.12), suggests something more along the lines of "terrified." Hence Gabriel's expected response, "Do not be afraid" (**vs. 30**). The angel then repeats an expression of "grace" or "favor," although still without delineating what if anything Mary had done to find such favor; the divine decision may be entirely "gracious" (Luke

---

[10]   See Michael L. Satlow, *Jewish Marriage in Antiquity* (Princeton: Princeton University Press, 2001), esp. 101–32; following Satlow, see Lynn Cohick, *Women in the World of the Earliest Christians: Illuminating Ancient Ways of Life* (Grand Rapids: Baker Academic, 2009), 119.

does like the term *charis,* as does Paul; the word does not appear in Mark or Matthew). Finally, Gabriel gives the message: she will conceive and bear a son whom she will name Jesus (**vs. 31**). The angel mentions nothing about the process by which she will conceive, but since Luke has already mentioned that Mary and Joseph are engaged, the uninformed reader would likely expect that Joseph would be the father. On the other hand, the biblically literate reader, or a reader familiar with Matthew's Gospel, might hear an allusion to Isa 7.14 *in the Greek,* where the prophet predicts that a "virgin (Greek *parthenos*) will conceive in [her] womb and bear a son." In Matthew, Mary's virginity remains in place prior to the birth of Jesus; in Luke, this is a possible but not necessary reading, as we shall see.

As with the other names in the text, the name Jesus is evocative. The name, which in Aramaic would be Yeshu or Yeshua, comes from the same Hebrew root as Hosea and Joshua, and it is also cognate to the term "Hosanna": the root meaning of all these terms is "save."

Luke adds to the child's identification: he like John will be "great" (vs. 15), but he also "will be called Son of the Most High" (**vs. 32a**). The title associates him with David (2 Sam 7.9), but adds to it. Mary's child not only will receive David's throne (**vs. 32b**), he will have an eternal kingdom (**vs. 33**). The challenge to Rome, which saw itself as the *imperium sine fine,* the "Empire without End" (Virgil, *Aeneid,* 1.279), is in place.

The earlier reference to Joseph as Mary's fiancé (vs. 27) coupled with Gabriel's statement that the "Lord God will give to him the throne of his ancestor David" (**vs. 32**) suggests that Jesus has "double paternity," both a divine conception and a human father.[11] Such double paternity was conventional in Greco-Roman biographies, as are the display of a child's wisdom and the ascension of the hero. Odysseus, Plato, Aristotle, Alexander the Great, Pythagoras, Augustus Caesar, and many others either claimed or were assigned divine paternity along with their earthly parentage. Ben finds that distinguishing Luke's story from these others is the lack of reference to a god and a human woman having intercourse; Amy-Jill notes that not all the Greek and Roman accounts actually depict sexual activity. For example, describing the hero Apollonius of Tyana, Philostratus writes, "To his mother, just before he was born, there came an apparition of Proteus ... She was in no way frightened, but asked him what sort of child she would bear. And he answered: 'Myself.' 'And who are you?' she asked. 'Proteus,'

[11] See Andrew T. Lincoln, "Luke and Jesus' Conception: A Case of Double Paternity?" *JBL* 132.3 (2013): 639–58, and primary sources listed there.

answered he, the god of Egypt'" (*Life of Apollonius* 1.4). Ben notes that there is good reason to think that Philostratus, writing in the early third century, is deliberately creating a counternarrative that reflects knowledge of the Gospel stories about Jesus, in order to suggest they are not so unique.

Luke's Gospel as well as Acts holds the two ideas together: Jesus has both a human father, Joseph, and a divine father, God. In Acts 2.30, Peter names David a prophet who knew that "God had sworn with an oath to him that he would put one of his descendants on his throne." The verse follows from 2 Sam 7.12, where God promises David, "When your days are fulfilled and you lie down with your ancestors, I will raise up your offspring after you, who shall come forth from your body, and I will establish his kingdom." That is, David's heir is to be David's biological descendant. Ben notes that Jesus, as Joseph's adopted child, has all the rights and responsibilities as any child he might have conceived; Amy-Jill notes the lack of sources to justify this claim and finds, instead, what appears to be a Christian adjustment to the original promise to David, just as the reading of John the Baptist as Elijah coming to announce the messiah rather than the messianic age and the later promise of the messiah's "second coming" are Christian adjustments. Her point is not that these adjustments are "wrong"; rather, it is to show in part why Jews and Christians today sometimes find gaps in understanding on the subject of messianic views.

Like Zechariah, Mary queries the details: "How can this be, since I am a virgin?" (**vs. 34**). Unlike Zechariah, she is asking about practicalities, not possibilities. Luke makes no mention of the Greek translation of Isa 7.14, which Matthew (1.23) cites in regard to the virginal conception. Nor does Luke give any indication of the timing of the marriage between Mary and Joseph. The angel vaguely responds that through the agency of the Holy Spirit, the power of God will overshadow her. Therefore, the child will be both "holy" and "called Son of God" (**vs. 35**). The title "Son of God," first used here in Luke, is more than a metaphor. Roman emperors either were proclaimed, or proclaimed themselves, sons of gods; the title has, in the first century, a natal as well as political connotation. The title fits within the motif of the Greco-Roman biography with its concern for divine paternity. For the Jewish world, all people are children of God (so Luke's genealogy, in which Adam is also a "son of God" [3.38]), so the title is more provocative in the Roman, gentile context.

As proof of the legitimacy of his words – as if an angelic appearance is insufficient – Gabriel tells Mary about Elizabeth's pregnancy (**vs. 36**). Here we learn that Mary and Elizabeth are related and thus that Mary too is from a priestly family. Their pregnancies are also related: first an infertile woman conceives; even more miraculous is a virgin bearing a child. As Gabriel explains: "nothing will be impossible with God!" (**vs. 37**).

According to the NRSV, Mary responds, "Here I am, the servant of the Lord" (**vs. 38** see also vs. 48). However, the Greek *doulē* literally means "[female] slave." While in the biblical tradition only free people identify themselves as slaves of God, the expression today – especially in light of slavery in our own histories and the ongoing devastation of human trafficking – renders the epithet problematic. Further, as Judith Lieu notes, "It is all too easy to draw from here a picture of Mary who passively submits, and to use it to exalt such passive submission as a virtue."[12] Indeed, "Mary can become a submissive figure, a model to be imposed upon others of passive acceptance of the impositions, and worse, of whatever is declared God's will, or of those with power."[13] Alternatively, Mary's self-designation can function as an ironic indicator of both personal freedom and complete devotion: the only master Mary has is God, and she willingly places herself in divine hands (we will return to the use of slave language in our discussion of the various parables in which disciples are depicted as slaves, e.g., 12.37). The epithet also associates Mary with celebrated fellow "slaves of the Lord" or, as the NRSV reads, "servants": Moses (Josh 1.1); Joshua (Judg 2.8); Samuel (1 Sam 3.9–10); Saul (1 Sam 14.41); David (1 Sam 12.10; Psa 18, 36); Zeubbabel (1 Esdr 6.27); and, from the New Testament, Paul (Tit 1.1) and James (Jas 1.1). Collectively, Israel's prophets are God's slaves as well (e.g., 2 Kings 9.7; Ezra 9.11; Amos 3.7). Mary thus situates herself among kings, prophets, apostles, and evangelists.

THE VISITATION

Luke 1.39–40, called the "Visitation," depicts Mary's hasty trip from Nazareth in Galilee to the Judean hills (**vs. 39**) to the home of Elizabeth and Zechariah. Luke indicates no traveling companion for the eighty miles or so, no means of travel (foot, donkey, cart, etc.), and no stopping points. The focus is entirely on Mary, and the lack of details hints at her independence and resourcefulness. Contrary to some recent speculation, her haste has nothing to do with her fear that, pregnant out of wedlock, she would

---

[12] Judith Lieu, *The Gospel According to Luke* (London: Epworth Press, 1997; reprinted Eugene: Wipf and Stock, 2012), 7.
[13] Ibid., 9.

be stoned. That idea comes from a misreading of John 8, the account of the woman accused of adultery. That woman's accusers are not about to stone her, and no one is carrying stones (scenes of men dropping the stones, one by one, come from Hollywood, not Holy Word). The men who brought the charges are attempting to trap Jesus: if he says, "Stone her," they would accuse him of barbarism; if he says, "Don't stone her," they would accuse him of going against Torah without an explanation. Regarding Mary, Luke indicates no scandal, and even in Matthew's account, Joseph decides to divorce Mary privately, and so without scandal. It is modern readers, not the ancient text, that see Jews willing to stone anyone who steps out of cultural convention.

Mary enters "the house of Zechariah," but she greets Elizabeth (**vs. 40**). The focus is on two pregnant Jewish women. The scene can recollect the household of Ruth and Naomi, two women of different generations who fully cooperate; it also provides an alternative to the more common biblical depictions of rivals in the same household, such as Sarah and Hagar, Leah and Rachel, Peninnah and Hannah, and even Luke's account of Martha and Mary (10.38–42) and the Parable of the Prudent and Prodigal Sons (15.11–32). Whereas these other scenes suggest competition, none is present here. Elizabeth yields to Mary's more glorious role, just as John yields to Jesus.

Mary's greeting prompts John to "leap," and Elizabeth feels herself full not only with a sixth-month-old fetus, but also with the Holy Spirit (**vs. 41**). The child John, in utero, recognizes Mary and so Jesus. Those who want to quibble about biblical inerrancy point out that in John 1.33, the Baptizer responds that he did not know Jesus, and so they find a contradiction. Amy-Jill sees Luke's hand in the visitation scene and so does not find an historical problem. Neither does Ben, especially if Luke's point is that the Holy Spirit in John recognizes who the unborn child in Mary's womb is.

Elizabeth's cry is both exultation and prophecy: "Blessed are you among women" (**vs. 42**). Before she mentions the child Mary carries, she blesses Mary. Mary thus takes her place alongside other women proclaimed blessed: Jael (Judg 5.24) and Judith (Jtd 13.18).[14] The connection anticipates Mary's hymn, which, like those of Deborah and Judith, celebrates God's redemption of Israel.

In Luke's narrative, Mary is blessed not simply because she is pregnant with an extraordinary child; Mary herself is blessed, and so she is more

---

[14]   Brittany E. Wilson, "Pugnacious Precursors and the Bearer of Peace: Jael, Judith, and Mary in Luke 1:42," *CBQ* 68.3 (2006): 436–56.

than simply a womb. Elizabeth continues to focus on Mary, the "Mother of my Lord" (**vs. 43**). Luke does not tell us when Mary actually conceived, but the combination of this title, the reference to the fruit of her womb, and Mary's own comment that God has "done great things" for her (1.49) all suggest that she is pregnant at the time of this visitation.[15] It is thus Elizabeth who announces Mary's pregnancy. The focus on pregnancy continues as Elizabeth now confirms what the narrator had mentioned in vs. 41: her baby kicked (**vs. 44**). Marcion would be appalled at such a scene; pregnant women who want their children (we note that not all pregnant women do) would understand the physical as well as emotional implications of the indication of quickening.

According to Elizabeth, Mary is blessed not simply because she conceived, but because she "believed" – she trusted – that the ancient prophesies would be fulfilled (**vs. 45**). The Greek term for "believed" is the verbal form of the noun *pistis*, usually translated "faith." To have faith is to trust. This is Luke's first use of the term, although Mary's belief remains consistent in Luke's account, for her last appearance is with fellow believers in Jerusalem, following the death of her son (Acts 1.14). Elizabeth here positions Mary as an active agent: she recognizes Mary's response to Gabriel's annunciation. Faith, or trust, in the divine is something that is not merely an internal position; it is something that others can discern.

"What was spoken" to Mary is, as far as Luke's narrative is concerned, the prediction of the conception and role of her son along with the notice of Elizabeth's conception. Mary will now fill in the blanks of what this prediction means. Her hymn, traditionally called the "Magnificat" from the Latin for "magnifies" (**vs. 46**) is, in a number of early Latin manuscripts, attributed to Elizabeth. The song is Mary's, but it could be sung by anyone who can celebrate redemption. It might particularly speak to, or be sung by, women, since the biblical tradition places songs of victory on women's lips. The first "Mary," Moses' sister Miriam, exulted, "Sing to the Lord, for he has triumphed gloriously" (Exod 15.21); Deborah encourages others to pick up the tune, "To the sound of musicians at the watering places, there they repeat the triumphs of the Lord, the triumphs of his peasantry in Israel" (Judg 5.11). Hannah celebrates God, who not only "raises up the poor from the dust; and lifts the needy from the ash heap" (1 Sam 2.8) but also, anticipating David and, for Luke, anticipating David's descendant Jesus, "will

---

[15]   David T. Landry, "Narrative Logic in the Annunciation to Mary (Luke 1:26–38)," *JBL* 114 (1995): 65–79 (esp. 75–76).

give strength to his king, and exalt the power of his anointed" (1 Sam 2.10). Judith, too, sings of divine victory, this time how the "Lord Almighty has foiled" Israel's enemies "by the hand of a woman" (Jtd 16.5). Women do not merely sing of God's victory; they are active agents in bringing it about.

Although Mary sings the song, it is not about her, but about the power of God. The verses are a pastiche of divine epithets. The first attribute is Mary's reference to "God my savior" (**vs. 47**). This is the Gospel's first explicit reference to soteriology. Mary's hymn makes clear that she is not speaking of salvation in terms of getting into heaven. She is speaking of human liberation, as did Hannah those centuries past. In Jewish sources of the period and subsequently, God saves primarily from earthly persecution, not for eternal life. The earthly focus of salvation can be found, for example, in Ps 25.5: "Lead me in your truth, and teach me, for you are the God of my salvation ..." Luke's Gospel, together with the Christian tradition, will come to understand "salvation" also as a matter of eternal bliss versus eternal torment.[16]

From this exultation of joy and delight, Mary offers an expression of her own "lowliness" (**vs. 48a**, Greek: *tapeinosin*), which can also be translated as "humiliation." She draws upon Hannah's self-designation in 1 Sam 1.11 LXX; the NRSV translates the same term as "misery." This concern for lowliness *may* be allusion to the so-called *anawim*, that is, the humble or oppressed who seek God's salvation (Ps 34; 69.32–36; etc.). It could also simply indicate that Mary is not among the elite, whether economically or genealogically. The NRSV's "servant" translates the Greek *doulē*, again, "slave" (see the previous comments on vs. 38).

Whether all generations will call her blessed (**vs. 48b**) depends on the religious orientation of that generation. Roman Catholics, Eastern Orthodox Christians, and Muslims all celebrate Mary; their traditions add various new stories to her biography, some about her sanctity, and others about her immaculate conception and bodily ascension into heaven following her death. Within some Protestant circles, songs about Mary have been silenced; given those developed stories in the Roman Catholic tradition, Mary became collateral damage in the Protestant Reformation. While Luther, Calvin, Zwingli, Wesley, and others retained deep appreciation for Mary, the tradition swung against her, and especially against all the

---

[16]   See the study on "salvation" language in Luke-Acts in Witherington, *Acts of the Apostles*, pp. 822–43, which demonstrates that Luke can use the terminology to refer to rescue from danger, or healing from disease or hurt; for example, "your faith has saved you," in the context of Jesus' ministry, means "your faith has healed you."

postbiblical stories of her life and death.[17] For the Magnificat to ring true, Mary should be celebrated by all Jesus' followers.

Mary's praise of God who "has done great things for me" (**vs. 49**) echoes Deut 10.21: "He is your praise; he is your God, who has done for you these great and awesome things that your own eyes have seen." The concern for the sanctity of the "name," already shown in the *Kaddish deRabbanan* cited in the Introduction, speaks to the ineffability of the Hebrew letters rendered into English as YHWH. "The name" – Hebrew *ha-Shem* – becomes a circumlocution for the God of Israel. The divine attributes of which Mary sings find a comfortable home in Jewish liturgy.

The comfort continues, as Mary speaks of how divine mercy traverses the generations (**vs. 50**). She is here paraphrasing Ps 103.17 (LXX 102.17), "But the steadfast love (Hebrew: *chesed*; Greek: *eleos*, "mercy") of the Lord is from everlasting to everlasting on those who fear him, and his righteousness to children's children." The concern for "generations" is part of Luke's effort to anchor the story of Jesus into the story of Israel. What the ancient Israelites sought is what, according to Luke, Jesus offers: salvation from enemies, freedom from want. The first form of salvation surfaces in the next verse, as Mary sings of scattering the proud (**vs. 51**). These "proud" here go undefined. A second reading of the Gospel may see their incarnation among the various characters who are identified as "rich" or powerful, but who do not realize that their wealth should be used, as Scripture mandates, to support the poor, the widow, the orphan, and the stranger (Deut 15.11; 27.19; Isa 10.2; Zech 7.10; etc.)

The Magnificat continues by speaking of the role reversal that occurs when the powerful are brought low and the "lowly" (again, Greek *tapeinous*) find themselves uplifted (**vs. 52**). This role reversal should create some exegetical difficulty: do we want a reversal of fortune, such that the previously privileged will face torment and the poor will enjoy power and wealth, or is this vision simply shifting deck chairs on the Titanic – same system, different suffering players? Should anyone be "exalted," and if such exaltation is necessary, what are the criteria?

The more visceral celebration, "He has filled the hungry with good things, and sent the rich away empty" (**vs. 53**), draws from Hannah's menu,

---

[17] See Beverly Roberts Gaventa and Cynthia L. Rigby (eds.), *Blessed One: Protestant Perspectives on Mary* (Louisville: Westminster John Knox, 2002); Scot McKnight, *The Real Mary: Why Evangelical Christians Can Embrace the Mother of Jesus* (Brewster: Paraclete Press, 2006).

"Those who were full have hired themselves out for bread, but those who were hungry are fat with spoil" (1 Sam 2.5). It also evokes Psa 107:9, "For he satisfies the thirsty, and the hungry he fills with good things." Although derivative in parts, all these songs are new songs, set in new times and sung by new voices. For those who suffer now, such role reversals are sustaining; for those who seek "justice," however defined, role reversal within a consistent system of "haves" and "have nots" cannot, in the long run, be good news.

The next verse turns to the subject of Israel's political identity. Mary speaks of God's "servant Israel," that is, the Jewish people (**vs. 54**). Isaiah had already marked Israel as God's servant, as we see in Isa 41.8–9, "And you, Israel, my servant, Jacob, whom I have chosen, the offspring of Abraham, my friend … You are my servant, and I have chosen you and not cast you off." The Church would come to see Jesus as Isaiah's "suffering servant," who "has borne our infirmities and carried our diseases; yet we accounted him stricken, struck down by God, and afflicted" (Isa 53.4), while the dominant Jewish view has been to regard the servant as Israel, taken into exile and then restored to the homeland. In this case, Christians can double-dip: they can see the servant *both* as Israel and as Jesus.

The Magnificat concludes with a final allusion to Israel's Scripture and history, from generation to generation, with Mary's confidence that the promises made not only to Abraham, but to Abraham's descendants (Greek *sperma*, "seed"), the Jewish people, will be fulfilled (**vs. 55**). The refrains of what God has done – shown strength, brought down and lifted up, filled and sent away, helped – are not only metaphors. The hungry who are filled are not just spiritual seekers; they are people who do not have enough to eat. The downtrodden are those who face oppression. Mary is thus issuing a political manifesto: when the promises of God come to fruition, people will have enough to eat; the rich will no longer exploit the poor.

Mary is also prophesying: the verbs in the hymn are in the aorist, or past tense: in Mary's imagination, God has already performed these social reversals. For Mary, the victory is already won. Although Luke does not explicitly name Mary a prophet, her self-designation of "slave of the Lord" together with the role of the Holy Spirit in her life, the women prophets of Israel's Scriptures (Miriam, Deborah, Huldah, Noadiah) and additional prophets named by the Rabbis (Sarah, Hannah, Abigail, Esther [*b. Meg.* 14a–b]), as well as Anna, whom we meet in Luke 2.36, and Philip's four prophesying virgin daughters (Acts 21.9), confirms her prophetic role.[18]

Mary stays until Elizabeth's ninth month (**vs. 56**), but she returns home before John's birth. Luke does not explain Mary's timing, but it does have a practical as well as pastoral import. Were the "Mother of [her] Lord" (vs. 43) to remain, Mary rather than Elizabeth and so John would be the focus of attention. The "home" also goes unspecified: we do not know if Mary returned to a home she herself owned, the home of her parents, or the home she shared with Joseph.

THE BIRTH AND NAMING OF JOHN

Luke returns focus to Elizabeth, who now bears her son (**vs. 57**). The birth prompts her rejoicing and that of her neighbors (**vs. 58**), as Gabriel had predicted (vs. 14). The neighbors recognize the divine mercy showed to Elizabeth, but ironically, they do not mention Zechariah. Elizabeth had been the one to seclude herself, so now any embarrassment or stigma she personally felt regarding her infertility is removed.

Again evoking Torah, Luke mentions the baby's circumcision on the eighth day (Gen 17.11–12) and so the "sign of the covenant" between God and the Jewish people (**vs. 59**). "They" (relatives? neighbors?) had planned to name the child after his father, but Elizabeth insists that he be named "John," according to the angel's instructions (1.13), which Zechariah, still mute, must have communicated to her (**vs. 60**). From late rabbinic times, the tradition developed that Jewish boys would be named at their circumcision; Luke appears to be the earliest attestation of this practice. Generally, children were named after grandparents rather than fathers (cf. 1 Mac 2.1–2), although naming a child after a parent was not unknown.

The mother's naming a child would not be unusual: Eve had named Seth; Rachel and Leah name their children. What is unusual, a break in tradition, is giving the child a name that "none of [his] relatives has" (**vs. 61**). Children's names are one way of remembering, even honoring, family members. The name, and so the memory, remains alive in Israel. John's name breaks with convention, even as it intimates a break in family

---

[18] Clayton N. Croy, "Mantic Mary? The Virgin Mother as Prophet in Luke 1.26–56 and the Early Church," *Journal for the Study of the New Testament* 34.3 (2012): 354–76, proposes that Luke withheld the title "prophet" from Mary lest readers associate her prophecy with the pagan view of the god as sexually penetrating the virgin prophetess (cf. Acts 16.16).

ties.[19] He will not be a priest in the Temple like his father; instead, he will assume the role of prophet.

The people then make signs to Zechariah, which suggests that his muteness also occasioned his deafness (**vs. 62**). If this is the case, then he could neither hear nor speak during Mary's visit with his wife. The readers are thus privileged to hear the women's words while the man in the household cannot. Zechariah confirms Elizabeth's announcement by writing the name "John" on a tablet: Luke thereby subtly indicates that the priest and at least some others in the gathering are literate (**vs. 63**). Later, Luke will indicate that Jesus also has the ability to read (4.17). Following this confirmation, Zechariah regains his speech (**vs. 64**) and so displays yet another miracle. Like Mary, he begins not with the notice of the child but with praise of God. The crowd's reaction is one of both of fear and of proclamation, for the story of the birth of John and the recovery of speech and hearing to his father spreads through the entire region (**vs. 65**). Similar proclamations about Jesus will be made, but they will spread far beyond the hill country of Judea.

There is always a gap between a sign and what it signifies. Elizabeth, the infertile woman, has borne a son; the son will be named "John" and not "Zechariah" or the name of any other relatives; the deaf-mute priest has regained his hearing and his speech. But what these miracles indicate remains unstated. Appropriately, the people who have heard this good news ponder its meaning, although they recognize that the meaning applies primarily to the baby: what will be his role, given that the hand of the Lord (Greek: *kyrios*; the title "lord" will later be applied to Jesus, as it is already by Elizabeth in vs. 43; here it refers to God) is with him? (**vs. 66**). From this reaction, the people in the story might conclude that John is to be a messianic figure; readers who know the story of Mary know that such a claim would be a misjudgment.

The formerly mute priest, filled like his wife with the Holy Spirit (**vs. 67**), then sings his own new song, traditionally called the "Benedictus," from the Latin for "Blessed be." Luke explicitly calls this song a "prophecy"; although the Magnficat does not receive this designation, the two hymns have the same function: to praise God who fulfills promises to Israel of liberation and redemption (**vs. 68**). The NRSV's "looked favorably on his people" (Greek: *episkeptomai*) is better translated, in this context, as "visited his people"; the divine involvement in the miraculous pregnancies is more than

---

[19] See Karl A. Kuhn, "Deaf or Defiant? The Literary, Cultural, and Affective-Rhetorical Keys to the Naming of John (Luke 1:57–80)," *CBQ* 75.3 (2013): 486–503.

simply a favorable look. Luke gives the impression of direct divine presence. More, like Mary, Zechariah renders this divine favor, this "redemption" of the people, as an event that has already occurred. Like Mary, he sees the victor and the redemption as a fact in history, not a promise yet to be fulfilled. Readers may see in his proclamation a recognition of Jesus' conception and its import.

Zechariah's initial celebration of the raising of a "mighty savior" (**vs. 69**) is, literally, "horn of salvation," a phrase found also not only in Psa 18.2, but connected to Hannah's song in 1 Sam 2.10; she too sings of the "horn of his anointed." The reference is not to Zechariah's own son John, but about Mary's son, Jesus, since Jesus is through Joseph of the "house of his servant David" (**vs. 69**). *How* Jesus and John will relate remains yet to be determined. Similarly, readers will need to continue through the Gospel to determine how Jesus will serve as "savior." This is Luke's first notice of the term.

The priest then links his song to Israel's prophets and thereby links both Jesus and John into Israel's history (**vs. 70**). As Mary evoked God's "servant Israel" (vs. 54) according to the covenantal promises made to "Abraham and his descendants forever" (vs. 55), so Zechariah sings of God's promises of salvation from enemies (**vs. 71**), the promise to the ancestors, and the holy covenant (**vs. 72**). In the same way the Gospel will need to explain the salvation Jesus provides, it also needs to explain what, exactly, these promises are and how they will be fulfilled. God's promises to Abraham and his descendants are detailed in Gen 22.16–18: "By myself I have sworn, says the Lord: Because you have done this, and have not withheld your son, your only son, I will indeed bless you, and I will make your offspring as numerous as the stars of heaven and as the sand that is on the seashore. And your offspring shall possess the gate of their enemies, and by your offspring shall all the nations of the earth gain blessing for themselves, because you have obeyed my voice." The promise here hints at the Christian universal mission, by which all the gentiles will also be blessed. Peter's confirms this focus when he tells the "Israelites," that is, the Jews, "You are the descendants of the prophets and of the covenant that God gave to your ancestors, saying to Abraham, 'And in your descendants all the families of the earth shall be blessed'" (Acts 3.25).

Luke does not, however, speak of the fulfillment of other promises, such as the promise of the land (Gen 12.7; 13.15–17; 15.18; 17.8; 26.3–4; 28.4, 13; 35.12; etc.). The Third Gospel, with its focus ultimately on the gentile mission, drops the promise of the land. Here we begin to see different messianic expectations of Jews and Christians. The traditional Jewish view of the messianic age includes a role for the land of Israel and for Jews to live there, including the return of the so-called "ten lost tribes" removed from northern Israel by the Assyrians in 722; the traditional Christian view, which does not retain a focus on ethnicity, did not start to speak of the land as "holy" or even as important until the time of Constantine, when the land came into Christian hands.

In speaking of the "oath" God swore to Abraham (**vs. 73**), Zechariah now focuses on being rescued from enemies and so serving God without fear (**vs. 74**). The reference to "serving" (Greek: *latreō*) carries a connotation of the Temple service; given Zechariah's priestly role, the connotation holds; given that Luke is well aware that the Romans destroyed the Temple, the connotation has to be adjusted to indicate any form of worship. Given that some followers of Jesus were persecuted *because* of their worship, Zechariah's hymn also looks forward not only to Jesus' own mission, but to its own fulfillment and thus universal redemption. That will be the time of "holiness and righteousness" (**vs. 75**).

Finally turning to his own son, Zechariah outlines how John fits into this pattern of fulfilled promises. John will be a prophet, and he will "go before the Lord to prepare his ways" (**vs. 76**). The verse takes its lyric from Isa 40.3, "A voice cries out, 'In the wilderness prepare the way of the Lord,'" but plays it in a new key. The "lord" referenced here is not God (the Father) but Jesus of Nazareth. The refrain will be heard again in 3.4, where Luke explicitly applies Isa 40.3 to John. Hints also of the Christian movement appear in the term "ways"; the underlying Greek is the word *hodos*, "way," the self-designation of Jesus followers (Act 9.1–2).

The common claims that prophecy had ended and therefore that John represents a new beginning do not quite match what the sources of the time tell us. While the prophetic canon was basically closed, Josephus considers himself a prophet and notes that many of the figures now known as messianic pretenders (Theudas, the Egyptian, etc.) considered themselves, and were considered by others, to be prophets (*Ant.* 20.97, 169) as he does Cleodemus the historian and the Hasmonean priest/king John Hyrcanus (*Ant.* 3.218, 322) as well as the Essenes (*War* 2.159). As Rebecca Gray summarizes, "In spite of the fact that Josephus seems to have believed that prophecy belonged, in some sense to the past, it can be demonstrated that he thought that there were still, in his own day, individuals who said and did very much the same sorts of things as the ancient prophets had said and done."[20] John's role is notable, but it is not unique for the period.

---

[20]   Rebecca Gray, *Prophetic Figures in Late Second Temple Jewish Palestine: The Evidence from Josephus* (New York: Oxford University Press, 1993), 8.

John's specific role will be to give "knowledge of salvation" (**vs. 77**). Based on Mary's Magnificat and the earlier content of the Benedictus, readers would be justified in seeing this knowledge as related to political liberation: food for the hungry; voice for the disempowered. But here the job description changes: the salvation is determined by "forgiveness of sins." The liberation is thus not (explicitly) from persecution or poverty, but from sin. Judaism already spoke of divine forgiveness, and Luke notes that such forgiveness could be found in sincere repentance (see 18.14; see also Isa 55.7; Psa 25.18). Thus, this type of forgiveness has to have a distinct meaning. The historical John baptized people as a sign that they had repented and so were prepared for the in-breaking of the messianic age (see comments on Luke 3). The Gospel will describe this forgiveness not only in terms of John's baptism, but in terms of Jesus' life, death, and resurrection.

The hymn concludes with a prediction: divine mercy will come to the people (**vs. 78**); this divine mercy that comes from on high will be incarnated in Jesus. He will come specifically to "those who sit in darkness and in the shadow of death" (**vs. 79**). The focus is becoming universal, since anyone can "walk in the shadow of death" (the King James Version has the well-known translation of Psa 23.4, "Yea, though I walk through the valley of the shadow of death ..."; the NRSV offers the less poetic "walk through the darkest valley"; see also Matt 4.16). The line may also suggest Psa 107.10,14, which speaks of people who "sat in darkness and in gloom, prisoners in misery and in irons," who repented of their rebellion against God and whom then God saved.

The chapter ends with John's growth from infancy to adulthood, and the notice that he was in the wilderness (**vs. 80**) until his public appearance as the Baptizer. Luke says nothing about a sojourn with the covenanters at Qumran; nor does Luke associate John with the Essenes. For the Third Gospel, John's role is to prepare for Jesus' messianic manifestation.

BRIDGING THE HORIZONS

1. The Stigma of Childlessness

Elizabeth speaks of the "disgrace" (**vs. 25**) that her infertility causes. Women today face the same stigma. Those who wish to conceive but cannot are objects of pity, and often advice that only makes the situation worse: "relax" or "pray harder." They may resort to expensive and invasive medical procedures even while given the message that what they are doing is unnatural, or even sinful. Women who choose not to have children are coded as selfish or unnatural.

Biblical interpretation that equates childlessness with sin makes the situation of the infertile woman all the worse. When women read, "What everyone knows, or knew in the Judean world of antiquity, is that childlessness is a consequence of a blameworthy life and so a sign of God's curse,"[21] they may internalize the critique; their friends and neighbors in turn may look at them not only with pity, but also with condemnation.

This common interpretation is a misreading of the Bible.[22] None of the texts typically cited indicates that infertility is a punishment for sin, or that the infertile woman is to blame for her condition. Instead, the text insists, repeatedly, that it is God who opens and closes wombs, and God does so for reasons both unexplained and inexplicable. It also acknowledges that women feel envy of those who can and do conceive. "When Rachel saw that she bore Jacob no children, she envied her sister; and she said to Jacob, 'Give me children, or I shall die!' " (Gen 30.1). When Elkanah asks, "Hannah, why do you weep? Why do you not eat? Why is your heart sad? Am I not more to you than ten sons?" (1 Sam 1.8), he does not realize that the answer is, "No, you are not." Psalm 127.4–5 associates fertility with a man's happiness: "Like arrows in the hand of a warrior are the sons of one's youth; Happy is the man who has his quiver full of them"; the converse is not sin, but sadness. The women who wish to but cannot conceive are not blameworthy, they are desperately sad.

Other stories provide small comfort. A number of admirable biblical women are childless, or at least no mention is made of their having had children. Miriam, Deborah, Esther, Ruth, Judith, and on to the New Testament figures of Anna (Luke 2), Mary and Martha, Mary Magdalene, Lydia, Priscilla, and Philip's four virgin daughters. The women who prophesy in Corinth are not described as mothers; neither is Phoebe the deacon or Junia the apostle of Romans 16. Thus, to be without children is not, for the biblical tradition, a curse. Jesus speaks of the ideal, angelic state as the time when "those who are considered worthy of a place in that age and in the resurrection from the dead neither marry nor are given in marriage" (20.35) and thus when there is no procreation. But such notices will not ease the heart of a woman who wants to have a child. Elizabeth's story raises, poignantly, the feelings of a woman struggling with infertility. Before we move

---

[21]   Green, *Gospel of Luke*, 4.
[22]   Moss and Baden, *Reconceiving Infertility*.

to the celebration of her child, we should pause to consider her situation. The response should not be judgment, or advice, but empathy and support.

2. The Virginal Conception and Christian Faith

Belief in the literal virginal conception – that Mary conceived Jesus "through" the agency of the Holy Spirit and without the presence of a male partner – has become somewhat of a litmus test of being a good Christian. Those who suggest the story is metaphor, let alone those who propose that Mary was seduced or raped, are vilified not only as "nonbelievers" but as evil. Jane Schaberg, the former nun whose 1987 volume, *The Illegitimacy of Jesus*, argued precisely as the title suggests, received death threats.[23] In turn, some liberals find belief in a literal virginal conception to be, like belief in a literal resurrection from the dead and a literal, bodily ascension into heaven, the stuff of fairy tales. Jesus becomes in this configuration at best yet another Greek demigod, like Hercules or Theseus or Perseus, with a divine father and a human mother. Some see the entire scenario as a fantastic invention; others posit that Luke received all the details about the annunciation by Gabriel, the visit with Elizabeth, the trip to Bethlehem, the shepherds, as well as the lyrics of the Magnificat, from Mary directly.

Discussion of the historicity of the Nativity appears in pretty much every commentary on Matthew and Luke, the two Gospels in which the stories appear. Most note that Isaiah 7.14 in the Hebrew mentions nothing about a virginal conception and that Matthew's proof-text (Matt 1.23) is from the Septuagint. Most mention the claim by the second-century pagan Celsus (Origen, *Contra Celsum* 1.32) that Mary committed adultery with a Roman soldier named Panthera, and a few note the first-century epitaph, found in Germany, of a fellow conveniently named Tiberius Julius Abdes Pantera.

The debates become precious; nothing new has been cited in years. Perhaps there are better ways of addressing Luke's account without the name-calling. Amy-Jill suggests that, like the resurrection, the virginal conception should be seen as a matter of faith, not history. If one's view

---

[23] Jane Schaberg, *The Illegitimacy of Jesus: A Feminist Theological Interpretation of the Infancy Narratives, Expanded Twentieth Anniversary* (Sheffield: Sheffield Phoenix, 2006; original 1987). See the helpful summary of the debate between Schaberg and Raymond E. Brown (author of *The Birth of the Messiah: A Commentary on the Infancy Narratives in the Gospels of Matthew and Luke*, new updated ed. [ABRL; Garden City: Doubleday, 1993]), by Frank Reilly, "Jane Schaberg, Raymond E. Brown, and the Problem of the Illegitimacy of Jesus," *JFSR* 21.1 (2005): 57–80.

of history includes miracles – by which we mean the direct, and singular, intervention of the biblical God into history to disrupt the course of nature – then one might well accept the reality of a virginal conception. At the same time, those holding the view of a supernatural break in history would need to determine if _only_ biblical accounts fit their view of history: for example, is Jesus' virginal conception a "fact," whereas the divine dictation of the Qu'ran to Mohammed is simply a legend? If one's view of history does not accommodate supernatural breaks in the natural world, then one should read Luke sympathetically (as one should do with anyone's Scripture) even if one does not find it historically credible. There are some historical events that "happened," such as the destruction of the Jerusalem Temple in 70; this fact is described by external (e.g., Roman, Christian) as well as internal (Jewish) texts and demonstrated by archaeological remains (such as the Arch of Titus and the Western Wall, the Kotel). Other events, especially the miraculous ones, fall into a different category.

Belief in supernatural events, especially those reported only by insiders, finally, has nothing to do with historical proof. Belief is not like Sudoku, in which sufficient logic, and an eraser, will yield the singular and correct answer. Belief is like love. And love has nothing to do with logic. Rather than condemn people for their beliefs, or their loves, the better move is for everyone to read Luke 1 and see what message occurs to them. For some, it will be the power and graciousness of the divine, who condescends to take on human flesh. For others, it will be the notice that the child of an unwed mother from a backwater village is, like every other child, a child of God.

For me (Amy-Jill), when I read the Lucan infancy accounts, I engage in what is called the "willing suspension of disbelief." That is, I read Luke as the Evangelist would have any ideal reader read, and so I am moved by the narrative. I don't have to believe that an actual angel spoke to a priest in the Temple or a virgin in the Galilee to see power and inspiration in the narrative. The text transports me to a different world, not one of my own, and in that world miracles can happen.

Ben suggests that a category distinction between faith and history doesn't much work, since when it comes to the virginal conception or bodily resurrection we are talking about faith that something happened _in history_. True enough, even credible evidence that something happened in ancient history doesn't amount to airtight proof it happened, but then we have no airtight proof that anything happened in antiquity, and in any case, "proof" in the scientific sphere is one thing, historical validity and likelihood is another. Applying scientific standard of proofs derived from chemistry or biology or the like to historical evidence is a category mistake, rather like trying to measure someone's weight with a sundial. Faith in the miraculous is not faith in faith; it is faith that various things happened in human history, and for that matter still happen today.[24] In addition, it is problematic to suggest that the God who set up the "laws of nature" in the first place would contravene them on a whim from time to time by intervening in the process. Better is the suggestion that miracles go beyond the known laws or scientific knowledge that we now have, rather than going against them. Faith and science do not need to be at odds with one another if faith and science both stay open to further evidence and correction of previously erroneous assumptions and conclusions.

---

[24] See Craig Keener, *Miracles: The Credibility of the New Testament Accounts,* 2 volumes (Grand Rapids: Baker, 2011).

Luke 2 Jesus' Birth and Childhood

¹ In those days a decree went out from Emperor Augustus that all the world should be registered. ² This was the first registration and was taken while Quirinius was governor of Syria. ³ All went to their own towns to be registered. ⁴ Joseph also went from the town of Nazareth in Galilee to Judea, to the city of David called Bethlehem, because he was descended from the house and family of David. ⁵ He went to be registered with Mary, to whom he was engaged and who was expecting a child. ⁶ While they were there, the time came for her to deliver her child. ⁷And she gave birth to her firstborn son and wrapped him in bands of cloth, and laid him in a manger, because there was no place for them in the inn.

⁸ In that region there were shepherds living in the fields, keeping watch over their flock by night. ⁹ Then an angel of the Lord stood before them, and the glory of the Lord shone around them, and they were terrified. ¹⁰ But the angel said to them, "Do not be afraid; for see – I am bringing you good news of great joy for all the people: ¹¹ to you is born this day in the city of David a Savior, who is the Messiah, the Lord. ¹² This will be a sign for you: you will find a child wrapped in bands of cloth and lying in a manger." ¹³ And suddenly there was with the angel a multitude of the heavenly host, praising God and saying, ¹⁴ "Glory to God in the highest heaven, and on earth peace among those whom he favors!"

¹⁵ When the angels had left them and gone into heaven, the shepherds said to one another, "Let us go now to Bethlehem and see this thing that has taken place, which the Lord has made known to us." ¹⁶ So they went with haste and found Mary and Joseph, and the child lying in the manger. ¹⁷ When they saw this, they made known what had been told them about this child; ¹⁸ and all who heard it were amazed at what the shepherds told

them. ¹⁹ But Mary treasured all these words and pondered them in her heart. ²⁰ The shepherds returned, glorifying and praising God for all they had heard and seen, as it had been told them.

THE PRESENTATION OF JESUS IN THE TEMPLE

²¹ After eight days had passed, it was time to circumcise the child; and he was called Jesus, the name given by the angel before he was conceived in the womb.

²² When the time came for their purification according to the law of Moses, they brought him up to Jerusalem to present him to the Lord ²³ (as it is written in the law of the Lord, "Every firstborn male shall be designated as holy to the Lord"), ²⁴ and they offered a sacrifice according to what is stated in the law of the Lord, "a pair of turtledoves or two young pigeons."

²⁵ Now there was a man in Jerusalem whose name was Simeon; this man was righteous and devout, looking forward to the consolation of Israel, and the Holy Spirit rested on him. ²⁶ It had been revealed to him by the Holy Spirit that he would not see death before he had seen the Lord's Messiah. ²⁷ Guided by the Spirit, Simeon came into the temple; and when the parents brought in the child Jesus, to do for him what was customary under the law, ²⁸ Simeon took him in his arms and praised God, saying,

²⁹ "Master, now you are dismissing your servant in peace,
      according to your word;
³⁰ for my eyes have seen your salvation,
³¹ which you have prepared in the presence of all peoples,
³² a light for revelation to the Gentiles
      and for glory to your people Israel."

³³ And the child's father and mother were amazed at what was being said about him. ³⁴ Then Simeon blessed them and said to his mother Mary, "This child is destined for the falling and the rising of many in Israel, and to be a sign that will be opposed ³⁵ so that the inner thoughts of many will be revealed – and a sword will pierce your own soul too."

³⁶ There was also a prophet, Anna the daughter of Phanuel, of the tribe of Asher. She was of a great age, having lived with her husband seven years after her marriage, ³⁷ then as a widow to the age of eighty-four. She never left the temple but worshiped there with fasting and prayer night and day. ³⁸ At that moment she came, and began to praise God and to speak about the child to all who were looking for the redemption of Jerusalem.

JESUS AND HIS PARENTS

[39] When they had finished everything required by the law of the Lord, they returned to Galilee, to their own town of Nazareth. [40] The child grew and became strong, filled with wisdom; and the favor of God was upon him. [41] Now every year his parents went to Jerusalem for the festival of the Passover. [42] And when he was twelve years old, they went up as usual for the festival. [43] When the festival was ended and they started to return, the boy Jesus stayed behind in Jerusalem, but his parents did not know it. [44] Assuming that he was in the group of travelers, they went a day's journey. Then they started to look for him among their relatives and friends. [45] When they did not find him, they returned to Jerusalem to search for him. [46] After three days they found him in the temple, sitting among the teachers, listening to them and asking them questions. [47] And all who heard him were amazed at his understanding and his answers. [48] When his parents saw him they were astonished; and his mother said to him, "Child, why have you treated us like this? Look, your father and I have been searching for you in great anxiety." [49] He said to them, "Why were you searching for me? Did you not know that I must be in my Father's house?" [50] But they did not understand what he said to them. [51] Then he went down with them and came to Nazareth, and was obedient to them. His mother treasured all these things in her heart.

[52] And Jesus increased in wisdom and in years, and in divine and human favor.

THE BIRTH OF JESUS

Luke sets the Nativity account at the time when the Roman emperor seeks to enroll "all the world" (**vs. 1**); immediately, Theophilus and so all readers are offered a choice between the realm of Caesar and the realm of God. Luke's hyperbole encourages this choice, since no census encompasses "all the world." As John Meier, states, "Attempts to reconcile Luke 2.1 with the facts of ancient history are hopelessly contrived."[1] The Roman census was a local affair conducted by local officials. Ben notes that all provincial governors or client kings were the ones who took the censuses and collected the taxes and they were under the authority and direction of Caesar. Amy-Jill adds

---

[1] John Meier, *A Marginal Jew: Rethinking the Historical Jesus*, 5 volumes (ABRL; New York: Doubleday, 1991), 1. 213.

that local authorities could collect taxes at their own discretion and that such collections were not universally imposed. Caesar will count the people for the purposes of taxation; Jesus will count for the purposes of serving others. The setting of Jesus' birth presents a second contrast, this one with John the Baptizer, who was born at the time of King Herod of Judea (1.5). In the step-parallelism pattern, John had a local impact while Jesus will have a global one.

That this census, according to Luke, took place "while Quirinius was governor of Syria" (**vs. 2**) has caused enormous debate. According to Matthew's Gospel, Jesus was born sometime before 4 BCE, the date of Herod's death and so prior to Quirinius's assumption of power. Josephus locates Quirinius as taking office in 6 CE.

There are four major solutions to this apparent discrepancy. First, we could translate **vs. 2** as: "this registration happened first (i.e., before) Quirinius was governor of Syria," although this approach strains the Greek.[2] Second, we could suggest that Josephus got his facts wrong, although the claim is unlikely given the governor's major role. Third, as we suggest in Chapter 1, we can regard Matthew's setting of Jesus' birth at the time of Herod the Great to be midrash rather than history, and we can take the "King Herod" of Luke 1.5 as a reference to Herod Archelaus. Or fourth, we can acknowledge the discrepancy but note that Luke is less concerned with dating than with making a political point. By mentioning a census and including the name Quirinius, Luke's readers would realize that Jesus is born into a family obedient to Rome's dictates even as their situation demonstrates the Empire's abuses.

In 6 CE, Quirinius – sent by Rome to take direct control over Archelaus's territory of Judea – did take a census, and his action sparked Judas the Galilean to lead a revolt. The rebels who rejected direct Roman rule gave rise to what Josephus calls the "Fourth Philosophy" or the Zealot movement in Galilee (*War* 2.8.2; 118; cf. *Ant.* 18.1). Descendants of Judas would lead the revolt in 66. In Acts 5.37, Gamaliel reminds his audience, "Judas the Galilean rose up at the time of the census and got people to follow him; he also perished, and all who followed him were scattered." Thus, Luke may have located Jesus' birth at the time of the census to indicate that Jesus'

---

[2]   See Brook W. R. Pearson, "The Lucan Census, Revisited," *CBQ* 61.2 (1999): 262–82 (esp. 278–82). Another grammatically feasible option is "this registration became most important (later) when Quirinius was governing Syria." See the detailed discussion in M. M. Culy et al., *Luke. A Handbook on the Greek Text* (Waco: Baylor University Press, 2010), 64–65.

movement was anything but Zealot-inspired. It did, however, occur not only at a time of Roman rule, but at a time when Rome controlled both money and movement.

One further notice both shows Luke's literary and apologetic talents even as it complicates historical reconstruction. Ps 87:6 (LXX 86) states, "The Lord records, as he registers the peoples, 'This one was born there,' *Selah*." That the Psalm was interpreted messianically cannot be ruled out.[3]

Luke's claim that everyone went to their "own towns" (**vs. 3**) creates another historical problem. The Roman census counted people where they lived because their taxes were related to where they owned property. The census also determined the number of men eligible for military service, so women generally were not counted. It is possible that Joseph owned property in Bethlehem. Matthew indicates that Mary and Joseph have a home in Bethlehem but has them relocating to Nazareth in Galilee after fleeing from Herod's troops to Egypt. Mark D. Smith, citing studies of Egyptian census data, notes that people who resided in major metropolitan areas (Greek *metropoleis*) received a tax reduction of as much as 50 percent; therefore, Joseph may have gone to "Bethlehem to maintain the legal status of his property as well as to take advantage of a tax loophole."[4] It is also possible that Luke uses the motif of the census as the mechanism by which Mary and Joseph arrive in Bethlehem so that Jesus can be born there.[5] For Luke, the focus is less on the mechanism of the census – Luke never recounts the enrollment – than on the connection of Joseph to "the city of David" because he was "descended from the house and family of David" (**vs. 4**). Continuing the motif of "double paternity" in Chapter 1, Luke establishes Jesus, through Joseph, as the heir to David's throne. Again, the challenge to Roman rule is implicit, but palpable. Ben notes that Rome did not consider client kings such as Herod Antipas, Herod Philip, or Herod Archelaeus as a threat to their rule unless they behaved badly, and there is no reason why the birth of a new Jewish king would inherently be seen as a threat. He sees Amy-Jill as overreading the contrast between the kingship of Jesus and the rule of Caesar, something Luke does not want to do.[6] On the contrast between the two reigns, here we agree to disagree.

3	François Bovon, *A Commentary on the Gospel of Luke 1:1–9:50* (Hermeneia; Minneapolis: Fortress Press, 2002), 83.

4	Mark D. Smith, "Of Jesus and Quirinius," *CBQ* 62.2 (2000): 278–93 (290).

5	See the detailed discussion in John Nolland, *Luke 1–9.20* (WBC 35a; Nashville: Thomas Nelson, 2000), 99–103 and the bibliography there.

6	See C. Bryan, *Render to Caesar. Jesus, the Early Church and the Roman Superpower* (Oxford: Oxford University Press, 2005).

Vs. 5 is an anodyne notice that while Mary is pregnant, she and Joseph are not yet married. Unlike Matthew, Luke records no potential problem regarding this situation. Nor does Luke discuss why Mary accompanied Joseph, when the two married, or even what Joseph's reaction was to her pregnancy. For Luke, the central concern is that Jesus, the "son of David," be born in Bethlehem, the home of David (**vs. 6**).

Arriving in Bethlehem, Joseph and Mary go not to an inn or hostel but rather to a private room, perhaps in the house of a friend or relative. The term in **vs. 7** translated "inn" (Greek: *kataluma*) refers to such a "guest room" or rented public space, as we see in 22.11, where Jesus instructs his disciples, "Say to the owner of the house, 'The teacher asks you, "where is the guest room (*kataluma*), where I may eat the Passover with my disciples?" ' " Luke's specific term for inn, *pandocheion*, appears in 10.34 (the location where the Samaritan rescuer took the wounded traveler). "No place for them in the *kataluma*" means that in this space, there was no room *for Mary to have a baby.* The stable provides a modicum of privacy. Mary and Joseph may even have had their child in the back portion of Joseph's ancestral home where, perhaps, animals would be fed, because the guest room in the family home was already occupied. Popular stories that the innkeeper rejected the couple because they could not pay, not only lack any basis in Luke's Gospel, they also reinforce false and negative stereotypes of greedy Jews. The recently surfaced claim that the innkeeper did not want Mary to give birth under his roof because she would create ritual impurity for all involved similarly introduces false and negative stereotypes about Jews and Judaism.[7] They have no place in any proclamation of the Gospel.

In Bethlehem, Mary "gave birth to her firstborn son" (**vs. 7**); the expression "firstborn" (Greek: *prōtotokos*) does suggest that she will have other children. Had Luke wished to note he was her only child, the word *monogenēs* (as in 7.12) would have been appropriate. Luke goes on to mention Jesus' brothers and sisters, so readers would likely presume Jesus was the first of Mary's several children.[8] By specifying Jesus as the firstborn, a point readers might have already presumed given that in Chapter 1 Mary had not yet "known a man" (1.34), Luke may be drawing a connection between Jesus and Israel as God's "firstborn" child (see Exod 4:22 LXX). New Testament readers can also

---

7   E.g., Michael Hesemann, *Mary of Nazareth: History, Archaeology, Legends* (San Francisco: Ignatius Press, 2016; translation of *Maria von Nazareth; Geschichte, Archäolgie, Legende* [Augburg: Sankt Ulrich Verlag, 2011]), 105.

8   See discussion in Alan Culpepper, "The Gospel of Luke," in Leander E. Keck (ed.), *The New Interpreter's Bible*, Vol. 9, *Luke-John* (Nashville: Abingdon, 1995), 3–490 (63).

draw connections to Jesus' role as firstborn of the new family of faith (Rom 8.29), of creation (Col 1.15), and of the dead (Col 1.18; Rev 1.5).

Mary wraps her firstborn in strips of cloth, a practice designed to keep the limbs of infants straight as well as to keep them warm (see Job 38.9; Ezek 16.4 LXX).[9] She then places him in a manger, that is, a feeding trough. The symbolism is often lost on modern readers, whose manger displays may be overpopulated with at least three kings, several shepherds, animals, a little drummer boy, the littlest angel, and perhaps a lobster; the crèche itself was a much simpler display originally created by Francis of Assisi in the thirteenth century. The import of the manger – minus the animals, the kings, and the commercialization – is that Jesus, who will give his body as food for his followers, is already found in the place where food is provided. Or perhaps Luke is emphasizing the vulnerability and true humanity of the one who would be the Savior of the world.

The symbolism may also extend to the clothes: "Can the threefold, deliberate phrasing in the Greek of 'wrapped him in cloth strips, placed him in a manger, because there was no place' perhaps anticipate the same threefold rhythm of 'wrapped him in linen cloth, placed him in a rock-hewn tomb, where no one had yet been laid' (23.53), so that the birth and burial mirror each other?"[10] We find leaving this thesis in question form appropriate. In any case, "laid in a manger" emphasizes the humble circumstances of Jesus' birth.

The episode about the shepherds in vss. 8–20 takes up more space than the discussion of the birth. The scene resembles the nativity accounts of Oedipus, Paris, and Romulus, who were attended by shepherds.[11] Once these images are in place, indeed once Luke mentions that there were shepherds in the region (**vs. 8**), readers may continue the connections: like Orpheus, Jesus will ascend from the dead; like Romulus, he will become known as the founder of a new kingdom. They may also think of the various shepherds in Israel's history: Rachel, Moses, and especially David.

Those ancient readers would not, however, view shepherds as "unclean and degraded persons" or "expendables."[12] Again, such claims misread history and distort the statements in the Mishnah and the Talmud.[13] The usually

---

[9]   See Johnson, *Gospel of Luke*, 50.
[10]   Ibid., 53.
[11]   Bovon, *Commentary on the Gospel of Luke*, 87
[12]   Green, *Gospel of Luke*, 11.
[13]   See the cogent discussion by Sarah Harris, "Why Are There Shepherds in the Lukan Birth Narrative?" *Colloquium* 44.1 (2012): 17–30.

cited text making such claims, *m. Kidd* 4.14, is a rambling passage in which individual sages express their quite conflicting comments about physicians, sailors, butchers, and shopkeepers as well as shepherds, with one rabbi of the bunch advising that men not teach their sons to be herders and another countering with "I should lay aside every trade in the world and teach my son only Torah." For these particular rabbis, writing at least a century after the time of Jesus, no activity is more important than attention to the Divine and to the Torah. One could just as easily cite, on the positive side regarding shepherds, Psalm 23, which begins "the Lord is my shepherd," or Philo, who states, "so full of dignity and benefit has the shepherd's task been held to be, that poets are wont to give to kings the title of 'shepherds of peoples,' a title which the lawgiver bestows on the 'wise'" (*Agr.* 10.41) and conclude that shepherds were exalted. The shepherds indicate not the degraded but the *ordinary* person outside the circles around Caesar. They range in symbolism from suggesting the birth of gentile gods to evocations of David and Moses to those outside the circles of power for whom a savior would be welcome (1.52; 4.18). Bethlehem was also one of the areas near Jerusalem where sheep were raised for the sacrifices in the Temple, although Luke does not make this point. As we continue to note: one does not need to create an ugly picture of Judaism in order to derive a beautiful picture of Jesus.

Angels (**vs. 9**) are harbingers of divine activity. Unlike Gabriel, who spoke to Zechariah (1.11) and Mary (1.26), this angel goes unnamed. This will be the last appearance of angels before they recur at the empty tomb (24.23). They serve to punctuate key events in the narrative as well as to signal the involvement of the supernatural in the Gospel; in Acts, they serve to arrange prison breaks (5.19; 12.7), promote the mission (12.7), and kill kings (12.23). The expression "angel of the Lord" can serve as a cipher for God, as we see, for example, in the stories of Hagar (Gen 16) and Moses and the burning bush (Exod 3). The figure first identified as an angel eventually becomes recognized simply as the Lord, or God. Luke here makes clear that Jesus is *not* this "angel of the Lord" and so diffuses any residual claims about Jesus' angelic status (on the connection cf. Gal 4.4; for the distinction cf. Heb 1.7).

Although frightened – the typical reaction – the shepherds receive "good news of great joy." This "good news" is, again, *euangellion*. The angel's reference to "all the people" (*pas ho laos*, **vs. 10**) has an indefinite application. It could include everyone, since Jesus' genealogy connects him to Adam and so to all of humanity, and since Acts describes the bringing of the "good news" to Samaritans and gentiles. Were the text in Hebrew, however, the expression "all the people" would have been *kol ha'am*, and it would have registered to listeners as a reference to the people Israel. The expression "all the people" appears frequently in the Scriptures of Israel, and almost always with Israel as the designation. This is the same Greek expression, by the way, that Matthew uses to describe the crowds that call for Jesus' death and who exclaim, "his blood be on us and on our children." When we speak of "all the people," let it always be for good news rather than finding it as an excuse for bigotry.

Luke then explains the content of the good news. The newborn "savior" (Greek: *soter*) (**vs. 11**) carries a title applied to major figures in the Hellenistic world, from heroes such as Hercules to healers such as Aesclapius. "Savior" is also a term of Roman propaganda: empirewide inscriptions referred to the "good news" (*euangelion*) of the Emperor Augustus, the imperial "savior" (*sōtēr*), a "son of god," and even "god from god" who "brought peace" to the "world" (so, e.g., the "Letter of the Proconsul to the Cities of Asia" sent in 9 BCE; the "Decree of the City Council of Ephesus concerning Caligula" of 38 CE). Luke is thus challenging the claims of the emperor as well as the imperial cult. Again, Luke gives readers a choice: which savior do you follow, and whose salvation do you want?[14]

The angel's phrasing, "is born this day," may have reminded Luke's readers of Isa 9.6, "For a child has been born for us, a son given to us; authority rests upon his shoulders; and he is named Wonderful Counselor, Mighty God, Everlasting Father, Prince of Peace." Isaiah's original message was about the son of the Davidic king currently on the throne; Christian readers took his comment as a prophecy concerning a future king to be born centuries later. The location of the birth, the "City of David," is Bethlehem, which the prophet Micah (5.2) proclaimed to be the place from which shall come "one who is to rule in Israel." Matthew explicitly cites the prophecy (Matt 2.6).

Despite the NRSV, Luke does not actually use the term "Messiah," a Hebrew term meaning "anointed one"; rather, Luke uses "Christ," the Greek

---

[14] There is a difference between challenging the claims that a Caesar should be worshiped, a new phenomenon in the first century CE, and challenging the claims that Rome can rule. It is the former that Ben sees as possibly being critiqued here. Also, Ben finds that the term *euangellion* likely comes into Christian discourse by way of Isaiah (LXX), as is clear in the earliest Christian documents, Paul's letters, not by way of later Emperor claims. If Luke is following Paul then one may question the allusion to Emperor claims here. See the essays in S. McKnight and J. Modica, eds., *Jesus Is Lord. Caesar Is Not* (Downers Grove: IVP Academic, 2013). Amy-Jill notes the prevalence of the term *euangellion* in Roman sources, including ones that predate the Christian era, and so she sees the use of *euangellion* in Luke's text as having a political valence.

equivalent. In this Gospel, "Christ" functions as a name for Jesus ("who is Christ, the Lord"), with "lord" (*kyrios*) being his title. The "sign" (**vs. 12**) or proof confirming the angel's words is not the heavenly display but the swaddled newborn in the feeding trough. The motif is reminiscent of the sign to Mary: she will know the truth of the angel's proclamation by finding her infertile cousin to be pregnant. Neither sign takes place on the universal stage; both involve pregnancy and childbirth, and both are intimately connected to women's bodies.

The necessary information conveyed, the angel together with the "multitude of the heavenly host" praises God for the good news that the baby will bring peace on earth for "peace among those whom he favors!" (**vs. 13–14**). One might have thought that this heavenly choir would have been the "sign." "Host" suggests an army of angels, but this army shows its power by praising God and singing about "peace." The Hebrew term for peace, *shalom*, indicates not only the cessation of violence, but a sense of wholeness or completion; in context here, it anticipates the messianic peace, when wars stop and people – or perhaps in Luke's more limited reading, only those of good will – are reconciled to each other and to God. The location of God in "the highest heaven" reflects the view that heaven has multiple levels. Paul speaks of being caught up to the "third heaven" (2 Cor. 12.2); since there were at least seven levels, Paul is being modest. Luke here is being theological: the "lord," "Christ," and "Savior" is in the manger, but God is in the highest heaven. Readers will need to understand Jesus' divine role in relation to that of God (the Father), just as they need to understand his double paternity. Luke has a high Christology (see 7.13) but distinguishes praises to God from praises to Jesus.

Who these people are whom God favors remains unstated; the Greek phrase translates "those whom he favors," *anthrōpois eudokias*, is more likely a way of speaking about "those upon whom God's favor rests" rather than about people who show good will to each other (see 1 QH 4.32–33; 11.9 and cf. Luke 3.22 and 10.21).[15] Longfellow's famous 1863 Christmas Carol, "I heard the bells on Christmas Day," proclaiming, "The words repeat of peace on earth, good will toward men" (relying on the King James Version), offers a less-precise translation. The disciples repeat the refrain of the angels' song, "Peace in heaven, and glory in the highest heaven!" when Jesus enters Jerusalem (Luke 19.38), and thereby Luke signals the continuity of Jesus' mission from his birth to his death. Luke also may be signaling already here

---

[15] Culy et al., *Luke*, 73.

a division among the people: there are those upon whom divine favor rests, and so there are those who do not receive it. The only other time a reference to this good pleasure (Greek: *eudokia*) appears is in 10.21, when Jesus, speaking in the Spirit, offers thanks to God the Father for having "hidden these things from the wise and the intelligent and having revealed them to infants; yes, Father, for such was your gracious will." The shepherds receive what others will not.

When the angels go into the heavens, the shepherds go to Bethlehem (**vs. 15**), and the subtle parallelism connects the two realms. The shepherds speak of what "the Lord" has revealed: they thus take the angelic announcement as representing divine proclamation. The angels speak for God. Jesus, as Luke will show, does the same, but his role is more than that of an angel or a prophet.

Hurrying, the shepherds find not just the baby in the manger (**vs. 16**), as the angels announced. Luke first mentions that they found Mary and Joseph: the child is part of a family. Then the shepherds become the first "good news givers" or "evangelists," as they report the angels' words to Mary and Joseph. To their news must be added the angel's comments to Mary and Zechariah's hymn. Different people have different insights into the meaning of this baby. Different people have different components of the good news: the shepherds heard from the angel about the baby's bringing peace and about the division among the people (**vs. 17**), a term earlier associated only with John the Baptizer (1.79). Mary knew about the conception and her son's role as son of David and son of God. The people hearing the shepherds' proclamation – at least Mary and Joseph, and perhaps more – are amazed (**vs. 18**). Luke says nothing, by the way, about anyone not believing the shepherds because they were impure or the dregs of society; nor does Luke express any concern about ritual impurity; therefore, nothing should be said along those lines by interpreters.

As the shepherds find Mary along with Joseph and the baby, so Luke returns to the Marian focus. Luke depicts Mary and Joseph as asking no questions; they receive the good news conveyed by the shepherds in silence. Nolland's translation captures the spirit of **v. 19**: Mary "stored up all these things, trying in her heart to penetrate their significance."[16] The Greek term *symballō*, usually translated "pondered," literally means "to throw together"; in colloquial terms, it suggests "mulling over." Gabriel had told her of wonders to come; now the shepherds add to this revelation. Luke says the

---

[16]   Nolland, *Luke 1–9*, 20, 97.

same thing about Mary again at 2.51. Mary's reaction takes place not in her head, however, but in her heart (Greek: *kardia*), the same heart that will be, as she will soon learn, pierced with a sword (vs. 35). The side-reference to Mary serves as an invitation to the reader: What does this good news mean, in practical terms? Is the world about to end? Will all the hungry be fed? Will economic resources be distributed? Will the blind see and the deaf hear? Will Satan be defeated?

Readers should ponder these questions as well as the scene ends with the shepherds not pondering but praising God (**vs. 20**). Their chorus complements that of the angels, who also sang praises to God (vs. 14). As Ben puts it, "those below and those above from the least to the most glorious are united." The verse also reminds us that Luke is concerned about confirmation of prophecy and describes the shepherds as basing the praise on "just as it had been told them." This oracle is not, however, from the Scriptures of Israel but is new testimony by an angel. The story of Jesus generates both fulfillment of old prophecy, and new prophecy and its fulfillment.

THE PRESENTATION OF JESUS IN THE TEMPLE

Luke now changes the time with the mention of eight days (**vs. 21**); Jews and anyone familiar with Jewish practice would know that Jewish boys are circumcised on the eighth day after their birth (cf. Gen 17.11–12). Circumcision is the sign of the covenant between God and Abraham as well as between God and Abraham's descendants. The practice of circumcision, called in Hebrew *brit milah*, "covenant of circumcision," is still performed for Jewish boys at the age of eight days as well as for men who convert to Judaism (there is a cognate practice also in Islam, since Muslims too claim descent from Abraham). Mary and Joseph, like Elizabeth and Zechariah (1.57–59), continue the covenant with Abraham. Jesus receives his name, as Gabriel had instructed (1.31), but without the problems attendant at John's naming. The name "Jesus" was relatively common, but Luke gives no indication that it is a family name for either Joseph (in his genealogy) or Mary (whose parentage and ancestry go unremarked).

Continuing to stress Mary and Joseph's fidelity to Torah, Luke next mentions "*their* purification" (**vs. 22**). Details here confuse, since Torah only mandates that Mary, who like all women is ritually impure following the birth of a child, participate in a cleansing. According to Lev 12.2–6, the purification of a new mother takes place forty days after the birth of a son. Impurity, which is not to be confused with sin, was a daily factor in Jewish life: one is impure because of menstruation or ejaculation, childbirth, or burial of a corpse. Purity marks matters of life and death. To regain the status of purity, which was needed to enter the Jerusalem Temple, people practiced certain rituals, such as bathing; in some cases, such as being cured from leprosy, sacrifice was also mandated. Attending to purity concerns allows practitioners to sanctify the body as well as to mark all times of either the beginning of life or its cessation. Such a sacrifice for the impurity created by childbirth applied only to the mother; the child was not regarded as ritually unclean; neither was anyone else associated with the mother.

Concerning the phrase "their purification," some scholars – attempting to prove the historicity of this irregular practice – suggest that Joseph helped with the delivery of Jesus, and thus he too was ritually unclean, but the citations usually offered (e.g., *m. Nid.* 5.1 cf. 2.5 and 1.3–5) do not support the claim. Others, noting both that there is no tradition of a man offering sacrifices after a child's birth and that Luke is perhaps ignorant of Temple practice, have enhanced the picture of Joseph's piety. Still others propose that Luke was aware of a later Second Temple practice that goes otherwise unattested.

The reference to the presentation of Jesus may also be a Lucan invention, a resonance of a practice no longer preserved, or an evocation of earlier material. By mentioning that Mary and Joseph "present" (**vs. 22**) Jesus to God, Luke mirrors the language of Samuel's presentation in the Temple at Shiloh (1 Sam 2.24). Luke is also referring to the practice called the "redemption of the firstborn." The quotation regarding the holiness of the firstborn (**vs. 23**) comes from Exod 13.2 (cf. Exod 13.11–15; 34.19; Num 18.15–16): "Consecrate to me all the firstborn; whatever is the first to open the womb among the Israelites, of human beings and animals, is mine." Since the Levitical priesthood served in the place of all firstborn males, Exod 13.13 goes on to state, "Every firstborn male among your children you shall redeem"; the symbolism relates to the salvation of the Israelites' firstborn children from the tenth plague at the time of the Exodus. This tradition, known as the *pidyon ha-ben*, is still practiced among Jews, with the redemption, traditionally five silver coins, paid to a Kohen (a priest), with the funds going to charitable purposes. However, Luke's "presentation" itself makes no mention of this practice.

For the purity offering and again in obedience to Torah, Mary and Joseph sacrifice two pigeons or turtledoves (**vs. 24**), the offerings of the poor. The Temple works on what might be considered a sliding scale: all people participated, according to their means.

Vss. 25–40 provide the stories of the Holy Family's encounters with Simeon and Anna, figures who resemble Zechariah and Elizabeth (1.5–25) in age, piety, Temple-centeredness, messianic hope, and the inspiration of the Holy Spirit. We first meet Simeon, whose name may be connected to the Hebrew root of "*Shema*" ("Hear! "Listen!"). He had been "looking for the consolation of Israel" (**vs. 25**), another Lucan expression reflecting Isaiah 40 ("Comfort, O comfort my people …" [Isa 40.1], cf. 52.9; 66.12, 13). Luke, who will again quote from this chapter in 3.4–6, does not detail the terms of the consolation. Given references to the census and so to Roman occupation, as well as to Caesar and Quirinius, consolation may well include national autonomy. Historically, a first-century Jew seeking divine consolation would have held traditional messianic hopes: the return of Jews in exile to the land of Israel; the end of death, poverty, disease, and despair; a general resurrection of the dead; a final judgment; and the eternity of the messianic age. Simeon summarizes the hope in **vs. 26**: the Holy Spirit had told him that he would not die until he saw the Lord's Messiah. The prophecy is a two-pronged one: Simeon will see the Messiah, but that sight indicates that his time of death is near. His reaction therefore could be dread, desire, or both.

Led by the Spirit, as the major figures in Luke-Acts are, Simeon enters the Temple (**vs. 27**). Mary and Joseph are in the process of presenting Jesus, which Luke describes, once again, in terms of faithfulness to Torah. Then Simeon receives the child into his arms (**vs. 28a**), a gesture of intimacy and trust on the part of the parents. Symbolically, the faithful of Israel embrace the Messiah, even as Luke indicates the passing of that earlier generation.

Praising God and so adding his voice to the choirs of angels and shepherds (**vs. 28b**), Simeon speaks the prayer known as the "Nunc Dimittis" (Latin for "now dismiss," the prayer's first words). Simeon asks that God "dismiss" his "slave" (the NRSV's "servant" is euphemistic)[17] to depart (**v. 29**); more bluntly, he is stating, "I can die now," but can die in the knowledge that he has seen, indeed touched, the Messiah. Thus, "I can die in peace." The term "release" (Greek: *apoluō*) also applies to the freeing of a slave, as Simeon's reference to God as "master" (Greek: *despotēs*, whence "despot") confirms. What he sees is God's "salvation" (**vs. 30**), that is, the Messiah. Jesus, whose name connotes "salvation," also embodies it.

Simeon's prayer then becomes prophetic, as it proclaims that this Messiah, this salvation, will impact "all peoples" (**vs. 31**), here indicating not only Jews but also Samaritans and gentiles. The gentiles require the

---

[17] See p. 37 in Chapter 1 on the use of the term "slave."

"revelation" of the God of Israel; the people Israel – represented by all the figures of the first two chapters – show the glory of covenantal continuity as well as the privilege of having God's Messiah as a member of these people (**vs. 32**). From references to the gentiles in terms of emperors and generals, the Gospel now locates them as people to be given the Good News. Since the scene is set, implicitly, in the outer court of the Temple – the "court of the gentiles" – we can imagine gentile visitors listening to this prophecy. It was the census prompted by a gentile, Caesar Augustus, for the sake of a gentile empire, that caused Mary and Joseph to be in Bethlehem; the mission of Jesus will reverse that census, as Luke suggests that all people are to be counted among the new family of God.

Simeon's prayer continues Luke's theme of universalism even as it expresses the Jewish eschatological hope that all nations would worship the one God; as Zechariah stated, "on that day ... the Lord will become king over all the earth; on that day the Lord will be one and his Name one" (Zech 14.9). This verse, by the way, closes the Hebrew prayer known as the *Aleinu* (from the first word: "It is upon us [to praise God]"), which is recited by traditional Jews three times daily at the close of the morning, afternoon, and evening service.

A CLOSER LOOK: THE CANTICLES IN LUKE 1–2

Speeches in works composed before recording devices need to be evaluated differently than we might evaluate them today. There is no evidence of scribes recording the words of Mary or Simeon, shepherds or angels. The ancient historian Thucydides explains how such songs, as well as speeches, came to be written. In his view, which was held by subsequent historians, an author should present the characters as saying what it seemed likely that they *did* say and if possible should adhere as closely to what he knew they actually spoke (*History of the Peloponnesian War* 1.22.1–2).

One could take a positivistic view and suggest that Luke had contact with someone like Mary, perhaps during the two years he was with Paul in Caesarea Maritima (this view presumes that Luke the writer of the Gospel and Acts was also the composer of the itinerary found in Acts). If this is the case, the Magnificat, the Nunc Dimittis, and the various other accounts all could have been told or sung to him. Less positivistic views suggest that Luke, who did not know Paul personally but, a generation or two later than Paul, sought to ensure that no one saw Paul, or anyone else associated with Jesus, as contravening Jewish Law, composed the hymns based on the building blocks provided by earlier hymns, such as Hannah's song in 1 Sam. Alternatively, Luke may have lifted some of these canticles from other sources. Whatever the origin of the songs, Luke has shaped the works in rhetorically effective ways according to the Gospel's overall historical and theological purposes.[18]

Mary and Joseph find Simeon's prophecy astounding (**vs. 33**), which is odd given that Gabriel told Mary about her child's eschatological role. Perhaps the astonishment simply involves Simeon's knowledge of Mary's personal experience. Or perhaps the astonishment is one of confirmation: hearing that one's child is the pivot on which the fate of the universe rests is an astounding message, even if it had been delivered earlier. A third possibility is the most likely: the astonishment comes from what Simeon next recounts, for his prophecy changes in tone from celebration to warning.

After blessing the family, Simeon offers a specific warning to Mary, the mother. First, he notes that the child will not only be welcomed, he will also be opposed. His mission will cause some in Israel to rise and others to fall (**vs. 34**). He thereby makes explicit the angel's notice about those who have divine favor and, implicitly, those who do not. Simeon continues by stating that because of this child, people's inner thoughts will be revealed (**vs. 35a**). What they think, as well as what they do, will matter. Finally, he tells her that suffering will come to her, personally (**vs. 35b**) as a sword will penetrate her own inner being. Although Jesus will suffer, the first notice of suffering in relation to this mission comes to Mary. Her suffering will be both personal and communal. Jesus' words to her at the Temple (2.41–52) and his strained relationship with his natal family (8.19–21) will test Mary's maternal role: she will need to let him be more than just her firstborn, and more than just Joseph's son.[19] Numerous controversies with fellow Jews will tear at her heart as well. And she will witness her son's torture and execution. Although all will call Mary blessed, her import is less for her trusting the angelic word

---

[18] R. Simons has demonstrated that the rhetoric of the hymns and speeches in Luke 1–2 shows numerous Greek oral and aural and rhetorical devices. His doctoral dissertation, supervised by John Nolland and Ben Witherington III at Trinity College Bristol, is summarized in *Tyndale Bulletin*, Vol. 60.1, May 2009.

[19] "Mary's struggle to 'let go' of her son likely accounts for part of the pain Simeon speaks of here …," Kuhn, "Deaf or Defiant?" 496.

and giving birth to Jesus than for her remaining faithful to him, despite the personal agony.

Reference to a second woman, herself apparently childless, adds to Mary's pathos as well as to Jesus' prophetic role. The only woman described in the New Testament (NT) as a "prophet" (**vs. 36**, though see Acts 21.9 on Philip's prophesying daughters), Anna stands in the line of Miriam, Deborah, Huldah, the daughters of Job, and Judith as speaking, and doing, the will of God. Her name should also remind readers of Hannah and so of Mary's own Magnificat. Like Simeon, Anna foreshadows the early followers of Jesus, gathered in Jerusalem, where they pray and fast (Acts 2.42, 46); her prophetic activity anticipates the pouring out of the prophetic Spirit in Acts 2. Textual variants create some confusion about her age: she could be about 105 but a widow for eighty-four years, or her widowhood extended a long time until now, when she is eighty-four. In either case, she is a widow, and she at least eighty (**cf. 37a**). She had been married seven years, and a widow for decades later. Like Simeon, she represents the "older generation" of Jewish piety.

Claims that Anna belongs to an order of widows who live in the Temple have no basis; nor could Anna, as a young woman and therefore likely having normal menstrual cycles, remain in the Temple unless, because of her fasting, her menstrual cycle ceased. Given that Luke is writing at a time when there were orders of Christian widows (see 1 Tim 5), mentions widows within the church (Acts 6.1; 9.39), and has an interest in celibacy, it is possible Anna foreshadows the fidelity of the women who are not dependent upon husbands or children. Anna's widowhood and continence conform to Luke's ideal of Christian behavior as well as to the Roman valuation of the *univira*, the once-married woman. Luke will continue to depict widows: the widow of Nain, whose son Jesus raises from the dead; the widow who confronts a judge in a parable; widows who are victims of scribes; a widow who puts her last coins into the Temple treasury; and so on. The book of Acts continues this interest in depicting the Hebrew and Hellenist widows in the Jerusalem Church as well as the widows who attend the corpse of the disciple Tabitha/ Dorcas. Amy-Jill finds their portraits to be consistent with the wishes of the author of the Pastorals: kind, generous, and basically silent. Ben is more optimistic about Luke's presentation of both widows and women. He is also doubtful that Luke has an ascetical agenda. He also thinks Luke wrote the Pastorals on behalf of Paul, hence the many connections between Luke-Acts and the Pastorals, including some forty words found only in Luke-Acts and the Pastorals.[20]

Despite Luke's pairing of men and women, the presentations are not the same. We hear Simeon's words; we do not hear directly from Anna. But we have more detail about Anna than we do about Simeon. We know her father's name, Phanuel; the name is the Greek transliteration of the Hebrew "Penuel" or "Peniel," meaning "face of God" (see Gen 32.31; Judg 8.8; 1 Kings 12.25); her sighting of Jesus thus makes her once again the daughter who has (seen the) face of God.[21] Her tribal identification, Asher, comes from a name mean "happy" or "rejoice." And we know that she functions, like the shepherds, as an evangelist: she may not speak to readers, but her words were, as Luke suggests, heard by any near her in the Temple (**vs. 38**). Ben sees a more-or-less egalitarian treatment of Simeon and Anna; Amy-Jill sees a silencing of women's voices. We will comment on the various other pairings of men and women, in narrative and parable, as we continue through the Gospel.

JESUS AND HIS PARENTS

Fulfilling their fidelity to Torah (**vs. 39** – the infancy materials continue to reinforce this fidelity), the family returns to Nazareth, their hometown. Jesus grows up as would be expected from the comments of Gabriel and Simeon: he is, like Solomon, filled with wisdom; he is, as the divine Son should be, filled with the favor or grace (Greek: *charis*) of God. Luke does not recount how Mary and Joseph coped with such a precocious child, although second-century Christian texts, such as the apocryphal *Infancy Gospel of Thomas*, suggest that their parental role was at best not easy. This latter text depicts Jesus as astounding his teachers with preternatural wisdom, making pigeons from mud and then turning them into real birds, helping Joseph in woodworking by miraculously stretching a board he had cut too short, killing his friends and then, when the parents protest, resurrecting them. Luke 2.41–52 is much more restrained.

[20] On which see Ben Witherington III, *Letters and Homilies for Hellenized Christians*, Vol. 1 (Downers Grove: IVP, 2014).

[21] See discussion in Andrés Garcia Serrano, "Anna's Characterization in Luke 2:36–38: A Case of Conceptual Allusion?" *CBQ* 76.3 (2014): 464–80 (esp. 468).

The note that Jesus "was filled with wisdom" (**vs. 40**) anticipates vs. 52, where Jesus increases in wisdom. Like any child, he learns. And his wisdom will, as 7.35 insists, be vindicated (see also 25.15). That he had God's "favor" indicates, among other things, that he takes after his mother (see 1.30).

The narrative in 2.41–52 is remarkable for many reasons, not the least of which is that it is the only canonical story about Jesus between infancy and adulthood. The scene is not, contrary to popular views, Jesus' "bar mitzvah" (literally, a "son of [the] commandment"; the term indicates when Jewish boys, at the age of thirteen, become recognized as adults – with all the rights and responsibilities of adults – in the community); such a ceremony did not exist in antiquity. Luke's scene rather evokes the stories of other extraordinary children, such as Samuel, who according to Josephus (*Ant.* 5.348) began his prophetic activity at twelve. Similar stories were told of Cyrus of Persia (Herodotus I, 114f.), Alexander the Great (Plutarch, *Life of Alexander* 5), and Moses (Josephus, *Ant.* 2.230; Philo, *Life of Moses* 1.21), and Josephus boasts: "when I was a child, about fourteen years of age, I was commended by all for the love I had of learning; on which account the high priests and principal men of the city came frequently to me together, to know my opinion about the accurate understanding of points of the law" (*Life* 9). For some in the ancient world, a person who accomplishes great things as an adult must have had both a prodigious childhood and a miraculous birth.

Again, stressing the piety of Joseph and Mary, Luke notes that they went to Jerusalem every year for the Passover (**vs. 41**), one of three pilgrimage festivals (along with Sukkot [Booths] and Shavuot [Weeks or Pentecost]). Their practice is a "usual" one (**vs. 42**); Luke indicates no financial hardship for such participation; the pilgrimage may have had the sense of a vacation as well as a holy endeavor; celebration and piety are not mutually exclusive. The family stayed for the eight-day festival and then began the return journey to Galilee; however, they did not realize that Jesus stayed behind in Jerusalem (**vs. 43**).

The loss of a child is every parent's nightmare. Simeon's prophecy is beginning to come true: the sword pierces the mother who believes she has lost her son. We need not accuse Joseph and Mary of bad parenting: huge crowds made the pilgrimage to Jerusalem for Passover, and many traveled in caravans with neighbors or with extended families (**vs. 44**). Yet the Passover that ends with the separation of mother and son anticipates Jesus' last Passover, when Luke does not note Mary's presence. Mary and Joseph look for Jesus but are unable to find him "among their relatives and friends." The scene foreshadows Jesus' creation of a new family, not based on biology or previous relationships, but based on their loyalty to him and to God (8.20–21). It also foreshadows Jesus' resurrection appearance, where his followers – thinking they have lost him – will find him on the road.

Mary and Joseph return to Jerusalem to search for their lost son (**vs. 45**), and on the third day they find him in the Temple (**vs. 46**). Luke's foreshadowing of Jesus' death (absence) and resurrection (finding) is not subtle. Jesus' parents find him among the teachers; his role is not one of a disciple but of full participant among those dedicated to the study and practice of Torah. Luke adds that all who heard him, including his parents, were stunned by his level of understanding, indicated not only by his questions but also by his answers (**vs. 47**). Being astounded at Jesus is a consistent response, as 8.56; 24.22 also indicate.

The parents, however, are sick with worry. Mary, already manifesting the sword piercing her heart, calls to him: "Child" (Greek: *teknon*; **vs. 48**). The father of the Prodigal uses the address for the elder son (15.31): this was the child the father realized he had lost. It is also the word Abraham uses for the Rich Man in the Parable of the Rich Man and Lazarus; in this case, the "child" is truly lost. Mary, speaking on behalf of both herself and Joseph, expresses her agonizing sense that she had lost Jesus. Her cry is that of a distraught mother. She has been "searching" for him in great "pain" (the NRSV "anxiety" does not fully capture her emotional state, or the sword in her heart). She and Joseph, "your father," have suffered on his account.

Jesus, sounding like a cocky adolescent, appears surprised at their worry (**vs. 49**). The Greek of his question reads, "Did you not know that I must be among the matters of my father?" A similar scene occurs in John 2, where Jesus appears initially to rebuff his mother's concerns. Jesus' role as Son of God does not eliminate his full embeddedness in this Jewish family. His concern, a necessity ("I must") is for everything related to God: the Temple, the Torah, the people. He recognizes his destiny, his calling. Here for the first time in Luke's Gospel, Jesus speaks of "my Father's house" and so identifies himself as God's Son. Mary speaks of "your father," meaning Joseph, but Jesus answers in terms of his (heavenly) Father.

Mary and Joseph, despite the annunciation by Gabriel, the good news from the shepherds, and the predictions by Anna and Simeon, cannot fully grasp what their son says or does (**vs. 50**). Whereas Jesus "understands" (vs. 47), his parents do not. For Luke, complete understanding of Jesus' identity and role is not yet possible. The depiction of Jesus' parents in the infancy narrative is very much like that of the disciples after Jesus' third passion prediction: "They did not understand any of these things, and this word … was hidden from them" (18.34). Understanding comes only when Jesus reveals himself (see 24:31), and understanding the full story requires hearing of the resurrection and ascension, and then rereading the Gospel in that light. A similar situation prevails with most parents of teenagers; what is obvious to the child is not at all clear to the parents, and vice versa.

In **vs. 51**, Luke stresses Mary's retention of what she has not yet understood and her continuing search to understand. The NRSV's "treasured all these things" is romantic and palliative; the Greek *diatēreō* simply means to "store" or "maintain"; she continued to ponder. "Treasure" is the wrong term for the message of a sword, and of tragedy.

This penultimate verse of the chapter also shows how the immediate crisis is resolved: Jesus returns with Mary and Joseph to Nazareth, and is obedient to them. The term for his obedience, *hypotassō*, appears in Eph 5.24; Col 3.18; Titus 2.5; and 1 Peter 3.1, all part of the genre known as "household codes"; there it describes the obedience of a wife to her husband. Here in Luke's account, Jesus models the filial piety expected of both Jewish and gentile children. Despite the claim that he is a "glutton and a drunkard" (7.34), which is the beginning description of the "rebellious son" (Deut 20.21), Jesus is neither glutton, nor drunkard, nor, formally, rebellious.

And as **vs. 52** states, he increased in wisdom, just as any child might. He is not static; he is not all wise, since he can increase in wisdom. He is, thus, fully human. Comparable are descriptions of Samuel (1 Sam 2.26) and Moses (Josephus, *Antiquities* 2.231; Philo, *Life of Moses* 1.19). Perhaps Luke also hints that Theophilus, or any one who loves God, would increase in wisdom by following this child as he grows to adulthood. The final verse of this chapter should be compared to the refrain at the end of other episodes in the infancy narrative at 1.80 and 2.40. Eventually, Jesus will display this wisdom and even be seen as an incarnation of it (Luke 11.49; 25.15). Luke also adds that Jesus grew in favor with God and human beings. The verb *prokoptō* elsewhere refers to growth in moral and intellectual life (cf. Gal 1.14; 1 Tim 4.15; and Lucian, *Hermotimus* 63).

BRIDGING THE HORIZONS

1. Luke's Infancy Materials and History

The Lukan birth and infancy stories, greatly loved and greatly debated, have profoundly shaped Church practice. Christ's mass, the origin of the term "Christmas," was only a minor celebration until 1223 when Francis of Assisi set up a scene of baby Jesus surrounded by Matthew's Magi, Luke's shepherds, and even live animals. Thereafter, there were ever-increasing additions to the celebration. St. Nicholas, a charitable bishop of Myra in Turkey who will eventually morph into Santa Claus, entered the festivities. Special confections were added, such as candy sticks in the shape of bishop's staffs (candy canes). The evergreen Christmas tree to which Luther apparently was the first to add candles, inspired by seeing stars shining through an evergreen when walking one winter night, was borrowed from pagan German celebrations of midwinter. Holly was added with the berries symbolizing Christ's blood and the leaves the crown of thorns. Mistletoe, which for the British Druids was a symbol of new life, entered the tradition as a sign of budding love, or an excuse for a kiss.[22] All this hoopla seems miles away from the story of a first-century Jewish family having to bring their first child into the world under less than ideal conditions.

To teach or preach this material requires an understanding of the message of the Gospel, apart from the tree and tinsel. It means understanding how Luke's initial readers would have heard the Gospel; to determine what the good news is for today, we need to know something about what it was two millennia ago. Bridging the horizons requires that one knows both what the characteristics of the two horizons are, and then be able to formulate a way of relating the two by analogy, example, parable, storytelling, similarity of human dilemma, or a host of other possible points or means of comparison. If we let the history go, we deny Jesus and Luke both their own social locations, and we ignore the people who first told these stories.

Luke's readers, likely gentiles, would have heard a very positive description of Jewish piety, the openness of the Torah to the poor, the piety expressed by both men and women in the Temple, and Jesus' engagement with Jewish teachers. Luke presents Jesus as fully embedded, and at home, in the Judaism of his time. The various rituals, by which Jews not only honored the covenant with Israel but also resisted assimilation against Rome, helped the community preserve its identity. Readers whether in the past or today who seek to divorce Jesus from his Jewish context, or who impose anti-Jewish stereotypes on the text, do a disservice to Luke and to the Gospel message.

---

[22]   See H. Clarke, *The Gospel of Matthew and Its Readers* (Bloomington: Indiana University Press, 2003), 15–23.

A second point concerns the political implications of this story: following Caesar's dictates, which disrupt families by sending them miles from their homes for the sake of getting more money from them, or following Jesus. The choice is between the values of the Empire of Rome and the values of the God of Israel. What might this story then say about the relationship between the Christian and the state?

A third issue concerns the role of age. Luke highlights the contributions that the elderly can make to the community: their wisdom is not to be overlooked. Nor should Jesus be seen as unique in his ability to talk with teachers. The account of the twelve-year-old in the Temple tells us not only that Jews were serious about educating their children, they were also serious about listening to them. Children are not to be "seen and not heard"; they are to be fully part of the family, and the community.

2. Luke, the Body, and Sexuality

Luke 1–2, with its emphasis on Jewish law, ritual practice, sexuality, and the body, would have struck some early second-century readers as peculiar if not perverse. Justin Martyr (ca. 150), Irenaeus of Lyon (ca. 185), and Tertullian (ca. 207) provide us information about Marcion, an early second-century teacher and the author of the *Antitheses*, a five-volume work. Marcion believed, inter alia, that the God of the "Old Testament" was a stupid, inept deity who created a flawed world marked by flawed materiality, such as the body. This jealous god wanted to keep people from having knowledge. Jesus, representing a different God, came to provide theological Truth. Tertuillian and his colleagues found this distinction between the God of the Old Testament and the God of the New to be heretical; as he states about Marcion's books: "The only air they have is fog, the whole year is winter, every wind that blows is the north wind. Water becomes water only by heating … The most barbarous and melancholy thing about Pontus is that Marcion was born there …" (*Against Marcion* 1.1).

Marcion appears to have been the first follower of Jesus to put together a list of books considered Scriptural and therefore having authority. He used the Gospel of Luke, but not the first two chapters. Luke's Gospel could easily start with 3.1–2: "In the fifteenth year of the reign of Emperor Tiberius, when Pontius Pilate was governor of Judea, and Herod was ruler of Galilee, and his brother Philip ruler of the region of Ituraea and Trachonitis, and Lysanias ruler of Abilene, during the high priesthood of Annas and Caiaphas, the word of God came to John son of Zechariah in the wilderness

..." We might think of what would be lost were we to dismiss Luke's Nativity. There is more here than the shepherds and the manger: there are the joys and struggles of parenthood, the growing pains of youth, the role of the Torah in determining the rhythms of life, the centrality of Jerusalem and the Temple, and the importance of personal piety.

Most notably, we would miss the importance of the body and sexuality: conception, birth, circumcision, ritual purity. Most of ancient Judaism resisted the mind/body split and the consequent denigration of the body. The tradition taught both that the body is in the image and likeness of the divine, and that we are but little lower than the gods (Psa 8.6 [Hebrew: *elohim*; the LXX reads *angelloi*, i.e., "angels"; cf. Heb 2.7]). This concern for the body in part underlies the Jewish concern for resurrection of the dead rather than for immortality of the soul; it is in the body that one enacts one's Jewish identity.

Matters will change as Christianity develops. The Church will promote a focus on virginity, celibacy, and continence whereas the rabbinic tradition increasingly emphasizes the expectations of marriage and children. In a related manner, the Church will praise those who sell all they have and give to the poor, while the rabbis refuse this practice since for a man to choose this lifestyle would put his wife and children in danger of poverty. As we continue through Luke's Gospel, we'll see the gradual move both toward celibacy and away from the natal family. Ben is not sanguine that Luke is particularly interested in advocating asceticism, but there is a strong and increasing focus on the family of faith rather than the natal family, and an emphasis on chastity if one is a single person.

3. The Census

In ancient Israel, a census served multiple purposes: to determine men eligible for military service (e.g., Num 1.1–3; 4.21–28; 26.1–4), to determine numbers of people available for Temple service (e.g., Num 4.2-3; 1 Chron 23.24–32), and to distribute land among the population (Num 26.52). The first biblical reference to a census is Exod 30.12–15, where God instructs Moses, "When you take a census of the Israelites to register them, at registration all of them shall give a ransom for their lives to the Lord, so that no plague may come upon them for being registered. This is what each one who is registered shall give: half a shekel according to the shekel of the Sanctuary (the shekel is twenty gerahs), half a shekel as an offering to the Lord. Each one who is registered, from twenty years old and upward, shall give the LORD's offering. The rich shall not give more, and the poor shall not give less, than the half shekel, when you bring this offering to the Lord to make atonement for your lives."

There is much to be noticed in this passage. First, the military aspect of the census appears in the notice of the age of the men: twenty years would be the age of conscription. Second, the insistence that everyone pay the same amount allows for an accurate count of the number of contributors; it also avoids the shame or honor that would be accrued for, respectively, being unable to pay enough or paying more than one's share. Third, the concern for ransom and expiation derives from the view that to count the people would be to expose them to danger (see 2 Sam 24.1–15 cf. 1 Chron 21.1–14). The tradition early developed that the people were not to be counted directly; rather, markers, such as shekels or ostraca, were counted instead. This practice also follows from the promise God made to Abraham that his descendants would be "as numerous as the stars of heaven and as the sand that is on the seashore" (Gen 22.17); therefore, as Hosea (1.10a [MT 2.1]) states, "Yet the number of the people of Israel shall be like the sand of the sea, which can be neither measured nor numbered." Josephus (*War* 6.9.3) states that when King Herod Agrippa (ruled 41–44) wanted to count the Jewish population, he counted the kidneys of the lambs sacrificed at Passover and multiplied by more than ten. Finally, the shekel for the Sanctuary (i.e., the Wilderness Tabernacle) is the origin of what becomes, by the first century CE, the Temple tax that Jesus advises paying (Matt 17.24–27).

The counting of people serves various ends. Benevolently, it can help in redistributing public funds. In the classroom, counting students ensures that no one has missed class because of external problems, and knowing they are counted at times encourages students to show up. But less benevolently, the counting of people is used for disciplinary purposes that dehumanize. Slaves on plantations were counted daily, to ensure none ran for freedom. Inmates in US jails are counted, sometimes six times a day. Subject populations or people in underserved areas are counted to determine how much food or medication will be distributed. How then do we ensure that people feel as if they count, rather than take the roll for self-interested purposes? These questions will return when we come to the parables in Luke 15.

Luke 3 John the Baptizer and Jesus' Genealogy

JOHN THE BAPTIST

¹ In the fifteenth year of the reign of Emperor Tiberius, when Pontius Pilate was governor of Judea, and Herod was ruler of Galilee, and his brother Philip ruler of the region of Ituraea and Trachonitis, and Lysanias ruler of Abilene, ² during the high priesthood of Annas and Caiaphas, the word of God came to John son of Zechariah in the wilderness.

³ He went into all the region around the Jordan, proclaiming a baptism of repentance for the forgiveness of sins,

⁴ as it is written in the book of the words of the prophet Isaiah,
> "The voice of one crying out in the wilderness:
> 'Prepare the way of the Lord,
>   make his paths straight.

⁵ Every valley shall be filled,
>   and every mountain and hill shall be made low,
>   and the crooked shall be made straight,
>   and the rough ways made smooth;

⁶ and all flesh shall see the salvation of God.' "

⁷ John said to the crowds that came out to be baptized by him, "You brood of vipers! Who warned you to flee from the wrath to come? ⁸ Bear fruits worthy of repentance. Do not begin to say to yourselves, 'We have Abraham as our ancestor'; for I tell you, God is able from these stones to raise up children to Abraham.

⁹ Even now the ax is lying at the root of the trees; every tree therefore that does not bear good fruit is cut down and thrown into the fire."

¹⁰ And the crowds asked him, "What then should we do?" ¹¹ In reply he said to them, "Whoever has two coats must share with anyone who has none; and whoever has food must do likewise."

¹² Even tax collectors came to be baptized, and they asked him, "Teacher, what should we do?" ¹³ He said to them, "Collect no more than the amount prescribed for you."

¹⁴ Soldiers also asked him, "And we, what should we do?" He said to them, "Do not extort money from anyone by threats or false accusation, and be satisfied with your wages."

¹⁵ As the people were filled with expectation, and all were questioning in their hearts concerning John, whether he might be the Messiah, ¹⁶ John answered all of them by saying, "I baptize you with water; but one who is more powerful than I is coming; I am not worthy to untie the thong of his sandals. He will baptize you with the Holy Spirit and fire. ¹⁷ His winnowing fork is in his hand, to clear his threshing floor and to gather the wheat into his granary; but the chaff he will burn with unquenchable fire."

¹⁸ So, with many other exhortations, he proclaimed the good news to the people.

¹⁹ But Herod the ruler, who had been rebuked by him because of Herodias, his brother's wife, and because of all the evil things that Herod had done, ²⁰added to them all by shutting up John in prison.

THE BAPTISM OF JESUS

²¹ Now when all the people were baptized, and when Jesus also had been baptized and was praying, the heaven was opened, ²² and the Holy Spirit descended upon him in bodily form like a dove. And a voice came from heaven, "You are my Son, the Beloved; with you I am well pleased."

THE GENEALOGY

²³ Jesus was about thirty years old when he began his work. He was the son (as was thought) of Joseph son of Heli, ²⁴ son of Matthat, son of Levi, son of Melchi, son of Jannai, son of Joseph, ²⁵ son of Mattathias, son of Amos, son of Nahum, son of Esli, son of Naggai, ²⁶son of Maath, son of Mattathias, son of Semein, son of Josech, son of Joda, ²⁷ son of Joanan, son of Rhesa, son of Zerubbabel, son of Shealtiel, son of Neri, ²⁸ son of Melchi, son of Addi, son of Cosam, son of Elmadam, son of Er, ²⁹ son of Joshua, son of Eliezer, son of Jorim, son of Matthat, son of Levi, ³⁰ son of Simeon, son of Judah, son of Joseph, son of Jonam, son of Eliakim, ³¹ son of Melea, son of Menna, son of Mattatha, son of Nathan, son of David, ³² son of Jesse, son of Obed, son of Boaz, son of Sala, son of Nahshon,

[33] son of Amminadab, son of Admin, son of Arni, son of Hezron, son of Perez, son of Judah, [34] son of Jacob, son of Isaac, son of Abraham, son of Terah, son of Nahor, [35] son of Serug, son of Reu, son of Peleg, son of Eber, son of Shelah, [36] son of Cainan, son of Arphaxad, son of Shem, son of Noah, son of Lamech, [37] son of Methuselah, son of Enoch, son of Jared, son of Mahalaleel, son of Cainan, [38] son of Enos, son of Seth, son of Adam, son of God.

JOHN THE BAPTIZER

John was born "in the day of King Herod of Judea" (1.5), and Jesus was born at the time when "a decree went out from Emperor Augustus that all the world should be registered" (2.1). Luke's concern with the political contexts, both Judean and Roman, remains in play when John begins to fulfill the prediction the angel Gabriel made to his father: "He will turn many of the people of Israel to the Lord their God" (1.16). Zechariah himself predicted that John would "give light to those who sit in darkness and in the shadow of death, to guide our feet into the way of peace" (1.79).

The causes of that deadly shadow appear in the beginning of Luke 3, where both local and imperial politics provide the setting for John's work. No longer are we in a time dated by the intimate and life-giving notice of months of pregnancy; now we are in the fifteenth year of Tiberius Caesar (**vs. 1**), the Roman emperor who ruled 14–37 CE and so in about 29 CE. Tiberius was a military genius who fought campaigns from Armenia to the Rhine to the Alps, and who conquered Dalmatia and sectors of Germania. This militarism, while good news for Rome, was not good news for the people killed or sold into slavery; it is consistent with Augustus Caesar's interest in taxation and conscription, and it is the antithesis of the Kingdom Jesus will proclaim.

That Pliny the Elder called Tiberius "tristissimus hominum," the "saddest of men," is one of several indications that this emperor was not well suited for the throne. More field marshal than political manipulator, Tiberius did not want the job of emperor and eventually decamped to Capri. He left in authority Lucius Aelius Sejanus, best known today for being the patron of Pontius Pilate. Sejanus made a run for the throne, and when Tiberius learned of his plotting, he had him arrested, tried, and executed for treason.

Eventually, Tiberius developed a reputation for killing any who challenged him, and worse. Although today historians question claims of Tiberius's cruelty and paranoia, at the time Luke was writing, many regarded Tiberius as both violent and perverse. According to the Roman historian Tacitus (56–120), Tiberius killed all suspected traitors, such that "here lay, singly or in heaps, the unnumbered dead, of every age and sex, the illustrious with the obscure. Kinsfolk and friends were not allowed to be near them, to weep over them, or even to gaze on them too long. Spies were set round them, who noted the sorrow of each mourner and followed the rotting corpses, till they were dragged to the Tiber, where, floating or driven on the bank, no one dared to burn or to touch them" (*Annals* 6.19). Suetonius (62–122) reports that the emperor "acquired a reputation for still grosser depravities that one can hardly bear to tell or be told, let alone believe"; he goes on, in great detail, to describe Tiberius's activities of sexual abuse of children and of women (*Life of Tiberius* 43–44). This would be the reputation Luke, and Luke's readers, would have known.

Luke would also have known that Tiberius had exiled the Jews from the city of Rome in 19 CE. Suetonius writes, "He abolished foreign cults, especially the Egyptian and the Jewish rites, compelling all who were addicted to such superstitions to burn their religious vestments and all their paraphernalia. Those of the Jews who were of military age he assigned to provinces of less healthy climate, ostensibly to serve in the army; the others of that same race or of similar beliefs he banished from the city, on pain of slavery for life if they did not obey" (*Life of Tiberius* 36).

Following the reference to the emperor, Luke mentions Pontius Pilate, appointed by Tiberius to the governorship of Judea (Pilate was in office 26–36 CE). Pilate, basically a middle-management bureaucrat, went on to achieve some notoriety of his own. The third figure Luke names, Herod in Galilee, is Antipas (ruled 4 BCE–39 CE), the tetrarch who would, as the chapter will soon reveal, execute John the Baptizer. By locating John in the context of Tiberius, Pilate, and Antipas, Luke demonstrates the shadow of death over the empire. The last two politicians Luke mentions in **vs. 1**, Philip and Lysanias, had comparably better reputations, which is not saying much. These latter references serve to reinforce the authority of the empire: wherever one would turn, Rome ruled.

Locally in Judea, a separate political system is in place; since no Jewish king is on the throne (Agrippa I receives the crown from the Emperor Claudius in 41 CE; see Acts 12.1), the high priest functioned as the representative of the people of Judea to Rome. Luke uses the singular reference to "chief priesthood" to refer to both Annas and Caiaphas (**vs. 2a**). Annas served as high priest from 6 to 15, and Caiaphas, his son in law, served 18–36.

Although Luke names neither of these men in the Passion Narrative, their presence here, along with that of Antipas, Pilate, and Caesar, foreshadows the fates of, respectively, John, Jesus, and Paul. By lumping all these political figures together, Luke not only shows that John and, subsequently, Jesus are players on the world's stage; the evangelist also indicates why Jesus instructed his follower to pray "your kingdom come" (11.2), for the present kingdom, international, national, and local, is found lacking. Luke, and some of Luke's readers, may well have been aware that the son of Annas, Ananus, executed James the brother of Jesus (Josephus, *Ant.* 20.9).

Into this political context, Luke introduces "John, the son of Zechariah" (**vs. 2b**). The first two verses could easily have served as the opening of the Gospel, and Mark's narrative indicates that a Nativity account is not necessary for the story of Jesus. Acts 1.22, wherein Peter emphasizes witnesses to the life of Jesus from the baptism to the Cross, can be seen as supporting the notion that Luke's Gospel originally began with the Baptist, since for Luke what is of utmost importance is Jesus' ministry and death, not his Nativity or his childhood. However, there are no otherwise complete manuscripts of the Third Gospel that lack the infancy accounts and many of the themes announced in Luke 1–2 are continued throughout the rest of the Gospel.

It is equally likely that Luke introduces John as the "son of Zechariah" both to recall Zechariah's own predictions of John's fate and to contrast John with other "sons" in the chapter: the children of vipers (vs. 7), those who claim Abrahamic sonship (vs. 8), the one for whom divine sonship is claimed (vs. 22), and the entire history of humanity, all of whom are "sons" or, better, "children of" Adam and so of God (vs. 38). Paternity in antiquity indicated not only one's lineage, it also indicated a legacy, a personality, and a place in society.

John's wilderness setting anticipates Jesus' wilderness trial in the next chapter even as it recalls Israel's time of purification in the wilderness following the Exodus from Egypt. The setting also establishes a contrast between the ascetic in the desert and both the kings in their palaces and the high priests in the Temple. The time of the first two chapters, of the faithful Jewish families going to the Temple, where they are warmly welcomed and where Jesus' teaching is appreciated by all, has past. Luke hints as well at the contrast between singular actor versus the entire political and priestly infrastructure. One voice, in the wilderness, can be as powerful as Caesar and Lysanias, Caiaphas and Philip.

This singular focus on John, rather than on his disciples or any community surrounding him, should check the popular tendency to associate John

with the Essenes or with Qumran and so the Dead Sea Scrolls. While such
a connection cannot be ruled out, and while John shares certain concerns
with the scrolls, from ritual immersion to a sense that divine justice will
soon replace human rule, there is no need to limit such views to one community. Moreover, were John to have been associated with Essenes and
Essenes, in turn, with the Scrolls, then Luke missed a good opportunity to
enhance John's reputation. The Essenes, at least according to Josephus, were
to be admired for their communal funds, honesty, and simple living,

Although people came to John to be baptized by him, Luke introduces
John by describing him as peripatetic: "he went into all the region around
the Jordan" (vs. 3). John reaches the people as best as he is able, given his
need for proximity to the river. His mission is to "preach" or "proclaim"
(Greek: *kēryssō*, a cognate to the term "kerygma") a "baptism of repentance
for the forgiveness of sins." John did not merely proclaim this baptism, he
practiced it. The term "baptism" comes from a Greek word meaning "to
dip" or "to dunk." The verbal aspect is the better way of introducing John,
such that he should be known not as John *the Baptist* (as if there were an
Albert the Baptist or Aretha the Baptist), but John *the baptizer*.

The rite of baptism is part of a cross-cultural pattern of ritual immersion.
What the rite signifies depends on the person performing it and the person
participating in it. It could signal rebirth, cleanliness or purity, forgiveness
or a change of status from outsider to insider, child to adult. Speaking on
behalf of the Deity, Isaiah proclaims, "Wash yourselves; make yourselves
clean; remove the evil of your doings from before my eyes; cease to do evil"
(Isa 1.16). According to Ezekiel, God promises, "I will sprinkle clean water
upon you, and you shall be clean from all your uncleannesses, and from all
your idols I will cleanse you" (Ezek 36.25). The Psalmist pleads, "Wash me
thoroughly from my iniquity, and cleanse me from my sin" (Psa 51.2).

In Jewish practice, immersion in a *miqveh* ("ritual bath") facilitates the
move from impurity to purity. A Jew in the Second Temple period might
immerse following menstruating or childbirth, ejaculation, or contact with
a corpse. The need to be in a state of ritual purity was primarily for worship
in the Jerusalem Temple, so most Jews were ritually impure most of the
time. Some people outside of the Temple's geographical proximity sought
to remain in states of ritual purity and thereby enact the roles of the priests
who served in the Temple; thus, they lived as if they were all members of a
"priestly kingdom and a holy nation" (Exod 19.6). Today, the *miqveh*, which
is usually connected to a synagogue, is used primarily by married women
at the end of each menstrual cycle, for part of the process of conversion to

Judaism, and for such life-cycle events as marriage and childbirth as well as, in some communities, for other moments in life for which a ritual of cleansing and reintegration might prove helpful, such as following a miscarriage or surgery.

Ritual impurity and moral impurity draw on the same language, but they should not be confused. Ritual impurity occurs because of normal bodily functions. Moral impurity occurs because of bad choices people make. No ritual washing can remove moral impurity; a bath cannot take away the sins of stealing or gossip. This distinction speaks directly to John the Baptizer's activities.

John's baptism draws from Jewish immersion practices concerning ritual purity and transforms them in three ways. First, he shifts the focus from ritual impurity to moral impurity. Instead of a regular purification process of immersion for normal human activity such as menstruation or ejaculation, John speaks about *a* baptism for the repentance of sins. The rite is not private, as would immersing in a *miqveh* be, but public. A person baptized by John would be comparable to a person who responded to an altar call or a public invitation to become a follower of Jesus: the community, witnessing the ritual, is placed in the position of holding the baptized person responsible for living the life the baptism signals. John's baptism was not, as far as we know, repeated by individuals; people did not go out after being immersed in the Jordan, sin during the week, and then present themselves for another immersion, as if John were running a get-out-of-hell weekly pass. Second, John associates his baptism with the in-breaking of the Kingdom of God; there is an eschatological focus to the ritual. John's baptism represented both the atonement of the baptized and their forgiveness in light of the coming Day of Judgment. Third, John plays a specific role as an officiant at a rite: one did not simply immerse; one *was immersed* by John.

Whether John's baptism washed away sin depends on the text one reads. For Luke, the details are not clear. Josephus, who mentions the respect with which John was held by his fellow Jews, states that John's baptism did not remit sin. Instead, according to Josephus, John was "a good man" who "commanded the Jews to exercise virtue, both as to righteousness towards one another, and piety towards God, and so to come to baptism; for that the washing [with water] would be acceptable to him, if they made use of it, not in order to the putting away [or the remission] of some sins [only], but for the purification of the body, supposing still that the soul was thoroughly purified beforehand by righteousness" (*Ant.* 18.117). For John, the immersion was the sign that the person had already repented and so been forgiven. *Or*, perhaps we should not read John's practice through the later lens of Josephus. Perhaps John really was suggesting immersion as an act of repentance and a recognition of the need for forgiveness. Josephus, an apologist as well as an historian writing, in part, to show Romans what splendid people Jews are, says nothing about John's eschatological program; nor does he say anything about the eschatology of the Essenes (here the question of whether the Dead Sea Scrolls are Essene texts complicates how we are to understand Josephus's comments on the sectarian groups).

These three points coupled with John's praise by Josephus indicate that John, historically, was not baptizing in opposition to the Temple system. One could be baptized by John as well as participate in pilgrimage or Temple sacrifice and prayer; similarly, today one can today go to a revival or visit a shrine and still attend a local church. Whether Luke sees John as in opposition to the Temple – John is, by paternal descent, a priest himself, but he does not serve in Jerusalem – remains an open question. But surely, Ben notes, some of the people must have been thinking that if they could get forgiveness as a result of John's immersion, then it would be unnecessary to go to Jerusalem and offer a sacrifice for atonement for sins. Here was an alternative means of forgiveness. Amy-Jill adds that because Josephus, a priest himself, saw no problems with John's baptizing, that at least for this priest, John worked in consonance with the Temple, not against it. Temple sacrifice was, for the people who directly participated in it, more for issues of purity and thanksgiving rather than sin.

Luke does not spend much time on the fine points of John's program. For Luke, John's major role is to prepare the way for Jesus. Following Mark's lead, Luke takes a quote from Isaiah, repunctuates it, and hints at different connotations of the terms. Isaiah, writing to the Jewish community in Babylon in the sixth century BCE, consoles the people by telling them that their exile is soon to end. "Get up," Isaiah the prophet insists, and get ready to go home: "A voice is shouting, 'In the desert, prepare the way of the Lord …'" Isaiah encourages the people, "Go out and build a highway, because you are going home." Ancient texts did not have commas and quotation marks; indeed, Hebrew even lacked vowels. Therefore, the same sentence could be understood in various ways.

Luke moves the comma. For Luke, Isaiah reads, "A voice is shouting in the desert …"; the reference is to John, in the desert (**vs. 4**). John is shouting, "prepare the way of the Lord." The Dead Sea Scrolls allow for the same translation, since the writers of the scrolls saw themselves as "in the desert" (i.e., at Qumran), where they were preparing for the Messianic age (cf. 1QS 8.12–16).

For Isaiah, the "way" is a road; for Luke, the term "way" (Greek: *hodos*, as in the English term "odometer") is the term the early followers of Jesus used as a self-reference; they did not call themselves "Christians" but "followers of the way" (Acts 9.2; 22.4; 24.14; see previous comments on 1.76). Thus, John's exhortation would be heard by Luke's readers as a reference to the Christian path. Finally, "the Lord" (Greek: *kyrios*), used by the Septuagint to translate the Hebrew Tetragammaton, the four letters that spell the name of the Deity, is in the New Testament usually a reference to Jesus. Isaiah's exhortation to the people to build a highway in the desert to show the end of exile becomes for Luke a description of John the Baptizer, in the desert, preparing people for the coming of Jesus.

Luke could have left Isaiah's quote with the point about the highway for the Lord; instead, Luke adds the next verse about valleys filled and mountains "made low" (**vs. 5**). The Greek for "made low" (*tapeinoō*) can also mean "humbled." The same term, in its noun form, appears in Mary's Magnificat in 1.52: "He has brought down the powerful from their thrones, and lifted up the lowly" (*tapeinous*). In speaking of the "humbling" or "humiliation" of the hills, Luke reminds readers of Mary's announcement and foreshadows Jesus' comments about reversal of roles in 6.21–26; 13.30, and 18.9–14; for Luke, the last will be first, and the first, last. The world itself will become, as Acts puts it, "topsy turvey" or "upside down" (Acts 17.6), in reversal of present social structures of rich and poor, emperor and peasant. This was the song Hannah had sung near the beginning of the Iron Age: "Those who were full have hired themselves out for bread, but those who were hungry are fat with spoil" (1 Sam. 2.5) and Isaiah sang during the Babylonian exile, and Mary sang at the turn of the era. The verses continue to resonate even as they are repurposed, as Luke does here.

The final line Luke records of Isaiah's prophecy concerns "all flesh" and the "salvation of God" (**vs. 6**). The verse moves readers from Isaiah's time to Luke's time to the present day, since all flesh has yet to see salvation. "Flesh" means human beings; "salvation" will have different connotations, as it does even in Luke's Gospel. It can mean salvation in the sense of final reward, eschatological redemption, or "getting into heaven"; for example, Jesus tells the man crucified next to him, "today you will be with me in Paradise" (23.43). However, the Gospel also suggests salvation indicates the comfort, hope, and healing that comes from Jesus' own teaching and actions. The first time the verbal form of the term for "salvation" appears in the Gospel, it is found on Jesus' lips when he says to the woman who was a sinner, "Your faith has saved you; go in peace" (7.50). To see the full complement of how this "salvation" functions, Theophilus and any "lover of God" will need to continue reading the Gospel and Acts as well.[1]

Such readers will realize immediately that for Luke, salvation is connected to ethical behavior. The crowds come to John for baptism, but Luke focuses not on immersion in the Jordan, but on the instruction of the Baptizer. John takes the offensive by referring to the people who approach him as a "brood of vipers" (**vs. 7**). This is not a compliment. The "brood" or "offspring" language continues the "sonship" focus of the chapter: one's parent determines one's status and one's actions. Vipers were thought to eat through the body of the mother and thus kill their parent; John's comparison can suggest that the people coming to him for baptism had killed the good tradition, represented by Zechariah and Elizabeth, Simeon and Anna, that gave them birth.

The "wrath to come" would include, for Luke's audience, the debacle of the Jewish revolt against Rome that began in 66 and ended in 70 with the destruction of the Temple. Rome blamed the Jews for engaging in revolt; the Jewish community blamed themselves, for no other explanation would make sense given the consensus that God is in control of history; the Church blamed the Jews for not accepting Jesus as Lord. Yet for Luke's readers, in the first century and the twenty-first, John's prediction and those that Jesus himself will make concerning the eschaton cannot be limited to past events. There is also for the Church a "second coming" including a final judgment. The Gospel's ethical teaching takes on heightened value when it is juxtaposed to that grand assize, for failure in ethics on earth will lead to damnation after death (see, e.g., 16.24).

John continues his attack by insisting that the people not rely on ancestral privilege; they need to act on their own. The appeal to "father Abraham" (**vs. 8**), again noting the theme of paternity, fits the Jewish idea, developed in the Rabbinic period and possibly in place earlier, that the community could appeal to the inexhaustible "Merits of the Fathers" (Heb: *Zechut Avot*): even were they to be lacking in righteousness, their ancestors were faithful and their merit could be tapped. We see hints of this idea in Moses' words to the people: "because He loved your ancestors, he chose their descendants after them. He brought you out of Egypt with his own

---

[1]   See the detailed study of Luke's use of salvation language in Witheringon, *Acts of the Apostles*, 821–43.

presence, by his great power" (Deut 4.37, cf. the appeal to the memory of the patriarchs in 32.13).

Judaism is a communal religion, which means that all members of the community are responsible for each other. If one person does something, for good or ill, that action has repercussions for everyone else. If one person sins, that sin impacts the community at large. And if one person engages in a meritorious act, the rest of the community can benefit from it. This view in part explains the cross: Jesus' faithful action impacts the entire community. However, whereas Judaism does speak of the Merits of the Fathers, such that past acts of righteousness evoke divine mercy on the present generation, it generally rejects the idea of what might be called the "sins of the Fathers": the present generations do not suffer for the sins of the past. The Talmud (*b. Sanh.* 27b) comments: "Are not children then to be put to death for the sins committed by their parents? Is it not written, 'Visiting the iniquities of the fathers upon the children' (Exod 34.7). There the reference is to children who hold in their hands the deeds of their parents (i.e., who follow their parents' footsteps)" (cf. *b. Ber.* 7a; *b. Mak.* 24a).

While the Merits of the Fathers are always available, appealing *only* to ancestral merit is insufficient. Each generation needs to add its own meritorious conduct. John the Baptizer puns by speaking of raising up "children" to Abraham from "stones," since the Hebrew term for "stone" (*eben*) is just one letter away from the Hebrew word for "child" or "son" (*ben*). Whether Luke or Luke's Greek-speaking readers would have recognized the pun remains unknown.

The more informed among Luke's readers also would have recognized the Baptizer's allusion to Isa 51.1–2:

> Listen to me, you that pursue righteousness,
>   you that seek the Lord.
> Look to the rock from which you were hewn,
>   and to the quarry from which you were dug.
> Look to Abraham your father
>   and to Sarah who bore you;
> for he was but one when I called him,
>   but I blessed him and made him many.

Looking to Abraham and so relying on ancestry is appropriate, but each generation, each person, needs to contribute.

John then alerts the people who have repented and have come to be baptized that repentance and baptism are also not enough: the ritual and the repenting must be followed up by good works. Neither the Jewish tradition *nor the Christian tradition* teaches that only correct belief makes one righteous. Unless that belief is accompanied by good deeds – or as John puts it, by "good fruit" (**vs. 9**) – it is worth nothing and so deserving of destruction. As the Epistle of James similarly insists, "Faith without works is dead" (Jas 2.26).

John is not presenting a new teaching. Isaiah had already warned, "The tallest trees will be cut down, and the lofty will be brought low. He will hack down the thickets of the forest with an ax, and Lebanon with its majestic trees will fall" (Isa 10.33b–34). John adds to this teaching with his eschatological threat not only of being chopped down but also of being "thrown into the fire." Encouraging repentance by threat of damnation may not be psychologically healthy, but it is often rhetorically effective.

To John's warnings, the crowds – men and women, poor and rich, sinners and saints – ask for guidance: "What then should we do?" (**vs. 10**). The same question will be repeated by specific groups: tax collectors (3.12), soldiers (3.14), a lawyer (10.25), and a ruler (18.18). The question is on one level unnecessary: the Jewish people already know from their Torah what is required of them. "Father" Abraham makes this very point in the Parable of the Rich Man and Lazarus (16.19–30) when he tells the rich man who seeks to save his brothers from hell: "They have Moses and the prophets; they should listen to them" (16.29).

But for these groups assembled around John, more information is needed: given the impending destruction, John proclaims, what should they do *now*? Perhaps each person, and each group, sought special instructions not explicit in Torah. There is no separate law code for tax collectors, soldiers, lawyers, or rulers. Moreover, all Torah requires interpretation, and new situations require new teaching. What is John's advice, in this time of Caesar, Pilate, and Caiaphas? What is John's advice, in light of the impending Day of Judgment?

John's answers are eminently practical. He gives no instruction on theological matters or doctrinal speculation; he offers no teachings on prayer or liturgy. Nor does he speak of supererogatory actions possible only for those who have no responsibility to others, such as "sell all you have …" (18.22). He speaks rather to matters of interpersonal ethics, that is, to the details of what it means to "love your neighbor as yourself" (Lev 19.18). According to John, people should share, whether material goods or food (**vs. 11**). The injunction is not just for the rich person who might have two coats; it is to any who might have a piece of bread that can be broken into pieces. John does not demand divestment, and he does not glorify poverty; he demands justice and fairness: When one person has two coats while another goes naked, and when one has feasts while another starves, that is unjust. Josephus summarizes John's teaching in a similar way by describing him as "a good man who commanded the Jews to exercise virtue, both as to righteousness towards one another and piety towards God" (*Ant.* 18.117).

The tax collectors (**vs. 12**) approach John with the title "Teacher" (Greek: *didaskalos*); the Hebrew equivalent would be *rabbi*. Teachers held positions of respect, as already seen in 2.46 when Jesus is found among the teachers in the Temple. Outside of the infancy material and this address to John, Luke attributes the title "teacher" only Jesus (3.2; 7.40; 8.49; 9.38; 10.25; 11.45; 12.13; 18.18; 19.39; 20.21, 28,39; 21.7; 22.11). Both John and Jesus are teachers, and both seek the repentance of the people, but Jesus will be more than a teacher; he is also "lord." Thus, for Luke, to limit Jesus to the role of teacher and so to dismiss the cross and its cosmic effects would be to misunderstand his mission. For the Gospel, the good news is more than ethical exhortation, and the message is more than one of secular humanism. Soteriology cannot be divorced, in Luke's view, from Christology, and ethics cannot be divorced from Jesus' death, resurrection, and ascension.

The tax collectors epitomize the type of sin that prevents community solidarity. Tax collectors took funds from the local population and gave it to the Romans. They were known for collecting more than the tax assessment, which is precisely the problem John addresses: "Collect no more than the amount prescribed" (**vs. 13**). He says nothing about repayment (contrast the generosity of Zaccheus the chief tax collector of 19.1–10) and nothing about giving to charity. John starts with a doable baseline: do no harm; do not take more than is your due. Interpreters who rush to associate tax collectors and the frequently paired "sinners" with matters of ritual, as opposed to moral, impurity again mistake how Jewish purity regulations function. Tax collectors however, in order to survive, had to collect more than the authorities required; otherwise, they had no salary. This system necessarily led to gouging.

To soldiers, John again offers the practical advice: do not extort; be satisfied with your wages (**vs. 14**). Although it is possible these soldiers were gentiles, the setting makes more likely the understanding that they are Jews serving in Herod's local force. Tax collectors and soldiers work with the support of, and to support, the government both imperial and local, and both are able to take advantage of their position. Luke does not find tax collecting or joining the army itself to be sinful, and indeed Luke will later present both tax collectors and army officers – still in their jobs – as models of righteousness.

The presence of tax collectors and soldiers – not the most beloved members of the population – coming to John prompted no small deliberation by the people of the region. The repenting of those known to do evil became for them a sign that, just perhaps, this John might be the Christ (**v. 15**; Luke uses this Greek term, *christos*, which the NRSV translates as "Messiah"). The Gospel has yet to provide a definition of the term, which had in the Jewish but not the pagan world connotations of divine commission, but with each use the connotations become more complex. The angel told the shepherds that the Christ has been born in Bethlehem and that he is "savior" and "lord" (2.11); Simeon, seeing the baby, announced that he had seen "the Lord's Messiah" (2.26). Now, in 3.15, the term receives additional details: the Messiah is someone who prompts tax collectors and soldiers to repent; the Messiah teaches ethical behavior and prepares people for the final judgment.

As the infancy narratives, with their step-parallelism, already indicated, John is not the Messiah. The next verse makes this point explicitly. Just as Jesus will demonstrate that he knows the thoughts of people before they express them, so John knows what is in the hearts of the people who have come to him. He responds in humility: a stronger one is coming; he is so great that John is not even worthy to serve as his slave by untying his sandal. Whereas John baptizes in water, this new figure will baptize with the Holy Spirit and fire (**vs. 16**). It is only in Acts 1.5 (cf. Acts 11.16) and then the Pentecost scene in Acts 2.1–4 that readers will recognize the full import of John's comment. In the context of Luke's narrative, John's announcement is mysterious: *How* is one dipped into fire? *How* is one dunked into the Spirit? If baptism in water relates to repentance, what does baptism in fire suggest?

John does not develop the discussion of baptism; instead, he returns to eschatological warning. Not only is his ax laid at the root, but this coming figure brings a winnowing fork to clear out the universal threshing floor following the final harvest (**vs. 17**). The wheat – to mix a metaphor, the people who bear good fruit – will be placed safely in barns; the chaff, those who bear nothing, will be consumed in unquenchable fire (the Greek term here is the source of the English word "asbestos"). For John, the end-time has begun and the judgment is under way. It is even possible that John saw the judgments as already completed: the wheat and the chaff have already made themselves known; the chaff cannot become wheat, any more than rocky ground can become fertile soil (8.8) or bad trees can bear good fruit (6.43).

John's message is, given his audience, one of comfort: people who have brought themselves to John and repented *are the wheat*; those who deny John and his baptism are the chaff. Hence Luke notes that John is proclaiming "good news" (**vs. 18**): the righteous who have sided with John will be rewarded; those who deny him will be burned.

In the next two verses, Luke abbreviates the story of a couple who represent the chaff: Herod Antipas and his wife Herodias. Whereas Mark and Matthew present a detailed account of Herod's banquet, at which Herodias's daughter danced and then demanded John's head on a silver platter, Luke simply remarks here that John had rebuked Herod "because of" his brother's wife as well as numerous unspecified evil actions (**vs. 19**) and that as a result Herod imprisoned John (**vs. 20**). The details of the marriage, including Herodias's divorcing Herod's half-brother and then, by marrying Herod, violating Levitical law (Lev 18.16), go unmentioned. Only in 9.9 does the reader learn that Herod also had the Baptizer beheaded

Luke takes the focus off John's death in order to move to Jesus' own experience at the baptism. At the same time, Luke makes it clear that Jesus and John were not engaged in rival movements; Jesus only began his mission after John had been imprisoned.

Turning to the baptism itself, Luke states that John had baptized *all the people* and adds, in the passive voice, that Jesus too *had been baptized* (**vs. 21**). The import is not the person performing the ritual, but that Jesus, together with the others at the Jordan, participated. One could even read Luke's Gospel and conclude that John did not baptize Jesus; John's Gospel suggests exactly that, since the Fourth Gospel has a baptizer, but no baptism of Jesus. Luke also says nothing about whether Jesus had repented, or even if he was sinful; only in the Epistle to the Hebrews (4.15) is Jesus said, explicitly, to be without sin.

Following his baptism, Jesus prays. The reference to prayer is Lukan; the comparative material in Mark (1.10) and Matthew (3.16) says nothing about prayer in the context of Jesus' baptism. Luke's Gospel will continue to stress Jesus at prayer (5.16; 6.12; 9.18; 11.1; 22.32), both to show Jesus' communication with his Father and to model the need for prayer to his disciples. Luke also reveals that the prayers are a form of communication: as Jesus prays, the heavens open. The reference connects Jesus to Ezekiel, who begins his prophecy by stating that "in the thirtieth year, in the fourth month, on the fifth day of the month, as I was among the exiles by the river Chebar, the heavens were opened, and I saw visions of God" (Ezek 1.1). Both Luke and Ezekiel offer a political context determined by date, the solidarity of the main figure among the people, a river setting, and the open heavens.

The *Holy Spirit* that descends in bodily form (**vs. 22a**) confirms what Luke's narrative has so far indicated: that Jesus is the beloved son of God. This is the same Spirit that inspired Elizabeth and Zechariah and by which Jesus was conceived; it is the same Spirit that will, according to Acts 2, descend on the followers of Jesus at Pentecost. The form of the dove reminds readers of Noah's ark, from which the dove was sent after the flood (Gen 8.8–12), although what exactly it symbolizes here remains opaque. The dove is not, in biblical literature, a sign of peace, and it is only in later Christian literature that it takes on this connotation. One comment in one Talmudic tractate (*b. Hag.* 15a) compares the "wind" or "spirit" (Heb. *ruach*; Gr. *pneuma*) of God that hovered over the deep (Gen 1.2) to a dove.

It would be anachronistic to read full-blown Trinitarian thought into Luke's reference, but from the perspective of later Christian theology it would be odd to avoid this association. What Luke intended to say, or what Luke's earliest readers heard, is not the sum total of what the Gospel means, or will mean. Further, the raw data from which one can construct Trinitarian theology can be found in the Gospels and elsewhere in the NT. Had Luke been asked whether the Holy Spirit was a divine person, and not merely a presence, a force, or a power, but a being, Ben is convinced his answer surely would have been yes. Ben further takes the analogy with the dove as meant to convey the idea that the Spirit, like the dove, is a living being. Amy-Jill would nuance the point. Yes, there are multiple divinities, as even Paul acknowledges in 1 Cor 8.5, "… there may be so-called gods in heaven or on earth – as in fact there are many gods and many lords"; but there is for Paul and the Corinthians he addresses "one God, the Father, from whom are all things and for whom we exist, and one Lord, Jesus Christ, through whom are all things and through whom we exist" (1 Cor 8.6). The issue then becomes not whether the Spirit is a "person" in "bodily form" but whether the Spirit is to be worshiped.[2]

The voice from heaven (**vs. 22b**) is called, in Hebrew, a *bat qol*, or "daughter of [the] voice"; it is a circumlocution for describing God's voice as it speaks from heaven. This same voice will return at the Transfiguration (9.35) with

---

[2]   See Paula Fredriksen, "Mandatory Retirement: Ideas in the Study of Christian Origins Whose Time Has Come to Go," *Studies in Religion/Sciences Religieuses* 35.2 (2006): 231–46 (esp. 241–43).

the same message, although there only Peter, James, and John will hear it. The *bat qol* is also known from rabbinic literature, and its origins trace back to the Bible, where a "voice" comes down from heaven (e.g., Dan 4.31, "a voice came from heaven," in this case, to King Nebuchadnezzar of Babylon). Resonant are statements that speak of hearing the divine voice but seeing no image, such as the voice of God at Sinai – "Then the Lord spoke to you out of the fire. You heard the sound of words but saw no form; there was only a voice" (Deut 4.12) – and the "still small voice" or "sound of sheer silence" after the storm that came to the prophet Elijah (1 Kings 19.12–13). According to the Tosefta (ca. 250 CE), the *bat qol* serves as a replacement for the ancient prophets upon whom the Holy Spirit rested (*t. Sot.* 13.2). Yet although the *bat qol* resounds through later Jewish literature to sinners as warnings and to saints as affirmation, it can also be debated.

The most famous rabbinic passage regarding the *bat qol* appears in the Babylonian Talmud (*b. B. Metz.* 58b–59a, and cf. *y. Mo'ed Katan* 3.1, 81 c–d). The passage concerns whether the oven of Aknai, which was constructed with layers of sand between each of its pieces, was kosher. R. Eliezer, who proclaims it kosher, "brought forward every imaginable argument, but they [the other rabbis] did not accept them. Said he to them, 'If the *halachah* [i.e, the legal decision] agrees with me, let this carob-tree prove it.' Thereupon the carob-tree was torn a hundred cubits out of its place – others affirm, four hundred cubits. 'No proof can be brought from a carob-tree,' they retorted." The debate goes on: Rabbi Eliezer prompts a stream of water to flow backward, and so on. Finally, he calls out, "If the *halachah* agrees with me, let it be proved from heaven.' Whereupon a heavenly voice cried out, 'Why do you dispute with R. Eliezer, seeing that in all matters the *halachah* agrees with him?' But R. Joshua arose and exclaimed: 'It is not in heaven ...'"

R. Joshua is alluding to Deuteronomy 30.12–14: "It [Torah] is not in heaven, that you should say, "Who will go up to heaven for us, and get it for us so that we may hear it and observe it?" Neither is it beyond the sea, that you should say, "Who will cross to the other side of the sea for us, and get it for us so that we may hear it and observe it? No, the word is very near to you; it is in your mouth and in your heart for you to observe." In other words, you gave us the Torah; let us determine how to interpret it.

The story continues: "R. Nathan met Elijah and asked him, 'What did the Holy One, Blessed be He, do in that hour?' 'He laughed [with joy], he replied, saying "My sons have defeated me, My sons have defeated me.'" We have here several differences between classical Christian thought and classical Jewish thought. As the traditions developed and came to separate,

Judaism stressed Torah interpretation and majority communal voices; Christianity stressed miraculous intervention and the charismatic authority of individuals.

At his baptism and his prayer, Jesus alone hears the message: "*You* are my beloved son." The term for "beloved" (Greek: *agapētos*) comes from the same root as the more familiar term *agapē*, meaning "love." A reference to a beloved child has multiple echoes in Israel's Scriptures. Isaac, the child Abraham almost sacrificed, is the "beloved son" (Gen 22.2 LXX); Israel also is God's "beloved son" (Hos 11.1). The closest reference to Luke's baptism scene is, however, Psalm 2.7, a royal psalm that proclaims, "I will tell of the decree of the Lord: He said to me, 'You are my son; today I have begotten you.'" In the "Western Text," also known as Codex Bezae or "D," Luke's verse reads, "You are my beloved son; *today I have begotten you,*" a quote from Psalm 2.7. Which reading was the original, or whether there ever was an "original" version of the Gospel as opposed to multiple contemporaneous written versions, cannot be determined.[3]

The voice adds another description to this beloved son: God is "well pleased" with him. Again, biblical echoes sound, with a striking chord in Isa 42.1, "Here is my servant, whom I uphold, my chosen, in whom my soul delights; I have put my spirit upon him; he will bring forth justice to the nations." The designation of "Messiah" thus gains new connotations: of being God's servant as well as son, and of proclaiming justice. Luke ends the scene with the voice, and not with Jesus' reaction. Although the voice offered no commission per se, the resonance of the *bat qol* with Isa 42.1 hints at the work to be done: proclaim justice. The earlier language of salvation also functions as a type of job description.

The last notice Luke provides is that Jesus was "about thirty" (**vs. 23a**) when all this happened. The age may be correct, although given the difficulties of the dating of Jesus' birth, it may be better regarded as symbolic. Joseph was thirty when he began to serve Pharaoh (Gen 41.46) and David was thirty when he began to rule (2 Sam 5.4). Dionysius of Halicarnassus, the Greek historian (60 BCE–ca. 7BCE), in speaking of Tarquin, noted in regard to the thirtieth year that "it is from this age onwards, as a rule, that the laws call to the magistracies and to the administration of public affairs those who desire such a career" *(Roman Antiquities* 6.3). John's Gospel suggests that Jesus might have been older: his opponents say to him, "You

---

[3]   On this textual tradition, see Ben Witherington III, "The Anti-Feminist Tendencies of the Western Text of Acts," *JBL* 103 (1984): 82–84.

are not yet fifty years old, and have you seen Abraham?" (John 8.57). There is a major difference in appearance between thirty and fifty.

The chapter ends with Jesus' genealogy according to Luke (**vs. 23b–38**). In Matthew's Gospel, the genealogy begins with Abraham and works its way down through to David, then the Babylonian exile, and then to Jacob the father of Joseph. That ending associates the Joseph of the Nativity with the earlier Joseph, son of Jacob, who also dreamed dreams and brought his family safely to Egypt. Luke begins with Jesus and works backward, and immediately a discrepancy occurs. For Matthew, the father of Joseph is Jacob; for Luke, the father's name is Heli. The genealogies will not agree again until King David. Attempts to make the lists correspond by suggesting that the Matthean genealogy offers throne names and the Lucan genealogy offers given names, or by making Luke's genealogy that of Mary rather than Joseph, mistake the purpose of the lists. Neither Matthew nor Luke is primarily interested in history here, and no actual history could be had, since following Zerubbabel at the end of the Babylonian exile, the names of Davidic descendants are lost. Israel would instead be ruled by priests until the beginning of the Hasmonean period in 164 BCE. Claims that families in the Davidic line retained the records cannot be substantiated. In his own autobiography, Josephus starts only with his grandfather (*Life* 3). While he does suggest that the priests kept genealogical records (*Contra Apion* 1.30–38) – and indeed Jews to this day recognize families in the priestly and Levitical lines – Josephus says nothing about the preservation of Davidic lineage.

It is better to regard the genealogies not as list of names that one can confirm or deny, but rather as serving Christological purposes. For Matthew, Jesus is the culmination of the story of Abraham and David, neatly divided into three series of fourteen generations each (Matthew makes the pattern fit by omitting a number of kings). For Luke, Jesus is connected to the royal household of David, a point already made by Gabriel's annunciation to Mary that her son would have "the throne of his ancestor David" (1.32) and confirmed by the birth in Bethlehem, the "city of David" (2.4). But his ancestor is not Solomon, as Matthew states, but another son, named Nathan. The name does not appear in any genealogies of David, but it does recall Nathan the prophet, the conscience of the court.

For Luke, the genealogy consists of seventy-seven names (or seventy-five, or seventy-two, etc., depending on which early manuscript we consult) and so suggests completion or perfection. The conclusion, or technically, the origin, connects Jesus to "son of Adam, son of God" (**vs. 38**). The verse indicates that all people, Jew and gentile, are children of God.

BRIDGING THE HORIZONS

1. The Baptist as Messiah

According to the Mandaens, a group based in Iraq and Southwest Iran and recently in the news because of persecution from ISIS, John the Baptizer is the Messiah and Jesus is an imposter. Their website describes them as "descended from Adam who was the first to receive the religious instructions of the Mandaeans," and it adds that their "last great teacher and healer was John the Baptizer."[4] The Mandaeans have an elaborate baptismal ritual, hold to strict dietary requirements, and are strictly aniconic, such that they have no images to which they pray. Their Sabbath is Sunday. According to Suhaib Nashi, general secretary of the Mandaean Association Union in Exile, "The most striking thing about the killings of Mandaeans in Iraq is that its [motives range] from monetary gain by the extremists to the more sinister reason of ethnically cleansing the population of Iraq to get rid of the entire population of Mandaeans."[5]

The plight of the Mandaeans today, persecuted because of their religious beliefs and ethnic distinctions, sends us back to the time of John the Baptizer. The Gospels intimate that there was a rivalry between John's followers and the followers of Jesus. In Mark's version of the baptism, John simply baptizes Jesus. In Matthew's rendition, "John would have prevented him, saying, 'I need to be baptized by you, and do you come to me?'" (Matt 3.14). In Luke's account, Jesus' superiority to John is already expressed when the two men are *in utero*, and John's mother calls Mary "the mother of my lord" (1.43). Finally, in John's Gospel, the Baptizer is neither associated with Elijah nor a messianic prophet (John 1.21) but is merely the "voice in the wilderness," and he is not depicted as having baptized Jesus. From the earlier texts to the later, John's role diminishes in relation to Jesus' messianic status.

Religious rivalries are nothing new. Whereas it is appropriate for adherents of one tradition to find their views superior to the views of others, the global histories of religious intolerance, and worse, should have taught us that claims of religious truth should not be debated at the point of a gun. Each group has its own logical sense. The Gospels bear witness that John the Baptizer had his own followers. Whether he would have regarded himself as the forerunner of the Messiah Jesus (as the Gospels present him)

---

4   www.mandaeanunion.org/component/k2/item/164-who-are-the-mandaeans.
5   www.ipsnews.net/2014/11/disciples-of-john-the-baptist-also-flee-isis/.

or whether he saw himself as the final prophet before the eschatological age will depend on the text one reads and the worshiper one asks.

How today do we proclaim the truths of our own religion without creating a system where those who hold another view are marginalized, demeaned, or oppressed? One way of proceeding is to recognize that different religions tell different stories with different Scriptures. The truth claims of each set of texts or each list of doctrines cannot be reconciled or, if you prefer, will not be reconciled until the culmination of the ages, the final judgment, the world to come, or whatever each group regards as eschatological markers.

Another way of addressing religious diversity is to see that faith is a matter of love rather than the result of logic. The Gospels are self-affirming texts, and Luke our evangelist has a particular agenda. The same can be said for Mandaean Scriptures. The task in interreligious conversation is not to explain why someone else has erroneous views – that would be no more successful than to explain why someone's love is not love. The task is to show how one's religious beliefs manifest themselves in the world. Here the Baptizer's ethical teachings, according to Luke, can be celebrated by all.

2. John's Ethics

John's advice to the general population as well as, specifically, to tax collectors and army personnel, is practical and direct: don't extort, don't take more than what you need; and be satisfied with your pay, make sure others who are in need have enough to get through the day. The exhortations, although simple, are almost impossible to implement. In today's culture, saving for the proverbial rainy day, let alone saving for one's children's college education, or for retirement so one will not be a burden on the children, precludes our giving away one of those two coats. With inflation as well as wage discrimination, raises may be all that keep us from falling through the social cracks. We do not live in light of an imminent eschatology; we fear to share, lest there not be enough for tomorrow, or the day after.

We also continue to rely on our parents, and their reputations. In some towns, "who's your daddy" makes all the difference, from getting a job to getting into a good school to joining a club. Life is not a strict meritocracy in which those who work the hardest make the most. Not every child has parents who express joy and love upon the birth; in the case of some pregnancies, the comments are less, "You look like you're glowing," than, "You'll have another mouth to feed," or, "You'll have to drop out of school to take care of the child," or, "You'll go stay with your aunt until the baby is born and then give it up for adoption."

John's warning speaks directly to people today who so rely on that privilege that they have even forgotten what it means. Caucasians in the United States do not recognize the privilege they have simply by being white. People born in one country or region do not realize the authority they have by speaking without what the native population perceives to be a foreign accent. John calls us to recognize that not all are, in fact, born equal. Not all have access to resources or power. If we recognized that we are all children of Adam and so children of God, we would be less inclined to rely on ancestral privilege, and we would be more inclined to recognize our responsibility to others, to clothe them and feed them. John's proclamation and Jesus' genealogy combine to reveal our interconnected worlds, and our interconnected ethical imperative.

Luke 4 The Wilderness, Nazareth, and Capernaum

⁴ Jesus, full of the Holy Spirit, returned from the Jordan and was led by the Spirit in the wilderness, ² where for forty days he was tempted by the devil. He ate nothing at all during those days, and when they were over, he was famished. ³ The devil said to him, "If you are the Son of God, command this stone to become a loaf of bread." ⁴ Jesus answered him, "It is written, 'One does not live by bread alone.'"

⁵ Then the devil led him up and showed him in an instant all the kingdoms of the world. ⁶ And the devil said to him, "To you I will give their glory and all this authority; for it has been given over to me, and I give it to anyone I please. ⁷ If you, then, will worship me, it will all be yours." ⁸ Jesus answered him, "It is written,

> 'Worship the Lord your God,
> and serve only him.'"

⁹ Then the devil took him to Jerusalem, and placed him on the pinnacle of the temple, saying to him, "If you are the Son of God, throw yourself down from here, ¹⁰ for it is written,

> 'He will command his angels concerning you,
> to protect you,'

¹¹ and

> 'On their hands they will bear you up,
> so that you will not dash your foot against a stone.'"

¹² Jesus answered him, "It is said, 'Do not put the Lord your God to the test.'" ¹³ When the devil had finished every test, he departed from him until an opportune time.

THE NAZARETH SYNAGOGUE

[14] Then Jesus, filled with the power of the Spirit, returned to Galilee, and a report about him spread through all the surrounding country. [15] He began to teach in their synagogues and was praised by everyone.

[16] When he came to Nazareth, where he had been brought up, he went to the synagogue on the sabbath day, as was his custom. He stood up to read, [17] and the scroll of the prophet Isaiah was given to him. He unrolled the scroll and found the place where it was written:

[18] "The Spirit of the Lord is upon me,
> because he has anointed me
>> to bring good news to the poor.
He has sent me to proclaim release to the captives
> and recovery of sight to the blind,
>> to let the oppressed go free,
[19] to proclaim the year of the Lord's favor."

[20] And he rolled up the scroll, gave it back to the attendant, and sat down. The eyes of all in the synagogue were fixed on him. [21] Then he began to say to them, "Today this scripture has been fulfilled in your hearing." [22] All spoke well of him and were amazed at the gracious words that came from his mouth. They said, "Is not this Joseph's son?" [23] He said to them, "Doubtless you will quote to me this proverb, 'Doctor, cure yourself!' And you will say, 'Do here also in your hometown the things that we have heard you did at Capernaum.'"

[24] And he said, "Truly I tell you, no prophet is accepted in the prophet's hometown. [25] But the truth is, there were many widows in Israel in the time of Elijah, when the heaven was shut up three years and six months, and there was a severe famine over all the land; [26] yet Elijah was sent to none of them except to a widow at Zarephath in Sidon. [27] There were also many lepers in Israel in the time of the prophet Elisha, and none of them was cleansed except Naaman the Syrian."

[28] When they heard this, all in the synagogue were filled with rage. [29] They got up, drove him out of the town, and led him to the brow of the hill on which their town was built, so that they might hurl him off the cliff. [30] But he passed through the midst of them and went on his way.

HEALINGS IN CAPERNAUM

[31] He went down to Capernaum, a city in Galilee, and was teaching them on the sabbath. [32] They were astounded at his teaching, because he spoke with

authority. [33] In the synagogue there was a man who had the spirit of an unclean demon, and he cried out with a loud voice, [34] "Let us alone! What have you to do with us, Jesus of Nazareth? Have you come to destroy us? I know who you are, the Holy One of God." [35] But Jesus rebuked him, saying, "Be silent, and come out of him!" When the demon had thrown him down before them, he came out of him without having done him any harm. [36] They were all amazed and kept saying to one another, "What kind of utterance is this? For with authority and power he commands the unclean spirits, and out they come!" [37] And a report about him began to reach every place in the region.

[38] After leaving the synagogue he entered Simon's house. Now Simon's mother-in-law was suffering from a high fever, and they asked him about her. [39] Then he stood over her and rebuked the fever, and it left her. Immediately she got up and began to serve them.

[40] As the sun was setting, all those who had any who were sick with various kinds of diseases brought them to him; and he laid his hands on each of them and cured them. [41] Demons also came out of many, shouting, "You are the Son of God!" But he rebuked them and would not allow them to speak, because they knew that he was the Messiah.

[42] At daybreak he departed and went into a deserted place. And the crowds were looking for him; and when they reached him, they wanted to prevent him from leaving them. [43] But he said to them, "I must proclaim the good news of the kingdom of God to the other cities also; for I was sent for this purpose." [44] So he continued proclaiming the message in the synagogues of Judea.

It is widely recognized that the sermon that Jesus gives in the Nazareth synagogue is programmatic for much of what follows in this Gospel. In fact, this sermon has the same rhetorical function in the Gospel as does Peter's sermon in Acts 2 for the Book of Acts.[1] Less often observed is that the opening narrative in Luke 4, the Temptation story, also sets up what follows, for only here does Jesus confront Satan during the ministry; Luke states that Satan departed *until an opportune time*, which turns out to be in 22.3, when Satan possesses Judas Iscariot. In between these two events, Jesus announces that he has seen Satan falling like lightning from heaven; Jesus' exorcisms, starting with the first healing in Capernaum, confirm his

---

[1] For numerous parallels, structural and otherwise, between Luke and Acts, and within each of those works, see C. H. Talbert, *Literary Patterns, Theological Themes, and the Genre of Luke-Acts* (Missoula: Scholar's Press, 1974).

victory. During his ministry as well, Jesus *will* make food appear miraculously, *will* proclaim a kingdom worth more than the earthly governments,
and *will* give up his life, but not in order to prove himself to Satan.
During Jesus' ministry, the Dominion of God is breaking into human history.[2] Readers thus know that when the Passion Narrative begins, when
Jesus once again faces Satan's agent in Jerusalem, that the battle has already
been engaged.

THE TEMPTATION

In Chapter 3, Luke sets John the Baptizer and Jesus in the context of international and local politics: Tiberius, Pilate, Herod, Caiaphas, and others
who hold authority on earth. With vss. 4.1–13, the "Temptation Narrative,"
Luke locates one possible source of their power: Satan, and it is Satan's
form of rule that Jesus resists. Yet the extent to which these authorities
gain their authority from Satan is debatable. Ben proposes that for Luke,
Caesar gains his power from God, although he grants that authorities can
misuse their power. Amy-Jill sees these governmental figures as operating
against the "kingdom" that Jesus proclaims, and she takes Satan's second
offer to Jesus of the glory and authority of all the kingdoms of the world,
as bona fide. In the Temptation Narrative, Satan offers Jesus power, acclamation, and immortality – all of which he will eventually gain – but on his
own terms.

Ben finds convincing Justo González's reading of the Temptation in
terms of a "double typology."[3] First, noting the genealogy's linkage of
Jesus and Adam (3.38), González sees the Temptation as a correction to
Adam's failure in Eden. Second, he sees it as correcting Israel's failure in
the wilderness: "The point is that the life of Christ begins the undoing
of the Fall, and indeed also the re-doing of the story of God's people.
But in order to undo the harm of the Fall and the sins of God's people
evil must be directly confronted and conquered."[4] For Luke, it is the

---

[2] Bovon, *Commentary on the Gospel of Luke*, critiques Hans Conzelmann's suggestion that
     the ministry of Jesus is a Satan-free time. To the contrary, the stories of the exorcisms
     show Jesus is battling and beating Satan by freeing his captives. See Bovon's Excursus on
     "Satan in Luke-Acts," pp. 141–42. For Conzelmann's still often-cited thesis, see his *The
     Theology of Saint Luke* (London: Faber and Faber, 1960; translation of the 2d ed. of *Die
     Mitte der Zeit: Studien zur Theologie des Lukas* [1957].

[3] Justo L. González, *Luke* (Belief: A Theological Commentary on the Bible; Louisville:
     Westminster John Knox, 2010), 56.

[4] Ibid., 57.

cross that will rectify the sins in Eden and the wilderness. Ben points out that this reading does correspond with Ps 51.5 LXX – "Indeed, I was born guilty, a sinner when my mother conceived me" – and Paul too taught that Adam's sin affected his descendants and so all humanity (Rom 5.12–21).

Amy-Jill sees this reading much as she sees Trinitarian readings of the Gospel: reading through the eyes of developed Christian faith, González's point holds; in terms of Luke's Gospel in its first-century context and in terms of what the Gospel records, she finds this reading less convincing. The idea of humanity's innate sinfulness is a very rare idea in both the Tanakh and Rabbinic Judaism. Contemporaneous Jewish sources do not emphasize a "Fall" (the term is a Christian one) in which, because of Adam and Eve's actions, humanity found itself in a state of alienation from God. For most Jews, sin can be conquered, as God early tells Cain, "Sin is lurking at the door ... but you must master it" (Gen 4.7). The Torah, given to Israel through God's gracious initiative, provides the guide by which one engages in right action and so overcomes temptation and the evil inclination. If one does sin, the Torah provides teachings regarding repentance and atonement, and both are possible, as the story of John the Baptizer indicates. Since the idea of a Fall and therefore a breach between heaven and earth does not characterize all of Israel's Scriptures or early Judaism; since Luke has depicted in the infancy accounts Jews "blameless" under the law; since the genealogy establishes no breaks between Adam and Jesus; since Luke does not speak of Adamic guilt or original sin; and since Luke, unlike Matt (20.28), and Mark (10.45), does not depict Jesus as dying to ransom humanity back, likely from Satan, she prefers the following alternative understanding of the juxtaposition of the genealogy and the Temptation.

That alternative view may be found in the genealogy's ending, "Son of Adam, son of God." Jesus' connection to all humanity indicates that just as he can resist temptation – and just as Abraham and Joseph and Job resisted temptation – so can anyone whose faith in the God of Israel and in the Torah is strong enough. Jesus' temptations differ in quality from normal human temptations: we cannot turn stones into bread, nor have we the confidence that angels will break our falls, nor do we have the chance to seize universal power. But everyone is tempted to engage in the quick fix rather than promote systemic change, to put self-interest ahead of communal need, and to worship the gods of this earth: money, power, fame, beauty, longevity. Thus, the temptations in Luke 4, although part of a cosmic battle, are also lessons for all people. As Jesus shows, knowledge and the use of Torah are one of the keys to overcoming demonic lures.[5]

Both Luke's Gospel (4.1–13) and Matthew's (Matt 4.1–11) present three temptations, but the accounts differ in order. Each begins with the temptation to turn stones into bread. Matthew's second temptation is for Jesus to throw himself down from the Temple parapet, whereas Luke reserves this for the third temptation. Matthew ends with the temptation of universal rule, and Luke ends at the Temple in Jerusalem. The Matthean version is more compelling in terms of the breadth of setting and the related escalation of power, from personal hunger in the wilderness to a show of divine protection in Jerusalem (which Matthew calls here the "holy city") to universal rule. Luke's order preserves the Gospel's focus on Jerusalem, where the text began as it introduced Zechariah in the Temple. The Third Gospel emphasizes Jesus' journey to Jerusalem (see 9.51; 13.13), and it is in Jerusalem where Jesus will face his final temptation. The Gospel ends with Jesus' followers "continually in the temple blessing God" (24.53).

For Luke, Jerusalem is the start of the good news of Jesus and the location of the birth of the Church (Acts 2). It is also the city that the narrative mostly leaves behind (though see Acts 21), as the Church moves outward to Samaria, the Diaspora, and finally Rome. Matthew also suggests both the importance and the problematic nature of Jerusalem: that Gospel's first reference to the city is the notice that Herod "and all Jerusalem" (Matt 2.3) are frightened by the Magi's news about the new "king of the Jews"; for Matthew, the mission of Jesus' disciples begins not in Jerusalem, but from a mountaintop in Galilee.

---

[5]   Ben notes that the ability to be law observant is not the same thing as the ability to avoid sin, especially the sins of omission (how many of us, for example, fully love their neighbor as themselves, and how often). Just because I keep all the laws of the city of Lexington, Kentucky, and am blameless in the sight of that law does not make me either sinless or even necessarily a righteous or good person. The point is that Luke certainly recognizes the "exceeding sinfulness of sin" and how humans can become so enmeshed in it, that they can even be possessed by dark powers. That he does not enunciate the full-blown later theology of original sin or the like is neither here nor there. As David Moessner has stressed in his longtime work on Luke-Acts, Luke has as one of his major concepts "the release from sins." See, e.g., D. P. Moessner, "The Script of the Scriptures in Acts: Suffering as God's Plan (*Boule*) for the World for the 'Release of Sins,'" in B. Witherington (ed.), *History, Literature, and Society in the Book of Acts* (Cambridge: Cambridge University Press, 1996), pp. 218–50. Amy-Jill agrees that humanity does not avoid sin; neither Judaism nor Christianity nor any other tradition has managed to put a stop to it. Yet both traditions provide teachings by which individuals can hold what Judaism calls the "evil inclination" (Hebrew: *yetzer ha-ra*) in check.

Luke 4 begins as the Spirit, which fills Jesus, leads him into the wilderness (**vs. 1**). Reference to the Spirit follows from the earlier chapters: the Spirit filled the Baptizer (1.15, 17; 80) and his mother Elizabeth (1.41), came upon Mary at the conception of Jesus (1.35), and inspired Zechariah's song (1.67) as well as Simeon's prophecy (2.26–27). John affirmed that Jesus would baptize with the Holy Spirit and fire (3.16), and the Spirit descended on Jesus at his baptism (3.22). That Jesus is both *full of the Holy Spirit* and *led by the Spirit* (**vs. 1**) should not surprise.

The Spirit enables Jesus to endure the Temptation even as it leads him to it. Luke's wording is less harsh than Mark's claim that the Spirit cast (Greek: *ekballō*, the same term used for exorcisms) Jesus out into the wilderness (Mark 1.12). Pastorally, Luke suggests that the Spirit never leaves Jesus, and therefore that Jesus faces his temptations using the same two resources available to his followers – the Spirit of God and the Word of God. Readers may also find here an anticipation of the familiar prayer, "lead us not into temptation" (11.4); the same Greek term underlying both references (*peirasmos*) can also be translated "test."

This test occurs *in the wilderness*, which was for Israel the site of its testing following the Exodus; it is also the place of new beginnings (Isa 40.3; Hos 2.14) as well of John's baptism (see 3.3). But whereas the people come out to the wilderness to be with John, Jesus will be alone with his thoughts, his hunger, his God, and Satan.

For some scholars, the events of the Temptation should be seen as less historical memory than something more akin to a dream, a vision, or what are called "altered states of consciousness."[6] The event did not happen in the sense that, had the technology been present, it could have been caught on camera. Anthropological speculation would locate Jesus, in the wilderness and having visions, as in a liminal state, detached from society's anchors (home, family, community, even his identity is put into question). His fasting (see the numerous fasts in the apocalypse 4 Ezra) is typical of vision quests and conducive to liminal states. Visions are the essence of apocalyptic literature (see the book of Revelation); in Luke's context, and in Jesus' context as well, such experiences were viewed as genuine revelations from God, often about heaven or of supernatural beings and their realm. We mention this reading especially for the sake of some of our students who are inclined to dismiss the mystical as wacko or as mythological nonsense,

[6] See John J. Pilch, *Visions and Healing in the Acts of the Apostles: How the Early Believers Experienced God* (Collegeville: Liturgical Press, 2004).

and for those who seek to appropriate Native American vision quests as a type of theological tourism. Such experiences are to be taken seriously and to be understood at least from the perspective of those who participate in them and from whose cultures they draw.

Another way of understanding the Temptation Narrative is to see Jesus in his role of cosmic warrior who defeats the forces of evil. This reading would encourage his followers, especially those undergoing persecution; it reminds them that the battle has been fought, and won, even as it tells them that Jesus, too, understands what it means to be hungry and to be tempted.

A third reading is to notice intertextual connections. Mark's version of this story mentions only that Jesus "was in the wilderness forty days, tempted by Satan; and he was with the wild beasts; and the angels waited on him" (Mark 1.12). The fasting for forty days connects Jesus to Moses (Exod 34.28; Deut 9.9), and the notice of his forty-day test mirrors Israel's time in the wilderness (Deut 8) as well as Elijah's flight, during a famine, to the mountain of God (1 Kings 19). The closest intertext is Deut 8.2: "Remember the long way that the Lord your God has led you these forty years in the wilderness, in order to humble you, testing you to know what was in your heart, whether or not you would keep his commandments." Connections to Moses and so the Torah, and to Elijah and so the prophetic tradition, alert readers that the keys to passing the test of fidelity are already present in Scripture.

Fasting and famished, Jesus begins his fight with "the Devil" (cf. 8.12; Acts 10.38; 13.10) (**vs. 2**), whom Luke also calls *Satanas* (10.18; 11.18; 13.16; 22.3,31; Acts 5.3; 26.18) and *Beelzebul* (11.15, 18, 19). "Devil" (Greek: *diabolos*) is the normal LXX translation of the Hebrew term *satan*. That term in turn derives from the Hebrew *ha-satan*, literally "the accuser." Originally a member of the heavenly court and functioning like a prosecuting attorney, the satan tests people's righteousness, with Job being the most famous of those brought to the test (Job 1–2). Eventually the definite articles (Hebrew: *ha*) drops out, and the figure's name becomes "Satan." By this point, sometime in the Second Temple period, Satan is less member of the heavenly court and more demonic opposition (see, e.g., 1 Chron 21.1).

The name Beelzebul derives from the Hebrew "baal" ("lord" or "prince" as well as the name of the Canaanite storm god) and "zevul" ("of the manor" or "of the palace")[7]; the more familiar expression "Baal-zebub" (2 Kings

---

[7]   On all this, see Michael S. Heiser, *The Unseen Realm: Recovering the Supernatural Worldview of the Bible* (Bellingham: Lexham Press, 2015).

1.2–3, 6, 16) is a pun on the name, translated "lord of the flies" (*zevuv* in the Hebrew language is a "fly"; the name is onomatopoeic). In the *Testament of Solomon*, a Jewish text dating anywhere between the first to the sixth century CE, Beelzebul is a chief angel who provides the following self-description: "I destroy kings. I ally myself with foreign tyrants. And my own demons I set on to men, in order that the latter may believe in them and be lost. And the chosen servants of God, priests and faithful men, I excite unto desires for wicked sins, and evil heresies, and lawless deeds; and they obey me, and I bear them on to destruction. And I inspire men with envy, and [desire for] murder, and for wars and sodomy, and other evil things. And I will destroy the world." His claims are inflated. The Jewish tradition did not question divine rule; Satan was never seen as having the ability to defeat God. "Among the Jews such ideas never developed so far as to question the ultimate sovereignty and final victory of God who represents truth, justice and faithfulness."[8]

Satan also has agents, such as demons (4.33) and unclean spirits (4.36; 6.18; 8.29; 9.42; 11.24; Acts 5.16; 8.7). The battle between Jesus and Satan therefore has implications for Satan's agents as well as for Jesus' disciples. Since the victor is already known, the temptations have to have an additional meaning. They tell us not simply that Jesus is more powerful than the Devil; they reveal the *type* of authority Jesus manifests and so what authority his followers are to manifest as well. The temptations are not arbitrary, for each one offers a desirable outcome: food for all, a better government, the demonstration of divine authority. The question then becomes first: how is one to achieve these goals? Second, the temptations ask the reader: what kind of authority do you worship?

Each temptation begins, "if you are the Son of God." Since the genealogy has just listed Adam and so all humanity as children of God, the temptations necessarily have implications for all humanity. However, the focus here is on Jesus. Luke does not view Jesus as simply another son of Adam. The devil already knew Jesus' identity; the supernatural realm already celebrated it in the annunciation to the shepherds (2.8–14). The testing thus is of Jesus *himself*: is he really the legitimate son or does he, like the Baptizer's audience (3.8), illegitimately claim his legacy? Ordinary mortals do not struggle with temptations to turn stones into bread, claim the rulership of all the world, or throw themselves off of tall buildings to see if God will rescue them.

---

[8]   Lieu, *Gospel According to Luke*, 30.

In recording the first temptation, the NRSV's *command this stone to become a loaf of bread* (**vs. 3**) misleads: the Greek simply says *artos*, "bread." The term opens to multiple associations, since the word "bread" occurs over three hundred times in the Bible (from Genesis to Revelation). For Luke, the term fits the motif of food, already hinted at with the baby in the manger (2.7,12,16). Luke will mention bread several more times, and each reference has implications for this first temptation: the bread of the presence permitted to the priests but which David and his men ate (6.4); the Baptizer's fasting by "eating no bread" in contrast to Jesus' feasting (7.33); the warning to the disciples not to take bread on their mission, for they should learn what it is like to be vulnerable and so be dependent on the hospitality of others (9.3); the prayer for bread (11.3); the parable of the friend who seeks bread at midnight (11.5); the reference to the messianic banquet where people will "eat bread in the kingdom of God" (15.16); the hunger of the prodigal son, who knows his father's laborers have "bread enough and to spare" (15.17); the festival of the Unleavened Bread (22.1,7); the bread of the Last Supper (22.19); and the bread at the Emmaus supper (24.30, 35). Jesus will eat bread, often, but on his own time, with his own followers.

In the background of this first test may also be Genesis 3, especially if one accepts González's perspective. The temptation to eat what is forbidden – whether by divine commandment or by divine commission – was also the temptation Adam faced, and failed. Since by the first century Satan had come to be associated with the snake in Eden, Jesus can be seen as the new Adam who does not lose access to paradise but rather opens its gates (see 23.43).

Jesus responds to the Devil by quoting from Deut 8.3: "One does not live by bread alone" (**vs. 4**). The quotation is part of a longer passage that relates the temptation to Jesus' present circumstances as well as to Israel's experiences in the wilderness. Moses tells the Israelites, "Remember the long way that the Lord your God has led you these forty years in the wilderness, in order to humble you, testing you to know what was in your heart, whether or not you would keep his commandments. God humbled you by letting you hunger, then by feeding you with manna, with which neither you nor your ancestors were acquainted, in order to make you understand that one does not live by bread alone, but by every word that comes from the mouth of the Lord" (Deut 8.2–3). Material goods, minus knowledge of their ultimate source and gratitude for them, cannot satisfy.

Jesus' rejection of the first temptation indicates more than his finding a successful proof-text. The problem with turning the stone into bread, which would be a great benefit for those who are hungry, is substituting the quick fix or the band aid for a problem that needs greater redressing. To redeem the world, systemic change is required; to tinker with one element such as feeding a hungry person bread, without looking at food production and distribution, cost, and accessibility, leads at best to a feel-good moment. To look to one miracle worker who says, "I can feed you," but not to recognize, again, interdependence – as Jesus insists his disciples recognize when he sends them out without bread – is to promote dictatorship. To pray for "daily bread" (11.13) alerts readers both that the eschatological banquet is yet to arrive and that bread comes to us not simply from above, but from the human hands that plant the seed, harvest the grain, mill it, knead it, and bake it.

As the Spirit had led Jesus to the wilderness, now the Devil leads him up, somewhere (**vs. 5**). In Matthew, the setting is a high mountain; in Luke, the setting is unspecified, and Jesus and Satan could be floating in the air. Literalists may choose to take Luke's version as indicating that the two were in outer space and watched the earth rotate; others may note that the scene is visionary; still others will conclude that Luke thought the earth was flat. The scene is reminiscent of Moses' overlooking the promised land (Deut 34.1–4). The time for Moses to enter was not at hand; the time for Jesus to receive his own kingdom will also have to wait.

Whether the Devil's offer of the *glory and all this authority* (**vs. 6**) of the kingdoms is bona fide remains an open question. If we begin with the presupposition that the world came into Satan's hands with Adam's fall, such that the authority has, as Satan puts it, *been given over to me*, the offer is legitimate. Or, we might see Satan as symbolically in control of "all the kingdoms," given the failure of Rome and its allies to bring about the golden age they proclaimed. In this case, human greed and desire for power allowed Satan to have control. Luke suggested that Augustus was in control over "all the world" (2.1); it turns out that Augustus has a superior, Satan. Jesus will warn, 'The kings of the Gentiles lord it over them; and those in authority over them are called benefactors. But not so with you ..." (22:25–26). This second temptation can therefore be read as a critique of any empire. The devil highlights "their glory" and "all this authority" – but glory and ultimate authority should, for Luke, belong to God, not to the state.

That Satan shows this glory and authority *in an instant* can suggest that the might of these kingdoms is both ephemeral and indistinguishable. The point is already demonstrated by the opening lines of Chapter 3: we may remember Tiberius, Herod Antipas, and Pilate, but Lysanias of Abilene is not, in most locations, a household name. Outside of the Christian tradition and outside the West, even the first three names may be unfamiliar. The imperial infrastructure disappears, empire after empire; the one who reigns today may be forgotten tomorrow.

Satan simply tells Jesus, *worship me* (**vs. 7**). The implication is that any who seek universal glory and authority are already worshiping Satan. We know who our gods are by the objects of our worship. As the covenant community was tempted by the sin of idolatry (see Deut 6.10–15), so Satan tempts Jesus to engage in false worship, and false politics.

Responding, Jesus does not say, "worship me," but, "Worship the Lord your God, and serve only him" (**vs. 8**). He is alluding to Deut 6.13: "The Lord your God you shall fear; him you shall serve, and by his name alone you shall swear." Again, the Torah provides the correct response to any test or temptation, as long as the text is interpreted correctly and then actualized. For Luke's readers, who know that Luke accords the title "Lord" (*kyrios*) to Jesus, worshiping the "Lord your God" could include the worship of Jesus. Ironically, then, especially when Luke is read through Trinitarian eyes, Jesus is suggesting that Satan ought to be worshiping him.

The third temptation, this one concerning false religion, takes place during another visionary experience: Satan places Jesus on the pinnacle of the Temple. Perhaps we are to think of the southeast corner of the Temple, which overlooked the Kidron Valley some 450 feet below. Josephus says that people standing there got dizzy and looking over the edge (*Ant.* 15.11.5). Satan then makes his pitch: "If you are the Son of God, throw yourself down from here" (**vs. 9**). This temptation is particularly subtle because it suggests that Jesus could demonstrate his total dependence on God by throwing himself off the Temple Mount. According to Eusebius, whose version of the account may have been influenced by the Temptation Narrative, James the brother of Jesus was thrown off the pinnacle of the Temple and killed (*Eccles. Hist.* 2.23.11).

Satan then adds enticement by quoting Scripture. Doubling up on textual leverage, he offers two verses from Psa 91 (vss. 11–12), a text that promises angelic protection for those who are God's own (**vs. 10**). Ironically, he overreads the Psalm: it says nothing about risking one's life or jumping off buildings; the phrase "so that you will not dash your foot against a stone" (**vs. 11**) is about stumbling while walking. Not all interpretations of Scripture are good interpretations. As Shakespeare (not the Bible) observes, "the devil can quote Scripture for his purposes" (*Merchant of Venice*, Act I, Scene 3). Ironically as well, the Psalm was used as a protection against Satan (11QApocryphal Psalms; *Tg. Psalm* 91; *y. Shabb.* 8b ["a song against demons"]).

Tempting the divine to suspend the laws of physics by saving one plummeting individual would produce a God known for show tricks. It would present Jesus as someone so invulnerable that he can jump off buildings and not be harmed. Jesus is, for Luke's Gospel, the Messiah and not Superman, and his own physical vulnerability to suffering and death – not his ability to be rescued by angels demonstrates his messianic role.

Jesus' final citation, "Do not put the Lord your God to the test" (**vs. 12**) comes from Deut 6.16. As with his second citation, readers are welcome to see "Lord your God" as a reference to Jesus. Luke has not told the reader that Jesus *is* God, but all the hints are there. As time passed, "gradually words in the OT spoken to or of God as 'Lord' were applied by the early Christians to Jesus."[9]

At the conclusion of the scene, Luke speaks of the devil as having "finished every test" (**vs. 13**); the phrase suggests these three temptations are illustrative of the numerous, various sorts of temptations Jesus faced over the forty days he fasted in the wilderness, or perhaps that humanity faces through the centuries. All our temptations can be seen as fitting into the three categories of tests that Jesus faced: temptations to self-interest and expedience; temptations of power and glory gained by false worship; and temptations of invulnerability, self-importance, and entitlement. They also suggest a threefold categorization of vice – love of pleasure, love of possessions, love of glory (Dio Chrysostom, *Orations* 4.84).[10] Given that these desires remain paramount, the message of the ability to overcome them with God's help remains pertinent. The point can be enhanced: with the knowledge of Scripture, Jesus defeats Satan. Therefore, his followers must recognize both that the Devil can cite Scripture, and that correct interpretation rests in their hands. **Vs. 13**, the Devil's departure, points forward to 22.3, 31–32, when the Devil will again test Jesus, but this time through Jesus' disciples, Judas and Peter. The image of Satan looking for an opportunity to strike makes clear that Luke sees Satan as a distinct being with intentions, not an impersonal evil force.

THE NAZARETH SYNAGOGUE

Passing his test, or overcoming the temptation, Jesus returns as he had left, filled with the power of the Spirit (**vs. 14**). He does not return alone,

---

[9]   Lieu, *Gospel According to Luke*, 29.
[10]   See Johnson, *Gospel of Luke*, 76.

for stories about him have begun to circulate. Luke's comment about this "report" spread about him holds the reader's interests, since Jesus has not done anything yet, publicly, to prompt such news. The witnesses of the shepherds, and Anna and Simeon, were decades ago. Luke here suggests that there are other miracles that Jesus did and teachings that he gave that are not recorded, or are recorded elsewhere (the Gospel's opening line indicates that "many have undertaken to set down an orderly account …"). The next scene tells us that Jesus has already done miracles in Capernaum and thus, on a second reading of the Gospel, we can fill in the blanks.

To this point in Luke's narrative, everything has gone well. Jesus teaches in "their synagogues." The pronoun need not be taken as distancing: Jesus is making the circuit in lower Galilee rather than remaining in his home-town of Nazareth. And he is doing well. The NRSV's comment, "Jesus began to teach" (**vs. 15**) is more accurately translated "he was teaching …," with the implication of repeated actions.[11] His teaching can refer to Scriptural exposition, but it need not: wisdom sayings, ethical maxims, midrashim, and such can all fit under the broad category. The "praise" (Greek: *doxazō*, whence "doxology") he receives has the connotation of glorification and even veneration in synagogues, since "glory" is usually given to God. The term is not anomalous here, although Luke may be implying something more than kudos.

Yet matters change when Jesus comes to his hometown of Nazareth, where he was "brought up" (literally, "nurtured") (**vs. 16a**). Comparing the synagogue scene to the descriptions of Jesus' Nazareth mission in Mark 6.1–6/Matt 13.53–58 suggests that Luke has rewritten an account of Jesus' unsuccessful visit. In Mark's version (6.3), the hometown congregation takes offense at Jesus, whom they regard as rising above his station. They ask, "Is not this the carpenter, the son of Mary and brother of James and Joses and Judas and Simon, and are not his sisters here with us?" Because of their unbelief, Jesus "could do no deed of power, except lay hands on a few sick people and heal them" (Mark 6.5), so he leaves voluntarily for other towns in the Galilee. For Luke, the congregation takes offense *because* Jesus refuses them the messianic benefits accorded others, and in Luke's version, the congregation seeks to kill him. One could claim that Matthew and Mark withheld that last bit of information; it seems more likely (at least to Amy-Jill) that Luke edited Mark's story for at least three reasons: to show Jesus as

---

11   Robert C. Tannehill, *Luke* (Abingdon New Testament Commentaries; Nashville: Abingdon, 1996), 90.

fulfilling Scripture, to anticipate the gentile mission, and to ratchet up the negative impressions of the synagogue congregation. The problem with this assessment, in Ben's view, is that Mark paints an almost equally negative picture of the hometown crowd.

Luke begins the scene by indicating that Jesus customarily went to the synagogue on the Sabbath; the observation continues the theme of fidelity to Jewish practice found in the first two chapters. For some readers, such as Ben, this loyalty signals Luke's respect for the Jewish traditions; for others, such as Amy-Jill, in Luke's narratives *only* Jesus and those connected to him, such as Paul, display fidelity, whereas the synagogue and the Temple are ultimately rejected as places of danger.

The accuracy of Luke's presentation of synagogue Sabbath activities in the late Second Temple period remains debated. The word "synagogue" is a Greek term meaning "gather together." Synagogues at the time of Jesus were congregations supported by "synagogue leaders" (see 8.41; 13.14) or patrons, and these rulers included women.[12] "Rabbis" known in the rabbinic tradition are associated with houses of study rather than with synagogues; only several centuries later did the title "rabbi" achieve today's sense of someone "ordained" as "clergy" to serve a congregation as a religious leader.

Luke omits what likely would have been the beginning of the Sabbath service, which would have involved the recitation of the *Shema* (Deut 6.4–9), the prayer that begins, "Hear (Heb: *shema*), Israel, the Lord our God; the Lord is one." Added to this prayer, following the first verse, is a doxology, "Blessed be the Name of His glorious kingdom for ever and ever." Jesus will echo this line when he instructs his followers to pray, "Hallowed be your name" (11.2). The *Shema* also has two other parts, Deut 11.12–21 and Num 15.37–41. The service would also, likely, include a reading from the Torah and probably a Psalm.

The date by which time congregations read a passage (the *haftarah*, from the Hebrew for "leaving" or "parting") from the Nevi'im or prophets

---

[12] Bernadette J. Brooten, *Women Leaders in the Ancient Synagogue: Inscriptional Evidence and Background Issues* (BJS 36; Chico: Scholars Press, 1982); Brooten, "Female Leadership in the Ancient Synagogue," in Lee I. Levine and Ze'ev Weiss (eds.), *From Dura to Sepphoris: Studies in Jewish Art and Society in Late Antiquity* (Portsmouth: Journal of Roman Archaeology, 2000), 215–23; see also Ross S. Kraemer, "A New Inscription from Malta and the Question of Women Elders in the Diaspora Jewish Communities," *HTR* 78.3/4 (1985): 431–38. For a nuanced assessment of these claims, see both Carrie Duncan, "Inscribing Authority: Female Title Bearers in Jewish Inscriptions," *Religions* 3 (2012): 37–49; and Ross S. Kraemer, *Unreliable Witnesses: Religion, Gender, and History in the Greco-Roman Mediterranean* (New York: Oxford University Press, 2012).

to accompany the Torah reading (much like a Christian lectionary in which an Old Testament reading, a Psalm, a Gospel reading, and a passage from the Epistles or Revelation provide four readings for each Sunday service) remains unclear. Philo hints that by the first century, both Torah and *haftarah* readings were in place. However, the *haftarah* readings in synagogues as they have been preserved do not include the passage from Isaiah that Jesus cites in Luke 4. Whether Jesus actually read this text, which serendipitously was the *haftarah* reading for the week, or whether the Jewish community, facing increasing persecution from the Christianized empire, dropped this reading from the liturgy remains an open question. Amy-Jill thinks Luke invents this entire scene as both a rewrite of the failed mission accounts in Mark and Matthew and as a programmatic passage for the Gospel in which synagogues are places of danger; Ben thinks that Luke is recording an historical incident. In either case, the verses from Isaiah suited the character of both Jesus' proclamation and his works of power.

Luke states that Jesus "stood up to read" (**vs. 16b**) and thus suggests Jesus was literate, something that could only be said of about 10 percent of the population of his time. One would need to stand, since a scroll of Isaiah is too large to hold. It would have been laid out on a table. It is possible that Luke had in mind not a scroll but a "book" in codex form. The verb translated "opening" could also mean "unfold," and the Greek says "book" rather than "scroll."[13]

Handed the Isaiah scroll, Jesus "finds the place" he will go on to cite (**vs. 17**), although Luke does not state that Jesus actually read the text. To this day, there are preachers who can find the correct spot (usually in the King James Bible) where a reading is to be found, but they are nevertheless functionally illiterate. Whether Luke has given Jesus an upgrade, or whether Jesus himself could read, will remain a matter of scholarly debate.[14] In remarking that Jesus "found" the text, Luke may be suggesting that Jesus chose these particular verses. Given the size of the Isaiah scroll (the one preserved from Qumran [1QIsaᵃ] is 734 cm high and is comprised of fifty-four columns), it might have taken him some time to roll the scroll to the correct passage. Or, perhaps the scroll was set for that day's *haftarah* reading.

13   Roger S. Bagnall, "Jesus Reads a Book," *JTS* 51.2 (2000): 577–88.
14   See Chris Keith, *Jesus' Literacy: Scribal Culture and the Teacher from Galilee* (Library of Historical Jesus Studies 413; London: T&T Clark, 2011); see also his *Jesus against the Scribal Elite: The Origins of the Conflict* (Grand Rapids: Baker Academic, 2014).

The text Jesus reads concerning anointing by the Spirit, good news to the poor, release to the captives, and sight to the blind (**vs. 18**) combines Isa 61.1a; 58.6; and 61.2a with Isa 42.7. Isaiah was speaking for himself when he said, "The Spirit of the Lord is upon me"; Jesus appropriates Isaiah's experience to himself. For Isaiah, the proclamation of release to the captives is not a prediction of the far future; it is the announcement that the Babylonian exile is about to end. For Jesus, reading half a millennium later, Isaiah is speaking about Jesus' mission. The Hebrew of Isa 61.1 is better translated "good news to the oppressed," whereas the Greek, which Luke follows, proclaims good news to the "poor." Finally, Jesus secures the connection between Isaiah's identification and his own by appropriating Isaiah's use of the term "anointed." The Hebrew term is *mashach*, which is connected to "messiah"; the Greek is a verbal form related to the term "Christ." This connection of Isaiah's proclamation and much later messianic expectation is not unique to Jesus: the Qumran text 4Q521 combines Isaiah 61 with Malachi's prediction (3.24) of the return of Elijah.[15]

The reading omits from Isa 61.1 the phrase "to heal (or 'bind up') the broken-hearted," and from Isa 61. 2 the phrase "and a day of vengeance." This is not how synagogue readings, from as far back as we can trace them, work. Unlike Christian lectionaries, synagogue readings from the Torah, the prophets, the Psalms, and the *Megillot* (or scrolls in the Writings) do not omit verses. What Jesus "reads," by combining verses and omitting others, is therefore not exactly what Isaiah writes. Further, the reading follows the LXX rather than the Hebrew text, as does his reference to the year of the Lord's favor (**vs. 19**). At the time of Jesus and in Judea and Galilee, synagogue readings would have been in Hebrew and then translated or paraphrased into Aramaic. The Targums, Aramaic paraphrases of the Hebrew dating from slightly later than the first century, may reflect earlier materials. Luke, whose knowledge of Hebrew or Aramaic is doubtful, would have used the Greek text.[16]

Numerous commentators suggest that Jesus omitted the line about the day of vengeance because he rejected a retributive system *that his Jewish*

---

[15] See John C. Poirier, "Jesus as an Elijianic Figure in Luke 4.16–30," *CBQ* 71.2 (2009): 349–63 (esp. 356–57).

[16] Ben notes that it is interesting that the Jewish honorific and grave inscriptions in Capernaum are about half in a Semitic language and half in Greek. Capernaum is near the border with Gentile lands. It is plausible that the reading of Scripture could have been done in more than one language. And the synagogue itself in Sepphoris, just over the hill from Nazareth, has Greek figures and Greek and Hebrew inscriptions right in the floor of the meeting room. Amy-Jill notes that the vast majority these inscriptions are from the fourth century and later, well after the time of Jesus.

brothers and sisters promoted.[17] That he also omits other good news is the first reason for rejecting this view of Jewish retribution. The second is that Jesus' sermon is on the benefits of the Kingdom, benefits that Jesus will not share with the people in Nazareth. Issues of divine justice, which includes punishment of sin, are not relevant given this emphasis. Similarly in error are those commentaries that claim Jesus incensed the people in the synagogue by proclaiming mercy to the "impure" or "dishonored" or "excluded." The issue in these verses is not Jewish exclusivity versus Christian mercy; Isaiah and Jesus are both speaking about human misery and divine grace.

By referencing these earlier passages from Isaiah, the sermon gives insight into the kingdom of heaven – a term, by the way, that Luke has not yet introduced: the blind will see; the captives will be released. "Jesus then proleptically enacts that kingdom by giving sight to the blind (7.21; 18.35–43). He tells the Baptizer's disciples, "Go and tell John what you have seen and heard: the blind receive their sight, the lame walk, the lepers are cleansed, the deaf hear, the dead are raised, the poor have good news brought to them" (7.22). Reference to giving sight in turn reinforces Jesus' connection to Isaiah, since another of the servant psalms speaks of the "servant of the Lord" who will "open the eyes that are blind, to bring out the prisoners from the dungeon, from the prison those who sit in darkness" (Isa 42:7).

Ironically, and tragically, Jesus does not release anyone from literal captivity, including John the Baptizer (see 3.20, where Luke noted that Herod had shut John up in prison; 7.21–22). The reference does, however, foreshadow the release of Barabbas, the three prison break scenes in Acts, and perhaps the releasing of people from demonic possession, as the next scene in the Gospel depicts. Taking the reference as a metaphor and as related to release from sin is another possible interpretation.

The "year of the Lord's favor" (or "acceptance" [Greek: *dektos*]) may allude to the Jubilee, the year when persons would be released from debts, slaves would be freed, and the land would lie fallow as it does in the sabbatical year (see Lev 25.10–13 – the Jubilee, the sabbatical of sabbaticals, is

[17] For example, Joachim Jeremias, *Jesus' Promise to the Nations* (London: SCM, 1958) 45 – a work that still remains a staple in biblical studies curricula – rewrites vs. 22 as "They [the synagogue congregation] protested with one voice and were furious, because he (only) spoke about (God's year of) mercy (and omitted the words about the messianic vengeance)." See discussion of this not atypical, negative view of Jews and Judaism in E. P. Sanders, *Jesus and Judaism* (Philadelphia: Fortress Press, 1985), 392–93 n. 14. See further discussion later in this chapter.

a once every fifty-year event, and so likely once in a lifetime). The Qumran scroll 11QMelchizedek (11Q13) explicitly associates Isa 61.1 with Lev 25 and the year of Jubilee.[18] Whether this tradition was actually put into practice is yet another open question; Amy-Jill doubts it, and Ben is a bit more optimistic. If this sermon is alluding to the Jubilee tradition, the allusion is faint. Nothing else in Luke's Gospel suggests attention to the economic issues so paramount in the Jubilee tradition. No slaves are remitted; no land is returned to its original owners; no monetary debts are forgiven. What would constitute for Luke a "favorable year," or an "acceptable year," needs to be discussed. John the Baptizer has already begun the description with his exhortations to avoid overcharging, to share food and clothing, and to be satisfied with one's wages. In his teachings and actions, Jesus will continue to explain, and to model, acceptability.

The reaction to Jesus' reading, the stares of the congregation (**v. 20**), have been interpreted as being attentive, impatient, and hostile; the attentive reading pays best attention to the words of Luke's chapter. There is nothing here to suggest hostility. Had the concern been that Jesus had read the words incorrectly, then those people in the synagogue with literacy skills would have corrected him (as people to this day do in synagogues when the Torah is chanted incorrectly). The synagogue congregation has heard good news, and they are anxious to hear more.

Jesus' first comment following the reading, "Today this scripture has been fulfilled in your hearing" (**vs. 21**), evidences a slight distinction from Matthew's Gospel. Matthew the narrator frequently notes that Jesus "fulfilled" this or that prophecy. In Luke's Gospel, Jesus makes the proclamation himself. Jesus' audience would have readily assented to the notion that God fulfills his promises: the idea that they were fulfilled on this day in this synagogue in the presence of this audience was another matter, and that required explication.

Favorably impressed, the congregation marveled at what he had to say. The NRSV's "they spoke well of him" (**vs. 22a**) does not quite capture the Greek *emartyroun autō*, with the verb derived from *martyreō*, "to witness" (whence eventually the term "martyr"). The congregation is literally "bearing witness" to him. The term for "gracious" is *charistos*, which appears in 2.52 to suggest that Jesus grew "in favor" with all. So far, so good.

---

[18]   Stephen Hultgren, *Narrative Elements in the Double Tradition: A Study of Their Place within the Framework of the Gospel Narrative* (BZNW 113; Berlin/New York: De Gruyter, 2002), 165.

The congregation's question, "isn't this fellow Joseph's son?" (**vs. 22b**), in context, cannot be anything but positive. They are proud of the hometown miracle worker and preacher. At this point in the Gospel, there is no reason for the congregation to think that Jesus is showing off or rising above his station. Yet in speaking of Jesus as "son of Joseph," they show that they do not have the same knowledge as the reader, for the reader knows of Jesus' double parentage; he is, in a unique way, also the Son of God.

It is Jesus, not the congregation, who goes on the offensive, just as earlier did John with those coming to him for baptism. He begins his explication by putting words in the mouths of the congregants: he would have them speak the proverb, "Physician heal yourself." The proverb suggests the duty of a doctor to treat family and friends first, before moving to the strangers. He then glosses the proverb's implications with a second command also put into the mouths of the congregation: "What we have heard happened in Capernaum, do also here in your native place" (**vs. 23**). That comment, which Luke labels a "parable," likely alludes to 4.14, which mentions the "report" that had gone out about him. Jesus, acting as a prophet, first presents his knowledge of the congregations' attitude before they express it, and, second signals that, as is the case with prophets, he will be rejected, for "Truly (Greek: *amen*) no prophet is accepted in the prophet's hometown" (**vs. 24**). The phrase "amen I say to you" is a hallmark of Jesus' speech (cf. 12.37; 18.17, 29; 21.32; 23.43); it may be the Semitic equivalent to "truly" (cf. "in truth I say to you" in 9.27; 12.44; 21.3). The use of "amen" (Hebrew for "so be it") normally comes after a statement; by validating his own speech, Jesus gives "unmistakable sign of prophetic self-consciousness."[19] The Greek for "accepted" is *dektos*, the same term used to describe the "acceptable" year of the Lord.

The comment about acceptability tips the scene from one of gracious appreciation to one of hostility. Jesus predicts what the congregation will do before they do, or even say, anything. Thus, the scene begins to fulfill Simeon's prediction to Mary that her child is destined for the falling and the rising of many in Israel, and to be a sign that will be opposed" (2.34). It also indicates more or less what, historically, happened in Nazareth and in Galilee more broadly to Jesus and his followers. Early sources do not indicate much positive reception of Jesus' ministry there: the Gospels record a failed mission in Nazareth as well as Jesus' curses against Galilean villages of Capernaum, Chorazin, and Bethsaida, which did not accept claims made

---

[19]   Johnson, *Gospel of Luke*, 80.

either by him or about him. Jesus' Galilean followers relocate to Jerusalem and then to the Diaspora.

Regarding the following vss. 25–30, which are mostly unique to Luke's Gospel, Ben and Amy-Jill continue to disagree on questions of historicity. We agree that Jesus may well have claimed for himself the fulfillment of messianic prophecies, and he may well have cursed the people of Nazareth for rejecting him, as he cursed the people of the other Galilean towns. But whether he read from the Isaiah scroll we debate; we also differ on whether he proclaimed that the messianic blessings would go only to the gentiles or even imagined a gentile "mission" as opposed to the turn of the gentiles to the worship of the God of Israel as accomplished not by missionaries but by divine fiat. Ben sees Jesus as establishing the Church's mission; Amy-Jill sees the Church writing in its own history here. Finally, Ben finds possible historicity in the depiction of the synagogue congregation's attempt to kill Jesus; Amy-Jill, because she finds the scene to be a Lucan invention, sees this synagogue reaction similarly to be part of Luke's apologetic designed to keep Jesus' followers out of synagogues and to cast synagogues as places of danger for them.

In his sermon, Jesus goes on to compares the synagogue congregation to the generations at the times of Elijah (1 Kings 17) and Elisha (2 Kings 5). The reference to Elijah in **v. 25** will remind readers of John the Baptizer, who acted "with the spirit and power of Elijah" in order to prepare "a people for the Lord" (1.17). The widow of Zarephath (**vs. 26**, cf. 1 Kings 17.8–24) finds her sisters among Anna, the faithful widow in the Temple (2.37) and the many other widows in Luke's Gospel and Acts. Although Zarephath is in Sidon (**vs. 26**), Luke does not present the story of the Syro-Phoenician woman (Mark 7.24–30, cf. the Canaanite woman of Matt 15.21–28) whom Jesus encounters in the region of Tyre and Sidon. Adopting a canonical perspective, readers will find fruitful a comparison between Elijah's widow and the Syro-Phoenician mother: a sick child, a reluctant healer, and the crossing of geographical and ethnic borders. Yet this comparison alerts us also to Luke's concern for gender. Luke omits (or perhaps did not know) the story of the woman who changes Jesus' mind about granting a healing for her demon-possessed daughter; similarly, Luke omits the strong characterization of the widow of Zarephath; in 1 Kings, she is active, vocal, and strong; in Luke, she is reduced to the object of Elijah's care and so an object of pity.

The reference to Elijah and the widow of Zarephath would also remind biblically informed readers of two forms of ministry the ancient prophet and Galilean teacher fulfill: as Elijah miraculously provides food for the widow, so Jesus will feed five thousand; as Elijah miraculously raises the widow's son from the dead, so Jesus will raise the son of the widow of Nain. Similarly, Elisha's cleansing of Naaman the Syrian military officer (**vs. 27**; cf. 2 Kings 5.1–14) anticipates Jesus' healing of the man with leprosy in the next chapter (5.12–13). With these allusions, Jesus locates himself firmly in the Scriptures of Israel: he shows his knowledge of them, appreciation for them, and his fulfillment of them. Ben notes that Jesus is presented as like the northern prophets of Israel, Elijah and Elisha, rather than like the Judean prophets who used the oracular formula "thus says Yahweh," a formula Jesus never uses.

Commentators typically interpret the references to the widow and the man with leprosy as designed to explode Jewish patriarchy, purity, xenophobia, and class consciousness. Joel Green states, "With these examples, Jesus underscores that 'good news to the poor' embraces the widow, the unclean, the Gentile, those of lowest status."[20] Robert McAfee Brown goes farther: "Jesus, not content to quit while he is ahead, points out that the gifts of God do not come automatically to those who attend the Temple [or synagogue] … And this is really too much! The idea that the message is for worthless outsiders rather than for us! The very notion that unbelievers will be the recipients of God's favor and we will not!"[21] Such misreadings give rise to replacement theology, that is, the notion that the covenant between God and the descendants of Abraham, Isaac, and Jacob has been abrogated, with the (gentile) followers of Jesus taking their place. As Green notes, "a number of interpreters regard the rejection of Jesus by those of his hometown as in some sense prototypical, signifying in a proleptic way the rejection of Jesus by the Jews and the consequent Gentile mission."[22]

Such triumphalistic readings negatively characterize the Jewish community even as they distort the Gospel message, for at least three reasons. First, the stories of the widow and Naaman are already part of the Jewish tradition, which also had a long recognition of the role of the righteous gentile. Second, there is no reason to presume that most Jews would have found outsiders as "worthless": these stories and the many others of righteous gentiles, the welcoming of gentiles into synagogues (the "Godfearers"), the presence of the Court of the Gentiles in the Jerusalem Temple, and even the

---

[20]   Green, *Gospel of Luke*, 218.
[21]   R. McAfee Brown, *Theology in a New Key* (Philadelphia: Westminster, 1978), pp. 94–95.
[22]   Green, *Gospel of Luke*, 208 n. 19, cf. Bovon, *Commentary on the Gospel of Luke*, 152, "Luke wants to make a programmatic statement that precisely his hometown of Nazareth – which, in the final analysis, appears here representatively for all Israel – hears the good news (in the Pauline sense) and resists it from the start."

Bible's notice that all people are in the image and likeness of the divine (Gen 1.26) make clear that no one is to be seen as "worthless." Indeed, Naaman the Syrian is the "commander of the army of the king of Aram," and the king advocates on his behalf; going to Elisha, Naaman takes "ten talents of silver, six thousand shekels of gold, and ten sets of garments" (and we think seeing a specialist is expensive). His status is hardly marginal. Third, there is no reason to bring in issues of purity; they have nothing to do with the widow on the one hand; on the other, Elisha cures the Syrian of leprosy and thus restores him to what would be a state of ritual purity.

For the original stories of the widow and the commander found in the Deuteronomic History, the motif is that of the "righteous gentile." Amy-Jill suggests that Luke, the (likely) gentile writer, critiques Jesus' Jewish contemporaries, and the Jewish contemporaries of Luke's own readers, for not believing in Jesus. Insider critique becomes outsider polemic. Ben offers a different perspective. First, he notes that Luke had presented very pious images of Jews in the first two chapters, so clearly Luke does not reject all Jews. Second, Ben regards Luke the author, so familiar with the LXX, as a (former) synagogue adherent, and so doubts Luke is engaging in polemics against former friends. (Amy-Jill simply adds here that the polemics of people who leave one religious tradition for another can be among the most vicious.) Third, Ben notes that Luke consistently portrays the Gospel as "for the Jew first" by depicting Paul as going to synagogue after synagogue with mixed results – some converts, some rejection. Finally, Ben proposes that some Jews, such as those in the hometown synagogue, did reject Jesus, and that is one of the causes that led to his demise. Amy-Jill thinks the rejection in Nazareth had nothing to do with Jesus' crucifixion. We agree that fair commentary on what happened is not polemic against Jews in general, nor is it a sign of a replacement theology;[23] determining what is "fair commentary" or "history" versus what is redactional invention remains a crux.

Although some commentators conclude that the people in the synagogue "are angry that Jesus would have spoken of the universalism of divine grace,"[24] that "The people of Jesus' hometown read the Scriptures as promises of God's exclusive covenant with them … their commitment to their own community boundaries took precedence over their joy that God had sent a prophet among them,"[25] and that "this ominous opening

[23] See, for example, Jakob Jervell, *Luke and the People of God* (Eugene: Wipf and Stock, 2002).
[24] Cf. Green, *Gospel of Luke*, 214–15 n. 41.
[25] R. Alan Culpepper, "Nazareth: Final Thought," on friarmusings (https://friarmusings.word press.com/2016/01/29/nazareth-final-thought/; posted January 29, 2016), and citing from

already suggests a reason why many Jews later on in Acts reject the Gospel, precisely because it is meant for all,"[26] such conclusions read Lucan apologetic as historical reporting. This exclusivity attributed to the hometown synagogue tracks neither with the Scriptures of Israel nor the synagogues nor the Temple nor day-to-day activities (as we see, e.g., in Luke 7). The problem is not Jesus' extension of grace; the problem is that Jesus denies the people of Nazareth what their own history promises. As Poirier notes, "The crowd's violent reaction ... has nothing to do with any sort of insularity or anti-Gentile sentiments ... but rather with Jesus' implying that the Nazareth crowd is the antitype to the Israel of Elijah and Elisha's day."[27] Ben agrees with this last quote, but not with the notion that Luke is retrojecting later Christian polemics into the story.

For Amy-Jill replacement theology coupled with the negative depictions of Jewish gatherings is part of Luke's literary strategy. For Luke, the synagogue is a place to be avoided; given Luke's likely gentile readership coupled with the allure synagogues had for gentiles – from the God-fearers of the first century to the Judaizers of the second century to Chrysostom's fulminations about his congregants visiting synagogues in the fourth century – the evangelist's concern is by no means hypothetical. Ben finds this reading a caricature of *Luke's* presentation, but not of the later anti-Jewish readings of Luke-Acts by Chrysostom and even some modern commentators. Ben highlights Luke's presentation of successful missions in the synagogues in Acts on multiple occasions from Paul's preaching, in Psidian Antioch, Iconium, Corinth, and elsewhere, and so he finds Luke's theology to be one of inclusion in Christ – Jews and gentiles united in Christ. Amy-Jill here is concerned about Luke's attitude toward those (majority) Jews who do not sign on to the program. Right to the end of Acts, Paul continues to talk to Jews about their Scriptures and about Christ. At no point in Acts is there a complete turning away from Jews to focus solely on gentiles, not even in Acts 28. Luke does not think God is finished with his first chosen people (and nor does Paul – see Rom 11). And Amy-Jill responds that Acts 28 ends with the citation of Isaiah concerning a people who will not listen as well as a direct turning to the gentiles; it is the *gentiles*, Luke tells us at the end, who will listen. The important point here, finally, is that we, Ben and Amy-Jill, are trying to listen, sympathetically, to each other. We see how we both came to our conclusions; we can

his "The Gospel of Luke." *New Interpreter's Bible*, Vol. 9 (Nashville: Abingdon Press, 1994–2004) 102–9.
26   Johnson, *Gospel of Luke*, 82.
27   Poirier, "Jesus as an Elijianic Figure," 363.

locate the source of the disagreement, and in the conversation can read with more sensitivity in the presence of those with whom we disagree. Ben agrees with Amy-Jill that stereotypes of early Judaism as a graceless religion or one opposed to inclusion of gentiles in contrast to the universality of the Jesus movement do no justice to early Judaism.

Back to the text: Some commentators who find Luke 4 indicative of "what happened" and so not a Lucan invention go on suggest that **vs. 29**, "They got up, drove him out of the town, and led him to the brow of the hill on which their town was built, so that they might hurl him off the cliff," indicates the practice of Jewish law, where the procedure for stoning requires the guilty party to be outside the city, pushed off a hill or cliff, and then to be stoned.[28] Problems here are manifold, from the factual observation that there is no cliff in Nazareth; the cliff, as such, is about 2.5 miles away from the location of the town, to the point that there is no indication of stoning in the scene, to the problem of building a historical context from one verse from a second century text, such as *m. Sanh.* 6.4, which includes an entire legal procedure missing from Luke's story, for determining practices in the late Second Temple period. Nor, finally, does Jesus say anything that would prompt the death penalty. Instead, as Judith Lieu perceptively notes, "We are left asking, perhaps uncomfortably, whether it is Jesus rather than their unbelief who has denied them the experience of salvation."[29]

Ben notes the story of the stoning of Stephen in Acts 7, but that scene represents not legal process but lynch mob. Not surprising, Amy-Jill has her doubts about the history of that incident as well, given its absence from early Church writings, when the Fathers are generally delighted to talk about martyrs, to the symbolic name *stephanos*, which means "crown," as was later associated with martyrdom. But that discussion is for another volume.[30]

A delicate balance is required to be fair to history and these texts. It is a *fact* that Jesus produced strong opposition from *some* of his own fellow Jews. This, however, provides no basis whatsoever for broad generalizations or caricatures of Jews and their views of Jesus then or later in history. All of Jesus' first followers were Jews, and much if not most of the NT was written

---

[28] See J. Blinzler, "The Jewish Punishment of Stoning in the New Testament Period," in E. Bammel (ed.), *The Trial of Jesus* (London: SCM Press, 1970), 147–61. For more recent examples, see Green, *Gospel of Luke*, 218.

[29] Lieu, *Gospel According to Luke*, 34.

[30] See Shelly Matthews, *Perfect Martyr: The Stoning of Stephen and the Construction of Christian Identity* (New York: Oxford University Press, 2010).

by Jews. Anti-Semitism is an ugly sin of which the Church has all too often been guilty, to this very day in some cases. But anti-Semitism should not be laid at the doorstep of Luke.

Luke depicts Jesus as slipping through the angry crowd (**vs. 30**) and goes on his way (cf. 22.3,53 and John 7.30; 8.59; 10.31,39). This "miraculous" conclusion adds, at least for Amy-Jill, an additional suggestion of invention rather than history. Ben disagrees. Were this the case it is inexplicable why Luke continues to portray followers of Jesus going to synagogues throughout Acts to share their beliefs about Jesus and sometimes winning sympathizers. While it is true that other than Christian sources, we have no indication that synagogues sought to kill Jesus' followers, Ben adds that this doesn't make the sources necessarily all wrong. We agree, however, that how we assess Luke's signature story is necessarily impacted by our knowledge of how demonization of enemies can only have tragic repercussions.

Similarly, we agree that there was strong opposition to the followers of Jesus by a variety of people in the first century, both Jews and gentiles, and sometimes this opposition resulted in violence. Jesus and Paul were killed by Rome, and Peter likely was as well. Luke reports that Herod Agrippa I killed James the brother of John. Josephus reports that an interim high priest prompted the execution of James the Just. If we forget or try to explain away the ugly parts of our shared past, even in a good cause, we do not do justice either to the cause of history or to the desire to foster better relationships between Jews and Christians.

HEALINGS IN CAPERNAUM

A variation on the scene in the Nazareth synagogue appears in vss. 31–37, where Jesus speaks at a synagogue in Capernaum (**vs. 31**), his home away from home where he had already done miracles (so 4.23). Luke again presents Jesus as "teaching," but the content of the teaching, or the possible underlying Scriptural texts, go unnoted. Rather, Luke focuses on the style of Jesus' presentation. The people are astounded (**vs. 32**) at his teaching because he spoke "with authority" (see Matt 7.29). Pharisees would cite the "traditions of the elders" and so locate their teachings within a broader, generational school; they operated within a communitarian basis and so arrived at consensus positions. Jesus, like the Teacher of Righteousness known from the Dead Sea Scrolls and like other charismatic leaders, makes pronouncements; his use of "amen" to prefigure them reinforces his personal authority.

The reference to the man with the unclean spirit who appears in the synagogue (**vs. 33**) indicates that the community welcomed not simply the healthy but also the disabled, for synagogues had no restrictions based on gender, physical health, or ethnic identity. Or, less likely, it could indicate that, for Luke, synagogues are places where Satan and his minions feel at home. It is our choice as to whether we want to offer a benevolent or malevolent reading.

The possessed man in the synagogue had multiple demons, for he shouts, "let *us* alone ..." These demons are on the attack: "What have you to do with us, Jesus Nazarene," or, literally, "what to us and to you?" (**vs. 34**). The same phrasing appears in John 2.4, where Jesus responds to his mother's notice of the lack of wine at the Cana wedding, "What to you and to me?" The demons are asking Jesus, in effect, "What business do you have with us?" Then, seeking power over him, they call him by name and title: "Jesus of Nazareth ... the Holy One of God." For the final irony: the demons know Jesus' identity; the people in the synagogue do not. At this narrative juncture, only supernatural beings, whether angels, the Devil, or demons – and Luke's readers! – know his identity.

Jesus silences the demons and then commands them to depart, which they do without harming their victim (**vs. 35**). Readers can see this exorcism as a partial fulfillment of the prophecy from Isaiah: Jesus has set a captive free. They may also remember that Jesus had rejected Satan's offer of "authority" in 4.6, and so see this exorcism as a reinforcement of Jesus' resistance. The exorcism then prompts the people to marvel (**vs. 36**) and news of his authority to spread (**vs. 37**) throughout the "region" (lower Galilee, if not farther). What the congregation in Nazareth had sought, according to Jesus, and what he refused to provide is here, in the synagogue in Capernaum, freely given.

This news of Jesus' authority and power may not have been entirely positive (gossip and hearsay, of any sort, rarely are). Exorcism in Jesus' day and Luke's time was sometimes seen as an act of magic (especially if charms or secret formulae were used).[31] The act can include knowledge of secret lore or by prayer and laying on of hands (1QapGen20.16–29); it can also require the piety of the exorcist (cf. *Prayer of Nabonidus*).[32] How one in antiquity distinguishes among miracle, medicine, and magic is often an act of perception: what is a miracle to one person is magic or medicine to another.

---

[31] Cf. *Paris Magic Papyrus* 3,007–85; Philostratus, *Life of Apollonius* 4.20; Josephus, *War* 7.185; *Ant.* 8.45–49.

[32] See discussion in Nolland, *Luke 1–9.20*, 204; and Graham Twelftree, *Jesus the Exorcist* (Tübingen: Mohr, 1993).

One often helpful test is the cost: medicine and magic require payment; free health care is a miracle. In Jesus' case, the exorcism also reflects that he is full of the Spirit and that he is able to overcome not only demonic but indeed cosmic opposition. He had already defeated Satan at the Temptation; the exorcisms are part of the mop-up operations. Yet the people may not know this; later others will accuse him of casting out demons in order to support Satan's agenda (11.15).

Since the Sabbath was (and is) a time for family gathering and enjoying a shared meal, Jesus leaves the synagogue and enters Simon's home (**vs. 38**). Luke's readers likely know that this Simon will be nicknamed "Peter" and will become the principal member of the Twelve Apostles. But in Luke's narrative, he is at this point simply a fellow whose home Jesus enters. We have here an indication of the Jewish tradition of inviting strangers for a Sabbath meal. Or, perhaps Simon, having seen Jesus' abilities, thought another exorcism might be possible. Simon's mother-in-law was suffering from a fever, and the people in the house "ask" Jesus about her. They do not request a healing, and thus do not treat Jesus as a healer-for-hire. Jesus "rebukes" (**vs. 39a**) the fever. The term can indicate a continuation of the exorcism theme, although it need not. Jesus also rebukes wind and waves (8.24), but he is not here engaging in exorcism. Luke's point is that Jesus has the power personally to address any force, natural or supernatural, and master it.

By rising and serving (**vs. 39b**), the woman does more than indicate the success of the healing. The term for rising (Greek: *anastasa*) can connote resurrection (24.46), and the term for serving (Greek: *diakoneō*) not only describes Jesus' own actions and commendations (22.26), but also is the origin of the word "deacon." The woman thus becomes the prototype for Jesus (22.26–27). Her service also anticipates the serving of Jesus' women patrons (8.1–3) and of the householder Martha (10.38–42). Similarly, the widow of Zarephath, mentioned in the synagogue sermon (4.26), can be seen as Elijah's patron, in that she provides him with food and lodging, much as the Great Woman of Shunem acts toward Elijah's successor, Elisha. However, whereas in 1 Kings 17.9, God commands Elijah, "Go now to Zarephath, which belongs to Sidon, and live there; for I have commanded a widow there to feed you," Luke keeps the focus on Elijah as the active participant. Whether Luke is to be seen as promoting women's leadership in the churches or relegating them to a patronage role wherein they support the male leaders but do not themselves lead is a question here asked but not yet answered.

Although Jesus heals Simon's mother-in-law, the Gospel tradition makes no mention of Simon's wife. It is possible he was a childless widower; perhaps the wife resisted her husband's fascination with the Nazarene teacher. Paul speaks of Peter as traveling with a "sister wife" (1 Cor 9.5 [the NRSV translates "believing wife"]), and later tradition depicts both Peter and his wife as martyred in Rome.

The setting sun (**vs. 40**) indicates the end of the Sabbath, when people could physically carry others to Simon's home. Luke notes that Jesus puts his hands on "each one" and healed them. Laying on of hands for healing is not mentioned in the OT, although the Qumran text 1QapGen.20.28–29 refers to Abraham laying hands on Pharaoh and exorcising a demon from him. Standard claims that by touching sick people, Jesus opens himself to impurity and thus rejects the purity laws misread both Luke (who never mentions the issue of purity) and Jewish purity laws: fevers, paralysis, deaf-muteness, and such do not make a person unclean, and Jesus violates no purity rules. However, his touching does indicate his compassion. Today, when fear of disease – the issues are contagion and in some cases personally revulsion at certain symptoms, not purity – prevents human contact, Jesus demonstrates the importance of physical touch.

Again, the demons identify Jesus, and again Jesus silences them (**vs. 41**). For Lucan Christology, Jesus is to be known not primarily as a miracle worker or exorcist; he is to be known primarily through his teachings and his fidelity. Simultaneously, Luke subtly suggests that while the demons can identify Jesus correctly, the people in Simon's house cannot. They need to learn this message for themselves and not through satanic delivery.

The following day, Jesus seeks solitude (**vs. 42**), but the crowds, knowing his miraculous powers, want to keep him with them. Jesus refuses: his task is to evangelize (**vs. 43**; "proclaim the good news," is the verb *euangelizō*) from city to city not about himself, but about the kingdom of God. He will do so in the synagogues of Judea. Whether the disaster of the Nazareth synagogue appearance will repeat itself or whether he will find welcome remains to be seen.

The phrase "kingdom/dominion of God" occurs for the first time in this Gospel at vs. 43; Luke will use the term thirty-one further times along with six references simply to "the kingdom." This expression, central to Jesus' preaching in the Synoptic Gospels, refers in part to the actions Jesus himself performs: the kingdom is present when demons are driven out and bodies are made whole. It indicates a future realm where salvation from all that prevents human wholeness and reconciliation prevails; therefore, it remains something for which people must pray, however "saved" they think of themselves. Jesus reflects early Jewish hopes for the restoration of God's people (see 17.20–21) and their views of a "world to come" (Hebrew: *olam ha-ba*) where there is an end to war, poverty, disease, and despair. The Kaddish prayer includes the verse, "May he establish his kingdom in your lifetime and in your days and in the lifetime of all the house of Israel, even speedily and at a near time."

BRIDGING THE HORIZONS

1. Testing and Tempting

The Greek term *peirasmos* can be translated either "testing" or "temptation." It applies to the "tests" by which God proves fidelity, and it refers to "temptations" by which the devil attempts to snare humanity. The same trial or crisis can be viewed either way. The difference is that a temptation intends to lure a person into doing something wrong, something sinful. It intends to destroy a person's character. The temptations Satan offers Jesus are real, because in each case – making food, creating a better government, demonstrating divine authority – there is a desirable outcome, what we might even call a "quick fix." However, the issue is the cost of accepting. In the story of Jesus' Temptation, Satan wants Jesus to stumble, that is, to commit idolatry. Helpful here may be Paul's admonition: "no temptation has overcome you that is not common to humanity, but God is faithful, such that he will not allow you to be tempted past your power to endure but with the temptation God can provide an adequate means of escape" (1 Cor 10.13).

Although the Temptation scene is a visionary battle with cosmic implications, the temptations Jesus faces have their mundane counterparts. We know the standard temptations: lust, greed, envy, and so on. But there are other temptations, equally sinful, but often ignored in church settings: self-satisfaction, sanctimoniousness, complacency, judging others, lording it over others. The temptation in Eden is to become like "the gods" or to think ourselves immortal, sinless, flawless, perfect. Our task is not to be divine; our task is to become fully human, to recognize our interconnectedness, the benefits and debits of our incarnated state, the yearnings of our souls and our bodies for connection and love.

The Epistle to the Hebrews (4.15) states that Jesus was "one who in every respect has been tempted as we are, yet without sinning"; however, as a human being, he had to have known the allure of the temptation and the

difficulty of the test. He also knew how to pass that test and avoid temptation. Jesus' quotes all come from Deuteronomy, whereas Satan draws from
the Psalms. Today, the bulwark of Church citations, especially in worship
contexts, comes from the Psalms, and the Law, the Torah, is seen as secondary. Without beginning with the Torah and so understanding the divine
will, the move to the Psalms, with their personal sense of comfort, can distort biblical appreciation. Indeed, the Torah presumes a communal audience, and readers of Luke would do well to look at the context of the quotes
attributed to Jesus.

Finally, the Temptation scene warns against proof-texting, that is,
against citing the biblical material out of context, for one's own purposes.
Jesus' quotations are all from the same section in Deuteronomy; he is not
divorcing them from their obvious meaning. The question is how to read
the Bible correctly. As the old adage goes, the Bible should be a rock on
which one stands, rather than a rock thrown to do damage.

2. Rejection in One's Hometown

Justo González offers a contemporary version of the synagogue episode:

> One can imagine in our day, a young man who becomes a famous athlete
> and signs a contract for millions of dollars. He then returns to his hometown,
> and all come to receive him and hear what he has to say. The town band
> goes out to greet him. The local papers praise him. The town gathers at the
> stadium for a welcoming ceremony. Everybody is excited. Some say: "It's dif-
> ficult to believe this is Joe, who grew up next door." When Joe finally comes
> to the speaker's stand, all are eager to hear what he has to say. They know
> that he has talked of the need for better schools and clinics, and that he has
> supported such institutions elsewhere. Now Joe stands up and says: "Do not
> think that because I grew up in Smallville you will receive any special favors
> from me. Actually, I've decided to support the school in Eastville and the
> clinic in Northville." There will be a chilled silence. Soon shock will turn to
> anger, and anger to hostility. "Who does he think he is? We don't need him!
> Run him out of town!"[33]

The analogy, while not uncommon, is not quite on target. The hometown
hero in Luke's story does not simply say that his benefits will go elsewhere.
He states that the hometown was *never* worthy. Nor does Jesus offer his
fellow congregants the option of visiting a clinic or a school nearby, since

---

[33]   González, *Luke*, 66.

he is not setting up institutions; he is performing miracles. Whereas we have no reason to think that the people of Eastville and Northville are any different ethnically or racially from those in Smallville, there are ethnic and religious distinctions underlying Jesus' examples. When we look at Luke's story with twenty-first-century eyes, we can see why the analogy fails. If we imagine the people in Smallville as religious, ethnic, or racial minorities and the folks in Eastville and Northville as in the majority, we begin to see the problem. When we observe that the people of Smallville have not, as far as we know, been victims of genocide perpetrated by the famous athlete's fans in the other cities, the analogy becomes all the more problematic. Finally, "run out of town" is not the same thing as "let's kill him," and so the murderous impression the reader has about the hometown folks. Luke presents a scenario that is much more disturbing, especially when read in the light of the past two thousand years.

3. Exorcism

John S. Mbiti describes a bright young African who went to the West for his education. "Finally he got what he wanted: a Doctorate in Theology... He was anxious to return home [to Africa] as soon as possible ... At home relatives, neighbors, old friends, dancers, musicians, drums, dogs, cats, all gather to welcome him back ... Suddenly, there is a shriek. Someone has fallen to the ground ... The chief says to him, 'You have been studying theology overseas for ten years. Now help your sister. She is troubled by the spirit of her great aunt.' He looks around. Slowly he goes to get Bultmann, looks at the index, finds what he wants, reads again about spirit possession in the New Testament. Of course, he gets the answer: Bultmann has demythologized it."[34]

This anecdote may make us smile, even as it alerts us to the fact that for some cultures, the inability to control the body is not a disorder created by an internal chemical imbalance but by an external, evil spirit. Rather than leave the interpretation at a cultural stalemate, sensitive exegesis can put the text into dialogue with both modern medicine and localized views. Emmanuel Oyemomi looks to Jesus the healer to reveal how illness "is both personal, social reality and largely a part of cultural construct."[35] He

---

[34]   John. S. Mbiti, "Theology in Context," in G. H. Anderson and T. F. Stransky (eds.), *Mission Trends No. 3: Third World Theologies* (Grand Rapids: Eerdmans, 1976), pp. 7–8.

[35]   Emmanuel Oyemomi, "The Challenges of the Concept of Medicine and Healing in the Gospel of Luke for the Church in Africa," *Ogbomoso Journal of Theology* 18.3 (2013): 113–27 (114).

concludes, "as there were sick people, institutions, administrations, in those days, so also there are sick people, sick governments, and sick institutions in our contemporary times. Hence, the church has the responsibility to rise up to the challenges ..."[36] Demythologizing can make for culturally poorer readings; ignoring historical-critical and scientific work can do the same.

---

[36]   Ibid., 123–24.

Luke 5 Disciples and Debates

CATCHING FISH; REELING IN PEOPLE

¹ Once while Jesus was standing beside the lake of Gennesaret, and the crowd was pressing in on him to hear the word of God, ² he saw two boats there at the shore of the lake; the fishermen had gone out of them and were washing their nets. ³ He got into one of the boats, the one belonging to Simon, and asked him to put out a little way from the shore. Then he sat down and taught the crowds from the boat.

⁴ When he had finished speaking, he said to Simon, "Put out into the deep water and let down your nets for a catch." ⁵ Simon answered, "Master, we have worked all night long but have caught nothing. Yet if you say so, I will let down the nets." ⁶ When they had done this, they caught so many fish that their nets were beginning to break. ⁷ So they signaled their partners in the other boat to come and help them. And they came and filled both boats, so that they began to sink.

⁸ But when Simon Peter saw it, he fell down at Jesus' knees, saying, "Go away from me, Lord, for I am a sinful man!" ⁹ For he and all who were with him were amazed at the catch of fish that they had taken; ¹⁰ and so also were James and John, sons of Zebedee, who were partners with Simon. Then Jesus said to Simon, "Do not be afraid; from now on you will be catching people." ¹¹ When they had brought their boats to shore, they left everything and followed him.

RESTORATION TO PURITY

¹² Once, when he was in one of the cities, there was a man covered with leprosy. When he saw Jesus, he bowed with his face to the ground and begged him, "Lord, if you choose, you can make me clean." ¹³ Then

Jesus stretched out his hand, touched him, and said, "I do choose. Be made clean." Immediately the leprosy left him. ¹⁴ And he ordered him to tell no one. "Go," he said, "and show yourself to the priest, and, as Moses commanded, make an offering for your cleansing, for a testimony to them."

¹⁵ But now more than ever the word about Jesus spread abroad; many crowds would gather to hear him and to be cured of their diseases. ¹⁶ But he would withdraw to deserted places and pray.

SICKNESS AND SIN

¹⁷ One day, while he was teaching, Pharisees and teachers of the law were sitting near by (they had come from every village of Galilee and Judea and from Jerusalem); and the power of the Lord was with him to heal. ¹⁸ Just then some men came, carrying a paralyzed man on a bed. They were trying to bring him in and lay him before Jesus; ¹⁹ but finding no way to bring him in because of the crowd, they went up on the roof and let him down with his bed through the tiles into the middle of the crowd in front of Jesus.

²⁰ When he saw their faith, he said, "Friend, your sins are forgiven you." ²¹ Then the scribes and the Pharisees began to question, "Who is this who is speaking blasphemies? Who can forgive sins but God alone?" ²² When Jesus perceived their questionings, he answered them, "Why do you raise such questions in your hearts? ²³ Which is easier, to say, 'Your sins are forgiven you,' or to say, 'Stand up and walk'?

²⁴ But so that you may know that the Son of Man has authority on earth to forgive sins" – he said to the one who was paralyzed – "I say to you, stand up and take your bed and go to your home." ²⁵ Immediately he stood up before them, took what he had been lying on, and went to his home, glorifying God. ²⁶ Amazement seized all of them, and they glorified God and were filled with awe, saying, "We have seen strange things today."

THE TAX COLLECTOR AND HIS FRIENDS

²⁷ After this he went out and saw a tax collector named Levi, sitting at the tax booth; and he said to him, "Follow me." ²⁸ And he got up, left everything, and followed him.

²⁹ Then Levi gave a great banquet for him in his house; and there was a large crowd of tax collectors and others sitting at the table with them.

³⁰ The Pharisees and their scribes were complaining to his disciples, saying, "Why do you eat and drink with tax collectors and sinners?" ³¹ Jesus answered, "Those who are well have no need of a physician, but those who are sick; ³² I have come to call not the righteous but sinners to repentance."

FASTING AND FEASTING

³³ Then they said to him, "John's disciples, like the disciples of the Pharisees, frequently fast and pray, but your disciples eat and drink." ³⁴ Jesus said to them, "You cannot make wedding guests fast while the bridegroom is with them, can you? ³⁵ The days will come when the bridegroom will be taken away from them, and then they will fast in those days."

³⁶ He also told them a parable: "No one tears a piece from a new garment and sews it on an old garment; otherwise the new will be torn, and the piece from the new will not match the old. ³⁷ And no one puts new wine into old wineskins; otherwise the new wine will burst the skins and will be spilled, and the skins will be destroyed. ³⁸ But new wine must be put into fresh wineskins. ³⁹ And no one after drinking old wine desires new wine, but says, 'The old is good.'"

At the end of Chapter 4, Jesus states his intention to proclaim the good news, and Luke affirms that he was "proclaiming the message in the synagogues of Judea" (4.44). Chapter 5 finds Jesus not in the synagogues, but on a boat, in a city, in the wilderness, at a banquet sponsored by tax collector, and finally in a private house. All of these places can be considered "synagogues" in the sense that they "gather together" people for common cause. Where Jesus is, people gather, and thus where Jesus is, synagogues are. Whether Luke is distinguishing Jesus from the synagogue, understood as both a communal and religious institution where Jews gather to hear the Torah read and interpreted, to sing Psalms, and to discuss communal issues, is an open question.

CATCHING FISH; REELING IN PEOPLE

The first setting for Luke 5 is the "Lake of Gennesaret," also called the "Sea of Galilee" (**vs. 1**). Luke 5 shares the location as well as the miraculous catch of fish and the commissioning of Peter with John 21, a chapter usually viewed as an appendix to the Fourth Gospel. Which if either was the original story cannot be determined. Amy-Jill thinks that John constructed a resurrection appearance from Luke's narrative, since she doubts that Luke would turn a report of a resurrection appearance into a simple commissioning. Ben thinks that while John knows the story Luke tells, the Fourth Gospel presents a different event but one that echoes the earlier one in some respects. We agree that Luke's story is about Jesus' commission of Peter while John's story is about restoring Peter, which *presupposes* the previous episode. In short, Ben sees Jesus using a similar miracle to restore Peter and others to the fold and recommission them after the resurrection; Amy-Jill sees John as repurposing a story known from the Synoptic tradition. One has to weigh the similarities as well as the differences between the two stories and then ask, "Is John's story a reappropriation of an earlier account, or is it a recapitulation involving two different episodes in the life of Jesus and Peter?"

In this setting, away from the town, the crowd comes to Jesus not for a miracle, but "to hear the word of God." This is Luke's first use of "word of God" language; it returns in 8.1 with the Parable of the Sower and twice more, in 8.21 and 11.28, where Jesus speaks of the importance of hearing the word and then actualizing it. Here, the word is proclaimed, but its contents are not given. Luke's immediate focus is not on the theology, but on the beginnings of discipleship and so, by extension, of ecclesiology, the growth of the Christian assembly. The account is not an allegory of later Christian life, but a looking back on the roots of the Jesus movement. At the same time, Luke tells the old story with one eye on the Gospel's audience so they can relate to it.

Ironically, not everyone was interested in Jesus' teaching; not all were pressing in on him. Jesus sees fishermen washing their nets (**vs. 2**) and, by implication, not listening to him. They are average workers doing average work, until Jesus intervenes. He gets into Simon's boat; this is the same Simon, soon to be called Peter, whose mother-in-law Jesus had just healed from a fever (4.38–39). Asking (not commanding, but simply requesting) Simon to pull out a little from the shore, Jesus sits down in the boat and continues his teaching (**vs. 3**). He sits not, contrary to so many commentaries, because rabbis sit when they teach: rabbis teach when they walk and when they stand as well. Jesus sits because, in a boat, sitting is the wiser position to take.

Teaching from a boat was not unique to Jesus. Describing his experiences as the leader of the revolutionary forces in the Galilee during the first revolt against Rome, Josephus recounts, "I gave order to the masters of the ships to cast anchor a good way off the land, that the people of Tiberias might

not perceive that the ships had no men on board; but I went nearer to the
people in one of the ships, and rebuked them for their folly, and that they
were so fickle as, without any just occasion in the world, to revolt from their
fidelity to me" (*Life* 167). The people did not listen to Josephus, but they did
listen to Jesus. Simon, in the boat with Jesus, is a captive witness. Following
this teaching, to which the crowds and Simon are privy but we the readers
are not (Luke thus lets readers know that the apostles have more to teach
than the words the Gospel records), Jesus tells Simon to head out to the
deeper water and drop his nets. The "your" in "let down your nets for a
catch" (**vs. 4**) is plural, and the pronoun suggests that Simon is not the only
fisherman in the boat with Jesus.

Simon, however, is the only one who demurs. Expressing his reluctance
to drop the net again (**vs. 5**) not only after he had just cleaned it, but also
after a night of unsuccessful fishing, Simon refers to Jesus not as "lord" or
"rabbi" but as "master" (Greek: *epistata*). The word appears in the New
Testament six times, but only in Luke's Gospel, and only in relation to Jesus.
It connotes a person in charge, as in the LXX, where it refers both to the
Egyptian "taskmasters" who supervise the Hebrew slaves (Exod 1.11; 5.14),
the men in charge of Solomon's corvée (1 Kings 5.16; 2 Chron 2.2), and army
officers (Jer 52.25). Peter positions himself thus somewhere between a slave
and a subordinate. Readers will need to determine the extent to which this
bureaucratic title, used both by disciples and by outsiders, is appropriate for
Jesus. Yes, Jesus has authority, but in each case the title is used, Luke shifts
the focus away from Jesus as military commander conscripting soldiers
or taskmasters imprisoning slaves to Jesus as healer and savior in need of
people who understand service, fidelity, and appropriate responses to the
divine call.

The term also appears in cases where people fail to understand Jesus.
Here, Peter will doubt Jesus' ability to provide fish. In 8.24, the disciples call
Jesus "master" when they fear they are about to drown, and thus they show
a lack of confidence. The next three uses, in 8.54, 9.33, and 9.49, show the
disciples' inability, respectively, to recognize that Jesus had been touched
and so had performed a healing, to understand that Moses and Elijah
would not be requiring housing for they will return to heaven while only
Jesus remains at the Transfiguration, and to realize that the casting out of
demons in Jesus' name benefits both the person released from the demon
and Jesus' mission itself. Finally, in 17.13, ten people with leprosy approach
Jesus, call him *epistata*, and ask for a healing. Jesus shifts aside the focus on
his own mastery to tell the supplicants, "Go show yourselves to the priests,"

even before their healing occurs (17.14). Only one of these sufferers returns to Jesus to express gratitude; not all who call Jesus "master" have mastered what that title means.

Although kvetching[1] about putting back out to the deep water and dropping the nets, Simon agrees. He had already seen Jesus do healings, including in his own house; he had already heard Jesus speak with authority. His complaint is a human response, but with Jesus making the request, the complaint is not warranted. Neither are claims that the Sea of Galilee in the late 20s and early 30s of the Common Era had been overfished and thus Jesus draws his initial disciples from starving people whose livelihoods had been destroyed by lack of environmental concern. This view has become popular among those interested in eco-theology. We applaud the interest in conservation; we prefer, however, that the Bible not be forced into false history. The end does not justify the means. Even in well-stocked lakes, fish do not always bite. Luke's story is about discipleship and not about conserving natural resources.

Simon, and whoever else was in the boat with him, obeys Jesus' command; the result is a catch yielding so many fish that the nets were straining (**vs. 6**). The Greek term for "they caught" (*synekleisan*) can also mean "shut up" or "make prisoner"; as an analogy for evangelism, the images of "caught fish" (the fish will suffocate and then be gutted) or of "being shut up" or "imprisoned" are not ideal. Therefore, as we shall see in a few verses, Luke changes the metaphor.

Given the enormity of the catch, Peter and his colleagues in the boat have to call for help from the other boats, and thus we learn that others also had rowed out to the deeper part of the lake. Whether these partners rejoiced in the size of the catch, or panicked in that the haul was causing the boats to sink, Luke does not say (**vs. 7**). On the metaphorical level, Luke shows that following Jesus can produce abundance, but as professionals in the fishing industry well know, it can also be dangerous.

Simon's reaction to the miraculous catch is striking for several reasons. First, although here (**vs. 8**) Luke introduces Simon's nickname, "Simon Peter" or "Simon the Rock," the disciple is anything but rock-solid. Luke never explains the origins of the nickname (contrast Matt 16.18); Theophilus the ideal reader, having received some instruction already, will have heard of this preeminent apostle. Second, while Theophilus may have heard of

---

[1]   Probably the first time this term, Yiddish for "complaining," has appeared in a Gospel commentary.

Peter's triple denial, which the other Gospels as well as Luke report, he may be unfamiliar with Peter's less-than-stellar early response to Jesus: "Go away from me, Lord, for I am a sinful man." The comment is marvelously ironic: where does Peter expect Jesus to go, given that the two are in a boat in deep water? Walk on the water? Third, Peter's wish that Jesus depart, coupled with his use of the term "Lord," sounds a bit like the demons who the previous chapter had exhorted Jesus, "Let us alone! What have you to do with us, Jesus of Nazareth? Have you come to destroy us? I know who you are, the Holy One of God" (4.34). And fourth, Peter refers to himself as "sinful" (Greek: *hamartōlos*).[2] He does not indicate the sort of sin of which he is guilty or whether this sinfulness is a long-term condition or the result of a single action. The same lack of detail will follow the "woman who was a sinner" in 7.36. Scholars have drawn a comparison between Peter and Isaiah, who upon having a vision of the divine throne and about to receive a commission to prophecy, exclaims, "Woe is me! I am lost, for I am a man of unclean lips, and I live among a people of unclean lips; yet my eyes have seen the King, the Lord of hosts!" Peter is not nearly as articulate as Isaiah. Nor is a fish-filled boat on the Sea of Galilee quite the same thing as the heavenly throne room. From a narrative perspective, at least, Peter anticipates the focus of Jesus' mission, since Jesus will state that he has not come to call the righteous but to call sinners (5.32).

Luke attributes Peter's reaction to amazement (**vs. 9**) at the size of the catch. Peter, having already seen Jesus heal his mother-in-law as well as all the healings recounted at the end of Chapter 4, should have been able to recognize Jesus' abilities to do miracles. Yet this catch comes as a surprise. Redaction critics might suggest that the pericope floated in from another source, and Luke has not well integrated it into the narrative. Theologians might respond that all miracles are amazing and wonderful, and we should be open to appreciate them.

Peter's amazement is shared by "all who were with him," including his business partners, the two sons of Zebedee (**vs. 10**). They may have been the others, to this point unnamed, in the boat with him. Our first introduction to the men who will be Jesus' primarily apostles marks them as "partners"; the Greek term (*koinōnoi*) provides us the origin of the term *koinonia*, well known from numerous sites of Christian gathering and fellowship. This plural form of the word, translated by the NRSV usually as "fellowship" (e.g., Acts 2.42; 1 Cor 1.19; 10.16; 1 John 1.3), becomes a hallmark of Christian

---

[2]   See also 5.8, 30, 32; 6.32–34; 7.34, 37, 39; 13.2; 15.1, 2,7, 10; 18.13; 19.7; 24.7.

living. As with terms like "evangelism/gospel," and "apostle," Luke takes a secular term and gives it a nuance appropriate to the developing church.

Along with masking the "fellowship" language, the English translation deforms the Greek of vs. 10 in additional ways. First, the name of John's brother is in Greek *Iakōbos*, which should translate into English as "Jacob." That is the English translation of the same name when it appears in the Septuagint (e.g., to refer to Jacob the patriarch). When *Iakōbos* appears in Matthew's genealogy to name Joseph's father, the NRSV has no problem translating the name as "Jacob" (Matt 1.15–16). Suddenly, when we get to the followers of Jesus, every Greek "Jacob" becomes "James."[3] Second, "you will be catching people" has, in the Greek, the sense of "catching alive" (*zōgrōn*, a combination word from the Greek for "alive" coupled with the word for "catch, prey"); the term is better suited to hunting than to fishing. Thus, Peter is no longer in the fishing business, and we learn shortly that James and John will join him in missionary work. Unlike Mark (1.17) and Matthew (4.19), however, Luke never mentions the pun about "fishing for people."

Returning to the shore, Peter along with James and John (who never actually receive a commission) "left everything and followed" Jesus (**vs. 11**). Jesus never told them to do so; Luke has no command to "follow" as does Matthew (4.19) and Mark (1.17). The commission for Luke is implicit. The disciples, soon to be apostles, know, in the presence of Jesus, what they are to do. The catch of fish is ignored, as the three men leave their lives on the sea, boats, and their families. Peter's mother-in-law – and her unmentioned daughter, Peter's wife – will no longer factor in his activities.

RESTORATION TO PURITY

The story of Jesus' healings and teachings continues with the next episode set in "one of the cities" (**vs. 12**). The use of "city" for communities in Galilee, such as Nazareth (2.4), is generous; Jesus' peripatetic mission is less from urban area to urban area but to comparably small towns in lower Galilee.

---

[3]   See on this linguistic shift Herschel Shanks and Ben Witherington III, *The Brother of Jesus* (New York: HarperOne, 2003; rev. updated ed. 2005). When the Greek was translated in various ways into European languages, the Spanish was sometimes Jaime rather than Santiago, and the older English translations such as the KJV transliterated the former Spanish name, for reasons not entirely clear. The same concern as we have seen can apply to the name Mary, which in light of Hebrew and Aramaic should have been rendered Miriam or at least Miryam.

Luke, likely writing outside the land of Israel, may not have a clear sense of the geography.

In this unnamed city, Jesus encounters a man with leprosy; the afflicted individual is not, contrary to Hollywood or popular preconceptions, confined to a cave or banished from the town; he has no bell around his neck, and he is not crying out "unclean, unclean." Although commentaries on New Testament texts that mention leprosy frequently evoke Leviticus 14–15, these ancient passages speak more about cleansing not only people but also garments and homes, and they are vague at best about the transmission of impurity by touch. And although commentaries frequently note that "leprosy" in antiquity was not Hansen's disease, a point supported by the references to clothes and homes, recently discovered archaeological evidence of the existence of Hansen's disease in Mediterranean antiquity indicates that the healing here may be of a disease more severe than psoriasis, seborrhea, or eczema.

Whatever the man's precise diagnosis, he is not suffering a mild case; he is "full of" the disease. Perhaps this is why, upon seeing Jesus – and so upon Jesus seeing him – he "bowed with his face to the ground," or, more literally, "falling upon his face." Were his features deformed, Jesus would not have to look at him.

The man begs Jesus for a "cleansing," which is the technical term for healing leprosy. His use of "If you choose" (literally, "if you wish") can indicate his humility: he is not putting a demand upon the miracle worker. More cynically, one could take the request less as a form of social politeness and more of a challenge: were Jesus to say, "I do not choose to cleanse you," he would be seen as either lacking in compassion or as incapable.

Jesus agrees to perform the cleansing, and in doing so he touches the man with leprosy (**vs. 13**). He does not violate any law in so doing[4]; to the contrary, Leviticus requires priests who diagnose either the presence of leprosy or its cure to touch the afflicted person. Some readers, still wanting to find a Jesus who rejects the purity laws, appeal to Josephus, who speaks to the matter of leprosy in his *Against Apion*. Responding to charges by Egyptian polemicists that Moses had leprosy, Josephus writes, "he forbade those that had the leprosy either to continue in a city, or to inhabit a village, but commanded that they should go about by themselves with their clothes rent; and declares that such as either touch them, or live under the same roof with them, should be esteemed unclean" (*Apion* 1.281). The passage,

---

4   *Contra* Green, *The Gospel of Luke*, 237.

which is about Moses and is a gloss on Leviticus, says nothing about first-century practice; it must also be read in conjunction with Josephus's apologetic goals. His comment about forbidding leprous people to appear in public is no more evidence of first-century practice than is Apion's own claims that the Jewish people are a leprous people. Indeed, by indicating that people *do* live "under the same roof" with those suffering from leprosy, Josephus demonstrates that not all, or even any, are banished. Luke's passage itself as well as the related passage concerning the healing of the ten with leprosy shows that people so afflicted had some freedom of movement.

The import of Jesus' touching the afflicted man is not violation of law and it is by no means undoing concerns with purity. We are not saying that purity was a nonissue in Jewish culture. There were concerns about ritual impurity, created by childbirth and death, menstruation and ejaculation. The Pharisees sought to move some of the purity practices of the Temple into the home, including ritual washing of the hands prior to eating. Jesus dismisses some of these Pharisaic teachings, but he does not undo purity laws. Even the scene in Acts 10, where Peter, in a dream, receives a command to eat unclean food, never results in Peter's eating anything unkosher. Rather, we learn that the dream concerns the entry of gentiles into the churches, apart from circumcision.

The problem here, with the man suffering from leprosy, is the psychological factor of touching a person whose physical state would likely produce revulsion in others. Jesus could have simply declared the man clean, as he exorcised the man with the demons (4.35); no touch was required. But Jesus reaches out and touches the man (vs. 13). The point is not antinomianism; it is compassion. Jesus touches him, connects with him, welcomes him. He also restores him to purity.

Jesus then orders the healed man to speak to no one: the NRSV's "tell no one" (**vs. 14**) misses the urgency of Jesus' command. The emphasis is not whether the man tells people that he has been healed; his emphasis is on his going to Jerusalem and making the requisite offering. This fact belies the standard claims that "No doubt, apart from Pharisaic scrutiny and with the temple far away in Jerusalem, legal requirements of this sort would have been relaxed on a local scale,"[5] let alone "perhaps the leper's actions are to spell the end of purificatory sacrifice, since Jesus is able to cleanse from leprosy without himself becoming unclean."[6] Lower Galilee at the time of

---

5   Green, *The Gospel of Luke*, 236.
6   C. F. Evans, *Saint Luke* (London: SCM), 295.

Jesus was a bastion of Jewish self-identity, with stone vessels, ritual baths, aniconic coinage, limited Greek graffiti, and no pig bones. There is no reason to think that adherence to the purity *mitzvot* was lax, or that Jesus himself was dismissive of the system. If he were, he would not bother to insist that the man's first responsibility is to go to the Temple. Indeed, for Jesus himself to go to the Temple, he would have had to be in a ritually pure state.[7] Jesus' agenda is *not* to do away with ritual purity; to the contrary, he is restoring people to states of purity.

The healing of the man with leprosy should remind readers of Jesus' synagogue sermon, where he spoke of Elisha's healing Naaman the Syrian of his leprosy (4.26–27). However, here the cleansed man is not a gentile but a Jew, and Jesus' insistence that the healed man make the offering in Jerusalem (the only place such an offering could be made) "as Moses commanded" reinforces his Jewish identity as well as his fidelity to Torah. This account thus corrects the view that the synagogue sermon indicated that Jesus would not heal any among his own people.

We include here a contemporary concern, since leprosy has not yet been eradicated. Several years ago, a dermatologist at Vanderbilt Medical Center, whom Amy-Jill met at a program at the local Church of Christ (strange things do happen in New Testament studies), advised her that people with leprosy do not want to be called "lepers," given the stigma of the name. They prefer, if the subject is their medical condition, simply to be called "people with leprosy," as we would describe people who have cancer or people who have heart disease.

The short interlude of **vss. 15–16** suggests a summary of Jesus' Galilean activities: healing and teaching, and then personal time, away from the crowds, for prayer. He is not, again *contra* numerous commentators, removing himself because he has become impure. Jesus does not need to go to the people who need healing; either he encounters them without seeking them out (4.33–34), or they come to him (e.g., 4.40–41), or others ask him about people in need of healing (4.38–39). Jesus has not yet "sought" those who are sick or possessed; instead, the sick and possessed, and their families and friends, seek him. The people's continual desire for him – to listen to his teachings, to touch him, to gain healing from him – tires him, and drains him. His need for prayer and solitude can be recognized by anyone

---

7   See the very helpful discussion, including summaries of scholarship on the purity laws, by Paula Fredriksen, "Did Jesus Oppose the Purity Laws?" *Bible Review* 11.3 (1995): 20–25, 42–47.

who works in health care, and particularly with people suffering chronic and painful conditions.

Jesus' withdrawing into the wilderness to pray reinforces Luke's complicated Christology: Jesus is lord/Lord, but Jesus is not God (the Father), for God (the Father) does not engage in personal prayer. Jesus is fully human: he tires, he requires solitude, he needs to rest. What the term 'God' means in these Gospel settings is the God of Israel, or as Christians would call him, God the Father. It is correct to say Jesus is *not* claiming to be God the Father, rather he prays to the Father. This prayer formula neither raises nor answers the question of whether Jesus saw himself as divine, or part of the divine identity, while at the same time being fully human.

Jesus' withdrawing also sets up an irony that will only be noticed at the end of the Gospel: there is a difference between withdrawing from the crowds in order to pray, and being deserted by the crowds as one is being tortured to death.

SICKNESS AND SIN

Readers familiar with the Gospel tradition know that most times "Pharisees" appear (**vs. 17**), they will challenge Jesus on legal matters, and Jesus will display his superior command of both Torah and rhetoric. **Vs. 17** marks the Pharisees' first appearance in Luke's Gospel (unlike Matthew's narrative [3.7], their presence at John's Baptism in Luke goes unnoted). Luke reinforces the connection between Pharisees and matters concerning the Torah – matters of utmost importance, since the Torah is the guidebook for Jewish living, and since differences in interpretation lead to different parties of Jews, such as Pharisees and Sadducees and the people who wrote the Dead Sea Scrolls. By associating Pharisees here with "teachers of the law" (Greek: *nomo-didaskaloi,* a term apparently coined in the NT [Luke 5.17; Acts 5.34; 1 Tim 1.7]), Luke does not say that the Pharisees and teachers had come specifically to meet Jesus, let alone to challenge him. Their gathering from throughout the Jewish homeland, "from every village of Galilee and Judea and from Jerusalem," suggests less a mass endorsement than a concerted assessment. Luke lets us know immediately that Jesus was in no danger from whatever challenge they might pose, since he had the "power of the Lord."

Before describing why all these Pharisees and teachers left their homes to see Jesus, Luke turns the reader's attention to several men (the Greek is gender-specific) carrying a paralyzed man on a bed (**vs. 18** cf. Matt 9.1–8;

Mark 2.1–12). Claims that they are acting like "slaves" and so risking their reputations find no purchase in the text:[8] carrying the disabled to Jesus, like bringing babies to Jesus, is what loving people do, and no negative reputation accrues to them. To the contrary, they are displaying faith.

Like all the others who had sought Jesus' healing, the paralyzed man and his friends seek contact with him. Unable to gain access to the house where Jesus was located – whether teaching, healing, or both, Luke does not say – they climb the roof and remove tiles; the Greek term is *keramos*, whence "ceramics"; unlike Mark 2.4, Luke images the tiled roof of a Roman estate; Matt 9.2–8 omits the roof episode entirely. The man's friends then lower him on his bed to Jesus (**vs. 19**).

Jesus' reaction is initially neither about property damage nor about the resourcefulness of the friends, nor even about their desperation; nor is it specifically about the paralyzed man. Jesus comments about "their faith," whether of just the friends or of all parties involved (**vs. 20**). The contents of this "faith" – the Greek *pistis* could also be translated as "belief" or "trust" – includes the certainty that Jesus, who had recently healed a man with leprosy and in whom there was power to heal, would heal the paralyzed man. Luke may also suggest that they had faith that their own efforts would be noticed, and appreciated.

Jesus could have said, "Great is your faith" (cf. Matt 5.28), but in what appears to be a non sequitur, announces, "Man (or person), your sins are forgiven you" (**vs. 20**). The NRSV's "friend" is an attempt at gender-inclusivity; the Greek is *anthrōpe*, "man," "person," or "human being." The issue is not friendship; it is humanity, with its vulnerability, needs, and faith.

Claims that Jews regarded paralyzed people or any people who today would be called "disabled" or "differently abled" as "sinners" and that the paralysis was the result of their sin are common. And they deserve to be called one thing – nonsense. Isaac was blind, but his blindness was not caused by sin. Jacob walks with a limp, but that came not from sin, but from a wrestling match. Jonathan's son Mehiboshet was "lame in both legs" (2 Sam 9.13; 19.27), but the text does not regard him as a sinner. Job had numerous ailments, but they were not the result of sin, despite the claims

---

[8]   *Contra* Craig Keener, *The Gospel of John: A Commentary*. Vol. 1 (Peabody: Hendrickson. 2003), who finds it "surprising … that the disabled person has with him four friends, who are willing to risk their own reputation by acting the part of the slave and bearing him to Jesus." Keener's view is cited by Mary Ann McColl and Richard Ascough, "Jesus and People with Disabilities: Old Stories, New Approaches," *Journal of Pastoral Care and Counseling* 63.3 (2009): Online.

made by his friends. Lev 19.14, the same chapter that mandates love of both the neighbor and the stranger, insists, "You shall not revile the deaf or put a stumbling block before the blind; you shall fear your God: I am the Lord." In the Jewish tradition, disabled individuals together with the poor, the widow, the orphan, and the stranger are under God's special protection, not because they are sinful, but because they are more socially vulnerable.

They are also the ones who will rejoice in the messianic age, for as Isa 35.5–6 states, "Then the eyes of the blind shall be opened, and the ears of the deaf unstopped; then the lame shall leap like a deer, and the tongue of the speechless sing for joy." Such verses also echo in Jesus' synagogue sermon heard in Luke's previous chapter (4.18). These details should eliminate the tendency to claim that Jews saw all sick people as impure and therefore avoided them and made them outcasts. The paralyzed man in this chapter is not an outcast; he is, quite literally, an *in-cast*.

Consequently, there is no necessary connection between the man's sins, whatever they may be, and his healing. It is up to us to make that connection, should we choose. Certainly, the linkage was available: it is this linkage that prompts the speeches of Job's so-called "friends." John's account of the man who is born blind, about whom the disciples ask Jesus, "who sinned, this man or his parents, that he was born blind?" (John 9.2; the question presumes some sort of connection), and Luke 13.1–5, in which Jesus asked if people killed in an accident were worse sinners than others, both show the connection. Jesus, in good Jewish fashion, disagrees both times when someone tries to link disability or tragedy and sin. However, in John 5.14, Jesus says to the paralytic whom he had cured: "See, you have been made well! Do not sin any more, so that nothing worse happens to you." John 5 and our passages should be read together, given the shared command to "Take up your bed/mat and walk" (John 5.8; Amy-Jill thinks this is a floating saying, from which the Synoptic and Johannine tradition constructed two different stories in which to fit it; Ben thinks that Jesus used the same saying on two separate occasions). Our concern here is the tendency of some interpretations to insist that "the Jews" saw a necessary connection and therefore mistreated or shunned the disabled, and Jesus disrupts this mistaken system. It is the interpretation that is itself mistaken, as this very account in Luke, with the fellow's friends who aid him, indicates.

In this narrative, Jesus is juxtaposing the two points, healing and forgiveness, to make a point about his abilities. He gets exactly the reaction he intended, as the scribes and Pharisees question whether Jesus might be blaspheming; they ask, "Who can forgive sins but God alone?" (**vs. 21**). The denotation of the Greek *blasphēmia* is unclear in a late Second Temple context. The Greek term means "slander" and in Rabbinic thought, its equivalent (the Hebrew *gadaf*) concerns using the divine name for nefarious reasons (e.g., *m. Sanh.* 7.5, which also mandates a precise trial to be sure of the person's guilt as well as awareness of the penalties), a reasoning that follows from the commandment, "You shall not make wrongful use of the name of the Lord your God, for the Lord will not acquit anyone who misuses his name" (Exod 20.7). *M. Sanh.* 6.4 associates blasphemy with worshiping idols (so also *m. Sanh.* 7.4; 9.3). Jesus has not invoked the name of God nor committed idolatry, so the Pharisees and scribes have a very broad, and otherwise unattested in Jewish sources, use of the term "blasphemy."

The Pharisees' comment about forgiving sins, as well as Jesus' offer of forgiveness, concerns only sins against God. People have the ability to forgive sins against each other; if they did not, Jesus' instruction to pray, "forgive us our sins, for we ourselves forgive everyone indebted to us" (11.4), and his mandate, "If another disciple sins, you must rebuke the offender, and if there is repentance, you must forgive. And if the same person sins against you seven times a day, and turns back to you seven times and says, 'I repent,' you must forgive" (17.3–4), would make no sense. This type of interpersonal forgiveness is also part of the Jewish tradition, as we see already in Sir 28.2, "Forgive your neighbor the wrong he has done, and then your sins will be pardoned when you pray."

Forgiveness of sins against God was available in Jewish tradition in multiple forms: along with Temple sacrifice, there was John's baptism (whether through the ritual of baptism or the repentance beforehand) and, especially, personal repenting. One Dead Sea Scroll, 4QPrNab, describes a Jewish miracle worker who forgives the sin of a man suffering a serious ailment.

Jesus designed his non sequitur to provoke a reaction, although the Pharisees issue him no public challenge. Instead, it is Jesus who is on the offensive, as he was also in the synagogue in Nazareth. He remarks that he is aware of their thoughts (**vs. 22**) and then poses a question: "Which is easier, to say, 'Your sins are forgiven you,' or to say, 'Stand up and walk?'" (**vs. 23**). The Pharisees do not answer, so the reader must. Ironically, in the narrative context, the easier thing to say is "your sins are forgiven." That pronouncement cannot be proved. Commanding a paralyzed man to walk and then having the man do so is the more difficult option. The form of argument is known in rabbinic literature as a form of the *qal v'homer*, from the lighter to the weightier, argument: if Jesus can make a paralyzed man walk, then surely he can forgive sins.

Alternatively, the discussion may be about the difference between what is easier to say and what is easier to do. Surely, it is easier *to say* "your sins are forgiven," not least because no one can tell whether it's true or not. But as to which is easier *to do*, if we are talking about sins against God, it is surely easier to cure someone's physical ailment than actually to cleanse someone of sin through divine forgiveness, something only God can do. There is a difference between being "the great Physician" and being "the great God."

In **vs. 24,** Jesus uses the title "Son of Man" (capitalized in the NRSV) for the first time: "so that you may know that the Son of Man has authority on earth to forgive sins ..." The title remains a major topic of New Testament studies, given its various nuances. It can refer to the supernatural figure mentioned in Dan 7.13–14, although readers of the NRSV would never make the connection. The NRSV translates: "As I watched in the night visions, I saw *one like a human being* coming with the clouds of heaven. And he came to the Ancient One and was presented before him. To him was given dominion and glory and kingship, that all peoples, nations, and languages should serve him. His dominion is an everlasting dominion that shall not pass away, and his kingship is one that shall never be destroyed." That "one like a human being" is, in Daniel's Aramaic, *bar enosh*, literally, "son of man." For Daniel, the title could refer to the angel Michael, or it could be a symbol of the Jewish people. The followers of Jesus saw in Daniel's vision a reference to their Lord. This apocalyptic redeemer figure, titled "son of man" or "human being," also appears in *1 Enoch* 37–71, where Enoch in chapter 71 himself takes the role. In both the New Testament and in *1 Enoch*, it refers to a particular human being, not an angel or a group of people.

Yet the title "son of man" does not have to carry apocalyptic or eschatological connotations. The Hebrew expression *ben adam*, literally, "son of man," appears more than one hundred times in the Tanakh, where it means, simply, "human being" or "mortal." The first use, Num 23.19, reads, "God is not a human being (*ben adam*), that he should lie, or a mortal, that he should change his mind." In Ezekiel's oracles, "son of man" is the form of address God uses for the prophet; the NRSV translates the Hebrew as "mortal." In Psalm 8.4 (LXX 8.5), the poet asks, "What are human beings (singular in Hebrew: *enosh*) that you are mindful of them, mortals (singular: *ben adam*) that you care for them?

Finally, the Greek expression used in the Gospels has the definite article before the phrase: Jesus is speaking of "*the* Son of Man." The definite article, which is not found in the texts from the previously mentioned Tanakh/ LXX, may indicate that Jesus is referring to a famous previous text and person – put another way, "the aforementioned Son of Man." In other words, Jesus is not running around speaking oddly in the third person about himself for no reason, or for the innocuous reason of indicating he is a human being. Rather, he is strongly suggesting that "he" is that aforementioned Son of Man mentioned in Dan 7, and the figure in Dan 7 is likely to be seen as some sort of supernatural being. One has to ask, what kind of person can rule forever in God's Kingdom?[9] When Jesus then speaks of the "son of man" (Greek: *ho huios tou anthrōpou*), his audience then, and now, needs to determine: is he claiming for himself the status of Daniel's apocalyptic redeemer figure? Is he speaking about the ability of human beings on earth to forgive sin (and so speak for the divine)? Is he pressing the question back on his audience to ask, "Who do you think that I am?"

Jesus claims the redemptory aspects of the title by ordering the "one who was paralyzed" to "stand up," and, "taking your bed, go home." The healed man does so, and in so doing glorifies God (**vs. 25**). We should not pass too quickly over what this scene would have looked like. It took several men to carry the man on his bed, but the man, alone, carries the bed back to his house. Not only can he walk, he has the strength to carry his bed. The bed serves as a sign of Jesus' ability to heal, and anyone seeing the man carrying it rather than prostrate upon it would know that a miracle has occurred. Were the man to be asked, "What happened?" he would respond, "Jesus healed me." For Luke's narrative, here, Jesus is again associated with God.

The people continue this glorification. "All of them" (**vs. 27**), including the Pharisees, scribes, and teachers of the Law, were amazed. Their conclusion is not, however, one of faith; rather, they speak of having seen "strange things." The Greek is *paradoxa*, that is, "paradoxes." They have seen a paralyzed man walk and more; they have seen a human being, Jesus of Nazareth, both heal and, apparently, forgive sin.

THE TAX COLLECTOR AND HIS FRIENDS

Strange things continue when Jesus next encounters a tax collector and, astonishingly, commissions him (**vs. 27**). First Peter, along with James and John, are called from their boats (5.1–11); now Levi is called from his toll booth. Miracles continue: a paralyzed man walks, sins are forgiven, and now an employee of the government leaves his job. Jesus gives him no reason to do so, other than his own authority. Luke does not indicate whether the tax

---

[9]   See Ben Witherington III, *The Christology of Jesus* (Minneapolis: Fortress Press, 1990).

collector had heard of any of the healings, or of Jesus' increasing popularity with the crowds.

The narratives of the unnamed paralyzed man (the Gospel tradition rarely gives names to people who are healed or upon whom exorcism is performed) and Levi the tax collector are connected by the reference to sin. Whereas the paralyzed man's sins are not named, Levi's sinful status would be apparent to all, for the reputation of tax collectors contained the stereotype that they were sinful; hence the Gospels frequently pair "tax collectors and sinners" (Matt 9.10–11; 11.10; Mark 2.15–16; Luke 5.30; 7.34; 15.1). Given the lower Galilean setting of this commission, Levi would likely be a customs agent working for Herod Antipas. Since Rome does not have direct rule over the Galilee, there is no reason to take him as a Roman agent or as indicating the eventual mission to the gentiles. Indeed, the name Levi marks him not only as a Jew, it connects him with Jacob's son Levi, the progenitor of the priests. By calling a tax collector, whose reputation would be one of overcharging the population in order to fill his own coffers, Jesus subtly asks, "at what altar do you worship?" Attentive readers will recall John the Baptist's advice to the tax collectors, "Collect no more than the amount prescribed for you" (3.13).

Levi gives up his day job: "He got up, left everything, and followed him" (**vs. 28**). Like the paralyzed man, Levi gets up; the same Greek term, *anastas* literally, "rising up," describes them both (5.25, 28). The paralyzed man takes his bed home; Levi will take Jesus into his home. Thus, the "everything" the tax collector left behind is the job, not his wealth. Levi then gives a "great banquet" for Jesus, and on the guest list is a "large crowd of tax collectors and others" (**vs. 29**). Levi keeps his wealth, but he now spends it on hospitality for Jesus and others. Perhaps he represents those householders, such as Mary, Martha, and, from the book of Acts, Mary the mother of John Mark and Lydia of Thyatira, who provide support for Jesus and for his emissaries.

Jesus does not name Levi among the Twelve Apostles commissioned in 6.14–16. The names of the Twelve vary from Gospel to Gospel. Mark 2.14 names the tax collector as "Levi son of Alphaeus"; Luke 6.15 mentions a "James son of Alphaeus." Amy-Jill finds the conclusion that this James (Greek: *Jacob*) is a nickname for "Levi" unconvincing. Ben thinks that there were certainly early Jews who had both personal names and nicknames, so perhaps that is the case here, but we cannot be sure one way or another. In Zeffirelli's classic movie *Jesus of Nazareth,* the matter is resolved as follows: Jesus asks the tax collector his name, and he says,"Levi, or Matthew,

I'm known by both names," and Peter, who despises tax collectors, chimes in with "and by others…"

Levi's banquet is the first of the numerous banquet scenes in the Gospel of Luke, and it has at least three different implications. First, Jesus, who is indiscriminate in his dining and who models open table fellowship, eats with sinners and tax collectors, crowds in the desert, and his disciples, and three times with Pharisees. In doing so, he is enacting the messianic banquet, where all recline together in comfort and peace, and where no one goes hungry. The meeting at table, called variously "communion," "Lord's Supper," "Eucharist," or "fellowship meals," serves as a foretaste of this heavenly dinner. However, ordinary table fellowship is not the same thing as a Passover meal, which was a family meal, and furthermore, the Lord's Supper, which is partially modeled on the Last Supper (whether it was a Passover meal or not), should not be confused or fused with later Christian *agape* meals or feasts. More discussion on the debate as to whether the Last Supper was a Passover meal appears later in this commentary when we get to Luke 22.

The second import of the banquet is that of the hospitality the followers of Jesus promoted. Homeowners would show hospitality to itinerant disciples, as Mary and Martha would later do for Jesus (10.38–42). Jesus will send out his disciples to proclaim the kingdom and to expect to receive hospitality: "Take nothing for your journey, no staff, nor bag, nor bread, nor money – not even an extra tunic. Whatever house you enter, stay there, and leave from there" (9.3–4, cf. 10.8–10). The irony that a tax collector epitomizes hospitality should not be lost.

Finally, Jesus is also, for first-century readers, participating in what they would recognize as a symposium. These formal meals, known most famously from Plato's *Symposium*, were opportunities for hosts to display their generosity, and for participants to display their knowledge and cleverness. The host serves as patron; the guests are either clients who will repay the host with public acclaim or services rendered, or they are friends of the same social circles who participate in a system of mutual reciprocity. Any host would anticipate that Jesus, known for his teaching as well as his healing, would be the ideal symposium guest. Jesus will continue to teach at meals ((7.36; 10.38; 11.37; 14.1,7,12,15), although as we shall see, he is a remarkably critical guest, for he holds the householder accountable to kingdom standards, not the basic patron–client relationships usually secured in formal banquet settings.

At the banquet, as if on cue, the Pharisees and their scribes appear again, this time to challenge Jesus' disciples about their dining companions (**vs. 30**). Just as this chapter earlier introduced the terms "word of God" and "Son of Man," here we first encounter the label "disciple." The numbers are not known, and aside from Peter, James, and John, Luke gives no names to the followers. Luke does tell us, however, that now there is an official group of sorts that affiliates itself with Jesus, and that they are distinguished from others. Jesus is gathering a group about him, and they will be known by their actions. Luke will shortly note that John the Baptizer also has disciples; the groups may be considered rivals, each loyal to a different teacher with a different understanding of how best to follow Torah, and how best therefore to live a righteous life.

The Pharisees, here complaining verbally rather than questioning in their hearts, ask the disciples, "Why do you eat and drink with tax collectors and sinners?" The setting for this conversation is not specified, although it appears that the disciples too were invited to the dinner. What the Pharisees are doing in the same setting is less clear: have they entered into a spacious hall, as a woman will do in Luke 7.36 when she anoints Jesus as he reclines at a Pharisee's table?

Their query is not, contrary to popular opinion, based on a concern for purity laws. Nothing suggests that the tax collector was serving unkosher food or food that has not been tithed. The issue is one of association, especially in a society in which one is judged by the company one keeps. Paul makes a similar case when he reminds the Corinthians: "I wrote to you in my letter not to associate with sexually immoral persons" (1 Cor 5.9). Parents do the same thing today when they warn their children about associating with drug dealers or shoplifters. Teachers – and Jesus is a teacher who has disciples – are expected to be moral exemplars. Finally, contrary to the prevailing view, Jesus is not dining "with sinners and other marginalized or outcasts of the society"[10] in the sense that these tax collectors are "marginalized" in the same way that we today speak of "marginalized people." Nor are they "outcasts"; to the contrary, they walked out of the common good for the sake of self-interest. We might take as modern equivalents the picture of Jesus as dining with arms dealers, drug pushers, pimps, loan sharks, and people who think they can, with impugnity, sexually abuse others.

On occasion, commentators will adduce, in order to describe Pharisaic views, select rabbinic references to the *amme-ha'aretz*, the "people of the land." The term as used in the Tanakh means simply that, people who live

---

[10]   Jason Valeriano Hallig, "The Eating Motif and Luke's Characterization of Jesus as the Son of Man," *Bibliotheca Sacra* 173.690 (April–June 2016): 203–18 (204; Hallig repeats the language of "outcasts").

in a particular area. In some Talmudic passages, the expression refers less to a "sinner" than to a person who is willfully ignorant of Torah teaching. It is often used in the Mishnah to distinguish individuals who are part of the rabbinic table fellowship (the *haverim*) from those who are not. If we must find a connection between an *am-* (singular) *ha'aretz* and this passage in Luke, *Pirke Avot* 5.13, on four human characteristics, would be appropriate: "(1) He who says, 'what is mine is mine and what is yours is yours' – this is the common type, though some say that it is the type of Sodom; (2) He who says, 'What is mine is yours and what is yours is mine' – he is an ignorant man (Hebrew: *am-ha'aretz*); (3) He who says, 'what is mine is yours and what is yours is your own' – he is a saint (Hebrew: *chasid*); and (4) He who says, 'What is yours is mine, and what is mine is mine' – he is a wicked man." Yitzkok Buxbaum explains, "The *am-ha'aretz* … is the kind of person who uses the property and possessions of others without permission, and thinks himself justified because he would not mind if they used his possessions."[11] The upshot is that the association of the tax collector and his sinful buddies with the rabbinic *amme ha'aretz* is both anachronistic and a category confusion.

The Pharisees' question was directed to the disciples, but Jesus responds on their behalf. In his first comment, he compares himself to a doctor, and the job of the doctor is to attend the sick, not those who are healthy (**vs. 31**). Here he accepts the label of "doctor" that he earlier had imputed to the people in the Nazareth congregation, when he proposed that they were thinking, "Doctor, heal yourself" (4.23; the same Greek term, *iatros*, appears in both verses). It is not Jesus who needs the healing. Tax collectors and sinners are, in his view, in need of healing; they are spiritually dis-eased, and their sickness can infect the larger community. At the same time, he suggests that there are others who are already healthy, and the Pharisees might be seen as members of that blessed group.

Jesus then makes clear why he visits those who are dis-eased: he states, "I have come to call not the righteous but sinners to repentance" (**vs. 32**). Judith Lieu notes, "It is sometimes suggested that in the eyes of the Pharisees the majority of the ordinary people, who by inclination or the realities of their daily lives were unable to follow the strict Pharisaic emphasis on purity, tithing or other aspects of the law, were 'sinners' to be avoided as sources of impurity" (cf. John 7.49). Yet, as she correctly observes, "for the most part

---

[11]   See Yitzhak Buxbaum, *The Life and Teachings of Hillel* (Lanham: Rowman and Littlefield, 1994), 179.

the Gospels do not see 'the sinners' as simply the ordinary people."[12] Jesus is dining not with the poor and destitute, he is dining with the rich, the exploiters, the abusers, the people who think of themselves and not of others.

In Jesus' analogy, the righteous then are the healthy; the sinners are the ones who are sick, and Jesus will be the physician who seeks to cure them. Luke's point is not that sinners and tax collectors stay in the state in which they are called; they are to repent, and in dining with them – in befriending them, in breaking bread with them – Jesus gives them the medicine they need.

Another group, an unidentified "they" also present at Levi's banquet, asks another question, and this time to Jesus directly: why do John's disciples, like the disciples of the Pharisees, fast, but your disciples eat and drink? (**vs. 33** cf. Mark 9:14–17; Matt 2:18–22). Perhaps they had noticed the relish with which Jesus' followers enjoyed the banquet. Notably, they do not ask Jesus himself about his fasting and feasting. Luke's focus thus is on the followers, Jesus' disciples in the Galilee in the late 20s and early 30s, as well as Christians at the time of Theophilus, considerably later.

Fasting was, in the Jewish culture, practiced for several reasons: certain fast days, such as Yom Kippur, the day of atonement, served to bring the people together, to humble them, and to prepare them for atonement. Lev 23.27 states, "Now, the tenth day of this seventh month is the day of atonement; it shall be a holy convocation for you: you shall deny yourselves and present the LORD's offering by fire" (cf. Lev 16.29–31; Num 29; see also the public fasts described in 2 Chron 20.3 and Ezra 8.21–23, where fasting is a form of prayer). Some groups, such as the Pharisees, fasted as a form of spiritual discipline, and Tacitus suggests that Jews were known for such practices (*Hist.* 5.4). Luke has already introduced Anna (2.37), the widow in the Temple, as engaging in such a discipline, Jesus himself fasted forty days in the wilderness under the guidance of the Holy Spirit (4.2), and his followers will fast as well (Acts 13.2–3; 14.23). Similarly, Judith the pious widow fasts as a discipline (Jtd 8.6), as do the people of her hometown of Bethulia, here as a form of prayer (Jdt. 4.13).

The conversation in Luke 5 is thus about spiritual discipline, not communitywide fasts mandated in Torah. Fasting can be, but is not necessarily, a form of asceticism. Periodic fasts for specific purposes do not make a person an ascetic. Jesus clearly did not abstain from food and wine as his

---

[12]   Lieu, *The Gospel According to Luke*, 45.

normal practice. Whether Jesus was a sexual ascetic is another matter. Ben notes that Jesus was not an ascetic, but like a normal pious unmarried Jew, he did abstain from sexual activity. This does not make him a sexual ascetic in his ethical outlook. Amy-Jill sees him as favoring sexual asceticism, as indicated by his pulling married couples apart. But we are not there yet.

In response to being challenged, Jesus adopts another analogy. Along with being a physician sent to heal the sinners of their sins and call them to repentance, he is the bridegroom sent to prepare his people for an eschatological wedding (**vs. 33**). In the presence of the bridegroom, at the time of celebration, one does not fast. Jesus here includes his disciples in the wedding party: they are as the NRSV translates, "the wedding guests" or as the Greek states literally, they are the "sons of the bridegroom," members of Jesus' own family. Being in the presence of Jesus requires special behavior, but after his ascension, patterns of fasting will return. Jesus tells his interlocutors that the disciples will fast, but only after the bridegroom is taken away (**vs. 35**). Meanwhile, he and his followers will eat and drink, enjoying their meals, as if they are at the messianic banquet. Of course, the "Son of Man has come eating and drinking" (7.34), because it is through table fellowship he calls the sinners to repent, he gathers disparate people together into a new family, and he anticipates the eschatological age.

The two parables that close the chapter conclude the food imagery as well as play upon the distinctions between the time of Jesus' presence and the time of his physical absence. There are also, for Luke's Gospel, other divisions of time: the times of Temple piety indicated by the infancy narratives, and the new time marked by the new covenant (22.20) established in Jesus' death. Different practices apply to each period.

Jesus first remarks that no one takes a swatch of cloth from a new garment and sews it onto an old robe; that would not only destroy the new garment, it would also create a mismatch with the old. Thus, both garments are ruined. Each piece should remain as it is, and so each can be worn (**vs. 36**). Similarly, no one puts new wine into old wineskins, because the new wine, as it continues to ferment, will destroy the old wineskins: the skins will burst, and the new wine will be spilled (**vs. 37**). The new wine belongs only in new wineskins (**vs. 38**). Despite the common view that Jesus is here rejecting old practices, such as fasting, the point of the parables is not that one or the other model, the new or the old, is rejected. Rather, each has its place. Fasting is practiced in the contexts where it is appropriate, just as feasting is practiced in its appropriate context. Nothing is eliminated and nothing is lost. Context matters.

Jesus is also affirming the practices of the Pharisees and of the Baptizer's disciples. Their cloth is appropriate to them, and so should not be appropriated by others. Jesus' followers also will fast, when the time comes. To secure this point, Jesus adds a final line: "No one after drinking old wine desires new wine, but says 'the old is good' " (**vs. 39**). Commentators frequently allegorize the old and new wine into the "good wine" of Jesus and his practices and the "plonk" of the Pharisees and the Baptizer's followers.[13] This allegorizing, in which Luke is seen to disparage the very practices in which Anna, Jesus, and the early Church will participate, is not necessary. We could equally argue that the better "old wine" is Torah understood through the interpretation of Jesus and, for Luke, those who appropriately carry his message.

Luke may well be arguing here against Christian communities that promote a libertine or antinomian approach to piety. Since Jesus is thinking eschatologically, in terms of a new covenant, he may also be intimating that new eras lead to new laws and responsibilities. For Ben, this new era involves leaving some old rules and practices behind. What is appropriate once the Kingdom breaks in doesn't make the old practices bad, but it can make some of them obsolete. Amy-Jill sees nothing in the Gospel indicating that a Torah-based practice is "obsolete." Sabbath is still observed, as is Temple piety in Acts by Jews such as Paul. Gentiles do not follow those traditions that keep Jews distinct, but they were never required to do so. Peter's comment in Acts 10.28 regarding a law preventing Jews from associating with gentiles is nonsense, as the Court of the Gentiles in the Temple indicates. Nor does Paul eat ham sandwiches or take long journeys on the Sabbath.

Ben says, we don't know that about Paul at least in regard to his travel on the Sabbath, and Peter is talking about laws that do indeed set Jews apart and limit their ability to *fully* associate with gentiles – for instance, by limiting their ability to participating in gentile religion, no small limitation for Jews in the first century – or to marry a gentile and then participate fully in his or her culture. Amy-Jill responds by noting that gentiles were, at the time, welcome to convert to Judaism should they wish, that participating in gentile religion – that is, worshiping the state gods or eating meat sacrificed to idols – was something many of the non-Jewish

---

[13] For example, Charles Talbert proposes, "In vs. 39, 'old' should be paraphrased 'good' and 'new' by 'inferior,' because here 'old' equals what Jesus brings – in contrast to 5:36–38 – and 'new' is the inferior system of the Pharisees and Baptists." Talbert, *Luke*, 65.

followers of Jesus ceased to do, and that intermarriage did occur, as we see for example in Acts 16.1.

1. Fasting

Fasting in antiquity was practiced by Jews, Samaritans, and gentiles. Related to the Greek concept of *askēsis* (whence "asceticism"), fasting was a form of training the body, and it served as well as a "spiritual discipline." It involved, and involves, stamina, self-sacrifice, self-control, temporary detachment from the normal way the world as well as our bodies work, and even a recognition of the bounty that we have, for one can only fast in the presence of food. For some people, then and now, fasting and other forms of ascetic activity serve to free individuals from the cares of the world and thus facilitate a union with the divine. For others, such as Daniel, limiting his diet was a means of resisting assimilation and proving the power of his God (Dan 1.6–16).

Several forms of fasting exist in religious traditions. Jewish fast days include not only Yom Kippur, but also, among others, Tisha b'Av, the fast of the ninth day of the month of Av (usually early August), in memory of the destructions of the Jerusalem Temple in 587 BCE and 70 CE (compare Jer 52.12–13); and the fast of Esther, which takes place the day before the holiday of Purim (see Est 4.16). Rabbinic literature and later Jewish practice adds other fasts, such as fasting on the anniversary of the death of a parent (*b. Ned.* 12a); brides and grooms are expected to fast on the day of their wedding, prior to the ceremony.

On the Islamic calendar, Muslims fast during daylight hours in the month of Ramadan, and fasting is one of the five pillars of Islam. Bahais fast during the month of Ala. Buddhist monks and nuns in the Vinyana branch of the tradition do not eat lunch (the noonday meal). Giving up a type of food for Lent is a form of fasting, as is fasting on the certain days during Lent on the Catholic calendar. Historically, Methodist clergy fasted on Wednesdays, in remembrance of the betrayal of Jesus, and on Fridays, in remembrance of his crucifixion. World Vision promotes a "40-Hour Hunger Famine" to teach those who have more than enough what those who have less endure day to day. Some people have chosen to fast one day a week, or to give up one meal, and dedicate the cost of the food they would have consumed to food banks. The Mormon church suggested that if everyone fasted one day a week, there would be enough food in the world to feed the hungry.

Today, fasting has other meanings. Political prisoners go on hunger strikes to protest injustice. The fast is designed to force others to take notice: justice is of such concern that individuals will forego eating, the very thing that keeps us alive, in order to call attention to its lack. Bobby Sands, after being elected to Parliament, went on a hunger strike in 1981 for Irish rights. After sixty-six days on a diet of water and salt, he died.

Today as well, churches that promote fasting need to consider its negative implications. Anorexia is not a voluntary fast but a psychological condition. For anorexics, the encouragement to fast is a danger rather than a blessing. For some congregations, there are starving people within the midst, but they hide their economic lack out of shame. For others, unless the food that goes uneaten can be given to people who lack daily bread, the fasting can create a sense of spiritual superiority that only serves to "puff up" (cf. Col 2.18) the pious rather than actually feed the hungry. Ludwig Feuerbach suggested that we are what we eat. The Gospel tells us to attend to our eating practices, and to know when to feast and when to fast.

2. Disabilities

To read Luke 5 is to encounter a number of example of disabilities, including skin disease and the inability to talk. Conventionally, we speak of "the leper" and "the paralytic," as if the limitations created by the physical conditions fully define the individual. That people healed by Jesus, with the exception of Lazarus and the women mentioned in Luke 8.1–3, are not named shows all the more the emphasis on the ailment. The same type of naming can appear in medical contexts – "take care of the stage 4 cancer in room 2, and I'll talk to the prostate problem in room 4."

We are more than our diagnoses, and descriptions of disability are more than a diagnosis. For Luke 5, disability also concerns friendship networks, access to health care, any perceived relationship between disability and sin, the place of the disabled within social networks, the recognition of the disabled by religious institutions, the identity of the person now healed from the disability, and so on. All of these issues require interrogation, as do any lessons to be gained from the passages.

It is not helpful to find the liberatory move in constructing a negative view of Jewish culture, wherein all disability is a sign of sin and so a prompt for stigma, and then Jesus arrives to announce that the disabled are God's children too. This includes claims such as "Forgiving sins here means removing the stigma imposed on him by a culture in which disabilities are associated with sin or where someone is ostracized as sinful and unworthy of his society's acceptance."[14] Jewish culture, as far as most of the sources indicate, recognizes that the disabled are under divine protection and so are to be supported, just as the friends bring the paralyzed man to Jesus, just as Jairus pleads with Jesus to save his daughter, just as Peter hopes that Jesus will heal his mother-in-law. The Gospel stories typically depict the disabled as within social structures that care for them rather than toss them into the streets or dismiss them as sinners. To classify the Gospel's disabled as "sinners" whom Jesus redeems from social stigma is to dismiss the real difficulties of physical disability, to use Judaism as a negative foil in order to make Jesus look good, and to ignore the responsibilities of Jesus' followers, today, to provide for people who cannot walk or who are suffering from debilitating illness the care that they deserve as fellow children of God.

[14] EDAN [Ecumenical Disability Advocates Network], A Church of All and for All, in *Interpreting Disability: A Church of All and for All* (Geneva: WCC, 2006), cited by Pauline A. Otieno, "Biblical and Theological Perspectives on Disability: Implications of the Rights of Persons with Disabilities in Kenya," Disability Studies Quarterly 29.4 (2009), online at www.dsq-sds.org/article/view/988/1164.

Luke 6 Teachings in Synagogues and on the Plain

¹ One Sabbath while Jesus was going through the grain fields, his disciples plucked some heads of grain, rubbed them in their hands, and ate them. ² But some of the Pharisees said, "Why are you doing what is not lawful on the Sabbath?" ³ Jesus answered, "Have you not read what David did when he and his companions were hungry? ⁴ He entered the house of God and took and ate the bread of the Presence, which it is not lawful for any but the priests to eat, and gave some to his companions?" ⁵ Then he said to them, "The Son of Man is lord of the Sabbath."

⁶ On another Sabbath he entered the synagogue and taught, and there was a man there whose right hand was withered. ⁷ The scribes and the Pharisees watched him to see whether he would cure on the Sabbath, so that they might find an accusation against him. ⁸ Even though he knew what they were thinking, he said to the man who had the withered hand, "Come and stand here." He got up and stood there. ⁹ Then Jesus said to them, "I ask you, is it lawful to do good or to do harm on the Sabbath, to save life or to destroy it?" ¹⁰ After looking around at all of them, he said to him, "Stretch out your hand." He did so, and his hand was restored. ¹¹ But they were filled with fury and discussed with one another what they might do to Jesus.

THE TWELVE APOSTLES

¹² Now during those days he went out to the mountain to pray; and he spent the night in prayer to God. ¹³ And when day came, he called his disciples and chose twelve of them, whom he also named apostles: ¹⁴ Simon, whom he named Peter, and his brother Andrew, and James, and John, and

Philip, and Bartholomew, ¹⁵ and Matthew, and Thomas, and James son of Alphaeus, and Simon, who was called the Zealot, ¹⁶ and Judas son of James, and Judas Iscariot, who became a traitor.

THE SERMON ON THE PLAIN

¹⁷ He came down with them and stood on a level place, with a great crowd of his disciples and a great multitude of people from all Judea, Jerusalem, and the coast of Tyre and Sidon. ¹⁸ They had come to hear him and to be healed of their diseases; and those who were troubled with unclean spirits were cured. ¹⁹ And all in the crowd were trying to touch him, for power came out from him and healed all of them.
²⁰ Then he looked up at his disciples and said:
    "Blessed are you who are poor,
        for yours is the kingdom of God.
²¹ "Blessed are you who are hungry now,
        for you will be filled.
    "Blessed are you who weep now,
        for you will laugh.
²² "Blessed are you when people hate you, and when they exclude you, revile you, and defame you on account of the Son of Man. ²³ Rejoice in that day and leap for joy, for surely your reward is great in heaven; for that is what their ancestors did to the prophets.
²⁴ "But woe to you who are rich,
        for you have received your consolation.
²⁵ "Woe to you who are full now,
        for you will be hungry.
    "Woe to you who are laughing now,
        for you will mourn and weep.
²⁶ "Woe to you when all speak well of you, for that is what their ancestors did to the false prophets.
²⁷ "But I say to you that listen, Love your enemies, do good to those who hate you, ²⁸ bless those who curse you, pray for those who abuse you. ²⁹ If anyone strikes you on the cheek, offer the other also; and from anyone who takes away your coat do not withhold even your shirt. ³⁰ Give to everyone who begs from you; and if anyone takes away your goods, do not ask for them again. ³¹ Do to others as you would have them do to you.
³² "If you love those who love you, what credit is that to you? For even sinners love those who love them. ³³ If you do good to those who do good

to you, what credit is that to you? For even sinners do the same. ³⁴ If you lend to those from whom you hope to receive, what credit is that to you? Even sinners lend to sinners, to receive as much again.

³⁵ "But love your enemies, do good, and lend, expecting nothing in return. Your reward will be great, and you will be children of the Most High; for he is kind to the ungrateful and the wicked. ³⁶ Be merciful, just as your Father is merciful.

³⁷ "Do not judge, and you will not be judged; do not condemn, and you will not be condemned. Forgive, and you will be forgiven; ³⁸ give, and it will be given to you. A good measure, pressed down, shaken together, running over, will be put into your lap; for the measure you give will be the measure you get back."

³⁹ He also told them a parable: "Can a blind person guide a blind person? Will not both fall into a pit? ⁴⁰ A disciple is not above the teacher, but everyone who is fully qualified will be like the teacher. ⁴¹ Why do you see the speck in your neighbor's eye, but do not notice the log in your own eye? ⁴² Or how can you say to your neighbor, 'Friend, let me take out the speck in your eye,' when you yourself do not see the log in your own eye? You hypocrite, first take the log out of your own eye, and then you will see clearly to take the speck out of your neighbor's eye.

⁴³ "No good tree bears bad fruit, nor again does a bad tree bear good fruit; ⁴⁴ for each tree is known by its own fruit. Figs are not gathered from thorns, nor are grapes picked from a bramble bush. ⁴⁵ The good person out of the good treasure of the heart produces good, and the evil person out of evil treasure produces evil; for it is out of the abundance of the heart that the mouth speaks."

⁴⁶ "Why do you call me 'Lord, Lord,' and do not do what I tell you? ⁴⁷ I will show you what someone is like who comes to me, hears my words, and acts on them. ⁴⁸ That one is like a man building a house, who dug deeply and laid the foundation on rock; when a flood arose, the river burst against that house but could not shake it, because it had been well built. ⁴⁹ But the one who hears and does not act is like a man who built a house on the ground without a foundation. When the river burst against it, immediately it fell, and great was the ruin of that house."

Luke 6 offers a variety of different narratives, in different genres, likely derived from different sources. According to the scholarly consensus, the first half of the chapter (a synagogue healing, the Apostolic commission, summaries of teaching and healing) derives from Mark's Gospel, and the second half (including blessings and woes, the command to love enemies, and several parables) comes from Q, that source of materials common to Luke and Matthew. In each case, Luke's redactional stamp is evident. This chapter shows Luke's tendency to de-eschatologize the material and to make it more user-friendly for his gentile audience.[1] Luke thereby does what theologians and ministers do: update material to the needs of the present generation and congregation. Among the tasks of the historian is to determine what the underlying material might have been and not only how, but why, authors adapted received material.

Such historical work on the Gospels is complicated by various factors. First, we cannot be certain that the source-critical consensus is correct. Luke may have had access to Matthew's Gospel, and Q may be a product of scholarly imagination rather than historical fact. Second, we do not know the extent to which Jesus himself changed his teaching, and there is no reason to presume that he said the same thing, the same way, to each group he encountered. Third, we cannot know if all the statements attributed to Jesus actually originated with Jesus; placing comments on the lips of others was not an uncommon practice in antiquity or, for that matter, today. For this chapter and for others, we grant Luke's position: either Luke thought the quotes came from Jesus, or Luke thought the quotes were something Jesus would have said.

SABBATH PRACTICES

Vss. 1–5, the account of the Pharisees in the grain field (cf. Mark 2.23–28; Matt 12.1–8) continues the question of eating practices that came to the table in Chapter 5. The issue here is whether it is permitted, according to Torah, to winnow grain and then eat it on the Sabbath. Stylistically, Luke continues to smooth out Mark's rough-edged account by omitting in **vs. 1** the Markan phrase "and they began to make a way" and by adding "and they were eating" to make clear what the disciples were doing. The scenario resembles Luke 5 in that it also combines questions of diet and discipleship. In 5.30, the Pharisees and scribes complain to Jesus' disciples about their dining companions; in 5.33, unidentified people ask Jesus about why his disciples, unlike those of John the Baptizer, eat and drink rather than fast; now the Pharisees, in a field rather than at a banquet, ask the disciples

---

[1]   See the discussion in Ben Witherington III, *The Gospel of Matthew* (Macon: Smyth and Helwys, 2005), 1–60.

about Sabbath restrictions related to winnowing grain. Their question, "why are you doing what is not lawful (literally, 'what is not permitted') on the Sabbath," addresses a plural "you," that is, the disciples (**vs. 2**).

In Exod 20.10, Moses instructs the people, "the seventh day is a Sabbath to the Lord your God; you shall not do any work – you, your son or your daughter, your male or female slave, your livestock, or the alien resident in your towns" (cf. Deut 5.12–13). The question then becomes: what constitutes work? The Mishnah (*Shab.* 7.2) lists thirty-nine categories of activities that count as "work," which is basically defined as the act of creating. Included in these forbidden activities are sowing, plowing, reaping, binding sheaves, threshing, winnowing, grinding, and sifting. Were such a list in place at the time of Jesus, or even at the time of Luke's composition, the Pharisees might have mentioned it. The disciples are doing something that looks like winnowing. Why Pharisees would be spending time in a grain field on the Sabbath remains a matter of scholarly debate: Ben perceives this narrative to be an historical reminiscence; Amy-Jill, who in thinking of the Pharisees popping up in the grainfields is reminded of the television show *Hee Haw*, in which actors popped up amid the corn to deliver clever lines, thinks the narrative more likely a later creation designed to further a legalistic, negative presentation of the Pharisees.

As he did with the question put to the disciples about their table fellowship (5.30), Jesus takes the initiative and answers for his followers. He argues, in good Jewish fashion, that human need overrides customs: if one is hungry, one should be able to obtain food on the Sabbath. He is in line with another statement found in rabbinic Judaism: attributed to R. Simeon b. Menasaya is the pronouncement, "To you [Israel] is the Sabbath given over, and you are not given over to the Sabbath" (*Mekhilta Ki Tissa* on Exod 31.14).

Then, still in good Jewish fashion, Jesus cites scriptural precedent for his disciples' behavior. Alluding to 1 Sam 21.1–6, Jesus asks the Pharisees, "Have you not read what David did …?" (**vs. 3**) and goes on to describe how when David and his companions were hungry, they "ate the bread of the Presence, which it is not lawful for any but the priests to eat" (**vs. 4**). The language of "taking," "eating," and "giving" also anticipates the Eucharistic descriptions in 22.19 of "take, give thanks, break, and eat." Jesus concludes that the "Son of Man is lord of the Sabbath" (**vs. 5**).

The problem here is that 1 Sam 21.1–6 does not say what Jesus claims. That passage, first, says nothing about hunger. Second, it has nothing to do with the Sabbath. Finally, no commandment is violated. The priest of Nob tells David, who had demanded five loaves, "I have no ordinary bread at hand, only holy bread – provided that the young men have kept themselves from women" (1 Sam 21.4). David assures the priest that his companions have been celibate, and the priest complies with David's demand. Thus, the bread was not forbidden to David and his men. It might be that readers are supposed to recognize the slips between what the text says and how Jesus refers to it. Jesus' question, "have you not read," puts the Pharisees on the spot. They are supposed to be the experts in legal precedent but, ironically, they do not respond to Jesus' *erroneous* citation. Luke may have known that there was a problem with the proof-text, in that Luke omits Mark's erroneous reference to "in the time of Abiathar the high priest." Thus, Jesus gives the Pharisees a false justification. Nor does the justification matter, because Jesus himself, Luke's Son of Man, determines what proper Sabbath observance is. It has been claimed that "David because of his special place in the purpose of God was free from the restraints of the law, and this freedom Jesus claims for himself and his followers."[2] However, the language of "restraint of the law" reinforces one Christian stereotype that views Torah as a problem to be solved rather than a blessing to be enjoyed. Nothing in 1 Sam suggests that David's behavior was illegitimate.

Read positively, the scene draws the connection between David and Jesus, whom Luke has identified as a "son of David." Jesus' response may also have served to legitimize later Christian Sabbath observance,[3] although how Luke envisioned gentile readers doing this, and what if anything the early gentile followers of Jesus did on the Sabbath, remains unclear. Paul, for example, never discusses Sabbath observance, despite his frequent references to what parts of Torah observance should be practiced by the gentiles in the local congregations and what part should not. Ben thinks Paul probably mentions Sabbath practice in Rom 14, and more certainly in Col 2.16, but Paul cautions against allowing anyone to judge congregants in regard to "new moons and sabbaths." The point is, for Ben, that Paul does not think even Jewish followers of Jesus are *required* to observe the Sabbath in light of the new situation in the new covenant. Paul Bradshaw argues that "Gentile Christians who adhered to St Paul's view of the Jewish law as no longer binding on them would have had no interest in keeping

[2]   Nolland, *Luke 1–9.20*, 257.
[3]   The practice of observing the Sabbath itself is not abrogated, according to Matthias Klinghardt, *Gesetz und Volk Gottes: Das lukanische Verständnis des Gesetzes nach Herkunft, Funktion und seinem Ort in der Geschichte des Urchristentums* (Tübingen: J. C. B. Mohr [Paul Siebeck], 1988).

any day of the week as the Sabbath."[4] Amy-Jill has her doubts as to whether Paul wrote Colossians; if he did, she sees him as attempting to prevent his gentile readers from participating in any practice that would mark them as Jews. She sees nothing in Paul's letters, which are addressed to gentiles, to suggest that *Jews* should not keep the Sabbath. She also is concerned that the language of "required" suggests that the Sabbath, and the other forms of *halakhah,* are burdens rather than both delights as well as the means by which Jews celebrated their identity. Ben points out that Paul had both Jews and gentiles in various of his congregations, as 1 Cor 16 and Rom 16 suggest to Ben; and when Paul wants to speak specifically or exclusively to gentiles, Rom 10–11 suggests he will make that clear. If Paul thought he was still obligated to keep the Sabbath, rather than it just being blessed option, he would never have spoken as he does in 1 Cor 9.20 when he says he "became the Jew to the Jew in order to win some." Here Amy-Jill reads 1 Cor 9.20 differently: she sees Paul not as speaking about his actions (he is not going to participate in nonlawful activities for the sake of peddling the Gospel). Rather, Paul is talking about the terms on which he makes his arguments: to Jews he speaks from the perspective of Torah; to gentiles he speaks from the perspective of Greek thought.

Pliny, *Letters* 10.96 (ca. 11–113) mentions that the Jesus followers "were accustomed to meet on a fixed day before dawn and sing responsively a hymn to Christ as to a god, and to bind themselves by oath, not to some crime, but not to commit fraud, theft, or adultery, not falsify their trust, nor to refuse to return a trust when called upon to do so. When this was over, it was their custom to depart and to assemble again to partake of food, but ordinary and innocent food." There are references to "the Lord's Day" in 1 Cor 16.2 and Rev 1.10, but the term is not associated with Sabbath observance or even clearly with worship. The same term appears in the *Didache* (ch. 14) and in the *Epistle to the Magnesians* of the early second-century bishop Ignatius of Antioch, but again, the references are not clear, and there is no compelling reason to associate any of this with Sabbath observance.

Ben suggests that in Jesus' view, the function of the Sabbath, whether ordinary or eschatological, was to give people rest from the things that plague them, whether it was disease or hunger or demons or something else. In his view, the Sabbath was the perfect time to release people from such needs or meet those needs. Ben finds that Jesus performed healings on

---

[4]   Paul Bradshaw, *Early Christian Worship: A Basic Introduction to Ideas and Practice*, 2d ed. (Collegeville: Liturgical Press, 2010), 83.

the Sabbath in light of the Kingdom that is coming, and not for the stated purpose of the Sabbath in the OT. It is Jesus, not the Sabbath, that gives rest from the things that plague us when it comes disease, decay, or death.

Amy-Jill would phrase the observation differently. The Sabbath is designed to encourage people to rest and to do so in the imitation of God. The point is not only to avoid what "plagues" us, for there is nothing necessarily plaguelike about our daily activities. God was not "plagued" by the work of creation, yet God rested on the seventh day. The focus of the Sabbath is not rest from hunger or demons; the Sabbath does not give rest from hunger – acquiring food does; the Sabbath does not give rest from demons – exorcism does. She finds that Jesus, as a Jew, would have celebrated the Sabbath and, as a Jew, would have debated with other Jews about how precisely this celebration should be engaged. Luke, not writing to Jews, or at least not writing primarily to Jews, has a different purpose.

The question of whether Luke expected *gentiles* to celebrate the Sabbath, in any way, must remain open. It was Constantine who, eventually, established Sunday as a holiday. If it is the case that Luke does not expect gentiles to celebrate the Sabbath, then the major, if only, force of this passage and the other Sabbath passages is to show that Jewish Sabbath observance is, for Luke's readers, not only irrelevant but potentially oppressive. Or, Ben suggests, the point is to report accurately the *Sitz im Leben* during Jesus' ministry, without ulterior motives.

Luke gives the story's conclusion a clear Christological focus by omitting Mark's "the Sabbath was made for human beings, not human beings for the Sabbath," and so focusing attention on the Son of Man as lord of the Sabbath. As with other pronouncement stories, this astounding claim silences the opposition and concludes the tale. González observes: "Jesus is not simply stating a commonly observable fact or a general principle. He is making a statement about himself and his mission as bringing creation to its intended order. What God intends for all human creation is fulfilled in Jesus."[5] A Jewish response might be that the Sabbath is precisely what God intends for human beings, but how it should be observed is a matter for the community to determine and not within the purview of an individual. How or even *if* Luke intended (gentile) readers to celebrate the Sabbath remains an open question. How people who follow Jesus today choose to celebrate the Sabbath remains a continual matter of debate within and across denominations.

---

5   González, *Luke*, 89.

The following account (vss. 6–11) records another Sabbath controversy, this time when Jesus heals a man with a withered hand in the synagogue (cf. Matt 12.9–14; Mark 3.1–6). To "on another Sabbath" (**vs. 6**), Luke adds to Mark's notice that Jesus entered a synagogue. Jesus' purpose in coming to the synagogue is not to heal but to teach. In Judaism, study and interpretation of Torah *are* forms of worship, for to honor God, one honors the text that reveals God. Torah study would be part of any Sabbath worship.

Present in the synagogue is a man with a withered hand, likely a member of the congregation rather than someone placed there by Jesus' opponents, for Luke says nothing about the man's presence in the synagogue as unusual. Jesus' reputation as a healer has become so secure that his opponents, like Luke's readers, know that a healing will take place. The variation on the theme – how Jesus will heal; what he will say; what his interlocutors will do – keeps the reader's interest.

From questioning his forgiving of sin, to querying his dining habits, to asking about the disciples' possible violation of community standards regarding Sabbath practice, the Pharisees retain their position as Jesus' narrative foils. Now they and the scribes watch Jesus to see if he would heal on the Sabbath (**vs. 7**). The Greek verb for "watch" here means "to spy out" or "to look at secretly, out of the corner of one's eye" (cf. Ps. 36.12 LXX). **Vs. 8** tells us that Jesus knew their agenda "but" (Greek: *de*, which can also be translated "and") he said to the man with the withered hand: "Get up and stand in the middle." He thereby sets up a public display in the center of the gathering; he does not speak quietly with those who would accuse him – he challenges them directly. He will both heal the man's hand and, given Luke's purposes, prove his points less about how to observe the Sabbath and more about this own identity.

By healing the man in the synagogue, has Jesus violated the Sabbath? The answer would depend on the person one asks. "Healing" is not one of the thirty-nine activities the Mishna proscribes for Sabbath observance. As far as we can tell, all Jews would agree that saving a life is appropriate, indeed, mandated, on the Sabbath.As the Mishna, *Yoma* 8.6, states: "And any matter of doubt as to danger to life overrides the prohibitions of the Sabbath." For a nonpainful chronic condition, the consensus view is that the healing, if it is a form of work (and health care professionals would know what constitutes "work" for them), should wait.

Luke's Jesus takes the position that the appropriateness of doing good on the Sabbath supersedes the need to avoid what might be called work. His question about whether it is "lawful" (the Greek is literally "whether it is permitted") to do good or to do harm on the Sabbath, to save a life or destroy it (**vs. 9**) is more rhetorical flourish than actual question in search of an answer: *of course* it is permitted to do good; *of course* it is permitted to save a life. There is, however, no actual "saving a life" in this context: the man with the withered hand is not at death's door. But he does not, in Jesus' view, have a full life, because he is deprived of the use of his hand. Only Luke mentions that the hand restored is the "right" hand, the hand used for work, gesturing, and greeting.[6]

Robert Tannehill develops Jesus' question: "The failure to do good is actually doing harm if an opportunity is lost. The healer who is present today may not be present tomorrow. In such situations, refusal to heal is an act with harmful consequences."[7] These arguments raise questions for those in church today. Should the orthopedist in the pew leave the service in order to attend to a nonpainful chronic condition? Should a pastor stop the service in order to replace one hearing-aid battery of the person in the pew whose other battery is working just fine? Does the chiropractor in the choir leave the anthem in order to massage a chronically stiff muscle? How, indeed, is the Sabbath to be observed, when those who can improve life for others need to take time for themselves? Moreover, if Jesus, and not the Sabbath, is the one who brings rest, why do his (gentile) followers need to celebrate the Sabbath at all? Ben adds here that Sunday is not the Sabbath, not even the Christian Sabbath, and such questions are irrelevant when it comes to the proper observance of the Lord's Day.

Jesus restores the man's hand to health. "'Stretch out your hand.' He did so, and his hand was restored" (**vs. 10**). Amy-Jill finds that no medicine was practiced; no work was engaged. The "divine passive" indicates that the hand was healed miraculously; Jesus himself could not be accused of "doing" anything. Not quite, says Ben. If the man stretched out his hand in the presence of Jesus, and the healing came from or through Jesus' presence, he certainly did something. Yes, Amy-Jill agrees: Jesus did something. But he performed no direct action that would allow his opponents to charge him with working on the Sabbath.

Their plans to accuse Jesus thwarted, the Pharisees "were filled with fury" (**vs. 11**).[8] Their irrational rage shows that they are, for Luke, out of control; Luke will continue to build a negative picture of Jesus' opponents: they are

6   Culpepper, "The Gospel of Luke," 134.
7   Tannehill, *Luke*, 111.
8   The Greek *avoia* indicates irrational anger, even pathological rage. See Bovon, *Commentary on the Gospel of Luke*, 204.

not loyal followers of Torah, but irrational, jealous, and intent on doing Jesus harm.[9] Luke does omit Mark's notice (3.6) that the Pharisees wanted to "kill" Jesus, perhaps because "Luke knows that the Pharisees are not part of the story of Jesus' death."[10]

Ben points out that scholars have difficulty maintaining the proper balance between, on the one hand, accusing Luke of fabricating the animus of the Pharisees against Jesus, perhaps retrojecting later controversies back into the ministry of Jesus, and on the other hand, doing too much apologetics defending the Pharisees in the Gospel accounts. For Ben, the historical facts are reasonably clear – there was opposition to Jesus' ministry on the part of various Jewish individuals and groups of his day, including the Jerusalem authorities. Were that not the case, it would be very hard to explain (1) the reason why the Gospel writers felt compelled to include so many controversy stories about specifically Jewish matters (Sabbath observance, corban, food laws, etc.) when by the time Luke was writing these issues were *not* likely hot button issues for the increasingly gentile Christian congregations; and (2) it would fail to provide a necessary historical background that helps explain what happened to Jesus during the last week of his life, especially vis-à-vis the involvement of some Jews in the demise of Jesus. *But* it may be true that the Gospel writers, including Luke, have overemphasized the degree or persistence of the opposition for the sake of emphasizing the tension that Jesus' ministry created and its relevance for dealing with later Church controversies with the synagogue. Amy-Jill agrees that apologetics, perhaps even her own, may enter the discussion. Yet she also sees these Sabbath stories as having nothing to do with the death of Jesus (thus doing away with Ben's second point). As for the controversies, their presentation of "bad Jewish practice and bad Jews" versus Jesus' Christological role as well as debate and healing abilities serves a purpose regardless of the details of the debates themselves (thus countering Ben's first point). One does not have to have an investment in the details of the argument as long as one is invested in the one who wins the debate, as contemporary responses to political debates abundantly demonstrate. Did Jesus and his fellow Jews debate Torah? Amy-Jill finds this to be most likely. Did Jesus' followers, both Jews and gentiles, debate the role of Torah's instructions regarding those practices that kept Jews distinct from gentiles? Of course. How much of the Gospel accounts reflects

---

[9]   Tannehill, *Luke*, 112.
[10]   Lieu, *Gospel According to Luke*, 48.

debates in which Jesus engaged and how much reflects the concerns of Jesus' second- and third-generation followers will remain, like the Torah itself, a matter of debate.

In 6.12–16, by distinguishing twelve men among his disciples to be "apostles" (the term derives from the Greek for "to send out"), the Lucan Jesus ensures that the legitimate tradition, based on eyewitness testimony (1.2), will continue. Whereas the number "twelve" remains constant across the Gospel tradition, and whereas the other Synoptics offer a commissioning of Jesus' disciples (Matt 10.1–4; Mark 3.13–19a), only Luke establishes this formal division between disciples and apostles.

The context in which Luke depicts this commissioning speaks to ecclesial organization. Luke remarks that, before choosing the Twelve, Jesus went to the mountain (no specific location is given) and spent the night in prayer (**vs. 12**). Mountains are, cross-culturally, locations where people perceive the divine presence; in Matthew's Gospel, seven scenes are set on mountains, including the famous "Sermon on the Mount" (Matt 5–7). Luke's symbolism regarding mountains is less easily mapped. Aside from the Transfiguration (9.28), Jesus does not ascend to mountains in this Gospel, and there are no mountain scenes in the Book of Acts. Indeed, the Sermon on the Mount in Luke becomes the Sermon on the Plain. Whether subtly associating Jesus with Moses on Mount Sinai, or Elijah on Mount Horeb, or indicating that Jesus, seeking intimate communication with God, needed a space away from those consistently making demands on him or testing him, or because that mountain is where Jesus, historically, went, Luke indicates *why* he went: "he spent the night in prayer." This is the only verse in the Third Gospel that states that Jesus prayed all night, and thereby Luke indicates the importance of the act to follow, the selection of the Twelve. In Acts, prayer accompanies the appointment of people to special positions (1.24; 6.6; 13.2–3; 14.23; cf. Luke 3.21; 5.16; 9.18, 28–29; 22.40–46).

According to Bovon, "the times at which Jesus prays are again and again connected to a decisive stage of the new age of salvation; in the prayers of Christians, the issue is usually the role of the individual or the congregation in the history initiated by God through Christ. For them, prayer means not to lose faith, to endure, not to surrender to temptation, and so on. In the case of Jesus, the salvation-historical issues predominate in prayer; but for the Christians, it is ethical issues …"[11] His observations raise several questions: To what extent does Luke see Jesus' prayer life as a paradigm for his followers? Should prayer also include praise of God, lament, or thanksgiving (the subjects in Jewish prayers from Tanakh through to the rabbinic period and on to the present), or can prayer be, "Please let me get an A on this test," or, "Please heal my cancer"? Are there inappropriate prayers? How is prayer related to ethics? In our increasingly secular age, we might also query prayer as a spiritual exercise: is it appropriate to pray if one does not believe in a transcendent deity who hears prayers?

Jesus' prayer in vs. 12 is less important in terms of its contents (which are not given) than its presence prior to the naming of the Twelve. That these followers will desert Jesus – three cannot keep watch with him; one denies him; another betrays him – brings additional pathos to this prayer. Jesus may be praying for his disciples; he may also be praying for himself.

When the night of prayer is over and day dawns, Jesus calls his disciples, chooses twelve, and calls them "apostles" (**vs. 13**). The term, already present in Koine Greek, had no particular religious connotation. Nor did the Hebrew word *shaliach*, from the root meaning "to send." An apostle was simply a messenger, sent usually by a patron to deliver a message.[12] For Luke, "apostle" is a technical term for the Twelve; the other Gospels do not use it (cf. 9.10; 11.49; 17.5; 22.14; 24.10 in comparison to Matt 10.2; Mark 6.30; John 13.16). Later, Luke will indicate that the apostles will have eschatological rule (Luke 22.29–30) and will be witnesses to all Israel (Acts 2.36). Acts 1.15–26 adds that requirements for being an apostle include being a witness to Jesus from the time of his baptism to his resurrection. Only Luke notes the choosing of a new twelfth apostle after Judas's demise (Acts 1.15–26), but when James the brother of John, the son of Zebedee, is executed by Herod Agrippa I, he is not replaced. For most Christians, the requirements indicate that the institution of "apostle" could not exist beyond the first generation of Jesus' followers. Others would take Paul's comment in 1 Cor 9.1, "Am I not an apostle? Have I not seen Jesus our Lord?" as opening up the apostolate to those beyond first-century Jews present in Galilee in the late 20s CE.

According to Acts 14.4, 14, Paul is also an "apostle," that is, one sent by Jesus himself. In Acts, Luke uses the term in its broader and more generic sense of "one sent"; Paul knows of "sent ones/apostles" of particular

---

[11] Bovon, *Commentary on the Gospel of Luke 1*, 208–9.
[12] See C. K. Barrett, *The Signs of an Apostle* (London: Epworth, 1970). On *apostellō* as meaning "sending with a commission," see 1.19, 26; 4.18, 23.

churches (see 2 Cor 8–9), and connects being an apostle with having seen the risen Lord (see 1 Cor 9.1). Paul sees himself as an apostle because he was "called by" and "sent by" Jesus (Rom 1.1; 1 Cor 1.1; Gal 1.1). Paul also applies the title to James the brother of Jesus and leader of the Jerusalem group of followers (Gal 1.19) and to Barnabas, his missionary companion (1 Cor 9.5–6). The Epistle to the Hebrews (3.1–2) calls Jesus an "apostle" because he was sent by God. Today, the Church of Jesus Christ of Latter-Day Saints (Mormons) has a quorum of Twelve Apostles. Therefore, when one speaks about "the Apostles," one does well to specify the text under discussion for names, numbers, and qualifications.

Luke's listing of the Twelve Apostles has little narrative value: with few exceptions, such as Peter and Judas Iscariot, other names could easily be substituted without compromising the plot. The number twelve may indicate that the apostles serve as a symbolic reconstitution of the twelve tribes of Israel, separated first by the rebellion of the Northern tribes against Rehoboam's rule in Jerusalem, and then severed by the Assyrian exile of the ten tribes comprising the Northern Kingdom of Israel. Jesus, the new son of David, is through his apostles, symbolically regathering the tribes. Anna, descendant of the tribe of Asher (2.36), shows the possibility of the regathering of the Northern people of Israel. Ben notes that to judge from the roles the Twelve play both during the ministry and at the eschaton, it seems more likely that they are intended to *free* the twelve tribes, not *be* the reboot of the twelve tribes. That is, they are supposed to minister to and have a judging function in relationship to the twelve tribes. Amy-Jill does not understand Ben's use of "free" here since they are not *qua tribal identification or membership of the people of Israel* enslaved, but she agrees on the evangelizing and judging function according to Luke (cf. 22.30).

Luke's order and naming of the Twelve here in Chapter 6 differ not only from the list in Acts 1.13; they also differ from Mark's list in several ways. First, Luke places Andrew second in the list, as does Matthew (**vs. 14**). This is Luke's first mention that Simon Peter had a brother. In John's Gospel (1.40–41), conversely, it is Andrew who first follows Jesus, and Andrew who introduces Peter to Jesus. Second, Luke alters, somewhat clumsily, Simon's nickname, and does not explain how the name "Peter" originated (see comments on 5.8). Given that the ideal reader, Theophilus, had some familiarity with the story being told, perhaps Luke did not find the need to detail the meaning of "Peter." Ben suggests that Luke has less interest than the other Gospel writers in promoting Peter as the leader of the movement following Jesus' death; that role goes to James the brother of Jesus (see Acts

15) and then, ultimately, to Paul. In Luke-Acts, Peter is less the "rock" of the church than he is for Matthew or John.[13] Third, Luke omits the nickname, "Boanerges" or "sons of thunder," accorded (Mark 3.17) to James and John, the sons of Zebedee. Consistently, Luke omits Aramaic phrases. Fourth, Luke omits Thaddeus and, instead, inserts Judas the son of James (**vs. 16**). If Peter and Andrew, and James and John, are seen as pairs, then we might also see Philip and Bartholomew as pairs. Philip, but not Bartholomew, appears in John 1.43–48; 6.5–7; 12.21–22; and 14.8–9. His Greek name connects him with Andrew; perhaps they had connections in the Hellenized city of Bethsaida (see 9.10; John 1.44; 12.21).

Luke lists Matthew and Thomas next (**vs. 15**). In the First Gospel, Matthew is the tax collector whom Jesus called and at whose house he banqueted. Luke, like Mark, identifies the tax collector as Levi (5.27). Whether this Thomas (the name means "twin" in Aramaic) is the same as the "disbelieving Thomas" of John 20, Luke does not say. Following James son of Alphaeus is Simon "called the Zealot."[14] The term "zealot" in relation to the political party opposed to Roman occupation surfaces in Josephus in relation to the First Revolt against Rome in 66–70. Given Luke's narrative setting, "zealot" in the political sense would be anachronistic; given Luke's actual time of composition, the term could easily indicate an anti-Roman agenda. The term as applied to Simon may also be used in its more traditional sense of someone who was especially pious or zealous for Torah observance. This Simon might have been a particularly zealous follower of Jesus, as Paul was a particularly zealous persecutor of Jesus' followers (Phil 3.6), or as Jesus himself, according to John, was zealous for the Temple (John 2.17).

We know nothing about "Judas of James" (**vs. 16**), who appears also at John 14.2. The final listing in this verse is Judas Iscariot. There are several conjectures the meaning of "Iskariot": (1) man of Keriot, a Judean village (thus Judas would be the only Judean among the Twelve); (2) a reference to the *sicarii*, the "daggermen" or hit men among the revolutionaries against Rome operative before and during the First Revolt; (3) a derivation from the Aramaic *s'qar*, meaning "the false one," and a slew of even less-likely etymologies. The various connotations are not mutually exclusive, and nowhere in the New Testament is the name explicated.

---

[13] The Western text of Luke and Acts inflates Peter's role, perhaps given his prominence in Matthew and John.

[14] Mark 3.18 offers "Simon *Kananaios*," a transliteration of the Aramaic term for "zealot."

Luke notes, laconically, that Judas "became a traitor." Luke's readers are already aware of opposition to Jesus: the congregation in the Nazareth synagogue; the Pharisees, scribes, and teachers of the Law; and now Judas. Opposition mounts. *How* and *why* Judas betrays Jesus or, as the Greek term *prodotēs* literally means, "hands [Jesus] over," remains yet unspecified. Ben notes that if Judas did indeed have revolutionary leanings, then Jesus' failure in the end to endorse or pursue such an approach might provide a historically plausible explanation for why Judas felt he had to betray Jesus. Judas may have believed Jesus had himself betrayed the cause of Jewish freedom and independence. Amy-Jill finds the revolutionary Judas thesis unconvincing for numerous reasons, from its complete lack of textual support to its historical improbability (had Judas wanted Jesus to respond militarily, a secret betrayal would not be necessary) to an overemphasized militarism in first-century Jewish apocalyptic speculation. But Judas's betrayal of Jesus was not a secret kept from Jesus, and furthermore, the activities of Jesus at the beginning of Passover week could have raised hopes of a military action in Jerusalem, hopes that were dashed later in the week when it became clear Jesus did not come to Jerusalem to assume the role of political ruler. Ben says that's precisely his point. Judas early in the week got his hopes up when he saw the Triumphal Entry and Temple action. They were dashed thereafter, which led to the betrayal.

Readers might also attend to Judas throughout the rest of the Gospel narrative to determine at what point, and why, he begins his disloyalty. Given Jesus' prayer prior to this appointing of the Twelve, Luke suggests that the naming of Judas was not a mistake. That Judas would become a traitor, but was not yet one, may suggest that this last-named apostle was until the Passion a faithful member of the newly formed community. Ben agrees, if by until the Passion we mean until near the end of Passion week.

THE SERMON ON THE PLAIN

Having named his Twelve Apostles, Jesus does not commission them or even send them out. Luke rather, simply, depicts the Twelve as accompanying Jesus as he descends the mountain. Jesus, the Twelve, and the other disciples now stand together with an enormous crowd from Judea and Jerusalem as well as Tyre and Sidon (**vs. 17**). If there are gentiles in this entourage, Luke does not make the point explicit. Listening are also Luke's

A CLOSER LOOK: THE SERMON ON THE MOUNT AND THE
SERMON ON THE PLAIN

The section beginning at vs. 20 and ending at 8.3, presenting a great
deal of material absent from Mark but found in Matthew, is sometimes
called the "little interpolation"; the title suggests that Luke was following
Mark's Gospel, and then added to it a chunk of material found in other
sources. The shorter section of twenty-nine verses, 6.17–49, is called
the "Sermon on the Plain," in contradistinction from Matthew's 106-
verse Sermon on the Mount, where similar material appears. Despite
their differences in size and form, the two sermons have the same
order, which suggests either that they are both drawing on a common
source or that one author is drawing on the other. All of the Sermon
on the Plain can be found in Matt 5–7, with three exceptions: the First
Evangelist includes no woes to balance the beatitudes; the saying about
the blind guide is found at Matt 15.14, and the saying about the dis-
ciple/teacher relationship is also found in Matthew's mission discourse
(Matt 10.24).

A comparison between the two sermons indicates each author's agenda.
For example, Luke has a concern for rhetorical balance, as seen with the
beatitudes and the woes, that is not reflected in Matthew. Rhetorically
neater (Matthew's sermon, especially if read aloud, give the sense of a
cobbling together of Jesus' greatest hits rather than a carefully crafted
development of ideas), Luke's sermon has a basic tripartite structure:
(1) blessings and woes (vss. 20–26); (2) paraenetic exhortations (vss. 27–
38); and finally (3) parables or proverbs (vss. 39–49).[15] Next, Luke lacks
some of the biblical material found in Matthew's Sermon (e.g., Matt 5.17,
19–20, 21–24, 27–28, 33–39a, 43; 6.1–8, 16–18; 7.6, 15 do not have Lucan
parallels), and especially notable in terms of absent materials are (1) the
concern for the permanence of the Torah and prophets; (2) the absence
of the formula "you have heard it said"; and (3) the Jewish practices of
prayer, fasting, and almsgiving. Likely, Luke has adapted traditional
material for a gentile audience less concerned with Torah's orthopraxy.
Conversely, Luke adds vss. 24–26, 27c, 28a, 34–35a, 37bc, 38a, 39a, most of
which address general ethics.

---

[15]   See the discussion in Culpepper, "The Gospel of Luke," 140–41.

readers, who would see themselves as among his disciples.[16] The people are present for different reasons: Jesus to teach; the apostles and disciples to be instructed; the crowds to be healed of diseases or exorcised from unclean spirits (**vs. 18**). Luke states that they sought to touch Jesus, "for power came out from him and healed all of them" (**vs. 19**). This notice of Jesus' power comports with earlier statements that Jesus was full of the Spirit; he is its conduit in that it flows through him. The same mediating function describes other ancient healers.[17]

To begin the sermon, **vs. 20** states that Jesus looked up, saw his disciples, and began to speak to them (the Greek literally says, "lifting up his eyes at his disciples"); this is the first place Jesus specifically addresses a group called "disciples." The address is to them, although the crowd, including the reader, overhears. It is up to the reader to determine: Am I among the disciples, or not?

The opening line, "blessed are the poor" (the NRSV's "you who are" is an editorial addition designed to clarify the address), forces listeners, then and now, to determine insider versus outsider status. Luke's "poor" preeminently means those suffering economic lack; Matthew offers "poor in spirit" and so deemphasizes the economic interest. Similarly, Luke offers a benediction to "you hungry" (**vs. 21**), whereas Matthew speaks of those who "hunger and thirst for righteousness." Matthew's interest in personal traits continues in the Sermon on the Mount's blessings of the meek, the merciful, the pure in heart, the peacemakers; these attributes do not appear in Luke's sermon. Ben suggests that, since there is so much evidence of Jesus' concern for the poor, it is likely that Luke, with the economic focus, is closer to Jesus' intent here.[18] Ben notes, for example, that the beatitudes in vss. 20b–23 take the personal form, "blessed are *you* poor," as compared with Matthew's "the poor in spirit,"[19] and that this formulation could suggest that, in Luke's view, Jesus sees at least some of his disciples as among the poor, hungry, mourning, and reviled. Amy-Jill would nuance the point: yes, Jesus is concerned about matters of justice, but she sees him as less directly

---

[16]   Lieu, *Gospel According to Luke*, 50.

[17]   See Witherington, *Christology of Jesus*, 156–78.

[18]   See Ben Witherington III, *Jesus and Money: A Guide for Times of Financial Crisis* (Grand Rapids: Brazos Press, 2010).

[19]   Fitzmyer, *The Gospel According to Luke I–IX: A New Translation with Introduction and Commentary* (AB; New York: Doubleday, 1970), 632, suggests that Luke introduced the "you" not only because of Luke's preference for the second-person plural, to match the "woe" formulations, but also because earlier sapiential sayings regularly used the third person.

involved with "the poor" themselves (the term does need elaboration, lest it become a cliché; most people of the time were "poor" in the sense of not being sure if there would be enough food to last the year; nor are "the poor" in the same category as "the homeless") than in how the rich treat the poor. The disciples are not among the destitute: four own boats; one is a tax collector. Indeed, because there is no change of address when Jesus begins the woes, the disciples to whom the sermon is addressed could just as easily be among the "rich" of vs. 24. Were the disciples among the destitute, then by calling them away from families, Jesus would leave those families in an even worse condition economically; were they among the destitute, then there is no reason to tell them not to bring money with them on the road.

Neither are the majority of the minor figures in the Gospel among "the poor": the ruler Jairus and his wife; the centurion with the sick child, Mary and Martha the householders, the various Pharisees as well as sinners and tax collectors with whom Jesus banquets, Zaccheus the chief tax collector, and so on. Nor does she think that all the people healed are poor. Jesus changes no systemic economic system. Theophilus, in the role of patron, is not poor, and Luke gives no indication that Jesus would want him to divest his holdings. Thus, what exactly this "good news to the poor" is, or what the "Kingdom" is that they inherit, requires further reading in the Gospel.

The term "blessed" (Greek: *makarios*) that begins the beatitudes has the sense of "good for you if ..." or "congratulations"; the Australian expression, "Good on you," and the Yiddish inflected, "Mazel tov," are cognate. Jesus is not suggesting in some masochistic fashion that destitution and starvation are desirable states. The beatitudes are a form of sapiential or wisdom speech (cf. Prov 8.34; Psa 1.1; 2.12; 34.8; 41.1; 84.4; 94.12; 119.2; Sir 14.1; 25.8, 9; 28.19), but these beatitudes draw upon not daily experience but Jewish eschatological hopes. Only the first beatitude speaks of what is true *now* ("yours *is* the Kingdom"); the rest speak of reversal of present lacks or difficulties. The import is that because God is fair, those who lack status or who are economically deprived will have enjoyment later (see, e.g., 16.23–25, the figure of Lazarus in the parable); for the poor, and who will likely remain poor, the knowledge of this reversal is already part of the Kingdom.

In **vs. 22**, the beatitudes change in focus from the universal social problems of poverty, hunger, and weeping to the particular mistreatment connected with the discipleship. The followers of Jesus may expect the same treatment as the master: they will be hated, excluded, reviled, and defamed. The reaction is related to the "Son of Man": as Jesus goes, so go his followers.

As he is rejected, so will they be. The claims are general rather than specific, so that seeking a particular social situation, such as the ever-popular but outside of John's Gospel unattested threat of being put out of the synagogue, is unhelpful. If one wanted to make the claim that Jesus could predict synagogue expulsion, he could just as easily predict rejection of gentile followers by those who found failure to worship the state gods a form of treason as well as impiety. Could Jesus have predicted that his followers would be rejected by some within their own households? Absolutely. Suggesting that they love him more than their parents (14.26 on "hating father and mother …") will likely result in rejection in kind.

Vs. 23, the corollary, stresses that the disciples should count it an honor to be mistreated for the sake of their message, for the prophets received the same mistreatment from their own ancestors. Eschatological joys, which will take place "in that day," are related to faithful living. To this point of consolation, Luke then adds the eschatological woes of vss. 24–26, which also may have had a consoling role. Not only will the fidelity of the disciple be rewarded, those who reject the disciples will be punished.

The woes, absent in Matthew's Gospel, address the opposite set of circumstances as found in the beatitudes. This use of the Greek *ouai*, "woe," is indebted to the prophetic warnings in the LXX (see, e.g., Isa 5.8–22); the term, something of an expletive, occurs fifteen times in Luke. Disciples who are rich, full, laughing, or much praised now may expect a reversal later; connections to the Parable of the Rich Man and Lazarus (16.19–31) are implicit. Luke's opening woe against the rich (vs. 24) follows the Gospel's theme of economic responsibility. The Gospel's ideal reader, Theophilus, is presented as a patron, and it is people in the patronage class whom Luke here addresses. Woes against the rich are standard fare throughout the Jewish tradition, as prophets such as Amos and Jeremiah make clear. The form continues into the Pseudepigrapha. For example, *1 Enoch* 94.8 reads: "Woe to you rich, for you have trusted in your riches, and from your riches you shall depart, because you have not remembered the Most High in the days of your riches."[20] That the rich have "received their consolation" indicates that they will have no eschatological reward, although Luke does not, yet, speak to any form of eternal torment.

The second woe addresses the well-fed now who will be hungry (vs. 25a). The reversal may sound satisfying to the hungry to watch the rich engage in the opposite of conspicuous consumption; problems emerge, however,

---

[20]   Cited in C. F. Evans, *Saint Luke*, 333.

when we wish upon others what we would not wish upon ourselves. The distinction between justice and vengeance (see comments on 18.3) is often a fine one.

This woe continues with the notice that the laughing will mourn (**vs. 25b**). The point is not that laughing in itself is to be avoided. John 11.35 notes that "Jesus wept," but it is highly likely that he had a good laugh or two on other occasions. The context of the woes suggests the type of laughter prompted either by self-satisfaction or by taking pleasure at the ills that others face (an extremely malicious *schadenfreude*). To laugh when others are starving, to laugh in the presence of injustice – not to mock injustice and so critique it through satire, but to find it funny – deserves its eschatological reversal.

The last woe suggests that praise received now is like the praise false prophets received in antiquity (**vs. 26**). The comment concerns the benefits, but ultimately debits, of rejoicing in a good reputation: if people speak well of you now, the verse implies, then you must be doing something to retain the status quo rather than challenge it. Jesus' comment about "their ancestors" at the end of the verse is odd, in that Jesus and his disciples are part of the same people as Isaiah and Jeremiah and those who opposed them.

The next section of the sermon, vs. 27–36, is framed by the theme of love and mercy.[21] Luke's introduction, "but to you who listen I say …" (**vs. 27**), again stresses that that message is for Jesus' disciples (cf. 6.18,47). The reference to listening calls upon not only the disciples and those in the narrative crowd, but Theophilus and then any who encounter the sermon through the centuries. The most important point to which ears should be attuned is that of extreme love, the love of enemies. The enemy is, in the context of the sermon, the one who hates, outlaws, denounces, and rejects those who follow Jesus (cf. the sixth antithesis in Matt 5.43–46).[22] Though there is some precedent in both Greek and Jewish literature for the sentiments expressed here (cf. *T. Benj.* 4.3; *T. Joseph* 18.2; Diogenes Laertius 8.1,23), only Luke and Matthew *command* love of enemies; this is an obligation for the disciple, not a charitable option. Jesus' call to love enemies was reiterated, even during the sporadic persecutions of the first two centuries (see *Didache* 1.3–5; Justin Martyr, *First Apol.* 15.9–10 cf. 14.3 and 16.1).

Earlier commentators suggested that the Greek presents a particular form of love: Jesus "recommends not merely a warm affection (*philia*) such

[21]   See discussion in Alan Kirk, "'Love Your Enemies,' the Golden Rule, and Ancient Reciprocity (Luke 6:27–35)," *JBL* 122.4 (2003): 667–86.

[22]   Fitzmyer, *The Gospel According to Luke I–XI*, 637.

as one might have for one's family, or a passionate devotion (*eros*) such as one might expect between spouses, but a gracious outgoing active interest (*agapē*) in the welfare of those persons who are ... antagonistic."[23] More recent study suggests that the division among the terms, especially between *philia* and *agapē*, is overstated. *Philia* also implies an active interest in the well-being of its object.[24]

Commentators have also frequently compared the command to love enemies with 1QS 2.2–17, the Qumran scroll that exhorts readers to bless their own members, but curse defectors or "the sons of darkness." Rarely, however, is the command to love one's enemies compared with the lack of love for enemies *shown in much of the New Testament and early Christian literature.* One should compare the best of one tradition to the best of another; to do otherwise is at best uncharitable; at it worse, it both inculcates prejudice and creates a sense of complacent superiority. The better move is not to contrast problematic comments in Jewish texts with positive statement in the Gospels, but to show Jesus in continuity with his own tradition, such as the injunctions on how to treat enemies. Jesus insists, "do good to those who hate you," and his Jewish tradition gives examples of what this good action might look like. For example, Prov 25.21 mandates, "If your enemies are hungry, give them bread to eat; and if they are thirsty, give them water to drink." Jesus requirement to love enemies is an intensification of the earlier Jewish material.

Luke gives two examples of what this love of enemies looks like in terms of verbal responses: "bless those who curse you, pray for those who abuse you" (**vs. 28**). Similarly, Prov 24.17 states, "Do not rejoice when your enemies fall, and do not let your heart be glad when they stumble." Amy-Jill does wonder if this concern for blessing and praying could have a sly implication: bless them, as Job's wife suggests regarding the one torturing him: "Bless God" (Job 2.9), the literal meaning of the Hebrew, has the opposite intent: "Curse God." For what one prays regarding the enemy is also

[23] Fitzmyer, *The Gospel According to Luke I–XI*, 638.
[24] Johnson states, "These elements can be found with equal concentration in such paraenetic texts as those of Pseudo-Isocrates (*Demonicus*), Epictetus (*Discourses*), and Dio Chrysostom (*Orations*)." *Gospel of Luke*, 115. On the love commandment, see especially Victor P. Furnish, *The Love Commandment in the New Testament* (Nashville: Abingdon, 1972); and Ceslaus Spicq, *Agape in the New Testament*, 3 vols. (Eugene: Wipf and Stock, 2006 [1966 original]). For a recent, concise treatment of how "love your neighbor" functions in Jewish thought, see Michael Fagenblat, "The Concept of Neighbor in Jewish and Christian Ethics," in Amy-Jill Levine and Marc Z. Brettler (eds.), *The Jewish Annotated New Testament*, 2nd. rev. ed. (New York: Oxford University Press, 2017), 645–50.

open to multiple possibilities. Amy-Jill is also reminded of the line from *Fiddler on the Roof*: in response to the question, "Is there a blessing for the Czar?" the rabbi of Anatevka responds, "May God bless and keep the Czar … far away from us."

On a more serious level, the question of what "loving the enemy" means is a difficult one. To bless and to pray for the enemy may not be sufficient responses, if the enemy is seen to blow up one's house of worship, or on the less dramatic level, harassing one's children. Love has an active force to it. It can include what we would call "tough love," but even here problems arise: what is the appropriate response to persecution?

The next three verses connect love of enemies with practical responses to personal attack and so begin to describe what this love looks like. **Vs. 29a** finds its more familiar form in Matt 5.29: "if someone strikes you on the *right* cheek." Matthew makes clear that the slap is a backhanded one, or a slap used by a master against a slave, or an officer against a peasant. Luke simply notes, "If anyone strikes you"; the class distinction of the backhanded slap is removed. Regardless of the status of the belligerent one, the victim is not to respond to violence with violence.

In the second part of the verse (**vs. 29b**), Luke speaks about the theft of a garment or perhaps seizure of it as goods demanded in a court case. Matthew (5.40) speaks of being sued for one's garment in a law court; Luke's focus is not on power differentials or on defeating an unjust suit, but only on nonviolent response. Luke then intensifies the nonviolence: disciples are not only to give to whomever begs of them, but even were someone to steal from them, they are not to ask for it back (**vs. 30**). Upper-class readers would not be left destitute if their shirt, or their purse, were stolen. Yet stealing food and clothing from the destitute would leave a family hungry and naked. Contemporary readers will have to make judgments on how best to follow these commands. Giving to anyone who asks anything is a quick way to impoverishment of oneself and one's family even as it reinforces the selfishness and acquisitiveness of others. Not reporting a crime can itself, depending on the crime (e.g., child abuse, rape), be grounds for prosecution. Contemporary readers again will have to make judgments on how best to follow these commands.

The fundamental principle undergirding these teachings appears in **vs. 31,** "Do to others as you would have them do to you." Luke places the "Golden Rule" (the title comes from the eighteenth century) here to connect it with love of enemies.[25] The commandment finds its antecedents

---

[25]   Culpepper, "The Gospel of Luke," 146.

in Tobit 4.15 ("Do not do to anyone what you hate"), and it is related to the "love commandments" of Lev 19.18, "Love your neighbor as yourself," and, especially Lev 19.34: "The alien who resides with you shall be to you as the citizen among you; you shall love the alien as yourself, for you were aliens in the land of Egypt: I am the Lord your God." In other words, the one who understands slavery should not enslave; the one who understands what it means to lack civil rights should not deprive others of those rights. From approximately the same time as Luke's Gospel is Aristeas's *Letter to Philocrates* 207: "As you wish that no evil should befall you, but to be the partaker of all good things, so you should act on the same principle toward your subjects and offenders." Later iterations include the Christian *Didache* 1.2 and the famous statement attributed by the Babylonian Talmud (*Shabb.* 31a) to Jesus' older contemporary Hillel, "What is hateful to you, do not do to anyone else."

Jesus' commandment is phrased in the positive ("Do to others …") whereas Hillel's is in the negative ("Do not do …"), and both forms are open to abuse. For some Christian missionaries, Jesus' love command formed the rationale for taking non-Christian children from their homes, forbidding indigenous populations to practice their religion or speak their own language since, as the missionaries rationalized, "we would not want to be pagans." The negative command could lead to a form of passivity, and that is why the context of Hillel's statement is important. Hillel's adage is a response to someone who asks him to summarize all of Jewish teaching "while standing on one foot." Following his summation, Hillel notes: "all the rest is commentary, go and learn." So also for Jesus – the Golden Rule is one part of a larger set of instructions.

The next three verses explicate that Jesus is talking about a love that goes beyond reciprocity. The commandment does not say "do to others … *so they* will do to you." It means that disciples should treat others as they would like to be treated, with no expectation of a cycle of reciprocity. One loves not simply to begin a relationship that will result in love, or loves simply because love has been offered (**vs. 32**), but because one should love. The same point holds for doing good; to do good in response, as reciprocity, is expected, ordinary (**vs. 33**). And it holds for lending (**vs. 34**): if one lends for the simple reason of expecting a return, then again, where is either the virtue or the risk? Because he notes that even sinners love and do good and lend, Jesus shows that he is not speaking about reciprocity or about patron/client networks that presume obligation. One should love, and do good, and lend, because that is the right way, in Jesus' view, to live.

The ethic Luke attempts to inculcate throughout 6.27–35 is a reciprocal one, but one that is determined neither by previous relationships nor by desire for personal gain.[26]

Jesus repeats, "love your enemies" (**vs. 35**) and, were his instructions not clear, he summarizes the point that love, doing good, and lending should not be part of a quid pro quo system. "Expect nothing in return," Jesus says, and the return will be given, in manifold form, by the God who also gives generously. God is the standard of proper behavior. As for those who eschew the social systems of reciprocity, they will find that God reciprocates their good works. As with the beatitudes and the woes, eschatological response brings earthly behavior to its proper reception.

The divine system is one based not on reciprocity, but on compassion (Greek: *oiktirmones*) or, as the NRSV reads, "mercy" (**vs. 36**). One does good, loves, and lends not only because these are the right actions to take, and not only because in such actions one models God, but because these actions display compassion. Compassion itself reflects the love commands: it is literally a form of co-suffering, of understanding, deeply, the needs of others and then doing what one can to fulfill them. The term reappears in the NT only in Jas 5.11, where, appropriately, the author writes, "… you have seen the purpose of the Lord, how the Lord is compassionate and merciful." A cognate appears in Rom 9.15, where Paul quotes Exod 33.10 LXX: "For he says to Moses, 'I will have mercy on whom I have mercy, and I will have compassion on whom I have compassion.'"

The topic of mercy neatly segues into the next two verses, since each is a variant on the concern for treating others with compassion. **Vs. 37** prohibits judging and condemning and enjoins forgiving; in each case, reciprocity is invoked negatively. One should give, love, and lend without expectation of return, but if one judges or condemns, one might be judged or condemned. Finally, Jesus insists on forgiving, with the response being that forgiveness will be granted. The next verse glosses this negative reciprocity system with the analogy of a good measure placed in one's lap (**vs. 38**). The "lap" (Greek: *kolpos*, which can also mean "breast" or "bosom") suggests grain caught in the fold of one's garment as it is poured out (see Ruth 3.15).[27] The measuring metaphor appears in later Jewish literature, such as the Babylonian Talmud, *Sotah* 1.7: "With the measure a person measures, it will be measured to him again." The image is not merely of a fair measure,

---

[26]   Kirk, ' "Love Your Enemies." '
[27]   Culpepper, "The Gospel of Luke," 148.

but a generous one. The idea is to impel the disciple not just to fairness but to generosity, kindness, compassion, and a nonjudgmental spirit. Luke's oral and aural rhetoric stands out: the Greek for "a good measure, pressed down, shaken together, running over," indicates a movement from "the shortest and the mildest to the longest and strongest so the listener feels the overflowing generosity in the words themselves."[28]

The brief proverb in **vs. 39** regarding the blind leading the blind, with the result that both stumble, exhorts disciples to refrain from attempting to lead before they have received instruction and, to continue the metaphor, had their own eyes opened. Yet we should not pass over the metaphor of blindness lest we stumble in reinforcing negative views of the sight-impaired. Blind people are entirely capable of guiding others; to suggest that they are helpless, let alone bad guides, is to fail to "see" how words, not intending to harm, nevertheless do so. Better metaphors are needed. For example, a mapmaker who fails to research the terrain cannot guide a pilgrim in the desert; they will both become lost. Ben points out that Jesus is *not* talking about literally blind people leading others. He is talking about the spiritually blind leaders leading others. Only if the words are taken out of context, which sadly they often have been, do we really need to change the metaphors. Amy-Jill worries that the metaphors themselves, even if they do not intend harm, nevertheless can create it. Using the language of disability – blind guides, lame arguments, deaf to the truth – is just as pernicious as language of ethnicity used to make negative comments: gyp (from "gypsies") people; Indian giver; and, yes, jew the price down. Lack of intention to insult and then *rejection* of the problem because of that lack does not resolve the problem; it makes it worse. At the same time, Ben notes that some people are too ready to take offense at something that is not merely not intended to hurt, but is innocuous. Do we really need to adjust our language and metaphors to people who are overly sensitive or too ready to find fault with anything that does not suit them? Somewhere in here there is a proper balance between caring deeply how one's words and actions come across to others, and thus speaking and acting with other-regarding love, and not catering to the hypersensitivity of some of one's audience. In a narcissistic age where people judge everything by how it makes them feel, it is hard to strike a balance in these matters.

The subject of guides moves the discussion to the teacher/disciple relationship. The next several sayings are strung together, like pearls that have

---

[28]   Tannehill, *Luke*, 121.

been collected from various sources and then placed together, so that the whole offers a greater impact than each saying would have individually. Each statement to the end of the chapter offers practical wisdom and encouragement.

Vs. 40 gives the disciples the good news that it is possible for them to be like their master, like Jesus (cf. Matt 10.24–25). Luke does suggest that a period of instruction is required for the student, in that the agenda of the Gospel is to teach Theophilus, and others, about the Good News.

Returning to the theme of not judging others, the next two verses focus on being self-critical. It would be hypocritical to be hypercritical (seeing the speck in the eye of the brother) of others while ignoring one's own need for improvement (ignoring the log in one's own eye) (**vs. 41**). Although the Gospels (see especially Matt 23) are known for associating Pharisees with hypocrites, **vs. 42**, an elaboration of the previous statement, indicates that hypocrisy is also a problem among Jesus' disciples, then and now. The NRSV's translation speaks of the "Speck in your neighbor's eye"; the Greek speaks of the "brother's [Greek: *adelphos*) eye." The critiques are not between social equals or external acquaintances; the critique is within the new family Jesus is in the process of creating. The practice of rebuking others known in Hebrew as *tokechah*, "rebuke" (see also comments on 17.3–4) is the means by which a family, or a society, can exist. As Gen 4 suggests, we are all our brothers and sisters' keepers. Lev 19.17 makes the point a commandment: "You shall not hate in your heart anyone of your kin; you shall reprove your neighbor, or you will incur guilt yourself." The next verse in Leviticus is the command to love the neighbor.

Another metaphor, that of the tree and its fruit in the next three verses, concerns character. Good trees bear good fruit, and vice versa (**vs. 43**). The proverbial metaphor that one is known by the fruits one bears is not an exhortation: thorn bushes do not produce figs, and brambles do not produce grapes (**vs. 44**); the verse has a hint of predestination to it. But it is also a prod: if one is a fig tree or a grapevine, or if one would so self-identify, then make sure the deeds are commensurate with that identification. Jesus challenges the disciples: if you think you are a good person, then what are you doing to show that your assessment is the correct one? Have you a log in your eye, or a stumbling block by your feet, or can you see for yourselves if your heart is producing good works (**vs. 45**)?

Luke's Sermon concludes with an exhortation to act and not merely pay lip service either to Jesus or to his teaching: don't call upon Jesus and so proclaim your piety when your actions belie your confession (**vs. 46**).

Don't claim the correct belief when you do not put your beliefs into prac-tice. This section finds a superb parallel in Jas 2.14–26: those who claim to be followers of Jesus must manifest love in action. To illustrate this pos-sible disjunction between self-identification and appearance to others, which is the same as the disjunction between thought and action, Jesus offers analogy or parable (**vs. 47**) about foundations (the heart, the belief, the proclamation) and the houses (the appearance, the action, the prac-tice) constructed on them. "Thus, just as the Sermon on the Plain began with a series of beatitudes and woes, so it now ends with a promise and a warning – a beatitude for the one who listens and acts, and a woe for the one who hears but does not act."[29]

Luke refers to a house built with a foundation on a rock as opposed to a house that is built on the ground and without a foundation (**vs. 48**). The comparison of weak and strong foundations is a conventional one, which finds a familiar echo in the story of the Three Little Pigs (a decid-edly nonkosher image). Evans cites a similar saying from *Avot* 3.22: "R. Eleazar b. Azariah used to say, 'Everyone whose wisdom is greater than his deeds, to what is he like? To a tree whose branches are many and its roots few; and the wind comes and roots it up and turns it over on its face … But everyone whose deeds are more than his wisdom, to what is he like? To a tree whose branches are few and its roots many, which, if all the winds that are in the world come and blow upon it, they move it not from its place.' "[30] Jesus expected his disciples to apply these principles or foun-dational teachings in the Sermon, and probably to amplify them in order to construct a way of living faithfully. The Sermon thus offers the foun-dation, but not the whole superstructure of proper ethics or orthopraxy.

BRIDGING THE HORIZONS

1. On the Sabbath

Amy-Jill notes that Jews and Christians both honor the Sabbath and keep it holy, despite the fact that we do so on different days. Jews, as well as the (Christian) Seventh Day Adventists, celebrate the day of rest from Friday evening to Saturday evening; the date is based on Gen 2.2–3: "And on the seventh day God finished the work that he had done, and he rested on the seventh day from all the work that he had done. So God blessed the

---

[29]   González, *Luke*, 96.
[30]   C. F. Evans, *Saint Luke*, 340.

seventh day and hallowed it, because on it God rested from all the work that he had done in creation." Jews have a second reason for celebrating the Sabbath: Sabbath rest is the challenge to slavery. Deut 6.15 mandates, "Remember that you were a slave in the land of Egypt, and the Lord your God brought you out from there with a mighty hand and an outstretched arm; therefore, the Lord your God commanded you to keep the Sabbath day." The followers of Jesus, keeping the idea of the Sabbath, shifted the date to Sunday, both because of the belief that their Lord was raised from the dead on Sunday and in order to differentiate their movement from that of Judaism.

Yet Ben notes that most Protestants do not regard Sunday as a Sabbath. It is rather the Lord's Day, the day of Resurrection. In Ben's view, the Sabbath commandment is the one commandment of the Ten Commandments that neither Jesus nor Paul reapplies to or requires of their followers. Indeed, it would appear that Paul in Col 2.16 warns against any Christian who would judge another in regard to Sabbath keeping, or require such Sabbath keeping. The question then arises for the churches: If Jesus and Paul both consider Sabbath observance irrelevant, should the followers of Jesus and Paul ignore the precedent of resting and the hallowing of the seventh day as God set in the act of creation? Should the followers of Jesus and Paul ignore the day of rest and therefore return themselves to slavery?

The Sabbath controversies in the Gospels – and we shall encounter more in Luke's narrative – generally present the Jews or their representatives as, at best, narrow, uncaring, and interested in the letter versus the spirit of the Law. It is often a helpful exercise to imagine what one's opponents would say about the same question. We learn from the Gospels that the Pharisees, like Jesus, take Sabbath observance seriously. They would likely be worried about a man who suggested that the Sabbath could be violated – that is, a man who suggested that people could, if not should, work on the Sabbath – simply on his say-so.

People who celebrate the Sabbath today need to determine what constitutes work, as well as who should be performing work. The same question holds for those who celebrate "the Lord's Day": what does the commemoration of Jesus' resurrection mean? Is it a form of Christian Sabbath in which one should rest and not work? Should Sunday morning worship be put aside in favor of miracle-working cures? Should medical doctors forego the service because someone with a nonpainful chronic condition might show up in the fellowship hall?

Jesus' Sabbath cures do not change the practice of Sabbath for Jews, and they cannot, since his miracle-working abilities were not common in his own time, or today. But if the only thing they do for today's reader is to develop the idea that when it comes to Sabbath observance, Jews are sanctimonious, or hypocritical or neurotic, then no good news is heard.

Perhaps one reading, on which we can all agree, is that these stories tell us that the human body is important. The human body feels pain, paralysis, and palsy, and if the opportunity for healing is present, it should be grasped. Yet we also learn from these stories that free health care is a miracle. In the absence of miracle workers but with the teaching that bodies are important, what then should followers of Jesus do? Some would say – keep praying for miracles of healing, they continue to happen. Ben points to the credible evidence for successful laying on of hands and faith healing today.[31] Amy-Jill is happy with prayer (might help; couldn't hurt), but she is not inclined to stop there either. Just as trees must bear good fruit, so prayers for healing should be accompanied by funds dedicated to medical research, personal attention to those in need of healing as well as to the ones who do most of the caregiving, and even recognition that prayers outside of Christian contexts may also be understood to prove efficacious. Ben agrees.

2. On Judging

Frequently misquoted or turned into a sound byte is the exhortation, "judge not." The command is not an excuse to avoid moral discernment. As Ben's grandmother once said, judging things and actions is required: "Don't be so open-minded that your brains fall out."

Jesus' words about judgment have two important components. First, they prevent any moral evaluation that deems another person as unredeemable, beyond help and hope. The eschatological context of Jesus' discussion of judgment needs to be remembered: we cannot know the future. Second, the "speck and log" argument warns against the tendency to be lenient in self-evaluation and harsh in evaluating others – this is what Jesus calls "hypocrisy." However, Jesus does not exhort followers to stop caring about sins. Catholic theology speaks of "sins of omission"; to fail to aid another is such a sin. Jesus expects that the members of the community will help each other with their shortcomings, oversights, and sins, not by pointing a finger, but by holding

---

[31] See Keener, *Miracles*.

out a hand to help, and speaking the truth gently, in love. G. K. Chesterton neatly summed up this teaching: "Now the mistake of critics is not that they criticize the world; it is that they never criticize themselves! They compare the alien with the ideal; but they do not at the same time compare themselves with the ideal; rather they identify themselves with the ideal."[32]

3. Blessed Are the Poor

Judith Lieu comments, "Luke's church does not see itself as the 'church of the poor,' for it awaits the reversal to come and does not campaign for it in the present, but the values it declares to be God's values may make that campaign inevitable."[33] Two thousand years later, despite Jesus' instructions – or centuries longer if we consider Deuteronomy – the world has not managed to attend sufficiently to questions of poverty.

Particular readings of the Gospel can serve to keep the present system in place rather than bring about systemic change. For example, Luke can be seen as romanticizing the poor: they are the ones who, even in the present, have the Kingdom of God. Pastors in well-manicured suburbs talk about the generosity of the poor (and it is true that lower-income people give a higher percentage of their funds to charity), and of how the spirit of Christ shines through areas of poverty because people have such strong faith. The congregation happily digs into their purses and wallets to support the collection, which will go to "the poor." The problem here is twofold. First, stereotyping reinforces rather than undermines injustice; romanticizing people with limited incomes as faithful and kind can be just as pernicious, and just as wrong as claiming that people are poor because they are lazy or stupid. But somewhere in between such stereotypes is a place where it is appropriate to praise the generosity of either a poor or a rich person, without pigeonholing them.

Second, Jesus – like his fellow Jews – calls people into community, and putting money in a collection plate is not forming community. The "neighbors" (so the NRSV) are really "brothers and sisters," members of the family. They should be supported "without expectation of return." At the same time, both those with funds and those without should be in relationship.

---

[32]   This quote appears in various forms and shapes in various of Chesterton's works. See www
.solemncharge.com/Library/chapter.aspx?key=GK-Chesterton-The-New-Jerusalem-
The-Philosophy-of-Sight-Seeing. It is a quote from *The New Jerusalem*, the chapter entitled "The Philosophy of Sightseeing," p. 1.
[33]   Lieu, *Gospel According to Luke*, 51.

4. On Forgiving, Part I

One of Ben's favorite true stories, and one he personally heard Corrie ten Boom tell in the late 1970s, is the following. He quotes it verbatim from her as reported both in her famous book *The Hiding Place* and later excerpted by *Guideposts Magazine*, which is the form of the story that follows:

> It was in a church in Munich that I saw him – a balding, heavyset man in a gray overcoat, a brown felt hat clutched between his hands. People were filing out of the basement room where I had just spoken, moving along the rows of wooden chairs to the door at the rear. It was 1947 and I had come from Holland to defeated Germany with the message that God forgives.
>
> It was the truth they needed most to hear in that bitter, bombed-out land, and I gave them my favorite mental picture. Maybe because the sea is never far from a Hollander's mind, I liked to think that that's where forgiven sins were thrown. "When we confess our sins," I said, "God casts them into the deepest ocean, gone forever ..."
>
> The solemn faces stared back at me, not quite daring to believe. There were never questions after a talk in Germany in 1947. People stood up in silence, in silence collected their wraps, in silence left the room.
>
> And that's when I saw him, working his way forward against the others. One moment I saw the overcoat and the brown hat; the next, a blue uniform and a visored cap with its skull and crossbones. It came back with a rush: the huge room with its harsh overhead lights; the pathetic pile of dresses and shoes in the center of the floor; the shame of walking naked past this man. I could see my sister's frail form ahead of me, ribs sharp beneath the parchment skin. *Betsie, how thin you were!*
>
> [Betsie and I had been arrested for concealing Jews in our home during the Nazi occupation of Holland; this man had been a guard at Ravensbruck concentration camp where we were sent.]
>
> Now he was in front of me, hand thrust out: "A fine message, Fräulein! How good it is to know that, as you say, all our sins are at the bottom of the sea!"
>
> And I, who had spoken so glibly of forgiveness, fumbled in my pocketbook rather than take that hand. He would not remember me, of course – how could he remember one prisoner among those thousands of women?
>
> But I remembered him and the leather crop swinging from his belt. I was face-to-face with one of my captors and my blood seemed to freeze.
>
> "You mentioned Ravensbruck in your talk," he was saying, "I was a guard there." No, he did not remember me.
>
> "But since that time," he went on, "I have become a Christian. I know that God has forgiven me for the cruel things I did there, but I would like to

hear it from your lips as well. Fräulein," again the hand came out – "will you forgive me?"

And I stood there – I whose sins had again and again to be forgiven – and could not forgive. Betsie had died in that place – could he erase her slow terrible death simply for the asking?

It could not have been many seconds that he stood there – hand held out – but to me it seemed hours as I wrestled with the most difficult thing I had ever had to do.

For I had to do it – I knew that. The message that God forgives has a prior condition: that we forgive those who have injured us. "If you do not forgive men their trespasses," Jesus says, "neither will your Father in heaven forgive your trespasses."

I knew it not only as a commandment of God, but as a daily experience. Since the end of the war I had had a home in Holland for victims of Nazi brutality. Those who were able to forgive their former enemies were able also to return to the outside world and rebuild their lives, no matter what the physical scars. Those who nursed their bitterness remained invalids. It was as simple and as horrible as that.

And still I stood there with the coldness clutching my heart. But forgiveness is not an emotion – I knew that too. Forgiveness is an act of the will, and the will can function regardless of the temperature of the heart. "… Help!" I prayed silently. "I can lift my hand. I can do that much. You supply the feeling."

And so woodenly, mechanically, I thrust my hand into the one stretched out to me. And as I did, an incredible thing took place. The current started in my shoulder, raced down my arm, sprang into our joined hands. And then this healing warmth seemed to flood my whole being, bringing tears to my eyes.

"I forgive you, brother!" I cried. "With all my heart!"

For a long moment we grasped each other's hands, the former guard and the former prisoner. I had never known God's love so intensely, as I did then.[34]

5. On Forgiving, Part II

The subject of forgiveness is a difficult one, and the subject of forgiving genocide particularly fraught. Corrie ten Boom can forgive the guard for what he did to her; whether she has the authority to forgive him for what he did to her sister, or to any of the others he brutalized, is a separate question. The noted Nazi-hunter, Simon Wiesenthal, tells the following story; the

[34] Excerpted from "I'm Still Learning to Forgive" by Corrie ten Boom from *Guideposts Magazine*. Copyright © 1972 by Guideposts Associates, Inc., Carmel, NY 10512.

summary comes from the "Facing History and Ourselves" website, under the subheading, "Exploring Dimensions of Forgiveness: The Sunflower."[35]

In *The Sunflower*, Simon Wiesenthal writes of an incident that occurred during the time he was a concentration camp inmate. One day, he and his work detail were sent to clean medical waste at a converted army hospital for wounded German soldiers. On the way, "Our column suddenly came to a halt at a crossroads. I could see nothing that might be holding us up but I noticed on the left of the street there was a military cemetery ... and on each grave there was planted a sunflower ... I stared spellbound ... Suddenly I envied the dead soldiers. Each had a sunflower to connect him with the living world, and butterflies to visit his grave. For me there would be no sunflower. I would be buried in a mass grave, where corpses would be piled on top of me. No sunflower would ever bring light into my darkness, and no butterflies would dance above my dreadful tomb."

Simon's work group arrived at the hospital. As they worked, a nurse came up to Simon and asked, "Are you a Jew?" When he answered "Yes," she took him into the hospital building, to the bedside of Karl, a 21-year old dying Nazi soldier. Karl's head was completely covered in bandages, with openings only for his mouth, nose and ears. Karl wanted to tell Simon his story. He began, "I know that at this moment thousands of men are dying. Death is everywhere. It is neither infrequent nor extraordinary. I am resigned to dying soon, but before that I want to talk about an experience which is torturing me. Otherwise I cannot die in peace ... I must tell you of this horrible deed – tell you because ... you are a Jew."

Karl talked about his childhood and described himself as a happy, dreamy child. His father was a Social Democrat and his mother brought Karl up as a Catholic. Karl joined the Hitler Youth and later volunteered for the SS. That was the last time his father spoke to him.

Karl went on to tell Simon about being sent to fight in Russia, and about coming, one day, to a village.

"In a large square, we got out and looked around us. On the other side of the square there was a group of people under close guard ... The word went through our group like wildfire: 'They're Jews' ... An order was given and we marched toward the huddled mass of Jews. There were a hundred and fifty of them or perhaps two hundred, including many children who stared at us with anxious eyes. A few were quietly crying. There were infants in their mothers' arms, but hardly any young men; mostly women and graybeards

---

[35] www.facinghistory.org/resource-library/exploring-dimensions-forgiveness-sunflower. For Weisenthal's extended treatment of this scenario, see Simon Wiesenthal, *The Sunflower: on the Possibilities and Limits of Forgiveness* (newly expanded paperback ed.) (New York: Schocken Press, 1998).

... A truck arrived with cans of petrol which we unloaded and took into a house ... Then we began to drive the Jews into the house ... Then another truck came up full of more Jews and they too were crammed into the house with the others. Then the door was locked and a machine gun was posted opposite ... When we were told that everything was ready, we went back a few yards, and then received the command to remove safety pins from hand grenades and throw them through the windows of the house ... Behind the windows of the second floor, I saw a man with a small child in his arms. His clothes were alight. By his side stood a woman, doubtless the mother of the child. With his free hand the man covered the child's eyes ... then he jumped into the street. Seconds later the mother followed. Then from the other windows fell burning bodies ... We shot ... Oh God! I don't know how many tried to jump out of the windows but that one family I shall never forget – least of all the child."

After that event, Karl's division moved on to the Crimea. One day, in the middle of a fight, Karl climbed out of his trench and he recalled, "in that moment I saw the burning family, the father with the child and behind them the mother – and they came to meet me. 'No, I cannot shoot at them a second time.' The thought flashed through my mind ... And then a shell exploded by my side. I lost consciousness ... It was a miracle that I was still alive – even now I am as good as dead ... So I lie here waiting for death. The pains in my body are terrible, but worse still is my conscience ... I cannot die ... without coming clean ... In the last hours of my life you are with me. I do not know who you are. I only know that you are a Jew and that is enough ... In the long nights while I have been waiting for death, time and time again I have longed to talk about it to a Jew and beg forgiveness from him. Only I didn't know whether there were any Jews left ... I know that what I am asking is almost too much for you, but without your answer I cannot die in peace."

Simon left the room without a word. When his group returned to the hospital the next day, the same nurse came to Simon and told him that Karl had died.

Over the next years of the war, time and again, through all his suffering, Simon thought of Karl and wondered if he should have forgiven him.

"Ought I to have forgiven him? Was my silence at the bedside of the dying Nazi right or wrong? This is a profound moral question ... The crux of the matter is, of course, the question of forgiveness. Forgetting is something that time alone takes care of, but forgiveness is an act of volition ..."

In his volume *The Sunflower*, Weisenthal poses this question to ethicists and theologians. Their answers vary. The answers will no doubt vary among the readers of this volume.

Luke 7 Healing, Debating, Forgiving

¹ After Jesus had finished all his sayings in the hearing of the people, he entered Capernaum. ² A centurion there had a slave whom he valued highly, and who was ill and close to death. ³ When he heard about Jesus, he sent some Jewish elders to him, asking him to come and heal his slave. ⁴ When they came to Jesus, they appealed to him earnestly, saying, "He is worthy of having you do this for him, ⁵ for he loves our people, and it is he who built our synagogue for us." ⁶ And Jesus went with them, but when he was not far from the house, the centurion sent friends to say to him, "Lord, do not trouble yourself, for I am not worthy to have you come under my roof; ⁷ therefore I did not presume to come to you. But only speak the word, and let my servant be healed. ⁸ For I also am a man set under authority, with soldiers under me; and I say to one, 'Go,' and he goes, and to another, 'Come,' and he comes, and to my slave, 'Do this,' and the slave does it." ⁹ When Jesus heard this he was amazed at him, and turning to the crowd that followed him, he said, "I tell you, not even in Israel have I found such faith." ¹⁰ When those who had been sent returned to the house, they found the slave in good health.

THE WIDOW OF NAIN

¹¹ Soon afterwards he went to a town called Nain, and his disciples and a large crowd went with him. ¹² As he approached the gate of the town, a man who had died was being carried out. He was his mother's only son, and she was a widow; and with her was a large crowd from the town. ¹³ When the Lord saw her, he had compassion for her and said to her, "Do not weep." ¹⁴ Then he came forward and touched the bier, and the bearers stood still. And he said, "Young man, I say to you, rise!"

[15] The dead man sat up and began to speak, and Jesus gave him to his mother. [16] Fear seized all of them; and they glorified God, saying, "A great prophet has risen among us!" and "God has looked favorably on his people!" [17] This word about him spread throughout Judea and all the surrounding country.

JOHN THE BAPTIST

[18] The disciples of John reported all these things to him. So John summoned two of his disciples [19] and sent them to the Lord to ask, "Are you the one who is to come, or are we to wait for another?" [20] When the men had come to him, they said, "John the Baptist has sent us to you to ask, 'Are you the one who is to come, or are we to wait for another?'" [21] Jesus had just then cured many people of diseases, plagues, and evil spirits, and had given sight to many who were blind. [22] And he answered them, "Go and tell John what you have seen and heard: the blind receive their sight, the lame walk, the lepers are cleansed, the deaf hear, the dead are raised, the poor have good news brought to them. [23] And blessed is anyone who takes no offense at me."

[24] When John's messengers had gone, Jesus began to speak to the crowds about John: "What did you go out into the wilderness to look at? A reed shaken by the wind? [25] What then did you go out to see? Someone dressed in soft robes? Look, those who put on fine clothing and live in luxury are in royal palaces. [26] What then did you go out to see? A prophet? Yes, I tell you, and more than a prophet.

[27] This is the one about whom it is written, 'See, I am sending my messenger ahead of you, who will prepare your way before you.' [28] I tell you, among those born of women no one is greater than John; yet the least in the kingdom of God is greater than he." [29] (And all the people who heard this, including the tax collectors, acknowledged the justice of God, because they had been baptized with John's baptism. [30] But by refusing to be baptized by him, the Pharisees and the lawyers rejected God's purpose for themselves.)

[31] "To what then will I compare the people of this generation, and what are they like? [32] They are like children sitting in the marketplace and calling to one another, 'We played the flute for you, and you did not dance; we wailed, and you did not weep.' [33] For John the Baptist has come eating no bread and drinking no wine, and you say, 'He has a demon'; [34] the Son of Man has come eating and drinking, and you say, 'Look, a glutton and a

drunkard, a friend of tax collectors and sinners!' ³⁵ Nevertheless, wisdom is vindicated by all her children."

THE WOMAN WHO LOVED MUCH

³⁶ One of the Pharisees asked Jesus to eat with him, and he went into the Pharisee's house and took his place at the table. ³⁷ And a woman in the city, who was a sinner, having learned that he was eating in the Pharisee's house, brought an alabaster jar of ointment. ³⁸ She stood behind him at his feet, weeping, and began to bathe his feet with her tears and to dry them with her hair. Then she continued kissing his feet and anointing them with the ointment. ³⁹ Now when the Pharisee who had invited him saw it, he said to himself, "If this man were a prophet, he would have known who and what kind of woman this is who is touching him – that she is a sinner."

⁴⁰ Jesus spoke up and said to him, "Simon, I have something to say to you." "Teacher," he replied, "Speak." ⁴¹ "A certain creditor had two debtors; one owed five hundred denarii, and the other fifty. ⁴² When they could not pay, he canceled the debts for both of them. Now which of them will love him more?" ⁴³ Simon answered, "I suppose the one for whom he canceled the greater debt." And Jesus said to him, "You have judged rightly."

⁴⁴ Then turning toward the woman, he said to Simon, "Do you see this woman? I entered your house; you gave me no water for my feet, but she has bathed my feet with her tears and dried them with her hair. ⁴⁵ You gave me no kiss, but from the time I came in she has not stopped kissing my feet. ⁴⁶ You did not anoint my head with oil, but she has anointed my feet with ointment. ⁴⁷ Therefore, I tell you, her sins, which were many, have been forgiven; hence she has shown great love. But the one to whom little is forgiven, loves little."

⁴⁸ Then he said to her, "Your sins are forgiven." ⁴⁹ But those who were at the table with him began to say among themselves, "Who is this who even forgives sins?" ⁵⁰ And he said to the woman, "Your faith has saved you; go in peace."

Chapter 7 begins with Jesus returning from the "Sermon on the Plain" (6.17–49) to Capernaum. Luke gives no reaction from either the disciples or the crowds to Jesus' teachings, but the several events depicted in Chapter 7 can be seen as glosses on the teaching. Given the enmity between Rome and many of the Jewish people – an enmity Luke's readers would know especially following Rome's destruction of Jerusalem and its Temple in 70 – the triple relationships in the story of Jesus' healing of the centurion's slave neatly demonstrates loving the enemy (cf. 6:27): the centurion shows love for the Jewish people and, by extension, the elders show their love for the centurion, and Jesus shows his love for all involved. The raising of the widow's son in Nain anticipates not only Jesus' own resurrection but fulfills his promise, "Blessed are you who weep now, for you will laugh" (6.21). The discussion with messengers sent from John the Baptizer both evokes and anticipates Jesus' healings, and Jesus' teaching about John can be seen as developing the model of the firm ethical foundation of 6.48–49. Finally, the conversation between Simon the Pharisee and Jesus about the woman who displays love for Jesus incarnates the import of Jesus' comment, "Don't judge" (6.37).

THE CENTURION AND THE JEWISH ELDERS

Sharing the same plot as Matt 8.5–13 and John 4.46–53 of a political superior who seeks Jesus' aid in curing his ailing son/servant/slave, Luke develops themes that sound throughout both the Gospel and Acts. Righteous gentiles and in particular centurions, Roman army officers, will continue to appear, and thereby fulfill Simeon's prediction that Mary's son will be "A light for revelation to the Gentiles" (Luke 2.32). This unnamed centurion at Capernaum and the unnamed centurion who stands at Jesus' cross in Jerusalem (24.47) will find the fulfillment of their anticipated roles in Cornelius, the centurion in Caesarea whom Peter baptizes (Act 10.1).

Jesus the healer, who had already performed miracles in Capernaum (4.23, 31–43), now expands his abilities by healing at a distance. Luke here offers a picture not only of Jewish/Roman cooperation but also of cooperation between Jewish leaders and Jesus. Here in Galilee, we are a far distance from the Passion Narrative.

Entering Capernaum (**vs. 1**), Jesus finds that his reputation as a healer has preceded him. Luke introduces a local centurion by title rather than name (**vs. 2**). A Roman army officer, this centurion would not be leading any major unit; there were no Roman troops stationed in the Galilee during Jesus' lifetime, though there were plenty of them just north of Galilee in what today we call Lebanon and Syria. Perhaps this centurion, like the more famous Cornelius of Acts 10, had retired to a land in which he had earlier fought. The other possibility is that the man is an auxiliary, and not of Roman descent but rather a gentile from this region, but given Luke's interest in Rome, this option is less likely.

The centurion in Matt 8.5–13 intercedes with Jesus on behalf of his *pais* (Matt 8.6); the term can be translated as either "son" or "servant"; the *pais* is paralyzed and in distress. For Luke, the person in need of intercession is not a child but a "slave" (Greek: *doulos*) who is "close to death" (**vs. 2**). The desperation parents face when their children are ill remains a trope throughout the biblical tradition, from the widow of Zarepath and the Great Woman of Shumen to the various parents in the Gospels who seek Jesus' gift of healing. Less common are the variations on the story where it is a slave, not a child, who requires healing, and a master rather than a parent who intercedes. The NRSV speaks of the centurion as having "valued highly" the slave, but the Greek literally means "to whom he was dear" or "precious" (Greek: *entimos*). The same term appears in 1 Pet 2.4,6 to describe Jesus himself as the precious living stone or cornerstone.

Assessing the Matthean version of the narrative, some New Testament scholars have proposed that the centurion approached Jesus not simply out of love for a subordinate, but because the subordinate was the centurion's lover. By extension, the paralysis noted in Matthew's version becomes a symptom of hysteria caused by sexual abuse. In this thesis, the reason the centurion does not want Jesus to come under his roof, again in Matthew's version, was that he did not want Jesus to know the details of his pederastic relationship to the *pais*. This imaginative reading lacks support both in the text and behind it. First, if the centurion is convinced that Jesus can do healing from a distance, he could also presume that Jesus would have known the particulars of the relationship. Second, that masters had favorite slaves – without any necessary sexual component – is part of Roman culture. Third, to invent a homosexual component, especially one that reads the slave's paralysis or sickness as caused by homosexual abuse, threatens to reinforce antihomosexual stereotypes. We are not denying that sexual abuse occurs, and we are not denying that this abuse can result in physical responses; we are concerned that this reading finds little historical purchase.[1]

---

[1] For intelligent discussions of the relationship of the account to questions of sexuality, see Theodore W. Jennings Jr. and Tat-Siong Benny Liew, "Mistaken Identities but Model Faith: Rereading the Centurion, the Chap and the Christ in Matthew 8:5–13," *JBL* 123.3 (2004): 467–94; and, in response, D. B. Saddington, "The Centurion in Matthew 8:5–13: Consideration of the Proposal of Theodore W. Jennings, Jr., and Tat-Siong Benny Liew," *JBL* 125.1 (2006): 140–42.

Unlike Matthew's centurion or John's ruler, both of whom approach Jesus directly, the Lucan officer never encounters Jesus face to face. For Luke, the time has not yet come for gentiles to receive the Spirit or to worship Jesus. The centurion, hearing about Jesus, sends "Jewish elders" to request that Jesus come and heal the slave (**vs. 3**). What power moves are involved in this request remain unstated. Perhaps the centurion thinks that Jesus, his "enemy," would be more receptive to a request from fellow Jews. Alternatively, perhaps the centurion did not want to face the awkwardness of having to subordinate himself directly to this Galilean healer. Perhaps he was concerned about making Jesus feel awkward in the crossing of cultural barriers: would Jesus come under his roof? Luke does not mention the centurion's motives.

Luke also does not mention the motives of the Jewish elders. They may be happy to help the centurion; as they tell Jesus, "He is worthy ..." (**vs. 4**). The verse will receive a counter in the centurion's own comments, sent through messengers: "for I am not worthy ..." (vs. 6). The elders continue: "he loves our people ... he built our synagogue for us" (**vs. 5**). The description will echo in Acts 10.22: "Cornelius, a centurion, an upright and God-fearing man, who is well spoken of by the whole Jewish nation, was directed by a holy angel to send for you to come to his house and to hear what you have to say." The comparison of Luke 7 and Acts 10 raises a question: Cornelius's messengers had no choice in speaking on his behalf; did the Jewish elders?

We may have another echo here, for Luke has already introduced a synagogue in Capernaum. In 4.33, in a Capernaum synagogue, Jesus encounters a man with an unclean spirit and performs an exorcism. From this event extends his reputation (4.37), perhaps to the centurion who paid for the building.

Luke does not describe the centurion as a convert or proselyte (contrast Nicolaus the "proselyte from Antioch" of Acts 6.5 and cf. Acts 2.10). Gentiles did become proselytes to Judaism, but others, known as "Godfearers," affiliated with the people and especially the synagogue without seeking full membership in the Jewish community. On occasion, gentiles served as synagogue patrons, as we see in inscriptional evidence. Often noted is the inscription from Acmonia in Phrygia, dating ca. 59–63 CE, when Julia Severa, whose name is first mentioned, served as the city's ruler (*archōn*): "This building was erected by Julia Severa, P(ublius) Tyrronios Clados, ruler of the synagogue for life (*archisynagōgōs dia biou*), and Popilios Zoticos, ruler (*archōn*), restored it with their own funds and with the money which had been contributed ... the synagogue (*synagōgē*) honored them with a golden

shield on account of their virtuous disposition, goodwill, and zeal for the
synagogue (*synagōgē*)."[2] The patronage would have brought both honor and
loyalty to Julia Severa from the Jews. The same system operates today when
people of one group offer financial support to another. Whether the patrons
are motivated by more than garnering the rewards of their patronage, or
whether the recipients move from a position of gratitude to one of trust or
friendship, can only be determined on a case-by-case basis.

Jesus agrees to the elders' request, but drawing near to the house, he is
stopped by the centurion's "friends" (Greek: *philoi*); whether these friends
are Jews or fellow gentiles cannot be determined (**vs. 6**). These friends
respectfully greet Jesus with the title "lord' (*kyrios*) and then make their
request: the centurion does not find himself sufficiently worthy to have Jesus
enter his home. The comment suggests that Jesus would have entered the
gentile's home, and thus it shows, as do numerous other examples, the error
of Peter's comment to Cornelius, "it is unlawful for a Jew to associate with
or visit a Gentile" (Acts 10.28). There is no such law. Ben proposes that the
opponents of Paul in Antioch (Gal 2.11–14) who came from Jerusalem seem
to have operated with some such concern or idea; Amy-Jill sees nothing
in this passage that suggests that it is unlawful for Jews to associate with
gentiles.[3] The issue here is table fellowship and distinct identities, which are
not the same things as visiting or friendship.

The centurion had served as patron to the synagogue, and therefore
the elders act on his behalf. Now he realizes that he himself is the client,
and he needs Jesus to provide for him. He has his friends give voice to his

[2]   For discussion and other examples, see Donald Binder, "The Synagogue and the Gentiles,"
in David C. Sim and James S. McLaren (eds.), *Attitudes to Gentiles in Ancient Judaism
and Early Christianity*, Library of New Testament Studies (London: Bloomsbury, 2013),
109 25.

[3]   Ben cites E. P. Sanders, *Paul. The Apostle's Life, Letters, and Thought* (Minneapolis: Fortress
Press, 2015), 443–99, in support of the idea that some Jews feared becoming involved in
idolatry if they were to enter a gentile's house and dine there. Gentiles regularly prayed
to pagan gods or invoked them over the meal. Thus, for Ben, it is conceivable that some
strict Jews thought it was unlawful to go there. Amy-Jill notes that what is conceivable
is not the same thing as saying that something is unlawful. Ben *notes that is not the
issue* – the issue is whether some strict Jews *thought* it was not merely inappropriate but
unlawful to do so, and the answer is yes, some did, however badly they understood their
own Law. In his notes on Acts 10 in "The Gospel of Luke," in Amy-Jill Levine and Marc
Z. Brettler, *The Jewish Annotated New Testament* 2d ed. ("New York: Oxford University
Press, 2017), 219–80 (244), Gary Gilbert offers a helpful compromise: "while some Jews
may have concurred with Peter's statement (e.g., Jub. 22.16), most would have had regular contacts with Gentiles, while probably taking care to avoid idolatry and prohibited
foods (e.g., *Ep. Arist.* 172–86; *m. Avod. Zar.* 3.4). Nonetheless, the idea that Jews did not
associate with gentiles is common (e.g., Philo, *Spec. Laws* 2.167; Tacitus, *Hist.* 5.1–13)."

subordinate status: he is unworthy and more, he would not presume to approach Jesus directly. Yet he knows that Jesus need only speak, and the slave would be healed (**vs. 7**). To support his self-subordinating position, the centurion notes that while he can command others, he is also under a higher authority (**vs. 8a**).

His comment resurfaces the moral question of the slave's position. Attempting to express his own subordinate status as well as his inability to command miracles, the centurion states, "I say to … my slave, 'Do this,' and the slave does it" (**vs 8b**). The problem here is twofold. First, the sick slave cannot obey these commands, so the centurion does not have complete authority over the slave's body. Conversely, the slave lacks this authority as well; his sickness, and not his will, prevents him from serving his master. Second, by healing the slave, Jesus will ensure that the slave will subsequently obey the centurion's commands. Perhaps the slave – perhaps a Jewish slave anticipating heavenly justice and resurrection to life – would prefer Jesus not intervene. Perhaps the slave will, upon being healed, find a better life. Or perhaps this slave, like the mantic slave whom Paul exorcises in Acts 16, will be treated worse than before. Reading Luke in light of our knowledge of how slavery functions, Amy-Jill notes that neither Jesus nor Luke critiques the system. Ben queries: why tell a story about the healing of a slave if you did not want to show Jesus' compassion not just for the centurion but also for the sick slave? Jesus treats them both as persons of sacred worth, and with respect.

When Jesus hears the centurion's comments regarding his place in the hierarchical chain of the Roman household, he marvels. To the crowd, although not to the centurion's friends, he remarks that "Not even in Israel have I found such faith" (**vs. 9**). "In Israel" here means among the Jewish people, since the story is set in the land of Israel. The motif evoked is that of the "righteous gentile," which is seen throughout Israel's literature. Pharaoh's daughter and the Egyptian midwives defy the genocidal commands of the Egyptian ruler (Exod 1); Rahab the prostitute proves more righteous than the spies Joshua sends to the land (Josh 2.6); Ruth the Moabite proves of more value to her mother-in-law than seven sons (Ruth 4.15); Achior the Ammonite general affiliates with Judith and her people and so denies his role as a member of Holofernes's army (Jdt 14.10).

What exactly the "faith" is that Jesus so praises remains yet another matter of dispute. It could be his belief that Jesus would heal at a distance, which is a more striking miracle than healing by touch or direct command. This type of healing appears as well in rabbinic literature; speaking of the first-century Galilean miracle worker, Rabbi Haninah ben Dosa, the Jerusalem Talmud (*b. Ber.* 34b) reports, "Once Rabban Gamaliel's son fell ill and he sent two students to R. Haninah b. Dosa in his town [to find out from him if his son would be cured]. He [Haninah] said to them [the students], 'Wait for me while I go up to the attic [to pray].' He went up to the attic, came down, and said to them, 'I am certain that Rabban Gamaliel's son has recovered from his illness.' [The students] made note [of the time of day that this happened]. [Later they confirmed that] at that very moment [when R. Hanina b. Dosa had finished his prayer, the son of R. Gamaliel was cured] and asked for food." Ben notes that the story in Luke about Jesus does not depict him needing to pray for God to intervene; he simply heals from a distance. Perhaps the faith is in the centurion's recognition that he is part of a chain of command of a powerful empire, and yet neither he nor the Empire can cure the sick; neither he nor the Empire can speak for God.

The centurion's fate remains unknown. Luke mentions that the ones who had been "sent" – the Jewish elders? the friends? – return to the home, they find the slave healthy (**vs. 10**). The centurion himself, so concerned about his slave at the beginning of the story, is not depicted as having any reaction to the healing. Readers here can use their imagination as to what happened to him: Did he become one of Jesus' many disciples? Did he move to Caesarea and was his name Cornelius? Was he the centurion who stood at the foot of the cross as Zefferelli depicted it in his film *Jesus of Nazareth*? We might also imagine what happened to the slave. Did his master free him? Did he become a follower of Jesus? Was he already?

THE WIDOW OF NAIN

Leaving Capernaum without having visited friends or family, Jesus goes to Nain; as before, the crowds follow him as do the disciples (**vs. 11**). Some follow because they are true disciples who follow Jesus' teachings; others may be questioning in their hearts or in their intellects whether this Galilean teacher has anything worthwhile or novel to say; still others may be seeking a healing, or a show. Not all who follow Jesus, yesterday or today, are to be counted as disciples.

By the gate of the city, Jesus sees the funeral procession of the "only son of his mother, and she was a widow" (**vs. 12**). They are likely heading out of the city to the cemetery. Luke's evocation of pathos is evident. As the centurion represented Roman power and as he had numerous subordinates, the widow, especially for Luke, represents the powerless and the pathetic. She will remind Luke's audience of the earlier widow, Anna, who epitomized silent faithfulness (2.36–37), and she anticipates the widow who puts her last two coins into the Temple treasury (21.2–3). She may also evoke the "real widow" who, "left alone, has set her hope on God and continues in supplications and prayers night and day" (1 Tim 5.5). Biblically literate readers will recall the dead son Elijah raised, the son of the widow of Zarephath whom Jesus mentioned in his synagogue sermon (4.26). 1 Kings 17.17 describes the situation as: "the son of the woman, the mistress of the house, became ill; his illness was so severe that there was no breath left in him."

Now there are two crowds: one following Jesus together with his disciples, and one with the widow in mourning. The first, in Luke's symbolic world, is following life; the second, in mourning, follows death. There is no question as to Jesus' reaction. Jesus "has compassion" (**vs. 13a**) on the widow; the term will reappear in other contexts of bringing the dead to life – the Samaritan in the parable has compassion on the man who fell among the robbers (10.33; the NRSV translates the same Greek term as "moved with pity"); the father in the parable has compassion on his younger son (15.50). Compassion is more than simply pity; it is a gut feeling, a sense of connection with the suffering person, and the move to help. Pity can remain at a distance; compassion requires a response.

Jesus responds to the widow "Do not weep" (**vs. 13b**). The command – and it is an imperative – may sound harsh. Amy-Jill notes that telling a bereaved mother that she should not weep for her only child can sound heartless. Whereas Jesus will raise the widow's son, children who die, today, remain dead. To tell grieving parents not to weep because they will see their loved ones in the resurrection is to fail to take seriously the reality of death. Those who weep will be blessed (6.21), but they need first to weep. To skip over the reality of death is both to deny the power of resurrection and to deny the loss that the ones left behind feel.

Ben says that while all this is a true and good observation, nevertheless from Luke's point of view, Jesus is about to raise the boy on the spot, not merely promise a future resurrection, so the woman's response is right and natural *up to the juncture* when the healer acts. After that, it's not appropriate. In short, this story is not meant to be applied to grieving parents nowhere near someone who can raise the dead. It is meant to glorify Jesus and his compassion. Amy-Jill agrees; her concerns is that she has heard more than one sermon and pastoral caregiver citing *this text* to tell grieving parents that their mourning is misplaced, because Jesus commanded the widow not to weep. We agree – that's a misuse of this text.

Jesus stops the procession, touches the coffin, and commands, "Young man, to you I say, rise" (**vs. 14**). The dead son immediately sits up and begins to speak (**vs. 15**). What he said, Luke does not record. The Gospel's focus is on the reality of death and resurrection, not the technicality of what "being dead" means. The focus is also on the restoration of the son to his mother. That Jesus "gave him to his mother" repeats the words the Deuteronomic Historian used to refer to the restoration of the widow's son by Elijah (1 Kings 17.21).

The immediately following conversation by and about the Baptizer reinforces Luke's comparison of John to Elijah. Whether John holds the role of Elijah or not, Jesus is superior to him. Jesus does what Elijah does, only Jesus does it better. Elijah raises the dead by praying and lying prostrate on the boy's body; Jesus can heal at a distance and heal by a word, without prayer.

The crowd and the disciples share a reaction not of joy but of fear (**vs. 16a**). The manifestation of the divine is frightening, even if the particulars, such as restoration from the dead, are positive. Anything that shakes up our worlds can be scary. The people respond, appropriately, by glorifying God. The people also respond, ironically, by determining that Jesus is a "great prophet"; they do not see that he is also more than a prophet. Just as Jesus is greater than John the Baptizer, a point Luke is about to reinforce, he is also greater than Elijah. Doubling the irony, the people speak of how this great prophet has "arisen" (Greek: *ēgerthē*) among them: "arisen" echoes Jesus' command that the young man "arise" (vs. 14) even as it anticipates his own resurrection. The scene ends with the acclamation that God has visited, or cared, for the people Israel (**vs. 16b**) as well as the notice that Jesus' reputation has spread throughout Judea (**vs. 17**). Capernaum and Nain are in the Galilee, but the news does not stop there.

JOHN THE BAPTIZER

Luke's connecting Jesus to Elijah via the healing of the widow's son segues into a discussion about John the Baptizer, the "new Elijah" of the Synoptic tradition. In the infancy accounts, Luke establishes the superiority of Jesus to John the Baptizer. Even when they are fetuses in utero, John acknowledges Jesus' superiority through his mother Elizabeth's proclamation (1.41–44). At the baptism, the cousins again demonstrate their relative rank: Jesus is superior to John (3.16). At the end of the baptism scene (3.19–20), Luke indicates that Herod had shut John up in prison. But here Amy-Jill finds an historical problem – while Jesus was going throughout Galilee and Judea, teaching and healing, the imprisoned John retained his own disciples. Had John believed Jesus to be the messiah, why keep his own followers? Ben does not find John's having his own disciples to be a problem: just because a master teacher shows up doesn't mean other teachers should stop having students and send them off to the superior one. Amy-Jill would agree, were Jesus for Luke *only* a master teacher. Ben adds that the question is what did John actually think about Jesus, and the tradition we are about to mention suggests that *in prison* and so late in his life he had asked "are you the One who is to come, or should we look for another?" In other words, he had doubts, and doubtless this affected his disciples' decisions too.

The scene begins with John hearing from his disciples the reports of Jesus' healings (**vs. 18**). Anticipating Jesus' sending his disciples, in pairs (10.1), to proclaim the kingdom of God (10.9), John sends two of his disciples to ask Jesus if he is the expected "One who Comes" (**vs. 19**). The opening of his question, "are you …" (Greek: *su ei*) draws upon the same language heard at the baptism, when the voice from heaven announces "you are/*su ei* [my son]." This "One who Comes" alludes both to Psa 118.26, "Blessed is the one who comes in the name of the Lord," and to Luke's own citation of this Psalm in 13.35, where Jesus tells Jerusalem, "See, your house is left to you. And I tell you, you will not see me until the time comes when you say, 'Blessed is the one who comes in the name of the Lord.'" The continuation of Chapter 7 suggests that John accepts Jesus' role; the continuation of the Gospel and into Acts leaves the fate of Jerusalem less clear. But note that Luke freely admits in Acts 19 that John still had "disciples" or followers long after his demise.

In the hour that John's disciples ask the question of Jesus, "are you (*su eis*) the one …" (**vs. 20**), Jesus had performed numerous healings and exorcisms (**vs. 21**) and so demonstrated himself to be, as Luke's narrative predicted, the one the Spirit anointed to proclaim the year of the Lord's favor (4.18). Such miracles would not, however, served as a sufficient justification that Jesus is the Messiah. Of the numerous statements from the Scriptures of Israel that were read in the first century as messianic predictions, and of the numerous figures – including John the Baptizer – who were regarded as messianic figures, *the performing of healings was not part of the messianic job description.* Others, including Jesus' own disciples, will perform healings and exorcisms, but these actions make them neither unique nor messianic. When Jesus tells John's disciples to report on the miracles – the blind see; the lame walk; the people with leprosy are cleansed; and so on (**vs. 22**) – he evokes his own sermon from the Nazareth synagogue. In Luke's narrative, Jesus fulfills prophecy and thus is the One who comes; historically speaking, however, the healings need not support the messianic claim. Others, from the ancient prophets to Jesus' followers to later rabbis, also did healings, but those healings do not grant messianic identity.

Jesus' next comment may hint at another question John has: if the Messiah is to "proclaim release to the captive," which was part of Jesus' synagogue sermon (4.18), John, in prison, has not seen his release, and he will not. By stating, 'blessed is anyone who takes no offense (literally: who does not find me to be a stumbling block/*skandalon*) at me" (**vs. 23**), Jesus may be alerting John and his followers not to doubt, even though Jesus will not free the Baptizer from prison. Jesus then speaks to the crowd around him about John. That crowd, knowing of John, and John's present circumstances, may have been asking the same question about releasing the captive.

Only when John's messengers depart does Jesus speak to the crowds about John's role. Had they stayed, the messengers might have taken issue with some of his comments. Jesus opens with several rhetorical questions. His opening query, "did you expect John to be a reed shaken by the wind?" (**vs. 24** cf. Matt 11.7–11), anticipates a negative answer: no, that is not what we expected. The next question about soft clothing (**vs. 25**) similarly anticipates a negative answer. Men in luxurious garb are in royal palaces, not the desert. With this second question, Jesus also hints at John's fate, for it will be a man in royal garb, in a palace, who will execute John. It is possible there is an implicit critique of Herod, who lived by a sea with reeds and wore such clothing in his palace in Tiberias, contrasting him with the man he imprisoned.

Turning from questions anticipating a negative answer to one anticipating a positive response, Jesus agrees with the crowd that John is a prophet; indeed, he is more than just a prophet (**vs. 26**): he is "the messenger" about whom Malachi spoke. Malachi (3.1) says: "Behold, I am sending my messenger (LXX: *angelos*, whence "angel") to prepare the way before me …" Luke changes the quote to "prepare *your* way *before you*" (**vs. 27**). The quote may remind Luke's listeners of John's earlier description in 3.4: "the voice of one crying out in the wilderness, 'Prepare the way of the Lord.'" Then comes the surprising news: as great as John is (**vs. 28a**), Jesus, and not only Jesus but all of his followers, are greater (**vs. 28b**). John's own disciples might beg to differ, but they are on their way back to John.

With vs. 28, Luke draws the line between John and all he represents, including the greatness of Israel's prophets, and the nascent Christian movement. John represents an ancient and respected line that, with the coming of Jesus, has itself come to an end; as Luke will later state, "The Law and the Prophets were in effect until John came; since then the good news of the Kingdom of God is proclaimed ..." (16.16). In Luke's account, the break between Jesus and the Jewish tradition is beginning, even as the road to Marcionism will be constructed by some of Jesus' followers, with Marcion himself later using Luke to accomplish such an end.

Luke continues by announcing that all the people (Greek: *pas ho laos*), and especially the tax collectors who came to John, had been baptized and then pronounced God righteous (Greek: *dikaioō*, also translated "justified") (**vs. 29**). The people agree with Jesus that John and his baptism were part of the divine plan. The Pharisees and lawyers, having refused the baptism, are therefore outside the desires and purposes of the divine (**vs. 30**). Fitzmyer writes, "Clinging to the Mosaic Law and not recognizing that John's baptism was a way to righteous status before God is seen here as a mode of frustrating God's own providence."[4] The comment is odd, especially since Luke described John's baptism in Chapter 3 but does not mention the Pharisees until Chapter 5. Fitzmyer has presumed the Pharisees' rationale for rejecting the Baptizer to be the "clinging to Torah" rather than explored any other reason they might have had, from rejection of his eschatological orientation, to rejection of his proclamation through threat, to concern that he was a political liability. Mosaic Law and the Baptizer's proclamation need not and should not be seen as in opposition. We could also observe that the point of Jesus' saying is about historical sequence, not about two opponents on the stage of history at the same time.

Jesus continues his speech by going on the attack, as he did in the Nazareth synagogue. His comments resemble those of John, who condemned the people coming to him as a "brood of vipers" (3.7). Jesus compares the people of this generation (**vs. 31**) – that the previous lines spoke of tax collectors and Pharisees suggests an inclusive "generation" – to children in the marketplace who are never satisfied with the games they play. If they have the flute played for them or, more broadly, if they are invited to celebrate, they refuse to dance; if they hear wailing or, more broadly, if they are called to mourn, they refuse to weep (**vs. 32**). Jesus will go on to associate John with fasting and so perhaps mourning, and he describes himself as eating and

---

4   Fitzmyer, *Luke I–IX*, 676.

drinking and so perhaps feasting and dancing. The people, this generation, are satisfied with neither activity, neither lifestyle.

Scolding the crowd as one might scold a child, Jesus tells even the ones who had followed John the Baptizer that they had misjudged him. They had called John the ascetic demon-possessed (**vs. 33**), and they called Jesus – here with the self-designation "Son of Man" – a "glutton and a drunkard" because he ate and drank (**vs. 34**). No behavior would have satisfied them, and no practice would have convinced them of righteousness or sanctity. Jesus is not simply speaking of a negative reputation regarding his dining practices; the comments about the children in the marketplace as well as the "son" create an intertextual allusion that anticipates the Passion. According to Deut 21.18–21, when parents have a "stubborn and rebellious son" who behaves as a "glutton and a drunkard," they are to bring him to the elders, who would then pronounce the death sentence upon him. The cautionary account in Deuteronomy (there is no evidence of anyone ever being convicted of this crime) indicates to the biblically literate reader that Jesus, the one accused of gluttony and drunkenness, will be put to death by the elders of the community. Despite the distinctions in the behaviors of John and Jesus, they do have one point in common, which Luke accentuates: they are both friendly with tax collectors (see comments on 5.30).

Jesus concludes his comments with a seeming non sequitur: "Wisdom is justified by all her children" (**vs. 35** cf. Matt 11.19). Personified Wisdom here evokes Prov 1–9 as well as Wis 7.27. Jesus may be associating himself with Wisdom incarnate, a point that underlies the famous prologue in the Gospel of John, "in the beginning was the Word." He may also be claiming from the crowds the role of the only adult in the scene: they are never satisfied, they misjudge, they condemn; but the wise person knows exactly what is needed, what is right, and what is just. This wisdom will become manifest in the next scene when the motifs of Pharisees, eating, inappropriate dining companions, and even posh settings versus desert asceticism, all come together.[5]

THE WOMAN WHO LOVED MUCH

Luke has just announced that the Pharisees rejected John's message, that Jesus sees John and his entire traditional past as at best outdated, and that

---

[5] On Jesus as Wisdom, see Ben Witherington III, *Jesus the Sage: The Pilgrimage of Wisdom* (Minneapolis: Fortress Press, 2000).

he himself represents Wisdom. Why a certain Pharisee then decides to invite him to a banquet remains unexplained (**vs. 36**). Why Pharisees will continue to invite him, for they will do so again in 11.37–54 and 14.1–24, remains equally speculative. Perhaps the Pharisee, hearing that Wisdom is justified by her children, sought to demonstrate himself a child of wisdom (he will fail in this attempt). Perhaps he wanted to hear more from Jesus, or perhaps he thought he had something to contribute to the topics Jesus had addressed. Luke gives no reason for suggesting that the Pharisee had pernicious motives; as elsewhere in the Gospel, Luke's image of Pharisees varies story by story. Indeed, Amy-Jill wonders whether Luke has crafted these three accounts of Pharisaic banquets; Ben thinks that Luke is recording historical events, but his choice of stories tells us something about his views.

Also, as elsewhere in the Gospel, Luke takes a story that had been circulating about Jesus – the story of Jesus' dining with various parties – and gives it a particular twist that highlights themes sounded elsewhere. Luke, more so than the other Gospels, is concerned about dining habits, especially among the rich; the topic not only sets up Jesus as a new Socrates who participates in symposium-style conversations at table, it is also directly relevant to the fellowship meals that Jesus's followers would continue to have. Next, Luke is concerned about the role of women and sometimes locates them as faithful but silent servants and patrons. Luke has an interest in Pharisees, who may represent members of the Jewish community of Luke's time who did not accept the Christian message and who therefore represent a challenge to the Gospel. Finally, Luke is concerned with the categories of repenting and forgiving. All four concerns unite in the account of the woman who enters the Pharisee's house and anoints Jesus' feet.

The canonical Gospels present a narrative with the same building blocks: a woman anoints Jesus, someone complains about the anointing, Jesus defends the woman. The blocks, however, come in different shapes and sizes: for Mark 14.3–9 and Matt 26.6–13, Holy Week begins when an unnamed woman anoints Jesus on his head. People at a dinner hosted in Bethany by "Simon the one with leprosy" complain that the woman had wasted the ointment: it could have been sold and the money distributed to the poor. Jesus tells them that the poor will always be with them, but he will not; the woman has anointed him for his burial. In John 12.1–8, the anointing occurs at the home of Lazarus; the anointing woman is Mary, the sister of Martha and Lazarus; the anointing is of Jesus' feet; and the complainant is Judas, who wanted to keep the money for himself. Luke's version, unlike the other three, is set well before the Passion Narrative, and since Jesus has not yet begun his journey to Jerusalem, the location may be somewhere in the Galilee. Luke's version has nothing to do with anointing Jesus for burial, and the complaint – which is heard only in interior monologue! – has nothing to do with the cost of the ointment. For Luke, the scene is about hospitality, judging, repentance, and forgiveness.

Amy-Jill thinks that Luke has rewritten the account in Matthew and Mark and, in doing so, recasts the woman into a sinner and not one who recognizes Jesus' death. She sees John, in turn, as further attempting to control the story by combining the Passion setting with the anointing of the feet and ensuring that the woman in the story is Mary the sister of Martha.[6] Ben notes that it is possible that Jesus was anointed more than once by a woman, and he finds no reason to think that Luke 7 records the same tradition as the other three accounts. Ben also notes that this story of the anointing enters Luke's account before the introduction of Mary Magdalene in 8.1–3 and Mary and Martha in Luke 10, and so the hearer of this Gospel would not assume this story has anything to do with either Mary Magdalene or Mary the sister of Martha. Although, as Amy-Jill adds, as soon as the reader meets Mary Magdalene in the very next scene, drawing a connection would not be surprising. Nor would it be surprising for later readers to connect the anointing woman, by Jesus' feet, with Mary, "who sat at the Lord's feet" (10.28). Ben and Amy-Jill agree that, at least in terms of Luke's narrative, the anointing woman is neither Mary Magdalene nor Mary the sister of Martha. Later Christian tradition blended the woman of Luke 7 with Mary Magdalene and sometimes also the woman caught in adultery in John 7.53–8.11 (see comments on 8.1–3).

Entering the Pharisee's house comes "a woman who was in the city, a sinner" (**vs. 37**). Commentators are quick to judge: the woman must be a prostitute, as if that is the only sin a woman is capable of committing. Luke recognizes that women are not so unimaginative: Sapphira along with her husband sins against the Church by withholding part of her pledge (Acts 5.1–10). Conversely, earlier in the Gospel, Peter identified himself as a sinner (5.8), and few would identify Peter's sin as prostitution. Indeed, the only time Luke mentions prostitutes is in the Parable of the Prodigal Son, in which the older brother accuses the prodigal of "devouring [the father's] property with prostitutes" (15.30). That is, the prostitutes in Luke

---

[6]   See Philip F. Esler and Ronald Piper, *Lazarus, Mary and Martha: Social-Scientific Approaches to the Gospel of John* (Minneapolis: Fortress Press, 2006).

exist only in the imagination of the elder brother and the reader. Luke lacks the comment from Matt 21.31–32 that prostitutes and tax collectors followed John the Baptizer and will proceed into heaven ahead of the so-called righteous.

The identification of the woman as a sinner says nothing about particular types of sin. It does, however, evoke Jesus' response to the Pharisees in 5.32, "I have come to call not the righteous but sinners to repentance." We might therefore see the woman as already repentant and thus coming to Jesus to express her gratitude. Like Zaccheaus in 19.7, this repentant sinner will be acknowledged before others who would judge her without knowing the full story.

The woman is carrying an "alabastron of myrrh," that is, expensive perfume. Commentators are also quick to offer a symbolic explanation of the myrrh: it represents incense and thus displays Jesus' body as the new altar (Exod 30.23); it associates the woman with the adulterous wife in Prov 7.17; it associates Jesus with another rescuer of the Jewish people, Queen Esther, who is marinated in myrrh for six months (Esth 2.12); it places Jesus in the role of the lover in Song of Songs (passim); it anticipates the opiate offered to Jesus on the cross (Mark 15.23, but not Luke); it reminds us of the gifts of the Magi (Matt 2.11); it anticipates his burial (John 19.39); and so on. Each reading will add nuance to the scene, but none is necessary. The woman is carrying the ancient equivalent of Chanel No. 5, but there's no reason to import comments about Coco Chanel or the French into the pericope.

Next, we do not know how the woman obtained the myrrh, or whether it represented all of her wealth or just a portion. We do not know if she had planned the visit or had a spontaneous reaction to learning that Jesus was dining locally. That she lives "in the city" may be a signal that Luke's audience, also urban dwellers, know of similarly wealthy women; that location returns in the Parable of the Widow and the Judge, where questions of economic status and gender return as well.

As Jesus reclines on a dining couch, the woman stands behind him, by his feet. Weeping, she drenches his feet first with her tears, and then with the myrrh. Finally, she uses her hair to wipe his feet, as she continues to kiss him (**vs. 38**). The scene is irregular, and sensual. Whether it is erotic, or immodest, or immoral, is a more difficult question. The fourth-century Church Father Asterius of Amasea saw the woman's unbound hair as a symbol of grieving; pagan women would unbind their hair in certain ritual settings to suggest a natural state; loose hair could indicate humility or mourning.[7] We see what we want to see.

The woman's actions are not necessarily erotic, and neither are they necessarily Christological. The word for her action, "anoint," is *aleipho*, not *christeo*, with its "Christ"-like resonances. While *aleiphō* is the term Mark (16.1) uses to describe the intent of the women who go to the tomb, there is no reason to import this intertext. The woman is simply anointing Jesus' feet. Claims that the foot anointing is meant to evoke Homer's *Odyssey*, in which Odysseus's nurse recognizes her true king beneath his beggar's guise, are imaginative. Luke's focus is on the exaggerated actions of the woman, with the exorbitant generosity of her behavior signaling the extent of her gratitude for the forgiveness granted to her.

The Pharisee – Luke accentuates the host's affiliation – then engages in internal monologue. For Luke, as well as for much of the ancient world, thinking to oneself is a negative indication: it suggests something one would be ashamed to speak openly, or a plot one connives.[8] Later, the prodigal son will engage in interior monologue in his planning on how best to return to his father to get the desired return. The Pharisee wonders: were Jesus a prophet, he would know "who and what kind of woman is touching him …" (**vs. 39**). One might wonder: how does *the Pharisee* know who she is?

Just as commentators are wont to identify the woman as a prostitute, so they are wont to see the Pharisee as concerned with a violation of purity laws occurring in his house when the woman touches Jesus. The issue is not purity. The Pharisee's inviting Jesus already indicates that at least this Pharisee did not see Jesus' affiliating with tax collectors to be a violation of purity. The better focus is on the Pharisee's question of whether Jesus was a prophet. The identification of prophet, already made in 1.76; 2.36; 3.4. 4.24, 27; 7.16, 26, applies finally to John the Baptizer. And as Jesus has just proclaimed, he, and his followers, are greater than John. Whereas earlier in this chapter, Luke reported that the people proclaimed, "A great prophet has risen among us!" and "God has looked favorably on his people!" (7.16), here the Pharisee comes up short, for Jesus is more than a prophet, as he is about

---

[7] See Charles H. Cosgrove, "A Woman's Unbound Hair in the Greco-Roman World, with Special Reference to the Story of the 'Sinful Woman' in Luke 7:36–50," *JBL* 124.4 (2005): 675–92.

[8] Michal Beth Dinkler, "The Thoughts of Many Hearts Shall Be Revealed: Listening in on Lukan Interior Monologues," *JBL* 134.2 (2015): 373–99.

to demonstrate. He not only knows the woman's condition of sinner, he has the authority to forgive her.

Responding to the Pharisee's interior monologue, Jesus poses a question (**vs. 40**). That he can respond to an unstated concern already demonstrates his prophetic ability. His response begins by naming his host "Simon," the same name of the fisherman who will become the preeminent apostle. The root of the name is Sh-M-A, whence the term *Shema*, the name of the Hebrew prayer from Deut 6.4, that begins, "Hear, O Israel …" Simon will need to hear, to listen. He also needs to learn. Although he addresses Jesus as "teacher" (Greek: *didaskolos*), which the tax collectors had used for John (3.12), he will need to learn that just as Jesus really is a prophet and more than a prophet, so Jesus too is a teacher, as one would find at a symposium, but also more than a teacher. Here Jesus, the teacher of parables, will instruct not only in the value of forgiveness, but on the one who can grant it.

Jesus poses a parable: there were two debtors, with one owing fifty denarii and one owing ten times as much (**vs. 41**). A denarius, a Roman silver coin, was the standard daily wage. The debts are not exorbitant, but neither are they inconsequential. Readers familiar with Matthew's Gospel would think of the prayer "forgive us our debts, as we forgive those who are indebted to us" (Matt 6.12); Luke's version speaks of forgiveness of "sins," for we ourselves forgive everyone indebted to us. (11.4). In Jesus' parable, when neither debtor has the funds to pay, the creditor forgives the debt; the Greek reads, literally, "to both he gave grace" (*echarisato*, from *charis*, **vs. 42a**). This is the same word Luke uses in 7.21, where the standard translation "had given sight" is actually "had given favorably" or "had given graciously."

The creditor's action surprises: those who lend money, from bankers to loan sharks, are not inclined simply to let the debt go. The response to such generosity should be love. The issue becomes one of degree: who will love him more (**vs. 42b**)? Substantively, the question cannot actually be answered. We do not know the specific needs of the debtors involved, who are themselves fictional characters. We do not know how small their income is, such that the forgiveness of the smaller debt may have had a greater impact on the family's income. Nevertheless, the view that the greater the forgiveness of the debt so the greater the love does sound logical.

Simon gets the right answer, although the NRSV's "I suppose the one for whom he canceled the greater debt" (**vs. 43**) misses the nuance of the Greek. Simon literally says to Jesus, "I lift up that for whom the greater (amount) is forgiven." The language of forgiveness allows the story to speak to both economic and personal issues, to forgiving a debt as well as to forgiving a sin.

The next several verses require the listener to continue with the mental image of the scene: Jesus is reclining on a dining couch, his head is likely at a slight angle to that of Simon, who is also reclining. The woman, still kissing Jesus' feet and wiping them with her hair, is standing at the back of Jesus' dining couch. Simon would have to lift his head a bit to see her. And that is exactly what Jesus wants. Jesus turns to face the woman, but he continues to talk to Simon. When he says, "You see this woman" (**vs. 44**), he is himself looking at her. His "you see" could be a question ("do you see?"), but the verb is a simple indicative: "you do see her." Now, really look. We first saw the woman through the narrator's eyes and then through Simon's eyes, and she appeared as a sinner. We see her now both as the model of hospitality and as the epitome of one who, having been forgiven, displays love.

As will prove typical for of Jesus, he is an odd dinner guest in that he insults his hosts. He lectures Simon: "You provided me no water for my feet" (**vs. 44a**). This notice of breach in etiquette becomes heightened by the even greater breach of a stranger providing what the host missed, and exorbitantly. The NRSV's bland "she bathed my feet" (**vs. 44b**) again misses the hyperbole. The woman is not giving Jesus a basic pedicure; Luke states that she "drenched" or "rained on" Jesus' feet with her tears. Whereas Simon did not offer a kiss of greeting, the woman again, lavishly, recuperates the loss.

This effusive kissing, while marking the woman's gratitude and love following her forgiveness, sets up several intertextual allusions. It will be with a kiss that the father of the famous parable greets his prodigal son. Both the woman and the prodigal spent lavishly, but the woman serves Jesus whereas the son acts for his own benefit; she was a sinner and he engaged in "dissolute living" (15.13). The kiss also creates an ironic contrast to 22.47–48, when at his arrest Jesus asks Judas, "is it with a kiss that you are betraying the Son of Man?" There will be, however, no kiss at the arrest.

From washing to kissing and now to anointing (**vs. 46**), Jesus points out to Simon how the woman plays the role of host. The accentuation of issues of hospitality flashes ahead to the story of Mary and Martha (10.38–42) where again, the host fails in the duties of hospitality. Martha, like Simon, will fail to attend to her guest. Like the woman at Jesus' feet in Chapter 7, so Mary – sitting at Jesus' feet – remains silent but proves herself the worthy disciple.

Finally comes the punch line that resolves the meaning of Jesus' parable even as it opens its own questions. The woman's sins, which were many, have been forgiven, and her love is the response (**vs. 47**). Alternatively, her love may have been what prompted the forgiveness. The love and the forgiveness are intimately related, with one prompting the other. Jesus then speaks not to Simon but, for the first and only time, to the woman directly: "Your sins are forgiven" (**vs. 48**). He may be informing her of her new status, or he may be reiterating or confirming what she already knew, or he may be making the comment for the sake of Simon and his other guests.

Whether directed to them or not, the other guests, the ones "co-reclining" with Jesus and Simon, engage in more interior monologue: "Who is this," they wonder "who even forgives sins?" (**vs. 49**). The question should extend beyond the "who" to the "how" and "which." As the divine representative, Jesus can forgive her sins against God. But for whatever sins she committed against others, Jesus' forgiveness requires explication. We might picture this scenario: a woman from the city robs a man at knifepoint. She then feels remorse, so she asks God to forgive her. Such an action, while commendable, does the victim no good. Her responsibility is to make restitution for him, and it is *his role* then to forgive her. How then can Jesus forgive, when the sin, or crime, was committed against a third party? The questions posed by Simon Wiesenthal in his *The Sunflower* (see pp. 191–93) recurs here.

We might imagine Jesus forgiving those sins she committed against others, for which she has repented, but for which she cannot receive forgiveness from her victims: a murdered associate? A vindictive neighbor who does not want to grant forgiveness? The mother of the son drawn by this woman into a life of sin? It is our role – according to both traditional Jewish and Christian teaching, to forgive the *repentant* sinner. According to *Midrash Tanhuma* (Hukkat 19), if the perpetrator asks the victim for forgiveness three times, and the victim still refuses to forgive, the victim is then seen to be at fault. More, victims themselves are required to pray for the forgiveness of the perpetrators (t. *B. Kam.* 9.29). Such generosity, consistent with Jesus' own drive to forgive, puts all of humanity into the image and likeness of the divine. Just as God is forgiving, so should we be forgiving (*b. Shabb.* 133b). Whether Jesus requires forgiveness prior to repentance, or without the possibility of repentance, remains a more difficult question.

Jesus dismisses the woman by stating that it was her "faith" that saved her: not any adherence to particular doctrinal views; not any action. "Faith" (Greek: *pistis*) is trust. The woman had the trust that, even if other people refused to forgive her and insist on seeing her as a sinner, Jesus would grant what they could not. Her repentance must be part of this faith, for the woman knew that God is always ready to forgive the repentant sinner. And so, she could do what Jesus commands: "Go in peace" (**vs. 50**).

The woman does not speak. Like Anna the prophet, the widow of Nain, Mary the sister of Martha, the widow who puts her coins into the Temple treasury, the daughters of Jerusalem who weep for Jesus, and many others, Luke's women may be moral exemplars, but they are generally silent ones.

BRIDGING THE HORIZONS

1. "I Am Not Worthy"

The centurion would not presume to come to Jesus; he was not "worthy." In turn, Jesus commends the centurion's faith. For a person with substantial social capital, recognition of a relative lack of worth can be a good thing: it takes away the sense of being all powerful or being fully in control. It prompts a recognition of limitations and dependence on others.

For the centurion's slave to speak of being "unworthy" is another matter entirely. To tell people whose self-worth is lacking, or people who have been socialized to think that their opinions and needs do not matter, who have been trained so fully to respect hierarchical differences that they would not presume to speak to their "betters," the centurion is not a helpful role model. To the contrary, this model of promoting a lack of worth would be harmful. If the centurion sees himself as "unworthy," we might wonder how he views his slave? Worthy of being healed, yes, but worthy in relation to him? How is human worth measured, and how do we see ourselves?

Society is generally hierarchical, and the centurion recognizes the chain of command. Yet his comment about not presuming to come directly to Jesus should raise questions. Why should we not "presume" to address someone in a higher position? Should the worker not have access to management, or – bringing matters closer to home – should assistant professors not be able to speak with the Department Chair or Dean without risking a negative tenure vote? We have known parishioners afraid to speak with their pastors or priests for fear of being a "bother" or a "nuisance" or, worse, labeled a "heretic" for asking questions. "The Pastor is too important to care about my problems," or, "Father is already overworked, so why bother him with this?" are not unfamiliar refrains. Surely if we are all in the image and likeness of the divine, we all have worth. Army rank, economic status, or educational privilege should not prevent communication.

Whether we are worthy in divine eyes is yet another issue the account raises. Do we approach God as "unworthy," as will, for example, the tax collector we find with the Pharisee in Jesus' parable (18.13: "But the tax collector, standing far off, would not even look up to heaven ...")? Several churches use language of "worth" liturgically, as in the response in the Roman Catholic Eucharist: "Lord, I am not worthy that you should enter under my roof, but only say the word and my soul shall be healed." Do we regard ourselves as craven sinners, never good enough? Do we emphasize Psa 144.3–4, "O Lord, what are human beings that you regard them, or mortals that you think of them? They are like a breath their days are like a passing shadow"? Or do we see ourselves in the image and likeness of the divine, just a little lower than the angels (cf. Heb. 2.6–7; see Psa 8.5)? And if the subject is approaching the divine, then we must do so not as "unworthy" outsiders but as loved children. We are all worthy.

We are all persons of sacred worth, created in God's image. This, however, is a different matter from saying we "deserve" or "merit" entering into the divine presence. Today, we live in a culture of entitlement. We think we are entitled to all sorts of things without having to work for anything or merit the desired benefit. Ben speaks of having to tell his students, repeatedly, "grades are not given and you are not *entitled* to A's, grades are earned."

While we have not "earned" the right (and it isn't a right, it's a privilege and a blessing) to enter God's presence or receive God's healing, we are all worthy of it precisely because of the way God has made us, creatures of sacred worth. Does the woman deserve to be forgiven? That is to ask the wrong question. It's not a matter of deserts or merit. Since all of us sin and fall short of God's highest and best for us, we could never "earn" forgiveness. Forgiveness is about grace, God's unmerited favor. And the woman in the story is emotional probably precisely because she realizes she has not merited the forgiveness she receives. People are not usually grateful when they just get what they deserve. They are grateful when they receive grace. As a preacher once said, "Justice is when you get what you truly deserve, mercy is when you don't get a punishment that you did deserve, and grace is when you get something positive like forgiveness you have not earned or deserved." To be worthy of something is one thing; to have earned it or deserved it is another.

Luke 8 Patrons and Parables, Healings and Exorcisms

¹ Soon afterwards he went on through cities and villages, proclaiming and bringing the good news of the kingdom of God. The twelve were with him, ² as well as some women who had been cured of evil spirits and infirmities: Mary, called Magdalene, from whom seven demons had gone out, ³ and Joanna, the wife of Herod's estate manager Chuza, and Susanna, and many others, who provided for them out of their resources.

THE PARABLE OF THE SOWER

⁴ When a great crowd gathered and people from town after town came to him, he said in a parable: ⁵ "A sower went out to sow his seed; and as he sowed, some fell on the path and was trampled on, and the birds of the air ate it up. ⁶ Some fell on the rock; and as it grew up, it withered for lack of moisture. ⁷ Some fell among thorns, and the thorns grew with it and choked it. ⁸ Some fell into good soil, and when it grew, it produced a hundredfold." As he said this, he called out, "Let anyone with ears to hear listen!"

⁹ Then his disciples asked him what this parable meant. ¹⁰ He said, "To you it has been given to know the secrets of the kingdom of God; but to others I speak in parables, so that 'looking they may not perceive, and listening they may not understand.'"

¹¹ "Now the parable is this: The seed is the word of God. ¹² The ones on the path are those who have heard; then the devil comes and takes away the word from their hearts, so that they may not believe and be saved. ¹³ The ones on the rock are those who, when they hear the word, receive it with joy. But these have no root; they believe only for a while and in a time

of testing fall away. [14] As for what fell among the thorns, these are the ones who hear; but as they go on their way, they are choked by the cares and riches and pleasures of life, and their fruit does not mature. [15] But as for that in the good soil, these are the ones who, when they hear the word, hold it fast in an honest and good heart, and bear fruit with patient endurance.

A LAMP UNDER A JAR

[16] "No one after lighting a lamp hides it under a jar, or puts it under a bed, but puts it on a lampstand, so that those who enter may see the light. [17] For nothing is hidden that will not be disclosed, nor is anything secret that will not become known and come to light. [18] Then pay attention to how you listen; for to those who have, more will be given; and from those who do not have, even what they seem to have will be taken away."

JESUS' TRUE RELATIONS

[19] Then his mother and his brothers came to him, but they could not reach him because of the crowd. [20] And he was told, "Your mother and your brothers are standing outside, wanting to see you." [21] But he said to them, "My mother and my brothers are those who hear the word of God and do it."

JESUS CALMS A STORM

[22] One day he got into a boat with his disciples, and he said to them, "Let us go across to the other side of the lake." So they put out, [23] and while they were sailing he fell asleep. A windstorm swept down on the lake, and the boat was filling with water, and they were in danger. [24] They went to him and woke him up, shouting, "Master, Master, we are perishing!" And he woke up and rebuked the wind and the raging waves; they ceased, and there was a calm. [25] He said to them, "Where is your faith?" They were afraid and amazed, and said to one another, "Who then is this, that he commands even the winds and the water, and they obey him?"

THE EXORCISM IN GERASA

[26] Then they arrived at the country of the Gerasenes, which is opposite Galilee. [27] As he stepped out on land, a man of the city who had demons met him. For a long time he had worn no clothes, and he did not live in

a house but in the tombs. ²⁸ When he saw Jesus, he fell down before him and shouted at the top of his voice, "What have you to do with me, Jesus, Son of the Most High God? I beg you, do not torment me" – ²⁹ for Jesus had commanded the unclean spirit to come out of the man. (For many times it had seized him; he was kept under guard and bound with chains and shackles, but he would break the bonds and be driven by the demon into the wilds.) ³⁰ Jesus then asked him, "What is your name?" He said, "Legion"; for many demons had entered him. ³¹ They begged him not to order them to go back into the abyss.

³² Now there on the hillside a large herd of swine was feeding; and the demons begged Jesus to let them enter these. So he gave them permission. ³³ Then the demons came out of the man and entered the swine, and the herd rushed down the steep bank into the lake and was drowned.

³⁴ When the swineherds saw what had happened, they ran off and told it in the city and in the country. ³⁵ Then people came out to see what had happened, and when they came to Jesus, they found the man from whom the demons had gone sitting at the feet of Jesus, clothed and in his right mind. And they were afraid. ³⁶ Those who had seen it told them how the one who had been possessed by demons had been healed. ³⁷ Then all the people of the surrounding country of the Gerasenes asked Jesus to leave them; for they were seized with great fear. So he got into the boat and returned. ³⁸ The man from whom the demons had gone begged that he might be with him; but Jesus sent him away, saying, ³⁹ "Return to your home, and declare how much God has done for you." So he went away, proclaiming throughout the city how much Jesus had done for him.

A GIRL RESTORED TO LIFE AND A WOMAN HEALED

⁴⁰ Now when Jesus returned, the crowd welcomed him, for they were all waiting for him. ⁴¹ Just then there came a man named Jairus, a leader of the synagogue. He fell at Jesus' feet and begged him to come to his house, ⁴² for he had an only daughter, about twelve years old, who was dying.

As he went, the crowds pressed in on him. ⁴³ Now there was a woman who had been suffering from hemorrhages for twelve years; and though she had spent all she had on physicians, no one could cure her. ⁴⁴ She came up behind him and touched the fringe of his clothes, and immediately her hemorrhage stopped. ⁴⁵ Then Jesus asked, "Who touched me?" When all denied it, Peter said, "Master, the crowds surround you and press in on you." [46] But Jesus said, "Someone touched me; for I noticed that power had gone out from me." [47] When the woman saw that she could not remain hidden, she came trembling; and falling down before him, she declared in the presence of all the people why she had touched him, and how she had been immediately healed. [48] He said to her, "Daughter, your faith has made you well; go in peace."

[49] While he was still speaking, someone came from the leader's house to say, "Your daughter is dead; do not trouble the teacher any longer." [50] When Jesus heard this, he replied, "Do not fear. Only believe, and she will be saved." [51] When he came to the house, he did not allow anyone to enter with him, except Peter, John, and James, and the child's father and mother. [52] They were all weeping and wailing for her; but he said, "Do not weep; for she is not dead but sleeping." [53] And they laughed at him, knowing that she was dead. [54] But he took her by the hand and called out, "Child, get up!" [55] Her spirit returned, and she got up at once. Then he directed them to give her something to eat. [56] Her parents were astounded; but he ordered them to tell no one what had happened.

The final scene of Chapter 7, the banquet at the home of Simon the Pharisee where the unnamed woman anoints Jesus' feet, appears, in retrospect, to foreshadow the multiple topics addressed in Chapter 8. First, Luke develops the broader issues of both hospitality and women's roles in mentioning the itinerant mission supported by women patrons. Continued as well are the hallmarks of the Gospel proclamation: the announcement of the Kingdom and its accompanying healings. Third, the banquet scene, with its Parable of the Two Debtors, also begins a more focused attention on Jesus' parables, with the famous "Parable of the Sower" as well as the metaphor of the lamp under a jar. Fourth, the question of insiders and outsiders, raised by Simon's thoughts concerning the propriety of Jesus allowing the woman to touch him, resurfaces in the discussion of Jesus' true relations: the natal family or those who hear the word of God. The stilling of the storm, the fifth connection, raises again Simon's questioning of Jesus' identity. The exorcism of the man from Gerasa, a sixth example, draws upon transitions of identity: as the woman goes from "the sinner" to "the one who loves much," so the man goes from actions of self-destruction to the proclamation of the Gospel. Example seven, a good biblical number, the final account of the hemorrhaging woman and the dead daughter of Jairus the synagogue ruler, returns to matters of women's status, Jewish leadership, faith, and Jesus' salvific role. What appears at first glance to be a series of disjointed stories in Chapter 8 thus emerges as a fulsome gloss on the previous pericope.[1]

THE WOMEN PATRONS

In his itinerant ministry through Lower Galilee, Jesus ventures into both cities and villages (**vs. 1**). Nowhere, however, does Luke mention the two major Galilean cities: Tiberias, the home of the court of Herod Antipas (see John 6.23), and Sepphoris, which is only a few hours walk from Nazareth. The vagueness of the geographical references also raises questions of the success of the Galilean phase of early discipleship. It is possible that Jesus deliberately avoided the two major cities in Galilee to eschew contact with Herod, a man whom he once called "that fox" (13.32). Although the Gospels speak of huge crowds following Jesus, with the feeding of the five thousand the most memorable, more Galilean cities and villages appear to have rejected Jesus rather than supported him. He is rejected in his hometown, although the story is depicted in different ways, from the synagogue scene in Luke's Gospel (4.16–30; and see Matt 13.54–58//Mark 6:1–8) to Jesus' announcement, "No prophet is accepted in the prophet's hometown" (4.24, cf. Matt 13.57//Mark 6.4//John 4.44). Both Matthew and Luke (and so the hypothetical Q source) record Jesus' cursing of the people of Capernaum (Matt 11.23//Luke 10.15), Chorazin, and Bethsaida (Matt 11.21//Luke 10.13). Jesus' followers eventually based themselves in Jerusalem, rather than in the Galilee, and antiquity leaves us little record of a prominent group of Jesus followers in Galilee prior to Constantine. Acts treats Galilee primarily as the home of the disciples rather than a place of any new mission (Acts 1.1; 9.31; 10.37; 13.31); Paul never mentions the region. There may well have been ongoing strong support for Jesus in the region, in places such as Nain and Capernaum as well as Cana (see John 2.1–10), but the communities in the Galilean cities were of less interest to Luke than the Jerusalem contingent and the extended gentile mission.

As Jesus proclaims the good news, he is accompanied by his Twelve (i.e., the ones named "apostles") as well as by other followers, whom we might call "disciples," although here Luke does not use the term. That term can be applied to women, as the description of Tabitha in Acts 9.36 demonstrates. Luke mentions some women among the group but defines them not in terms of witness but of having been "cured of evil spirits

---

[1]   Nolland, *Luke 1–9.20*, 370 suggests that 8.1–3 prepares for the whole section 8.4–9.20.

and infirmities" (**vs. 2a**). To this point in the Gospel, the only identified woman to have received such a cure is Peter's mother-in-law, although women would have been among the crowds who came to Jesus. The description[2] separates the women from the Twelve: the men are explicitly "with him"; the women grammatically are distanced. Jesus commissioned the Twelve; the women follow because of their healings. This distinction will remain consistent in Luke-Acts: the men take the leadership positions and the women provide ancillary, or patronage, support. There are exceptions, however. For example, according to Acts 18.26, Priscilla and Aquila both instruct the Christian teacher Apollos (Amy-Jill would have been happier had Luke depicted Priscilla as providing the instruction on her own).

But Ben notes that in Luke 23–24 these selfsame women are depicted as disciples who "remembered" Jesus' earlier teaching, in this case about his coming demise and resurrection. Further, they meet the criteria mentioned in Acts 1 for being a viable ongoing witness to and about Jesus, for they have been with him from the early days of the ministry onward, and Acts 1.14 indicates the meeting in the upper room is not an all-male affair, any more than the meeting at the house of John Mark's mother in Acts 12 is an all-male affair. And Peter, in Acts 2, publicly indicates that the prophetic Spirit of God was going to be an equal opportunity employer of women and men to get the message out, a fact confirmed by Philip's prophesying daughters. In short, Ben does not think that Luke has as an agenda of reinforcing a male leadership hierarchy, relegating the women to the hospitality brigade. Amy-Jill grants Ben's points; she would have been happier had women been in the running for the apostle to replace Judas and had their prophetic voices been heard. Ben would too. Rom 16 tells us that Junia was a noteworthy apostle, and Junia could be the Latin equivalent of the name "Joanna," so it would not be impossible for Luke to have included a woman among the candidates to replace Judas.[3]

Before describing what these women do, Luke names them. "Mary, called Magdalene, from whom seven demons had gone out" (**vs. 2b**), is the one witness consistent across all four Gospels to the cross and to the empty tomb. Only Luke describes her as having been possessed, and severely so.

---

[2]   See Witherington, "On the Road with Mary Magdalene, Joanna, Susanna, and Other Disciples: Luke 8.1–3," first published in *ZNW* 70 (3–4, 1979): 242–48; reprint in Levine with Blickenstaff (eds.), *Feminist Companion to Luke*, 133–39.

[3]   See E. J. Epp, *Junia: The First Woman Apostle* (Minneapolis: Augsburg Fortress, 2005).

Luke does not, however, detail her symptoms; the import is less that she was possessed than that she had been healed and she is now a fellow traveler with Jesus.

Joanna, the wife of Herod's administrator, had status in reference to her husband (**vs. 3a**). Although Luke lacks the story of John the Baptizer's execution at the instigation of Herodias (3.19; 9.9), the Gospel and Acts have an interest in Antipas and his court. Acts 13.1 mentions Manaean, "a member of the court of Herod the ruler," as among the "prophets and teachers" in Antioch. Joanna's presence confirms not only that some well-connected women were part of the movement, a point Luke reinforces in Acts, it also reminds readers that Jesus' mission does not take place in a political vacuum. Herod Antipas will kill John the Baptizer, may seek to kill Jesus (some Pharisees announce this threat [see the discussion of 13.31]), and according to Luke plays a role in Jesus' Passion (23.11).

Susanna, the third woman mentioned by name, is otherwise unknown. Since Mark (16.1) and Matthew (27.56) also list three named women, but the names differ across the Gospels, it is possible that the Church remembered that there were three major women in the movement, but aside from Mary Magdalene, the names were less important than the cohort of three, who parallel the inner circle of disciples: Peter, James, and John.[4] In two cases, Peter and Joanna, married individuals leave their spouses to follow Jesus; a third example, the "wife of Zebedee," appears in Matthew's Gospel (20.20; 27.56, where she is one of the three women at the cross). Joanna thus anticipates Jesus' later comments about the breakup of households (e.g., 18.29 on leaving "house or wife or brothers or parents or children for the sake of the Kingdom ..."). Ironically, whereas 18.29 might be taken to suggest that only men are disciples, since it says nothing about wives leaving their husbands, the first clear separation of a married couple is of the wife, Joanna, who has separated from her husband at least in terms of support for Jesus (see the discussion of 18.29).

The language and syntax of **vs. 3b**, translated in the NRSV as "... and Susanna and many others, who provided for them out of their resources," offers several interpretive possibilities.[5] First, *diakoneō* could indicate a ministerial focus, especially since Luke lived at a time when "deacons" had already become an established Church office (see comments on 4.39). Thus,

---

4   See Lieu, *Gospel According to Luke*, 60.
5   Esther de Boer, "The Lukan Mary Magdalene and the Other Women Following Jesus," in Levine with Blickenstaff (eds.), *Feminist Companion to Luke*, 140–60.

the better translation would be "served" or even "ministered." Luke will use the same verb to describe the ministry Martha, the sister of Mary, will provide for Jesus in 10.38–42. Second, grammatically, it is indeterminate whether the "many others" served Jesus, the Twelve, *and the three named women*, or whether the named women and the "many others" were the ones who served. Third, if there is a grammatical break such that the three named women are among those who were served by the others, then the three named women should be grouped with Jesus and the Twelve, who also evangelized.[6]

Finally, the service itself goes undetailed. Something more than cooking and cleaning is likely involved. Their service could have been paying for whatever the entourage needed – food, housing, footwear, and so on – as well as perhaps using social capital to open doors (cf. Phoebe the "deacon" in Rom 16.1–2). This type of patronage does not require that the women be "rich" per se; it does indicate that they had access to their own resources.

Luke 8.1–3 locates the women as patrons, and it locates the women and Jesus in a system of reciprocity. Their response to Jesus could be seen as a form of reciprocity: he healed them, and they served him in response. In this configuration, Jesus is the patron and they are the clients; their job, as clients, is to praise the patron. Conversely, as patrons of the movement, the women provide support for Jesus and others, and Luke in turn praises them by recording their names. Recognizing the women as patrons and acknowledging their names also moves the focus away from their having suffered possession and illness: healing stories and parables rarely provide the names of either men or women (e.g., neither the widow of Nain nor her son, nor the centurion and his slave, is named).

That women would be both patrons and disciples of a charismatic teacher is not anomalous. According to Josephus, the Pharisees had women patrons; in *Ant.* 17.41–42, Josephus, no fan of this movement (he finds them to have overstepped their station by teaching the people, the role Josephus, himself a priest, thinks belongs to people in his class), states: "for there was a certain sect of men that were Jews, who valued themselves highly upon the exact skill they had in the law of their fathers, and made men believe they were highly favored by God, by whom this set of women were inveigled. These are those that are called the sect of the Pharisees, who were in a capacity of greatly opposing kings ... Accordingly, when all the people

---

[6] Quentin Quesnell "The Women at Luke's Supper," in Richard J. Cassidy and Philip J. Scharper (eds.), *Political Issues in Luke-Acts* (Maryknoll: Orbis, 1983), 59–79 (68).

of the Jews gave assurance of their good will to Caesar, and to the king's government, these very men did not swear, being above six thousand; and when the king imposed a fine upon them, Pheroras's wife [Herod the Great's sister-in-law] paid their fine for them." Rabbinic literature (*t. Nid.* 5.2–3) confirms women's support for Pharisees. In less petulant sections, Josephus records that the Hasmonean queen Salome Alexandra (ruled 76–67 BCE) supported the Pharisees (*War* 1.107–19; *Ant.* 13.398–432). Josephus also notes that Simeon bar Giora, one of the leaders of the Revolt in 66–70, had women followers (*War* 4.505).[7]

H. Flender concludes, "Luke expresses by this arrangement that man and woman stand together and side by side before God. They are equal in honor and grace; they are endowed with the same gifts and have the same responsibilities ..."[8] Ben suggests that Luke's interest in women is part of his larger interest in the liberation of the captives and the oppressed of all sorts, and so reflects the realizing of the prophetic agenda outlined in Chapter 4 and based on Isaiah 61.[9] Ben is convinced Luke is not attempting to relegate women to hospitality duties, nor is he treating them as second-class disciples.

Amy-Jill again would rephrase: Luke does not depict women *qua* women as part of an oppressed group: Luke is aware that women are both oppressed and oppressors, both sinful and saints. Whether Luke offers good news particularly for women, or whether Luke offers a "double message" by which women are recognized and at the same time relegated to supporting roles rather than leadership positions will remain a debated issue.[10]

A CLOSER LOOK: MIRIAM OF MIGDAL

Although famed in Western culture as a repentant prostitute and more recently as Jesus' lover and even wife, Mary Magdalene appears in the New Testament as neither prostitute nor paramour, but as a faithful disciple. Prior to the cross, she is found only once in the Gospel tradition: Luke's notice that she had been possessed by seven demons and

[7] See Tal Ilan, "Gender," in Amy-Jill Levine and Marc Z. Brettler (eds.), *The Jewish Annotated New Testament*, 2d ed. (New York: Oxford University Press, 2017), 611–14.
[8] H. Flender, *St. Luke – Theologian of Redemptive History* (London: SPCK, 1967), 9–10.
[9] See the discussion in Witherington, *Women in the Earliest Churches*, 129–30.
[10] The classic study is Turid Karlsen Seim's aptly titled *The Double Message: Patterns of Gender in Luke-Acts* (London: Bloomsbury T&T Clark, 2004). See also the Introduction and essays in Levine with Blickenstaff, eds., *Feminist Companion to Luke*.

that she and other women provided Jesus support. In all four Gospels, she is present at the cross, and she is the sole consistent witness to the empty tomb.

Second- and third-century Christian accounts such as the *Gospel of Mary* depict her as the keeper of Jesus' special revelations; she appears in opposition to Peter, who represents ecclesiastical authorities who resist her leadership and so all women's leadership in the burgeoning communities. In the final saying (114) of the *Gospel of Thomas*, Peter exhorts Jesus, "Make Mary leave us, for females are not worthy of life." Jesus responds, elliptically, "Look, I will guide her to make her male, so that she too may become a living spirit resembling you males. For every female who makes herself male will enter the kingdom of Heaven."[11] The text's interest in asceticism is likely promoting that Mary, and so women, become "male," physiologically. *Thomas* may be suggesting that women engage in extreme fasting that will stop the menstrual cycle; decrease breast tissue; and, with testosterone replacing estrogen, create facial hair. Women thus become ersatz men.

The *Gospel of Philip* (probably third century) describes Mary as Jesus' "companion" (the phrase could mean either "life companion" or "companion in intercourse"), "sister," "mother," and "friend"; it also states "Jesus loved Mary more than the other disciples [so also the *Gospel of Mary*], embraced her, and kissed her on the ....": at this point, there is a lacuna in the text. The metaphors are sexually coded, but the meaning is also one of asceticism. Jesus and Mary model the *syzygy*, the primal unity divided and now rejoined, according to what has come to be known by the catch-all term "Gnostic" thought. Otherwise put, the language is that of the *heiros gamos* or sacred wedding/bridal chamber, but the program is world- and flesh-denying.

In the fifth century, Pope Gregory V associated Mary Magdalene with the female lover in Song of Songs who seeks her beloved at night. He also associated our Mary with Mary of Bethany, the sister of Martha (Luke10. 38–42; see also John 11–12); thus, Mary Magdalene becomes the model of the contemplative life, while Martha represents the active life. Since Mary the sister of Martha anoints Jesus' feet according to John 12.3, Mary Magdalene then becomes the anointing woman, and so

---

[11]   Translation by Stephen Patterson and Marvin Meyer, *The Gnostic Society Library* (www.gnosis.org/naghamm/gosthom.html), from Robert J. Miller (ed.), *The Complete Gospels: Annotated Scholars Version* (Sonoma: Polebridge Press, 1992, 1994).

becomes associated with the anointing woman of Luke 7. In the Eastern communions, Mary becomes known as the myrhh-bearer (Matt 28.1; Mark 16.1; cf. John 20.1), whereas in the West her reputation becomes that of the redeemed sinner. Because Luke names Mary Magdalene immediately after the story of the anointing woman, and because the Western tradition understood this woman to be a prostitute, so Mary Magdalene became known as a prostitute.

The eighth-century *Golden Legend* (1.374–83) calls Mary the "apostle to the apostles" (the title is based on her revelations to the disciples in John 20). She is said to be the beautiful, long-haired daughter of wealthy parents and the sister of Martha and Lazarus; here we see the conflation of Mary of Bethany with Mary Magdalene. Following the proclamation of Jesus' resurrection, she goes first to Ephesus, and then, along with Martha and Lazarus, to Marseilles. Alternative medieval traditions describe Mary as engaging in thirty years of penance near Marseilles or seven years of penance at Sainte-Baume. After having received final communion from angels and then dying, she was interred at Vezelay in Burgundy, where her shrine and her corpse became a prime source of relics.

Although Mary is not, at least in the earliest sources, identified as a prostitute, some of this reception history, colorful and ahistorical though it is, should not be disparaged. Today there are programs, such as the Magdalene House in Nashville, designed to help women move out of the sex industry.[12] For many of these women, the idea that Jesus would favor a prostitute rather than dismiss her is incentive to remain in the program.

Stripping away the legend, we can venture some historical conclusions about Mary Magdalene. First, her name was not "Mary" but "Miryam" or "Miriam"; she bears the same name as the sister of Moses (see Exod 15.20–21), and, perhaps, her name could be associated with Mariamme, Herod

---

[12] See www.thistlefarms.org/index.php/about-magdalene. According to a 2011 *Huffington Post* article on the program and its founder, Episcopal priest Becca Stephens, "In its 14-year history, Magdalene has had more than 150 graduates, about three-quarters of whom were still clean two and a half years after entering the program. When Stevens started Magdalene, there were five women; now Magdalene has six houses and about 30 women at a time. There are currently 100 women on the waiting list." By 2017, there were more programs, more women who have successfully completed them, and more women on the waiting list. See Melinda Clark, "Magdalene and Thistle Farms Offer Prostitutes a Chance for Regrowth," *Huffington Post*, Impact April 26, 2011, updated December 23, 2012, www.huffingtonpost.com/2011/04/26/magdalene-and-thistle-farms_n_854130.html.

the Great's Hasmonean wife.[13] Second, the designation "Magdalene" is not a last name. Just as Jesus was known as "Jesus of Nazareth," so Mary was known as "Mary of Migdala" or Migdal, a town on the northwest corner of the Sea of Galilee known for its processing of salt fish. The name "Magdal" (Aramaic) or "Migdal" (Hebrew) comes from the Hebrew/Aramaic root G-D-L meaning "big," and the term specifically indicates a "tower." The Greek name for the village was Tarichaea ("salted fish"). Archaeological investigations, which have only recently begun, reveal a synagogue with stone benches, an ornately carved reading table for the placement of scrolls (the "Magdala Stone") and (so far) four *miqva'ot* (ritual bathing pools).[14]

Only Luke suggests that Mary had been possessed. How one understands the reference will depend on one's theological beliefs. Amy-Jill finds the reference to "possession" to be catch-all language for a variety of illnesses, ranging from what the local society considers aberrant behavior, to fever, paralysis, deaf-and-mute symptoms, blindness, and so on. She also wonders whether the notice of the possession and the exorcism serves to discredit the women as leaders (much as today a stay in a psychiatric facility serves, in the eyes of some, to disqualify a person from serving in a public office), or, conversely, if her exorcism makes her a more credible speaker because she has fought with demons and won the battle. Ben finds credible cross-cultural testimony to the reality of evil spirits and therefore to the credible practice of exorcism over many centuries, including our own. Ben further diagnoses occult and astrological practices, from the time of Jesus to today, to be precisely what lead to spiritual problems in the lives of the practitioners. Thus, Ben sees Miriam as perhaps such a practitioner who dabbled in the occult and believed in the powers of darkness. Amy-Jill sees no reason to view the symptoms of possession as caused by occult practices and sees nothing in Mary's recorded history to suggest such practices. She further worries that people today who consider themselves "possessed" or who are considered "possessed" by others, if associated with "occult practices," will be blamed for their own condition. "Blaming the victim,"

[13]   See our discussion of the name "Mary," pp. 34–35.
[14]   For a popular discussion, see Marcela Zapata-Meza, "Magdala 2016: Excavating the Hometown of Mary Magdalene," Bible History Daily (07/07/2016) at www .biblicalarchaeology.org/daily/archaeology-today/magdala-2016-excavating-the-hometown-of-mary-magdalene/. See also Jane Schaberg with Melanie Johnson-Debaufre, *Mary Magdalene Understood* (New York and London: Continuum, 2006).

especially when the victim is a child so diagnosed, can only exacerbate the unfortunate situation.

Luke is the only evangelist to mention both Mary's possession and her presence prior to the cross. Mark 15.41 says she was one of the traveling disciples in Galilee. Matt 27.55 states that several women, including our Miriam, traveled with Jesus and the Twelve up to Jerusalem from Galilee for the Passover celebration. According to Mark 15.40–41, a group of women watched the crucifixion from afar, and the first person mentioned in the list is Miriam of Magdala. While the male disciples had all denied, deserted, or betrayed Jesus, the female disciples, or at least these three, remained faithful. Mark 15.47 states that the two Miriams saw where Jesus was buried. Immediately thereafter is the brief reference at Mark 16.1 to their coming to the tomb on Sunday morning. Amy-Jill finds that the story here becomes historically questionable: the women's expectation, according to Mark, was to anoint the body. However, once tombs are sealed, they are not opened for such purposes; the women's notice that they lacked someone to help them move the large stone seal reinforces the unlikelihood their plan. Ben disagrees. Tombs with rolling stones in trenches in front of them could be rolled back, and regularly were in the case of family tombs where multiple people are buried in the same place on different occasions. The tomb of Joseph of Arimathea was surely a family tomb. Amy-Jill says Mark had already announced that Jesus' body was anointed for his burial (see Mark 14.8), so the women's actions at the tomb would be redundant. Ben disagrees. The action of the woman in Mark 14 was before the crucifixion and would not have ruled out the felt need to embalm the body and add spices in the winding sheet after the devastations of crucifixion. Then again, one person's act of devotion to the dead does not make other people's actions superfluous if they also want to honor the dead.

Perhaps by naming Mary Magdalene and the other women at the tomb, Mark wants to make a point about discipleship: Mark pairs three named women (Mary Magdalene, Mary the mother of James, and Salome) who go to the tomb, but who will then flee with the three named men (Peter, James, and John), who fail Jesus at Gethsemane. It is the unnamed anointing woman in Mark 14 and the unnamed centurion at the cross in Mark 15 who offer the correct response to Jesus. The unnamed outsiders may be better bearers of the Gospel than those who would see themselves as the privileged insiders.

Matthew's rewritten version has "Mary Magdalene and the other Mary" come to "see" the tomb (Matt 28.1), which makes more historical sense.[15] Rather than fleeing the tomb in fear and remaining silent as they do in Mark's account, they proclaim Jesus' resurrection to the eleven male disciples. Luke, as we will see, offers an unnamed group of women, whom the disciples do not believe. Amy-Jill thus sees Luke as lessening the women's role. Ben disagrees. The women are mentioned in Luke 23.49,55–56 and these very same women are mentioned again immediately thereafter at 24.1 and then *explicitly* named at 24.10. The listener to Luke's Gospel would hear Luke 23 and 24 together and draw the appropriate conclusion. Amy-Jill notes that Mary Magdalene appears alone, unaccompanied by other women, at the tomb according to John 20. Ben replies that this is probably not correct. Mary herself says, "*we* don't know where they've put him," suggesting that while the focus in John 20 is on her as an individual, the presence of other women with her is mentioned indirectly. Amy-Jill sees that comment as an indication that John knows the Synoptic tradition but suppresses the presence of the other women in order to focus on Mary.

C. H. Dodd once said that the Johannine account was the most self-authenticating of all the Easter narratives because, he asked, who would invent the notion that Jesus appeared first to a little-known woman from Magdala?[16] The question can be answered in part. First, women did visit tombs, so their presence would not be unusual. Second, Amy-Jill notes that scene in John could suggest literary fiction just as much as it can suggest historical authenticity: John's depictions of mistaken identities, the recognition scene, and the reunion of the man and woman, even empty tombs (see Chariton's *Chaireas and Callirhoe*) are all part of the convention of the Hellenistic romance. Then John, as he typically does with literary conventions (cf. the meeting of a man and a woman at a well in John 4), makes the familiar very strange and so explodes the convention. The story works because readers know the convention and then delight in the shifts.

---

[15]   Thomas M. R. Longstaff, "What Are Those Women Doing at the Tomb of Jesus? Perspectives on Matthew 28.1," in Amy-Jill Levine with Marianne Blickenstaff (eds.), *A Feminist Companion to Matthew*, FCNTECW 1 (Sheffield: Sheffield Academic Press, 2001), 196–24.

[16]   C. H. Dodd, *The Interpretation of the Fourth Gospel* (Cambridge: Cambridge University Press, 1953).

Ben counters that John's tomb story has nothing to do with such romantic plot lines. Mary calls Jesus rabbouni, "my master" (i.e., teacher) there, not "my spouse." Furthermore, such fictional romance stories do not have a disciple meeting her teacher in a graveyard, so the suggested parallels don't work! There is no romance element in the story in John 20, which is the essential element in fictional romances. Drawing an analogy with Hellenistic romances is a genre mistake. Even when John repeats the convention of the man and the woman who meet at a well and who are regularly expected to marry (as in John 4), John immediately defies convention and takes the story in a more theological, more profound direction.

The NT tells us nothing more of the story of Miriam. Paul makes no mention of her; neither does the book of Acts. We know nothing of her family, or whether she was married or had children. We do not know how she met Jesus; suggestions that she was an associate of Peter and Andrew, James and John, through the fishing industry (Migdal is about six miles from Capernaum) are conjecture. She may have been a business person, like Lydia (see Acts 16), which could explain her financial independence. According to Celsus, she was a hysteric; according to the Gospel tradition, she was the first to proclaim the resurrection of Jesus. Luke follows the story of these women with the Parable of the Sower (8.4–15). To see continuity between the women's generosity and the parable's surprising results of sowing the Word in profligate fashion would not be inappropriate.

THE PARABLE OF THE SOWER

This material is taken from Mark 4.1–20 (cf. Matt 13:1–23), which Luke condenses by omitting Mark 4.13 (Jesus' exasperation at the disciples' inability to understand parables) and Mark 4.33–34 (the comment on Jesus' speaking to the crowds in parables but explaining the meanings to his disciples). As is typical for Luke, compared to Mark the disciples get an upgrade, and compared to Mark as well, the Lucan Jesus is a teacher of the people.

Vs. 4 introduces the audience of the parable: a "great crowd." Jesus' speaking is public, rather than reserved for the select few. The crowd would have understood his speaking to them "in a parable" as his telling them a story meant to provide a challenge or, potentially, reveal a mystery.

For the Parable of the Sower, as in any parable, the listener needs to decide where to enter the story: as the sower? As the seed? As the

---

A CLOSER LOOK: PARABLES

Parabole is a term for a comparison or comparative illustration. In his *Rhetoric* (2.20.1ff.), Aristotle treats parables as a subclass of comparative proofs that he calls paradigms (*paradeigma*). Parables are distinguished from fables (*logoi*) in that they are typically shorter and draw upon common experience. Quintilian agrees with Aristotle that a *parabole* is a subcategory of paradigms drawn from common experience and used as an auxilliary to inductive proofs. His view is that they are most effective when they have few or no metaphorical qualities, but rather speak in plain language (*Inst. Or.* 5.1.30ff). Quintilian likewise dissociates parables from metaphors and links them closely with historical analogies (*Inst. Or.* 4.1.70; 6.3.61–62). Thus, parables are not allegories; they do not require an answer key to determine equivalences between elements in the story and elements in experience. Luke's unique lengthier story-form parables (e.g., the Good Samaritan, the Prodigal Son, the Pharisee and the Tax Collector, the Rich Man and Lazarus) follow the Greek rhetorical conventions about such parables in a way and to a degree not true of most of those found in Matthew and Mark.

Although today they are frequently treated as children's stories – and it is true that children can find meaning in them – parables are designed for adults. They should be understandable to anyone, but understanding requires also an interrogation of one's own views. Parables help us to see the world in a different way; they shake up our status quo, and because they do, listeners may find themselves resisting what they have to say.

---

ground? The parable describes how numerous seeds did not take root. Some were trampled or eaten by birds (**vs. 5**); some fell on the rock and withered (**vs. 6**); some fell in the thorns and were choked (**vs. 7**). So far, matters are not looking good for the sower or for his crops. Finally, the seed that fell on good soil produced an amazing hundredfold return (**vs. 8a**). In terms of the result, typical yields were between seven- and fifteenfold, although Varro comments on hundredfold yields in nearby Gadara (*De re rustica* 1.44.2). Jesus tells the parable, then issues his invitation: listen! (**Vs. 8b**).

In its original context, apart from Jesus' explanation (as discussed in the following), the parable (vss. 5–8) likely served to let the disciples know that not everyone would be receptive to their message. The focus is not on the failures, however, but on the positive result. Amy-Jill thinks that the explanation of the parable that follows, in which Jesus explains what the elements mean allegorically, was not part of the original materials. She sees the explanations to the parables, here and elsewhere (see the discussion on Luke 15), as material added by the evangelists or perhaps the oral tradition upon which they drew. Ben accepts the explanations as also coming from Jesus since other early Jewish parables do often come with explanations.

In Luke's narrative, the parable explains *why* something happens; it is therefore not a morality tale. The determining factor needed for assessing the parable is the soil, not the seed and not the sower. The seed is scattered profligately, and it is possible that a tenant farmer might scatter grain on every scrap of land available in hopes for a good crop. But it is the condition of the soil that determines whether there will be growth or not. Readers who take the parable as an incentive to yield good crops therefore miss the focus on the soil: a soil cannot change its nature, any more than a tree can transform from an oak to an elm, or, to use Jesus' own language, a bad tree can yield good fruit. As Luke 6.43 noted, "No good tree bears bad fruit, nor again does a bad tree bear good fruit."

The disciples inquire as to the parable's meaning (**vs. 9**); for Mark, the disciples are unthinking, but Luke makes their question legitimate. They ask what the parable means, but Jesus changes the subject. Instead of beginning with his explanation, he explains the purpose of speaking in parables: they are meant to befuddle hearers. His paraphrase of Isa 6.9–10 (**vs. 10**) follows Mark 4.12, but Luke omits Mark's comment that the parables were designed to condemn those who were not disciples. Yet his paraphrase does suggest a separation: those who resist the parables, who will not see and not hear, will not understand. They could not, since they are like the rocky soil or thorny patch. This separation of insiders and outsiders will continue throughout the Gospel and Acts, even to the end of Luke's story, where Paul repeats the Isaiah quote in reference to the Jews in Rome who refuse his message (Acts 28.26–27).

The disciples can take comfort in that they have the explanations of the "secrets" (Greek: *mysteria*, whence "mysteries") of God's plans (cf. Dan 2.18–19, 47; 1 Cor 2.1,7), but the comfort is limited. Jesus then unpacks the parable, and in doing so turns it into an allegory. Perhaps the allegory, in which the seed is the word of God (**vs. 11**), the ones on the path are prevented by Satan from salvation (**vs. 12**), the ones on the rock are fickle (**vs. 13**), and the ones among the weeds are choked by their wealth (**vs. 14**), came from the early followers of Jesus and not from Jesus himself. However, rabbinic parables often have allegorical elements them, and sometimes come with explanations as well.[17]

In the end, this parable serves as a frank commentary on Jesus' ministry. There were many failures, as well as outstanding successes; Jesus spoke to all, even to those who were not likely to yield to his message or who would follow and then fall away. Jesus was not an advocate of "once saved, always saved" soteriology.

A LAMP UNDER A JAR

Jesus continues his teaching with a series of individual sayings that appear directed not to the crowds but to his disciples, the last-mentioned audience. From the subject of mysteries and so what is hidden, Jesus segues into another parable of sorts at vss. 16–17 (cf. Matt 4.21–25), with application at vs. 18. This cryptic couplet regarding the lamp placed on the stand rather than in a jar or under the bed (**vs. 16**) suggests that sharing the Good News means to shed light, not obscure it. The next comment (**vs. 17**) alerts listeners that there is more to come. The parables reveal only a part of the Kingdom message as well as a part of knowledge of the one who tells them. Attentive listening is also required (**vs. 18**), and those who hear and heed will be rewarded with even more information. The comments are both teasers and incentives: Jesus has more to teach, and the disciples thus have more to learn. But if they do not grow in their knowledge, and if they do not continue to act, they will lose whatever knowledge, or power, they have. This last remark closes the entire discussion in 8.1–18.[18] For Luke, deciding for or against Jesus is a zero-sum situation: the good soil will yield, and yield spectacularly, but the bad soil will have nothing.

JESUS' TRUE RELATIONS

Luke's narrative shifts from the sower in the field to the lamp in the home and now to the household and family. The household can function as one's

[17] Brad H. Young, *The Parables: Jewish Tradition and Christian Interpretation* (Grand Rapids: Baker, 2008); Reuben Zimmermann in cooperation with D. Dormeyer, G. Kern, A. Merz, C. Münch, and E. E. Popkes (eds.), *Kompendium der Gleichnisse Jesu* (Gütersloh: Gütersloher Verlagshaus 2007).
[18] See I. Howard Marshall, *The Gospel of Luke* (New International Greek Testament Commentary; Grand Rapdis: Eerdmans, 1978), 327.

"soil": nurturing parents, access to good education, economic security, sufficient food and health care, freedom from bullying or abuse, and so on
give children advantages in later life. Jesus' relationship with his own family,
depicted in the first two chapters, appears to be one of caring, piety, and
nurturing. In this passage, he redefines the family from the basis of biology
to the basis of care.

Condensing Mark 3.31–35 (cf. Matt 14.46–50), Luke paints a more receptive picture of the Holy Family than is found in Mark. Luke retains the
notice that Mary and her other children came to Jesus (**vs. 19**) and were
standing outside (**vs. 20**): given the crowds, they are unable to get close to
him. Luke omits Mark 3.21 which suggests that Jesus' family thought he was
crazy (see also John 7.3, 5). Luke also omits Mark's reference to Jesus' sisters,
as well as Jesus' question, "Who are my mother, brothers and sisters?" and
his gesture of pointing to the disciples and so distinguishing his natal family
from those belonging to the family of faith.

Luke knows the outcome: Jesus' family would eventually be part of his
program (see Acts 1.14). One could even read **vs. 21** as suggesting that it is
Jesus "mother" and 'his brothers" – Mary and her sons (and daughters) –
who exemplify discipleship by "coming" to Jesus. Yet we never see Jesus here
as actually speaking to this family. Mary may well at this point have felt that
sword Simeon predicted would wound her (2.35). Her son is constructing a
new family in which she will have a role, but he will not leave the crowds to
be with her. She has to let him go, and be.

JESUS CALMS A STORM

Jesus leaves the crowd with the question of whether his natal family ever
reached him left undecided, and together with his disciples he gets into a
boat to sail across the Sea of Galilee (**vs. 22**). For several of the disciples,
who were in the fishing business, handling a boat well should be expected.
These "disciples" may include the women listed in 8.1–3 and even Mary and
the siblings. (Ben and Amy-Jill like to think this is the case.)

Jesus falls asleep in the boat (**vs. 23**), and the biblically alert reader will
recall Jonah falling asleep in the ship heading to Tarshish (Jon 1.5). This
allusion is strengthened when Luke reports a great storm that threatened
to swamp the boat. The same scenario presented itself in Jonah 1. Jesus
remains undisturbed, but the disciples – some of whom should have been
masters at sailing – panic. Whereas Mark (4.34–36) speaks of more than
one boat carrying disciples, Luke only has the single vessel, which obviates

the problem of whether the disciples in the other boats were also in danger. Instead of doing what they know how to do, the disciples who had previously made their living on the sea wake up Jesus and tell him that they are perishing (**vs. 24a**). Calling him "master" (*epistata*), the disciples remind readers of Simon Peter's earlier comment from a boat: we've worked all night but there are no fish (see 5.5). Disciples, in a boat, with a problem: we've seen the scene before, and we the readers know that a miracle is about to occur.

The disciples, on the other hand, lack trust: Jesus has already performed enough miracles to let the disciples know that they are safe. More, the disciples lack faith in their own abilities. To mix the metaphor, the wind and the sea function as the rocky soil; to continue the allusions to that parable: Jesus is about to reveal to them another mystery, whose full explanation will not be realized until his resurrection and ascension.

Jesus answers their prayer. He rebukes the wind and the waves (**vs. 24b**). He then, more gently, rebukes the disciples for their lack of faith (**vs. 25a**). The disciples, in turn, marvel, and they wonder about the mystery of Jesus' true identity (**vs. 25b**). This miracle account would have had particular resonance with Luke's gentile audiences, for they had heard stories of how gods and those very close to them (kings, sages, miracle workers) controlled natural elements (cf. Porphyry, *Life of Pythagoras*, 29). Closer to Luke's narrative are the stories of Jonah as well as of Moses, Joshua, and Elijah, who exercise control over nature (cf. Exod 14.15–16; Josh 3.10–13; 2 Kings 2.8). But the disciples' question is more than the attempt to understand Jesus in terms of ancient heroes or even Greek or Roman gods. Whereas the God of Israel has control over nature (e.g., Psa 89.9 proclaims: "You rule the raging of the sea; when its waves rise, you still them"; Psa 107.29 repeats, "He made the storm be still and the waves of the sea were hushed"), now the disciples see Jesus as manifesting divine traits. They ask who he is. The reader, ideally one who has been listening, is to provide the answer. They have encountered the presence of God in Jesus. This story thus anticipates Peter's confession in 9.20.

From 8.24 (Jesus' stilling the storm), until the confession in 9.20, Luke keeps the focus on Jesus' deeds: the present text and 9.10–17 are nature miracles, and sandwiched between them are two healings or exorcisms. Although retaining the accounts of the demon-possessed man in Gerasa and the conjoined story of the woman suffering hemorrhages and the raising of Jairus' daughter, Luke omits *all* of Mark 6.45–8.27a (Jesus' walking on water, controversies with Pharisees, the Syro-Phoenician woman and her demon-possessed daughter, the healing of a deaf man by use of the

Aramaic term *ephphata* [which likely sounded to a Greek-speaking audience like "abra cadabra" or some other magical incantation], the feeding of the four thousand, and the healing of the blind man of Bethsaida). Instead, Luke includes a number of accounts distinct to the Third Gospel.

THE EXORCISM IN GERASA

The boat having safely made its passage to the other side of the Sea of Galilee, Jesus arrives in Gerasa (**vs. 26**). Thus, begins, in 8.26–39 (Matt 8.28–9.1; Mark 5.1–20), the most detailed and dramatic of the New Testament exorcisms found in the other Synoptic Gospels and in Acts (there are no exorcisms in John's Gospel). The manuscript tradition across the Synoptics is inconsistent on the name of the location: Gadara, Gergesa, or Gerasa. The territory of Gadara extended to the southern side of the Sea of Galilee, and Gerasa/Jerash was one of the cities of the Decapolis, and so likely near the very southern end of the lake. Either one was "opposite Galilee"; either location situates the exorcism in a predominantly gentile area. That there were pigs in the area indicates gentile territory (cf. Lev 11.7 and Deut 14.8).

To Amy-Jill, the name also hints at the allegorical nature of this story. The Hebrew word *gerash* means to expel, as Adam and Eve were expelled from Eden (Gen 3.24). The city is thus "expelledville" or "exorcismburg." Such allegorical play continues with the name of the demon, "Legion," and its resonance with Roman troops. Ben doubts there is any allegorical play with the town name, since it actually existed with that name at the time.

In Gerasa, Jesus encounters a demon-possessed man (**vs. 27**) who epitomizes abjection: he is naked, homeless, and disabled. From the chaos of the raging sea and wind, the narrative thus turns to the chaos created by possession. Although well-meaning homilists sometimes describe the man as an "outcast," the term is not apt for any of his Synoptic depictions; to the contrary, the people in the town attempted to prevent him from injuring himself (8.29), but he, or his demons, were too strong to contain or constrain. It is the demons who cast the man out, not society.

In **vs. 28**, the possessed man or, more accurately, the demons possessing him, identify Jesus; calling him "Son of the Most High God," they provide the answer to the disciples' question in the previous story. At the same time, the title can suggest a polytheistic setting where the God of Jesus is the "most high" within the pantheon.

Luke plays with narrative time in **vs. 29**: we hear the demons' response to Jesus, and his title, before we know that Jesus had commanded them to leave the possessed man. Luke then develops the depiction of the man's chaotic state: the people had attempted to chain him up for his own protection, but no bond would hold him. His power was supernatural.

In **vs. 30**, Jesus and the demons engage in conversation. By demanding the demon's name, Jesus demonstrates his authority. The name "Legion" refers to a Roman army unit containing five thousand to six thousand men. One could conclude that the demons symbolize Roman authority; just as the demons possess the man and strip him of his resources, so do the Romans possess the lands and people and take what they want.

According to **vs. 31**, the demons plead that they not be sent into the abyss. That the demons would bargain with their exorcist is a familiar convention: The Jewish pseudepigraphon called the *Testament of Solomon* (1.6) also recounts a request by a demon for a concession under similar circumstances.

The demons, not displaying the most intelligent response, then ask to be sent into pigs feeding nearby (**vs. 32**). Luke laconically indicates that Jesus permitted them to do so. The pigs immediately stampede and, like lemmings, hurl themselves over the bank and drown (**vs. 33**). What the disciples feared would be their fate becomes the fate of the pigs, and the demons in them. This death is further ironic in that demons do not like water: they prefer the dry areas. The expulsion of demons and their descent into the "abyss" (that is the Greek term used in vs. 31) thus functions as another sign of the in-breaking of the Kingdom of God. According to one early Jewish and Christian way of thinking about things (cf. Jude 6; 1 Pet 3.19; 2 Pet 2.4; Rev 20.1–2), that descent would be their eschatological fate.[19]

The herders, having lost the pigs and so their livelihood, report far and wide what had happened (**vs. 34**). Luke does not tell us how the report went: options range from praise of Jesus for performing an exorcism to condemnation of Jesus for wrecking the economic infrastructure of Gerasa.

When the townspeople find the man clothed, in his right mind, and assuming the posture of a disciple at the feet of Jesus, they do not rejoice (**vs. 35**). Their reaction is rather one of fear. Even when they hear the details of the exorcism (**vs. 36**), they continue to "fear a great fear" (**vss. 35;** cf. 37). The response is not what Jesus had received in Galilee, where people flocked to him for healings. Rather, *all* the people ask Jesus to leave the area (**vs. 37**). A person with the power to exorcise the demons, and who had so little regard for their property, was frightening rather than comforting.

---

[19]   See Ben Witherington III, *Jesus the Seer* (Minneapolis: Fortress Press, 2104), x–xii.

There's an ironic contrast in this account to Luke's signature story of Jesus in the Nazareth synagogue. There, Jesus recounted how two gentiles had gratefully received healings from Israel's prophets (4.25–26), but the people sought rather to hurl him off a cliff (4.29). Readers might have expected the gentiles to receive Jesus joyfully, but for Luke, the time of the gentile mission will not take place until the Book of Acts.

This point about the mission timing is reinforced in the last two verses of the scene. The formerly demon-possessed man begs Jesus to allow him to remain with him (**vs. 38**). Whether the man's motives were interest in learning more, desire to take his place among the disciples, or fear of the demons' return, Luke does not state. Instead, Jesus commands the man, "return to your home" (**vs. 39**). The mention of a home suggests that the man had property, and perhaps a family, in the town. The man returns to Gerasa, with the proclamation of what had been done for him. Yet he changes Jesus' instructions. Jesus spoke of proclaiming "how much God had done" for him. The man speaks of how much *Jesus* had done. In so doing, he anticipates both the gentile mission and the recognition that Jesus is divine.

A GIRL RESTORED TO LIFE AND A WOMAN HEALED

The remainder of Chapter 8 retells the Markan stories of the synagogue leader Jairus, his dead daughter, and the hemorrhaging woman (cf. Matt 9.18–26; Mark 5.21–43). Preserving Mark's technique of intercalation – of sandwiching one story within another – Luke shortens both accounts to highlight both Jesus' power and Jairus's pathos. That Luke limits Mark's accounting of the woman's unhappy experiences with doctors (cf. Mark 5.26) provides some support for those who want to identify the author of the Third Gospel as "the beloved physician." By eliminating the Aramaic "Talitha cum" in Mark 5.41, Luke eliminates as well any sense that Jesus might have issued a magical formula. Luke, however, eliminates all traces of Aramaic, which can suggest he simply did not know the language and did not think his audience did either. While the Gerasene man returned to his home to proclaim the good news, Jesus returns to Galilee to find crowds waiting for him (**vs. 40**). The contrast to his rejection by the crowds in Gerasa is palpable, as will be, later in the Gospel, his rejection by the people in Jerusalem. But in this part of the narrative, Luke emphasizes the successful mission. Readers will need to determine how many of these people who here seek Jesus will turn out to be thin or rocky soil.

From demons inhabiting a naked, wounded man who fall at Jesus' feet and beg Jesus to leave them alone, Luke turns to their opposite: a "leader of the synagogue" (*archisynagogos*) who falls at Jesus' feet and entreats him to heal his daughter. The scene is one of a powerful man who has not the power to heal his daughter. Luke brings forward from Mark's version of the story the notice of the girl's age: she is an only child, about twelve, and she is dying (**vs. 42**). Instead of thorns choking the father (cf. 8.14), he is being choked by the crowd.

And he is hindered again by the appearance of a woman who had been bleeding for twelve years. The connection to the dying child is immediate: a girl on the verge of menarche, and a woman who is unable to control her irregular bleeding. While Luke does not locate the source of the woman's hemorrhaging, the Greek suggests a vaginal or uterine flow. Although commentators rush to speak of the woman's ritual impurity, following Lev 15.25–30 on irregular bleeding, that is not the heart of the story. Rather, the focus is on her desperate medical condition. She had lavishly spent her money on physicians, but neither they nor anyone else was able to cure her (**vs. 43**). Luke's focus is not on purity issues, but on the woman's physical health – her disability[20] – and her economic condition.[21]

The woman approaches Jesus from behind, unlike Jairus, who falls at Jesus' feet. She touches his "fringe," that is, his ritual "fringes" or, in Hebrew, *tzitzit*, worn by Jewish men to indicate their fidelity to Torah (Num 15.38). Her action results in her healing, as "immediately" the bleeding ceased. He has restored her to health, and to ritual purity.

Jesus asks "who touched me?" – he had felt the power flow out of him (**vs. 45**). Peter, unaware of the miracle, responds that an answer would be impossible to determine, for the crowds were pressing in on Jesus; in his calling Jesus "master" (*epistata*), readers by now realize that Peter has once again missed the boat, as it were (see 5.5). But Jesus recognizes his own physical reactions: he is as much in the body as the hemorrhaging woman: as she felt blood flow from her, so he felt the power flow from him (**vs. 46**).

---

[20]   See Candida Moss, "The Man with the Flow of Power: Porous Bodies in Mark 5:25–34," *JBL* 130.4 (2011): 643–62.

[21]   Amy-Jill Levine, "Discharging Responsibility: Matthean Jesus, Biblical Law, and Hemorrhaging Woman," in D. R. Bauer and M. A. Powell (eds.), *Treasures Old and New: Recent Contributions to Matthean Studies.* Symposium Series 1 (Atlanta: Scholars Press, 1996), 379–97; reprint in Levine with Blickenstaff (eds.), *Feminist Companion to Matthew*, 70–87.

His question about the one who touched him is an honest one. Luke depicts Jesus as living a genuinely human life: he can ask who touched him; he can feel power flow from him; he can hunger and thirst, and die. He can also, as 2.52 puts it, grow in wisdom over time. Jesus' life is not a charade. He is not pretending not to know something here; he is genuinely asking for information. Jesus' genuine humanity involves partaking of limitations of knowledge, and time, and space, and power, and mortality, the five limitations all humans experience.[22]

The woman recognizes that she has to acknowledge her actions. She falls down before Jesus, as had the man from Gerasa and Jairus, but whereas the first begged Jesus to leave him alone and the second begged Jesus to heal his daughter, this woman makes a public declaration of her miraculous healing. She announces to all the people both *why* she touched him and *how* she received a healing (**vs. 47**).

Jesus affirms her healing and her testimony by calling her "daughter," a label that highlights her own relationship to Jesus (**vs. 48a**), who had not that long ago noted, "my mother and my brothers are those who hear the word of God and do it" (8.21). Here a daughter is added to the family. The term does not, however, signal that she had been earlier removed from the family of Israel or that she was an outcast. Jesus will also call the woman who had been bent over a "daughter of Abraham," and on his way to his death he consoles the "daughters of Jerusalem." The term also has a strong literary function, since the woman's actions had interrupted Jesus' journey to the home of Jairus and his dying daughter.

The woman had come to Jesus in hopes of being healed; Jesus confirms that her "faith" or "trust" (Greek: *pistis*) has saved her (**vs. 48b**). This faith is certainly in Jesus' ability to do the healing; it may also incorporate a sense of her faith in herself. She had the courage to approach a miracle worker, who could just as easily have killed her as cured her. At the end of her story, Jesus dismisses her. She receives no commission, like that of the healed man in Gerasa. Unlike the women healed in 8.1–3, she does not, as far as we know, become a disciple. Perhaps she returned to her home and experienced, for the first time in twelve years, what it felt like to be healthy.

The delay prompted by the woman's healing and subsequent testimony was fatal for the little girl. Even while Jesus was speaking, a messenger reports to Jairus that his daughter had died. Then, as if seeing that Jesus'

[22] The New Testament Epistle to the Hebrews says that Jesus experienced all natural human limitations, including temptations, but without sinning (Heb 4.15).

needs were more important than the death of a child, the messenger advises Jairus not to "trouble the teacher" (**vs. 49**). There is no word of consolation; just a notice to stop bothering Jesus. The messenger, perhaps unaware of Jesus' abilities and absent during the woman's healing and testimony, does not know what the reader knows, namely, that Jesus has the power to raise the dead. The story of the son of the widow of Nain has already indicated this power (7.11–17). Although Luke had reported that this story had "spread through all of Judea and the surrounding country" (7.17), apparently this messenger, in Galilee, missed the news. Jesus reassures Jairus: if he too has faith, like the healed woman, his daughter will be saved (**vs. 50**). Jesus' earlier comments to the hemorrhaging woman (vs. 48) echo in his assurance to the ruler: faith and healing can come together.

Entering the ruler's house, Jesus takes, together with the father and mother of the dead girl, the three disciples in his inner circle, the ones who will witness the Transfiguration in the next chapter and who will eventually fail him at his arrest (**vs. 51**). Faith can be fragile, as the Parable of the Sower indicates. At the same time, the faith of the outsider, whether the hemorrhaging woman or the synagogue ruler and his wife, can be stronger than those who had witnessed other miracles or received Jesus' special teaching. The people weeping outside (**vs. 52**) may have included other disciples and other members of the Twelve – faith and grief are not mutually exclusive; belief in resurrection does not obviate the pain one feels on the death of a loved one. As Mark's Gospel shows poignantly in the account of another devastated father, the cry, "I believe; help my unbelief" (Mark 9.24) has its place.

When Jesus says that the child is not dead but sleeping (**vs. 52**; see 1 Thess 5.10 for "sleep" as a euphemism for "death"), the people outside laugh (**vs. 53**). They are not ridiculing Jesus; the laugh is the laugh of bitterness; it is not dissimilar to the (male) disciples' later dismissal of the women's proclamation of the resurrection (24.11). Assurance of resurrection, even for those who believe, is not always enough.

Jesus takes the girl's hand and calls to her, "Child, arise" (**vs. 54**). The same scene will replay in Acts, when Peter will say to the disciple in Joppa, "Tabitha, get up" (Acts 9.40). The two scenes are connected not only through the resuscitation of a corpse, but through tradition history as well. In Mark's Gospel, when Jesus raises Jairus's daughter, he says to her, in Aramaic, "Talitha cum," which Mark (5.41) translates as "Little girl, get up." Luke, as we've seen, drops Aramaic phrases. But perhaps Mark's Aramaic is meant to be heard, quietly in the background, in the story of Tabitha. The name "Tabitha" and the Aramaic term "Talitha" are distinguished by only one letter.[23]

The child rises, and Jesus commands that she be given something to eat (**vs. 55**). The issue here is less concern for her hunger than demonstration of the reality of the raising. Ghosts do not eat; living bodies do. The child's eating shows she is back among the living, just as Jesus' eating at the end of Luke's Gospel (24.42–43) proves that he is not a ghost. To eat is to live, and in the later Church contexts, to eat is also to celebrate the resurrected Christ and to anticipate one's own resurrection and participation in the heavenly banquet. Luke tells us that the parents were astounded (**vs. 56a**). Just as having faith does not preclude mourning, so too it does not preclude surprise. Faith is not something that predicts order in the world; it does not override emotions.

The chapter concludes with the motif of the "messianic secret" known from Mark's Gospel: Jesus commands the people present not to report the healing (**vs. 56b**). There are several explanations for this command to secrecy. It is possible that Jesus is not interested in drawing attention to himself, although given mass public healings and feedings, including the earlier raising of the widow's son in Nain, this sudden move away from self-promotion would be odd. The silence does contrast with the public proclamation by the healed woman and the command to the man exorcised of demons to proclaim his healing, and who healed him.

More skeptical scholars, from the time of Wilhelm Wrede, proposed that the followers of Jesus invented this motif in order to explain why belief in Jesus was not prominent among the Jews in Galilee and Judea. This explanation too fails to account for all the healings and miracles done in public. The claim that Jesus is seeking to keep a low profile given Rome and its client kings' antipathy to popular teachers fails by that same argument. The claim that Jesus does not want to be known as a miracle worker but as one who suffers and dies, so that he silences most miracle recipients and speaks in parables to the crowds, but announces his suffering "plainly" (see Mark 8.32), fits Mark's Gospel better than it does Luke's narrative.

Perhaps the concern here is for the child: an adult is in the better position to handle the attention and to respond by proclaiming the Gospel (so, e.g., the man from Gerasa healed of demon possession or the woman healed of bleeding). Jesus elsewhere displays particular concern for children (e.g., 9.47–48; 18.16).

---

[23]   See Amy-Jill Levine, "Tabitha/Dorcas, Spinning Off Cultural Criticism," in Harold W. Attridge, Dennis R. MacDonald, and Clare K. Rothschild (eds.), *Delightful Acts: New Essays on Canonical and Non-canonical Acts* (WUNT 391; Tübingen: Mohr Siebeck, 2017), 41–65.

Or perhaps the evangelists do not want to publicize Jesus' doing a healing for a *synagogue* ruler. For a movement defined in opposition to synagogues, as that signature scene in Luke 4 and most of Luke's other references to synagogues suggest, the news of this healing would compromise the opposition. But Ben doubts Luke has such an agenda. An agenda to show the Jesus movement is distinct and stands somewhat *apart* from the synagogue is not the same thing as an agenda to define one's movement *over against* the synagogue. Whatever the reason for the command to secrecy, the command has, obviously, been broken, since the story is recorded in all three Synoptic Gospels.

BRIDGING THE HORIZONS

1. On Labels

Luke identifies the woman who anoints Jesus as "a sinner," and readers frequently move to the classification of the woman's sin as "prostitution," as if women are capable of no other type of sin, and as if the only way the woman could obtain her expensive perfume was by selling her body. Labels matter. Barbara Reid suggests that the woman should be called "the woman who loved much" rather than "the sinner," for that is how Jesus understands her.[24] How we label people, indeed how we label biblical accounts, may tell us more about our own sense of priorities than about what the biblical narrative actually suggests.

Similarly, we may call the possessed man in Gerasa the "Gerasene demoniac," or the "healed man in the Decapolis" or "Legion." The Parable of the Sower could just as easily, and perhaps more accurately, be called "The Parable of the Different Soils." The "hemorrhaging woman" could be "the woman who seeks medical care for herself" or even "the woman who displays courage and faith." Jesus in the next chapter asks his disciples, "Who do you say that I am?" (9.20). Labels matter.

2. On Possession

Luke tells us that Mary Magdalene had been possessed by seven demons. Whether we see in the demons the seven deadly sins (pride, avarice,

---

[24] Barbara E. Reid, "'Do You See This Woman?' A Liberative Look at Luke 7.36–50 and Strategies for Reading Other Lucan Stories Against the Grain," in Levine and Blickenstaff (eds.), *Feminist Companion to Luke*, 106–20. For a review of the relationship between the woman's identity and the sin, see in the same volume Teresa Hornsby, "The Woman Is a Sinner/The Sinner Is a Woman," 121–32.

gluttony, lust, jealousy, laziness, and anger), count up the number of forms possession can take according to ancient views (e.g., muteness, deafness, blindness, paralysis, fever, self-injury, injuring others), or simply take the number "seven" as indicating the severity of her condition, Mary's situation is dire. Today, it is not unusual to see the equation of ancient demon possession with what we would call issues of mental health. The simplistic equation is more than unscientific; it is dangerous. It denies what we have learned about how our minds and bodies function; it stigmatizes those who are suffering; and in extreme cases it can lead to abusive forms of treatment.

Today, people who have been diagnosed with mental illness or even who have been under the care of a psychologist or psychiatrist can be regarded as at best untrustworthy. In antiquity, being healed by a major figure could, conversely, indicate status or credibility. For example, Jesus tells the man healed in Gerasa, "return home and declare how much God has done for you" (8.39). Thus, the exorcism stories open up the possibility not only of healing, but of respecting the voices of those who had been healed.

The story of Legion introduces another subject worth discussion: the causes of mental health issues. Contemporary studies of the effects of violence – in the household, in the country – show that mental health disorders can accompany trauma. The most well-known diagnosis in this category is posttraumatic stress disorder (PTSD). Graham Twelftree, author of a major study of exorcism accounts in the New Testament and who himself questions this diagnosis, nevertheless notes: "It is currently popular to argue that possession and mental illness was caused or at least exacerbated by social tension, and was a socially acceptable form of oblique protest against, or escape from, oppression."[25] Legion's name signifies the incursion of foreign troops into an area; the violence the man does to his own body, together with his superhuman strength, suggests that he is acting out what the Empire had done to his land and his people.

Yet Legion's case is a distinct one in the Gospels. All the other exorcism accounts concern people who are embedded in apparently healthy familial and community systems. Next, life in Gerasa, at least as far as Luke indicates, was not one of traumatic foreign incursion: the people were doing just fine, until Jesus showed up and killed off their livelihood. Thus, the name "Legion" may be more symbolic of the devastation of the man's condition than actually indicative of Roman troops destroying the social

[25]   Graham Twelftree, *Jesus the Exorcist: A Contribution to the Study of the Historical Jesus* (Tübingen: Mohr//Peabody, MA: Hendrickson, 1993), 143.

infrastructure of the Decapolis. And yet, that very name must speak to the view of the Empire. Were a person today to speak of the demonic power as "my name is drone," we might have a near-equivalent.

Finally, the stories of exorcisms invite us to consider how we judge alternative ways of viewing the world. Some of Jesus' detractors, seeing that he is behaving in a manner that could be construed as socially aberrant (e.g., encouraging followers to leave their homes and families, associating with agents of the occupation government such as tax collectors, speaking of himself as the means by which the kingdom of God is breaking in) accuse him of having a demon. Mark 3.21 has "those with him" – likely Jesus' family – claim that Jesus is "beside himself" (the Greek term here is the basis of the word "ecstasy"). The next verse depicts the charge that Jesus "has Beezebul" (i.e., is possessed by a demon). John 8.48 and 10.20 both recount the accusation that Jesus is possessed. These charges accrue, cross-culturally, to visionaries: Abraham, Moses, Jesus, Mohammed, and so on. Celsus asked about the resurrection of Jesus, "But who says this? A hysterical [or crazed] female, as you say, and perhaps some of those who were deluded by the same sorcery?" (Origin, *Contra Cels.* 2.55). What is insanity to one person is Gospel Truth to the other.[26]

3. On Christology

It is one of the besetting problems of the conservative Christian community (whether Catholic, Protestant, or Orthodox) that it tends to devalue or even ignore the humanity of Jesus. Jesus is seen as sort of 90 percent divine and 10 percent human. But Docetism, along with Gnostic portrayals of a Christ without a real human body and human nature, was quite rightly condemned by the early Church as heretical. The formula agreed upon by the wiser early Church writers was "truly human, and truly divine," or as we might say, 100 percent both. From a Christological point of view, how do the writers of the NT convey this idea?

One early answer is found in Phil 2.5–11, which speaks of the preexistent Son of God, who had equality with God and was in very nature God. Nonetheless, he did not take advantage of that, but instead stripped himself, limited himself, and took on a human nature and life. In other words, Phil 2 presents a divine condescension where the divine Son accepts limitations of

---

[26]   See the classic study by Michel Foucault, *Madness and Civilization: A History of Insanity in the Age of Reason* (New York: Random House/Vintage Books, 1965).

time and space and knowledge and power and mortality without ceasing to be the divine Son. Ben suspects that Luke operates very much with the same paradigm that we find in Phil 2.5–11 in his understanding of the relationship of the human and the divine in Jesus. Amy-Jill suggests both that Luke does not have a systematic Christology: Jesus may be *conceived or born* as divine (1.35), or as Acts 2.36 puts it, he *is made* both "Lord and Christ," or becomes divine, after his death and resurrection.

In Ben's view, Luke carefully avoids having Jesus called "Lord" (with a capital "L") in dialogues in the Gospel before the resurrection, but in the narrative framework the term appears (as we see in the widow of Nain story in Luke 7). Amy-Jill is not convinced by this argument. Since Jesus' interlocutors frequently address him as "lord," it is up to the reader to determine the import of the title.

Ben concludes that Luke knows that Jesus' roles during his earthly ministry were not the same as he was believed to take on thereafter. Jesus did not assume the role of risen Lord until after Easter. This is why, for example, Acts 2.36 has Peter remark, 'This Jesus whom you crucified, God *has made* both Lord and Christ." In short, Luke is careful in portraying Jesus before and after Easter, approaching the matter not only as a convinced Christian, but also as a historian who wants to do justice to the humanity of the historical Jesus.

Luke 9 Mission, Transfiguration, and Predictions of Death

MISSION OF THE TWELVE AND THE DEATH OF THE BAPTIZER

¹ Then Jesus called the twelve together and gave them power and authority over all demons and to cure diseases, ² and he sent them out to proclaim the kingdom of God and to heal. ³ He said to them, "Take nothing for your journey, no staff, nor bag, nor bread, nor money – not even an extra tunic. ⁴ Whatever house you enter, stay there, and leave from there. ⁵ Wherever they do not welcome you, as you are leaving that town shake the dust off your feet as a testimony against them." ⁶ They departed and went through the villages, bringing the good news and curing diseases everywhere.

⁷ Now Herod the ruler heard about all that had taken place, and he was perplexed, because it was said by some that John had been raised from the dead, ⁸ by some that Elijah had appeared, and by others that one of the ancient prophets had arisen. ⁹ Herod said, "John I beheaded; but who is this about whom I hear such things?" And he tried to see him.

¹⁰ᵃ On their return the apostles told Jesus all they had done.

FEEDING FIVE THOUSAND (PLUS)

¹⁰ᵇ He took them with him and withdrew privately to a city called Bethsaida. ¹¹ When the crowds found out about it, they followed him; and he welcomed them, and spoke to them about the kingdom of God, and healed those who needed to be cured.

¹² The day was drawing to a close, and the twelve came to him and said, "Send the crowd away, so that they may go into the surrounding villages and countryside, to lodge and get provisions; for we are here in a deserted place." ¹³ But he said to them, "You give them something to eat." They

said, "We have no more than five loaves and two fish – unless we are to go and buy food for all these people." [14] For there were about five thousand men. And he said to his disciples, "Make them sit down in groups of about fifty each." [15] They did so and made them all sit down.

[16] And taking the five loaves and the two fish, he looked up to heaven, and blessed and broke them, and gave them to the disciples to set before the crowd. [17] And all ate and were filled. What was left over was gathered up, twelve baskets of broken pieces.

JESUS' IDENTITY AND ITS RELATIONSHIP TO DISCIPLESHIP

[18] Once when Jesus was praying alone, with only the disciples near him, he asked them, "Who do the crowds say that I am?" [19] They answered, "John the Baptist; but others, Elijah; and still others, that one of the ancient prophets has arisen." [20] He said to them, "But who do you say that I am?" Peter answered, "The Messiah of God." [21] He sternly ordered and commanded them not to tell anyone, [22] saying, "The Son of Man must undergo great suffering, and be rejected by the elders, chief priests, and scribes, and be killed, and on the third day be raised."

[23] Then he said to them all, "If any want to become my followers, let them deny themselves and take up their cross daily and follow me. [24] For those who want to save their life will lose it, and those who lose their life for my sake will save it. [25] What does it profit them if they gain the whole world, but lose or forfeit themselves? [26] Those who are ashamed of me and of my words, of them the Son of Man will be ashamed when he comes in his glory and the glory of the Father and of the holy angels. [27] But truly I tell you, there are some standing here who will not taste death before they see the kingdom of God."

TRANSFIGURATION

[28] Now about eight days after these sayings Jesus took with him Peter and John and James, and went up on the mountain to pray. [29] And while he was praying, the appearance of his face changed, and his clothes became dazzling white. [30] Suddenly they saw two men, Moses and Elijah, talking to him. [31] They appeared in glory and were speaking of his departure, which he was about to accomplish at Jerusalem.

[32] Now Peter and his companions were weighed down with sleep; but since they had stayed awake, they saw his glory and the two men who stood

with him. ³³ Just as they were leaving him, Peter said to Jesus, "Master, it is good for us to be here; let us make three dwellings, one for you, one for Moses, and one for Elijah" – not knowing what he said. ³⁴ While he was saying this, a cloud came and overshadowed them; and they were terrified as they entered the cloud. ³⁵ Then from the cloud came a voice that said, "This is my Son, my Chosen; listen to him!" ³⁶ When the voice had spoken, Jesus was found alone. And they kept silent and in those days told no one any of the things they had seen.

HEALING THE CHILD SUFFERING SEIZURES

³⁷ On the next day, when they had come down from the mountain, a great crowd met him. ³ Just then a man from the crowd shouted, "Teacher, I beg you to look at my son; he is my only child. ³⁹ Suddenly a spirit seizes him, and all at once he shrieks. It convulses him until he foams at the mouth; it mauls him and will scarcely leave him. ⁴⁰ I begged your disciples to cast it out, but they could not."

⁴¹ Jesus answered, "You faithless and perverse generation, how much longer must I be with you and bear with you? Bring your son here." ⁴² While he was coming, the demon dashed him to the ground in convulsions. But Jesus rebuked the unclean spirit, healed the boy, and gave him back to his father. ⁴³ᵃ And all were astounded at the greatness of God.

INABILITY TO UNDERSTAND

⁴³ᵇ While everyone was amazed at all that he was doing, he said to his disciples, ⁴⁴ "Let these words sink into your ears: The Son of Man is going to be betrayed into human hands." ⁴⁵ But they did not understand this saying; its meaning was concealed from them, so that they could not perceive it. And they were afraid to ask him about this saying.

⁴⁶ An argument arose among them as to which one of them was the greatest. ⁴⁷ But Jesus, aware of their inner thoughts, took a little child and put it by his side, ⁴⁸ and said to them, "Whoever welcomes this child in my name welcomes me, and whoever welcomes me welcomes the one who sent me; for the least among all of you is the greatest."

⁴⁹ John answered, "Master, we saw someone casting out demons in your name, and we tried to stop him, because he does not follow with us." ⁵⁰ But Jesus said to him, "Do not stop him; for whoever is not against you is for you."

REJECTION IN SAMARIA

⁵¹ When the days drew near for him to be taken up, he set his face to go to Jerusalem. ⁵² And he sent messengers ahead of him. On their way, they entered a village of the Samaritans to make ready for him; ⁵³ but they did not receive him, because his face was set toward Jerusalem. ⁵⁴ When his disciples James and John saw it, they said, "Lord, do you want us to command fire to come down from heaven and consume them?" ⁵⁵ But he turned and rebuked them. ⁵⁶ Then they went on to another village.

⁵⁷ As they were going along the road, someone said to him, "I will follow you wherever you go." ⁵⁸ And Jesus said to him, "Foxes have holes, and birds of the air have nests; but the Son of Man has nowhere to lay his head."

⁵⁹ To another he said, "Follow me." But he said, "Lord, first let me go and bury my father." ⁶⁰ But Jesus said to him, "Let the dead bury their own dead; but as for you, go and proclaim the kingdom of God."

⁶¹ Another said, "I will follow you, Lord; but let me first say farewell to those at my home." ⁶² Jesus said to him, "No one who puts a hand to the plow and looks back is fit for the kingdom of God."

Just as the accounts of the desperate father with a dying daughter and the equally desperate woman with a chronically severe medical condition are sandwiched together or "intercalated" in Luke 8, such that one story helps to interpret the other, so the account of the mission of the Twelve and the confirmation of John's death are intercalated. The import is one of warning: proclaim your truth, and you may be put to death by the powers-that-be. The authority one has over personal distress, whether demons or disease, granted by Jesus, is greater than the authority that any earthly power holds. Yet those earthly powers still have their strength.

Chapter 9 continues to juxtapose the earthly with the heavenly. Interplays of the question of Jesus' identity and the role of the disciples show the connections between heaven and earth even as they reveal new mysteries, epitomized by the Transfiguration. The glories of the divine contrast with the desperation of a father with a suffering child; the miracles of healing and the models of humility contrast with the disciples' desire for personal advancements and the refusal of hospitality to Jesus. Chapter 9 also begins Jesus' journey to Jerusalem, and the road is found already to be rough.

MISSION OF THE TWELVE AND THE DEATH OF THE BAPTIZER

Jesus summons the Twelve, including Judas Iscariot, who so far appears to be a successful disciple. Yet Luke has already identified him as Jesus' betrayer. The warnings the Parable of the Sower issues about infertile soil and thorns lurk in the background. Questions of loyalty and insider versus outsider status will continue in the chapter: who is the loyal one and who the traitor? Who is on "our side" and who is the "outsider?" Of what value, if any, have such labels? To the Twelve, Jesus gives "power and authority" (Greek: *dynamis* and *exousia*) over demons and disease (**vs. 1**). The authority is not for their self-aggrandizement, but for "curing" people. Their role is not only to be "fishers" but also "healers," of body and mind. Jesus shares his gifts with his disciples, as is appropriate, for they will be the ones to represent him following his ascension. In the previous chapter, he had performed healings and exorcisms; like a teacher training his students, he showed them the "how"; now, with the authority and the power he also grants them, they can move from the watching to the doing.

Such authority begins with the Twelve, but it is not to be limited to them. On the one hand, Judas will leave the group; on the other, followers such as Saul of Tarsus will have this same authority. Whether followers who lived past the apostolic age continue to have this authority to heal and to exorcise, or whether it as well as other charismatic gifts (cf. Acts 2) ceased with the close of the New Testament story, depends on the teachings of each denomination. There are, however, plenty of early Church stories about the continuation of such gifts and miraculous activities well past the apostolic age. When anyone provides healing of body and spirit, one could claim that the divine message is present: healing the weak is part of the proclamation of the Kingdom (**vs. 2**). If the healings brought people to listen to the disciples or made them more curious about the source of their power, so much the better for the Church.

The hemorrhaging woman had spent all her funding on physicians (8.43); Jesus' disciples, in the role of healers, will not accept monetary payment for their works. To the contrary, they are to model their dependence on others. Jesus sends them into the harvest with nothing to protect them, and so no signs of status. There will be no staff to ward away animals or thieves; they will have no bag, for there is nothing they need to carry; they will have no food, and so they must rely either on the bounty of nature or the generosity of strangers; they have no funds to purchase bread or a room for the night; they have one garment only (**vs. 3**). Despite having nothing, they were never at a loss; Jesus later asks them: "When I sent you out without a purse, bag, or sandals, did you lack anything?" They respond, "Not a thing" (22.35). There was the system of standing hospitality that could be relied on in one village or another in the land of Israel, but the people had to be willing to provide it for the disciples of a controversial teacher.

Jesus did not expect *all* his followers, let alone the global population, to divest and become itinerant missionaries. Mary and Martha, whom we meet in the next chapter, indicate the importance of followers able to provide hospitality to the missionaries. The lesson is rather one of mutual support and gift exchange: householders provide the itinerants hospitality; itinerants provide the houses not only healing and fellowship, but also an image of interdependence, a demonstration that material possessions need not determine who we are, or "choke" us of our responsibilities (the Parable of the Sower again). For those who have the calling, the vocation, to become an itinerant, Jesus shows another way of being in the world: the primary duty of these disciples is not marriage and family, but living as if they had a foot already in the Kingdom.

Having one foot in the Kingdom does not mean jumping from house to house. Jesus instructs the disciples to stay in the home that welcomes them (**vs. 4**). The injunction has at least three practical values. It prevents the disciples from seeking better accommodations; it prevents the possible embarrassment to the members of the household should the disciples leave; and it allows the disciples to work with the householders to establish a new basis for the mission. The modern term for this system would be something on the order of "franchising." The house where the disciples stayed might become known as a place that welcomes strangers. In fact, the Greek word often translated "hospitality" is *xenophilia*, which means kindness to or love of strangers.

Despite the high value placed on hospitality, not all householders would be thrilled with the idea of a wandering charismatic sharing accommodations with the family; nor would all people find warnings of eschatological tribulation, let alone familial disruption, welcome. Thus, Jesus reminds the disciples of what the parable of the various soils already indicated: not all missions take root (**vs. 5**). The disciples will be rejected. However, they are not to curse those who reject them, but neither are they to leave without any symbolic gesture. They should shake the dust off their feet "as a witness" or "testimony" against those who did not receive them. One does not force the Kingdom upon others, but neither should the rejection of the mission go unnoted. With the dust shaken off and thus a "clean start," the disciples prepare to go to the next house, the next village.

Luke records an entirely successful initiative. The Gospel is proclaimed; healings are performed (**vs. 6**). No notice is given of the length of time the mission took, or where exactly the disciples went, or how many people were evangelized or healed. No record other than the Gospels exists for this successful mission. In Matthew's Gospel, although there is a full missionary discourse (ch. 10), there is in fact no mission. For Luke, while the narrative of a successful mission indicates the transferal of part of Jesus' authority to his followers, it also has another purpose: to show that the mission can be dangerous.

Suddenly, Luke introduces Herod the Tetrach. Readers might have anticipated this appearance: Luke earlier noted that John the Baptizer had condemned the ruler not only for marrying his brother's wife and thus violating Torah, but also for "all the evil things" he had done (3.19). Herod remains a danger to John, to Jesus, and to those who would follow them. Herod had heard what had been occurring – stories about Jesus had been widely circulating, and now the disciples were repeating the stories and performing actions to accompany them. Herod's first reaction is to think that John the Baptizer, whom he had beheaded, had returned from the dead (**vs. 7**). The irony is that it will be Jesus, not John, who will return. Others, hearing about the healings, presume that Elijah has reappeared; thereby, Luke reminds readers of Jesus' synagogue sermon, wherein he evokes Elijah as the one who visited the widow of Zarepath (4.26). Since Elijah had never died, and since he was expected by some to usher in the messianic age, such speculation is logical. Still others think that another ancient prophet, or a prophet like Moses (Deut 18.15), had appeared (**vs. 8**). But Luke has made clear that Jesus is not Elijah, or an ancient prophet; he is something greater. The story of the Transfiguration (9.28–36) will secure this point.

But Luke has here, pardon the expression, gotten ahead of the story, for the account of John's death has not yet been told. The next verse fills in the gap. Herod admits that he had John decapitated (**vs. 9a**). Luke omits the account of Herodias and her daughter, the banquet, the dance, and the head on the silver platter (Mark 6). Explaining why something is *not* present inevitably requires guess work. Luke's sources may have lacked the story; Luke may avoid portraying women in positions of any authority; Luke may wish to focus on the Herodian rulers – Antipas, Agrippa I (Acts 12), Agrippa II (Acts 23) – and the challenge Jesus, Peter, and Paul pose to their authority; Luke may want to downplay John in the role of hero, and so on.

Herod's appearance in Luke 9 ends with a question about Jesus: "Who is this one?" (**vs. 9b**). As the Gospel continues, readers are increasingly able to provide an answer. Herod will have the chance to ask his question directly later, in a story unique to Luke's Gospel (23.6–13), but he never gets the right answer.

This section of Luke's narrative ends with its own subtle answer: in response to Herod's question, the disciples – here called "apostles," the ones "sent out" – return to Jesus and report on the success of the mission. Jesus withdraws to Bethsaida (**vs. 10**), out of Herod's control and in the region of Gaulanitis ruled by Herod Philip. The time has not come for him to risk direct political confrontation, but the threat remains.

FEEDING FIVE THOUSAND (PLUS)

In Bethsaida, Jesus repeats what he had instructed his disciples to do: proclaim the Kingdom and perform healings (**vs. 11**). Those tasks will never be fully completed until the eschaton arrives. As the day comes to a close, the Twelve advise Jesus to send the crowds to the neighboring villages so that they can find food and lodging (**vs. 12**). They thereby advise him to tell the crowds what he had told them earlier: rely on the hospitality of others. Given Jewish hospitality practices, just as the disciples could find a place to rest among the people, so could the crowds.

The reciprocity system is about to change. Instead of sending the crowds out, Jesus orders the disciples to feed them. Since they also had brought no provisions with them, the disciples are incredulous: they have limited resources; they are not about to purchase food for the thousands of people surrounding them; and they are in the wilderness, not the marketplace (**vs. 13**). Five loaves and two fish do not go very far. Unless they do.

Jesus advises the disciples to have the crowds sit in groups of fifty (**vs. 14**), which they arrange (**vs. 15**). This is already a minor miracle, as crowds are not usually given to orderly placement. There would be one hundred sets of people, and likely more than fifty per group, as Luke does not appear to have counted the women and the children (see Matt 14.21). Then Jesus takes the bread and the fish, looks to heaven to show his continual relationship to his Father, blesses the food, breaks it into pieces, and distributes it to the disciples so that they can distribute it to the people (**vs. 16**). The verse will remind Luke's readers of the Eucharist, the communion or memorial meal, in which Jesus took bread, blessed it, broke it, and distributed it (22.19; cf. 24.30). It should also remind biblically literate readers of the manna that fed the children of Israel when they too were in the wilderness (Exod 16.22). To this day in traditional Jewish households, at a meal a blessing is said and the bread distributed to the people at the table. On the Sabbath, the practice usually finds two loaves of *challah*, braided egg-based bread, because of the double portion of manna given in the wilderness so that collection was not required on the day of rest. Jesus' actions are thus entirely normal for a Jewish meal and, given the number present and the ability of the disciples to feed them all, entirely extraordinary. The thousands eat to satisfaction, and the disciples take up twelve baskets of leftovers (**vs. 17**). A number of readers see in this scene the miracle of sharing, and sharing can have miraculous import. But that is not what the Gospel writers are suggesting. For Jesus' early followers, the bread and fish are multiplied no more and no less miraculously as the blind are granted sight and the dead are raised.

This miraculous feeding is the one miracle, aside from the resurrection of Jesus, recounted in all four Gospels, but each evangelist provides a distinctive presentation. Whereas in John 6.14–15, the crowd reacts with the acclamation that Jesus is "the prophet who is to come into the world" and then acts on this acclamation by seeking to make Jesus the king, Luke laconically ends the scene with the notice of the leftovers. It is up to Luke's readers to draw their own conclusions regarding what they have just been told.

JESUS' IDENTITY

The scene shifts, with Jesus somehow having removed himself from the crowds (how he did this is not Luke's concern). He prays – praying is a Lucan theme that will return in 9.28–29 – and then he asks his own question to the disciples: what is the crowd saying about him (**vs. 18**)? What does one say about someone who can facilitate the feeding of thousands of people with limited resources?

The disciples provide the answers, which resemble Herod's own suspicions recorded in 9.7–8: John the Baptizer or Elijah or a prophet (**vs. 19**). Luke repeats the list of candidates in order to show that these answers are incorrect. Then Jesus changes the question: what do the disciples think? That is, have they been able to move beyond popular acclamation or public rumor and get to the heart of the message? Peter, answering for his companions, gets the right answer: "The Messiah (Greek: *Christos*) of God" (**vs. 20**). The answer is correct, but it is also partial. The term "Messiah" or "Christ" had multiple connotations at the time: the Messiah could be a military leader such as Cyrus of Persia, called "the Lord's Messiah" or "the Lord's anointed" in Isa 45.1. He could be a prophet, or a shepherd, a king, or a priest. For the Gospels, the concern is not "is Jesus the Messiah?" – the evangelists all agree that he is. The question is, "what kind of Messiah is he?"

Jesus here provides another partial answer to this question. He begins by repeating the command to secrecy (**vs. 21**), such as the one he gave to the synagogue ruler, his wife, and the disciples who witnessed the raising of the dead girl (8.56). For the Gospels, the meaning of Jesus' being the Messiah cannot be fully understood apart from the cross. Miracles do not make a Messiah; no early Jewish text aside from the Gospel accounts suggests that one of the messianic signs was the performing of healings and exorcisms. To have authority over demons and to cure ailing bodies and minds are traits not limited to Jesus, so these are not to be taken as messianic signs, or at least they are not *distinctively* messianic in character.

What determines, in part, Jesus' messianic identity is that he will suffer and die, and on the third day, be raised (**vs. 22**). This was also not part of common messianic beliefs. The "Son of Man" was a known title, but he was not one who suffered. Luke had used this title earlier to speak of what the "son of man" signified: the Son of Man had authority to forgive sins (5.24) and was "lord of the Sabbath" (6.5); the disciples had heard that they would be persecuted "on account of the Son of Man" (6.22); the Son of Man was himself accused of being a drunkard and a glutton (7.34) – but nothing about death and then resurrection. Unlike Mark 8/Matt 16, where Peter rejects this teaching, here the disciples are silent. These silent disciples include the women, since 24.6 makes clear that they too had heard, from Jesus, that he would be crucified and then raised.

They continue to remain silent when Jesus predicts not only his suffering, but theirs. Not only Jesus would suffer, but so would his followers, as he had already indicated in the beatitude (6.22; cf. 21.12). To follow means not only to participate in Jesus' authority to heal and exorcise, and not only to proclaim the Kingdom, but to put the mission ahead of any personal interests. To be a follower means to deny oneself. "You must take up your own cross," Jesus tells them (**vs. 23**). But Luke adds "daily" or "day by day" to the injunction: the point here is not to submit to capital punishment; it is to act as if one has already given up one's life. The focus is on willingness to sacrifice for others – rather than on the self. At the same time, those who "take up the cross" are imitating their Lord.

Jesus restates his injunction in the next verse: self-interest will lead to destruction; denial of the self in service to others results in salvation (**vs. 24**). A person can gain all the goods in the cosmos, but lose the eternal rest (**vs. 25**). The title "Son of Man" then returns, when Jesus proclaims his own heavenly authority: he will return in glory, as the eschatological judge, and the terms of his judgment are people's response to him and his message, his identity, and his teaching (**vs. 26**). The stress on his "words" means that to be a disciple is not only to proclaim his resurrection or his Lordship, but to attend to his Kingdom message regarding how one lives in the world. The shame and pain of the cross will be transformed into the glory of the resurrected Jesus, accompanied no longer by sinners, but by angels.

This difficult section ends with an even more difficult message: the kingdom will come before some of the disciples hearing Jesus' teaching will die (**vs. 27**). The verse is a crucible of interpretations. For some readers then and now, the Kingdom has not yet come, since Jesus has not yet returned, and therefore he was wrong: everyone listening to his words that day has been long dead. For others, Jesus is speaking to all readers at all times and so teaching that at some point – perhaps in the reader's own time – the Kingdom will break in fully. Meanwhile, the teaching about it must continue. Or perhaps Luke saw the kingdom manifest on earth with the growth of the Church, such that the spread of the mission throughout the earth, or at least to Rome, is indicative of the Kingdom. Or again, perhaps we can all see the Kingdom present, if we have eyes to see. Three disciples will soon see Jesus transfigured and so have a glimpse of the Kingdom. But that glimpse is also afforded to those who are healed, who are shown and show hospitality, who risk death for the sake of others. The Kingdom may be in the future, but it is also present; as Jesus will later teach, "The Kingdom of God is among you" (17.21).

TRANSFIGURATION

Among those present for Jesus' declaration that they would see the Kingdom were Peter, James, and John. These three apostles, who had just seen Jesus raise Jairus's daughter from the dead and so witnessed the Kingdom proleptically, now see Jesus "transfigured" – the Greek states that the "outward form of his face became other" (Greek: *heteros*). This vision comes eight days after Jesus' first passion prediction. The number could indicate the "new week" or "new time" he inaugurates. It also anticipates the resurrection, because the "first day" of the week is also the "eighth day" if one begins the count from the week before. More subtly, the eighth day is the day infant Jewish boys are circumcised, so covenantal language provides part of the background. Jesus had spoken about his death, and about his being raised. The Transfiguration makes visceral both conditions.

Jesus takes the disciples who had witnessed the raising of Jairus's daughter to a mountain to pray (**vs. 28**). Although tradition since the time of Origen (185–254) claims that the site is Mt. Tabor (and some think Mt. Hermon, the tallest mountain in the area, makes better sense), Luke is uninterested in geographical precision. Mountains, symbolically, suggest a place closer to the divine (e.g., Exod 19.16–19; 34.2–9; 1 Kings 19.11–13), just as pits, trenches, and the abyss suggest a distance from heaven. The motif of prayer continues, for prayer facilitates a connection with the divine.

Jesus' change in appearance takes place while he was praying, and by noting this fact, Luke reinforces the relationship between the Kingdom and prayer. The change itself cannot be fully described; words fail in the attempt to describe something otherwordly. Luke states that Jesus' face "became other"; whatever he had looked like previously – the Gospels never provide a physical description of him – he now looked different (**vs. 29**). Alternatively, we might take the "face" as representing our outward appearance, with the otherness becoming a glimpse of the true self.[1] Matthew (17.2) and Mark (9.2) actually state that Jesus underwent a "metamorphosis" (that is the Greek term they use). That expression might remind readers of the classics such as Ovid's turn-of-the-era *Metamorphosis*, but Luke avoids any connection between Jesus and the Greek gods. It might also remind readers of the more recent text, Franz Kafka's *Metamorphosis*, and so bring out the terror of the scene, the inability to understand what is happening, the fear that something can happen to one's body.[2]

His clothing too had changed, to a perfect white, flashing as does lightning. Such changes occurred before in biblical tradition. Moses' face became so radiant when he was in direct conversation with God that he needed to put a veil over it before speaking to the people (Exod 34.29–35). The white clothes suggest an angelic appearance, as seen in Dan 12.3 and will be seen in this Gospel's description of the "two men in dazzling clothes" at the tomb (24.4).

The vision of the Kingdom continues with the appearance of Moses and Elijah (**vs. 30**). Although traditional readings see Moses as the representative of Torah and Elijah as the representative of the Prophetic texts, this allegorical reading is not necessary. Representatives are not needed, since Luke has already cited material from both collections as authoritative. The two figures from antiquity do represent the tradition, but their appearance at a Transfiguration has a deeper implication: together with Jesus, Moses and Elijah are people whose bodies cannot be found. Deut 34.6 states of Moses, "He was buried in a valley in the land of Moab, opposite Beth-Peor, but no

---

[1]   See George Aichele and Richard Walsh, "Metamorphosis, Transfiguration, and the Body," *Biblical Interpretation* 19.3 (2011): 253–75 (262).

[2]   Ibid., 253.

one knows his burial place to this day." Elijah left the earth accompanied by a whirlwind and a fiery chariot (2 Kings 2.11). Jesus' body will first be absent from the tomb and then ascend into heaven. The bodies of all three are marked by the miraculous: Moses from a living being to a buried corpse and yet, in bodily form, appearing at the Transfiguration; Elijah, remaining in human form, and descending from heaven; and Jesus, transfigured here, soon to be both a corpse and a resurrected body.

These three glorious beings do not speak of Torah or prophets; they speak to and of Jesus, and specifically about his departure (the Greek term is his "exodus"), to be "fulfilled" in Jerusalem (**vs. 31**). For biblical readers, the term "exodus" cannot be unchained from its connection with the liberation from Egypt and so the Passover.[3] Subtly, Luke has linked Jesus' Passion and death with both the escape from slavery and the protection, through the blood of the Passover lambs, of Israel's firstborn. Jesus has already announced that he is going to be crucified; "departure" sounds at first like a euphemism (e.g., "she passed away" rather than "she died"), but the term "exodus" coupled with the presence of Moses shows that the meaning is deeper. The language of "fulfilled" confirms the symbolic import of Luke's description. Jesus' death is no more an accident or arbitrary than was the Passover. It had, as far as Luke is concerned, been indicated already in the Scriptures of Israel. It was divine will.

Luke turns attention now to the disciples, "weighed down with sleep, but being awake" (**vs. 32**). This description is entirely apt: the Transfiguration of Jesus coupled with the appearance of Moses and Elijah would be something one might see in a dream, or in those moments of coming to consciousness upon waking up. They do not see Jesus but "his glory," the term associated with the God of Israel. In Hebrew, the term usually used to express this glory is *kavod*, which also has the connotation of "heaviness," as in "a weighty argument" or "gravitas." In Hebrew, the verse would have made a great pun: the weight of sleep versus the gravitas of the divine. Complicating this waking vision is their seeing the "two men" with Jesus. Only the four ascended the mountain; how the other two men came to be there is left to the disicples' imagination.

As soon as the disciples see them, Moses and Elijah begin to depart: to where, or how, Luke does not explain. Peter finally says something, but not

---

3   Susan R. Garrett, "Exodus from Bondage: Luke 9:31 and Acts 12:1–24," *CBQ* 52.4 (1990): 656–80, suggests, "Luke regarded the death, resurrection, and ascension as an 'exodus' because in these events Jesus, 'the one who is stronger,' led the people out of bondage to Satan" (659).

what others might have said. He does not say to Jesus, "What happened?" or, "You look splendid," or even, "My Lord!" Instead, he suggests building tents, one for each. Luke, again aptly, notes that Peter "did not know what he was saying" (**vs. 33**). Tents? Really? Perhaps Peter wanted them to remain, but the lesson is that the bodies of the three do not remain; we do not have access to them. What remains are the stories about them, and the guarantee from the Gospel that all three will return in bodily form.

How Peter recognizes Moses and Elijah goes unstated. But that earlier attention to bodies – dead and alive; present and absent – may provide a clue. Moses may be recognized either by his veil (a motif known elsewhere among Jesus' followers; cf. 2 Cor 3.13) or by the "shining" that shown from him (Exod 34.35); Elijah may be recognized by his clothing; as 2 Kings 1.8 notes, he was a "hairy man, with a leather belt around his waist." Whereas Matthew (3.4) and Mark (1.6) identify John the Baptizer as wearing a leather belt and so add to the connections they draw between the Baptizer and Elijah, Luke downplays that connection by omitting that description.

While Peter was speaking, a cloud overshadows them: whether the "them" is the disciples or Moses, Elijah, and Jesus, the grammar of the text does not say (**vs. 34**). However, biblical tradition does. Earlier, Luke had used the same Greek term translated "overshadow" to refer to the Holy Spirit, who will "overshadow" Mary (1.35). The term suggests mystery, and it also suggests, through this double usage, a change in the body. For Mary, it means new life in her womb; for Moses, Elijah, and Jesus, it means the transformation from living body, to corpse, to resurrected life. And the cloud means more than that: since it indicates divine presence (e.g., Exod 24.15–18; Ezek 1.4; 10.3–4), it serves here to hide and then claim the bodies of Moses and Elijah, as well as to provide the transition of Jesus from transfigured back to his familiar state. The disciples are terrified: if the cloud represents the divine, and if Moses, Elijah, and Jesus are all connected with the transition between life and death, then the disciples too have something to fear. Biblically literate readers will be reminded of the frightening theophany at Sinai (Exod 19–20), further referenced in Heb 12. 18–21.

From the cloud comes a voice, the voice of God. The voice – disembodied, unlike Moses, Elijah, and Jesus – announces that the disciples must focus not on Moses, not on Elijah, but on Jesus, "my son, the elect one"; to him they must listen (**vs. 35**). One could hunt through Israel's Scriptures for allusions or intertexts to help unpack this verse. For example, "chosen" or "elect" language can suggest Isa 42.1 ("Here is my servant ... my chosen ... I have put my spirit upon him; he will bring forth justice to the nations").

"Listen to him" could remind readers of Deut 18.15 ("The Lord your God will raise up for you a prophet like me [Moses] from among your own people; you shall listen to such a prophet"). This approach allows readers to interpret the divine voice as showing Jesus as the epitome and fulfillment of both the Prophets represented by Elijah and the citation from Isaiah and the Torah represented by Moses and the citation from Deuteronomy. Moreover, since the voice from heaven necessarily relates to the earlier voice from heaven heard at the baptism – "You are my Son, the beloved; with you I am well pleased" (3.22) – at the Transfiguration the meaning of Jesus' sonship develops. It is a sonship in complete agreement with Moses and Elijah. The Law and the Prophets no more disappear with the bodies of Moses and Elijah than the Gospel disappears with the ascended body of Jesus. Law, Prophets, and Gospel are all in continuity; the bodies are absent, but the words remain.

Remaining after the cloud departs is Jesus. Although the heavenly voice commanded the disciples to listen to Jesus, here Jesus remains silent. The disciples who witnessed his Transfiguration say nothing to anyone (**vs. 36**). Jesus did not command them to remain silent; here the choice is theirs. How the story was eventually told, and how it came to be recorded, no Gospel writer indicates. The author of 2 Peter hints at the process by which it came to be known: distinguishing between the "cleverly devised myths" (2 Pet 1.16) and the story of Jesus, he speaks of how "we ourselves heard this voice come from heaven while we were with him on the holy mountain" (1.18).

In 2 Cor 3.18, Paul speaks of how he and his congregation, "with unveiled faces, seeing the glory of the Lord as though reflected in a mirror, are being transformed [Greek: *meta-morphe*, whence "metamorphosis") into the same image from one degree of glory to another ..." What this transformation "looks" like will depend, until the eschaton, on the imagination of the listener. Dorothy Lee comes close to getting the picture: "The presence of such beauty at the transfiguration is palpable in the body of Jesus as it becomes translucent, redolent with light, depicting the union of divine and human, glory and flesh. The transfiguration is the epitome of incarnate beauty."[4] To describe a heavenly body, to describe what the "Kingdom of God" looks like, is a task finally for poets and artists; the words of narrative or history necessarily fail.

---

[4]   Dorothy Lee, "On the Holy Mountain: The Transfiguration in Scripture and Theology," *Colloquium* 36.2 (2004): 143–59 (154).

HEALING THE CHILD SUFFERING SEIZURES

On the "next day," the disciples are back to reality; they have the vision of the Transfiguration, but they also have in front of them the power of Satan. One cannot stay on the mountain forever (**vs. 37**). The crowd that greets the four who descend may have been waiting for Jesus. Before he took his disciples up the mountain, he had fed five thousand people. Perhaps the crowds are the same people, having waited those nine days for Jesus to return to them.

From the crowd, a man's shouting is heard: "Teacher," he calls out, "I have an only child, a boy ..." (**vs. 38**). Readers know what comes next: we have seen before the desperate parent, Jairus, seeking healing for his sick daughter; we have seen Jesus raise both Jairus's daughter and the son of the widow in Nain. The Gospel reinforces the pain of parents who witness their children in distress. In antiquity, infant mortality rates were high. This child's malady is not death but possession. A "spirit takes him" and "tears him apart" so that it "breaks him" (**vs. 39**). Speculation about the symptoms is common in the literature: epilepsy, autism, and so on. For Luke, the cause of the ailment is "a spirit." The Holy Spirit had "overshadowed" Mary, but this spirit is destroying a child; the face of Jesus had been transfigured into glory; the face of this child is foaming at the mouth. Images of the Kingdom of God and images of hell exist in the world.

The father does what any desperate parent would: he looks for help wherever he might find it. Jesus is absent on the mountain and Peter is worried about building tents; down below, on the ground, the father has been begging the remaining disciples – who were given "power and authority over all demons" (9.1) – to help him. And they were not able (**vs. 40**).

Jesus does not respond with the compassion he had for the widow of Nain or with the assurance he gave to Jairus and his wife. As if his face is now "made other" by anger, he addresses – whom? The crowd following him and demanding from him healings, exorcisms, and food? The father, seeking favors? The disciples, unable to perform the exorcism? Them all? – as a "faithless and perverse generation," and he speaks of how being with them is unendurable (**vs. 41**). Jesus, fully human, experiences his own emotional transformation. To go from the sublime experience of his changed body and encounter with Moses, Elijah, and the divine voice to the muck of human desperation proves almost to be too much. But the outburst does not last. He cannot but heal the child, so he tells the father to "bring your son."

The horror of the situation becomes evident as the demon throws the boy into seizures. But Luke notes curtly that Jesus "rebuked the unclean spirit." Then he hands the boy back to his father (**vs. 42**). No conversation is recorded between Jesus and the demon, no words of exorcism are pronounced. And no comment is made by the son or the father; as with the Transfiguration, words here fail. The son's face is no longer foaming; his body is no longer convulsing. For the father, the child has been transfigured, and what the father sees now, a healthy child, is an image of the Kingdom. The account ends with the notice that the people were amazed "at the greatness" of God (**vs. 43**). It would not be inappropriate to see Luke as suggesting that Jesus, in defeating the demon and healing the child, represents God on earth.

Before we leave this story, one loose end remains: why were the disciples unable to heal the child? In Mark's much longer version of this account (Mark 9.14–29), Jesus explains that with such demons, "This kind can come out only through prayer" (Mark 9.29). The impression is that for Mark, the disciples were first-year medical students who did not know what type of antibiotic to administer. In Matthew's version (Matt 17.14–20), the disciples failed because of their "little faith." Matthew then has Jesus state, "if you have faith the size of a mustard seed, you will say to this mountain, 'Move from here to there,' and it will move; and nothing will be impossible for you" (Matt 17.20). Neither diagnosis is helpful for Jesus' followers, or medical practitioners, who are dealing with certain cases. Not all healings happen. Luke does not seek to make excuses; just as well. Telling parents of ailing children that they need a better prayer, or a larger amount of faith, may worsen their situation. Should the child then fail to thrive, not recover, or die, then the parents will blame themselves for their insufficient prayer, their insufficient faith. Luke is more honest here. There is evil in the world, and until that Kingdom fully comes, attacks on the body and the mind will remain.

INABILITY TO UNDERSTAND

The second passion prediction comes in the context of the marveling over the exorcism (**vs. 43**). Not all evil has been eradicated, and nor does "marveling" over a miracle necessarily lead to bearing good fruit. Jesus tells his disciples, "Put into your ears these words," or, bluntly, "Pay attention." Hearing is to be active; they are not simply to listen to the words, but to understand them, to make them register. Luke is also talking to the readers, for they too are disciples or at least potentially disciples. The miracles and exorcisms are not as important as the cross (**vs. 44**). In this second prediction, Jesus does not mention his resurrection; the focus is on his being handed over (the Greek *paradidōmi* can also be translated "betray"). From the previous prediction, given to the apostles immediately after the epiphany on the mountain, they should know what "handed over" means.

But the disciples are not able to grasp the message. Anticipating the events on the road to Emmaus, where two disciples are unable to recognize the resurrected Christ and only in the breaking of bread realize his resurrected presence, Luke notes that the disciples could not understand his words, for the meaning "was hidden" from them. Nor did they have the courage to ask him what he meant (**vs. 45**). This short sentence is filled with both meaning and mystery. First, Luke does not explain what prompts their inability to understand. Was it the incongruity of knowing that a man who can control the sea, raise the dead, and exorcise demons could be arrested and killed? Was it a divine act (the verb "it was hidden" or "it was concealed" is in the passive voice) that prevented the disciples from knowing what would happen, so that they would not try to prevent it? Can we only fully grasp the truth of a death, let alone a resurrection, when it actually happens, and even then we might miss the meaning – as Matthew notes regarding the eleven disciples who first saw the resurrected Jesus, "some doubted" (Matt 28.17)? And second, the disciples' fear goes unexplained. Should one fear to raise questions? Were they afraid of showing their own ignorance, especially after Jesus' outburst about the "faithless and perverse generation" (vs. 41)? How does one move from fear to righteous action?

From lacking understanding and fearing to asks questions, the disciples devolve into engaging in petty squabbles. Ears that should have listened to Jesus' messages of service and compassion and self-denial have been closed. The irony is tragic: Jesus is talking about his death, and the disciples are arguing about their relative rank in their movement (**vs. 46**). Jesus does not ask them about this conversation directly: they are afraid to inquire about his passion; he, knowing their thoughts, has no need of questions.

Needed is a lesson, this one visual rather than given only in words (**vs. 47**). Jesus takes a child, places the child by his side, and then makes two pronouncements. First, he makes clear that the more important question is not "Who is the greatest," but "What should you do?"[5] The disciples are not to argue about rank; they are to welcome this child – any child – in

---

[5]   See Jerome Kodell, "Luke and the Children: The Beginning and End of the Great Interpolation (Luke 9:46–56; 18:9–23)," *CBQ* 49.3 (1987): 415–30, on Luke's changing the Marcan order of these statements.

Jesus' name, and thus they "welcome" or "receive" (the Greek bears both meanings) him (**vs. 48a**). Jesus is going away; one way of keeping his presence alive is to welcome those who lack power and authority, the most vulnerable, the ones most susceptible to attack. Next, he tells the disciples that in receiving him, they receive his Father, for it is the Father who sent the Son. The Greek word for "sent" is the same root as the term "apostle." Jesus is sending these disciples into the world as God had sent him. There is a relationship among them all, and that connection is all the status they need (**vs. 48b**).

Jesus concludes this instruction by returning to the question of rank: the least among them is the greatest (**vs. 48c**). The most important person – the one who most deserves our attention, our compassion – is the one who is the weakest and most vulnerable. This teaching is what liberation theologians refer to as the "preferential option for the poor." Whereas some commentators seek to draw a contrast here with Jewish teaching, which they see as regarding children as the ones who are to show obedience and need discipline,[6] there is no contrast at all. Jesus' teaching is fully in line with Deuteronomy, where the people particularly under divine protection are the poor, the widow, the orphan, and the stranger, and it is to these most vulnerable that people with resources should attend.

Changing the subject from the little child back to status, John – one of the three insiders who together with Peter and James witnessed the raising of Jairus's daughter and the Transfiguration, and who therefore may well have thought himself to be greater than the other apostles and the uncounted other disciples of Jesus – raises a question about a rival exorcist. He informs Jesus that they saw someone, not among the disciples, casting out demons by invoking Jesus' name. (**vs. 49**). John is concerned with who gets to use Jesus' name; he is not concerned with the healing of people possessed by demons. He's completely missed the message of the little child. He wants to restrict this power to the in-group, to those who "follow with us." Therefore, he and the other disciples sought to prevent the other exorcist from casting out demons.

Jesus' response is consistent with his exemplar of the little child. If the rival exorcist is doing the same work as the disciples, if the rival exorcist is also casting out demons, and if the rival exorcist is using the name of Jesus to do good, then he is on the right side. If he's not against you – indeed, if he's doing what you are doing, or *should* be doing – let him be (**vs. 50**). Judith

[6]   So, e.g., C. F. Evans, *Saint Luke*, 428.

Lieu states that Jesus "prohibits any attempt to claim exclusive rights to his authority."[7] It is not only the Twelve who can claim to be Jesus' followers. Given their own failures, this is a point they, and those who claim today to be their heirs and therefore have a lock on discipleship, need to take seriously.

REJECTION IN SAMARIA

With **vs. 51**, Luke begins Jesus' journey from Galilee to Jerusalem. The journey will take nine chapters (9.51–19.28), in which Jesus will provide more teaching to his disciples, and more brief glimpses through his miracle-working ability, into what the Kingdom looks like. The entire journey takes place under the shadow of the cross, for the time has come for his "taking up": his being crucified, but also his being raised and his ascension.

The opening of the journey is not an auspicious one. Whereas the Gospel of John (ch. 4) depicts Jesus' welcome in a Samaritan village, Luke depicts his rejection. Jesus sent messengers to find lodging for him in Samaria, the country between Galilee and Judea (**vs. 52**). He could have avoided Samaritan territory, but this was the direct route from Galilee to Judea, and it was not uncommon for Jews to cross Samaria. Yet the route could also be dangerous. Samaritans and Jews had rival Temples, rival priesthoods, rival claims to be heirs of the patriarchs, and rival messianic views.

According to the Gospel of Matthew, Jesus instructs the disciples to avoid Samaritan territory (Matt 10.5); Mark ignores them entirely. Josephus makes several comments about Samaritans, which are generally noncomplimentary. He records that in the early years of direct Roman rule of Judea, when Coponius was governor (6–9 CE), Samaritans hid themselves among the Jews going to the Jerusalem Temple for the Passover and then strewed human bones in the sanctuary in order to make it ritually unclean (*Ant.* 18.29–30; the modern analogy, although not quite a parallel, would be the hate crime of putting the head of a pig in a synagogue or mosque). Then, during the governorship of Cumanus (48–52), Samaritans killed a number of Jewish pilgrims who attempted to cross Samaria on their way from Galilee to the Jerusalem Temple (*War* 2.232–35; *Ant.* 20.118).

Jesus had talked about "receiving" or "welcoming" a little child, and how such reception indicates receiving both him and the one who sent him. The Samaritans refuse to "receive" him because "his face was going to Jerusalem"

---

[7]   Lieu, *Gospel According to Luke*, 79.

(**vs. 53**). He was heading not to their Temple, and he was not acting as their Messiah. Attentive readers may recall Jesus' rejection in his hometown, where he spoke of the miracles performed for gentiles (4.24–27); here the scene replays, with the Samaritans rejecting Jesus because his focus is not on them but on Jerusalem.

John speaks up again, this time with this brother James. Having yet to learn not to abuse their status, having missed the teaching that they are to "love your enemies" and "do good to those who hate you" (6.27), and having failed to see that the expulsion of demons in Jesus' name advances the Kingdom, the two disciples fail again. Their reaction to the rejection is not to leave, as Jesus left Nazareth, but to fight by using the supernatural power they claim. They want to call down fire from heaven; that is, they want to use the power Jesus had given them to destroy, rather than to heal, to exorcise, or to show divine love. Commentators, correctly, associate their appeal with 2 Kings 1.9–12, the scene where the prophet Elijah calls down fire from heaven to destroy his opponents. The previous references to Elijah (9.8, 19, 30) reinforces this connection. Also, underlying their call is Gen 19.24, the destruction of Sodom and Gomorrah. According to Ezekiel, these two cities were destroyed because of their failure to care for the weak: "This was the guilt of your sister Sodom: she and her daughters had pride, excess of food, and prosperous ease, but did not aid the poor and needy" (Ezek 16.49).

As if James and John were demons, or the chaotic sea, Jesus "rebukes" them (**vs. 55**) and then heads to another village (**vs. 56**). Destruction of one's enemies is God's eschatological role, not the role of Jesus or his disciples. Dale Allison demonstrates how Jesus' rejection of violence is part of a larger Jewish tradition that takes Elijah's actions as a negative exemplar.[8] One does not respond to a lack of hospitality with napalm. The disciples will continue to fail; Jesus' response will be one of forgiveness.

DEMANDS OF DISCIPLESHIP

The journey continues. Jesus is accompanied by the Twelve, by other disciples including the women from Galilee, and by people from the local towns – some seeking healing, some questioning Jesus' credentials, some curious. On the road, a potential disciple promises to follow Jesus wherever he will go (**vs. 57**). Jesus has already announced that to follow him means to

---

[8] See, e.g., Dale C. Allison Jr., "Rejecting Violent Judgment: Luke 9:52–56 and Its Relatives," *JBL* 121.2 (2002): 459–78.

take up the cross daily. It means to be rejected and persecuted. It will later mean, at least for some, to reject home and family. Whether "on the road" this potential disciple understood fully what it means to "follow Jesus" cannot be determined. Jesus responds, metaphorically, that to follow him may mean to become homeless; the "Son of Man," unlike the foxes and the birds, has no place to rest (**vs. 58**). The failure to find hospitality in Samaria makes evident the case. Luke may be hinting at political persecution as well as homelessness: the mention of a "fox" reappears in 13.32 in reference to Herod Antipas. We do not know if this potential disciple joined the group or, if he did, if he will prove to be rocky or thin soil.

Repeating as if a refrain the language of "following," Jesus now calls another to "follow" him. This time, the potential disciple is the one to hesitate: he wants first to bury his father (**vs. 59**). Luke does not indicate whether the father has just died and the son needs to attend to his interment, as would be expected then, and now. Or perhaps the son wished to care for his father and, when the father died, perform the customary funerary rites.

As Tobit tells his son Tobias: "My son, when I die, give me a proper burial. Honor your mother and do not abandon her all the days of her life. Do whatever pleases her, and do not grieve her in anything" (Tob 4.3; cf. 6.15). Or again, given that Jews in the late Second Temple period practiced secondary burial, in which after a year in the tomb, the bones of the dead were collected and placed in ossuaries, perhaps the potential disciple sought to wait at home until this rite could be completed.

The potential disciple's demurral makes sense in his culture, and it should in the twenty-first century as well. But Jesus is here fully countercultural, for his role consists of disrupting some families. Harshly he states, "Let the dead bury their own dead." Reading his comment as calling those who do not follow him as already "dead" would not be inappropriate. For Jesus, the moment is urgent; the role of the disciple is not to attend to domestic duties, but to "proclaim the Kingdom of God" (**vs. 60**). As with the first would-be disciple, we do not know if this second man, called directly by Jesus, responded by becoming a follower.

For a third time, Luke uses the language of "follow" as another would-be disciple seeks to split the difference between "follow always" and "let me first bury my father." He simply wants to say good-bye to those in his house (**vs. 61**). The request to most people sounds reasonable. Again, Jesus demands an immediate response. Evoking Elijah for the last time in the chapter, Jesus tells the man that if he places his hand on the plow – if he joins the movement – and then looks back, he is not fit for the Kingdom (**vs. 62**). He is alluding to 1 Kings 19.19–21, where Elijah finds Elisha plowing in the field and commissions him. Elisha asks, "Let me kiss my father and my mother, and then I will follow you," and Elijah gives him permission. Elijah called down fire from heaven whereas Jesus rejects the violence. Elijah allowed his disciple one last kiss with his mother and father whereas Jesus rejects the biological bonds in favor of the Kingdom message. For a third time, we do not know whether the would-be disciple joined the movement or returned to his home.

BRIDGING THE HORIZONS

1. The Disciples as Leaders

The disciples, who are unable to understand Jesus' prediction of his Passion, unable to overcome petty squabbles over rank, unable to see the importance of focusing on the child rather than on their own status, and happy to destroy towns, are not at this point encouraging paradigms for Church leadership. Throughout Chapter 9,[9] Jesus explains what discipleship entails; foremost, it does not mean exaltation of the self. Disciples are to attend to the most vulnerable members of the community, those who are unable to offer reciprocity for attention. Second, disciples are not to respond to rejection with violence; they are to love their opponents, not bomb them. Third, their role is not one of self-aggrandizement but of self-sacrifice.

In Church leadership, in politics, or in any organization, the temptation to place one's own needs over those of the group is omnipresent. Jesus insists on focusing on the needs of those with the least amount of power and the least likelihood of paying back in kind. At the same time, leaders need to be aware of their own power and authority, and to use it wisely. Finding the balance between giving all to the Kingdom and recognizing one's personal talents is not easy, but it is necessary.

2. On Becoming "Other"

The "Transfiguration" takes its name from the Greek term "metamorphosis," which is found in Matthew and Mark's version of the account but

---

[9] On the unity of the chapter, see Robert F. O'Toole, "Luke's Message in Luke 9:1–50," *CBQ* 49.1 (1987): 74–89.

not in Luke's. Luke describes, as best as one can describe, this transcendent event, by stating that Jesus' face "became other" (9.29). We might therefore attend to what we see, and how we are seen. Is the face we present to the public, or even in the mirror, an image of our true self? Do we worry about hair and makeup, acne scars or crooked teeth, or do we seek more to present a face to the world that displays concern, or joy, or interest? Is our true self the body we inhabit, or the ideal body we seek in the gym, or the resurrected body where everything looks better than we can imagine?

If we look closely, and if we are lucky, we will see this "other" face, this transcendent face. Look at the faces of parents welcoming a newborn; look at the face of the child who is loved. At times, the glow is incandescent. We see this and we smile. Look at the face of the child who survived the bombing, or the elderly veteran seeking care. The othering of the image of God into despair cannot be avoided. We see this and we weep. Or, do we close our eyes, or change the channel?

The Transfiguration story also raises another major issue, an issue that will come up in the Lukan Parable of the Rich Man and Lazarus in Chapter 16. Even stupendous miracles and transformations of human form do not necessarily produce faith or understanding in the observer. One cannot be "wowed" into the Kingdom of God; there must openness, a willingness to receive, some faith. The amazement of crowds or of disciples is not the same thing as a response of faith. That aforementioned parable dramatically concludes with the rich man in Hades saying, "No, father Abraham; but if someone goes to them from the dead, they will repent." Abraham said to him, "If they do not listen to Moses and the prophets, neither will they be convinced even if someone rises from the dead." Seeing doesn't necessarily lead to believing, but believing can lead to seeing and understanding even if one only hears the Word, but sees no miracle.

Nor does the belief come from the will. One can no more will to believe than one can will to love. There is, for both belief and love, a transcendent, mysterious quality.

Luke 10 Instructions for the Seventy, the Lawyer, and Martha the Householder

¹ After this the Lord appointed seventy others and sent them on ahead of him in pairs to every town and place where he himself intended to go. ² He said to them, "The harvest is plentiful, but the laborers are few; therefore, ask the Lord of the harvest to send out laborers into his harvest. ³ Go on your way. See, I am sending you out like lambs into the midst of wolves. ⁴ Carry no purse, no bag, no sandals; and greet no one on the road. ⁵ Whatever house you enter, first say, 'Peace to this house!' ⁶ And if anyone is there who shares in peace, your peace will rest on that person; but if not, it will return to you. ⁷ Remain in the same house, eating and drinking whatever they provide, for the laborer deserves to be paid. Do not move about from house to house. ⁸ Whenever you enter a town and its people welcome you, eat what is set before you; ⁹ cure the sick who are there, and say to them, 'The kingdom of God has come near to you.' ¹⁰ But whenever you enter a town and they do not welcome you, go out into its streets and say, ¹¹ 'Even the dust of your town that clings to our feet, we wipe off in protest against you. Yet know this: the kingdom of God has come near.' ¹² I tell you, on that day it will be more tolerable for Sodom than for that town. ¹³ Woe to you, Chorazin! Woe to you, Bethsaida! For if the deeds of power done in you had been done in Tyre and Sidon, they would have repented long ago, sitting in sackcloth and ashes. ¹⁴ But at the judgment it will be more tolerable for Tyre and Sidon than for you. ¹⁵ And you, Capernaum, will you be exalted to heaven? No, you will be brought down to Hades. ¹⁶ "Whoever listens to you listens to me, and whoever rejects you rejects me, and whoever rejects me rejects the one who sent me."

REVELATIONS TO THE DISCIPLES

¹⁷ The seventy returned with joy, saying, "Lord, in your name even the demons submit to us!"

¹⁸ He said to them, "I watched Satan fall from heaven like a flash of lightning.

¹⁹ See, I have given you authority to tread on snakes and scorpions, and over all the power of the enemy; and nothing will hurt you. ²⁰ Nevertheless, do not rejoice at this, that the spirits submit to you, but rejoice that your names are written in heaven."

²¹ At that same hour Jesus rejoiced in the Holy Spirit and said, "I thank you, Father, Lord of heaven and earth, because you have hidden these things from the wise and the intelligent and have revealed them to infants; yes, Father, for such was your gracious will. ²² All things have been handed over to me by my Father; and no one knows who the Son is except the Father, or who the Father is except the Son and anyone to whom the Son chooses to reveal him."

²³Then turning to the disciples, Jesus said to them privately, "Blessed are the eyes that see what you see! ²⁴ For I tell you that many prophets and kings desired to see what you see, but did not see it, and to hear what you hear, but did not hear it."

THE LAWYER'S QUESTIONS AND ANSWERS

²⁵ Just then a lawyer stood up to test Jesus. "Teacher," he said, "what must I do to inherit eternal life?"

²⁶ He said to him, "What is written in the law? What do you read there?"

²⁷ He answered, "You shall love the Lord your God with all your heart, and with all your soul, and with all your strength, and with all your mind; and your neighbor as yourself."

²⁸ And he said to him, "You have given the right answer; do this, and you will live."

²⁹ But wanting to justify himself, he asked Jesus, "And who is my neighbor?"

THE PARABLE OF THE MAN WHO FELL AMONG THE ROBBERS

³⁰ Jesus replied, "A man was going down from Jerusalem to Jericho, and fell into the hands of robbers, who stripped him, beat him, and went away, leaving him half dead. ³¹ Now by chance a priest was going down that road; and when he saw him, he passed by on the other side. ³² So likewise a Levite, when he came to the place and saw him, passed by on the

other side. [33] But a Samaritan while traveling came near him; and when he saw him, he was moved with pity. [34] He went to him and bandaged his wounds, having poured oil and wine on them. Then he put him on his own animal, brought him to an inn, and took care of him. [35] The next day he took out two denarii, gave them to the innkeeper, and said, 'Take care of him; and when I come back, I will repay you whatever more you spend.'

[36] Which of these three, do you think, was a neighbor to the man who fell into the hands of the robbers?" [37] He said, "The one who showed him mercy." Jesus said to him, "Go and do likewise."

MARY AND MARTHA, AND JESUS

[38] Now as they went on their way, he entered a certain village, where a woman named Martha welcomed him into her home. [39] She had a sister named Mary, who sat at the Lord's feet and listened to what he was saying. [40] But Martha was distracted by her many tasks; so she came to him and asked, "Lord, do you not care that my sister has left me to do all the work by myself? Tell her then to help me." [41] But the Lord answered her, "Martha, Martha, you are worried and distracted by many things; [42] there is need of only one thing. Mary has chosen the better part, which will not be taken away from her."

Chapter 10 blends material unique to Luke (vss. 29–42) together with an adaptation of Mark's report of the mission of the Twelve, which Luke had already taken over in 9.1–6.[1] In both stories about the disciples' mission, the emphasis lies on the instructions and not their enactment; for the mission itself, readers have to wait until Acts. That Luke gives more attention to the return of the seventy-two than to the return of the Twelve (9.10) anticipates the role that people outside the apostolic circle of the Twelve will have.[2]

GATHERING THE HARVEST

The chapter begins with Jesus appointing seventy (or seventy-two) of his followers to serve as advance parties into every town and village (**vs. 1**). That the manuscript tradition records both seventy and seventy-two suggests

---

[1] For detailed source criticism, see Darrell L. Bock, *Luke 9.51–24.53* (Grand Rapids: Baker Academic, 1996), 986–92.
[2] Tannehill, *Luke*, 173.

that early scribes did think of the number as symbolic.[3] Determining what it symbolizes cannot, however, be done with mathematical precision. The number seventy itself shows up seventy-seven times in the Christian Bible (NRSV), and any text can be seen as informing this scene, whether Luke intended the allusion or not. The number seventy recollects the seventy members of Jacob's family (Gen 46.27b mentions that "all the persons of the house of Jacob who came into Egypt were seventy") and so can suggest that the disciples reflect the people of Israel. According to Exod 24.9, seventy elders accompanied Moses and Aaron to see God on Mt. Sinai. The Mishnah, *Sanh.* 1.6, states that the "Great Sanhedrin," the Jerusalem court, had seventy-one members. It derives the seventy-one from Num 11.16, where God commands Moses to appoint seventy elders. The elders, plus Moses, total seventy-one. Num 11.16-30 goes on to note that the elders were filled with the Spirit, but then two more receive the gift as well – Eldad and Medad. Luke's seventy-two could then allude to the people who saw God on Mt. Sinai, or who were filled with the Spirit in the wilderness, or who served as leaders of the earlier community. Josephus states that the Zealots, whose primary purpose was to expel Rome from the land of Israel, had seventy judges (likely in imitation also of Num 11; see *War* 4.336). Luke, who may have been familiar with Josephus's writings, can be seen as offering a counterrevolutionary model: Jesus' seventy are not to engage in violent struggle; theirs is another model for another Kingdom.

Alternatively, the seventy might suggest the traditional view that there are seventy nations of the world (Gen 10.2–31; see also *Jubilees* 44.34; the Septuagint states that there are seventy-two nations), and the *Letter of Aristeas* 46–50 records that seventy-two scribes translated the Torah into Greek, so the Third Evangelist, or copyists, who knew the Septuagint may have adapted the number to fit the Greek texts and so anticipate the gentile mission. The book of Numbers (31.38) states regarding the gains from the attack on Midian, "the oxen were thirty-six thousand, of which the LORD's tribute was 72." We do not see a connection between this reference and the manuscript tradition regarding vs. 1. Sometimes a number may be just as number. Or again, Luke may have been looking for a number that suggested fullness or completion, or even critical mass.

Readers with imagination might eventually develop seventy or seventy-two different explanations for the number, and some might simply state,

[3] See Bruce Metzger, *A Textual Commentary on the Greek New Testament (Ancient Greek Edition)* (New York: United Bible Societies, 1971), 128.

"Luke says seventy because that's how many there were." Historians will debate whether Jesus did in fact send out seventy missionaries: there is no external confirmation of this mission, even in the other Gospels; nor does Luke depict Jesus as going to these locations. Ben sees no reason to doubt Luke's report; Amy-Jill finds more symbolic value than historical reporting here.

The verb for "appointed" (Greek: *anadeiknumi*) refers to an official commissioning. Like the Twelve, the seventy-two are sent out two by two, perhaps because the testimony of two witnesses was required to validate the truthfulness of the message (Lev 19.17; Deut 19.15),[4] or this may have been simply a safer way to travel. Today, "two by two" reminds people of the animals entering Noah's ark (Gen 7.9, 15); with this intertextual allusion, the seventy can be seen as those who are prepared for the eschaton, or who are called out of a doomed world.

According to Luke, Jesus sends the seventy (or seventy-two) with a commission based on a metaphor: there is much to harvest but few laborers to work the field (**vs. 2a**; cf. Matt 9.37). The harvest imagery, already suggested by the Parable of the Sower, has an eschatological quality. The time is short, and the grain needs to be gathered. The next line, wherein the seventy (or seventy-two) are to ask the "Lord of the harvest" to send (more?) laborers (**vs. 2b**), must be a reference not to Jesus but to God: if Jesus is the "Lord of the harvest," then he has no need to tell followers to ask him to send more. The line fits uneasily into the context, since the emissaries do not pray for more workers, and there is no indication that they were unable on their own to accomplish their commission. Jesus himself has chosen seventy out of what Luke suggests is a larger number.

The metaphors continue, as Jesus warns these emissaries of the dangers on the road. Whereas in John's Gospel Jesus is the primary "lamb" (e.g., John 1.29, 36), in the Synoptic tradition the disciples are the lambs endangered by surrounding wolves (**vs. 3**; cf. Matt 10.16). In the appended chapter 21 of the Gospel of John, Jesus, similarly, will command Peter, "Feed my lambs" (21.15) as a sign that Peter loves him. Here in Luke, what started as the laborious but generally safe work of harvesting has now become a threatening situation. The vulnerable followers, like the Twelve before them (9.3–5), are to carry no money and wear no shoes (**vs. 4a**). They are not merchants peddling goods, or well-off travelers going to meet family or friends. They will look like beggars, which in fact they will be. Like lambs, they are

---

4   See R. T. France, *Luke* (Teach the Commentary Series; Grand Rapids: Baker, 2013), 178.

vulnerable and defenseless. The instructions will resonate in the parable to follow, where a man on the road is accosted by robbers.

Nor are these followers to engage in conversation on the road (**vs. 4b**). Luke Timothy Johnson suggests that because the mission will be in Samaria, hostile territory, engagement with people on the street might be dangerous,[5] although it is by no means clear that Jesus is enjoining a Samaritan mission. That will come in Acts 8. Darrell Bock sees a relation of the command to 2 Kings 4.29, where the prophet Elisha tells his servant Gehazi to accompany the Great Woman of Shunem to her house and there to raise her son from the dead: "Gird up your loins, and take my staff in your hand, and go. If you meet anyone, give no greeting, and if anyone greets you, do not answer; and lay my staff on the face of the child."[6] Both views are possible, although given the earlier mission of the Twelve as well as Luke's (and Jesus') focus on the household, the simplest explanation is that Jesus wants these emissaries to head straight for the houses, which will be their base of operations. It is in the house where the greeting is to be given, as Jesus is about to make explicit. To continue to mix the metaphors, it is in the home where the harvesting is done and the lambs are safe. The time for conversing on the road will come much later, after the cross, on the road to Emmaus (24.13). And even there, the fullness of revelation remains not on the road, but at the table.

These followers, eschewing comforts during their travels, show some similarities to the Cynics, a philosophical school that promoted freedom, self-sufficiency, bold and frank speech, and the critique of social norms. However, unlike the Cynics, Jesus' emissaries are embedded in a system of reciprocity. Jesus tells them to enter a house, whatever house, and greet it with "peace" (**vs. 5**). The greeting is not a simple, "Hello there," or, "How're ya doin?'" "Peace" (Hebrew *shalom*; Greek *eirēnē*) is a palpable thing; it connotes reconciliation, calm, and wholeness. It is something that one can actually "give" to another, as we find in cases where someone's presence or words serve not just to end hostility, but to create a feeling of *shalom*. The greeting takes place not on the road, where relationships are ephemeral; it takes place in a home, where natal and marital families are disrupted and a new family connected through loyalty to Jesus and through hospitality is created.

The next verse demonstrates that this "peace" is more than an abstract concept. It is something that can be both given and received, and even

5   Johnson, *Gospel of Luke*, 167.
6   Bock, *Luke 9.51–24.53*, 997.

shared. The peace the disciples convey can "rest" on (**vs. 6**), even as it can bring rest to, the receptive householder. But if the peace is rejected, the emissary regains it. Thus, peace never leaves the followers: it is theirs to distribute, and to share.

Under the canopy of peace, these emissaries remain in the same house (**vs. 7a**), as did the apostles sent out in 9.3–5. They are not to search for better lodgings, accept the invitation of the highest bidder, or shame the initial host by leaving. The concern that they eat and drink (**vss.7b- 8**) whatever is provided has multiple implications. First, they are not to complain about the food, whether the taste or the quantity. Second, Jesus notes that the food is payment, for laborers – the emissaries – are entitled to a wage. The payment seals the reciprocity. Third, the food hints at the eschatological banquet, when all people will recline together at table. There is a hint of the Eucharist here with the concern for food in the context of a household, discipleship, and peace. To break bread together is an indication of peace and friendship (cf. Acts 2.43–47; 4.32–37). Finally, since they are only visiting Jews – the gentile mission has not yet begun – they can be assured that the food they will receive is kosher. There are no pork chops on the menu in lower Galilee, as archaeologists have noted. They need not concern themselves with issues of sectarian practice related to either washing before meals or the precision of what produce had been tithed.

Like the Twelve, these emissaries are to cure the sick, and they are to proclaim the nearness of the Kingdom (**vs. 9**).[7] The combination of peace, proclamation, healing, and food within the household gives the impression of a house-church. Luke's readers may have recognized themselves in the roles of missionaries or householders, a recognition reinforced in the story of Mary and Martha, which concludes the chapter.

Should they be rejected, the emissaries are to shake the dust off their feet (**vs. 10**; cf. 9.5). The rejection is not simply of a household, but of an entire town. Jesus' instruction thus suggests that in some towns, no one will be receptive of their mission and message. As harvesters, they know that not all seed takes root. But just as the emissaries retain the peace that they found with Jesus and obtained from him, so they retain the good news of the Kingdom. Even if an entire town rejected them, they still know the Kingdom is near (**vs. 11**).

---

[7] Culy et al., *Luke*, 47–48 note that *eggiken* means "near," not "here," in this text. This same verb is used in Matt 3.2 and Mark 1.15 by John the Baptizer to announce the coming of the Kingdom.

The next verse does suggest a bit of *schadenfreude*: the towns that rejected the Kingdom message will be destroyed by the Lord of that Kingdom. Jesus states that devastation will be so great that what happened to Sodom will seem more tolerable (**vs. 12**). His allusion is to Gen 19.24, which describes how "the Lord rained on Sodom and Gomorrah sulfur and fire from the Lord out of heaven" (cf. Isa 3.9); the redundancy of the verse could allow early followers to see Jesus as the referent of the first "lord" and God (the Father) as the referent of the second. Regarding the sin of Sodom, which prompted the destruction, the prophet Ezekiel makes clear that Sodom was destroyed because of lack of hospitality, an allusion already prompted by the rejection of Jesus in Samaria (9.54), when James and John wanted to call down fire from heaven. Since Jesus' statement appears in the context of households either accepting or rejecting the disciples, the concern for Sodom's hospitality is here also invoked.

Jesus next specifies the cities that will suffer a fate worse than that of Sodom: he begins with Bethsaida and Chorazin, both on the north side of the Sea of Galilee (**vs. 13;** see Matt 10.15; 11.24). Proposing that his miracles, his "deeds of power," should have demonstrated the legitimacy of his movement, he adds that had those miracles been done in the pagan cities of Tyre and Sidon, the people would have repented (**vs. 14**). A rhetorical question, introduced by the Greek word *mē*, as here in reference to Capernaum, requires the answer, "no." The comparison has biblical precedent. The book of Lamentations also draws upon the destruction of Sodom to set up a comparison to the destruction of Israel: "For the chastisement of my people has been greater than the punishment of Sodom, which was overthrown in a moment, though no hand was laid on it" (Lam 4.6). The argument of vs. 14, however, is not compelling; miracles need not indicate messianic presence. Religions across the globe have claimed that their founders and their saints performed miracles; no one tradition has more legitimate claims to these miracles than another. Nor does Luke mention what these "deeds of power" were, for Luke depicts no mission in Chorazin or Bethsaida. For those who experienced a healing or an exorcism in the name of Jesus, the message of the nearness of the Kingdom might prove compelling. For others, including those who found no healing, it does not.

Similarly, Jesus condemns the city of Capernaum (**vs. 15**), where he performed those initial deeds of power known to the synagogue in Nazareth (4.23), and where he had already taught (4.31). Capernaum will suffer the same fate as her sister cities; rather than be exalted, perhaps as the place where Jesus originally preached, Capernaum too is damned. For all those preachers who talk about an "Old Testament God of Wrath and a New Testament God of Love," such verses should serve as a corrective.[8] The "woes" here, like the "woes in 6.24–26, are eschatological threats, where the destruction is eternal. Yet we might inquire into the rhetorical function of such hyperbolic warnings or pronouncements: is Jesus stating what will happen, or what might? Presumably if these warnings were heard and heeded, the outcome could be different. The town of Capernaum was not, as far as our archaeological and textual records show, directly impacted by the revolt against Rome.

Unlike Sodom, which not only refused to aid the poor but also, from the youngest to the oldest, men and women, attempted to rape the visitors who sought shelter with Abraham's nephew Lot (Gen 19), the sin of these towns is their rejection of Jesus. **Vs. 16** makes this point explicit: to follow the disciples is to follow Jesus; to reject the disciples is to reject not only Jesus, but the "one who sent" him, God. The reciprocity system that the disciples create in the household has a cosmic implication. Those who reject Jesus will be rejected by him and his Father. To reject Jesus is, consequently, a worse sin than the sins of Sodom combined. Otherwise put, to reject Jesus is worse than to oppress the poor or to rape. The analogy is hyperbolic and, especially to victims and the impoverished, potentially offensive.

For some scholars, the invectives found in Matthew and Luke, stemming according to one solution to the Synoptic problem from the hypothetical document Q, lack authenticity; that is, they do not come from the historical Jesus. In this reconstruction, the apocalyptic warnings were pronounced not by Jesus, but by his followers, whose proclamation was rejected. Jesus and his movement did not, as far as history can tell us, gain much traction in the cities of lower Galilee. The followers of Jesus relocate to Jerusalem, as both Acts and Paul tell us. Acts says almost nothing about any sort of Christian mission or presence in Galilee (cf. Acts 8.1, 9.31). Lower Galilee instead became a home in the late first and early second century (the time Luke is writing) to the rabbinic movement. The hyperbole of Luke's invective may be the reaction of Jesus' followers to the failure of the mission, if not the reaction of Jesus himself. Neither of us (Ben and Amy-Jill) finds this argument compelling. It rather serves to protect Jesus from saying anything that goes against contemporary approval, such as threats of hell, even as it assigns the problematic statements to the "Jews" in the movement.

---

[8]   Jesus has more to say about the reality of Hell (which he calls Gehenna) than Paul, or any other NT writer, save John of Patmos in Revelation.

REVELATIONS TO THE DISCIPLES

Luke records no failure of the mission. Instead, the seventy (or seventy-two) joyfully return with good news: they were able to perform exorcisms (**vs. 17**); that is, they defeated Satan's soldiers. They say nothing, however, about the proclamation of the Gospel, the change in the households, or the acceptance of the Kingdom message.

Their announcement prompts Jesus to exclaim that he saw Satan fall (**vs. 18**). The imagery should be taken literally: Jesus had a vision. If one can exorcise a demon, one can surely see the master of the demons fall. The vision also has good precedent, from the "sons of God" in Gen 6.2, who become the "fallen angels" or "watchers" of Second Temple Judaism to Isaiah's notice of seeing the "Day Star" fallen from heaven (Isa 14.12).[9] In the worlds of ancient Israel and Second Temple Judaism, the border between the natural and the supernatural world is porous, and visionaries can see beyond the mundane. Jesus' vision has cosmic import: Satan may be the "ruler of the world," as the Temptation Narrative suggests (4.6), but his rule is ending.[10] The exorcisms are proof of that. On the one hand, Jesus' vision assures the disciples that the victory is already won: Satan has fallen and evil has been defeated. On the other hand, Satan remains on earth, and his powers are still strong. Luke here foreshadows Satan's ongoing presence and power, from binding a woman Jesus will encounter in a synagogue (13.16) to possessing Judas Iscariot (22.3).

The good news to his followers continues as Jesus grants them authority over the dangerous elements of the natural world, the snakes and the scorpions, as well as over Satan, the "enemy" (**vs. 19a**). While it would have been better news had they had this authority prior to their mission, the assurances Jesus grants them will now apply to the next mission his followers undertake, which will be the outreach prompted by Pentecost (Acts 2) and the resultant persecution of the movement. In assuring the followers that they are invulnerable (**vs. 19b**), Jesus also takes away the fear that the initial image of "lambs amidst wolves" might have created. At the same time, he wants to prevent them from boasting in their powers. The matter of import is not that they can survive a snakebite, or even that they can cast out demons. Luke issues no invitation to "pick up snakes" or drink poison (Mark

---

[9]   Jon Carman, "The Falling Star and the Rising Son: Luke 10:17–24 and Second Temple 'Satan' Traditions," *Stone-Campbell Journal* 17.2 (2014): 221–31. On the historical Jesus as a visionary, see Witherington, *Jesus the Seer*.
[10]   González, *Luke*, 136.

16.18 is a later non-Markan addition to the earliest manuscripts) in order to demonstrate power or bring others to the movement. What is important is that in their welcoming Jesus, Jesus has welcomed them, and therefore their names are inscribed, as in a guest registry, in the heavenly books (**vs. 20**). Psa 69.29 speaks of the "book of the living" or the "book of life" (Hebrew: *sefer chayim*) in which the names of the righteous are inscribed (cf. Exod 32.33; Isa 4.3). Leslie Baynes suggests, "Just as the 'chosen people of old' were written in a book of life that functioned as a citizenship list, so it seems that the seventy constitute a citizenry, one that does the work of Jesus."[11]

Ben sees Jesus' struggle and that of his disciples as not mainly with "flesh and blood" but rather with supernatural powers and principalities.[12] Amy-Jill agrees that there is a cosmic dimension to the narrative, but she does not rank these struggles: rather, she sees Jesus as equally invested in how one lives in the world, how one finds peace in the household, and how one follows the commandments of God. Ben reads the Greek of vs. 19 as saying, "in nothing will he hurt you," and so sees this verse not referring to actual venomous creatures; rather, Luke is speaking of spiritual protection (cf. Luke 11.11–12; 2 Cor. 11.3; Rev. 12.9,14–15; 20.2, where Satan is called a snake), for like Jesus, some of these followers likely will suffer physically.[13] Amy-Jill agrees that some of the disciples will be hurt – according to Acts, James the brother of John is executed by Herod Agrippa I (Acts 12.2). However, she reads the Greek as saying, "nothing will hurt you": if one can exorcise a demon, one can survive a snake bite. We both agree that the verse is related to the eschatological vision of Isa 11.8, "The nursing child shall play over the hole of the asp, and the weaned child shall put its hand on the adder's den," and to Acts 28.3, when Paul survives a viper bite.

The reference to the heavenly inscription, like Jesus' vision of the fall of Satan, is to be taken literally. The idea of heavenly record books was common in early Judaism (cf. Dan 12.1; Ps 69.28; Ex 32.32; *Jubilees* 19.9; cf. Rev. 3.5). To this day, in Jewish practice, one of the greetings for Rosh Ha-Shanah, the new year, is "*Ketivah v'chatima tovah*," "May you have a good inscription and sealing," for on the new year the book of life is opened. Ten days later, on Yom Kippur, when the book is closed, the greeting is "*Gemar chatimah tovah*," ("May you have) a good final sealing."

---

[11] See Leslie Baynes, *The Heavenly Book Motif in Judeo-Christian Apocalypses* (Supplements to the Journal for the Study of Judaism 152; Leiden and Boston: Brill, 2012), 139.
[12] See Witherington, *Jesus the Seer*, 279–80; and idem, *The Christology of Jesus*, 145–55.
[13] See Tannehill, *Luke*, 179.

At the notice that the disciples' names are secure (to this point, Judas's treachery mentioned in 6.16 has yet to manifest itself, but the references to Satan are an ominous reminder), Jesus himself rejoices. Inspired by the Spirit and so again indicating the cosmic dimensions of his mission, he offers a prayer of thanksgiving to God, the true lord of heaven and earth (**vs. 21a**; on this address, see Tob 7.17; Jdt 9.12), and here he reveals his own cosmic secrets. The disciples, compared to "infants" (cf. Matthew's "little ones") are the ones who have heavenly knowledge.[14] The "wise and intelligent" remain unenlightened (**vs. 21b**). Accepting the Kingdom message may not be a matter of personal choice but a matter of predestination. God chooses to whom to reveal heavenly truths. The piling up of vocatives makes the statement emphatic.[15]

Further, Jesus takes full part in this predetermined sharing of secrets. He has received them from his Father, and he in turn will choose to whom to reveal them (**vs. 21c**). The secrets he holds concern the correct knowledge of God. Otherwise put, if one does not follow Jesus, one cannot follow God; more, if one is not chosen by Jesus to receive the secrets, one cannot have correct theology. This dualistic thinking, more normally associated with the Fourth Evangelist, restricts to Jesus and his followers any proper knowledge of the divine. Yet as Judith Lieu remarks, "It could hardly be said that so far no one had known God, for the OT is founded on God's self-revelation to Israel and her responsive 'knowledge' in obedience."[16] For Luke, the issue here is not just any kind of divine knowledge but a saving knowledge of God available through Jesus and the proclamation about him.

The last two lines of this brief, private revelation to the disciples again assure them that they are chosen and that they have a truth others lack. They have seen and heard what others – prophets and kings – have not (**vss. 23–24**). Prophets such as Elijah and Isaiah (cf. Isa 6) had visions of heaven; kings had access to power. The disciples, in Jesus' estimation, have seen something more than imperial power or the heavenly throne; they have seen God's Messiah, and they have been chosen to proclaim his Gospel of the Kingdom.

---

[14] See Witherington, *Gospel of Matthew*, 237–39. Luke, unlike Matthew and John, does not present Jesus primarily as a sage, but Luke knows this tradition. See also Witherington, *Jesus the Sage*.

[15] Culy et al., *Luke*, 356.

[16] Lieu, *Gospel According to Luke*, 85.

A CLOSER LOOK: SAMARITANS

The biblical tradition records that after King Solomon's death, a rebellion broke out among the northern tribes. By 1 Kings 12.20, "When all Israel heard that Jeroboam had returned, they sent and called him to the assembly and made him king over all Israel. There was no one who followed the house of David, except the tribe of Judah alone." Some from among the tribe of Benjamin joined Rehoboam, and they with the Judahites, in the South, continued the Kingdom of Judah. The Northern Kingdom took the name Israel and established its capital in the city of Samaria. That is where the court of Queen Jezebel and King Ahab – the opponents of Elijah – was located.

In 722 BCE, the Northern Kingdom of Israel was conquered by the Assyrians. As was common in antiquity, empires resettled the courts, the elite, and the intelligentsia of conquered nations. The Assyrian emperor Sargon II claimed that he had taken 27,290 people from the Kingdom of Israel into exile (this is the beginning of the legend of the "Ten Lost Tribes" who, according to some Jewish messianic speculation, will return when the Messiah comes); Sargon likely inflated the number of people he exiled. According to Josephus (*Ant.* 11.297–347; cf. 2 Kings 17. 6–24), the Samaritans were primarily descendants of peoples whom the Assyrian Empire resettled in Israel ca. 721 BCE. Josephus overstates this resettlement as well; the majority of the Israelite population remained in the land.

Samaritans and Judeans, the latter called "Jews," were thus siblings, both claiming descent from Abraham, Isaac, and Jacob. They were also, as biblical siblings often are, bitter rivals. Josephus states that the Samaritans claimed to be Jews when the latter group was prospering, but claimed they were a separate group when things were not going well for Jews (*Ant.* 9.291). Positive relations between Samaritans and Jews included the marriage of Herod, who insisted on defining himself as a Jew, and the Samaritan Malthace; she was the mother of Herod Antipas and Herod Archelaus.

Conflicts between Jews and Samaritans – which went in both directions –were over the proper place of worship and priesthood, proper Scriptures, and proper interpretation of Torah (the Samaritan Pentateuch differs from the Torah in certain places). Following the return of portions of the southern population from Babylonian exile sometime around 525 BCE, relations between Samaria and the Persian colony of Yehud, the former Kingdom of Judah, deteriorated. Neh 4.1–2 states that both Sanballat, the governor of Judea appointed by the Persian emperor Darius, and the "army" of Samaria opposed the rebuilding of Jerusalem's Temple and city walls (cf. Ezra 4). A little over a century later (ca. 388), the Samaritans built their own temple on Mt. Gerizim, which in turn was destroyed by the Hasmonean king John Hyrcanus in 128 (*Ant.* 13.254–56). On the basis of Deut 18.18, Samaritans spoke of a *Taheb*, a restorer prophet, who would be like Moses, and who would come and restore true worship on Mt. Gerizim. To this day, Samaritans, who claim descent from the "Joseph" tribes of Manasseh and Ephraim as well as from the tribe of Levi, still celebrate the Passover sacrifice on Mt. Gerizim, the site of their original temple.

Rabbinic comments on Samaritans, all postdating the first century, vary from approval to disapproval. Occasionally, Christian commentators will find the most negative rabbinic statements, make them normative for all Jews, and retroject back to the first century in order to show how Jesus rejects "Jewish" teaching or stands on the moral high ground above it. For example, several studies insist that "the Jews" thought the land of Samaria was unclean and should be avoided and that Samaritan women were menstruants from the cradle (*m. Niddah* 4.1) and so perpetually unclean. The problem with traveling through Samaria was not ritual purity; it was fear of bandit attack. The Mishnah passage cited goes on to associate Sadducees with Samaritans, which indicates that the subject is a sectarian one and thus by no means the view of "all Jews"; it also states regarding these women, "But those [who have contact] with them are not liable for entering the sanctuary and do not burn heave offering on their account, because their uncleanness is a matter of doubt." According to *m. Ter.* 3.9, a Samaritan's offering to the Jerusalem Temple is acceptable; *m. Dem.* 7.4 discusses Samaritan wine purchased by Jews. The early rabbis have differing views on Samaritans, and select citations from later sources should not be used as a negative foil in order to make Jesus look good.

Luke's previous chapter indicated the antipathy Samaritans had toward Jesus in that he was heading to Jerusalem; regarding correct worship, Jesus tells a Samaritan woman, "You worship what you do not know; we worship what we know, for salvation is from the Jews" (John 4.22). Jesus is not much interested in interfaith dialogue or multicultural affirmation. In the early years of the first century, Samaritans desecrated the Jerusalem Temple by scattering human bones in it (see our comments on Luke 9.51–56). For Jesus to tell a story in which the Samaritan is the hero would have sounded absurd to his Jewish audience. The phrase "good Samaritan" would have been an oxymoron.

THE LAWYER'S QUESTIONS AND ANSWERS

The Parable of the Good Samaritan (10.25–37) is, together with the Parable of the Prodigal Son (Luke 15), the most beloved, and most belabored, of all of Jesus' parables. Since the Patristic Era, the parable has been overread and allegorized: the man leaving Jerusalem was Adam, expelled from Eden; the robbers are Satan and his minions; the "stripping" is Adam's loss of immortality; the Priest and the Levite represent the failure of the Law and the Prophets to save; the Samaritan is Jesus; the oil and wine are baptism and the Eucharist, or Old Testament and New Testament, or the gifts of the Spirit; the inn is the Church; the innkeeper is Paul; the coins are the sacraments; and so on.[17] Such allegorical interpretations denude the parable of its Jewish character and context, and they turn it into a story about later Christian ideas, institutions, and practices. All parables can be read from the subject position of the reader; we can always ask, "what does this text mean *to me*?" But if we want to know what the text might have meant to Jesus' original audience or to Luke's readers, then we are asking a different question.

Luke's story begins (**vs. 25**) with a lawyer seeking to "test" Jesus. The term "lawyer" (Greek: *nomikos*) appears in Luke's Gospel also in connection with Pharisees (7.30; 11.45–52). Elsewhere in the New Testament, *nomikos* appears only in Matt 22.35, where again a "lawyer" seeks to "test" Jesus, and in Titus 1.13, where a lawyer named Zenas receives the author's commendation. In the Septuagint, 4 Macc 5.4 mentions the righteous Eleazar, "a man of priestly family, a *nomikos*, advanced in age, and known to many in the tyrant's court because of his philosophy" who will die a martyr's death for sanctification of the divine name and fidelity to his Jewish tradition. Claims that the lawyer of Luke 10 was in the employ of the Pharisees, or of the Temple, find no purchase in the text itself and are speculations that

---

[17]   See Craig A. Evans, *Luke* (NIBCNT 3; Peabody: Hendrickson, 1990), 178. On the many allegorical readings, see R. H. Stein, *The Method and Message of Jesus' Teaching* (Philadelphia: Westminster, 1978), 45–55.

serve only to disparage both group and institution. The lawyer does, however, fit the category "wise and intelligent" (10.21), those who are not privy to heavenly truths. By being among the intellectual elite, the lawyer, at least according to Luke's narrative, has lost the case before he ever entered the court.

That the lawyer stands in opposition to Jesus is also signaled by Luke's rhetoric: "testing" is what Satan had done with Jesus in Chapter 4; the term "to test" in Greek (*peiradzō*) can also be translated "tempt." Thus, the lawyer is in Satan's role; that he and Jesus will speak about verses from Scripture further connects the two scenes.

The context of "testing" also alerts us to the nuances of the lawyer's address. He might have addressed Jesus as "lord" (Greek: *kyrios*), as did the man with leprosy (5.12), the centurion (7.6), James and John (9.54), and a number of others. Instead, he calls Jesus "teacher" (Greek: *didaskalos*), which is usually a term of respect, as it is in the address to John the Baptizer by the tax collectors in 3.12. Yet the title is insufficient when addressed to Jesus. "Teacher" is used by Simon the Pharisee in 7.40 just before Jesus tells the Parable of the Two Debtors and then condemns Simon for his judging the anointing woman. The people who know that Jairus's daughter is dead and therefore suggest he no longer "trouble" Jesus refer to Jesus as "the teacher" (8.49); they do not think that Jesus will be able to raise the girl. In the previous chapter, the man with the possessed son addresses Jesus as "teacher," and it is then that Jesus complains about the "faithless and perverse generation" (9.38–41). The lawyer's address to Jesus along with his goal of testing and his membership among the elite give him his first three strikes.

If there were four strikes, the lawyer would have them. His question about "inheriting eternal life" (**v. 25**) could under other circumstances be seen as innocent. In Luke 18.18, a "ruler" will also address Jesus as "teacher" and ask exactly the same question. But the ruler does not seek to "test" Jesus. The ruler wants information from a trusted teacher; the lawyer's motives are more likely designed to trip Jesus up, since in early Judaism, eternal life was not a commodity to be inherited but a gift freely given. In the context of Luke's narrative, the lawyer's question could be a response to Jesus' remark, "For I tell you that many prophets and kings desired to see what you see, but did not see it, and to hear what you hear, but did not hear it" (10.24). The lawyer may well wonder how Jesus came to have such knowledge, or why he would approve of predestination and not, by implication, of free will. Luke does not state whether the "ruler" who called Jesus "teacher" became a disciple, but his discipleship is unlikely. For Luke, Jesus cannot simply be "teacher," he must also be "Lord"; the concern for this title will reappear at the end of the chapter, in Luke's account of the sisters Mary and Martha.

Jesus responds to the questioning lawyer by asking a question of his own: "What is written in the Law; what do you read there?" (**vs. 26**) speaks to the lawyer's textual expertise (the Torah) and his professional expertise (he is literate). Although the rabbinic texts suggest that all Jewish boys by the age of five could read Scripture – "Judah ben Tema used to say, 'At the age of five, [a boy is prepared] for Scripture. At ten, for Mishnah … At fifteen, for Talmud'" (*Avot* 5.21) – they are reflecting a different culture than the late Second Temple period.[18] Judah ben Tema was also being generous. Most people did not require the skill of literacy: books were expensive and rare in the small towns of the Galilee. Not even the Pharisees are shown as actually reading from texts: their knowledge of Torah practice may have been traditional rather than, as we find in rabbinic texts that do suggest general access to books, based on close readings of the words of Scripture.[19]

The question reinforces the lawyer's position among the "wise and intelligent." The "infants" (vs. 21) among Jesus' followers, listening to this story, already know who will pass the test. The question also, ironically, already answers the lawyer's question. The Law, or Torah, is what gives life, as Deut 8.1 cf. 28.1–14 attests, and postbiblical Judaism recognizes the Torah as the "tree of life" (Hebrew: *etz chaim*; see Prov 3.18). The lawyer is asking an eschatological question, not about "life" now as available through the study of Torah, but about everlasting life when one dies or at the eschaton. Ben sees the two forms of "life" – now and then – as distinct. Amy-Jill sees a continuity.

The lawyer responds by citing Deut 6.5 on love of God and Lev 19.28 on love of neighbor (**vs. 27**). This combination of texts already existed in early Judaism, as the *Testament of Issachar* 5.2-3 and the *Testament of Dan* 5.3 indicate. In the Gospels of Matthew (22.37) and Mark (12.29–31), Jesus himself is depicted as combining these texts into what has come to be called the "Greatest Commandment." The lawyer's answer also comports with later Jewish teaching: Rabbi Akiva, martyred by Roman authorities ca. 135, is quoted as saying that Lev 19.28 is the "greatest teaching" in the Torah (*Sifre* on Lev 19.18), and Deut 6.5 was already recognized as Israel's signature belief. Jesus tells the man he answered correctly; he had. Jesus then adds,

---

[18] See Catherine Hezser, *Jewish Literacy in Roman Palestine*, TSAJ 81 (Tübingen: Mohr Siebeck, 2001) as well as the critical essay review by Meir Bar-Ilan, "Literacy Among the Jews in Antiquity," *Hebrew Studies* 44 (2003): 217–22; Keith, *Jesus' Literacy*.

[19] See Paul Mandel, "Scriptural Exegesis and the Pharisees in Josephus," *JJS* 58.1 (2007): 19–32.

"Do this and you will live" (**vs. 28**), which may be an allusion to Lev 18.5, "You shall keep my statutes and my ordinances; by doing so one shall live: I am the Lord." Whether Jesus' response concerns eternal or eschatological life or whether Jesus is shifting the lawyer's question from eschaton to ethics, or whether it combines both concerns, remains an open question.

The story could have concluded at this juncture, but the lawyer is still seeking to "test" Jesus; now he is also seeking to "justify himself," that is, to make himself look right and ordered correctly (as in the expression "justified margins"). His conversation with Jesus has become a public challenge, with the honor and reputation of each man at stake. The lawyer asks his second question: who qualifies as "neighbor" (**Vs. 29**). Tannehill proposes, "the term translated 'neighbor' (Greek: *plēsion*) means one who is near. That would render his question as actually asking, "Who is close enough to me that I must respond with love, as the commandment says?'"[20] Were the lawyer asking, "Whom must I love?" then his question is not legitimate, since the same chapter in Leviticus that requires love of neighbor goes on to say, "When an alien resides with you in your land, you shall not oppress the alien. The alien who resides with you shall be to you as the citizen among you; you shall love the alien as yourself, for you were aliens in the land of Egypt: I am the Lord your God" (Lev 19.33–34).

The lawyer's question asks for a boundary definition, and so necessarily also asks, "Who is not my neighbor?"[21] However, contrary to a number of commentators who find "who is my neighbor?" an offensive question, it is not. All peoples need to determine who is the neighbor and who the stranger. Neighbors have citizen rights (neighbors can vote in local or national elections; strangers cannot) and liturgical roles (neighbors, fellow Jews, can have the honor of an *aliyah* in the synagogue, whereas non-Jews cannot in many congregations; neighbors, fellow Christians, can participate in Eucharistic practices or communion celebrations in churches; strangers, the nonbaptized, cannot according to some Christian groups). The question of the Samaritans is precisely one of neighbor (insider) versus stranger (outsider). Samaritans are not gentiles; they worship the God of Genesis, that is, the God of the Jews; they follow the laws of Torah; they claim the same ancestry. Whether they are in or out was a debated question among Jews.[22] *However*, when it comes to whom to love, whether one is

---

[20]   Tannehill, *Luke*, 182.
[21]   Bock, *Luke 9.51–24.53*, 1028.
[22]   See Fagenblat, "The Concept of Neighbor."

an insider or an outsider, a neighbor or a stranger, does not matter: love is indiscriminate. The lawyer asked about eternal life, and Jesus shifted the question to how one lives, ethically, in the present. The lawyer asks about insiders and outsiders; Jesus shifts to the more important question: who manifests compassion?

THE PARABLE OF THE MAN WHO FELL AMONG THE ROBBERS

Our title reflects the early title given the parable. Where we enter and how we see ourselves in the story will influence our interpretation of it. For Jesus' audience, and for Luke's readers, the ideal identification should be, at least initially, with the fellow who fell among the robbers. We are with him in the ditch, and through our half-dead eyes, we are watching for someone to come to the rescue.

Our title also seeks to avoid the offensiveness that the traditional title, "Parable of the Good Samaritan," implies, even though most people today do not see the offense. Were we to call the parable the "Parable of the Good Jew" (which, had Jesus been a Samaritan, might have been the title it received), we can begin to see the offense. The title presumes that "Good Samaritan" is unexpected. "He's a good immigrant" or "she's a good Muslim" might help get at the offense. The traditional title presumes that all members of the group are, with this one exception, to be negatively regarded.

The parable begins with "some fellow" (Greek: *anthrōpos tis*); he is likely a Jew (**vs. 30**) since this is a story set in Judea and Jesus identifies the Samaritan as such, the one person in the story who is not a Jew. The fellow is going down the serpentine, dangerous road from Jerusalem to Jericho. The road is the normal commuter route that priests and Levites, among others, regularly took, because some of them – likely those who could not afford to live in the high-rent district on Mt. Zion – lived in Jericho. The distance is some 17 miles, but the journey could be made on foot in a day, especially since it was quite literally all downhill. The road drops approximately 3,300 feet in elevation from Jerusalem to Jericho. The turns and hills along the way made this journey perilous, for bandits could easily waylay someone on the road (so Josephus, *War* 4.451–475). One always, by the way, *goes up* to Jerusalem and *down from* Jerusalem; the idiom signals the centrality of the city according to the Bible and subsequent Jewish literature.

The poor fellow, whoever he is, is attacked by bandits (Greek: *lēstēs*). Despite attempts by some commentators to import the model of "social banditry" (as in *Robin Hood*) and identify the bandits as dispossessed peasants attacking the rich, that is not Luke's point. Luke elsewhere uses the term *lēstēs* in the quote from Jeremiah regarding the Temple as a "den of robbers" (19.46): the "robbers" for Luke are the Temple authorities and any who practice the ritual without the required fidelity to God or change of heart, not dispossessed peasants. The only other use of the term in Luke's Gospel is in 22.52, when Jesus asks the "chief priests" and the "elders" if they are arresting him as they would *a bandit*. Listeners would identify not with the bandits in the parable, but with the man in the ditch. He is at this point "everyone" or at least "every man," for he is no longer marked by clothing and so by status. He is wounded, naked, and half-dead.

Along the road comes first a priest and then a Levite (**vss. 31–32**), and both pass by the victim. Commentators frequently propose that the priest and Levite refuse to aid the victim because of concerns regarding corpse impurity. The text underlying this interpretation is Lev 21.1–4, which teaches that the "priests, the sons of Aaron," shall not come into contact with a corpse unless it is the body of an immediate relative. The text is not relevant for our parable, for several reasons.

First, had the priest been going *up* to Jerusalem, where purity was required for Temple service, then he might have been concerned that he would have to wait a week before fulfilling his priestly duties. But he is going *down* and so not about to participate in Temple service. Second, the rule concerning corpses is *not* applicable to Levites, so the presence of the Levite disrupts any connection to Lev 21. Third, in the book of Tobit, the titular hero is like a funny Jewish Antigone who spends the first few chapters burying the unclaimed bodies of strangers. Jews would have expected fellow Jews to attend not only to victims of attack, but to unburied corpses. Fourth, Josephus, our first-century historian, insists that Jews take care of unattended corpses and follow Torah's command "not to let anyone lie unburied" (*Apion* 2.211 cf. *Ant.* 5.317; *War* 3.377; 4.317). Fifth, the Mishnah, *Nazir* 7.1, even enjoins a high priest "to contract corpse uncleanness on account of a neglected corpse." The priest and the Levite were not following Torah, and laws of purity provide them no excuse.[23] Indeed, both priest and Levite *should* have stopped to help, as Jewish literature from before Jesus through to Rabbinic literature indicates. Likely Jesus' audience, and Luke's, would have been not only surprised but appalled by the priest and

---

[23]   Lieu astutely notes, "in particular [the parable] does not say, as commentators have been too quick to, that temple duties and hence the obligations of the Law were what kept them from obedience to the law of love." *Gospel According to Luke*, 87.

the Levite. Jews would have expected the priest and Levite to stop, because that was the right thing to do.

The reason the priest and Levite are mentioned has nothing to do with Temple purity. It has everything to do with Jewish expectations. In Judaism, then and even today, three categories have survived through the centuries. A Jew is either a priest (descended from Aaron, the brother of Moses), a Levite (descended from Moses' ancestor, Levi, the third son of Jacob and Leah), or an Israelite (descended from Jacob's other sons; a Jew-by-choice is considered an Israelite as well). The naming of the first two sets up the expectation of the third, just as, in a church context, to say, "Father, Son ..." anticipates "Holy Spirit."

It is not the expected Israelite who stops, but the unthinkable Samaritan who attends to the victim (**vs. 33**). To go from priest to Levite to Samaritan is tantamount to going from Father to Son to Satan. Samaritans were the enemy; Jesus' audience, identifying with the man in the ditch rather than the Samaritan, might think to themselves, "that Samaritan coming near is going to kill me."

The Greek term for "compassion" – used also to describe Jesus' reaction to the widow of Nain, and the response of the father to his "prodigal" son – indicates feelings that come from the innermost part of one's being, literally the bowels. The NRSV's "moved with pity" does not quite get at the nuance of the Greek. From compassion, the Samaritan moves to action. The explanations that he used oil to soothe the hurt of the bruises, and wine, with its alcohol, to clean the cuts are as good as any (**vs. 34**). After bringing the injured man to an inn in Jericho, he guarantees that the innkeeper will continue the care; he offers two denarii (two days' wages) as well as his promise to pay whatever additional cost accrued. The depiction of the Samaritan is thus consistent with Luke's concern for aiding the poor (as Margaret Thatcher said in 1980, "Nobody would remember the Good Samaritan if he had only good intentions. He had money as well).''[24] The promise is both generous and threatening (**vs. 35**): the Samaritan coming back to check on the victim.

Biblically literate readers should be reminded here of 2 Chron 28.8–15. In this earlier text, a Judean (Jewish) prophet named Oded condemns Samaritan leaders for their attack on their Judean neighbors, and the Samaritans respond with mercy: they clothed the naked, gave them food and drink, anointed them, placed the injured on donkeys, and brought

[24]   www.bbc.com/news/uk-politics-10377842.

them to Jericho. The Samaritans may be enemies, but even enemies can do the right thing, and even enemies can become friends. The cycle of violence can be broken.

Following the parable, Jesus changes the lawyer's question. The lawyer had asked, "Who is my neighbor?" but Jesus asks him, "Who proved neighbor?" or, "Who showed himself to be a neighbor?" (**vs. 36**). As Michael Fagenblat summarizes, "In the end, the parable does not answer the lawyer's question 'Who is my neighbor?' but illustrates how to love. It shows the Jewish questioner what a neighbor does but does not redefine who a neighbor is."[25] The lawyer again answers correctly, "The one who showed him mercy," though he answers reluctantly; he may be loath to voice the explicit "Samaritan." Jesus concludes this test by telling the lawyer: "Go and do likewise" (**vs. 37**). Whether the lawyer learned to ask the right question is never noted; like the centurion and his slave, Jairus and his daughter, and many others, his story is not continued in Luke's narrative.

"Divine mercy does not ask the worth of the recipient. It only sees the need,"[26] is a good but insufficient summary of the parable. A better summary is, "It is one thing to learn that the command to love encompasses anyone who is in need, even the outsider or enemy; it is far more disturbing to have to acknowledge that the enemy or outsider may be more quick to show love than those who are certainly fellow 'insiders.'"[27] But the shock and the challenge is even greater. Not only might the outsider, the enemy, show compassion, but we must realize that only when we can accept this possibility will we ourselves be able to live.[28]

MARTHA AND MARY, AND JESUS

Luke 10.38–42 turns from "a certain man" or "some fellow" of the parable to "a certain woman"[29] (**vs. 38**), as the next scene takes place in the home of two of Jesus' female disciples. The presence of these patrons was anticipated by the notice of the women patrons in 8.1–3 and the instructions to the seventy-two to enter homes; here Jesus takes the role of one of his disciples

[25] Fagenblat, "Concept of Neighbor."
[26] Frederick W. Danker, *Jesus and the New Age: A Commentary on St. Luke's Gospel* (Philadelphia: Fortress Press, 1988), 133.
[27] Lieu, *Gospel According to Luke*, 87.
[28] For more commentary on this parable, see Amy-Jill Levine, *Short Stories by Jesus: The Enigmatic Parables of a Controversial Rabbi* (New York: Harper One, 2014), 71–106.
[29] Culpepper, "The Gospel of Luke," 231.

by entering a home and bringing peace to it. The same scene reappears in Acts 16.14–15, when "a certain woman named Lydia" welcomes Paul into her home. For an earlier account of a woman providing for a man in her house, we may recall the widow of Zarepath, who served Elijah, and perhaps Peter's mother-in-law, who served Jesus. When Martha "welcomes" or "receives" Jesus into her home, she is doing what householders greeting disciples do (10.8).

Luke has an interest in women patrons: what Luke expects those patrons to do, however, remains a matter of debate. Luke may be locating women in leadership roles as presiders over house-churches; alternatively, Luke may be asking women to put their resources in the service of the Church but to allow men to determine resource allocation and to make other leadership decisions. Ben is more sanguine about women's leadership in Luke's narrative than is Amy-Jill. Ben also thinks that the message that Mary has chosen the good or best option here suggests Luke does not see women merely as patrons, but as those who should prioritize learning Jesus' teaching.

Luke does insist that anyone can show, and should show, hospitality. Following the Parable of the Man Who Fell among the Robbers, the story of Martha and Mary echoes both the hospitality shown by the Samaritan and the disruption in daily routine. In the parable, the Samaritan stops his journey not only to tend the victim's wounds but also to find him care in Jericho. His "one needful thing" was to aid a fellow human being in trouble. Mary too stops whatever she was doing; her "one needful thing" is to listen to Jesus.

The personalities of Mary and Martha as portrayed in 10.38–42 match their Johannine depictions: in John 11–12, Martha is the more verbal, outgoing, and critical one, and Mary the more silent: traditionally she is viewed as the more introspective.[30] It is John (11.1, 18) who tells us that Mary and Martha live in Bethany, which is near Jerusalem. Later tradition saw Martha as representing the active life and Mary the (preferred) contemplative (see Gregory's *Homily on Ezekiel* 2.2.9).

Once again, commentators are wont to contrast Jesus' teaching with select rabbinic statements. Sometimes they cite the early third-century CE *mishnah*, *Avot* 1.5, wherein Yose b. Yochanan of Jerusalem says, "Don't talk too much with women," and the sages add, "He spoke of a man's wife; all the more so is the rule to be applied to the wife of one's fellow. In this regard

[30] See Witherington, *Women in the Ministry of Jesus*, 100–3.

did sages say, 'So long as a man talks too much with a woman, he brings trouble on himself, wastes time better spent on studying Torah, and ends up an heir of Gehenna.'" Granted, the passage is not a feminist anthem. Nor, however, should it be read as normative for late Second Temple Jews. It is in-house rabbinic banter, undercut consistently by examples of men and women speaking with each other in rabbinic literature. Were they not talking, even in the rabbinic period, such advice as R. Yose's would not be needed. The society was homosocial, but there was no law preventing men from talking to women; such a law would make no sense, especially in the context of friends gathered together in a home owned by a woman patron. Missing in the standard citations of this *mishna* in the context of Jesus and women is the verse that comes immediately before: "Yose b. Yoezer says, 'Let your house be a gathering place for sages, and wallow in the dust of their feet, and drink in their words with thirst" (*Avot* 1.4). The sages should be so lucky that this becomes general practice.

The disruption in this scene is not a breach of Jewish law; it is a breach of household routine. Jesus, apart from his entourage, enters the home of a woman named Martha, and she welcomes him (**vs. 38**). He is the itinerant, and she the householder. Readers might expect, based on the commissions of the Twelve and of the seventy (or seventy-two), that there will be a healing in the home, a message about the Kingdom, food served and eaten, and peace throughout. Luke will now disrupt these expectations.

Although the home belongs to Martha, the narrative turns immediately to Mary, Martha's sister (**vs. 39**). Luke does not specify the details of their relationship, but given that Martha owns the house, she is likely the elder. The presence of two sisters in the same household evokes the motifs of both women's rivalry and sibling rivalry found in Israel's Scriptures. Women in the same household are frequently at odds, and at odds over a man's attention: Sarah and Hagar are Abraham's co-wives, Leah and Rachel vie for Jacob's attention, Peninah and Hannah are co-wives in competition regarding childbearing. The similar pattern of sibling rivalry between and among brothers – Cain and Abel, Ishmael and Isaac, Esau and Jacob, Zerah and Perez, Joseph and his brothers, Solomon and his brothers – also underlies this story. That motif will reappear in Luke's Parable of the Prodigal Son. Ruth and Naomi break the pattern, as do Mary and Elizabeth in Luke's own narrative. Mary and Martha reinstantiate it, at least at the beginning of the scene. Whether they remain in opposition or come to be together with Jesus is the part of Luke's story readers can fill in, or that the author of the Fourth Gospel does for them.

Martha is the host and patron, but Mary is one who sits at Jesus' feet and listens to his teaching. To sit at one's feet is to take the role of a disciple. In terms of visualization, Mary is closer to Jesus than is Martha. The import of her position is further enhanced by Luke's language; it is not just "Jesus" or "he" by whose feet she sits, but "the lord." The scene is therefore more than just a narrative about hospitality; the teaching is a matter of revelation.

While Mary listens to Jesus, according to the NRSV, Martha is "distracted by her many tasks" (**vs. 40a**). The Greek literally reads, "distracted by much ministry." The word translated "tasks" is *diakonia*, the root of the English term "deacon." It ranges in meaning from "service" to "ministry." Tannehill suggests, "in this setting of hospitality, *diakonia* means caring for one's guests, especially through providing a meal. According to some commentators, it does not refer to an established 'ministry' of preaching and leadership. Whereas some observe that the verb *diakoneō* in Luke's Gospel can refer to domestic service such as providing food ... something that women or slaves were expected to do (4.39; 8.3; 12.37; 17.8)."[31] There is no reason to presume that Luke 8.3, a reference to patronage, indicates domestic service.

Moreover, the term is also predicated of Jesus and the disciples (22.26–27), who are by no means limited to kitchen duties. Warren Carter notes that "Partnership with others in the acts of ministry pervades all eight texts" where the Greek term [*diakoneō*] appears in Luke's Gospel.[32] The office of "deacon" was well established in the churches at the time Luke wrote, as the mention of Phoebe the "deacon" in Rom 16.1–2 demonstrates. Luke's readers would have known this office, and therefore likely saw Martha in the context of a house-church. They may have also recognized Mary as her "sister" in ministry. The connection of Martha's concern with ministry is finally enhanced by her concern that she has been left alone to do the work (**vs. 40b**). Jesus had sent his disciples out in pairs; ministry requires support.

The role of a disciple is not simply to listen; it is to ask questions, to be actively engaged in learning. Mary is silent, but Martha is not. Her comment to Jesus is one of both respect, in that she calls him "Lord," and one of exasperation: "Do you not care?" is the language of critique. Martha is stating, not too subtly, that he *should* care that Mary is not working and that he *should* encourage her to help in the service. Martha also wants Jesus to

---

[31]   Tannehill, *Luke*, 185–86.
[32]   Warren Carter, "Getting Martha out of the Kitchen: Luke 10:38–42 Again," *CBQ* 58.2 (1996): 264–80 (271); reprinted in Levine with Blickenstaff (eds.), *Feminist Companion to Luke*, 214–31.

provide the instruction or, better, fix the problem: she and Mary, like Sarah and Hagar, never speak to each other (in contrast to John 11).

Ben suggests that since "lord" here is in the vocative as Martha's form of polite address, and not in the narrative framework where Luke the Christian is talking to his own audience, we should not envision Martha as speaking like a post-Easter follower would about Jesus. Luke knows enough about the historical circumstances to know that no one saw or addressed Jesus as "the risen Lord" before Easter, nor did Jesus refer to himself that way in the aforementioned saying. The reference to the "Lord" in vss. 39 and 41 is Luke speaking as the Christian narrator, not Martha. There is a difference. Amy-Jill finds the literary effect of the narrative to include not only the lifetime of Jesus but also the time of the Church. Thus the Christian hearing the Gospel of Luke would hear Martha's address as implicitly containing confessional import. Martha thereby represents to the listener both the pre-Easter friend of Jesus and the post-Easter well-off woman in the Church.

Luke retains the emphasis on Jesus' authority by referring to him in the next verse, for the third time in this vignette, as "lord." Jesus' repetition of the name, "Martha, Martha" (**vs. 41a**), like his repetition of the name "Simon" (i.e., Peter) in 22.31, is an indication of concern as well as a warning. Martha's worry and distraction are not based on minor matters, such as fluffed pillows or parsley garnishes. The worries and distractions *of ministry* are substantial: ensuring people have enough food, shelter, health care, companionship. Jesus is not belittling Martha's situation. He is, rather, establishing priorities.

The final line of the account (**vs. 42**) is textually difficult: the tradition ranges from "one thing is necessary" to "a few things are necessary" to an omission of the phrase entirely in the Old Latin tradition. Our text sets us up to expect a contrast between the many things about which Martha is concerned, and something else. Mary is engaged in only one thing: listening to the "word" of Jesus. The contrast is between hearing "the word" and anything else. One cannot do ministry until one is catechized; hearing comes before doing, learning comes before action, and instruction in the word is required before running a house-church. As Deut 8.3b states, a person does not live by physical food alone, but by everything that proceeds out of the mouth of the Lord (Deut 8.3b).[33] Jesus had quoted that verse to the devil (4.4).

---

[33]   C. A. Evans, *Luke*, 177.

We might better understand Jesus' critique of Martha by considering her role as householder. Throughout the Gospel, Jesus finds himself at dinner settings, and he consistently critiques the host (as we saw already with Simon the Pharisee in Luke 7). Martha, the (wealthy?) householder, similarly receives criticism because she has misplaced her focus. Distracted by all her "ministry," she is pulled away from what should be the center of her attention.[34] In her role of host, she must be attentive primarily to her guest. Jesus' critique of Martha concerns hospitality and catechesis, not gender. At the same time, whereas Mary has chosen the better part – to listen to Jesus – there is potential danger in her choice as well. Only to listen and not to act is to fail to thrive as a disciple. "Mary manifests yet another possible danger, that disciples may be so intently centered on the Lord's teaching (10:39–40) that they do not *do* or *pass on* the teaching (cf. 8:21; 11:28)."[35]

Finally, we see here that Jesus is not setting himself up as a mediator.[36] A scene similar to that of the two sisters reinforces this point. In 12.13–15, a fellow from the crowd commands Jesus, "Teacher, tell my brother to divide the family inheritance with me" (12.13), just as Martha had commanded Jesus, "tell her to help me." In both cases, Jesus rejects the command and, gently, critiques the speaker. Jesus opens up the possibility of reconciliation: it is up to the estranged people to make the matter right. Luke does not tell us if Martha and Mary reconciled, or even if this was the one moment of disagreement in an otherwise healthy relationship. John, who may have known Luke's story, assures readers that all is well between the siblings.

BRIDGING THE HORIZONS

1. Concentration of Power

The potential for abuse is always great when power is concentrated in the hands of a few. In his instructions to the seventy-two, Jesus takes certain kinds of power out of their hands. They are not to take resources with them when they itinerate. They are to rely on local hospitality and to stay with the household that initially welcomed them, rather than climb the social ladder and so shame their original hosts. They are not to rejoice over their power over demons; rather, they are to rejoice that they have a place in

---

[34] Carter, "Getting Martha out of the Kitchen," 268.
[35] Ibid., 279.
[36] See Bock, *Luke 2: 9:51–24:53*, 1041.

the Kingdom of God. Sathianathan Clarke remarks concerning some missionaries today, "Those who arrive with purses full of currency and credit cards to circumvent dependence on the host community, with bags capable of containing weapons to overpower the people that welcome … are more likely to be wolves."[37] This, Ben says, is an unfair comment, indeed a caricature, if it is meant to be a *generalization* about all self-supporting Christian missionaries. Amy-Jill finds Clarke's comment to ring true *in some cases*, since she has been in conversation with numerous people, especially women from the two-thirds world, who recount stories of missionaries who evangelize on the basis of economic superiority. This approach can turn the Gospel into a commodity, even as it can function to demean the people whom the missionary evangelizes.

Ben recounts the following story:

> Sheryl had been my friend for many years. We grew up in the same neighborhood in High Point, North Carolina, but there was a difference between the two of us. She was part of an observant Jewish family, and I was a part of an observant Christian one. I had had the privilege to attend synagogue once in a while and to celebrate with Sheryl when she became a bat mitzvah. She and her family welcomed me in their synagogue and in their home. There came a day when Sheryl asked me if I would take her to a dance for high school students at the local country club. I told her I would be honored to do it. I had not realized that that club was restricted: Jews and African Americans were barred from membership, and even attending functions. Sheryl knew this, and she wanted to be sure I understood that bringing her to the club could be awkward, or costly.
>
> We went to the dance and had a grand time, and I learned more that night than just new dance steps. I learned in a small way how to see the world through the eyes of a person who regularly experienced prejudice. Jesus encouraged his disciples to prioritize love and mercy and compassion, regardless of the cost. Perhaps the day will come when those who claim to be his followers, such as those "good Christians" who belonged to that country club and who, most likely, all went to church on Sunday, will all do the same.

Amy-Jill appreciates Ben's compassion and recognition of prejudice. She also sees there the possibility of the envy of the other for the good things they have. Did Sheryl envy those who were going to the dance and feel herself left out? Is that how some people feel when missionaries – loaded with

[37] Sathianathan Clarke, "Global Cultural Traffic, Christian Mission, and Biblical Interpretation: Rereading Luke 10:1–12 Through the Eyes of an Indian Mission Recipient," *Ex Auditu* 23 (2007): 162–78 (169).

goodies – arrive at the borders or on the shore? What did Sheryl's parents do to make her comfortable in her own identity? Do we seek assimilation, or the denial of our own identities, because it is the easier path or the path to material gain? What is the missionary offering, and at what price?

2. Predestination and Salvation

Jesus states in 10.22 both that the only way to know the God of Israel is to be his follower and that he himself holds the lock on who can know and who cannot. In one verse, Luke restricts salvation to the followers of Jesus and damns people who follow a different path. It's an easy move from this claim to the bigotry that marks the claim of "I'm saved and you're not."

This view of salvation, known as predestination, takes responsibility for belief out of the hands, and hearts, of the individual and locates it with God. In one respect, the predestinarian claim makes psychological sense. Most people do not "believe" in theological claims because of empirical evidence or scientific proof. Paul himself admits that the salvation gained by Jesus' death is not a logical conclusion; to the contrary, he states, "we proclaim Christ crucified, a stumbling block to Jews and foolishness to Gentiles" (1 Cor 1.23). Belief is not a matter of logic and nor is it a matter of knowledge. It has nothing to do with intelligence (it can indeed bypass the well-educated, as Luke 10 also observes), and it cannot be compelled. It is, rather, like love. It comes unbidden.

Some Jews at the time did believe in predestination. The Community Rule (1QS 3.15–21; 4.18–20) from Qumran asserts that God has "appointed for humanity two spirits in which to walk until the time of his visitation: the spirits of truth and injustice. Those born of truth spring from a mountain of light, but those born of injustice spring from a source of darkness. All the children of righteousness are ruled by the Prince of light and walk in the ways of light, but all the children of injustice are ruled by the Angel of Darkness and walk in the ways of darkness ..." Josephus states that the Essenes "declare that fate is the mistress of all things, and that nothing befalls people unless it be in accordance with her decree" (*Ant.* 13.172). The Gospel of John moves in a similar predestinarian direction.

This was not the only view at the time, and a text that looks predestinarian in one place can look open to both fate and free will in others. Various early Jews, including Paul and the Pharisees, held together a belief in both predestination or God's providence and also free will. Describing the Pharisees, Josephus states that they found "certain events are the work of fate, but not all; as to other events it depends on ourselves whether they shall take place or not" (*Ant.* 13.172, cf. 18.13; *War* 2.162–63). *Pirke Avot* 3.16 offers a quote traditionally attributed to the famous Rabbi Akiva, "All is determined, but free will is given." The technical term for this is "compatibilism." Thus, finding this combination of ideas in Luke's writings is possible. As E. P. Sanders observes, it seems to be modern people who have trouble holding these ideas together in tension without affirming just one or the other.[38]

The predestinarian pronouncements would be good news to those disciples who shook off more dust than received hospitality. The rejection of the message was not their fault: rocky soil and thorny soil cannot change. Perhaps others can change it, but that is not what the parable says. Predestinarian impulses coupled with hidden wisdom also made sense in a first-century context, as it is a mark of apocalyptic thinking (cf. the instructions to Daniel: "Keep the words secret and the book sealed until the time of the end" [Dan 12.4]) and Paul's comment, "We speak God's wisdom, secret and hidden, which God decreed before the ages for our glory" [1 Cor 2.7]).

Recognizing that belief is more like love than it is like logic should help Christian missionaries today, well meaning though they are, stop attempting to "prove" to Jews or anyone else that Jesus is their messiah. No citation of a text from the Tanakh is going to "prove" that Jesus is Lord. Rather, if one begins with the belief that Jesus is Lord, one will find his presence in Israel's Scriptures. More, such recognition should stop other missionaries from telling Jews and Muslims, Hindus and Buddhists, atheists and agnostics, "Unless you believe the following doctrinal statements, you will go to hell." Adults can usually brush off such claims: if we do not accept the presupposition of a deity who arbitrarily damns people, then we are not going to be worried about the damnation itself. However, children do not always have this theological sophistication. It is psychologically offensive to threaten children with hell if they do not "believe" something that is by all logical views a folly and a scandal, and it is theologically inconsistent to proclaim a "God of love" who is only loving to some, but a sadistic bully to others.

Ben notes that there is another way to read Luke's statements about revelations that are hidden from one group and revealed to another. This is apocalyptic language about revelation offered during the ministry of Jesus.

[38] Sanders, *Paul: The Apostle's Life, Letters, and Thought*, 52, and at various other places in this lengthy study. See for an extended discussion of compatibilism in early Jewish sources Jonathan Klawans, "Josephus on Fate, Free Will, and Ancient Jewish Types of Compatibilism," *Numen* 56 (2009): 44–90.

It is not statements about people's eternal salvation. Luke is talking about who receives and understands the teaching of Jesus when he offers it, and who does not. And the point of such remarks is to indicate who will become Jesus' first disciples and witnesses. Disciples of Jesus are not already "born again" Christians. In other words, the focus is not about the eternal destiny of those who receive the message of Jesus, it's about their calling and equipping for ministry. And as for the soils in the Parable of the Sower, Ben sees that soils can be changed. The rocky soil can be denuded of its rocks. The soil with brambles can be cleared and made serviceable. The parable is not about predestination by God to be this or that kind of soil, but about who was and wasn't receptive to Jesus's message and call to follow him, *in their current condition*. But conditions can change, and so can people.

Luke 11 Prayer, Petitions, Parables, and Polemic

TEACH US TO PRAY

[1] He was praying in a certain place, and after he had finished, one of his disciples said to him, "Lord, teach us to pray, as John taught his disciples."
[2] He said to them, "When you pray, say: Father, hallowed be your name. Your kingdom come. [3] Give us each day our daily bread. [4] And forgive us our sins, for we ourselves forgive everyone indebted to us. And do not bring us to the time of trial."

PARABLE OF THE PUSHY PAL

[5] And he said to them, "Suppose one of you has a friend, and you go to him at midnight and say to him, 'Friend, lend me three loaves of bread; [6] for a friend of mine has arrived, and I have nothing to set before him.' [7] And he answers from within, 'Do not bother me; the door has already been locked, and my children are with me in bed; I cannot get up and give you anything.' [8] I tell you, even though he will not get up and give him anything because he is his friend, at least because of his persistence he will get up and give him whatever he needs.
[9] "So I say to you, Ask, and it will be given you; search, and you will find; knock, and the door will be opened for you. [10] For everyone who asks receives, and everyone who searches finds, and for everyone who knocks, the door will be opened.
[11] Is there anyone among you who, if your child asks for a fish, will give a snake instead of a fish? [12] Or if the child asks for an egg, will give a scorpion?
[13] If you then, who are evil, know how to give good gifts to your children, how much more will the heavenly Father give the Holy Spirit to those who ask him!"

DEFEATING SATAN

¹⁴ Now he was casting out a demon that was mute; when the demon had gone out, the one who had been mute spoke, and the crowds were amazed. ¹⁵ But some of them said, "He casts out demons by Beelzebul, the ruler of the demons." ¹⁶ Others, to test him, kept demanding from him a sign from heaven. ¹⁷ But he knew what they were thinking and said to them, "Every kingdom divided against itself becomes a desert, and house falls on house. ¹⁸ If Satan also is divided against himself, how will his kingdom stand? – for you say that I cast out the demons by Beelzebul. ¹⁹ Now if I cast out the demons by Beelzebul, by whom do your exorcists cast them out? Therefore they will be your judges. ²⁰ But if it is by the finger of God that I cast out the demons, then the kingdom of God has come to you.

²¹ When a strong man, fully armed, guards his castle, his property is safe. ²² But when one stronger than he attacks him and overpowers him, he takes away his armor in which he trusted and divides his plunder.

²³ Whoever is not with me is against me, and whoever does not gather with me scatters.

AN EMPTY MIND IS THE DEVIL'S PLAYGROUND

²⁴ "When the unclean spirit has gone out of a person, it wanders through waterless regions looking for a resting place, but not finding any, it says, 'I will return to my house from which I came.' ²⁵ When it comes, it finds it swept and put in order. ²⁶ Then it goes and brings seven other spirits more evil than itself, and they enter and live there; and the last state of that person is worse than the first."

COMPARATIVE BLESSINGS

²⁷ While he was saying this, a woman in the crowd raised her voice and said to him, "Blessed is the womb that bore you and the breasts that nursed you!" ²⁸ But he said, "Blessed rather are those who hear the word of God and obey it!"

SIGNS AND WHAT THEY SIGNIFY

²⁹ When the crowds were increasing, he began to say, "This generation is an evil generation; it asks for a sign, but no sign will be given to it except the sign of Jonah. ³⁰ For just as Jonah became a sign to the people of Nineveh, so the Son of Man will be to this generation.

³¹ "The queen of the South will rise at the judgment with the people of this generation and condemn them, because she came from the ends of the earth to listen to the wisdom of Solomon, and see, something greater than Solomon is here! ³² The people of Nineveh will rise up at the judgment with this generation and condemn it, because they repented at the proclamation of Jonah, and see, something greater than Jonah is here!

³³ "No one after lighting a lamp puts it in a cellar, but on the lampstand so that those who enter may see the light. ³⁴ Your eye is the lamp of your body. If your eye is healthy, your whole body is full of light; but if it is not healthy, your body is full of darkness. ³⁵ Therefore consider whether the light in you is not darkness. ³⁶ If then your whole body is full of light, with no part of it in darkness, it will be as full of light as when a lamp gives you light with its rays."

TABLE TALK INVECTIVE

³⁷ While he was speaking, a Pharisee invited him to dine with him; so he went in and took his place at the table. ³⁸ The Pharisee was amazed to see that he did not first wash before dinner. ³⁹ Then the Lord said to him, "Now you Pharisees clean the outside of the cup and of the dish, but inside you are full of greed and wickedness. ⁴⁰ You fools! Did not the one who made the outside make the inside also? ⁴¹ So give for alms those things that are within; and see, everything will be clean for you.

⁴² "But woe to you Pharisees! For you tithe mint and rue and herbs of all kinds, and neglect justice and the love of God; it is these you ought to have practiced, without neglecting the others.

⁴³ "Woe to you Pharisees! For you love to have the seat of honor in the synagogues and to be greeted with respect in the marketplaces.

⁴⁴ "Woe to you! For you are like unmarked graves, and people walk over them without realizing it."

⁴⁵ One of the lawyers answered him, "Teacher, when you say these things, you insult us too." ⁴⁶ And he said, "Woe also to you lawyers! For you load people with burdens hard to bear, and you yourselves do not lift a finger to ease them.

⁴⁷ "Woe to you! For you build the tombs of the prophets whom your ancestors killed. ⁴⁸So you are witnesses and approve of the deeds of your ancestors; for they killed them, and you build their tombs. ⁴⁹ Therefore also the Wisdom of God said, 'I will send them prophets and apostles, some of whom they will kill and persecute,' ⁵⁰ so that this generation may

be charged with the blood of all the prophets shed since the foundation of the world, [51] from the blood of Abel to the blood of Zechariah, who perished between the altar and the sanctuary. Yes, I tell you, it will be charged against this generation.

[52] "Woe to you lawyers! For you have taken away the key of knowledge; you did not enter yourselves, and you hindered those who were entering."

[53] When he went outside, the scribes and the Pharisees began to be very hostile toward him and to cross-examine him about many things, [54] lying in wait for him, to catch him in something he might say.

The previous chapter ended with Jesus in Martha's home; Chapter 11 begins with Jesus "praying in a certain place" (Amy-Jill would like to think that the place is the courtyard in front of Martha's house) and teaching his disciples how to pray. The prayer then sets the agenda for the next several sections of the chapter. The parable usually called "The Friend at Midnight" concerns matters of bread, relationships, and hospitality; single sayings about need and response follow the prayer's concern for reciprocity as well as divine paternity. Jesus is tested regarding whether he is in league with Satan, and so he is "brought to the test" as he had been in the Temptation Narrative. A woman calls out to him to bless his mother's womb and breasts, but Jesus refocuses the blessing on those who do what God would want.

As the crowds increase, the topics change. Jesus turns from blessing to warning: the sign of Jonah, the question of whether one walks in the light or the dark, the excoriations of Pharisees for following proper ritual but not following through on justice and love, and finally the hyperbolic charge against "this generation" for murder, from Abel to the present. Following these vilifications, Luke notes, laconically, that the Pharisees "began to be very hostile toward him."

TEACH US TO PRAY

Both Ben in North Carolina and Amy-Jill in Massachusetts recited the Matthean version of what John Dominic Crossan calls "The Greatest Prayer"[1] in elementary school every morning, along with saying the Pledge of Allegiance and singing the "Star Spangled Banner." Neither of us thought

---

[1]   John Dominic Crossan, *The Greatest Prayer: Rediscovering the Revolutionary Message of the Lord's Prayer* (New York: HarperOne, 2010). See also Ben Witherington III and L. Ice, *The Shadow of the Almighty* (Grand Rapids: Eerdmans, 2002).

praying in public settings was strange. For Ben, the prayer was already familiar, as he had heard it every Sunday in the United Methodist Church. Amy-Jill, who did not hear this prayer in the synagogue, nevertheless found it familiar, because it sounded Jewish themes: God as father, the special nature of the divine name, something about food. "Lead us not into Penn Station" also made sense to her, since she knew this was a busy place where children could get lost. She is not sure when she first realized the prayer was associated with Jesus of Nazareth, and when it was called the "Lord's Prayer," that the "lord" in question was Jesus. She thought it was a fully Jewish prayer, and she was right. Public recitation of the prayer ended in US public schools in 1961, at least officially (it went on for a while longer in parts of the South).

In Matthew's Gospel (6.9–13), Jesus delivers the prayer to the disciples as part of the "Sermon on the Mount": it comes as a form of general instruction. In Luke's Gospel, Jesus is in an unidentified "some place" where, typically in this Gospel, he is at prayer. One of his disciples, politely waiting until he had stopped, addresses him as "lord" (*kyrios*) and asks for instructions. The disciple does not ask for Jesus to share his own prayers (which to this point have been silent), but to teach his disciples as John taught his own followers (**vs. 1**).

This opening immediately raises several issues. First, the disciples already know how to pray. They are all Jews (the gentile mission has not yet begun), and they would all to some extent be familiar with the Psalms as well as typical blessings for food, morning and evening prayers, and so on. Their tradition also promoted personal prayer, as we see especially in Second Temple literature: the Additions to the Book of Daniel (the "Song of Azariah" and the "Prayer of the Three Young Men in the Furnace"), the major Greek version of the books of Esther, Judith, and so on, all display personal prayers. From Qumran come numerous personal prayers, including 1QH (H for *hodayot*, or "prayers"), likely to be the prayers of the founder of the community, the Teacher of Righteousness. Thus, they do not need instruction on *how* to pray. Second is the concern for the rivalry between Jesus and John. Even following John's beheading, his disciples continued to follow the Baptizer's teachings rather than affiliate with Jesus and his followers. Third, what exactly Jesus' disciple asks is not clear. Does he request a specific prayer that would mark the disciples as Jesus' followers, or does he want Jesus to teach his disciples the prayer that John had taught? The Greek for "just as" (*kathos*) could lead in either direction. Fourth, Luke does not make clear whether this prayer would replace other prayers or supplement them.

Finally, and of greatest import for disciples of Jesus today, is the formulation itself. Luke's version of the "Lord's Prayer" is different from the version in the Sermon on the Mount. No other versions of this prayer appear in the New Testament, although there are some similar sounding verses. Rom 8.15 and Gal 4.6 both contain the reference to God in Aramaic as "Abba, Father," which may echo the prayer, but it may also recall Jesus' prayer in Gethsemane, which in Mark's version contains this same Aramaic address (Mark 14.36). The early Christian text called *The Teaching of the Twelve Apostles* or the *Didache* contains a variant of the prayer. The text instructs, "And do not pray as the hypocrites, but as the Lord commanded in his Gospel, pray thus: 'Our Father, who is in Heaven, hallowed be your Name, your Kingdom come, your will be done, as in Heaven so also upon earth; give us today our daily bread, and forgive us our debt as we forgive our debtors, and lead us not into trial, but deliver us from the Evil One, for yours is the power and the glory for ever.' Pray thus three times a day."

The wording passed along from Jesus to his immediate followers to the Gospel writers, which includes the translation from Aramaic to Greek, is not consistent. For these disciples, and those who would walk in their footsteps, the ideas rather than a verbatim recollection were what mattered. The ideas – the naming of the divine as "father," the sanctification of the Name, the yearning for the Kingdom, the concern for bread today and tomorrow, forgiving of sins/debts, and eschewing of temptation – could be expressed in different words. But in all versions of the prayer, brevity rather than babble is preferred, as Tertullian's *Tract on Prayer* and Cyprian's *On the Lord's Prayer* had noted early on.[2]

Without any question as to the necessity of such instruction, Jesus responds, "Whenever you pray ..." (**vs. 2**). Thereby, he sets up the prayer as *something to be repeated*. The opening, "Father" lacks Matthew's famous "Our" (Matt 6.9); the address thus lacks the emphasis on the communal relationship. For Luke, the prayer begins with the personal, not the congregational. Nevertheless, Jesus' instructions hint at the communal: "Whenever you (plural) pray ..."

The prayer is addressed to "father"; the Greek reads *pater*, the standard term for "father." The underlying Aramaic would be *abba*. The editor of the *Theological Dictionary of the New Testament*, Gerhard Kittel, who contributed the article on the term *abba* to that dictionary, asserted that "Jesus' usage shows how this Father-child relationship to God far surpasses any

---

[2] Evans, *Luke*, 477.

possibilities of intimacy assumed in Judaism, introducing indeed something which is wholly new."[3] Kittel's claim was then developed by the German biblical scholar Joachim Jeremias. First, Jeremias proposed that *Abba* was the term by which children would address their fathers and so a form of "baby talk."[4] When faced with evidence to the contrary, he retracted this view, although he continued to insist, "It would have seemed disrespectful, indeed unthinkable, to the sensibilities of Jesus' contemporaries to address God with this familiar word."[5] Marianne Meye Thompson correctly observes, "Jesus did not scandalize his contemporaries by the application of 'baby talk' to God."[6] Nevertheless, "abba-daddy" versus "anything Jews would say" remains a staple in Christian preaching.

The word *abba* in modern Hebrew can have the connotation of "daddy" (Hebrew-speaking children today refer to their parents as *abba* and *imma* [daddy and mommy]), but that is not the meaning of the Aramaic. *Abba* means "father" (Greek *pater*), which is how Mark and Paul both define the term.

Nor is the address unique to Jesus. Jews then, and now, address God as "father." The address already appears in late biblical material such as Sir 23.1 ("Lord, Father and Master of my life") and 51.10 ("Lord, you are my Father"); Tob 13.4 ("He is our Father and he is God forever"); and Wis 14.3 ("it is your providence, O Father, that steers its course"). In the Jewish liturgy, it is familiar especially from the phrasing *avinu malkhenu*, "Our father, our king ..." (*b. Ta'an* 25b, a prayer ascribed to Rabbi Akiva). From the Dead Sea Scrolls, we find the following intimate prayer, "For my father did not know me and my mother abandoned me to you. Because you are a father to all the [son]s of your truth. You rejoice in them and like her who loves her child, and like a wet-nurse you take care of all your creatures on (your) lap" (1QH 17.29–36). Similarly, 4QApocryphon of Joseph (4Q372) reads, "And he [Joseph] said, "My father and my God, do not abandon me

---

3   Gerhard Kittel, "Abba," in Idem (ed.) *Theological Dictionary of the New Testament*. 10 vols (Grand Rapids: Eerdmans, 1964), I, 5–6; (ET of the German original [1933]). For a full discussion of the use of "abba" as well as "father" language for God in early Judaism, see Mary Rose D'Angelo, "*Abba* and Father: Imperial Theology in the Contexts of Jesus and the Gospels," in Amy-Jill Levine, Dale C. Allison Jr. and John Dominic Crossan (eds.), *The Historical Jesus in Context* (Princeton: Princeton University Press, 2006), 65–78.

4   Joachim Jeremias, *The Prayers of Jesus*, Studies in Biblical Theology 2d Ser. 6 (London: SCM Press, 1967), 58–60.

5   Joachim Jeremias, *New Testament Theology* (London: SCM Press, 2012), 67. See James Barr, "*Abba* Isn't Daddy," *JTS* 39 (1988): 28–47.

6   Marianne Meye Thompson, *The Promise of the Father: Jesus and God in the New Testament* (Louisville: Westminster John Knox, 2000), 28.

to the hands of the Gentiles ... do me justice, so that the poor and afflicted do not perish." In 3 Mac. 6.2–3, the righteous priest Eliezer prays, "Almighty king, God most high, all-ruler, since you govern all the creation with mercy, look upon the seed of Abraham, upon the children of the sanctified Jacob, the people of your sanctified portion, perishing as strangers in a strange land – father!" The Amidah prayer (also called the "Shemonah Esreh" or "Eighteen" [benedictions] or simply Tefillah, [the] Prayer, which is part of Judaism's daily liturgy, entreats "favor us our Father" (benediction 4) and "forgive us, our father" (benediction 6).

In Ben's view, while it is certainly true that *abba* means "father" and is not baby talk, the study of the actual usage shows that it is a term of intimacy something like "father dearest," and more importantly it is a term, so far as we know, not used before Jesus in prayer to address God directly. *It is not the simple Aramaic equivalent of Ab, the proper Hebrew term for father.*[7] Luke omits the Aramaic, as is Luke's tendency, but keeps the correct translation.

Amy-Jill finds this reading to be clinging to the attempt to make Jesus' usage unique. She also notes, as Ben taught her to say, that "absence of evidence is not the same thing as evidence of absence." We have very few Aramaic prayers to begin with, and in the "our father," the term *abba* does not appear, but the previously cited list of "father" language suggests that to address God, intimately, as "father" is a staple in early Judaism. She argues instead that Jesus used an address already known in his Jewish culture. Then, Jesus' disciples continued the "father" language beyond his original instruction: the address appears with increasing frequency as we move from the earlier sources such as Mark (four appearances) and perhaps Q (nine appearances in four passages), to the later sources: nineteen appearances in Luke, forty-two in Matthew, and a remarkable 109 in John's Gospel.[8] Ben notes that something has to account for the infrequency of the use of "Father" in prayer language before the time of Jesus, and the increasing frequency of the usage in the Gospels, climaxing in the Fourth Gospel. In Ben's view, Jesus, without denying that Jews before him could have per-sonal relationships with God, was suggesting that through a relationship

---

[7]   See Ben Witherington III and L. Ice, *The Shadow of the Almighty*, in which every use of *"abba"* in early Judaism is examined. Ben finds that the term was used by disciples of their teacher, a teacher such as Honi the Circle Drawer, but the issue here is its use of God, which appears unprecedented. Jeremias was not *totally* wrong. And yes, whether used of God, a favorite teacher, or a parent, it is a term of affection or intimacy. In early Christian practice (see Rom 8), it is a Spirit-prompted term of intimacy and affection.

[8]   D'Angelo, *"Abba* and Father," 65.

with Jesus himself, one could draw especially close to God, and indeed even address God as Jesus himself did.

The address "father" can expresses intimacy as well as genealogy (see 3.38, where Adam is explicitly called a "son of God," which makes God the father of Adam and so of all of Adam's descendants); it can also suggest politics. In 2 BCE, the emperor Augustus accepted the title *pater patriae*, "father of the fatherland, a title similar to the American appellation of George Washington as "father of the country" or the expression "founding fathers." To call the God of Israel "Father" thus indicates that the emperor of Rome is not the "father" to whom one prays or on whom one relies. Ben proposes that this may explain the plethora of "father" language in the Gospel of John, likely composed late in the first century CE, but it is unlike to explain the early usage by Jesus and his disciples, who in Galilee are unlikely to have run into this claim very often, if at all, in the first three decades of the first century CE. Amy-Jill again has her doubts. Roman imperial theology had already penetrated not only Judea but also the Galilee and Samaria well before the destruction of the Temple. It would have been known by coinage, experienced in trade as well as travel including pilgrimage to Jerusalem, and present in areas such as Caesarea Philippi and Bethsaida.[9] Thus, on Jesus' lips, the address may have had a political valence.

The hallowing or "making sacred" of the divine name refers to the "four letters" (Greek: *tetragrammaton*) that comprise the name revealed to Moses in Exod 3.13–14. From the burning bush, God commissions Moses to set the free the Israelites enslaved in Egypt. Moses inquires, "If I come to the Israelites and say to them, 'The God of your ancestors has sent me to you,' and they ask me, 'What is his name?' what shall I say to them?" God said to Moses, "*eheyeh asher eheyeh*," Hebrew for "I will be what I will be." The LXX translates these Hebrew words as *ego eimi*, "I am." Then God said further, "Thus you shall say to the Israelites, 'I will be/I am (*eheyeh*) sent me to you.'" God speaks in the first person, "I will be." When others would then speak of God or for God, they would use the third person of the same verb, "he will be." The letters spelling out "he will be" in Hebrew are *yod-heh-vav-heh*, and these letters come into English as YHWH.

The name is ineffable; it cannot be pronounced. The pronunciation "Yahweh" is a guess; "Jehovah" is an attempt to use the letters of the Tetragrammaton but with the vowels of the term "Adonai," literally "my

9 See Michael Peppard, *The Son of God in the Roman World: Divine Sonship in its Social and Political Context* (New York: Oxford University Press, 2011), esp. 24–25.

lord." To hallow or make sacred this divine name, and to affirm its inability to be pronounced, reminds the faithful that God is free, beyond full human comprehension, ultimately unknowable even as God is intimate, as a father. The sacredness, and the mystery, are components of the divine. To profane the divine name (see, e.g., Ezek 36.20–28) is to act in such a way that God would be blasphemed among the nations. Just as even today, the actions of children reflect on their parents, so the actions of Israel reflect on the God they worship. To hallow the divine name requires people act in accordance with the father's desires.

The next line, "Let your kingdom come," suggests to Ben that Jesus uses Kingdom language in a positive and eschatological way in keeping with earlier apocalyptic uses, for example in Dan 7.13–14, where the issue is not the Roman emperor but rather God's everlasting Kingdom. He finds not only Jesus' response to the question about paying taxes to Caesar but also his comment, "my kingdom is not of this world" (John 18.36), to indicate that Jesus did not offer teaching on the Kingdom with one eye on the false king, the emperor, unless one is thinking of a contrast with *all merely human kings,* including figures such as Herod Antipas. In Amy-Jill's view, Ben's suggestion about the Danielic use is not mutually exclusive to political interests. The language of "Father," like the language of "Kingdom," proclaims that the Kingdom presently in place is not the one God desires. There is another Kingdom, ruled not by the emperor of Rome but by the God of Israel, the "Father of compassion" (Heb: *av ha-rachamim*).

Related to compassionate rule and the heavenly Kingdom is the idea of the messianic or heavenly banquet, when the righteous recline together with the ancient patriarchs (Amy-Jill adds the matriarchs as well) and when hunger is no more. Across time and space, eating has always been more than a means of taking nourishment. With whom we eat, what, when, and how mark us as members of a family or community. Jesus typically meets people at table, whether as a guest or as the host. Luke's phrasing of the prayer, literally, "Our bread, the next day, give to us according to [the] day" (**vs. 3**) has usually been understood as "Give us each day our daily bread" (so the NRSV). The problem with this translation is its redundancy: if the bread is "daily," then of course it would be "each day." The simpler "Give us our daily bread" would mean the same thing. The problem is the term translated "daily" (Greek: *epiousios*). It shows up nowhere else in contemporaneous literature, and even Origen (*Concerning Prayer* 27.7) comments on its lack of earlier reference. We get the translation "daily" from Jerome, whose Latin rendition offers *contidianum*. The underlying

Aramaic may have been *mahar*, which has the connotation of "tomorrow," and this reading both eliminates the redundancy and makes sense of the verse. "Give us tomorrow's bread today" would be, Amy-Jill proposes, a prayer for that heavenly banquet, when the righteous dine together with the patriarchs. Or, Ben suggests, it is the prayer of the needy, who, if they don't have tomorrow's bread the night before, will not eat before working in the morning.

The imagery of the messianic banquet does not exhaust the meaning of this "bread." John's Gospel (6.31) speaks explicitly about the manna in the wilderness, provided for the Israelites on their way from slavery in Egypt to freedom in the promised land (Exod 16), and Luke's prayer could evoke this imagery of divine providence and freedom as well. References to distributed bread further anticipate the Last Supper and the ending of the trip to Emmaus, where two disciples recognize their resurrected Lord in the breaking of bread. Finally, the prayer should draw attention to those who lack bread; to pray for bread – eschatological, Eucharistic, or otherwise – and to ignore people who are starving is to fail to hallow the divine name.

To sit at table with others is to construct a family, and a family requires certain maintenance systems to allow it to thrive. The maintenance model for the family Jesus is constructing, the family that addresses God as "father," includes the forgiving of sins. Jesus teaches his disciples to pray, "forgive us our sins, for even we ourselves forgive everyone indebted to us" (**vs. 4a**). Matthew's parallelism, "forgive us our debts ... forgive our debtors" is missing here: for Luke's version, God is the one who forgives sins, whereas the disciples forgive debts. In Aramaic, the same word (*hob*) can be translated "sin" or "debt." The expression relates to the idea that to sin is to create a debt in one's heavenly account. When one sins, the account goes into deficit; when one acts as God wants, the balance grows as "treasures are laid up in heaven" (see 12.33; 18.22).[10] Luke, who is very interested in economic concerns, may have recorded the prayer in such a way as to stress debt forgiveness on the part of the disciples. For God to forgive their sins, the disciples must display the generosity of God, who gives freely.

If one does not hold debts, one is less likely to be tempted, and so we come to the last line of Luke's version of the prayer. "Do not bring us to the time of trial" is better translated "do not bring us to a test" or a "temptation"

---

[10]   See the very interesting study on sin language and how the debt concept of sin predominated in the NT era by G. A. Anderson, *Sin: A History* (New Haven: Yale University Press, 2010).

(**vs. 4b**). The same Greek term for "test" or "trial" appears in the Temptation Narrative (4.1–13), where the devil "tempts" or "tries" Jesus. In the context of the prayer, the verse may have an economic import: disciples are ideally to hold all in common (see Acts 2.44; 4.32) and to support each other through the shared gifts of healing and hospitality (see 10.38–42). Forgiveness will not come from God to people who are tempted to hoard what they have, including daily bread. Luke will pick up this idea again in the Parable of the Pushy Neighbor, which follows the prayer.

The image of trial and testing has yet another connotation, for testing is what God does to the righteous. God tested Abraham, and the test was, "Take your son, your only son, the son whom you love, Isaac, and offer him as a burnt offering" (Gen 22.2). Jesus' followers also recognize that they will face testing, or trial.

Given the political undertones of the prayer, from the address "father" to the desire for God's Kingdom, this last line may also have political import. In the Parable of the Sower, Jesus spoke of the seed that lands on rocky soil: it represents the ones who "in a time of testing fall away" (8.13). Jesus came to a time of trial, as did his followers: the Book of Acts records the trials, whether legal or trumped up, of Peter, John, Stephen, and Paul. There was no empirewide persecution of Jesus' followers until the mid-third century, but their testing – rejection of their good news by friends and family who did not accept Jesus' teachings; rejection of gentile followers by locals who found their refusal to worship the gods of the empire or to eat meat offered to those gods as tantamount to treason (Acts 15.29) – may have been a daily matter.

PARABLE OF THE PUSHY PAL

Unique to Luke, the parable usually called "The Friend at Midnight" should be interpreted, in its literary context, as a commentary on the prayer. Connecting prayer and parable are motifs of bread, of temptation, and of community. Confusing the connection are the vague pronouns of the parable, such that the identity of the "friend" shifts: the friend of the disciples ("who among you will have a friend"), the person from whom the friend begs food, the friend of the one making the request, or all three. The vagueness of the address confounds the reader even as it indicates that the events are happening in a friendship circle: everyone is friend to everyone else.

The scenario of the parable appears to be as follows: two friends live in a town. The first (we'll call him "Mr. Host") has just welcomed a traveler, much as Mary and Martha would welcome Jesus; Jesus had already told his disciples, the seventy or seventy-two sent out, that they could expect local hospitality (**vs. 5**). Mr. Host, however, does not have food on hand for the visitor. It is midnight, the stores are closed, and he needs to feed his guest. He approaches a friend who lives in the neighborhood and calls out to him "Friend …" This is what friends do: they depend on each other for provision. So, Mr. Host asks his friend if he can borrow food (**vs. 6**). Mr. Sleepy, as we shall call him,[11] is not inclined to respond: it's late, he's in bed as are his children, and the door is already closed (**vs. 7**). His temptation is to stay in bed, warm and comfortable, rather than to get up at midnight to provide food for someone's guest.

But friendship trumps convenience. Jesus states that Mr. Sleepy, despite his disinclination to get up and wake the rest of his household, will rise to the occasion. Mr. Sleepy will do the right thing, both because it is his "friend" who asks, and because of that friend's persistence (**vs. 8**). Indeed, Mr. Host too has likely been awakened by his traveling friend. He too got out of bed to provide hospitality.

Mr. Sleepy knows Mr. Host very well, and Mr. Sleepy is well aware that Mr. Host is not going to stop knocking. Friends aid friends; friends do not let friends want for bread. There's an old saying, "the enemy of my enemy is my friend." The parable plays on this idea, but here, "The friend of my friend is also my friend."

From a canonical perspective, the parable has a meaning beyond indicating what friends do. Mr. Host bears some resemblance, in his persistence and his apparent lack of shame, to the importuning widow of 18.1–19; just as Mr. Sleepy does not want trouble (vs. 7), so the judge speaks of the widow as creating trouble for him (18.5).[12] According to Rev 3.20, it is the Christ who stands at the door and knocks: "Listen! I am standing at the door, knocking; if you hear my voice and open the door, I will come in to you and eat with you, and you with me." Mr. Pushy does not knock; he just calls out, and it's likely the neighbors will hear his shouting. The friend at midnight might be a shameless neighbor who understands that friendship is stronger than sleep or convenience and so who is willing to risk annoying in order to feed the hungry. A friend has no choice but to rise to the occasion.

---

[11] The naming of the figures is based on a suggestion by Professor Melanie Trexler.

[12] Klyne Snodgrass, *Stories with Intent: A Comprehensive Guide to the Parables of Jesus* (Grand Rapids: Eerdmans, 2008), 440.

Luke concludes this parable with a floating statement by Jesus that could be applied to a number of sayings. "Ask and it will be given to you" (**vs. 9**) does summarize the parable. Although the traditional reading of the saying is that God provides what we need, in Luke's context, the saying is more about the relationship among disciples: they will not withhold what they have, they do not keep debts, and they provide when people need bread. All a follwer needs to do is ask. "Ask and you will receive" reflects a community where immediate need is immediately met. Among the disciples, those who ask for friends to be fed will receive food; those who knock in search of hospitality will be received (**vs. 10**).

Matthew records the same statement in the Sermon on the Mount (Matt 7.7), and there as well the focus is not heavenly generosity, but earthly response. Both Matthew and Luke then record the analogy that glosses Jesus' statement regarding request and reception. Jesus explains this saying by speaking of parental response to the needs of the child: if the child asks for a fish, the parent will not give a snake; if the child asks for an egg, the parent will not give a scorpion (**vs. 11–12**; cf. Matt 7.8–9). The point reinforces the opening prayer, with its address to "Father."

The narrative section concludes with a return to theological issues. Jesus states that just as human beings are far from perfect but nevertheless understand how to love their children, by analogy, the heavenly Father, who is perfect, will care for all children. As parents may give fish or eggs, the heavenly Father will give the Holy Spirit to those who ask (**vs. 13**). The fathers, both earthly and heavenly, give because it is the right thing to do, and not because of any desire for reciprocation. Children cannot pay their parents back for fish or eggs, any more than humanity can pay God back for the gift of the Spirit. Parents provide what is needed, just as God will provide what is needed. But there is one requirement: children need to ask for what they want, and so do disciples. Prayer is the medium by which the disciples make their requests to God. But friends also should know that they can ask other members of their friendship circle for what they need. The door will be open by friends, and by God.

DEFEATING SATAN

We next find Jesus in the process of casting out a demon who had caused its victim to be mute; the exorcism proves successful when the possessed man begins to speak (**vs. 14**). Given the verbal cues of the past verses – the prayer that should be spoken aloud; the friend who speaks up on behalf of one who is hungry – the opening the mouth of one who had been possessed by a demon that causes muteness is appropriate.

The subject then changes to the matter of authority: some unnamed accusers claim that Jesus' exorcisms indicate not his returning people to health, but his being in league with the devil (**vs. 15**). The name Beelzebul is one of Luke's few nods to an Aramaic original. "Beel" would be, in Hebrew, "Ba'al," meaning "lord"; "zebul" means "of high places," and together the name is a title of the Canaanite god Baal. Changing "zebul" to "zebub" is a parody that comes originally from 2 Kings 1.2, which refers to the "god of Ekron" as "Baal-zebub." The word "zebub" or "zevuv" in Hebrew means "fly" (the name is onomatopoeic, since "*zvvvvv*" is the sound a fly makes). This is the origin of the familiar expression "lord of the flies."

By accusing Jesus of being in league with Satan, of working his exorcisms by Satanic power, Jesus' opponents show that they accept the success of the exorcisms. Rather, they question their source. This question of Jesus' authority continues as others seek from him a sign from heaven (**vs. 16**). To the skeptic, the miracle can be explained by science, or by demonic power; to the believer, the miracle is an act of the divine. The distinction among miracle, medicine, and magic is a fragile one, although generally, the miracle is free of charge whereas medicine and magic come at a cost. As Amy-Jill has already observed, free health care is a miracle. As Ben puts it, magic is a bottom-up human attempt to manipulate a deity to do what one wants or needs, whereas miracles are top-down phenomena. Believers can only pray for miracles; they cannot twist God's arm to make it happen.

Jesus responds to the accusation that his so-called miracles indicate his authority comes from the devil with the logical claim that divided kingdoms cannot stand (**vs. 17**). To exorcise a demon is to work *against* Satan, and therefore to defeat Satan's kingdom. If Jesus casts out demons by the authority of Satan, then Satan's kingdom must be divided, and a divided kingdom cannot stand (**vs. 18**). Were one to quibble, one might note that a sacrifice of a pawn can lead to the capture of the king, but Luke is not a chess player. Luke rather is contrasting the "Kingdom" for which the disciples pray with the kingdom of Beelzebul; the Kingdom of God the Father will prevail over the kingdom of Satan.

Following the logic of the argument regarding a house divided, Jesus offers a second explanation for why his work is on the side of God rather than of Satan. Jesus is not the only exorcist in Judea or Galilee; others are also engaged in the battle against Satan, and they too are healing the afflicted. Therefore, Jesus asks how these other exorcists do their work (**vs. 19**).

Although the NRSV speaks simply of "your exorcists," the Greek has Jesus ask, "If I by Beelzebul cast out the demons, [then] your sons, by whom do they cast out?" Several commentators suggest that the "sons" (Greek: *huioi*) refers to Jesus' disciples, who will judge Israel (22.30) since "your" exorcists suggests a more personal relationship of these sons with his interlocutors. Jesus' accusers may have a personal investment in closing down his activities: he poses a threat to their children's business. Faint echoes sound here of 9.49–50, where John the Apostle complained about the exorcist who was casting out demons in the name of Jesus. Jesus concludes this part of his retort by stating that these very sons will judge the accusers. The theme of division in the family, with the younger generation supporting Jesus and the older one rejecting him, continues.

According to Matt 12.28, Jesus announces that he casts out demons by the "Spirit of God"; Luke has Jesus speak of the more anthropomorphic "finger" (**vs. 20**). The expression echoes Exod 8.18, where Pharaoh's magicians, unable to recreate the plague of gnats, regard Aaron as displaying the "finger of God." If Pharaoh's magicians can see the divine hand at work with Aaron, surely the opponents can see the divine at work in Jesus. In Deut 9.10, Moses speaks of the "two stone tablets written with the finger of God"; thus, Jesus may also be alluding to his divine authority: his words have the status of Torah. More, by his demonstration of power, by his casting out Satan, he manifests God's Kingdom. This Kingdom is one of self-possession rather than demonic possession; it is one in which evil, of any sort, human or supernatural, is cast out.

Jesus offers an analogy, in continuity with the image of the house divided, to describe his work. The strong man (**vs. 21**) is Satan. Whereas the NRSV speaks of his guarding his "castle" and notes that "his property is safe," the Greek speaks of his guarding his "courtyard" and states that his property is "at peace." The reference to "courtyard" (Greek: *aulē*) reappears in Luke only once more, in 22.55, in reference to the courtyard of the High Priest, the courtyard where Peter warms himself by the fire while Jesus is under direct fire from his accusers. Satan will no more be at peace than Caiaphas, as the peace of Jerusalem will soon give way to the Roman War of 66–70. Jesus in this analogy is the "stronger" man, who overpowers Satan, strips him of his armor, and divides his spoil (**vs. 22**). Whereas Jesus does not have a divided house, he himself will divide Satan's realm. John the Baptizer had already referred to Jesus as the "stronger one" (3.16); here Jesus, the stronger one, shows how much power he, and so his followers, have, for they too cast out demons.

This section ends with Jesus' assertion of a division among the people: those who are for him and so are gathering others into the Kingdom, and those who are against him and so scattering the people (**vs. 23**). The imagery is one of sowing seed, but the context is cosmic warfare.

AN EMPTY MIND IS THE DEVIL'S PLAYGROUND

The next three verses continue the topic of demonic activity, but they shift in focus from those who act with or on behalf of Satan to those whom Satan and his staff, the "unclean spirits," possess. Whereas Josephus claims that King Solomon was able to effect permanent exorcisms, such that the spirits never returned (*Ant.* 8.45), Jesus indicates that such spirits can return.

Upon returning to the person from whom it had departed, the unclean spirit – as opposed to anything holy – finds a neat and tidy space, as if ready for company (**vv. 24–25**). The stepping-stone construction from the earlier stories begins to become evident: the friend who visits and needs bread; the house stormed by the stronger one; now the house empty and ready to be possessed by others. Having welcoming space to maneuver, the evil spirit invites seven more evil spirits to cohabitate. The afflicted person is left in a worse condition (**vs. 26**).

Commentators frequently suggest that this enigmatic scenario indicates that removal of demons of any sort, whether spiritual powers or addictive behaviors, requires a replacement to fill the gap. For many a therapist or pastoral counselor, that something else is God or Jesus, or a higher power, or prayer. More skeptical readers might see here an explication for a failed exorcism: yes, the demons can return, and yes, the relapse is worse than the initial condition. This is sometimes the case with "miraculous" healings today, where following the euphoria of belief in a healing, the reality of the cancer or the depression returns with a crash.

Perhaps the passage indicates that one must respond to the gift of exorcism. For Jesus, exorcism is a miracle; it is neither medicine nor magic. Jesus takes away the demons; it is the responsibility of the dis-possessed individual to find a new identity, a new spiritual center. Survivors of possession must be identified by something other than their demons.

Or perhaps the parable is a warning: compulsions to keep things neat and tidy can be demonic. The more we try to pick up every crumb, straighten every line, and avoid the untidiness that is human life, the less comfortable we are, the less able we are to offer hospitality or take a break in our schedule. Accepting a bit of messiness may be a good way of avoiding demons.[13]

COMPARATIVE BLESSINGS

A woman responds to these various comments about the defeat of Satan by praising Jesus' mother for giving him birth and breastfeeding him (**vs. 27**). References to Jesus' mother may remind readers of her *Magnificat*, which speaks of the defeat of the forces of evil: "He has shown strength in his *arm*; he has *scattered* the proud … He has brought down the powerful …" (1.51–52). The divine arm relates to the finger of God by which Jesus defeats Satan (so 11.20); the scattered proud are those who reject Jesus (so 11.23).

Along with these intratextual allusions are intertextual ones, for in Israel's Scriptures, breastfeeding signifies more than the provision of nourishment to the child. Breastmilk indicates the imbibing of both ethnicity and ethos.[14] For Amy-Jill, the woman's accolade associates Mary with other biblical scenes of lactation, from Moses' mother (Exod 2.7–10) to Naomi (Ruth 4). Mary therefore proves to be one of the sources of Jesus' wisdom even as she reinforces his membership in the people of Israel. But Ben adds, this cannot be Luke's sole view. He reads 2.41–52 as indicating that young Jesus grew in a wisdom and with a stature that did not come from Mary and to some degree was at odds with Mary's own views.

According to the NRSV, Jesus contradicts the woman's beatitude with a mild "Blessed rather …"; the Greek is harsher: "On the contrary" (Greek: *menoun*), says Jesus. Hearing the divine word and not merely "obeying" it but actually *guarding* it are more important (**vs. 28**). To guard is more than to obey: to guard indicates that one ensures that the word itself is protected from misuse. The verse about Mary's womb and breast is consistent with Luke's emphasis, likely derived from Jesus, on celibacy and so not on the mechanics of parturition and lactation. It also indicates that Mary is to be praised – for all generations will call her blessed (1.48) – not (only) because of her gynecological attributes, but because she herself guarded the word, both her child and his teachings.

[13] Suggested by Scout McFall (Vanderbilt Divinity School, fall 2016).
[14] Cynthia R. Chapman, *The House of the Mother. The Social Roles of Maternal Kin in Biblical Hebrew Narrative and Poetry* (ABRL; New Haven and London: Yale University Press, 2016), cites numerous ethnographical studies "of multiple societies that considered breast milk to be the substance that transmitted ethnic identity and social status" (15; see also 135).

SIGNS AND WHAT THEY SIGNIFY

As the crowds gather, Jesus anticipates their desire for a sign (**vs. 29a**). Readers may be reminded of his criticism of Simon the Pharisee, who thinks to himself that Jesus cannot be a prophet given his acceptance of the ministrations of the woman who loved him much (see 7.36–50). The exorcisms alone do not provide such a sign, since as Jesus' opponents had noted, an exorcist may be on Satan's team: deceiving through good deeds is not an impossibility. Jesus knows they want a sign of his divine authority, something that will be universally convincing: general resurrection of the dead; the ingathering of all the Jews dispersed to foreign lands; a final judgment; peace on earth. These would be the signs of the messianic age. Yet he refuses to grant them this, and he accuses them of evil before they voice their concerns.

According to Mark 8.12, Jesus insisted, "no sign will be given to this generation"; for Luke, a sign, of sorts will appear. Jesus speaks cryptically of the "sign of Jonah" (**vs. 29b**). The sign is ambiguous. Jonah can be interpreted in various ways: as a prophet who convinces the gentile nation of Assyria to repent and so as representing the gentile mission; as a prophet who symbolically was swallowed by death and then came to life again (Matt 12.40 states, "For just as Jonah was three days and three nights in the belly of the sea monster, so for three days and three nights the Son of Man will be in the heart of the earth"); as a symbol of divine protection (3 Macc 6.8 notes, "Jonah, wasting away in the belly of a huge, sea-born monster, you, Father, watched over and restored him unharmed to all his family"); as a reference to a "dove," since this is what the name "Jonah" means in Hebrew, and so of peace; as an indication of the threat of destruction lest the people repent; and so on. Jesus makes the first option explicit: Jonah represents God's judgment on the Ninevites as well as divine acceptance of their repentance; so, for Luke, the gentiles will repent at the message of the Son of Man. Yet whereas the Assyrians repented in sackcloth and ashes, the majority of the people who hear Jesus' words and witness his exorcisms will not accept his messianic role (**vs. 30**).

The sign is an ironic one, just as the Book of Jonah is ironic. The very Ninevites who repented at Jonah's proclamation will be the ones who, in the next generation, destroy Jonah's country. The original Jonah ben Ammitai, mentioned in 2 Kings 14.25, lived at the same time as the prophets Amos and Hosea (ca. 786–746 BCE). His original message was a positive, nationalistic one (an ancient "Israel first" proclamation) of political expansion. The

Assyrians, with their capital at Nineveh, destroyed the Northern Kingdom of Israel in 722. Those who repent and are forgiven in one generation may turn and destroy God's people in the next generation.

Jesus then continues on the offensive by negatively contrasting his own people's rejection of him with the acceptance, by foreigners, of earlier representatives of Israel and Israel's God. The queen of the South – that is, the Queen of Sheba (1 Kings 10.1–10; according to Josephus [*Antiquities* 8.165], she ruled Egypt and Ethiopia) – listened to Solomon; the Ninevites listened to Jonah (**vs. 31**). Resurrected, both the ancient Queen and the Assyrian people will condemn Israel. The claim overstates, since nothing in earlier Scripture casts the Queen of Sheba as a sinner, or casts Solomon as a prince of repentance (**vs. 32**), but the general point about faithful outsiders and unfaithful insiders holds. The Scriptures of Israel as well as postbiblical Judaism recognize "righteous gentiles" such as Pharaoh's daughter, who rescues Moses; Rahab the Canaanite, who rescues Joshua's messengers; Ruth the Moabite, who proves her loyalty to Naomi and Boaz; and from the Deuterocanonical books, Achior, the faithful Ammonite, who anticipates Judith's salvation of Israel. These figures and others often prove more faithful than do many of the insiders.

Imagery requiring Jesus' interpretation continues in the next two verses with his references to light and dark. Jesus starts with the obvious point that to light a home, one places the lamp not in the crypt, but on a lampstand (**vs. 33**; see comments on 8.16, which records the similar statement, "No one after lighting a lamp hides it under a jar or puts it under a bed, but puts it on a lampstand, so that those who enter may see the light"). Then the discussion moves into an inexact allegory, and the awkwardness of the discussion may signal the evangelist's attempt to develop a more complicated message from a simple analogy. First, Luke compares a person's eye to a lamp (**vs. 34**); the references to an unhealthy eye could be allusions to the notion of the "evil eye" and so the desire to curse others. In this configuration, the eye is not merely a receptor but also the source of light as well as darkness. Then the analogy breaks down with the question of whether one's light is not in fact darkness (**vs. 35**). The discussion concludes with the prosaic point that a body filled with light is like a lamp that dispels the darkness (**vs. 36**).

Jesus' comment in John 8.12, "*I am* the light of the world," makes sense metaphorically, especially considering John's extensive use of light and dark imagery. Matthew offers an alternative message when, in the Sermon on the Mount, Jesus tells his disciples, "*You* are the light of the world" (Matt 5.14). This verse immediately precedes Jesus' comment about not hiding a lamp but allowing its light to shine for others. Luke's version focuses on internal light.

The chapter ends with another burst of invective against lawyers and Pharisees. In context, the lawyers and Pharisees are those who bring Jesus' followers to the test (11.4), side with Satan, and compare negatively with the Ninevites: the lawyers and Pharisees are filled with darkness, have the evil eye, and will be condemned. The scene also both recapitulates (7.36; 10.38) and anticipates (14.1) other meal scenes in which Jesus condemns the householder, such as Simon the Pharisee and Martha the sister of Mary, for improper hospitality.

Innocently enough, at first, a Pharisee invites Jesus to his home to share a meal, and Jesus, accepting, reclines at table with the host and his friends (**vs. 37**). Given the events of Chapter 7, where Jesus reclines at table with Simon the Pharisee, readers can anticipate that Jesus will criticize the host. In the earlier scene, the woman anoints Jesus' feet while the Pharisee gave him no water for his feet (7.44). Continuing the reference to washing in the context of violation of the ethos of the home, Jesus here does not use the water available. Rather than following Pharisaic practice, Jesus does not first wash before he eats (**vs. 38**). The term translated "wash" (Greek: *baptizō*, literally "dip") would remind readers also of John's baptism, something that the Pharisees had rejected. While not dipping with John, Pharisees had practiced washing their hands as well as certain vessels in accord with their general view that all of Israel was a priestly kingdom and a holy nation (so Exod 19.6; cf. 1 Pet 2.9). All meals become meals in the divine presence, and they are eaten in gratitude for divine bounty. Just as the priests washed their hands before coming into contact with the sacrificial offerings (the same practice can be found today in certain Christian denominations where the presider washes hands before touching the elements of Communion or Eucharist), so should all of Israel. Jesus, again knowing what his Pharisaic host was thinking (see 7.39–40), goes on the offensive. He accuses all the Pharisees of participating in external washings whereas inside they are filled with corruption (**vs. 39**). The concern is not with Pharisaic practices per se; rather, the practices serve as a launching pad to engage in anti-Pharisaic invective.

Jesus' first accusation is that the Pharisees are full of greed and wickedness. This focus on greed, which anticipates Jesus' charge that Pharisees are "lovers of money" (16.14), a point found nowhere else in ancient literature but a stereotypical charge, contributes to the stereotype, still present today, that Jews are more interested in money than compassion, greed as opposed to generosity. Next, after calling the Pharisees "fools," he accuses them of ridiculous behavior: why wash the outside and not take care of the inside, since God made them both (**vs. 40**)? Then, once again, the rhetoric breaks down as Luke seeks an allegorical reading. Comparing, somewhat awkwardly, the inside of the cup and the person, **vs. 41** exhorts that the Pharisees, and so by extension everyone, should give alms, and it is therefore not through ritual washing but through supporting the poor that one obtains cleanliness.

Judith Lieu observes, "The picture that has often been drawn of the ordinary people of Jesus' day as weighed down by the joyless imposition of legalistic niceties through self-righteous religious leaders has no support from the Jewish sources."[15] To this claim, Ben counters that Jesus is in the same tradition as the polemics of the ancient prophets about these very kinds of things: various forms of hypocrisy and injustice by the leaders of God's people are critiqued. The intent of Jesus or Luke to critique actual misbehavior is one thing. The use of such a critique by later Christians wrongly to stereotype Jews in general is another, and can rightly be called anti-Semitism. Ben insists that we not caricature a whole people of being guilty of what only some among them could rightly be accused of, or worse, caricature sincere religious praxis as mere superficiality or legalism that misses the mark. Amy-Jill, again, wants to nuance this observation. Jesus as a Jew speaking to other Jews engaged in invective, and in so doing he was not being anti-Jewish. *However*, when that invective gets taken up by people outside the Jewish community and placed in the canon of a movement that comes to define itself over and against Judaism, words that originally were not anti-Jewish become so. Ben adds that the dictum, "the abuse of something does not rule out its proper use," applies here. The words do not *become* anti-Semitic just because Christians later *misused* them. The words still mean what they originally meant in their original context. But stripped of that context, and without understanding the rhetorical nature of early Jewish insider invective, including prophetic invective, this material is all too easily abused.

Jesus' claim uses the language of ritual impurity to speak about moral lack. Purity and compassion do not function on the same register. One can

---

[15]   Lieu, *Gospel According to Luke*, 96–97.

be in a ritually pure state but lack compassion (so the high priest in the Temple); one can be both pure and compassionate (so Anna and Simeon in the Temple); one can be impure but epitomize compassion (so both Elizabeth and Mary after they give birth to their sons). Jews, including Pharisees, understood the importance of giving alms, just as Christians do today (whether people practice what they understand is another matter). As the Book of Tobit, just one of many examples, makes clear, "Give alms from your possessions, and do not let your eye begrudge the gift when you make it. Do not turn your face away from anyone who is poor, and the face of God will not be turned away from you ... Give some of your food to the hungry, and some of your clothing to the naked. Give all your surplus as alms, and do not let your eye begrudge your giving of alms. Prayer with fasting is good, but better than both is almsgiving with righteousness. A little with righteousness is better than wealth with wrongdoing. It is better to give alms than to lay up gold. For almsgiving saves from death and purges away every sin. Those who give alms will enjoy a full life" (4.7, 16; 12.8–9). This concern for almsgiving continues to this day in Jewish practice. It is based on the commandment from Deut 15.11: "Since there will never cease to be some in need on the earth, I therefore command you, 'Open your hand to the poor and needy neighbor in your land.'" We mention these verses, among numerous others, to correct Christians who have expressed to us the idea that Jesus invented care for the poor.

The invectives continue as Jesus condemns the Pharisees for tithing spices and herbs but neglecting justice and love of God. The critique is of a both/and rather than either/or nature: people should *both* tithe *and* engage in justice as well as love God (**vs. 42**). Next, he accuses them of conceit: of loving the first seats in the synagogues and similar signs of public respect (**vs. 43**). That they have such respect, however, may suggest that they've earned it. Josephus finds that the people in general were following Pharisaic and not priestly teachings; this response, for Josephus the priest, indicates that the Pharisees have overreached their station. Both Ben and Amy-Jill are reminded here of those churches where the "leading men" of the congregation sit behind the pulpit, in the seats of honor.

By calling Pharisees "unmarked graves" (**vs. 44**), Jesus returns to the matter of purity. Corpses have the highest degree of impurity. This does not mean that people should not bury corpses or attend memorials at their graves, as we discussed previously in Luke 10, in our comments on the excuses attributed to the priest and the Levite in the Parable of the Good Samaritan. Graves were marked by whitewashing, so that people going to

Jerusalem would not inadvertently come into contact with a grave, become ritually impure, and so have to wait a week before participating in Temple practice (see Num 19.11–22). Today the expression "whitewash" means "erase the guilt" or "exonerate based on false facts."

Responding to this tirade, one of the lawyers, remarkably calmly, addresses Jesus respectfully as "teacher" and states that by insulting the Pharisees, Jesus insults the lawyers also (**vs. 45**). Members of the groups are associated, as the lawyer's presence at the dinner party indicates. Jesus does not disagree. Again, he advances by charging the lawyers with their own inappropriate priorities. They load burdens on others but don't lift a finger to ease them (**vs. 46**). Commentators tend to take these "burdens" as a reference to the "thirty-nine classes of work that one could not do on the Sabbath lest the third commandment be violated."[16] Aside from this association being based on an anachronistic claim, it is also one that disrespects Jewish tradition. Within Judaism, Torah is not a burden from which one needs to be relieved but a blessing for which one gives thanks. Ben proposes that Jesus is talking, as he does elsewhere, about burdensome fees the lawyers charge for services rendered (see 20.46–47).

Jesus then returns to the theme of tombs, this time not as places of ritual impurity but as sites that honor the prophets there interred. He tells the lawyer, "your ancestors killed" those prophets, but you built their tombs (**vv. 47–48**). The term "ancestors" (the Greek literally means "fathers") cannot refer to all Jews, since Jesus' ancestors too were Jews. The term "fathers" must be taken as indicating "those in the same profession as you," that is, fellow lawyers, and particularly *your* type of lawyer. The critique is rhetorical: lawyers in general are not responsible for the construction of tombs; building a tomb for prophets would suggest condemnation of their deaths rather than complicity in them.

Before burying Jesus too deeply in this rhetorical ploy, Luke changes the subject. Using the phrase "Wisdom of God" as self-referential; Jesus speaks in the voice of Lady Wisdom, who called consistently to the people to repent. He attributes to her not the direct call, but the sending of ancient prophets to the people of Israel. By adding that Wisdom also speaks of sending "apostles" (Luke 6.13, where Jesus speaks of distinguishing his apostles from the larger group of disciples), Jesus aligns himself with Wisdom even as he aligns his ambassadors with the ancient prophets. None of Jesus' apostles has yet been killed or even persecuted, although both persecution and, for

[16] Fitzmyer, *Luke*, ad loc.

some, death will be their fate (**vs. 49**). By equating those who persecuted Amos, Jeremiah, and others of ancient Israel's prophets with those who reject Jesus and his followers, Luke sets up the model of the Pharisees and lawyers as perpetual murderers, responsible for every criminal death "since the foundation of the world" (**vs. 50**). To charge lawyers and Pharisees with the death of Cain is exaggerated; to charge them with the death of Zechariah is confusing (**vs. 51**). The reference is probably to the priest Zechariah, who under the influence of the Holy Spirit said to the rulers of Judah, "Thus says God: 'Why do you transgress the commandments of the Lord, so that you cannot prosper?' Because you have forsaken the Lord, he has also forsaken you'" (2 Chron 24.20b). King Joash then orders his stoning, and an unidentified "they" stone Zechariah in the Temple (2 Chron 24.21). Josephus, *War* 4.330–44, describes how two Zealots murdered a prominent citizen named Zechariah, accused but acquitted of supporting Vespasian, in the Temple. Luke, perhaps familiar with Josephus' work, could have been alluding to both, and thereby extending the charges against the lawyers and Pharisees from Abel to the destruction of the Temple and thus into the time of the Church.

Jesus presses on by charging the lawyers with taking away the "key of knowledge," that is, awareness of correct Torah interpretation. They not only prevent the people from understanding the divine word, they mislead others who seek this understanding (**vs. 52**). The underlying point may be one of literacy: lawyers, along with scribes, are the literate members of the population; they can read the Torah, but they do not open up the text to others, and they prevent those outside their circles from gaining the knowledge to study the text for themselves. This charge too is overstated, given that the Torah was read to the congregations (synagogues) every week.

The chapter ends with a masterpiece of understatement, as Luke notes that the people Jesus has just charged with murder are "very hostile" (**vs. 53**). They lie in waiting for him to say something either ignorant or blasphemous or both. They will have to wait a very long time.

BRIDGING THE HORIZONS

1. On Hyperbole and Anti-Judaism

It is important to remember the clearly and intentionally hyperbolic nature of invective or polemics. The intent of such exaggerations is not to state the bare facts, but to sound an alarm that something is terribly wrong and that the audience needs to wake up and deal with it. Like the exaggeration, "If you keep lighting matches in the house you will burn the whole house down," the hyperbole is intended to force the audience to see that something is seriously wrong, and to stop doing it and go in a different and better direction. The failure to understand how this sort of rhetoric works has sadly led to all sorts of anti-Semitic misuse of these texts by later Christians.

Ben and Amy-Jill agree that it is inaccurate to charge Jesus with being anti-Jewish. We disagree on whether the charge can be laid at Luke's feet. Ben says the charge is inappropriate. Amy-Jill finds that Luke can be read – and certainly has been read – as having anti-Jewish views. However, the charge is usually a nonstarter. The claim that Luke is anti-Jewish gets no traction from many readers who are invested in the sanctity of the sacred text. But to claim that there is no problem leaves the problematic texts unaddressed. We do agree that a number of interpretations have steered Luke's Gospel into anti-Jewish waters, and those sailings need to change course.

2. On Forgiving Trespasses and Forgiving Debts

In Matthew's Gospel (6.12), Jesus speaks about forgiving debts, a subject Luke also addresses in the context of the parable told to Simon the Pharisee (7.42). For Luke, the prayer Jesus teaches his disciples asks for the forgiving of trespasses. The same Aramaic word underlies both translations. What did Jesus intend: personal reconciliation or economic reform? There is no reason to presume an either/or answer; Jesus may well have intended a "both/and" response, but each has a stopping point.

Asking forgiveness and granting it become a means of establishing reconciliation within the community. However, granting forgiveness to a person who continually offends can become a sign of abuse rather than reconciliation. Nor are all people capable of granting forgiveness: such response does not come easily to the abused spouse, the rape victim, the mother of a murdered child. John's Gospel recognizes this difficulty by affirming, "If you forgive the sins of any, they are forgiven them; if you retain the sins of any, they are retained" (John 20.23; see commentary on 23.34).

Acts 2.44–45 claims that the followers of Jesus, gathered together in Jerusalem after the death of their leader, "had all things in common," and that the members of the group "would sell their possessions and goods and distribute the proceeds to all, as any had need." This system too, however, can suffer abuse. Ananias and Sapphira withhold funds promised to the

Church, and rather than be reconciled, following the exposure of their lies, both drop dead (Acts 5.1–11). This account is more than a cautionary tale about lying to the Church; it indicates that the communitarian model is difficult to sustain. Luke does not depict this model of holding all things in common as prevailing in the rest of the Book of Acts, and it does not mark any of the Pauline churches.

In teaching at Riverbend Maximum Security Prison several years ago, with a class comprised of students from both Vanderbilt Divinity School and Riverbend insiders, Amy-Jill suggested that it was easier to forgive a sin than a debt. Should someone trespass against her, she could summon the will to forgive, but if someone owed her $100,000 and she needed to put two children through university, obtain health insurance, and pay the mortgage on her house, she would want the money. One Riverbend student eloquently noted how the family of his victims had, after months of participation in a victim-offender mediation program, forgiven him. He then suggested that the reason she found sin easier to forgive than debt was because she did not understand sin. And because she did not understand sin, she could not understand forgiveness.[17]

3. Shamelessness and Friendship

In vs. 8, the narrator concludes the parable usually called "The Friend at Midnight" by stating, in the NRSV, "I tell you, even though he will not get up and give him anything because he is his friend, at least because of his persistence he will get up and give him whatever he needs." The verse presents several problems. First, "persistence" is not a good translation of the Greek term *anaideia*.[18] It means "shamelessness" or "dishonorable behavior," as Clement of Alexandria and John Chrysostom long ago noted.[19] Second, nothing in the parable suggests persistent shouting or knocking; rather, Mr. Host shouts once, and Mr. Sleepy, despite his protests, provides the needed bread. And third, we do not know who, exactly, is the one lacking shame.

---

[17]   See Levine, *Misunderstood Jew*, 49–50.
[18]   Alan F. Johnson, "Assurance for Man: The Fallacy of Translating *Anaideia* by 'Persistence,'" *Journal of Evangelical Theology* 22.2 (1979): 123–31.
[19]   Herman C. Waetjen, "The Subversion of the 'World' by the Parable of the Friend at Midnight," *JBL* 120.4 (2001): 703–21 (703); Klyne Snodgrass, "*Anaideia* and the Friend at Midnight (Luke 11:8)," *JBL* 116.3 (1997): 505–13, gives a helpful lists of various English translations and, citing the *Thesaurus Linguae Graecae* database, finds all 258 occurrences of the term, except Luke 11.8 and texts dependent on it, to be negative (506).

It could be Mr. Host, who is shouting to his friend at midnight and who is already in the awkward position of not having sufficient food for his guest; it could also be Mr. Sleepy, who by providing Mr. Host the bread avoids any label of shame from the neighbors.

If we apply "shameless" to Mr. Sleepy, we may find, according to Herbert Waetjen, that "Friendship is indeed the reality that is being subverted by this parable."[20] This subversion becomes evident when we realize we cannot determine Mr. Sleepy's motives. He may be providing the bread because that is what friends do, or he may provide aid because to fail to do so would prove injurious to his reputation. The reading does prompt provocative questions about friendship, altruism, and the import of reputation. Alternatively, we may find Mr. Host to be the shameless one and so conclude that the parable is set up as a *qal v'homer* (from the lesser to the greater) lesson: "The whole point of the parable, however, is that God is *not* like the sleeper in that God is not reluctant but is eager to respond. In this way, it is a parable of contrast," for "The parable teaches the certainty of a God who hears prayer and responds."[21]

Or perhaps the parable, like those of the Widow and the Judge and the Pharisee and the Tax Collector of Luke 18, traps us. The parable complicates our view of what is right, and it teases us at the same time by asking questions. We do not know with whom in the parable we are to identify: Mr. Host, Mr. Sleepy, the visitors? No one in this parable is behaving well. Mr. Host should have had food on hand; his visitors could have come with provisions rather than expect to be fed; perhaps both Mr. Host and his visitors could have waited until morning, or at least made do with whatever food was in the home. Mr. Sleepy, with whom we readers may well empathize, contravenes the idea of friendship by complaining rather than immediately providing bread. More, Mr. Sleepy winds up rewarding Mr. Host's shamelessness. If he refuses to help, he may damage his reputation in several ways: by showing himself unwilling to engage in hospitality; by undermining the meaning of friendship; by allowing people to go hungry; by setting up a situation in which Mr. Host will find other friends, also tucked in for the night, to disturb. Like the innkeeper in the Parable of the Good Samaritan, like the businessowner whose accounts were finagled by the unjust steward, Mr. Sleepy is stuck. But Mr. Sleepy is trapped into doing a good thing.

---

[20] Waetjen, "Subversion of the 'World,' " 711.
[21] Snodgrass, "Anaideia," 512, 513; emphasis in the original.

4. The Sign of Jonah

On the afternoon of Yom Kippur, the Day of Atonement, Jews read the Book of Jonah, and we find messages of repenting, of God's care for the world, of the stay of the decree of destruction, and even for some congregations a word of resurrection. The tradition of reading the scroll on Yom Kippur has been in place at least since the early Rabbinic period (*b. Megillah* 10b). There is no formal place in the Christian tradition where the entire book is read in one liturgical setting although portions of Jonah do appear in Christian lectionaries. In some Christian settings, Jonah is primarily a book read, in abbreviated form, to children, because it's a nice story with some resemblance to *Pinocchio*.

How we read the book (in whole, in part), where (in Church, in synagogue, in a library or classroom or home), and when (on Yom Kippur, for an assignment) will all influence the message that we take from it. For parts of the Jewish mystical tradition, as Jonah is rescued from the "belly of Sheol," so Jonah becomes a symbol for resurrection. Similarly, Jonah starts in the fourth century to become a symbol of resurrection on Christian sarcophagi. St. Jerome allegorized Jonah to the incarnate Christ who leaves his father's house and becomes flesh. John Calvin saw Jonah as an allegory for the human soul that requires discipline. The Zohar, a medieval book of Jewish mysticism, proposed that Jonah is the soul that descends from heaven to earth. One author took the book to be an allegory of a nervous breakdown. We do with Jonah what we want.

Here's one more reading worth considering, if the setting in which we read Jonah is one of today's news. The ancient city of Nineveh, the capital of the Assyrian Empire, as well its modern counterpart, is located east of the Tigris River, opposite the city of Mosul, which has been much in the news given the civil war in Syria. Under present US law (2017), the inhabitants of Nineveh, the very people to whom God sent Jonah, would not be allowed entry into the United States. What sign are we then conveying? Is this a sign we want to support, in light of biblical concerns regarding hospitality?

Luke 12 Proverbs, Provocations, and Preparations

¹ Meanwhile, when the crowd gathered by the thousands, so that they trampled on one another, he began to speak first to his disciples, "Beware of the yeast of the Pharisees, that is, their hypocrisy.
² "Nothing is covered up that will not be uncovered, and nothing secret that will not become known. ³ Therefore whatever you have said in the dark will be heard in the light, and what you have whispered behind closed doors will be proclaimed from the housetops.
⁴"I tell you, my friends, do not fear those who kill the body, and after that can do nothing more. ⁵ But I will warn you whom to fear: fear him who, after he has killed, has authority to cast into hell. Yes, I tell you, fear him! ⁶ Are not five sparrows sold for two pennies? Yet not one of them is forgotten in God's sight. ⁷ But even the hairs of your head are all counted. Do not be afraid; you are of more value than many sparrows.
⁸ "And I tell you, everyone who acknowledges me before others, the Son of Man also will acknowledge before the angels of God; ⁹ but whoever denies me before others will be denied before the angels of God. ¹⁰ And everyone who speaks a word against the Son of Man will be forgiven; but whoever blasphemes against the Holy Spirit will not be forgiven. ¹¹ When they bring you before the synagogues, the rulers, and the authorities, do not worry about how you are to defend yourselves or what you are to say; ¹² for the Holy Spirit will teach you at that very hour what you ought to say."

ECONOMIC ADJUDICATIONS

¹³ Someone in the crowd said to him, "Teacher, tell my brother to divide the family inheritance with me." ¹⁴ But he said to him, "Friend, who set me to be a judge or arbitrator over you?"

¹⁵ And he said to them, "Take care! Be on your guard against all kinds of greed; for one's life does not consist in the abundance of possessions." ¹⁶ Then he told them a parable: "The land of a rich man produced abundantly. ¹⁷ And he thought to himself, 'What should I do, for I have no place to store my crops?' ¹⁸ Then he said, 'I will do this: I will pull down my barns and build larger ones, and there I will store all my grain and my goods.' ¹⁹ And I will say to my soul, 'Soul, you have ample goods laid up for many years; relax, eat, drink, be merry.' ²⁰ But God said to him, 'You fool! This very night your life is being demanded of you. And the things you have prepared, whose will they be?' ²¹ So it is with those who store up treasures for themselves but are not rich toward God."

²² He said to his disciples, "Therefore I tell you, do not worry about your life, what you will eat, or about your body, what you will wear. ²³ For life is more than food, and the body more than clothing. ²⁴ Consider the ravens: they neither sow nor reap, they have neither storehouse nor barn, and yet God feeds them. Of how much more value are you than the birds!

²⁵ "And can any of you by worrying add a single hour to your span of life? ²⁶ If then you are not able to do so small a thing as that, why do you worry about the rest? ²⁷ Consider the lilies, how they grow: they neither toil nor spin; yet I tell you, even Solomon in all his glory was not clothed like one of these. ²⁸ But if God so clothes the grass of the field, which is alive today and tomorrow is thrown into the oven, how much more will he clothe you – you of little faith!

²⁹ "And do not keep striving for what you are to eat and what you are to drink, and do not keep worrying. ³⁰ For it is the nations of the world that strive after all these things, and your Father knows that you need them. ³¹ Instead, strive for his kingdom, and these things will be given to you as well. ³² "Do not be afraid, little flock, for it is your Father's good pleasure to give you the kingdom.

³³ "Sell your possessions, and give alms. Make purses for yourselves that do not wear out, an unfailing treasure in heaven, where no thief comes near and no moth destroys. ³⁴ For where your treasure is, there your heart will be also.

PREPARATIONS

³⁵ "Be dressed for action and have your lamps lit; ³⁶ be like those who are waiting for their master to return from the wedding banquet, so that they may open the door for him as soon as he comes and knocks. ³⁷ Blessed are

those slaves whom the master finds alert when he comes; truly I tell you, he will fasten his belt and have them sit down to eat, and he will come and serve them. ³⁸ If he comes during the middle of the night, or near dawn, and finds them so, blessed are those slaves.

³⁹ "But know this: if the owner of the house had known at what hour the thief was coming, he would not have let his house be broken into. ⁴⁰ You also must be ready, for the Son of Man is coming at an unexpected hour."

⁴¹ Peter said, "Lord, are you telling this parable for us or for everyone?"

⁴² And the Lord said, "Who then is the faithful and prudent manager whom his master will put in charge of his slaves, to give them their allowance of food at the proper time? ⁴³ Blessed is that slave whom his master will find at work when he arrives. ⁴⁴ Truly I tell you, he will put that one in charge of all his possessions. ⁴⁵ But if that slave says to himself, 'My master is delayed in coming,' and if he begins to beat the other slaves, men and women, and to eat and drink and get drunk, ⁴⁶ the master of that slave will come on a day when he does not expect him and at an hour that he does not know, and will cut him in pieces, and put him with the unfaithful. ⁴⁷ That slave who knew what his master wanted, but did not prepare himself or do what was wanted, will receive a severe beating. ⁴⁸ But the one who did not know and did what deserved a beating will receive a light beating. From everyone to whom much has been given, much will be required; and from the one to whom much has been entrusted, even more will be demanded.

INTERPRETATIONS

⁴⁹ "I came to bring fire to the earth, and how I wish it were already kindled! ⁵⁰ I have a baptism with which to be baptized, and what stress I am under until it is completed! ⁵¹ Do you think that I have come to bring peace to the earth? No, I tell you, but rather division! ⁵² From now on five in one household will be divided, three against two and two against three; ⁵³ they will be divided: father against son and son against father, mother against daughter and daughter against mother, mother-in-law against her daughter-in-law and daughter-in-law against mother-in-law."

⁵⁴ He also said to the crowds, "When you see a cloud rising in the west, you immediately say, 'It is going to rain'; and so it happens. ⁵⁵ And when you see the south wind blowing, you say, 'There will be scorching heat'; and it happens. ⁵⁶ You hypocrites! You know how to interpret the appearance

of earth and sky, but why do you not know how to interpret the present time?

⁵⁷ "And why do you not judge for yourselves what is right?

⁵⁸ Thus, when you go with your accuser before a magistrate, on the way make an effort to settle the case, or you may be dragged before the judge, and the judge hand you over to the officer, and the officer throw you in prison. ⁵⁹ I tell you, you will never get out until you have paid the very last penny."

Luke 12 focuses on the positive behaviors disciples are to cultivate.[1] Whereas Matthew presents these teachings in the Sermon on the Mount, Luke disperses them into Chapters 6, 11, and 12. Whether the Sermon on the Mount (Matt 5–7) is the First Evangelist's collection of Jesus' statements, or whether Luke found the sayings gathered in Matthew's Gospel and dispersed them throughout the Third Gospel, or whether the common statements come from a hypothetical source (Q) shared by Matthew and Luke remains an open question. Our focus is less on the materials behind the text than it is on how these various statements can be interpreted within the context of Luke's Gospel.

In Chapter 12, Jesus speaks primarily to his disciples, although nondisciples do listen in (cf. vss. 1, 22, 29, 41 to disciples, and vss. 13 and 54 to the crowds). As the great homiletician Fred Craddock observed, "All can listen in, learn what it means to be a disciple, and take a place at the feet of Jesus if they so desire."[2] Only Luke's Parable of the Rich Fool (vss. 13–21) and the saying on watching and waiting (vss. 35–40) are unique to this Gospel.

REVELATIONS

Shifting scenes from the previous chapter, Luke observes that huge crowds (literally, a *myriad*) came to hear Jesus' teaching (**vs. 1a**). Perhaps Luke has given Jesus an upgrade: we have no external confirmation that Jesus was gathering huge crowds. Should he have done so, the local political authorities would have noticed. According to Josephus, John the Baptizer was executed because of his popularity: Herod worried that, should John encourage revolt, the entire populace would engage in an uprising. Luke's concern here is to show Jesus as the legitimate teacher over and against the Pharisees, or, for Luke's audience, against those Jews who did not accept Christian proclamation. The notice that the people were trampling on one another (**vs. 1b**)

---

[1]   See C. A. Evans, *Luke*, 193.
[2]   Fred B. Craddock, *Luke* (Louisville: Westminster/John Knox, 1990), 160.

suggests that the people themselves are out of control. Hence, Jesus speaks not to them, but first to his disciples.

In Mark 8.15, Jesus advises the Twelve to beware of the leaven of the Pharisees and of Herod. The disciples, who had seen Jesus feed five thousand with limited resources, then say to one another, "It is because we have no bread" (Mark 8.16). The men are incapable of recognizing a metaphor, even were it to hit them on the head. Depicting the same scene, Matthew (16.11) highlights their denseness by having Jesus ask, likely with some exasperation, "How could you fail to perceive that I was not speaking about bread? Beware of the yeast of the Pharisees and Sadducees!" The literal reading is not always the correct one.

For Mark, the metaphor is a broad one anticipating anything Jesus' opponents could cook up; Matthew defines the yeast as representing Pharisaic teaching (Matt 16.2). Luke preempts any possibility of misunderstanding by having Jesus explain his metaphor: yeast refers not to bagels but to hypocrisy.

This "leaven" is what we today know as sourdough starter. It is not the exact same thing as yeast. Yeast is a healthy rising agent, leaven, a left over bit of a previous batch of raised bread, which if left too long can become moldy and so experience corruption. The Bible uses the same term for both however, since it does not speak of yeast apart from its role as a leavening agent. A staple of the ancient diet, yeast and leaven offer multiple metaphoric connotations. Drawing upon the Passover tradition, when all leavened products are removed from the home and when Jews for eight days eat unleavened bread (*matzoh*), Paul advises the Corinthians, "Your boasting" – that is, your being puffed up, like dough that rises when the yeast is activated – "is not a good thing. Do you not know that a little leaven leavens the whole batch of dough? Clean out the old leaven so that you may be a new batch, as you really are unleavened. For our Paschal Lamb, Christ, has been sacrificed" (1 Cor 5.6–7). The image of leaven reappears in 13.21, where Jesus tells a parable about yeast that a woman hid in three measures of flour. As we will discuss, readers who regard leaven as a "contagion" puff up the evidence. The point here is hypocrisy, not impurity or toxicity.

Luke may be suggesting that hypocrisy can puff up: we become so secure in our own righteousness that we take pride in something that does not in fact exist. Or, perhaps Luke's readers would see the Pharisees as outwardly righteous, but Luke warns that what looks good, such as fresh-baked bread, is really a trap. Such a reading would fit the Book of Acts, where Luke depicts Pharisaic members of the Church as suggesting the wrong approaches (e.g., in Acts 15.5, Pharisees insist on circumcising male gen-tile affiliates). The Pharisees would no doubt beg to differ regarding Luke's caricaturing of them.

Jesus then extends the metaphor to warn that what one attempts to con-ceal will be proclaimed publicly (**vs. 2**). The concern is both eschatological as well as practical and ethical. At the final judgment, hypocrisy will be unmasked, for God knows what is in our hearts.[3] Practically speaking, most secrets eventually come out. The verse also anticipates the discussion later in the chapter about witnessing: disciples need not conceal their affiliation with Jesus and his community, since that information is bound to be made public. They should proclaim their loyalty no matter what the repercussion.

Then, directly addressing the disciples, Jesus tells them that whatever they say in the dark or behind closed doors (**vs. 3**) will be revealed. Fred Craddock speaks of hypocrisy that involves pretending *not* to be something, rather than pretending to be something. In this reading, whispering behind closed doors may have to do with avoiding a public witness.[4] Alternatively, Jesus may simply be warning his disciples: don't gossip; don't dissemble. As he states, "let your yes be yes and your no be no" (Jas 5.12; cf. Matt 5.37).

Craddock's suggestion of secrecy during times of persecution receives support from the next nine verses, all of which deal with the dangers of public testimony. Jesus begins this section by calling his disciples, for the first and only time in Luke, "friends" (**vs. 4**).[5] The Greek *philoi* (cf. John 15.13–15; 3 John 15) immediately evokes the parable in the previous chapter, where Mr. Host rouses Mr. Sleepy, his "friend," from his sleep. To be a friend of Jesus does not mean sleeping late, or taking the easy path; it could mean being put to death. Yet to be a friend of Jesus also means that the death of their bodies is not the cessation of their message or the erasure of their exis-tence. After killing the body, one's enemies can do no more. Jesus' obser-vation is consistent with the Stoic ideals found in 4 Macc 13.14–15: "Let us not fear him who thinks he is killing us, for great is the struggle of the soul and the danger of eternal torment lying before those who transgress the commandment of God."

The power and authority that should concern Jesus' friends belong to God – the one who can create never-ending torment (**vs. 5**). The fear of God may be the beginning of knowledge (so Prov 1.7); it is also the only true

---

3   See Marshall, *Gospel of Luke*, 512.
4   Craddock, *Luke*, 161.
5   Johnson, *Gospel of Luke*, 194.

fear, since only God can damn for eternity. Hell, in Greek, *Gehenna*, takes its name from the Valley of Hinnom, a place of the abomination of child sacrifice (Jer 7.31–34; 19.4–13; cf. 2 Kings 23.10). Only here does Luke use *Gehenna*; elsewhere the Gospel speaks of *Hades* (10.15; 16.23; cf. Acts 2.27, 31). The parallel in Matt 10.28 puts the case more vividly: no earthly power can kill the *psyche*, the human spirit or soul.

Jesus mitigates the harshness of this saying, in part, by reassuring his disciples that God has no wish to damn them. On the contrary, God remembers even sparrows, small birds easily trapped, as precious (**vs. 6**). The analogy of the persecuted disciple to the sparrow is not simply a sympathetic one; sparrows, especially when in a flock, can also do damage, as anyone who has read or watched *Game of Thrones* knows. Less provocative language appears in the next verse, where Jesus assures the disciples that God attends to them, each of them, directly, even to each hair on their heads (**vs. 7**). Scott Spencer helpfully notes, "The hope of renewed bodies heightens the value of bodily existence and lessens the fearful sting of death (and receding hairline)."[6] The theme of attention to every individual and so of counting will recur in the three parables, of one hundred sheep, ten coins, and two sons, in Luke 15.[7]

To the consternation of theologians who seek to displace anthropocentric values, Jesus concludes these comments with the notice that the disciples are more valuable than the sparrows. Humanity is, for the Bible, the culmination of creation. Humans, not animals, are in the image and likeness of God (Gen 1.26–27). This comparison in valuation does not mean, however, that the sparrows are devalued. To the contrary, they have to be of value, because otherwise the comparison to the value of human beings would be irrelevant. In turn, it is the responsibility of humanity to care for the sparrows, and the rest of God's creation, for with value and authority comes responsibility.

The disciples are more than sparrows; they are witnesses to Jesus. Their role is not to speak behind closed doors or in the dark, but to acknowledge their lord in public. When they do so, Jesus will reciprocate by proclaiming their testimony before angels, which means in the heavenly court (**vs. 8**). Conversely, those who deny him will find themselves denied in that same courtroom (**vs. 9**). The first verse of the couplet is positive; Jesus himself,

---

[6] Scott F. Spencer, "To Fear or Not to Fear the Creator God: A Theological and Therapeutic Interpretation of Luke 12:4–34," *Journal of Theological Interpretation* 8.2 (2014): 229–49 (236).

[7] See later comments on 21.18; cf. 1 Sam 14.45; Acts 27.34.

reigning as Son of Man, affirms his followers' fidelity. The unfaithful ones "will be denied" – passive voice. The form is the "divine passive" and expresses God's verdict. The lack of subject subtlety indicates that God does not want to damn any part of creation. Jesus does not condemn those who deny him directly, but their fate is secured, as Jesus had already noted in 9.26: of "those who are ashamed of me and of my words, of them the Son of Man will be ashamed when he comes in his glory and the glory of the Father and of the holy angels." The promise and threat both follow from the previous assurances regarding being brought to trial. Witnesses on earth who seek to save themselves by denying Jesus will find themselves lost in the eschatological trial; earthly faithfulness results in eschatological reward.

In a gloss to these comments about the damnation of deniers, **vs. 10a** states, keeping the voice in the divine passive, that speaking against the Son of Man is a forgivable offense. Such denying is precisely what Peter will do as Jesus faces his own trial at the court of the High Priest (22.34, 61). Followers, fearful in the face of persecution, may say whatever they can to save themselves from prison or the cross, and God will forgive them. This is the same viewpoint expressed in 1 Pet: "For the Lord's sake accept the authority of every human institution, whether of the emperor as supreme, or of governors as sent by him..." (1 Pet 2.13–14a). In other words, go through the motions of honoring the emperor by pouring out a libation to his statue, or eating meat offered to idols: God knows what is in your heart, and God does not want you to die.

However, blasphemy against the Holy Spirit is unforgiveable (**vs. 10b**). "Blasphemy," a term that appears in Tob 1.18 as well as Isa 52.5 (LXX) and Dan 3.29 (LXX), lacks a formal definition in early Judaism. The earlier sources suggest it means speech intended to do evil. For Tobit, the reference to "blasphemies" accompanies the description of how King Sennacherib of Assyria put many Israelites to death. Isaiah similarly puts "blasphemy" in the context of foreign nations who persecute Israel. In Daniel, the concern for blasphemy against the God of Israel is pronounced by the Babylonian king. The term "blasphemy" appears less often in the Hebrew texts compared to the Deuterocanonical literature and the New Testament. In these later works, it carries the general connotation of speaking against a divinity or acting in such a way as to cause an outsider to think that the actor's God is lacking in morals. For a modern analogy, for a self-avowed Christian to act in a way that would cast a negative light on the Christian community (embezzling funds, committing a sexual indiscretion, and so on) would be to blaspheme the Christ.

Because Luke only uses the term here, the connotations remain speculative. Following Daniel and Tobit, the term could have something to do with the taking of a life, especially by foreign powers. The Church Fathers proposed that those who blaspheme against the Son of Man are the gentiles who have yet to be instructed in Christianity, while these who are not forgiven are Church members who, following their baptism, commit apostasy.[8] Bock suggests, "The difference between blaspheming the Son of Man and blaspheming the Spirit is that blaspheming of the Son of Man is an instant rejection, while blaspheming of the Spirit is a permanent decision of rejection."[9] But nothing in this saying suggests that one of these acts of blasphemy is a one-time deal, and the other ongoing and insistent.

Ben suggests the verse could refer to those who say negative things about Jesus, the human being, because they do not realize his divine status whereas they already know that God's Spirit is part of the divine identity, but for Amy-Jill, the appeal to the Spirit in order to make a point about Jesus seems convoluted. Jesus' proclamation of this "unforgiveable" sin has given rise to no small degree of anxiety on the part of some Christians. Some among the faithful fear that doubting is the same thing as blasphemy and thus fear that their eternal souls are in danger. Doubt is not the problem; indeed, doubt may be part of considered belief. Matthew (28.17) tells us that of the Eleven who saw the resurrected Jesus, some "doubted"; doubting Thomas of John 20 is still an apostle. In class one night at Riverbend Maximum Security Institute, one of Amy-Jill's students, convicted of child abuse, defined "blasphemy against the Holy Spirit" as believing that God could not love a person like him. To limit a sense of divine love, or mercy, may well be such blasphemy, as it limits divine capacity.

A catchword system connects the reference to the Spirit to the next two verses (**vss. 11–12**), which return to the question of public testimony. Jesus assures his followers that the Spirit will inspire those "led into temptation" so that they need not fear to speak truth. Rather than blaspheme against the Spirit, followers are to rely on the Spirit to give them words to testify to their Lord and their faith. The same idea recurs in 21.14–15, "So make up your minds not to prepare your defense in advance; for I will give you words and a wisdom that none of your opponents will be able to withstand or contradict." These references to the Spirit then point forward to the disciples'

[8]   C. F. Evans, *Saint Luke*, 518–19.
[9]   Bock, *Luke 9.51–24.53*, 1143.

roles after Pentecost. They will be brought before several audiences who find their claims range from the silly to the dangerous.

One could conclude from these verses that Luke lived in a time when Christians were consistently being hauled to courts, judicial and governmental. The popular view that in the first and second centuries persecution was pervasive and martyrdom was common overstates. Empirewide persecution of the Church happened first under the Emperor Decius in 250. Decius mandated that all residents of the Empire, with the exception of the Jews, had to sacrifice to the Roman gods and to obtain a certificate indicating that they had performed the ritual. Christians had to choose whether to go through the motions of this public display of patriotism or reject it. Yet some of Jesus' followers did find themselves persecuted, such as Nero's scapegoating of the community in the city of Rome for the great fire in 64 and Pliny's arraignment of Christians in Bithynia in 110–113. At the time Luke was writing, persecution was local rather than empirewide, and sporadic rather than regular. While the persecution was not systematic, or done empirewide due to some official decree in the first century, it was nonetheless real.

Already in Paul's letters "persecution" occurs. Paul states, "Five times I have received from the Jews the forty lashes minus one" (2 Cor 11.24), a form of synagogue discipline. In 2 Cor 11.25, Paul adds that he had three times suffered the Roman punishment of being beaten by rods (see, e.g., Acts 16.22; Josephus, *War* 2.14.9). That Paul was persecuted is not in question; he writes letters while under arrest; Acts records his Roman imprisonment. Paul does not explain *why* the discipline was applied or why he was arrested. Paul's proclamation of Jesus as Lord itself should not have created the problem: there is nothing in Judaism of the time that would make a messianic proclamation offensive. Even calling Jesus "divine" might have made sense to Jews in the first century, where divinity was a relatively fluid concept. "Multiple divine personalities are native to ancient monotheism. John could (and did) designate Christ as *theos* and still be an ancient monotheist, because of the hierarchical arrangement of his heaven: *logos* is subordinate to *ho theos*, just as "son" is to "father."[10]

Perhaps Paul was interrupting the synagogue meetings with his outbursts; perhaps he was telling gentile god-fearers that they could not eat food offered to idols and so dine at a gentile friend's table. Most likely, at least in Amy-Jill's view, is that Paul's gentile followers had ceased to worship the state gods and so others in their cities perceived them to be

[10]   Fredriksen, "Mandatory Retirement," 243.

at best unpatriotic if not actually endangering the common welfare; such unpatriotic actions done in the name of a crucified Jew put the local Jewish community in danger.

Luke's Gospel does not suggest that Jesus' followers are in imminent danger; the Book of Acts, which depicts Paul's arrest but not his execution, is written retrospectively. Ben accepts Luke's account of the stoning of Stephen (Acts 7) as historical; Amy-Jill, concerned that Stephen is not mentioned by Paul or the early Church fathers, that his Greek name means "Crown" and so symbolizes the crown of martyrdom, and that his speech reads like a Lucan composition, wonders if he is a Lucan construction designed to explain the lack of a strong Christian presence in Jerusalem (see comments on 4.29). However, Stephen's name does appear in the list of the Seven Hellenists chosen to serve the Hellenistic widows in Acts 6.1–5. It is thus unlikely, especially as far as Ben is concerned, that Luke has made up a person named Stephen. In any case, celebrations of the martyrs of the faith bind the community together as well as reinforce the view that their tradition is worthy of loyalty unto death.

ECONOMIC ADJUDICATIONS

In vss. 13–34, the subject turns from public testimony to private temptations. Teachings on fidelity, proclamation, courage, and perseverance are interrupted by a fellow in the crowd who, accepting Jesus' authority, asks for a legal ruling. "Teacher," he calls out, and then orders Jesus to settle a familial economic dispute (**vs. 13**). The form of his demand and its connection with family responsibilities recapitulates Martha's demanding Jesus, "Lord … Tell her to help me" (10.40). The scene also anticipates the Parable of the Prodigal Son, wherein the younger brother demands, "Father, give me the share of the property that will belong to me," and the father complies by dividing "his property between them" (15.12). Each story helps to interpret the others. In all three cases, biological families appear as dysfunctional. For Luke, the only true family is the family of faith. Jesus will shortly insist, "Whoever comes to me and does not hate father and mother, wife and children, brothers and sisters, yes, and even life itself, cannot be my disciple" (14.26).

Jesus again refuses to involve himself in domestic disputes. The NRSV's translation of the opening of **vs. 14** as "friend" does not capture the connotations of the Greek *anthrōpe*, which is better rendered in today's English, as "man" (as in "hey man …"). The *Gospel of Thomas* 72 gets the essence of the line: Jesus "turned to his disciples and said to them, 'I am not a divider, am I?'" His rhetorical question in Luke's version, "who set me to be a judge or arbitrator over you?" risks an evident answer from anyone who has been following Luke's narrative. The answer is, "God did." The petitioner might have gone in this direction, but he does not. Readers informed of the Scriptures of Israel may catch a hint of Exod 2.15, in which Moses' fellow Israelites challenge him: "Who made you a ruler and judge over us? Do you mean to kill me as you killed the Egyptian?" Jesus, like Moses, is not going to give such a questioner the opportunity to continue the attack. Instead of fleeing as did Moses, Jesus launches into a colorful teaching about the dangers of greed.

He issues to "them" (the crowd? the disciples? the importuning man and his associates?) a warning against both greed and possessions (**vs. 15**). The eschewal not only of greed but also of possessions, that is, "lots of stuff," can be regarded as wisdom speech, which often utilizes hyperbole to make its points. If read as hyperbole, Jesus' negative comments about possessions are warnings against materialism. The comments can also be regarded as consistent with Jesus' overall dismissal of personal property, a subject introduced with the warnings and woes against the rich (1.53; 6.24; 8.14) and continuing in the immediately following parable (see also 12.21; 14.12; 16.19–31; 18.23, 25; 21.1–3). As much as Luke speaks about the poor, the addresses of the Gospel, epitomized by the presumed patron "Theophilus," appear to be among the wealthy. Judith Lieu observes, "despite all [Jesus'] sympathies for the impoverished and excluded of society, it is the attitudes and assumptions of the wealthy which form his starting point, perhaps suggesting that they constituted a significant element within his own community."[11] Luke is thus nudging Theophilus, and those like him, toward self-sacrificial living.

To reinforce his saying, Jesus tells a parable, unique to the Third Gospel, about a financially secure rich man with fertile lands (**vs. 16**). Lucan parables that speak of "rich men" usually show the instability or ultimate poverty of their investments.[12] The "rich man" anticipates other parables such as the rich man whose estate manager squanders part of his estate and then cooks the books by deleting part of the debt (16.1), and the rich man who refused to care for poor Lazarus (16.19). In each case, the rich man will learn that

---

11   Lieu, *Gospel According to Luke*, 101.
12   See Witherington, *Jesus the Sage*, on stock characters in Wisdom literature like the "fool" and the "sluggard."

his money cannot buy happiness but rather will entrap him. Alan Sherouse observes that the Lucan expression *Anthrōpos tis en plousios*, "there was a rich man," signals to the Gospel's readers "connotations of superfluity, self-ishness, and separation from the poor."[13] That the rich man did not himself create the wealth but that "the land ... produced abundantly" already shows that his own self-centeredness is misplaced.[14]

As soon as Jesus states that the rich man was thinking to himself, we again encounter a familiar theme. Interior monologue in the Gospels is not a sign of wise circumspection but of self-centered plotting: Simon the Pharisee begins the motif by wondering to himself about Jesus' knowledge of the woman who was kissing his feet (7.39); the prodigal son will wonder to himself about how to regain his place at his father's table (15.17); the dishonest manager will silently plot how to retain economic leverage (16.3); and a judge will think to himself that the wiser course is to adjudicate in favor of a tenacious widow rather than risk her hitting him (18.4). The Greek *dialogidzomai* behind the NRSV, "he thought to himself" (**vs. 17**), might here be rendered as "calculated"; the rich man is engaged in cost-benefit analysis.

His conclusion to the question of what to do with his abundance is to knock down his old silos and construct larger ones to store not only his grain, but also his other possessions (**vs. 18**). Narcissistically, he speaks of "*my* fruit, *my* barn, *my* goods, and even *my* soul."[15] He does not realize that just as his soul is in the hands of God, so his surplus should be in the mouths of those who are hungry. His plans are also not wise on the practical level: the smarter approach would be to build newer buildings first, or extend the originals, rather than begin with destruction.

Conversely, wise persons would know that given economic disparity, it is the responsibility of the rich to care for the poor, as Deuteronomy insists. Readers may even find that watching the rich man continue to deliberate what to do with his abundance is like watching a trainwreck. On the other hand, the rich man's desire to rest, eat, drink, and cheer (**vs. 19**) is itself

[13] Alan Sherouse, "The One Percent and the Gospel of Luke," *Review and Expositor* 110 (Spring 2013): 285–93 (285).

[14] Spencer notes, "God implicitly plays the lead role throughout as Creator of all (land, grain, humanity) and Lord of life and death. And the part of best supporting actor is played by the earth endowed with God's creative energy" ("To Fear or Not to Fear the Creator God," 241).

[15] Bock, *Luke 9.51–24.53*, 1152; see also Rachael Oliphant and Paul Babie, "Can the Gospel of Luke Speak to a Contemporary Understanding of Private Property? The Parable of the Rich Fool," *Colloquium* 28.1 (2006): 3–26; emphasis added.

not illegitimate. His interior monologue recollects Eccl 8.15: "So I commend enjoyment, for there is nothing better for people under the sun than to eat, and drink, and enjoy themselves, for this will go with them in their toil through the days of life that God gives them under the sun." Reinforcing the point, Ecclesiastes continues: "The living know that they will die, but the dead know nothing; they have no more reward, and even the memory of them is lost … Go, eat your bread with enjoyment, and drink your wine with a merry heart; for God has long ago approved what you do. Let your garments always be white; do not let oil be lacking on your head. Enjoy life with the wife whom you love, all the days of your vain life that are given you under the sun, because that is your portion in life and in your toil at which you toil under the sun" (Eccl 9.5–9). For this ancient Wisdom text, the world is to be enjoyed, life is to be lived to the fullest. Appreciating the good gifts we receive is not the same thing, however, as hoarding them. Luke does not expect all the wealthy who read the Gospel to sell all they have; the expectation is rather that they will provide their surplus to those who need it, and perhaps even make sacrifices for the poor.

The rich man is trapped. He has no community, no wife, and no children, as far as we know. His only conversation partner is his own soul – until, that is, God speaks to him. The conversation is not a pretty one. Calling him a "fool" (Greek: *aphrōn*), God tells the rich man that his life is over. This is the only time God speaks directly in a parable; the irony here is that in its translation of Psa 14.1, the LXX asserts that "The fool (*aphrōn*) says in his heart, 'There is no God.'"[16] For Luke, there most certainly is a God, and that God does not have much patience with rich fools. In asking about the distribution of his property – "whose will they be?" – God may well be indicating that the man has no children, no heirs, no friends. He lived an insular life, hoarding when he should have been generous, and he will die in that insularity (**vs. 20**).

Jesus ends the parable with the warning that one "store up treasures" (**vs. 21**) not on earth but in heaven (see 12.33; see Tobit 4.5–11; *1 Enoch* 97.8–10). The metaphor of a heavenly rather than earthly treasure suggests not only that God takes account of our actions, but that there are actual accounts. To put food into the hands of the hungry is tantamount to laying a gift on the altar of God, and thus to lay up treasures in heaven. To sin is to draw down from that heavenly account. To give to the poor is to increase one's account; to hoard, to lay up treasures on earth, is to draw down against that account

16   Sherouse, "One Percent and the Gospel of Luke," 291.

(cf. Matt 6.19). This point reappears later in this chapter, when in vss. 33–34 Jesus speaks about the best treasure, and its location.

The issue is not the dreaded "works righteousness" that makes some Protestant readers squeamish; one does not do good deeds to earn divine love or a place in heaven. One lays up treasures in heaven because that is what a faithful person does; to fail to act according to one's confession means that the confession itself is worthless. As the Epistle of James 2.17 insists, "faith by itself, if it has no works, is dead." The hapless brother who served as the catalyst for this discussion by asking Jesus to divide the family property got more than he bargained for, but not, perhaps, what he wanted.

Turning to his disciples, Jesus changes the subject from the impropriety of self-centered hoarding to the concern for daily bread. Vss. 22–34 continue the conjoined themes of economics and anxiety. Given Luke's emphasis on providing instruction to the rich, the advice about the cares of the day may be taken as more profitably addressed to them. To tell rich people not to worry about food or clothing is fine: they have closets and pantries. To tell people on public assistance who need to feed their children not to worry is cruel. Similarly, to tell a healthy person not to worry about adding an hour is easy; to say "don't worry" to the person with stage-four cancer or heart failure, who seeks just one more hour to tell a spouse, "I love you," is cruel. One needs to understand the nature of wisdom speech. Both Jesus and his disciples would have realized that this sort of advice was not meant to be taken to be always and in every situation true, any more than the wisdom speech in the book of Proverbs is.[17]

Jesus begins by exhorting disciples not to worry about food or clothing (**vs. 22**). In an eschatological context, the instructions are easier to accept; for a life that will continue through the generations, disciples may have difficulty with Jesus' demands. Whether read with an eschatological lens (the world is about to end, so we do not need to have property to keep us safe or comfortable in the future) or with a sapiential lens (we should be focused on the Kingdom, not on material possessions), Jesus' words can provide valuable instruction as long as they are not heard apart from the very real needs of the poor. For some, life is food, for the alternative, starving to death, occurs daily in parts of the globe. Concern for clothing is also a pressing issue, especially for the homeless in colder climates.

By telling his disciples that food and clothing are not of ultimate import (**vs. 23**), Jesus is not issuing a call to be careless or stupid. His call is to

---

[17] On the nature of wisdom speech see Witherington, *Jesus the Sage*.

replace fear with faith, anxiety with trust, greed with generosity. Because the call is communal, he places responsibilities on everyone, rich and poor alike. As the Jewish community insisted on sustaining the poor, and as Rome had a public dole, so the followers of Jesus are to put their trust in God even as they know that others will do the same, and in so doing, will provide support for all. The call is idealistic, but it is also practical and an offer of hope.

Disciples must provide for those who have less, so that they need not worry. They should also know that God seeks their provision; using a *qal v'homer* (from the lesser to the greater) argument, Jesus asks, "Consider the ravens" (vs. 24): if God is concerned for the birds, how much more so should God be concerned with those who are in the image and likeness of God? His point reflects back on 12.6–7: if the sparrows and the hairs on one's head all find divine attention, so surely human beings are under divine care. For the followers of Jesus, as for the Jewish community in general, to be under divine care means to be cared for within the human community. It also means that life should be one of mutual reciprocity. Adriana Destro and Mauro Pesce point out that despite there being places where people can lodge (e.g., the "inn" where the Samaritan brings the wounded traveler [*pandoxeion*, 10.34]), the disciples depend on home-hospitality, such as shown to Jesus by Mary and Martha (10.38–42): "The support mechanism for travelers (via hospitality) should be understood as the practice of reciprocal aid rather than as pure generosity. To the extent to which hospitality was granted, one could hope to eventually receive it in return."[18]

Torah teaches that God "executes justice for the orphan and the widow" and that God "love[s] the strangers, providing them food and clothing," and therefore God's people should do the same (Deut 10.18–19). To read Jesus' words out of context might lead to the conclusion that "God will provide"; to read them in the context of the Bible and the Jewish tradition, we find that this divine provision requires us to act in the image of the divine.

Jesus parallels the concern for food and body with the concern for life. A product of his time, he speaks of not being able to add an hour to one's life (vs. 25). Today, we can prolong life by various artificial means. From a theological perspective, however, his point holds: whatever we do is ultimately in God's hands. Therefore, whatever we do, we do not need to worry

---

[18]   Adriana Destro and Mauro Pesce, "Fathers and Householders in the Jesus Movement: The Perspective of the Gospel of Luke," *Biblical Interpretation* 11.2 (2003): 211–38 (228).

(**vs. 26**). If everything works as it should, the hungry receive food, the naked receive clothing, and the dying receive compassion. Worry is not necessary, and worry does nothing to prolong life, let alone to make us faithful.

In effect, Jesus is advising his followers to determine what is of ultimate import for their lives. The Stoics would call this focus a concern to rid themselves of *adiaphora*, the incidentals. This is the approach Paul takes in his Letter to the Philippians: it does not matter that to him, and it should not matter to the Philippians, that he is in chains and may be executed. In light of his proclamation of and belief in the Christ, he can be at peace. If the lilies of the field are more glorious than Solomon (**vs. 27**), and if the grass alive today is tossed into the oven for fuel tomorrow, then surely God, who cares more about humanity than about local flora, will care for human beings (**vs. 28**). Having faith that all will be well – whether on earth or, for Jesus and his followers, in the eschatological age – allows the disciple to navigate the world in a state of joy, as Paul discovered and exhorted: "Therefore, my brothers and sisters, whom I love and long for, my joy and crown, stand firm in the Lord in this way, my beloved" (Phil 4.1).

In the midst of exhortations to confidence and hope, Jesus calls the disciples "you of little faith"; the Greek *oligopistos* is especially frequent in Matthew's Gospel (e.g., Matt 6.8,30; 8.26; 14.31). Jesus knows his disciples will weaken and doubt, and at the same time he assures them of divine love and provision. Doubt and fear are not necessarily signs of bad faith or lack of sanctification. Jesus' focus here is on combating lack of faith that manifests itself in anxiety and that ignores the generosity to be found, somewhere.

Jesus repeats his points in the next several verses: do not strive and do not worry (**vs. 29a**). The term here translated "worry," *meteōridzomai*, has the connotation of soaring up on high (as in "meteor"). We might think of worrying about not reaching the mark, the pay raise, the A+, the gold star. He adds to his advice by reminding the disciples that this attitude of trust, coupled with the recognition that Jesus' followers will provide, places them in a distinct position compared to the nations of the world. The gentiles, who at this point in the narrative represent those yet to be evangelized, do not have the comfort that Jesus' followers have (**vs. 29b**). In **vs. 30**, Luke adds to this material also found in Matthew the note that "the nations of the world," that is, the gentiles, are characterized by worry about life's necessities (cf. Matt 6.25).

In the Sermon on the Mount (Matt 6.3), Jesus tells his disciples, "Strive first for the kingdom of God and his righteousness, and all these things will be given to you as well." Luke offers a shorter statement without ranking: there is no "first" here. Luke focuses on encouraging the disciples to "strive for his kingdom" (**vs. 31**). The striving suggests living with the focus on aiding others, and to have the assurance that others will provide aid as well. That assurance means that Jesus' disciples, the "little flock," need not fear, for God their shepherd will protect them. God wants people to experience the Kingdom, as anyone who now looks at grace, ravens, or lilies will know (**vs. 32**). The Kingdom is thus neither an impossible dream nor an ideological construct; it is a reality.

From comforting words, Jesus turns to what may be uncomfortable exhortation. He tells his disciples, the inner circle of his followers, to liquidate their material assets and give the proceeds to those in need (**vs. 33**), an exhortation not found in the Matthean parallel. Luke presupposes the audience – represented by the patron Theophilus – has resources to sell. By supporting the poor, disciples obtain wallets that are never empty and that can never be robbed; that is, they have treasures in heaven. In turn, if they have these heavenly treasures, their heart is directed toward heaven and they no longer will have the cares of the world (**vs. 34**). The call to divest everything does not apply to all the disciples. Tabitha, called a "disciple" in Acts 9.36, did not divest all; instead, she used her wealth in her devotion to good works and to giving charity.

A similar idea appears in Jewish sources. *Mishnah Peah*, which concerns the requirement that landowners leave the corners of their fields for the poor, the widow, the orphan, and the stranger, that is, for society's most vulnerable, begins (1.1): "These are things which have no [specified] measure: [the quantity of produce designated as] *peah*, (2) [the quantity of produce given as] first-fruits, (3) [the value of] the appearance offering, (4) [the performance of] righteous deeds, (5) and [time spent in] study of Torah. These are things the benefit of which a person enjoys in this world, while the principle remains for him in the world to come: [deeds in] honor of father and mother, (2) [performance of] righteous deeds, (3) and [acts which] bring peace between a man and his fellow. But the study of Torah is as important as all of them together." As the rabbis suggest, one sets one's heart on God through the understanding of the divine Word, and by acting on it. Jesus exhorts his followers to set their hearts on that treasure in heaven. Some are called to divest everything; all are called to put their resources in service to others.

Fully divesting, giving everything to the poor, and then becoming among the poor oneself is a practice that drops out of Judaism but remains within some forms of Christianity.[19] When a culture recognizes celibacy as a way of life, personal divesting will more likely be recognized. The celibate who divests has no personal responsibility to a spouse or children. As the followers of Jesus began to move away from their Jewish roots and increasingly find a home in gentile culture, parts of their movement also increasingly turned to an emphasis on celibacy, virginity, and continence.

PREPARATIONS

Only some people have the spiritual gifts, the personal fortitude, or the psychological makeup to forego marriage, children, and property and so rely on the good will of others. Jesus' instructions in vss. 35–48 now change to a more general focus on how disciples should live in the world as they await Jesus' return. The wait will be long, and fidelity is the watchword in the interim.

On the one hand, disciples are not to worry about what they wear; on the other, they are to be (metaphorically speaking) "dressed for action" (**vs. 35a**, cf. Exod 12.11 as well as 1 Kings 18.46; 2 Kings 4.29; Isa 59.17; Job 38.3). The King James Version offers, "Let your loins be girded." The image is one of tying up of the robe with a belt so that the legs and feet are free,[20] and the implication is that discipleship is not the easy life of the master in robes of linen and purple but the hard life of the slave who works both day and night. Having their lamps lit (**vs. 35b**), these slaves are not themselves the "light of the world" as they are in Matthew's Sermon on the Mount (Matt 5.14; Luke does not have this verse): they are rather the slaves of Christ who stand ready for his return. Thus, their roles are both friends (see vs. 4) and slaves. Amy-Jill is reminded of the several Jewish prayers that begin *Avinu malkeinu*, "Our Father our King"; our relationship to the deity is one of both intimacy and obedience.

Luke makes the slave status of the disciples explicit in the next verse. As slaves in the master's house (**vs. 36**), they are to be prepared at all times to serve the master. Today any positive association with the term "slave" is obviated by what we recognize to be this terrible sin of human history. The term in antiquity could, however, have a positive connotation, as we have already seen in Mary's Magnificat (1.48). Irmtraud Fischer points out,

---

[19] See Amy-Jill Levine, "'This Poor Widow …' (Mark 12:43): From Donation to Diatribe," in Susan Ashbrook Harvey et al. (eds.), *A Most Reliable Witness: Essays in Honor of Ross Shephard Kraemer* (BJS 358; Providence: Brown University Press, 2015), 183–94.

[20] See Johnson, *Gospel of Luke*, 203.

"As for the self-designation 'slave,' 'female slave,' or 'maidservant,' it is taken from the diplomatic code. Only free people in the courtly context designate themselves with it in the Hebrew Bible; these are free people who want to honor their counterpart. The self-designation is never used by people in a subjected state."[21] Whether the term "slave" could or even should be recuperated will remain a subject of debate.

For Matthew, the wedding banquet is the site where Jesus the bridegroom celebrates with his followers, and the place of division where those who do not prove faithful or who come unprepared are cast out. Only Matthew (25.1–13) has the Parable of the Wise and Foolish Virgins, in which the bridegroom refuses half of the women entry into the banquet; only Matthew (22.12–13) describes how a man lacking a wedding garment is ejected from the celebration and cast into the outer darkness. For Luke, the eschatological focus is *not* the wedding banquet. In Luke's parables, Jesus is not a bridegroom. The only time Luke speaks of bridegrooms is in 5.34–35, where Jesus speaks of himself as the bridegroom, present with his disciples prior to the cross. After his crucifixion, he is Lord and Master, not bridegroom. Whereas in Matthew, the foolish virgins are the ones who knock on the door of the wedding, for Luke, it is Jesus the master returning from the wedding who knocks. The slaves – that is, the disciples – must be awake so that they can allow him entry.

To state that these prepared slaves are blessed when the master returns is an obvious point (**vs. 37a**): were they not prepared, they would be beaten. How ironic, how tragic, that the state of *not being beaten* can be seen as being blessed. The verse also helps those who are free realize how precious their freedom is, even as it helps free people recognize the horrors of slavery. Finally, the verse challenges any self-complacency the Church might have, as the institution becomes more permanent and as eschatological concern fades. The delay in Jesus' return should not, must not, lead to lack of vigilance. An old rabbinic proverb attributed to Rabbi Eliezer states, "Repent

[21] Irmtraud Fischer, "Déjà-vu for Proving Soteriological Pertinence: Gender-Relevant Reception of the Hebrew Bible in the Narrative Texts of the New Testament," in Mercedes Navarro Puerto and Marinella Perroni (eds.) and Amy-Jill Levine (ed. English translation), *Gospels: Narrative and History* (The Bible and Women: An Encyclopedia of Exegesis and Cultural History; Atlanta: Scholars Press, 2015), 69–96. See also Irmtraud Fischer, "Die Rede weiser Menschen ist höflich: Über die Umgangsformen von Weisen in den Davidserzählungen und dem multikausalen Bias in der Exegese derselben," in Andreas Vonach und Georg Fischer (eds.), *Horizonte biblischer Texte: Festschrift für Josef M. Oesch zum 60. Geburtstag* (Orbis Biblicus et Orientalis [OBO] 196; Freiburg/Schweiz: Academic Press Fribourg, 2003), 2–38.

one day before you die" (*Pirke Avot* 2.10): the urgency of maintaining fidelity to one's tradition underlies these Lucan images as well.

The normal master/slave scenario now enters a new dimension. Those alert slaves find themselves being served by their master (**vs. 37b**). The scene is better known from John's depiction (13.4-11) of Jesus' washing the disciples' feet; whereas the Johannine Jesus displays his servant leadership at one of his final meals with the disciples, for Luke, the master will serve his disciples upon his return. Since the disciples are to imitate the master, the lesson in both Gospels is that the leader is a slave to all. Perhaps John, knowing this Lucan saying, adapted it into the Last Supper scene.

The next three verses read like an amalgamation of traditional material. Luke starts by speaking of the master's return at night or near dawn (**vs. 38**), the times when all members of the household would be asleep. Then, with "night" as catchword, Luke moves to the image of the thief in the night (**vs. 39**), which appears throughout early Christian literature as a description of Jesus' Second Coming (cf. 1 Thess 5.2-4; 2 Pet 3.10; Rev 3.3; 16.15). The image was one means by which Jesus' followers, and perhaps Jesus himself, talked about the inbreaking of the Kingdom of God, the heavenly action whereby all of Satan's forces are defeated, sickness and death are no more, and the dead rise. The image of the thief is a difficult one for at least two reasons. First, the coming of the Kingdom should be a time of great joy for the faithful, but the image of having a house burgled is not one that most look upon with fond anticipation. Second, the standard Christian image winds up comparing Jesus to a thief, and the negative connotations do not fit either the person or his mission. Jesus is "stealing" nothing. People rather are to give freely, as Jesus himself does. That Jesus would use such provocative language surprises neither Ben nor Amy-Jill. Ben points out that the analogy is not, finally, between Jesus and a thief; it is between the coming of a thief at a surprising time and the coming of Jesus at a surprising time.

Luke takes care of both potential problems with the imagery. Although vs. 39 draws on the traditional "thief in the night" imagery, Luke combines this imagery with the earlier comments about the stronger man who plunders the home of Satan (11.21-22). With this textual echo, Luke advises readers that Satan did not know when Jesus would break into his house, explains that Jesus is not actually a thief but is one who takes back what Satan himself had stolen, and changes the imagery from Jesus as a thief to Jesus as the Son of Man who returns from the heavenly banquet at an assured but unknown time (**vs. 40**). The reference to the Son of Man brings the discussion full circle, as Jesus had just been talking with this followers about multiple roles of the Son of Man: 11.30 in relation to the Sign of Jonah; 12.8 concerning public testimony; and 12.10 concerning eschatological judgment.

Ben finds that to talk about Jesus' "delay" is therefore inappropriate, since "delay" only applies if a date has been set, something that is specifically denied in Mark 13.32, and in the thief in the night imagery. It is not the timing but rather the certainty about the return that provides the eschatological sanction and motivates the ethical advice here. Amy-Jill agrees with Ben's reading of Luke's emphases, but she nevertheless finds "delay" an appropriate term, given the two millennia since the promise of return was proclaimed. Finally, concerning this timetable, Luke makes clear that any who would seek signs, interpret texts, or proclaim personal revelations of the timing is not to be believed. Eschatological date setting – no matter how popular it has been over the past two millennia – is, simply, wrong.[22] As Luke's Jesus says in Acts 1.7, "it is not for you to know the times or periods the Father has set by his own authority."

At **vs. 41**, Peter asks Jesus about the audience of the parable: does it apply only to the Twelve, or to insiders in the Church, or to the world? The import of this verse, which lacks a Matthean parallel, remains obscure, but obscurity is not a hindrance to exegetical imagination. Peter may be thinking that Jesus will serve only those among the first followers at that eschatological moment; for Luke, it is more likely any slaves of Jesus – that is, any faithful members of the church – will receive the rewards commensurate with their behaviors. The narrative presupposes an audience broader than just the disciples, for in vss. 54–56 Jesus speaks directly to the crowd. As if dismissing Peter's question as unworthy of a slave who is to serve others rather than to keep the rewards to himself, Jesus offers in vss. 42–48 a variant on the earlier parable.

Rather than answering Peter's question directly, Jesus responds with a rhetorical question concerning the faithful and prudent manager who, although also a slave, has the authority to provide provisions for fellow slaves (**vs. 42**). These managers are the leaders of the movement, such as Peter and John, or perhaps Mary and Martha, others who will oversee the Church. The household manager has multiple tasks, but Jesus focuses on feeding fellow slaves: one need not worry about what one will eat if all those who serve the right "master" (**vs. 43**) are properly fed. The reward for such faithful and obedient service is not rest, but more work; the faithful

---

22 See Ben Witherington III, *Jesus, Paul, and the End of the World* (Downers Grove: IV Press, 1992).

manager will be "put in charge of all his possessions" (**vs. 44**), that is, all who belong to the Son of Man.

Conversely, if the slave, encouraged by the master's delay or, for Luke, the extended interim time before the *Parousia*, abuses others in the household and eats, drinks, and gets drunk while others go hungry (**vs. 45**), eschatological punishment awaits. The language is visceral: the master "will cut him in pieces" (**vs. 46**) and consign him to damnation. Jesus' judgment is not limited to sins of commission or deliberate wrongdoing; **vs. 47** indicates that sins of omission, of failing to act, will also be judged. Deliberate wrongdoing leads to being cut into pieces; failing to act leads to a beating. There are no bystanders in Luke's Gospel (cf. 1 Cor 3.10–15 for a different metaphorical presentation of the same idea about what happens to ministers). The depiction of God as a master who would beat his slaves, and so the violence of Jesus' language, will disturb some readers. It should. By the twenty-first century, we should have developed the sense that violence only begets more violence, and that to describe the divine as violent risks encouraging the faithful of whatever sort to take up arms in conformity. Yet for some, the idea of divine violence provides comfort: it tells them that those who abuse them, or their own authority, will suffer appropriate penalties.

Vs. 48 reflects the Lukan theme that ignorance is a mitigating factor in soteriological judgment. In Luke 23.34, the crucified Jesus cries out concerning those executing him, "Father, forgive them, for they do not know what they are doing"; in Acts 3.17, Peter tells his Jerusalem audience, "And now, friends, I know that you acted in ignorance, as did also your rulers ..." The Torah (e.g., Num 15.27–31) had already accounted for intentional versus unintentional sin.

The section ends with Jesus' notice that, as Joseph Fitzmyer puts it helpfully, "Much will be required (by God) of the gifted servant, and even more of the really talented one."[23] To serve the divine is less an occasion for immediate rest than it is the notice that competence and fidelity are rewarded – the better term may be "consigned" – to more work. The point holds not only for theology, but for any system in which some do more work than others.

INTERPRETATIONS

Commentary on judgment segues in vss. 49–59 into the challenges, and the threats, of discipleship. From demands for proper service and assurances

---

[23] Fitzmyer, *Luke X–XXIV*, 992.

that lack of fidelity will result in lack of divine grace, Jesus turns to settings in which service will create not peace, but divisiveness. In stating that he has come to bring fire (**vs. 49**; cf. 3.16; *Thomas* 82), Jesus speaks of the refiners' fire that melts away the dross and presents the pure burnished metal. The image of fire also refers to divine judgment, as Jeremiah had announced with the same metaphor (cf. Jer 5.14 and especially 23.29, "Is not my word like fire, says the Lord, and like a hammer that breaks a rock in pieces?") and the Baptizer had announced in 3.9. For Jesus, the urgency of eschatological deliverance increases as he comes closer to the cross; he wants the dross burned away and the purified people delivered.

Using the language of baptism, which connotes water, to refer instead to fire, Jesus intimates the new life that will emerge from the destruction of evil. His own "baptism," which he describes metaphorically, is his death. Marshall finds that **vs. 50** "conveys the idea that the death envisioned by Jesus ... is not mere fate or accident but a destiny to be fulfilled; cf. 13.32;22.37... The thought is thus 'How I am totally governed [constrained] by this until it is finally accomplished!' "[24] The "stress" mentioned should be accentuated; he feels, deeply, for both the pain he himself will face and the struggles his followers will face as well.

As Jesus is agonizingly distressed, so will some of his disciples be. Vss. 51–53, which draw on Micah 7.6 (cf. Matt 10.35–36), describe the disruption Jesus creates in the family. Comparable is the Qumran Hymn Scroll, 1 QH 2.14–15, which states: "I became a man of dispute for those who mouth error, and [a man of pe]ace for all who look upon the right." The divisions for Jesus are generational, with the younger generation shifting their focus from what might be called "family values" (care for aging parents, appreciation for family traditions, family land, family business) to Kingdom values, with the new focus more on the family of faith, one's "brothers and sisters in Christ." A similar type of familial disruption occurs whenever an individual affiliates with a religious tradition other than that of the natal household: the Southern Baptist son who converts to Roman Catholicism, the United Methodist daughter who converts to Orthodox Judaism.

Warnings of eschatological as well as present distress continue. In **vss. 54–56**, Jesus criticizes his audience: they can read the signs of the weather but not the eschatological signs of the time. The analogy works on the premise that those who are wise enough to interpret earthly signs should be wise enough to see what is coming on the horizon. We might

---

[24]   Marshall, *Luke*, 547. See the discussion in Witherington, *Christology of Jesus*, 123–24.

also think here of the difference between clock time (Greek: *chronos*) and eschatological time (Greek: *kairos*, the word used in **vs. 56b**). Jesus calls the crowd "hypocrites," an insult he uses frequently (see especially Matt 23): the implication is that the crowd sees itself as wise when it is really foolish. For Luke, the foolishness of the crowd is its inability to recognize Jesus as their Messiah; for the majority of the people in Jesus' time, and for the majority of the Jewish people since, the response is not foolishness but entirely understandable. Because there is no messianic age and no general resurrection of the dead, final judgment, or peace on earth, then the Messiah has not come. For Jesus' followers, that he is the Messiah and that his death creates a reconciliation between heaven and earth and a general forgiveness of sinners is self-evident.

The final section of the chapter, **vss. 57–59**, moves from familiar disruption to communal dysfunction. These verses about being taken to court appear in Matthew's Sermon on the Mount (Matt 5.25). Although the comments can be read with an eschatological flavor and with God as the judge, the nonallegorical, practical interpretation better fits the literary context for both Luke and Matthew. "Having begun this section with an exhortation to courage in the face of tribulation, and continued with a warning against avarice in the face of fear, Luke has Jesus finish his sayings to the disciples with parables that explicitly raise the issue of judgment."[25] The theme of the final section is judging what is right (**vs. 57**). Jesus exhorts, "Make peace with your opponent" (**vs. 58**), lest the law case embroil you in a worse situation in which extrication is impossible (**vs. 59**). The lines anticipate, but in a complicated way, the Parable of the Widow and the Judge (18.2–5), wherein the widow litigator achieves in the court exactly what she wants while the judge is the victim, or perhaps the beneficiary, of her machinations. In either case, her opponent loses.

BRIDGING THE HORIZONS

On Greed

Fred Craddock, master homilist and exegete, said of Jesus' Parable of the Rich Fool:

> The parable calls covetousness folly. It could also have said it was a violation of the law of Moses (Ex. 20.17) and of the teachings of the prophets

---

[25] Johnson, *Gospel of Luke*, 209.

(Micah 2.2). Even so, it seems to have been a widespread problem in the church (Rom. 1.29; Mark 7.22; Col. 3.5; Eph. 5.5; 1 Tim. 6.10). This craving to hoard not only puts goods in the place of God (in Pauline theology, covetousness is idolatry, Rom. 1.25; Col. 3.5) but is an act of total disregard for the needs of others. The preacher will want to be careful not to caricature the farmer and thus rob the story of the power of its realism. There is nothing here of graft or theft; there is no mistreatment of workers or any criminal act. Sun, soil, and rain join to make him wealthy. He is careful and conservative. If he is not unjust, then what is he? He is a fool says the parable. He lives completely for himself, he talks to himself, he plans for himself, he congratulates himself. His sudden death proves him to have lived as a fool. "For what does it profit a man if he gains the whole world and loses or forfeits himself?" (9.25).[26]

The issue Luke addresses is not material possessions "simpliciter" but our tendency to hoard them. Johnson, seeing this point, stresses: "It is out of deep fear that the acquisitive instinct grows monstrous. Life seems so frail and contingent that many possessions are required to secure it, even though the possessions are frailer still than life. Only the removal of the fear by the persuasion that life is a gift given by the source of all reality can generate the spiritual freedom that is symbolized by the generous disposition of possessions ... [L]ife cannot be secured by possessions, existence is a gift outside human control."[27]

On Hell

The Aramaic term *Gehenna*, found in 12.5 but more frequently in Matthew, likely derives from the Hinnom Valley in Jerusalem, which was according to Jeremiah a place of child sacrifice. The prophet records that some residents of Judah who would soon face Babylonian exile "go on building the high place of Topheth, which is in the valley of the son of Hinnom, to burn their sons and their daughters in the fire – which I did not command, nor did it come into my mind" (7.31; see also Jer 32.35; 2 Chron 28.3; 33.6; *1 En.* 90.26–27). Jeremiah records how desperate people take desperate action. One irony here is that the Gospel celebrates God's allowing his own "beloved son" to go to the cross. Although biblical literature has little to say about postmortem rewards or punishments, the various cultural influences on Israel, from Persian to Greek to Roman,

---

[26]   Craddock, *Luke*, 163.
[27]   Johnson, *Gospel of Luke*, 201.

prompted a development in views of what we today call "heaven" and "hell."

The Jewish tradition never developed doctrinal views of eternal damnation. Indeed, the more the Church focused on salvation and damnation, the more the Jewish community focused on sanctification found in the way one lives. At the time of Jesus, the predominate view among Jews in the land of Israel was one of resurrection followed by a final judgment; we see this idea promoted in the New Testament as well as in early rabbinic literature. Martha's assertion about her dead brother, Lazarus, reflects popular Pharisaic teaching: "I know that he will rise again in the resurrection on the last day" (John 11.24]. Similarly, the Mishnah, *Ber.* 5.2 states, concerning the daily prayer known as the *shemoneh esreh* [Eighteen Benedictions], "They refer to the 'wonder of the rain' in [the blessing concerning] 'the resurrections of the dead' [the second benediction]"; see also *m. Sanh.* 10.1; *Pirke Avot* 4.22). Rabbi Akiva stated that the punishments of hell, "the judgment of the wicked in Gehenna is twelve months" (*m. Eduy* 2.10). This idea of limited suffering, comparable to the Christian idea of Purgatory, prevailed.

Whether there are postmortem punishments cannot be determined by historical analysis or philosophical argument, any more than these approaches can prove the existence of God. Ben firmly believes in hell; Amy-Jill likes the idea (there are people she would like to see assigned there) but finds the idea of any torture, even of the most heinous of people, unacceptable (see "On Heaven and Hell, Again," in Chapter 16). This is why even some conservative Christians through the ages have promoted the idea of extinction or ceasing to exist when it comes to those who reject God as their savior.

On Divine Care

"His Eye Is on the Sparrow," a hymn written ca. 1905, was immortalized by Ethel Waters, the great African American singer; both Ms. Waters and her song advanced the cause of justice and compassion. Billy Graham asked her to sing it in his early crusades, to great effect on the crowds. The assertion that God cares for everyone should function not only as a source of comfort, but also as a source of provocation. Since we are in the image and likeness of the divine, we should also display this care.

Luke 13 Repentance, Healing, and Salvation

DEATH AND SIN

¹ At that very time there were some present who told him about the Galileans whose blood Pilate had mingled with their sacrifices. ² He asked them, "Do you think that because these Galileans suffered in this way they were worse sinners than all other Galileans? ³ No, I tell you; but unless you repent, you will all perish as they did. ⁴ Or those eighteen who were killed when the tower of Siloam fell on them – do you think that they were worse offenders than all the others living in Jerusalem? ⁵ No, I tell you; but unless you repent, you will all perish just as they did."

PARABLE OF THE FIG TREE

⁶ Then he told this parable: "A man had a fig tree planted in his vineyard; and he came looking for fruit on it and found none. ⁷ So he said to the gardener, 'See here! For three years I have come looking for fruit on this fig tree, and still I find none. Cut it down! Why should it be wasting the soil?' ⁸ He replied, 'Sir, let it alone for one more year, until I dig around it and put manure on it. ⁹ If it bears fruit next year, well and good; but if not, you can cut it down.'"

SATAN AND OSTEOPOROSIS

¹⁰ Now he was teaching in one of the synagogues on the Sabbath. ¹¹ And just then there appeared a woman with a spirit that had crippled her for eighteen years. She was bent over and was quite unable to stand up straight. ¹² When Jesus saw her, he called her over and said, "Woman, you are set free from your ailment." ¹³ When he laid his hands on her, immediately she stood up straight and began praising God.

¹⁴ But the leader of the synagogue, indignant because Jesus had cured on the Sabbath, kept saying to the crowd, "There are six days on which work ought to be done; come on those days and be cured, and not on the Sabbath day." ¹⁵ But the Lord answered him and said, "You hypocrites! Does not each of you on the Sabbath untie his ox or his donkey from the manger, and lead it away to give it water? ¹⁶ And ought not this woman, a daughter of Abraham whom Satan bound for eighteen long years, be set free from this bondage on the Sabbath day?"

¹⁷ When he said this, all his opponents were put to shame; and the entire crowd was rejoicing at all the wonderful things that he was doing.

PARABLES OF MUSTARD SEED AND YEAST

¹⁸ He said therefore, "What is the kingdom of God like? And to what should I compare it? ¹⁹ It is like a mustard seed that someone took and sowed in the garden; it grew and became a tree, and the birds of the air made nests in its branches."

²⁰ And again he said, "To what should I compare the kingdom of God? ²¹ It is like yeast that a woman took and mixed in with three measures of flour until all of it was leavened."

LESSONS ON SALVATION

²² Jesus went through one town and village after another, teaching as he made his way to Jerusalem. ²³ Someone asked him, "Lord, will only a few be saved?" He said to them, ²⁴ "Strive to enter through the narrow door; for many, I tell you, will try to enter and will not be able.

²⁵ When once the owner of the house has got up and shut the door, and you begin to stand outside and to knock at the door, saying, 'Lord, open to us,' then in reply he will say to you, 'I do not know where you come from.'

²⁶ Then you will begin to say, 'We ate and drank with you, and you taught in our streets.' ²⁷ But he will say, 'I do not know where you come from; go away from me, all you evildoers!'

²⁸ There will be weeping and gnashing of teeth when you see Abraham and Isaac and Jacob and all the prophets in the kingdom of God, and you yourselves thrown out. ²⁹ Then people will come from east and west, from north and south, and will eat in the kingdom of God.

³⁰ Indeed, some are last who will be first, and some are first who will be last."

PASSION PREDICTIONS

[31] At that very hour some Pharisees came and said to him, "Get away from here, for Herod wants to kill you." [32] He said to them, "Go and tell that fox for me, 'Listen, I am casting out demons and performing cures today and tomorrow, and on the third day I finish my work. [33] Yet today, tomorrow, and the next day I must be on my way, because it is impossible for a prophet to be killed outside of Jerusalem.'

[34] Jerusalem, Jerusalem, the city that kills the prophets and stones those who are sent to it! How often have I desired to gather your children together as a hen gathers her brood under her wings, and you were not willing! [35] See, your house is left to you. And I tell you, you will not see me until the time comes when you say, 'Blessed is the one who comes in the name of the Lord.'"

As Jesus draws closer to Jerusalem, the subjects of Satan and sin, death and resurrection, become heightened. The chapter opens with a notice of outrages committed by Pontius Pilate; it ends with warnings concerning Herod Antipas. In 3.1, the Gospel makes its first reference to Pilate, along with its first reference to Herod Antipas. Here, in Chapter 13, Luke begins instruction on the need for redemption from such rulers. The extent to which we readers are to see either or both as aligned with Satan remains a matter of debate. In this chapter as well, the Pharisees make an ambiguous appearance. Whether they are seeking Jesus' welfare, or seeking to stop his mission, also remains an open question.

DEATH AND SIN

In material unique to the Third Gospel, Luke uses events that occurred during the governorship of Pontius Pilate (26–36 CE) as illustrations of the arbitrariness of death: for Galileans and Judeans, sinners and saints; caused by political murder, human error, or an accident of nature. Repeating the theme of repentance, which is prominent in the Gospel of Luke, cause of death is a lesser concern than whether the people who died had repented of their sins.

The chapter opens with some among the crowd informing Jesus that Pontius Pilate had ordered the murder of Galileans who had come to Jerusalem to offer sacrifices (**vs.1**). This is not the first time that Galileans, Jerusalem, sacrifice, and warning appear together. Luke earlier depicted the trip made by Mary and Joseph from Galilee to Jerusalem to present Jesus at the Temple. There, Simeon had predicted to Mary both that her son Jesus would be the cause of dissension in Jerusalem and that a sword would pierce her own soul (2.34–35). In 22.59, Luke will refer to Peter as a "Galilean," and in 23.6, Pilate recognizes Jesus as a Galilean; on a second reading of the Gospel, the mention of Pilate's murdering Galileans takes on an even more ominous connotation.

Pilate's lack of concern for Jewish sensibilities is recorded by numerous historians. Although this particular incident of murdering Galileans in the Temple does not appear in external sources and therefore could be, especially given the Lucan themes that surround it, a redactional invention, it is consistent with Pilate's other activities, including bringing Roman standards into Jerusalem, raiding the Temple treasury for funds to construct an aqueduct (*War* 2.9; *Ant.* 18.3), and massacring Samaritans (*Ant.*18.4.1). There is no reason to presume that these Galileans did anything to deserve their fate: they were pilgrims offering sacrifices; Luke does not associate them with political revolutionaries like Judas the Galilean of Acts 5.37 (cf. *War* 2.118). Their closer association is with Mary and Joseph, who also came to Jerusalem to worship in the Temple and offer sacrifice there.

Jesus responds not with sympathy for the victims, even though he is a fellow Galilean, but with a response to a question his informers did not ask. His concern is not Pilate's injustice, but the victims' actions. He asked whether the crowd thought that the murdered Galilean pilgrims were worse sinners than others from their region (**vs. 2**). The implied answer should be: "No, these pilgrims were not worse sinners. There is no reason to presume that they were any morally different than anyone else."

Then Jesus shifts from a question about sin to a pronouncement concerning repentance. Should the people not repent, they too will die as did the Galilean pilgrims (**vs. 3**). Ben sees Jesus as correcting the assumption that if something terrible happened to a person or group of people, one then has the right to assume they were worse sinners than others. He finds support for this reading in John 9, when Jesus denies that the man born blind is blind because he or his parents sinned. In Jesus' teaching, there is no infallible connection to be made between suffering and sinning. Sometimes there is a correlation, but often there is not. Amy-Jill notes that commentators typically suggest that Jesus is correcting the dominant Jewish view that suffering is punishment for sin. For example, Charles Talbert writes, "As any good Jew knows, trouble is God's punishment for sin, while tranquility is a sign of God's blessing. Our lives are tranquil; there is no disaster. Why should we repent?"[1] That Deuteronomic idea is itself already mitigated by numerous other biblical and postbiblical texts, from the Book of Job to Tobit's misfortunes to Daniel's travails to the deaths of the Maccabean martyrs. She sees nothing in the comment here in Luke 13 to indicate that the people thought those Galilean pilgrims were morally problematic. To the contrary, the people informing Jesus seem to her more interested in highlighting Pilate's barbarism.

Jesus uses the example to make a point about repentance, and so he turns from Pilate's actions to eschatological judgment. His comment about repenting resonates with the saying of Rabbi Eliezer in _Pirke Avot_ 2.10, "Repent one day before you die." The verse receives a gloss in _b. Shabb._ 153a: "His disciples asked: 'Does a person know on which day he will die?' Rabbi Eliezer said to them: 'Therefore, a person should repent today, for perhaps tomorrow he will die; hence, all his days are passed in a state of repentance. Indeed, so said Solomon in his wisdom: At all times, your clothes should be white, and oil should not lack from your head'" (the citation is to Eccl 9.8).[2]

Jesus' instruction on unexpected death and the need for repentance receives a second example that is also unattested in external sources. Jesus mentions eighteen people killed by the collapse of the tower of Siloam in Jerusalem (**vs. 4**). Here he speaks not of "sin" but of "debt" (the NRSV's "offenders" masks the Greek _opheletai_, "debtors"). Although in the Greek language, references to "debt" specifically indicate monetary debt, the verse functions here according to its Aramaic equivalent for "debt," _hob_, which can also mean "sin or trespass." The concern is not that the people killed owed money; it is that they, like everyone else, have a heavenly bank account for which sin depletes the treasury and good deeds refill it.[3] Thus, the term "debtors," especially in this context, indicates that "repentance" is not merely an intellectual or even spiritual state. It means making amends with those one has hurt, either by direct action or by inaction. Repentance means restoration of relationships. Without this restoration, eschatological suffering awaits (**vs. 5**).

The reference to the eighteen who died when the tower collapsed receives an echo in the story of the women bent over for eighteen years (13.11), which

[1]   Talbert, _Luke_, 145.
[2]   See, for _Pirke Avot_ and glosses, the Chabad website, www.chabad.org/library/article_cdo/aid/2011/jewish/Chapter-Two.htm.
[3]   See discussion in Anderson, _Sin: A History_.

will appear shortly. The connection indicates that neither the people killed in the accident nor the woman are to be seen as punished for sin. Rather, changing the subject, Jesus again insists that repentance is required or eschatological punishment will follow.

The reference to the number eighteen may have yet another implication aside from a catchword between the two narratives; it may symbolize, for both accounts, the tragedy of loss of life. All Hebrew letters have numerical equivalents, with *aleph* (a) equaling 1, *bet* (b) equaling 2, and so on. The letters *chet* (8) and *yod* (10), which together add up to the number eighteen, also spell the word *chai*, meaning "life" (whence the phrase, "l'chaim," "to life"; there is no association with chai tea). Both the people killed in the accident and the woman bent over are lacking full "life." Given the context of repentance, the idea that life will be restored to the victims is not an impossible interpretation of their stories. That the bent-over woman is restored, is returned to full life, confirms this reading.

PARABLE OF THE FIG TREE

In its narrative context, the Parable of the Fig Tree (13.6–9) is a commentary on the two disasters in Judea; for Luke, the tree is an allegorical representation of the person who needs to repent. If no repentance happens, then the gardener will cut it down. To state the need for repentance, however, does not require a parable; the two examples of Pilate's murders and the tower's fall already served that purpose. Weeding out unnecessary connections, adducing other biblical references to barren fig trees, and considering Jesus' other parables containing surprising details yield much more challenging messages than "repent."

Jesus begins the parable by describing a man who plants a fig tree in his vineyard, but he finds no fruit on it (**vs. 6**). Matters are confused. First, since the next verse tells us that the vineyard owner had a gardener, it is not clear why the vineyard owner himself is doing the planting. That is not his job. He may be micromanaging, or he may have planted the tree incorrectly, by burying the roots too deep, not providing sufficient irrigation, or not considering the amount of sunlight. Second, he has planted a fig tree in a vineyard, which is where one would expect not figs, but grapes. Should one argue that vines use fig trees for support, as does Pliny the Elder (*Natural History* 17.35.199–200),[4] then the owner's concern about the lack of figs

---

[4]   Snodgrass, *Stories with Intent*, 260.

would be irrelevant to the function of the tree. Third, the tree is not yielding its figs. Something has gone wrong, but at this stage, we cannot tell if the problem is the vineyard owner himself, the soil, the weather, or the tree.

We start with weeding out some of the allegories. Commentators from the Patristic period onward are often quick to provide allegorical interpretations. The vineyard is usually Israel, given Isaiah's famous Parable of the Vineyard (Isa 5.1–7 cf. Psa 80.8–13, which compares Israel to a vine). Klyne Snodgrass, in his comprehensive study of Jesus' parables, uses Augustine's interpretation of the fig tree, along with that of the Good Samaritan, to epitomize the allegorical approach: the three actions the owner takes correspond to the presence of God before the giving of the Law, the time of the Law, and the time of Christ's mercy.[5] Cyril of Alexandria (*Homiletic Commentary*) proposed that the tree represented Judaism/the synagogue, and it would be cut down so that the gentile church could be planted. According to the eminent early German biblical scholar F. C. Baur, "The fig tree, finally cut down after such a long time of unfruitfulness, is a picture of the Jewish people and their guilt."[6] Or, the fig tree is the Temple. The gardener is Jesus, since Mary Magdalene mistook him for a gardener in John 20.15; that Mary was mistaken does not appear to have influenced the connection some commentators make between Luke's Parable and Mary's comment. The owner of the vineyard is God (the Father), who also planted a garden in Eden.

Or, the owner and the gardener are the two sides of God, one representing justice and the other mercy. The three years the owner has waited for fruition represent the three years of Jesus' public activity (according to one reading of John's Gospel). Or, they may represent the extra time God gives humanity to repent (2 Pet 3.8–9 proposes that a day to God is like a thousand years, with the delay of the Final Judgment designed to encourage repentance). The fig tree is the Temple, the Jewish people, or the recalcitrant Christian. The manure represents prophetic teaching (a potentially unfortunate, or humorous, image). Augustine concluded that the fig tree represented humanity while the manure represented humility. These readings have their own internal logic, and parables will speak to each generation anew. While such interpretations are not "wrong," they are also

---

5   Ibid., 4.
6   See Joseph B. Tyson, *Luke, Judaism, and the Scholars: Critical Approaches to Luke-Acts* (Columbia: University of South Carolina, 1999), 25, citing F. C. Baur, *Kritische Untersuchungen über die kanonischen Evangelien, ihr Verhältniß zu einander, ihren Charakter und Ursprung* (Tübingen: Fues, 1847), 508.

unlikely to be what either Jesus' audience (we are accepting the parable as coming from Jesus) or Luke's readers would find.

Concordance searches yield other fig tree references (Judg 9.10–11; 2 Kings 18.31; Isa 34.4; Jer 8.13; 24.1–10; Hos 9.10; Prov 27.18; Song 2.3; and so on) that are similarly less productive for interpreting Luke's parable in its narrative or historical contexts. The best connection may be to Mic 7.1–2, in which the prophet (speaking for God) laments, "there is no first-ripe fig for which I hunger," since "the faithful have disappeared from the land." Yet the parable's plot does not fully support this allusion, since the tree in the parable still has the potential to yield fruit.

Still others see the parable as Luke's rewriting of the narrative of the withered fig tree found in Mark 11.12–21. In this intercalated narrative Mark presents, Jesus finds a fig tree without fruit, curses it, enters the Temple, disrupts normal activity, and leaves Jerusalem. The next morning, the disciples find the tree withered. Matthew condenses the miracle by having Jesus curse the tree, and then the "fig tree withered at once" (Matt 21.19). For Mark, the destruction of the tree foreshadows the destruction of the Temple. For Matthew, the fig tree is an illustration of the miraculous might of the faithful, who can wither trees and move mountains (Matt 21.20–22). Luke has neither of these ideas in mind. The scene is not set in relation any more to the Temple than to the Tower of Siloam; the parable has nothing directly to do with the disciples' miraculous abilities to create ecological disasters. For Luke, there is a fig tree in a vineyard.

The vineyard owner consults the gardener: because the tree has had three years to produce figs and, so far, has produced nothing, he orders that it be cut down. It is wasting soil or, literally "leaving the ground idle" (**vs. 7**). He planted the tree, but he is not willing to cut it down. One might be reminded of the rich and powerful, who will take responsibility for planting an idea, or a business, but will not be present when the business fails and the assets need to be liquidated, but this too is an unnecessary although plausible reading.

The greater problem is the presence of the gardener. Arland Hultgren proposes, "The caretaker intercedes for the tree."[7] Yes, and yet: it is his job to ensure that the plants thrive. If the tree had been absorbing the nutrients needed by the vines, the gardener should have noticed the problem and

7 Arland J. Hultgren, *The Parables of Jesus: A Commentary* (Grand Rapids: Eerdmans, 2000), 244.

addressed it. His intercession may be as much for himself as for the tree, for the parable opens the possibility that the gardener has not been doing his job. That possibility is reinforced by the next line, in which the gardener asks for another year's delay in order for him to dig around the tree and fertilize it (**vs. 8**). The gardener had three years to cultivate the tree, and for three years, as far as we know, he simply let nature take its course. He is only now doing his job and tending the tree.

The gardener complicates the scene even more with his final comment: if the tree remains unproductive, you (second-person singular) – that is, you, the landowner – can cut it down (**vs. 9**). The gardener shifts the burden of responsibility back to the man who planted the tree originally: you planted it; if it bears no fruit, you pull it down. The job of the gardener, at least here, is to tend the plants and not to uproot them.

We do not know what happens with the owner, the gardener, or the tree. The tree could still be growing, or the owner could have cut it down. Its future is open, as are our interpretive possibilities. For Luke, the interpretation is constrained by the context: the tree is the sinner who must repent or suffer eschatological uprooting. Its job is not to support grapevines, but to "bear good fruit" (3.9; 6.49; 8.15).

The parable, abstracted from its context, offers the following additional possibilities. Perhaps it is about responsibility: who plants, who tends, who uproots? Perhaps it prompts questions of the stewardship of nature: our task is not to blight trees but to ensure they have the nutrients they need; to have dominion over God's creation is to care for it. Or perhaps the parable offers a teaching, like the Parable of the Sower, for prophets and missionaries: one can only do so much, after which the fate of the plant, or the person, is in divine hands. Or again, the parable may be heard to question what we expect of the natural world: the tree can support vines, or it can provide beauty and shade, or it can produce fruit. Does every tree, let alone every person, serve the same purpose? Finally, the parable asks us listeners, what we would like to see happen. Do we want the tree preserved, or uprooted? Do we want the gardener to be successful, even if he failed to care for the tree for three years? Is tending assiduously, after three years, enough after ignoring the tree day after day, month after month? Should the one who planted the tree have done more himself than simply look for figs? Whose fault is it, if it is anyone's fault, that the tree has not yielded figs? That final question is a good guide for anyone who seeks, personally, to bear good fruit.

SATAN AND OSTEOPOROSIS

The scene changes from outside to inside, from a barren fig tree to a woman who is incapacitated from bearing all the fruit that she could, given her physical limitations. The day is the Sabbath, and Jesus is again teaching in one of the local synagogues (**vs. 10**). Given the disaster in the first synagogue appearance, where the assembled people from Nazareth turn from their delight in his words to their desire to kill him, we may be prepared for another unpleasant encounter. Yet Jesus had also performed a healing in the synagogue on the Sabbath (6.6–11, the man with the withered hand), so we might expect another miracle. Finally, Jesus had recently warned about trials in synagogues (12.11), so an argument regarding behavior in the assembly could also be expected. Our expectations are not disappointed.

The anticipated healing finds its foreshadowing in the next verse. A woman, bent over for eighteen years and therefore unable to stand upright, appears (**vs. 11**). Her problem is that she is physically disabled. Commentators then impose additional disability and pain on her by insisting that she is marginalized in her Jewish context. Joel Green, for example, comments: "in our present text, Sabbath and synagogue function as symbol of Jewish exclusivity ... Whether the woman was in a state of ritual impurity, or under what conditions a woman might have been present in the synagogue – these are issues marginal to the narrative ... These loci of the sacred, Sabbath and synagogue, actually segregate this needy woman from divine help."[8] Women would have been present in synagogues; there is nothing remarkable about her presence. There is no reason to question her state of ritual purity, or Jesus' state for that matter. These questions are not "marginal" to the pericope; they are completely irrelevant. Nor is the woman excluded in her Jewish context. To the contrary, the synagogue is a place where disabled people are welcome, as the Gospels themselves demonstrate. She is not on a second-story ledge overlooking the men in the congregation; she is not behind a screen.

The category in which our woman is best understood is that of "disabled person in the synagogue," where she takes her place alongside the man with the withered hand. She is *not* exemplary of any "far-reaching emphasis on the inclusion of outsiders within the circle of Jesus' followers, e.g., tax collectors and sinners, women, lepers, and the demon-possessed,"[9] because

---

[8] Joel B. Green, "Jesus and a Daughter of Abraham (Luke 13:10–17): Test Case for a Lucan Perspective on Jesus' Miracles," *CBQ* 51.4 (1989): 643–54 (649).

[9] Ibid.

these categories are illegitimate. There are no demon-possessed or leprous people in Jesus' circle, because he has healed them; there are no tax collectors in the inner circle, save for Levi, who appears to have given up his day job. The sinners have, ideally, repented. And the women stay women, outside the inner circle of the apostles, providing ministry to Jesus and support to his followers. Ben notes that this notice does not suffice as a description of how Luke views Mary Magdalene and the other women mentioned in 8.1–3. They are also the ones who "remember" what Jesus taught them at the crucial juncture at the empty tomb in 24.6–8. They were not outsiders simply serving as the hospitality brigade for the twelve men. Thus, Ben sees the women as more than outsiders; Amy-Jill sees them as outside *leadership* roles. We do both note, however, that Mary Magdalene, like Peter, is always listed first among the women disciples. Perhaps she is so listed because she is the leader of the women disciples, just as Peter is of the male disciples.

Our woman, like all figures in Luke's healing narratives, is not named. The focus is on her features that she may share with others: her presence in the synagogue; her ailment; her membership in the family of Abraham; her vulnerability to Satan; and, for the Gospel, the light she sheds on Christology. Our woman is, like the numerous women, even today, disabled by osteoporosis or other forms of curvature of the spine. We have no details on her economic circumstances or familial status. That she is in the synagogue in the Land of Israel tells us that she is most likely a Jew.

Whether she can see anyone from her vantage point cannot be determined. Jesus, and we, can see her. He calls to her with the generic address "woman" and then proclaims her liberated from her disability (**vs. 12**). The address is familiar from the Gospel of John, where Jesus refers to his mother (2.4; 19.26), the Samaritan woman (4.21) at the well, the woman accused of adultery (8.10), and Mary Magdalene (20.15 cf. 20.13, where the angels use the term) all as "woman" (Greek: *gynē*). This is the only place in Luke's Gospel where Jesus uses this address, although Peter will use the same term to address a woman who accuses him of being Jesus' associate (22.57). The address does not therefore have the same comparative import in the Third Gospel as it does in the Fourth.

Unlike the hemorrhaging woman who approaches Jesus, here Jesus takes the initiative. He pronounces the disabled woman free, and the healing comes when he touches her. As soon as he places his hands on her, she rises up. More, she praises God (**vs. 13**). Since this is what one does in the synagogue, she is fully engaging Sabbath worship. Whereas Green insists "these loci of the sacred, Sabbath and synagogue, actually segregate this needy woman from divine help,"[10] the opposite is the case. Were the woman not in the synagogue, Jesus would not have seen her. It is in the synagogue that she receives her healing.

The conflict is not with the synagogue either as institution or as congregation; it is rather with the synagogue leader (Greek: *archisynagogos*, the same title applied to Jairus, the father of the girl Jesus raises [8.41]), who complains to the congregation that Jesus violated the Sabbath day (**vs. 14**). The man has a point. Saving a life would be permitted, indeed mandated, as *m. Yoma* 8.6 also states: "And any matter of doubt as to danger to life overrides the prohibitions of the Sabbath." But medical practitioners today can expect that on Sunday morning they would not be asked between the first hymn and the sermon to provide therapeutic aid to people with nonpainful chronic conditions.

Jesus offers a counterpoint to the synagogue ruler. Although he answers only him, his address is in the plural, "You hypocrites" (**vs. 15**). The implication is that the synagogue ruler was not the only one to find the healing, under the circumstances, problematic. Using a standard *qal v'homer* (from the lesser to the greater) argument, he notes that if the people will bring their animals to a watering trough on the Sabbath, then surely, they would see the value in the release of a woman from Satanic bondage. The comparison of the woman to an ox or donkey is not a particularly congenial one, but the point holds.

Better is Jesus' labeling the woman a "daughter of Abraham" (**vs. 16**). References to Abraham appear in several other places in Luke's Gospel, with most sounding a theme of liberation. Mary speaks of the promises made "to Abraham and to his descendants forever" (1.55) and Zechariah of the oaths made to Abraham (1.73) regarding salvation from "the hands of our enemies" (1.74). Luke has turned from these manifestly political connotations to a different form of salvation, where the issue is Satanic occupation, not military conquest. Conversely, John the Baptist decries the claim by some of having Abraham as one's father (3.8), since personal action rather than ancestral privilege matters. In our chapter, it is precisely ancestral privilege that Jesus invokes. Various other roles for Abraham, increasingly in terms of eschatological salvation, pervade later passages (13.28; 16.22–30; 20.37).

The title "daughter of Abraham" finds yet one more connection in the Gospel: Jesus refers to Zaccheus, the short tax collector, as a "son of Abraham" (19.9). Here the discussion revolves around the righteousness

---

[10]   Ibid.

of a tax collector, not the physical health of a woman in the synagogue. Zaccheus, up a tree rather than in a synagogue, has no community, and it is to a community that Jesus restores him by giving him the public forum to express his true practices. The woman already has the community; Jesus gives her the healing needed to participate in it with her full life (see the previous discussion of the number eighteen).

By noting that the woman was bound by Satan, Jesus obviates any judgment that she is bent over by sin, or by the Law. The problem is Satan, and the problem of supernatural evil is a real one for Jesus and for Luke. The healing is a defeat of Satan, not a critique of Judaism or the synagogue as an institution. It is also a miracle. Momolu Armstrong Massaquoi observes, "The tendency of the modern mind to create a division between the 'natural' and the 'supernatural,' has promoted a distortion in popular opinion with regard to miracles."[11] We may seek a rational explanation for the healing, or turn the miracle into an allegory regarding religious movements or institutions. In this case, the healing is precisely that, a healing, and therefore worth celebrating.

The congregation agrees with Jesus' assessment. Those who opposed his presumed violation of the Sabbath, although he did no actual "work" other than touch the woman, celebrate not only this healing, but also other unnamed "glorious things" he had been doing (**vs. 17**).

A SECOND CLOSER LOOK: THE KINGDOM OF GOD IS LIKE ...

In introducing the Parable of the Sower in Luke 8, we offered a few comments on parables. We here develop that discussion in light of the formula, "The Kingdom of God is like."

Luke, along with Matthew and Mark, is our first interpreter of parables aside from an unrecoverable oral tradition. For a number of these parables, Luke tells the reader the meaning: the Parables of the Lost Sheep, Lost Coin, and Lost Family Members in Chapter 15 are about repenting and forgiving; the Parable of the Feisty Widow and Uncaring Judge in Chapter 18 is about praying always and not losing heart; and the Parable of the Dishonest Manager in Chapter 16 is about "making friends with dishonest mammon" (16.9). For some scholars, most notably John

---

[11]   Momolu Armstrong Massaquoi, "Jesus' Healing Miracles in Luke 13.10–17 and Their Significance for Physical Health," *Ogbomoso Journal of Theology* 18.1 (2013): 98–123 (98).

Meier, a number of the parables, including the famous Good Samaritan and Prodigal Son, come from the hand of Luke and not from Jesus.[12] We are proceeding in this volume as if Jesus told the parables Luke records; Ben and Amy-Jill do disagree, however, on whether or not several interpretations of the parables come from Luke (so Amy-Jill) or from Jesus (so Ben). Amy-Jill finds that the Lucan interpretations all require allegory, and they all require a special answer key to understand the details in the parables, so much so that one might wonder, "How would anyone have gotten *that* message?" Ben finds the interpretations consistent with the rest of Jesus' message and plausibly understood by anyone following Jesus. He adds that early Jewish parables often did have allegorical elements, and sometimes explanations as well.[13]

The parables Jesus employs typically use mundane images, of yeast and seed, parents and children, loss and finding. Interpreting these images became the job of evangelist and homilist, or of any reader who asks, "what does this story mean to me?" with each generation imposing its own symbolism on the images. The parables, like all literature, like all metaphors and similes, are open to multiple interpretations. Metaphors and similes, like art and music, sometimes better help us express profound concepts, like love or peace, the idea of God, or the notion of the kingdom that is not what we have but for which we yearn. Any analogy will be inexact, and each will only capture part of the fuller meaning.

We are not claiming that Luke, the Fathers, or readers today are "wrong" in their interpretations (save when those interpretations impose lessons that are anti-Jewish, racist, sexist, etc.; some interpretations are not good interpretations). We are claiming that the parables will take on different meanings inside and then outside of Luke's contextualization. By choosing where to place a parable and by appending a meaning, Luke promotes Luke's own agenda, as all writers do. By imagining the parables as they existed behind the text, additional messages, perhaps coming from Jesus himself, can be heard.

[12] See John P. Meier, *A Marginal Jew: Rethinking the Historical Jesus.* Volume 5, *Probing the Authenticity of the Parables* (ABRL; New Haven: Yale University Press, 2016). Meier finds that only four parables fit the criteria of authenticity: Mustard Seed (Mark/Q overlap), Evil Tenants (embarrassment), and Talents/Pounds and Great Supper (M/L overlaps).

[13] On other early Jewish parables, see discussion in Levine, *Short Stories by Jesus*; and B. H. Young, *The Parables: Jewish Tradition and Christian Interpretation* (Grand Rapids: Baker Academic, 2008).

The Kingdom parables do more than describe this mysterious realm that is both present and future, on earth and in heaven, fully accessible and always ephemeral. They also function to challenge us. They do not only tell us something about the kingdom, they also make us part of the kingdom by changing us. C. H. Dodd famously said, "At its simplest, the parable is a metaphor or simile drawn from nature or common life, arresting the hearer by its vividness or strangeness, and leaving the mind in sufficient doubt to its precise application to tease the mind into active thought."[14] They challenge, they indict, they open up our hearts and prick our consciences. They are wisdom sayings that defy easy explanations even as they are simple stories that even a child can begin to understand.[15]

PARABLES OF MUSTARD SEED AND YEAST

The two parables that follow the synagogue healing are only tangentially connected to the preceding narrative. Mustard seed and yeast are both domestic items; both are small, both grow inside other mediums (respectively, soil and dough); both change their own form and can change the form of other things; both produce new materials that can be used for food and for medicine; and both benefit when humans catalyze them so that they can fully manifest their latent capabilities. Both, finally, have been used by scholars, once again, to set up Judaism as a negative foil over and against which Jesus and Christianity can appear worthwhile. Such readings are not only dependent on and promulgators of anti-Jewish teaching, they are not necessary in order to find profound meaning in the parables.

Jesus begins this short teaching, apparently still in the synagogue, by asking for a comparison by which to understand the Kingdom of God (**vs. 18**). The comparison, like all comparisons, will be inexact. Several parables about the Kingdom show us that the concept itself is too broad, too multifaceted, to be embraced with a single comparison. Each kingdom parable is necessarily partial.

The first comparison casts the Kingdom next to a mustard seed sown in a garden. The seed grows not simply into the expected mustard plant, but into a giant tree in which birds nest (**vs. 19**). As with the Parable of the Fig

---

14   C.H. Dodd, *The Parables of the Kingdom* (New York: Charles Scribner's Sons, 1961), 5.
15   For example, see Amy-Jill Levine and Sandy E. Sasso, *Who Counts? 100 Sheep, 10 Coins, and 2 Sons* (Louisville: Westminster John Knox, 2017), for a children's version of the parables in Luke 15.

Tree, something has gone very wrong. Mustard does not grow into giant trees; birds do not nest in mustard plants, because the plants are too close to the ground and so to animals with a taste for eggs. The images are sufficiently unsettling to set the imagination to work. Ben adds that the comparison is not meant to be fully true to life but rather true to the Kingdom.

Complicating any immediate move toward imagination is the presence of different versions of this same parable in three other texts. Mark 4.30–32 lacks reference to a garden and mentions "the greatest of all shrubs" rather than a tree. For Mark, the birds nest not in the branches, but in the shade. Matt 13.31–32 comports with Mark's version, but Matthew offers the setting of a field, not a garden. In the *Gospel of Thomas* 20, Jesus tells the parable in response to the disciples' question, "Tell us what the kingdom of the heavens is like?" In *Thomas*'s version, the seed falls on plowed ground, puts forth an enormous branch, and the branch provides shelter for the birds.

The parables share more in common than display differences. They all emphasize the smallness of the seed, an emphasis secured by the contrast to the large plant the seed produces. From this distinction, commentators draw numerous conclusions. Those interested in theology and church offer familiar readings. For some readers, the parable is about a church with small beginnings but universal import, such that the gentiles, represented by the birds, find shelter in it. Therefore, the parable is designed to encourage the disciples. For others, it is about the importance of faith. As Jesus states in Luke 17.6, "If you had faith the size of a mustard seed, you could say to this mulberry tree, 'Be uprooted and planted in the sea,' and it would obey you" (Matt 17.20 offers the variant, "Amen, I tell you, if you have faith the size of a mustard seed, you will say to this mountain, 'Move from here to there,' and it will move; and nothing will be impossible for you'"). Still others see a reference to the relative weakness of the human body and the assuredness of the resurrection. In 1 Cor 15.36–48, Paul states, "What you sow does not come to life unless it dies." Supporting this view is an appeal to Jesus' statement in John 12.24: "Amen, Amen, I say to you, that unless a grain [Greek: *kokkos*, literally, "seed") of wheat falls into the earth and dies, it remains just a single grain; but if it dies, it bears much fruit." Therefore, the parable is about the mystery of the resurrection. All of these readings work. None, however, is particularly ethically challenging, socially disruptive, or even all that imaginative.

Current political readings of the parable appeal to readers seeking a countercultural Jesus. As detailed in Amy-Jill's book on parables,[16] commentators

[16] Levine, *Short Stories by Jesus*.

regard the seed as "a 'despised and rejected' weed"[17] or a "dangerous infesting weed" that threatens to "destroy" the garden by taking it over.[18] A few claim that the parable is an apt image for describing Jesus' "association with the unclean"[19] and for his Kingdom as welcoming the "unclean" gentile nations into the Church. Extending this obsessive interest in finding antipurity legislation, another claims: "Jesus depicts a kingdom not of the righteous but of the impudent rule-breaking sinners … The kingdom of God will be open to the undesirable."[20] At the same time, the birds serve to issue warnings to "the upper classes who live off the toil of the poor cultivator," since their "ventures pose a challenge to oppressive systems of power just as mustard run wild can overtake cultivated fields."[21] In these readings, the garden is the status quo, the empire, Judaism, or everything that is not in agreement with the Gospel. The first problem with these readings is that the parable shows nothing destructive. The second is that numerous texts from antiquity affirm the value of mustard as spice, as medicine, and as ornamental plant. The third is that mustard has nothing to do with impurity. And the fourth is that the seed does not take over the garden: one tree does not preclude other plants from sprouting. The upshot of these approaches is one that primarily makes biblical scholars feel good about their liberationist politics.

Related to such readings are the anti-imperialist claims. Because the Bible sometimes describes empires as trees that are chopped down, so the mustard tree is the alternative to Assyria, Babylon, or any colonialist, expansionist governmental system.[22] Ezek 31.3–14 depicts Assyria as a cedar of Lebanon that sheltered birds until destroyed by divine decree, and Dan 4.11–12 picks up this theme. Luke's version of the parable lacks this anti-imperial slant. Mustard is not cedar. Claims that the "birds of the sky"

---

[17] David Buttrick, *Speaking Parables: A Homiletic Guide* (Louisville: Westminster John Knox, 2000), 77; "despised and rejected" is an allusion to Isa 53.3, the "suffering servant," understood in Christian interpretation to be Jesus

[18] Barbara Reid, *Parables for Preachers, Year A* (Collegeville: Liturgical Press, 2001), p. 16, following John Dominic Crossan, *The Historical Jesus* (San Francisco: HarperSanFrancisco, 1991), pp. 276–80.

[19] Reid, *Parables for Preachers Year A*, p. 105

[20] Buttrick, *Speaking Parables*, p. 78

[21] Barbara Reid, *Parables for Preachers, Year C* (Collegeville: Liturgical Press, 2000), pp. 297, 304, following Douglas E. Oakman, *Jesus and the Economic Question of His Day* (Lewiston/Queenston: Edwin Mellen, 1986), 125.

[22] Robert W. Funk, "The Looking Glass Tree Is for the Birds," *Interpretation* 27.1 (1973): 3–9 (4), and following numerous commentators, including Bernard B. Scott, *Re-Imagine the World: An Introduction to the Parables of Jesus* (Santa Rosa: Polebridge Press, 2001), 38–40; see also Reid, *Parables for Preachers Year A*, 104–5; Buttrick, *Preaching Parables*, 77 on subverting the "dream of triumph."

represent gentiles also overstate. The Tanakh uses this phrase forty times, and in the vast majority of cases, the birds are exactly that, winged creatures that fly and nest. The birds in the Parable of the Sower (8.5) may be allegorical references to something external, but they need not be seen as gentiles eating up the faithful. The birds with nests whom Jesus compares to foxes who have holes (9.58) are birds, not gentiles; the same point holds for the ravens who neither sow nor reap (12.24).

If we weed out the concerns for purity and political transgression, the parable opens up to multiple, inspirational, and challenging readings. It speaks to potential, to the unexpected, to small beginnings and gigantic ends; to transformation, to the move from the mundane to the marvelous.

These same concerns infuse the next parable, in which Jesus compares God's Kingdom (**vs. 20**) to yeast – we should think of sourdough starter – that a woman "hid" (that is the Greek term used) in three measures of flour (**vs. 21**). Again, commentators insist that the parable is about uncleanness. Ben notes that yeast could become "corrupt" due to the ongoing bacterial processes. He finds "yeast" to be a new healthy rising agent whereas leaven is a leftover piece of bread with the rising agent still producing chemical processes in it. Put another way, leaven is "old yeast in bread." The term the Gospel uses is *zyme*, which can be translated either "yeast" or "leaven." Ben sees an intrinsic metaphor for corruption; Amy-Jill does not. The "yeast" or "leaven" becomes corrupt only when it is paired with something else suggesting corruption. Ben notes that if by "something else" one means or includes bacteria, then it is in order to note that bacteria is an *inherent* part of the fermenting process after a period of time, hence the negative associations of leaven as yeast gone bad.

That Jews remove all leavened products for Passover indicates that they are happily using leaven the other fifty-one weeks of the year, and that they are not associating their bread with corruption. This Passover imagery is the background to Paul's comment in 1 Cor 5:6–8: "Do you not know that a little yeast leavens the whole batch of dough? Clean out the old yeast so that you may be a new batch, as you really are unleavened ... Therefore, let us celebrate the festival, not with the old yeast, the yeast of malice and evil, but with the unleavened bread of sincerity and truth." Because of the Passover connection, yeast can have a negative connotation. Jesus speaks of the "leaven of the Pharisees" (12.1) as representing hypocrisy. But this connection does not pervade the parable.

Alternatively, a rabbinic text, *Derekh Eretz Zuta* on Lev 26.6 (citing R. Jehoshua b. Levi), states: "Great is peace, for it is as the leaven to dough.

If the Holy One had not given peace to the world, sword and beast would devour up the whole world."

Whereas neither the *Gospel of Thomas* nor the Gospel of Mark pairs the mustard seed and the yeast, Matthew's Gospel does (Matt 13.31–33), and this connection helps us interpret Luke's parable. Seed and yeast share several factors: they are domestic, small, transform, work on their own without too much human fussing, and give rise to something both tasty and therapeutic. Both parables also play on the idea of exaggeration: the giant tree; the three measures of flour that will yield sixty pounds of dough. Both contain a hint of the uncanny or at least unexpected: mustard does not grow into a tree; bakers do not "hide" yeast but "mix" it or "knead" it into the dough.

This parable too opens to multiple interpretations. Ryan Schellenberg, who does a superb job at cleaning out the various claims made about the seed and the dough, concludes: "The use of leaven as a cipher for the kingdom of God makes it clear that here leaven represents the pervasive power of something good."[23] The mustard and the leaven both reveal the surprise of the kingdom: from a seed, an unexpected tree that provides shelter; from hidden dough, enough food to feed a village. Both reveal the presence of the Kingdom in what might seem ordinary, small, or utilitarian.

For Luke, the seed and the yeast are gender coded. It is a man (Greek: *anthrōpos*) who tosses the seed into the garden; it is a woman (Greek: *gynē*) who hides the yeast in dough. The *Gospel of Thomas* makes the gender-coding explicit. Whereas Luke speaks of yeast that a woman hid, *Thomas* 96 compares the "kingdom of the Father" to a "woman who took a little leaven." The Kingdom potential is in the garden and the kitchen. And it is in each one of us, as we become something unexpected, something extraordinary.[24]

LESSONS ON SALVATION

Concluding the two parables but providing neither interpretations of them nor audience reaction, Luke offers the summary that Jesus taught from town to town as he headed toward Jerusalem (**vs. 22**). In an unnamed village, Jesus receives what is for Luke the correct address, "lord," as well as a question about the numbers to be "saved" (**vs. 23**). Luke does not tell

---

[23]   Ryan S. Schellenberg, "Kingdom as Contaminant? The Role of Repertoire in the Parables of the Mustard Seed and the Leaven," *CBQ* 71.3 (2009): 527–43 (542).

[24]   Amy-Jill Levine and Sandy E. Sasso, *The Marvelous Mustard Seed* (Louisville: Flyaway Books, 2018).

us why an anonymous individual would either address Jesus with this title rather than "teacher" or ask him about the quantity of those to be saved. Missing as well is the follow-up detail: saved *from what*? For the earlier biblical material and generally in Jewish thought, "salvation" is from earthly crises: slavery, military conquest, death. For Luke's Gospel, salvation primarily concerns the afterlife, although it sometimes has the sense of "healed" or "rescued" from something.

This distinction in emphasis continues into Jewish and Christian history. Rabbinic teaching and, following from it, much of today's Judaism, generally, speak of salvation in the present even as it focuses on sanctification in earthly life. For example, *Unetanah Tokef* ("we shall ascribe holiness"), a *piyyut* (hymn) antedating the eleventh century, fragments of which were found in the Cairo Genizah, speaks of the Day of Judgment as being annual rather than simply eschatological; the liturgical refrain proclaims: "But repentance, prayer and righteousness avert the severe decree." The Christian tradition has come to focus less on sanctification through following Torah than on salvation dependent on belief in Jesus as Lord, although Ben notes that the Methodist tradition has a very strong focus on sanctification and good works in this life.

Jesus' response concerns striving for eschatological or heavenly salvation, and he proclaims that only few will enter (**vs. 24**). Missing is the contrast in Matt 7.13–14, where Jesus speaks of the wide path's appeal; Luke's focus is those who will be saved, and what they must do. Commentators frequently insist that the "striving" is not to be an indication of "works righteousness," such that people attempt to "earn" their salvation. They sometimes continue by contrasting Christian grace with Jewish law and presume that Judaism does insist on a works-righteousness soteriology. The first part of this formulation requires nuance: the Gospel is not constructed on a "believe and you are saved" program; it requires action. Without the bearing of good fruit (3.9 cf. 6.43; 8.15; 13.9), the belief is at best self-serving. Judaism foregrounds orthopraxy over orthodoxy, but it does not function on a works-righteousness model. Instead, it begins with the presupposition of divine grace, and one follows Torah in response to that divine initiative.

The language then shifts to the household setting. In a recapitulation of several earlier sayings, the householder, here Jesus or God, has shut the door, and now the listener is Jesus' audience and Luke's readers: we are the ones who might find ourselves standing outside, knocking on the door, and hearing the condemnation: "I do not know you or your background" (**vs. 25**). The verse stands in contrast to 11.9b–10, where Jesus states: "knock, and the door will be opened for you. For everyone who asks receives, and everyone who searches finds, and for everyone who knocks, the door will be opened." It also contrasts with the Parable of the Pushy Pal (11.5–8), where insistent requests prompt the positive response. Finally, it anticipates the Parable of the Rich Man and Lazarus (16.19–31), with its images of gates, the afterlife, and the importance of works.

Like the Pushy Pal, the hypothetical importuners believe they can prevail on their relationship with the householder: they shared table fellowship with him; they recognized his teaching (**vs. 26**). But eating and drinking, whether at a Eucharistic table or agape meal or even with other followers, and even knowledge of the teaching, prove insufficient. The householder states that he never knew these people, calls them evildoers (literally, "workers of unrighteousness"), and demands they leave (**vs. 27**). The setting is domestic; the implications are soteriological and eschatological. References to weeping and gnashing of teeth and to the patriarchs and prophets in the Kingdom (**vs. 28**) indicate that the "Kingdom" here is one not (only) found on earth, but found both/either in heaven/at the end of time. Inclusions of people from all the compass markers to recline at this heavenly banquet (**vs. 29**) secure the eschatological setting. The geographical markers, in Luke's Gospel, hint at the gentile mission; should the comment go back to Jesus, he might have been speaking primarily of "the ingathering of the exiles," the return of Diaspora Jews to the covenant community in the Land of Israel. Commentators who see these diners as gentiles who *replace* Jews read ungenerously.

The scene ends with the floating saying concerning the reversal of roles for last and first (**vs. 30**) and so reminds attentive readers of the details Mary sets out in the Magnificat: bringing down the powerful and lifting the lowly; filling the hungry and sending the rich away empty (1.52–53). The verse does not distinguish the (first) Jews from the (last to be first) gentiles; its focus, given the context of the Gospel, is on economics: rich and powerful, privileged and undersourced. For those who consider themselves the "have nots," the slide down the social ladder of those who have may be desirable. Nor can the privileged understand the needs of the economically marginal without actually experiencing, fully, that marginal status. However, the shifting of first to last and vice versa can also create a sense of *schadenfreude* if not a fantasy of revenge. Proclamations of reversal such as this and the related comments about the humbling of the exalted and the exaltation of the humble (18.14) can both comfort and condemn, depending on how we apply them.

PASSION PREDICTIONS

As Jesus continues his travels to Jerusalem, a contingent of Pharisees issues an ambiguous warning that he leave Galilee, since Herod seeks his life (**vs. 31**). It is not clear if the Pharisees are seeking to trick Jesus into silence by manufacturing a threat or if these particular Pharisees care about his safety. Nor is it clear if Herod wants to kill Jesus: his actions in 9.6–7, when he mistakes Jesus for a risen John the Baptizer, suggest no murderous intent. Nor does his encounter with Jesus in 23.8 indicate murderous views; to the contrary, he was "very glad" to see Jesus because he "was hoping to see him perform some sign." These other references to Antipas in the Gospel tip for Amy-Jill the balance toward seeing the Pharisees here as malevolently intended: they are trying to trick Jesus into stopping his activities. Ben favors a more benevolent reading. He stresses that Luke does not have an agenda to paint all Pharisees as bad or as hypocrites.

Jesus does not take the bait, or the warning. Calling Herod a "fox," which is not a compliment, he trumpets his exorcisms and healings and next, to the reader who knows the full story, foreshadows his death and resurrection with a reference to "the third day" (**vs. 32**). Then, finally, he announces his death directly: he is a prophet, and he must be killed in Jerusalem (**vs. 33**).

The Gospels' presentation of Jerusalem varies from "the holy city" (Matt 4.5; 27.53; Rev 11.2, cf. Num 11.18; Isa 48.2; Psa 46.4; Tob 13.9; 1 Macc 2.7) to the place where prophets are stoned. In Jesus' lament over the city, he implicitly includes himself among the prophets who are killed (**vs. 34**). The prophets, sent to warn the people to repent, to behave in an ethical manner, and to return to proper worship of God, are themselves killed by those to whom they had been sent. The Pseudepigraphal texts entitled *Lives of the Prophets* (*Deaths of the Prophets* would have been more apt) and *The Martyrdom and Ascension of Isaiah* depict these deaths as the authors imagined them, and thus begin the process of turning prophets into martyrs. By accusing "Jerusalem" of this persecution, Jesus indicts the city and so, by implication, its Jewish residents rather than its Roman overlords. Jesus thus echoes Jeremiah, who made similar predictions in light of the forthcoming Babylonian conquest (Jer 22.5).

Ironically, the claim that "It is impossible for a prophet to be killed outside of Jerusalem" not only undervalues Jesus' role, in that he is more than a prophet, but it also undercuts the role of John the Baptizer. Herod had John beheaded in Machareus, the fortified hilltop palace located in Jordan 25 kilometers (16 miles) southeast of the mouth of the Jordan River.[25]

Whereas Jesus had wished to gather the people, as a hen gathers its chicks, the city refused his maternal (or galline) care. He proclaims Jerusalem's "house" as "left." Although most scholars take the "house" as a reference to the Temple, Luke's broader use of the term (Greek: *oikos*) could indicate a focus less on the place than on the people inhabiting it or even the leaders, the ones who rule the household. A similar saying appears in Matt 23.37–39, but there in the context of the woes against the scribes and Pharisees and following the Temple incident. Luke dissociates this saying from the Temple and so preserves a positive image of the institution. This relatively positive view of the Temple reappears in Acts, where the apostles as well as Paul continue to worship there. The positive view receives reinforcement in the Parable of the Pharisee and the Tax Collector, since it is in the Temple that the tax collector finds restoration of relationship with God (see 18.10–14).

Some manuscripts attempt to bring clarity to the statement by adding "desolate" to the verse and so both bring Luke into line with Matthew's version and indicate that the divine presence has forsaken Mount Zion. Although this focus on the Temple and on judgment as opposed to personal lament can be derived from the context, these readings are not necessary and not fully consistent with Luke's own agenda.[26]

Jesus also offers the city hope: when the people proclaim him as God's agent, they will see him, and by implication the presence of God, again (**vs. 35**). The people's anticipated response, "Blessed is the one who comes in the name of the Lord," derives from Psa 118.26. The Psalm is one of the Hallel Psalms sung by pilgrims to Jerusalem, and so both echoes Jesus' own journey to Jerusalem as well as the importance of the Temple as a site of proper worship, community unity, and divine presence. The "one coming" is Jesus the Messiah, as Luke had intimated with John the Baptizer's words, "one, who is more powerful than I, is coming" (3.16), as well as the question John's disciples pose to Jesus, "are you the one who is coming?" (7.19). Jesus' own disciples confirm this role of the coming king in 19.41–44.

This event will be an eschatological one, for Jerusalem does not welcome Jesus into its heart, and Luke the evangelist knows that the vast majority of the people in Jerusalem did not accept the Gospel of Jesus. In Luke's

---

[25] See the report of the excavator of Machareus by G. Voros, "A Palace-Fortress with Multiple Mikva'ot," *BAR* 43.4 (2017): 30–39, 60.

[26] See Francis D. Weinert, "Luke, the Temple, and Jesus' Saying about Jerusalem's Abandoned House (Luke 13:34–35)," *CBQ* 44.1 (1982): 77–90.

version of the Triumphal Entry, it is "the whole multitude of the disciples" (19.37) and not the people who welcome him. It is the disciples who proclaim, "Blessed is the king who comes in the name of the Lord" (19.38), and not the local rulers. To the contrary, some Pharisees attempt to stop the disciples' acclamation (19.40). In 19.41–44, when Jesus finally arrives at the city, he weeps and then predicts the city's destruction by the Romans. Eschatological hope remains alive, but Luke knows the history of the city. Luke knows that Rome will destroy Jerusalem and burn down its Temple. One could read Luke as blaming this destruction on the Jewish population that refused to acknowledge Jesus as lord and king. Or, more charitably in light of what follows in this Gospel, one could say the blame falls upon those Jewish leaders of Jerusalem who reject and plan to kill Jesus, not the Jewish population in general.

BRIDGING THE HORIZONS

1. Jerusalem

Throughout the centuries, Jerusalem has been the city of peace, the holy city, a pilgrimage site, and a place where many feel the divine presence in a stronger, more personal way. It is a sacred site for Judaism, Christianity, and Islam, which refers to the city by the Arabic term, *Al Quds* ("the Holy"). It is also a locus of war, of divisions among and even within religious groups, a place whose history is contested. Today, both some Israelis and some Palestinians claim the city as their capital; today, the city is divided.

Jerusalem and the extended areas that now go by the terms "Israel," "Judea and Samaria," and "Palestine" remain contested sites. Some Christian denominations favor BDS (boycott, divest, and sanction) policies designed to put economic and cultural pressures on Israel so that the state will withdraw from all territories claimed by the Palestinians and so allow this population to have its own state. The goal of some proponents of BDS is elimination of the Jewish state entirely; the goal of others is a two-state resolution. Other Christians see Jerusalem as the eternal Jewish capital and so, although varying in their view of the borders or even existence of a separate Palestinian, Muslim-majority state, promote the view of Jerusalem as Israel's capital. In the United States, in July 2016, the Republican Party platform omitted earlier references to Palestine and referred to Jerusalem as Israel's "undivided" capital. On December 6, 2017, Donald Trump proclaimed Jerusalem the capital of Israel. On December 21, 2017, the United Nations

General Assembly voted, 128 to 9, with thirty-five nations abstaining, to condemn President Trump's recognition.

In reading about Jesus' lament, Christians might consider how much they know about present-day Israel. No matter what political conclusion they draw, churches need to be wary of the tendency to put all the blame for the lack of peace on any particular group. Jewish control in antiquity, then Roman control, Christian, Muslim, Ottoman, British, Israeli, Jordanian, and so on, has not yielded peace in the city. Meanwhile, modern-day prophets are still being murdered. Members of the Egyptian Islamic Jihad on October 6, 1981, assassinated Anwar Sadat, the president of Egypt who brokered an Egyptian–Israeli treaty. Yigal Amir, a right-wing extremist Jew, assassinated Israel's Prime Minister Yitzhak Rabin on November 4, 1995, at a rally for Shalom Achshav (Hebrew: "Peace Now"), an Israeli organization opposed to settlement expansion and in favor of a two-state resolution. Bombings and stabbings, rock-throwing and shooting, assassinations and imprisonments, are daily tragedies in the land Christians call "holy."

Jerusalem's people, Jewish, Christian, Muslim, Bahai, Druze, Samaritan, and more, still wait for that day of peace. Those who see that peace as related to Jesus, whether ethically or eschatologically, or both, do well not only to pray for the peace of Jerusalem, but also to inform themselves of the city's history, the present-day political situation, and the role religion has played and might play in the city's tragic history. The goal should not be to make the first last and the last first, and nor should it be to sit back and wait for the *Parousia*. Any individual, like a mustard seed or a pinch of yeast, can advocate for change, for mutual recognition of both Jewish and Palestinian claims to the land, and for peace.

Luke 14 Banquets Earthly and Eschatological

¹ On one occasion when Jesus was going to the house of a leader of the Pharisees to eat a meal on the sabbath, they were watching him closely.
² Just then, in front of him, there was a man who had dropsy. ³ And Jesus asked the lawyers and Pharisees, "Is it lawful to cure people on the sabbath, or not?" ⁴ But they were silent. So Jesus took him and healed him, and sent him away.
⁵ Then he said to them, "If one of you has a child or an ox that has fallen into a well, will you not immediately pull it out on a sabbath day?" ⁶ And they could not reply to this.

DINNER ETIQUETTE

⁷ When he noticed how the guests chose the places of honor, he told them a parable. ⁸ "When you are invited by someone to a wedding banquet, do not sit down at the place of honor, in case someone more distinguished than you has been invited by your host; ⁹ and the host who invited both of you may come and say to you, 'Give this person your place,' and then in disgrace you would start to take the lowest place. ¹⁰ But when you are invited, go and sit down at the lowest place, so that when your host comes, he may say to you, 'Friend, move up higher'; then you will be honored in the presence of all who sit at the table with you. ¹¹ For all who exalt themselves will be humbled, and those who humble themselves will be exalted."
¹² He said also to the one who had invited him, "When you give a luncheon or a dinner, do not invite your friends or your brothers or your relatives or rich neighbors, in case they may invite you in return, and you would

be repaid. ¹³ But when you give a banquet, invite the poor, the crippled, the lame, and the blind. ¹⁴ And you will be blessed, because they cannot repay you, for you will be repaid at the resurrection of the righteous."

THE GREAT BANQUET

¹⁵ One of the dinner guests, on hearing this, said to him, "Blessed is anyone who will eat bread in the kingdom of God!"

¹⁶ Then Jesus said to him, "Someone gave a great dinner and invited many. ¹⁷ At the time for the dinner he sent his slave to say to those who had been invited, 'Come; for everything is ready now.' ¹⁸ But they all alike began to make excuses. The first said to him, 'I have bought a piece of land, and I must go out and see it; please accept my regrets.' ¹⁹ Another said, 'I have bought five yoke of oxen, and I am going to try them out; please accept my regrets.' ²⁰ Another said, 'I have just been married, and therefore I cannot come.'

²¹ So the slave returned and reported this to his master. Then the owner of the house became angry and said to his slave, 'Go out at once into the streets and lanes of the town and bring in the poor, the crippled, the blind, and the lame.'

²² And the slave said, 'Sir, what you ordered has been done, and there is still room.' ²³ Then the master said to the slave, 'Go out into the roads and lanes, and compel people to come in, so that my house may be filled. ²⁴ For I tell you, none of those who were invited will taste my dinner.'"

LESSONS ON DISCIPLESHIP

²⁵ Now large crowds were traveling with him; and he turned and said to them, ²⁶ "Whoever comes to me and does not hate father and mother, wife and children, brothers and sisters, yes, and even life itself, cannot be my disciple. ²⁷ Whoever does not carry the cross and follow me cannot be my disciple.

²⁸ For which of you, intending to build a tower, does not first sit down and estimate the cost, to see whether he has enough to complete it? ²⁹ Otherwise, when he has laid a foundation and is not able to finish, all who see it will begin to ridicule him, ³⁰ saying, 'This fellow began to build and was not able to finish.'

³¹ Or what king, going out to wage war against another king, will not sit down first and consider whether he is able with ten thousand to oppose

the one who comes against him with twenty thousand? [32] If he cannot, then, while the other is still far away, he sends a delegation and asks for the terms of peace.

[33] So therefore, none of you can become my disciple if you do not give up all your possessions.

[34] "Salt is good; but if salt has lost its taste, how can its saltiness be restored?

[35] It is fit neither for the soil nor for the manure pile; they throw it away. Let anyone with ears to hear listen!"

Luke Chapter 14 contains material mostly unique to Luke, with a few verses (from Q?) toward the end. Thematically, the chapter coheres through the motif of the banquet and so of the responsibilities of hosts and guests. Vss. 1–24 are set at the home of a "ruler of the Pharisees" (cf. 22.66); the rest of the chapter concerns disruption in households and the cost of discipleship. The synagogue healing of the man with dropsy that begins the chapter (vss. 1–6) has the same structure as the synagogue healing of the bent-over woman in the previous chapter (13.10–17). Both healings are followed by lessons on humility, and both chapters end with warnings to those who believe they are secure in their relationship with God.[1]

In Luke's Gospel, Jesus dines with Pharisees three times (cf. 7.36–50; 11.37–54). The setting along with references to banqueting with sinners and tax collectors (cf. 5.29–39) suggests a symposium and thus presents Jesus as a philosopher. Luke is presuming elite readers as well as those who can imagine what the wealthy do. The Gospel's banquet scenes, whether hosted by tax collectors or Pharisees, indicate that Jesus dines with people with resources and influence. Theophilus and people like him, Luke's ideal wealthy readers, are directly addressed.

Meals in antiquity, as well as in many settings today, both reinscribe social roles and separate insiders from outsiders. Fancy restaurants and weddings immediately proclaim the ranking: the "head table" and tables set near the head hold more prestige than table 24 near the kitchen. Luke 14 recognizes that convention and then seeks to correct it toward a more socially equitable system. However, the insider and outsider distinction remains.

The symposium setting is conventional and so stereotypical, as is Luke's depictions of Pharisees, and a negative *stereotype* it is. Pharisees were not generally among the socially elite; Josephus notes that they worked in crafts and in business just as Paul, a Pharisee, remained a leather-worker. Simon

---

[1] González, *Luke*, 178, following Culpepper, "The Gospel of Luke," 283.

the Pharisee, with whom Jesus dined, seems to have been socially more elite, although Luke may have given him a status upgrade. Likely writing to a predominantly gentile audience located outside the land of Israel, and certainly read by gentile audiences outside Israel, Luke tells readers what to think about this Jewish group, and Luke's negative emphasis has had a tragic legacy through the centuries. While Luke does not depict the Pharisees in an exclusively negative light,[2] the negative images have been the ones to prevail. In some current Christian preaching, the term "Pharisee" and the term "hypocrite" are seen as synonymous, even as some Christians presume that all Jews, like Luke's Pharisees, are rich (Amy-Jill sardonically replies, "we should be so lucky"). Negative use of the term "Pharisee" does no justice to many Pharisees of that era, including Saul of Tarsus.

The common scholarly view is that Jesus is fully inclusive in his dining practices.[3] The argument overstates. Jesus does not dine with gentiles, and there is no evidence that he dines with anyone who is likely to violate Jewish practices regarding kosher food, unless, Ben adds, tax collectors and sinners are examples of Jews who were not consistently Torah-true when it came to food. He does not invite outsiders to private meals that he hosts.[4] Even the feeding of the five thousand is not premised on Jesus' inclusivity: the meals do not symbolize universalism or indiscriminate table fellowship; they symbolize the eschatological banquet. As Andrew McGowan deliciously puts the case: "They depict Jesus as an impressive caterer, not as inclusive host."[5] Mark's feeding of the four thousand (Mark 8.1–10) may tell a more inclusive tale since it takes place on the border of or within the Decapolis, where gentiles would be present, but Luke lacks this account.

HEALING THE MAN WITH DROPSY

The opening six verses of Luke 14 contain the Gospel's last Sabbath controversy. Ben suggests that the "leader of the Pharisees" (**vs. 1**) indicates a Sanhedrin member and therefore sees the setting as a Jerusalem residence; Amy-Jill sees no reason for either the Pharisee's Sanhedrin membership or

2   See Amy-Jill Levine, "Luke and the Jewish Religion," *Interpretation* 68.4 (2014): 389–402, and "Luke's Pharisees," in Jacob Neusner and Bruce Chilton (eds.), *In Quest of the Historical Pharisees* (Waco: Baylor University Press, 2007): 113–30. The Neusner/Chilton volume treats Pharisees in their various appearances in ancient literature.
3   See France, *Luke*, 242.
4   Andrew McGowan, "The Hungry Jesus," *Bible History Daily* 3/18/25 www.biblicalarchaeology.org/daily/biblical-topics/bible-interpretation/the-hungry-jesus/.
5   Ibid.

the Jerusalem setting. Jesus has not yet arrived in the city; further, 22.66 mentions only chief priests and scribes at the Sanhedrin meeting; the Pharisees are conspicuously absent. Because the term translated "leader" is *archōn*, "ruler" or, literally, "first one," the verse anticipates Jesus' consistent critique both of people in authority and of householders. The image is Luke's; the Pharisees did not have formal "leaders" or rulers,[6] although Josephus (*Life* 21) mentions "the first of the Pharisees," which indicates there is a de facto pecking order.

Luke does not tell us why the Pharisees have invited Jesus to dine. Perhaps they had encountered Jesus in a synagogue on the Sabbath and were impressed by his teaching. Perhaps they recognized that he was a stranger in their town and, in standard practices of hospitality, invited him to a Sabbath meal. That they are seeking to trap him is a possible reading, but not a necessary one. They may have been interested in his teachings; they may have wanted to talk with him about his associations with sinners and tax collectors. Was he attempting to convince them to repent and make restitution to any they had cheated or betrayed? Was he affirming their lifestyles? Was he expressing support for Roman taxation? Or was he setting a pattern by which table hospitality could become the site for reconciliation along with repentance and reform? What indeed was the outcome of such dinners, other than a good meal?

Although the "they" of "they were watching him closely" (the verb *paratēreō* has the nuance of hostile observance; cf. 6.7; 20.20; Acts 9.24) is not explicated, given that such dinners in Luke are frequented by other Pharisees and their sympathizers, readers are correct to see Jesus' dining companions as skeptical about his agenda. Since the meal setting evokes again the symposium scene, readers will also expect debate.

The presence of the man with dropsy (i.e., edema, retaining of fluids) also goes unexplained (**vs. 2**). It is unlikely he was set up by the host to test Jesus, because Jesus does not treat him as part of any conspiracy. Nor was he likely to have been a dinner guest, since Jesus sends him home. Nor again is he presented as a sinner in need of forgiveness, so the association of sin and disability presumed by many Gospel readers (if not the text itself or the Jewish context behind it) is not present. He may have had heard, as did the anointing woman (7.36), that Jesus was dining at the Pharisee's house, and he had therefore come to seek healing. The man may also have followed Jesus and the Pharisees from the synagogue to the home. Commentators

6   Lieu, *Gospel According to Luke*, 113.

who presume that the man was "unclean" or "impure"[7] impose a less likely context, for not only are sources lacking regarding edema as an indicator of ritual impurity, the text itself belies the claim. Luke elsewhere associates Pharisees with issues of purity; that the host and his other guests do not find a purity issue here signals that neither should readers.

A subtext may concern the association of dropsy with insatiable craving. The Greek term translated "dropsy" is formed from the word for water (*hydōp*) and means something like "waterlogged." Amanda Miller details how "Cynic and Stoic philosophers commonly used dropsy as a metaphor for avarice, symbolized particularly by the parallel between dropsy's insatiable craving for more water and greed's acquisitive desire for more honor and wealth."[8] That the conversation will turn to matters of economics is therefore the prognosis.

Knowing he is being watched, Jesus asks the Pharisees about whether it is lawful to heal on the Sabbath (**vs. 3**). No laws *forbade* healing on the Sabbath. However, the Sabbath is also the time for rest, not work. As we have noted in our comments on the bent-over woman in Chapter 13, were people with non-life-threatening ailments to come into church on a Sunday morning and, during the service, request medical attention from the physician in the next pew, it is likely the request would be deferred. Jesus' question, because it is phrased in the abstract, cannot be easily answered. One would need to know the details of the medical condition. One would also need to know if the healing comes by miracle, rather than medicine or magic. Much like the challenges posed to him by other trick questions, such as "should we pay taxes?" (20.22), Jesus' question is designed to trip the interlocutors.

The others at table, are silent (**vs. 4**). Ironically, the term for silent (Greek: *hēsychadzō*) can also mean "at rest," which is appropriate to the Sabbath. Were the story told by rabbinic Jews, there would likely be a discussion of what acts of healing would be appropriate and what would not

---

[7]   Johnson proposes, "if his edema was so obvious as to be noticed, he would be regarded as impure because of the Levitical strictures concerning 'swellings' that were associated with leprosy (Lev 13:2)." That verse speaks not to swellings in general but to the telltale white spots associated with leprosy: "When a person has on the skin of his body a swelling or an eruption or a spot, and it turns into a leprous disease on the skin of his body, he shall be brought to Aaron the priest or to one of his sons the priests."

[8]   Amanda Miller, "Bridge Work and Seating Charts: A Study of Luke's Ethics of Wealth, Poverty, and Reversal," *Interpretation* 68.4 (2014): 416–27 (422), following John T. Carroll, *Luke: A Commentary* (New Testament Library; Louisville: Westminster John Knox, 2012), 296–97. See also Chad Hartsock, "The Healing of the Man with Dropsy (Luke 14:1–6) and the Lukan Landscape," *Biblical Interpretation* 21.3 (2013): 341–54.

be. For any who seek both to honor the Sabbath and keep it holy, and to love one's neighbor, such questions require discussion.

Jesus, who displays no indication of engaging in medicine or magic, "took him and healed him." Here we see the difference between what Jesus does and the practice of healing: Jesus, exceptionally, produces a miracle; doctors and nurses must work. This healing does not, however, settle the issue of whether Jesus' observers would have considered this act a violation of Sabbath rest.

Following the healing, Jesus dismisses the healed man. The dismissal indicates that the man was not a dinner guest, and no one, including Jesus, makes any attempt to ask him to stay. He serves rather as a foil for the discussion. Ben and Amy-Jill like to think that the dismissal is Jesus' way of allowing the man to return to friends and family and, with them, to celebrate his healing. But again, Luke does not provide the details.

In discussing the Sabbath healings in the Gospels, commentators typically list rabbinic restrictions on Sabbath healing (e.g., *b. Shabb.* 18a; 53b; 75b; 108b; 111a; 128a; 140a) to suggest a contrast to Jesus' miracle working. Rarely do they actually cite these texts, so that readers have to use their imagination to determine how strict these rules are. Rarer still is the note that the rabbinic comments postdate the New Testament and are descriptive of what the rabbis think people should do rather than descriptive of what they do; a similar point can be made about Jesus' teachings on discipleship and possessions in this chapter. Then, *against* rabbinic restrictions on healings on the Sabbath, they present Jesus' compassion for the suffering. The comparison is a category confusion, for Jesus is doing miracles and the healings listed are not miracles. Ben notes that the comparison Jesus uses with the rescuing of an animal or a child from a pit (**vs. 5**), which does not involve a miracle, should tell us that Jesus is not distinguishing between miraculous acts of compassion and other sorts of acts of compassion. Amy-Jill focuses on the miracle itself, which does not appear to be any form of "work," however defined.

By comparing the healing of a person on the Sabbath to rescuing a child or an animal that had fallen into a pit, Jesus produces another *qal v'homer* ('from the lighter to the heavier') argument. By including the "child" in his example, he tips the question toward an affirmative answer. One scroll associated with the Qumran cache, CD 11.13–17, advises against "assisting a beast in giving birth on the Sabbath day. And if it should fall into a cistern or pit, he shall not lift it out on the Sabbath." Whether the Qumran covenanters actually practiced this hypothetical scenario cannot be determined. Whether

Pharisees would have agreed with this notion is also another question. If they had preserved the teaching that an animal should be left in a pit or left unassisted in giving birth, they make no mention of it here. Reading the Qumran Community Rule as normative for first-century Judaism is no more appropriate than is reading the Rule of St. Benedict normative for all of Christianity.

This scene ends with the silence of the Pharisees (**vs. 6**) to Jesus' question. The open question thereby becomes an occasion for discussion, by Luke's readers then and through the centuries. Whereas Jesus can do miraculous cures on the Sabbath, such miracles are today few and far between. What is the medical professional to do, in a worship setting or a private home? Do doctors ever have a day of rest? Are nurses always on call? How is a non-Jewish follower of Jesus to celebrate a "day of rest," if at all?

DINNER ETIQUETTE

Robert Tannehill observes that the person who suffers from dropsy, while swollen with fluid, also suffers from unquenchable thirst. Hence dropsy became a metaphor for insatiable desire, viewed as a moral failing. Jesus cures a man with dropsy, and then turns to the Pharisees and lawyers, whom Luke depicts as driven by an insatiable desire for places of honor.[9] The instructions about dining can therefore be seen to hinge around the question of whether Jesus can heal the Pharisees from greed as he healed the man from edema.

The reading is not inconsistent with Luke's presentation of Pharisees as Jesus' opponents. Given Luke's address to Theophilus the elite patron, the advice on dining practice is less designed to cure any Pharisaic compulsion than it is to warn Jesus' followers not to exalt themselves. Given Luke's classification of the Pharisees as "lovers of money" (16.14), readers, putting this description together with the associations of dropsy with greed, will find a focus not only on honor, but also on the accumulation of wealth.[10] Ben notes that this conclusion is to get ahead of Luke's narrative, which would have likely been read out orally in the order in which we find it. Amy-Jill figures that the story would have been told more than once, and each successive reading would reinforce earlier images. That the man with dropsy is cured by Jesus' miraculous abilities in turn indicates that

---

[9]   Tannehill, *Luke*, p. 228.
[10] See Hartsock, "Healing of the Man with Dropsy," 347.

"when it comes to greed, wealth, and selfishness, Jesus seems to suggest that it is a disease whose only cure is not simple renunciation but miraculous healing."[11] Alternatively, Luke may be suggesting that the changing of the human heart is, like a miraculous healing, the result of God's gracious intervention. Thus, the question of fate versus free will can be seen to underlie the narrative.

The scene starts with Jesus' noticing how the guests chose places of honor (**vs. 7a**), which would be the places nearest to the host. The conceit is odd, given that it was usually the host who determined the seating. Jesus does not immediately tell a "parable" (**vs. 7b**) in the sense of a short narrative with a connection to behavior or a challenge to the status quo, but with plain advice that would apply directly to the elite. He advises that anyone invited to a wedding banquet, and by extension to any banquet, should avoid places of honor, for the guest risks being asked by the host to cede the seat to some more distinguished person (**vs. 8**). The result of being asked to move would be public humiliation (**vs. 9**). This piece of wisdom draws from Prov 25.6–7: "Do not put yourself forward in the king's presence or stand in the place of the great; for it is better to be told, 'Come up here,' than to be put lower in the presence of a noble." Matt 23.6, in a chapter replete with anti-Pharisaic invective, speaks of Pharisees as wanting the places of honor at banquets; Luke's presentation of the same subject is less antagonistic, which again suggests, to Ben, that Luke is not interested in stereotyping all Pharisees.

One could claim that Jesus sought to counter the stratifying game of banquet seating; instead, he reinforces it by advising *how* a person might obtain a seat of greater honor: "sit down at the lowest place, so that when your host comes, he may say to you, 'Friend, move up higher'; then you will be honored in the presence of all who sit at the table with you" (**vs. 10**). The one displaying humility is honored.[12] For Jesus this is not (merely) a social strategy; it is also an eschatological reversal, for the last becoming first occurs as the Kingdom breaks into human history. Divine saving activity produces reversals of normal expectations about social stratification. The observation would be very good news to the disciples, especially those whose teaching is rejected.

---

[11]   Ibid., 353.

[12]   On assigning places at a banquet according to honor, see *Letter of Aristeas* 183–87; Plutarch, *Moralia* 615–19; Petronius, *Satyricon* 38,70; Juvenal, *Satires* 5.16–19; 11.129–32. For an adaptation of Jesus' teaching on this matter see Jas 2.1–3 and the discussion in Ben Witherington III, *Letters and Homilies for Jewish Christians* (Downers Grove: InterVarsity, 2007).

Luke does not tell us where Jesus was sitting; had he been speaking from a dining couch far from the host, his words would have greater impact. That possibility opens new readings of the scene, which helpfully complicate its message. For the host to move a person already seated and eating so that someone else may be elevated would itself be rude and shameful behavior: it suggests that the host did not have initial control over the seating. To ask a guest to vacate a seat would be shameful not only for the guest but also for the host and potentially for everyone else involved. Should the concern for honor be maintained, perhaps the one being elevated might demur: "No, thank you, I'm quite fine where I am." If the concern is to eschew honor, why change seats at all?

The floating logion of **vs. 11** regarding humbling and exaltation does not dismiss the honor code; instead, it reverses the assigning of humiliation and honor. To state that the "last shall be first and the first shall be last," a variant on this verse, still leaves hierarchy, and so the potential for abuse, in place.[13] Commentators frequently adduce Ezek 21.26 as an intertext: "Thus says the Lord God: 'Remove the turban, take off the crown; things shall not remain as they are. Exalt that which is low, abase that which is high.'" The problem with this connection is that Ezekiel is speaking of a punishment that results in destruction rather than an eschatological reward, much less a preferred seat at a banquet.

Jesus continues his instructions on banquet behavior in the next three verses. First, turning to the one who had invited him, he advises variation on the guest list so that the cycle of reciprocity would be broken. Banquets and luncheons, then and today, are typically populated with friends and family. Those on the guest list today will be tomorrow's hosts (**vs. 12**). Instead, Jesus advises that the Pharisee "invite the poor, the crippled, the lame, and the blind" (**vs. 13**), because they are not in the position to reciprocate. Rather, reciprocation will occur at the heavenly banquet, at the "resurrection of the righteousness" (**vs. 14**; cf. 13.29; Acts 23.6; 24.15; Dan 12.2–3; Josephus, *War* 2.163). The phrase does not indicate that only the righteous would be resurrected. Jewish teaching varied on the afterlife and on eschatological judgment.[14] The view that earthly action would result in a heavenly repayment continues the theme of laying up treasures in heaven. Jesus' advice anticipates the Parable of the Rich Man and Lazarus (16.19–31). It

---

[13]   Cf. Rom 12.16; Eph 4.2; Phil 2.3; Col 3.12; Acts 20.19; Jas 4.6.

[14]   See the detailed discussion of ideas in early Judaism in Richard Bauckham, *The Fate of the Dead* (Leiden: Brill, 1998); Alan Segal, *Life After Death: A History of the Afterlife in Western Religion* (New York: Doubleday, 2004).

also matches Luke's overall concern that the rich attend to those who lack resources.

Yet the statement is ironic in this narrative context, since the host had already gone beyond inviting only his friends and relatives: he had invited Jesus. It can be argued that Jesus' words indicate, "Those who invite family and people of status are exalting themselves by proclaiming their place in this group. Those who invite the poor and crippled are humbling themselves."[15] We could go as far as to claim that: "Closely related to the ethics of wealth, poverty, and possessions in the Gospel of Luke is the theme of status reversal, the idea that the current power structure and values of this world will be turned upside down by the reign of God."[16] Luke's presentation is more subtle. The patron/client system in antiquity was both reciprocal and nonegalitarian. The host who invited those unable to repay in kind expected his guests to repay with honor. The "poor, the crippled, the lame, and the blind" invited to dinner would proclaim the host's generosity, and thereby they would contribute to his honor. Social stratification is modified by Luke's program, but it is not fully inverted. Patrons continue to support clients; the rich continue to support the poor.

Commentators frequently note that with the exception of the poor, the people on this second guest list were those excluded from the Jewish priesthood (Lev 21.17–21) and at Qumran from the messianic banquet (1QSa 2.5–6).[17] They continue by noting that "the Jews" would have found the poor and the disabled as deserving of their condition: they are being punished by sin. They conclude that dining with the poor or the blind would violate purity laws. For an example of such common preaching, we cite a major homiletical commentary on this pericope:

> [Jesus' teaching] would have sounded quite strange to the ears of many of Jesus' contemporaries. To their way of thinking the poor, the crippled, the lame, and the blind are those from whom God has withheld his blessing. In all likelihood, it was thought that their afflictions were the result of sin (cf. John 9.1–3). These people, along with the Gentiles, would be the last people to enter the kingdom of God. Why should anyone invite them to a feast? To eat with such people could result in religious defilement. Therefore, the pious Israelite would quite naturally desire table fellowship with others of similar piety. Jesus, however does not share this narrow self-righteous view. His

15   Tannehill, *Luke*, 230.
16   Miller, "Bridge Work and Seating Charts," 417.
17   Buttrick, *Parables*,158; Hultgren, *Parables*, 337.

proclamation declares that even the lowly and the outcast may be included in the kingdom of God.[18]

Such conclusions, which have nothing to do with Luke's passage, serve only to reinforce a negative view of Judaism and a distancing of Jesus from his Jewish environment. First, the evocation of priestly criteria is gratuitous. Luke is talking about present-day behavior, not the eschatological guest list. Second, disabled priests still received support from the Temple, even though they could not preside at the sacrifice. Third, the Scriptures of Israel and their Jewish interpreters *consistently* insist that God cares about the poor, the widow, the orphan, and the stranger; that is why the people are both legally required and prophetically exhorted to care for them. From the blindness of Isaac to the blindness of Tobit to the travails of Job, Jews well knew that disability was not necessarily the result of sin. Nor did they think of the blind and the poor, or the disabled, as either "outcast" or "unclean," for disability is not in the same category as ritual purity. The numerous prophetic condemnations of the rich made it very clear to them that wealth was not a sign of righteousness.

If we take the eschatological reading, we could also claim – although we will not, because it would be the same sort of negative reading that sets Jesus against Judaism this commentary eschews – that Jesus himself excludes the disabled from that messianic banquet: he does so by healing people rather than welcoming them "as is." Jesus heals people's bodies and, in cases where impurity would be a factor (the man with leprosy; the woman with a vaginal or uterine hemorrhage), he restores them to ritually pure states.

Finally, we should be wary about the conclusion that people who are poor or people with disabilities lack resources. This view creates another negative stereotype. One can invite guests, regardless of funds; those who are poor, however defined, can also extend hospitality. Nor is physical disability incompatible with material wealth. Nor again is it helpful to regard any outside elite circles as pitiable and in need of handouts.

Ben notes that Proverbs makes a positive correlation between wealth and wisdom and wealth and piety, as does the depiction of Solomon in various places in the OT. It is not surprising, then, though it is also not justified, that some then also assumed that there is a negative correlation as well, that the poor were poor because they were at fault: they refused to do hard work (see the sluggard in Proverbs), or they lacked piety. Luke counters

---

[18]   C. A. Evans, *Luke*, 223.

this stereotype in the Parable of the Rich Man and Lazarus, for it is pious Lazarus who is homeless and poor who ends up in Paradise with Abraham. Amy-Jill grants the point about Proverbs, but she offers two corollaries to Ben's view. First, Proverbs also disentangles wealth and righteousness and consistently urges kindness and generosity to the poor, so clearly Proverbs does not see the poor as sinners (e.g., Prov 14.21, "Those who despise their neighbors are sinners, but happy are those who are kind to the poor"; Prov 21:13, "If you close your ear to the cry of the poor, you will cry out and not be heard"; Prov 22:16, "Oppressing the poor in order to enrich oneself, and giving to the rich, will lead only to loss"; and, especially Prov 28:11, "The rich is wise in self-esteem, but an intelligent poor person sees through the pose"). Second, there is nothing in the parable about Lazarus's "piety." Ben counters that there is indeed an indication of Lazarus' piety in that parable – he is taken to heaven, to the very "bosom of Abraham." But this discussion must wait until we get to Luke 16.

THE GREAT BANQUET

The chapter's next section, vss. 15–24, continues the theme of the dinner party, both earthly and messianic. When a dinner guest, apparently in sympathy with Jesus, offers the beatitude, "blessed is anyone who will eat bread in the kingdom of God," Jesus offers a parable (variants of which appear in Matt 22.2–10; cf. *Thomas* 64). Matthew's version describes a royal wedding; Luke continues the subject of the wealthy host. Both versions are usually taken to be about the eschatological banquet; however, Luke's details suggest that the focus is less on dining in a future Kingdom and more on dining in the here and now, where the Kingdom can be enacted.

The host of our Lucan banquet is *anthrōpos tis* (**vs. 16**), that is, "some fellow"; the same term describes the man going down the Jerusalem-to-Jericho road (10.32), a rich man with abundant crops (12.16), a man suffering from edema (14.2), a father with one prudent and one prodigal son (15.11), and so on. In Luke's version, the dinner is just a dinner: no wedding, no bride and groom, no bridesmaids and groomsmen. There is therefore no reason to jump to an allegorical reading, in which the host is God or Jesus and the guests represent soteriological categories.

The guests have accepted the original invitation, as the host's sending a slave to summon the guests indicates (**vs. 17**). Yet those on the guest list make excuses for why they cannot attend. None of the excuses is compelling: one fellow states that he has to inspect recently purchased land (**vs. 18**).

He should have inspected it prior to the purchase. Another indicates that he has to try out some recently purchased oxen (**vs. 19**); he should have tried them out before the purchase, and a second check can wait. The third begs off: he has just married and therefore cannot attend (**vs. 20**), although why a recent marriage would prevent attending a banquet goes unstated. After all, the man has the rest of his life to spend with his wife.

Commentators regularly compare the excuses to Deut 20.5–7 – the passage concerns exemptions from military service: "Has anyone built a new house but not dedicated it? He should go back to his house, or he might die in the battle and another dedicate it. Has anyone planted a vineyard but not yet enjoyed its fruit? He should go back to his house, or he might die in the battle and another be first to enjoy its fruit. Has anyone become engaged to a woman but not yet married her? He should go back to his house, or he might die in the battle and another marry her" (*m. Sotah* 8.2–6 qualifies the list). The connections are not strong, and they are also unnecessary. In Luke's Gospel, the excuses are newly bought land, newly bought livestock, and recent marriage. Triple excuses do not a direct allusion to Holy War make. For Luke's initial audience, the host is a man, the dinner is a good meal, and the guests are soon to be off the A list.

For Luke's audience as well, the folkloric "rule of three," in which the first two items set up the third, is in evidence. This same motif is what grants the Parables of the Good Samaritan and the Prodigal Son their punch. Missing from most commentaries is the humor of the excuses, which the "rule of three" creates. The first two guests describe property they have acquired and the desire to inspect that property. The third, who has "just been married" says nothing about "trying out" the bride, although listeners attuned to the rule of three would fill in the missing note and chuckle.[19] The details, and the joke, are earthly (and the third is sexist); they also disrupt the move to allegory and so to the messianic feast.

The parable continues as a slave reports the excuses to the master, who grows angry. He demands that the slave bring to the banquet "the poor, the crippled, the blind, and the lame" (**vs. 21**). When that command is fulfilled and the banquet hall is not yet full (**vs. 22**) – one wonders just how large the banquet hall is! – the master issues a second order, "go into the roads and lanes and compel people to come in" (**vs. 23**). The parable concludes with

---

19   See Bruce W. Longenecker, "A Humorous Jesus? Orality, Structure and Characterisation in Luke 14:15–24, and Beyond," *Biblical Interpretation* 16 (2008): 179–204.

the host stating that no one on the first guest list will taste the dinner (**vs. 24**), an ironic comment at best, since these guests had sent their regrets.

Once again, commentators are quick to point out that the people in the second and third invitation are unclean and outcast, not qualified for priesthood and denied a place at the messianic banquet.[20] Or, the third group invited represent gentiles, that is, the people "the Jews" despise. Thus, the parable is about a surprising reversal.[21] The issue here is neither Jewish ritual nor ethnic diversity; it is rich versus poor, social hierarchy, and the reciprocity system.

Were the parable about the messianic banquet, then there would be no poor or disabled, because the messianic age is the time when all suffering, physical and economic, is ended. We would be not at a dinner table with any who suffer. Isaiah (24.6–10) gives an early description of this banquet: "On this mountain the Lord of Hosts will make for all peoples a feast of rich food, a feast of well-aged wines, of rich food filled with marrow, of well-aged wines strained clear ... He will swallow up death forever. Then the Lord God will wipe away the tears from all faces ... It will be said on that day, 'behold, this is our God; we have waited for him, that he might save us.'" It's a lovely image, but it is not what Luke is describing.

Indeed, were the messianic age to be in place, there would be no slaves. While the move to make the parable about heavenly rewards – about who gets in to the dinner and who is left outside – is not surprising, it is also a form of domestication. It allows readers to feel good about themselves ("surely I, the follower of Jesus, am on the guest list," or, "we the gentiles" are the ones who accepted the invitation while all those "rich Jews" [the expression taken as tautological] are damned"), to dismiss the need for health care and relieving of poverty ("surely the poor and those in need of health care can get into heaven later, so I do not need to worry about them now"), and to rejoice at the fact that they are in and others are out ("surely those folks, who denied the invitation, are to be condemned").

Surely, we can do better. The parable is a narrative extension of the advice Jesus gave in vs. 13. Just as a guest can be humiliated by being asked to move to a lower seat, so can a host be humiliated by having dinner invitations declined. In each case, Jesus offers advice that will both prevent any

---

[20]   Commenting on Matthew's parable, Buttrick states, "Obviously, national pride and ritual purity had begun to control the guest list" (*Parables*, 158;) see also Young, *Parables*, 185; Hultgren, *Parables*, 337.

[21]   Discussion in C. A. Evans, *Luke*, 224–25.

humiliation and add to honor: take the lower seat; invite those who cannot reciprocate in kind but who will sing your praises in the streets.

There is also some humor in the host's move to fill the banquet hall. "Compel them" to come (vs. 23) is sometimes explained as indicating that the "unclean" would not feel comfortable in the home of a wealthy person. Again, the explication misses both the particulars of Jewish purity laws and a second punch line of the parable. No hungry person would turn down a banquet; compulsion is hardly needed. Here we see the host's desperation: he wants the filled hall, and so the chance to reclaim his honor.

In the end, everyone benefits: the feast is well attended, the hungry are well fed, and the host – who is inevitably analogized to God but for Luke's Gospel need not and probably should not be – is well honored. Even the final line, that the ones invited will not taste the dinner (**vs. 24**), contributes to the irony, for the ones invited had no wish to partake. Not only do they get exactly what they want, the host precludes them from a taste: the people filling the hall will ensure that there are no baskets of loaves and fishes left over.

Yes, this parable can be read as about acceptance of John and Jesus. It can be read as a story of rejection, the rejection of the invitation to the Kingdom, first offered presumably by John, but then clearly by Jesus. It can also be a story about acceptance, the acceptance of surprising dinner guests at the messianic banquet and the exclusion of those originally invited. In this allegorical reading, the host is the gracious God who wants his "house" to be full of guests and who accepts all comers.

The messianic banquet interpretation is not the only or even the best interpretation of the parable. The narrative can also be read as a piece of practical wisdom: the open invitation to the poor provides the hungry sustenance and the host honor. Everyone benefits. The joke may finally be on those who declined the invitation: they had sought to humiliate the host, but the tables are turned when the host, it turns out, will turn out to have a hall overflowing with grateful diners. Those who declined the invitation do not know what they are missing.

LESSONS ON DISCIPLESHIP

The remainder of the chapter clusters an assortment of discrete sayings addressed by Jesus to the "large crowds" traveling with him (**vs. 25**). The audience can indicate a type of recruitment speech: Jesus invites followers, but he does not paint a rosy picture of living the Gospel. Rather, he cautions the crowds about any initial enthusiasm: you may want to join, but here are the costs you need to calculate.

The first two verses speak to the cost of being his follower. In **vs. 26**, Jesus shockingly states that a disciple must hate his parents, children, wife (the statement presumes that only men are disciples), siblings, and even life. Claims that the apparently hyperbolic statement is typical of Jewish wisdom literature or that they represent a Semitism indicating not "hate" but "love less" are plausible. Matthew's parallel saying, "Whoever loves father or mother more than me is not worthy of me; and whoever loves son or daughter more than me is not worthy of me" (10.37), indicates that discipleship is a matter of priority: both domesticity and discipleship are commended. Yet for Luke, discipleship does not appear to be a both/and; it is rather an either/or. Everything that is not directly related to discipleship is to be rejected: to hang on to earthly life will be giving up the heavenly one, just as piling up treasures on earth depletes the heavenly treasury. Jesus had already voiced this need for total commitment in 9.62, "No one who puts a hand to the plow and looks back is fit for the Kingdom of God." And yet there are stay-at-home disciples of Jesus such as Mary and Martha in Luke 10 as we have already seen. Not all disciples are asked to give up everything and become itinerant.

Luke's view of the family is complicated. The Gospel promotes hatred of father and mother, and it also affirms the commandment "honor your father and your mother" (18.20, citing Exod 20.12; Deut 5.16). Jesus himself "honored" Mary and Joseph by his obedience to them (2.51). Honoring parents can take the form of dedicating one's life to Jesus. Or, honoring "father and mother" could, for Luke (and Jesus), refer to the honoring of those in the new "family of faith" (8.21; the "father" is God; "my mother and my brothers are those who hear the word of God and do it").

The teaching then moves from hatred of life to taking up the cross, for taking up the cross is exactly what those who "hate life" – that is, those who are able to give up everything related to life's attachments – do (**vs. 27**). Jesus' teaching reinforces his comment in 9.23, "If any want to become my followers, let them deny themselves and take up their cross daily and follow me." One is not to suffer for the sake of suffering; rather, one should be able to ask the questions, "For what or whom would I give up my life? For what or whom would I give up everything?" with the response, "for the kingdom and for Jesus." The lectionary reinforces this interpretation by pairing these verses with Phil 3.7–9, where Paul, in chains and facing possible execution, stoically states, "Yet whatever gains I had, these I have come to regard as loss because of Christ. More than that, I regard everything as loss because of the surpassing value of knowing Christ Jesus my Lord. For his sake, I have suffered the loss of all things, and I regard them as excrement, in order that I may gain Christ and be found in him." Such total dedication is therefore not compatible with the dedication shown by those who would, in the name of God, blow up federal buildings or shopping malls, buses and trade centers. To take up the cross means to give up one's own life rather than to take the lives of others.

The next several verses attempt to mitigate the starkness of the previous two statements. The first test case concerns a builder who, before erecting a tower, estimates the cost (**vs. 28**). Again, the audience presumes people who have the money for the land, the materials, and the workers. To peasants, the analogy, "if you plan to build a skyscraper," has little immediate pertinence. Jesus is not here talking to peasants, although they too easily understand the analogy. Returning to the subject of shame, which surfaced in the image of the diner being asked to give up his seat and the host who may have an empty banquet hall, Jesus notes that anyone who builds the foundation but runs out of funds before completing the project will face ridicule (**vs. 29**). The term the NRSV translates as "able" (Greek: *ischuō*) is better rendered as "is strong enough"; Luke's listeners may have recalled the seeker who is not "strong enough" to enter the narrow door (13.24). The concern is not ability, but fortitude and perseverance. Jesus then quotes what people will say of such a builder: "he could start, but he could not finish" (**vs. 30**). Today, where cost overruns are common and bankruptcy is a momentary distraction for those able to secure million-dollar loans, the issue of shame may be lessened.

There may also be here a foreshadowing of Jesus' own commitment. As Arland Hultgren points out, the term for "ridicule" (Greek: *empiazō*) or "mock" is only here applied to a person other than Jesus.[22] This term reappears in the Passion Narratives, where Jesus is the object of mocking (18.32; 22.63; 23.11; 23.26). To those who thought that the cross was the end of his life and thus indicated a failure to complete the messianic mission, Luke provides a correction with the resurrection and then with ongoing mission in Acts.

The relation of the image to the mission can appear inexact: Jesus calls people to follow him, and they are to respond without hesitation. This builder, conversely, does a cost estimation before beginning his project.

---

[22]   Hultgren, *Parables*, 139.

Alternatively, Jesus may be speaking of those disciples who would join him but then not carry through to the end. To return from being one of Jesus' followers to one's own household, whether Jewish or gentile, could be seen as shameful: the apostate neither understood the task nor was able to complete it. As Jesus stated in 9.62, "No one who puts a hand to the plow and looks back is fit for the Kingdom of God."

Jesus next offers a comparable image of a king who determines if his fighting force of ten thousand is strong enough to withstand his opponent's army of twenty thousand (**vs. 31**). The cost-benefit analysis yielding the conclusion that he has insufficient strength, the king eschews battle in favor of sending a delegation to ask for the terms of peace (**vs. 32**). Shame plays a role here too: the king with the weaker army is in the weaker position. This king may receive honor yet, should his negotiating strategies, like his advance planning, prove viable. He can recuperate his reputation, save the lives of thousands, and perhaps achieve whatever goal prompted the war.

The final verse in this section, which limits the role of "disciple" to those who give up all their possessions (**vs. 33**), continues the theme of divestment. It may also indicate that Luke is presenting a narrow definition of "disciple." Followers who remain with their families, maintain their homes (such as Mary and Martha), or have treasures on earth (such as Joseph of Arimathea) are also found worthy, but they are not in the inner circle. Acts describes the community of Jesus' followers as having all things in common and thus of entrusting their wealth to the apostles for distribution. The economic model is designed to ensure that no one is in need, and it is based on a theology that all property belongs to God. What is given to each depends on the need of each person. The "all things in common" principle is implemented on the basis of who has the resources and who has the need.[23] That system breaks down quickly, first with Ananias and Sapphira's withholding promised funds (Acts 5.1–11), and then with the Hellenistic widows overlooked in the daily distribution (Acts 6.1). The rest of Acts, and the rest of the New Testament, do not presume that followers would engage in divestment. Instead, those with resources are to aid those who lack them.

The chapter's final two verses, paralleled in Matthew's Sermon on the Mount (Matt 5.13–14), wrap up the concern for discipleship with an indication of what happens when the singular focus on Jesus and the Kingdom becomes diffused. Salt that loses its savor (**vs. 34**; the Greek literally says "if the salt becomes foolish" [*mōranthē*, whence 'moron']) means salt that has

---

[23] See Witherington, *Jesus and Money*.

become diluted. The image appropriately follows from the singular focus of the previous verses. As diluted salt is not even good enough for a pile of fertilizer, so the individual who is held back from total commitment by love of life, or love of family, is unworthy of being called a disciple. The numerous symbolic values of salt – as a preservative, medicine, seasoning, and such – enhance the primary meaning of the saying: diluted salt cannot preserve, heal, or enhance life.

1. On Election

The Parable of the Banquet has been interpreted as not only instructions to the elite, but also as a warning to the "elect" who decline the invitation. Because the term translated "invited" (Greek: *kaleō*) literally means "called," some interpreters see the first "called" as the Jews, those who are the (apparently) *chosen* or *elect* people of God and then see the ones compelled to enter as the gentiles. They conclude that the (gentile) church replaces the Jews. To read the parable as about soteriology rather than social behavior can set up a Jewish versus Christian reading that would be antithetical to Jesus' views, for Jesus never thought that Israel had ceased to be God's people.

Was this Luke's view? Ben thinks this is a very unlikely reading of Luke's Gospel and Acts; Amy-Jill, who observes that the only faithful "Jew" left in Luke's two-volume corpus is Paul, is less sanguine about Luke's presentation, but she would like to think that Ben's more optimistic, inclusive view is correct. After all, Ben queries, weren't Simeon, Anna, Elizabeth, Zechariah, Mary, and Joseph faithful Jews? Indeed they were, Amy-Jill agrees, but they are also all members of that earlier generation. Readers will thus need to determine how to address a text that is open to supersessionist interpretations.

2. On Taking Up the Cross

Today the idiom of "taking up the cross," or, "we all have our crosses to bear," has lost its shock value. Fanny Crosby's hymn, "Keep Thou My Way," with its famous line, "Gladly the cross I'd bear," has devolved into "Glady, the cross-eyed bear" in a children's misunderstanding of a Sunday school teaching. All too often, we confuse ordinary suffering with cross-bearing.

To speak of "extending the arm for the lethal injection" or "standing before the firing squad" may recover at least part of the shock of the statement.

Physical pain may well be a thorn in the flesh, but it is not a cross. Suffering from cancer or heart disease is neither something one chooses. Nor need it be redemptory. Cross-bearing as a metaphor for discipleship has to do with a chosen course of life, not something that happens. The question facing the one who would be a disciple becomes, "For what would I give up my home and my family, and my life?"

The second thing to be said about cross-bearing is that Jesus does not call us to bear *his* cross. Rather, he talks about picking up our *own* crosses. This means that there is no room for Christians developing messiah complexes as if they could save the world. To take up one's cross *daily* and follow Jesus indicates a commitment to live with the singular goal of living the Gospel, no matter what the cost. Jesus had made the same point in 9.23 by stating, "If any want to become my followers, let them deny themselves and take up their cross daily and follow me."

Missionaries who have lost their lives in service to others – the Evangelical Jim Elliott; the Catholics Jane Donovan, Dorothy Kazel, Maura Clarke, and Ita Ford; and countless others – show what cross-bearing means. So too do those prophets who are killed in Jerusalem, and in Memphis, and in New Delhi, and elsewhere, for speaking words of peace that others did not want to hear.

3. On Social Practice

Luke's continual criticism of hosts, whether Simon the Pharisee in Chapter 7 or the two unnamed Pharisaic hosts in Chapters 11 and 14, or even Martha in Chapter 10, functions as practical wisdom. For the rich among Luke's readers, then and now, the message is both practical and merciful. To invite those out of one's social circle to dinner and to treat them as honored guests rather than either objects of charity or opportunities for entertainment is a type of hospitality rarely practiced. We tend to invite our friends, not strangers, to our homes. Indeed, with some good reason, we are hesitant to invite strangers: they might just as easily steal from us as dine with us. "It is an entirely different experience, for example, to eat a meal at table with homeless women, men, and children than to hand them groceries once a month."[24] Nor is it easy to cross social lines: what do "we the well-off" say to "them the poor" without sounding patronizing, elitist, or clueless?

[24]   Miller, "Bridge Work and Seating Charts," 427.

Church-based meals become a good opportunity for such interaction to develop. The dinner is at the church, where everyone is welcome and one pays what one can. By having the payment given in envelopes, those who cannot afford even the few dollars do not have to be embarrassed by their limited contributions; the same point should hold for the collection plate passed down the pews during the worship service. The conversation already has several good starting points: Christology, ethics, Church history, one's personal understanding of a parable or a psalm. At such tables, all should be welcome, and all are welcome as equal participants in the Kingdom project.

Luke's hosts will benefit from their welcoming of people off the A list, for those people will praise the hosts' hospitality and generosity. Were people to praise the hospitality and generosity of the Church – today's "host" – so much the better. And were the rich in the Church to subsidize the food for the poor, without insisting on public notice of their contribution, then they would both shift the patronage system from individual honor to community recognition. Thereby, they lay up treasures in heaven even as they facilitate a type of heaven on earth.

Luke 15 Parables of Losing and Finding

¹ Now all the tax collectors and sinners were coming near to listen to him.
² And the Pharisees and the scribes were grumbling and saying, "This fellow welcomes sinners and eats with them." ³ So he told them this parable:

THE LOST SHEEP, OR THE COUNTING, SEEKING, FINDING, CELEBRATING SHEEP OWNER

⁴ "Which one of you, having a hundred sheep and losing one of them, does not leave the ninety-nine in the wilderness and go after the one that is lost until he finds it? ⁵ When he has found it, he lays it on his shoulders and rejoices. ⁶ And when he comes home, he calls together his friends and neighbors, saying to them, 'Rejoice with me, for I have found my sheep that was lost.'
⁷ Just so, I tell you, there will be more joy in heaven over one sinner who repents than over ninety-nine righteous persons who need no repentance.

THE LOST COIN, OR THE COUNTING, SEEKING, FINDING, CELEBRATING COIN OWNER

⁸ "Or what woman having ten silver coins, if she loses one of them, does not light a lamp, sweep the house, and search carefully until she finds it?
⁹ When she has found it, she calls together her friends and neighbors, saying, 'Rejoice with me, for I have found the coin that I had lost.'
¹⁰ Just so, I tell you, there is joy in the presence of the angels of God over one sinner who repents."

THE LOST SON, AND THE FATHER WHO FORGOT TO COUNT

[11] Then Jesus said, "There was a man who had two sons. [12] The younger of them said to his father, 'Father, give me the share of the property that will belong to me.' So he divided his property between them. [13] A few days later the younger son gathered all he had and traveled to a distant country, and there he squandered his property in dissolute living. [14] When he had spent everything, a severe famine took place throughout that country, and he began to be in need. [15] So he went and hired himself out to one of the citizens of that country, who sent him to his fields to feed the pigs. [16] He would gladly have filled himself with the pods that the pigs were eating; and no one gave him anything.

[17] But when he came to himself he said, 'How many of my father's hired hands have bread enough and to spare, but here I am dying of hunger! [18] I will get up and go to my father, and I will say to him, "Father, I have sinned against heaven and before you; [19] I am no longer worthy to be called your son; treat me like one of your hired hands." ' [20] So he set off and went to his father.

But while he was still far off, his father saw him and was filled with compassion; he ran and put his arms around him and kissed him. [21] Then the son said to him, 'Father, I have sinned against heaven and before you; I am no longer worthy to be called your son.'

[22] But the father said to his slaves, 'Quickly, bring out a robe – the best one – and put it on him; put a ring on his finger and sandals on his feet. [23] And get the fatted calf and kill it, and let us eat and celebrate; [24] for this son of mine was dead and is alive again; he was lost and is found!' And they began to celebrate.

[25] "Now his elder son was in the field; and when he came and approached the house, he heard music and dancing. [26] He called one of the slaves and asked what was going on. [27] He replied, 'Your brother has come, and your father has killed the fatted calf, because he has got him back safe and sound.' [28] Then he became angry and refused to go in.

His father came out and began to plead with him. [29] But he answered his father, 'Listen! For all these years I have been working like a slave for you, and I have never disobeyed your command; yet you have never given me even a young goat so that I might celebrate with my friends. [30] But when this son of yours came back, who has devoured your property with prostitutes, you killed the fatted calf for him!'

[31] Then the father said to him, 'Son, you are always with me, and all that is mine is yours. [32] But we had to celebrate and rejoice, because this brother of yours was dead and has come to life; he was lost and has been found.'"

The parables of Luke 15 are traditionally read as stories about sin, repentance, and restoration. This interpretation stems from Luke's two glosses. Taken on their own, without the evangelist's allegorical connection of sheep to sin and coins to calumny, Jesus' listeners would focus on the three main figures – the sheep owner, the woman, and the father – as well as the move from one hundred lost to ten to one and so on, and then the parables trap them, as parables are wont to do. It first appears that the younger son is the lost one, but it turns out that the older is lost as well, and he is the one for whom the father must seek. Allusions to older and younger brothers from the Scriptures of Israel undergird the reference to a father with two sons and so both add to the import of the third parable and complicate interpretations derived from it.

In the following discussion, we take seriously both Luke's interpretation of the parables and the meaning we derive from looking at the parables detached from the allegories of sin and repentance.[1] One word of reminder is in order: parables often have allegorical elements in them, some have more, some have less, so there is inherent encouragement to interpret these parables allegorically. For example, "vineyards" signal Israel; "kings" can signal "God," but there is a difference between a parable with allegorical elements and an overly allegorical interpretation of a parable that no one would understand without an answer key. We may debate whether Luke's editorial activity illuminates or obscures the original meaning of the parable. In Ben's view, it highlights certain elements already present in the parables; Amy-Jill sees how, reading through Luke's lenses, which are tinted with concerns for repenting and forgiving, the allegorical readings make sense. She doubts, however, that Jesus' audience would have interpreted the parables in the same way Luke does.

LUKE'S SETTING FOR THREE PARABLES OF COUNTING, SEEKING, AND FINDING

Jesus likely told the same parable on more than one occasion. Matthew, Mark, and Luke then determined where to place them in the context of Jesus' life,

---

[1]   See detailed discussion in Levine, *Short Stories by Jesus*, 25–70.

what the audiences were, and in some cases what the parables meant. Thus, the Gospel writers are not simply recording what Jesus did and said, they are already in the process of interpreting his actions and his teachings. That is what homilists and historians do. Each generation, each reader, provides new interpretations, and thereby the stories remain alive and relevant.

Luke sets the three parables in the context of Jesus' associating with tax collectors and sinners (**vs. 1**). This association is familiar, as Luke has mentioned Jesus' association with this contingent several times (e.g., 5.29–32; 7.29, 34; cf. 5.27; 7.37, 39; 18.10–13; 19.2, 17). "Sinners and tax collectors" are not "outcasts"; rather, they have violated the welfare of family and community and thus walked out of home and community. We typically today do not use the term "outcast" to speak of arms dealers, loansharks, insider traders, or collaborationists with occupation governments, but they would be the modern equivalents of Jesus' audience. "Sinners" can also refer to the immoral in general, and the sexually immoral in particular.[2] These individuals saw in Jesus, or heard about his teaching, a welcoming presence. In the parables that follow, Luke provides an interpretation that speaks directly to their situation: God rejoices when they repent.

The response to their approach is also typical of the Third Gospel: the Pharisees and scribes grumble because Jesus both welcomes tax collectors and sinners and eats with them (**vs. 2**). The Pharisees may be presuming Jesus is overlooking the harm his table companions have done to home and community. Luke's interpretation of the parables makes clear that Jesus does not condone sin, nor does he focus on the details of it. Jesus' concern is repentance and the forgiveness that comes with it. His concern, further, is on the reintegration to community that repentance prompts. The Pharisees and scribes do not know this. Only gradually does Luke reveal the response of Jesus' audience: the tax collectors either leave their toll booths (5.27–28) or reveal to the community that they are righteous (19.2–10). Jesus comes "to seek out and to save the lost" (19.10). Whether the tax collectors and sinners have the strength to follow him, or whether they will be like seed that does not take root, is a matter that goes unanswered. The hope remains.

It is in the context of this double audience that Luke sets the three parables to follow. Readers in Church contexts frequently conclude that the "prodigal son" in the third parable represents sinners and tax collectors, or faithful (gentile) Christians,[3] welcomed home by the gracious Father-God. The

---

[2] See E. P. Sanders, *Paul and Palestinian Judaism* (Minneapolis: Fortress Press, 2017).
[3] Reid, *Parables for Preachers, Year C*, 65.

father is seen as displaying a gracious love unheard of in Judaism, whether that be love of an actual father for his son or love of the gracious God to all sinners. The older brother is then cast as the Pharisees, or all Jews, who function according to a works-righteousness theology, resent the inclusion of gentiles in the Church, and do not understand grace. Comments such as "The main theme [of the parables in Luke 15–16] would seem to be the opposition of the Pharisees, in their self-justification and hardness based on their observance of the law, to the message of repentance,"[4] find their basis less in the parables themselves than in Luke's contextualization of them. Then standard anti-Jewish polemic kicks in. For example, Eduard Schweizer writes: "those who nailed [Jesus] to the cross because they found blasphemy in his parables – which proclaimed such scandalous conduct on the part of God – understood his parables better than those who saw in them nothing but the obvious message, which should be self-evident to all, of the fatherhood and kindness of God, meant to replace a superstitious belief in a God of wrath."[5]

Amy-Jill sees some of these readings as following from Luke's contextualization. In the context of Luke's Gospel, reading the younger brother as a "gentile" is possible although not necessary. Ben argues that Luke is not interested in ethnic stereotypes; Luke is interested in repentance and genuine faith whether displayed by Jews or gentiles, and there are plenty of Jews about whom unique stories are told in this Gospel that reflect this concern, for example the story of Zacchaeus. We agree, however, that the negative stereotypes of Jewish theology and practice need to be challenged. Although John Wesley saw the older brother as representing the Pharisees, Ben also notes that as many times as he has heard the Parable of the Prodigal Son preached in the Methodist Church, not once has he ever heard the notion that the younger brother was a gentile, or that the older brother represented stern Pharisees.

THE LOST SHEEP, OR THE COUNTING, SEEKING, FINDING, CELEBRATING SHEEP OWNER

Parables do not come with names attached, and how we label the stories influences how we read them. The first parable is traditionally called the "Parable of the Lost Sheep," which puts the focus on the lost animal.

---

4   C. F. Evans, *Saint Luke*, 582; see also Johnson, *Gospel of Luke*, 242.
5   Eduard Schweizer, *Jesus* (London: SCM, 1971), 29, cited in Young, *Parables of Jesus*, 132.

Intertextual associations then abound, for the identification of the covenant community as "sheep" under both the watchful eye of the good shepherd and the exploitative eye of the bad shepherd is a standard biblical trope. Since Jesus is elsewhere identified as the "good shepherd" – John 10.11 depicts him saying, "I am the good shepherd. The good shepherd lays down his life for his sheep"; in John 10.14, Jesus states, "I am the good shepherd. I know my own and my own know me" – readers naturally associate Jesus with the sheep owner and themselves with the lost sheep. This reading, consistent with Luke's interpretation of the parable, provides comfort. Sinners find the love of God extended to them, and they respond to that love by repenting.

This interpretation works best when details of the parable are ignored. Taking Jesus at his word, we find an additional reading of the parable that functions primarily as a setup to the third parable in the chain. That reading promotes the importance of counting, a point already made in Jesus' comment in 12.7: "But even the hairs of your head are all counted. Do not be afraid; you are of more value than many sparrows."

Jesus begins by addressing his audience: "Which of you, having a hundred sheep" (**vs. 4**). The main figure of the parable is not a shepherd; it is a sheep owner. Again, Luke, and Jesus, describe an audience of some means. Nevertheless, commentators immediately jump to several conclusions. Some, presuming that a man who owns one hundred sheep is a shepherd, insist that Pharisees could never identify with a shepherd since Jews generally classified shepherds among a "class of proscribed trades,"[6] the "outcast,"[7] the "unclean,"[8] and the objects of "contempt."[9] There is nothing in the opening line that justifies such readings. The parable functions as an invitation to the audience with its opening "which of you … ?" Listeners have no reason *not* to identify with the main figure, just as they have no

---

[6]   Kenneth E. Bailey, *Poet and Peasant/Through Peasant Eyes: A Literary-Cultural Approach to the Parables in Luke* (Grand Rapids: Eerdmans, 1983), 147; Idem, *Finding the Lost: Cultural Keys to Luke 15* (Concordia Scholarship Today; St. Louis: Concordia Publishing, 1992), 65, Joachim Jeremias, "ποιμήν," *TDNT* 6 (1974): 488–89; and Bernard Brandon Scott, *Hear Then the Parable: A Commentary on the Parables of Jesus* (Minneapolis: Augsburg Fortress), 413–14. See also Hultgren, *Parables of Jesus*, 57–58. Following Jeremias, *Jerusalem in the Time of Jesus* (London: SCM, 1969), 303–5, 310, is Reid, *Parables for Preachers, Year C*, 84: "It is a shock for respected religious leaders to be asked to think of themselves as lowly shepherds."

[7]   Scott, *Hear Then the Parable*, 414.

[8]   Snodgrass, *Stories with Intent*, 102.

[9]   Citing Jeremias is also Ralph F. Wilson, "Shepherds in Bethlehem (Luke 2:8–20)," at *Jesus Walk*, www.jesuswalk.com/lessons/2_8-20.htm.

reason *not* to identify with the woman who lost her coin or the father of the two sons.

On the other hand, commentators regard the man who lost a sheep as a symbol for God. This interpretation fits Luke's agenda, but it does not fit the details of the parable. The man *lost* the sheep (**vs. 4**). Since God does not lose us, Amy-Jill concludes that the sheep owner cannot be God. Ben notes that this conclusion depends on what "lost" means in the parable. If it is referring not to losing track of someone but rather to persons who have spiritually lost their way, then yes, God could indeed lose such a person. Matthew's version of this parable (Matt 18.12–14; see also *Gospel of Thomas* 107) describes the sheep as having "gone astray" (the Greek *planaō* has the connotation of being deceived), and so conforms the parable to the requirement of church leaders that they keep their flock from false teaching. Matthew reinforces this reading by setting the parable not in the context of Jesus' dining with sinners and tax collectors, but as part of the fourth major section, the ecclesiastical discourse, where Jesus explains to the disciples how to run a church.

Nor are we, Jesus' listeners, immediately to identify with the lost sheep in the parable, despite Psa 119.176 – "I have gone astray like a lost sheep; seek out your servant, for I do not forget your commandments." Again, the owner *lost* the sheep. The title, "Parable of the Lost Sheep," might be better replaced with a focus on the frantic sheep owner searching for the one sheep that he has lost.

The search is an all-out endeavor. Leaving (Greek: *kataleipō*[10]) the ninety-nine in the wilderness, the owner seeks the lost. Were the owner a shepherd, he would have been an inept one. Leaving ninety-nine sheep to their own devices would likely leave the owner, at the end of the day, with only the lost sheep he found. Amy-Jill's friend Deborah, reporting on teaching in Tanzania, noted that according to her friends there, when a sheep goes astray, they shoot it. Otherwise, the rest of the flock might follow. The search of the sheep owner is exaggerated.

Granted, parables are not necessarily true to ordinary life. They are meant to be true to Kingdom values. The parable therefore immediately asks: are we like the sheep owner seeking and saving the lost one? This is what Jesus does in his table fellowship with sinners and tax collectors. This reading is a start, but it still omits the full challenge of the parable. That

---

[10]   Hultgren, *Parables of Jesus*, 54.

challenge becomes most apparent when all three parables in Luke 15 are read together.

The sheep owner, rejoicing that he has found the lost sheep, hoists it over his shoulders (**vs. 5**). This is an easier way to move a sheep than to call out, "Here, Fluffy," and hope that it will follow. Bringing the sheep home, he summons friends and neighbors to a party in celebration of finding the sheep (**vs. 6**).

Whether the sheep owner has listened to Jesus is another matter. Not that long ago, Jesus advised, "When you give a luncheon or a dinner, do not invite your friends or your brothers or your relatives or rich neighbors, in case they may invite you in return, and you would be repaid. But when you give a banquet, invite the poor, the crippled, the lame, and the blind" (14.12–13). This parable has a compatible message, but the message is not yet clear.

So far, the parable has set up an outline to be repeated in the next two stories: something lost, a search, something found, a celebration. Because the story began with a full complement of one hundred sheep from which one was lost, readers should also expect one out of a full complement to be lost in the second and third stories. Listeners in Jesus' time would have realized the import of that full complement, for the only way the sheep owner knew that he had lost the sheep was by counting. He would have passed the sheep through a sheepfold and numbered them as they moved. Based on the folkloric "rule of three," this story should prime listeners to expect a similar pattern in the second story, and a reversal of the pattern in the third. The parables do not disappoint.

There is some evidence that Jesus told parables in pairs, the first featuring a man and the second a woman. We see this model with the mustard seed and the yeast, and we see it again with the sheep and the coin. Given this tendency, Ben proposes that the third parable, that of the lost son, was probably placed here by Luke and therefore was not part of an original triad. Amy-Jill sees the three parables as mutually interpreting, given that they have the same structure, the same concern for one missing out of a larger number, and the same plot line. That Jesus also tells numerous parables with a "rule of three" basis – the three types of soil, the three dinner guests who decline the invitation, the three potential helpers on the road to Jericho, and so on – she sees no reason to doubt that Jesus told all three parables together. (Here, oddly, Amy-Jill sees Luke as more accurately recording Jesus' teachings whereas Ben sees redactional placement; one never knows). Ben's point, however, is that the rule of three applies *within the parables*, not to a series of parables. It's the rule of two in regard to a series of parables that Jesus himself paired, as the examples Amy-Jill cites show.

At the end of the first parable, Luke offers an allegorical interpretation: the sheep has become the repentant sinner, and the rest of the flock are the ninety-nine who do not need to repent (**vs. 7**). By implication, the sheep owner, transformed into the "good shepherd," symbolizes God. Ben finds this a plausible interpretation, consistent with both Jesus' ministry and Luke's themes. Amy-Jill finds a Lucan imposition on earlier material: sheep do not repent; nor had the sheep need of repenting, for the sheep did nothing wrong. To the contrary, it was the sheep owner who lost the sheep, discovered the loss while counting the flock, searched for the sheep, found it, and then celebrated. We do, however, agree that people can go astray from God; they can wander off the right path. This parable is not a lesson about animal behavior, but rather about human choices. Ben sees an allegorical element to the story as inherent, and it is the case that all parables can have allegorical elements. Amy-Jill agrees that the parable can be read, and has been read, as about sin and repentance. But she remains concerned with both the words of the parable: the man lost the sheep and with the parable's connection to the account of the lost coin. Sheep can wander off; coins are, necessarily, lost rather than independent agents that deliberately wander away from wallets.

THE LOST COIN, OR THE COUNTING, SEEKING, FINDING, CELEBRATING COIN OWNER

The second parable follows the same outline as the first, and the commentators follow their same outline as well. Jesus speaks of a woman having ten silver coins (**vs. 8**), and again the commentators race to find a negative Jewish background against which they can set Jesus. Some express surprise that Jesus would tell a story about a woman,[11] given what they presume to be the overpowering misogyny of Jewish culture. Snodgrass, for example, states, "She is evidence of … Jesus' sensitivity toward women … something new, even surprising,"[12] Such readers apparently missed the books of Ruth, Esther, Judith, and Susannah, along with the songs of Deborah and Miriam, the matriarchs, and countless other women who appear in Jewish

---

[11]   Hultgren, *Parables of Jesus*, 64, following Bailey, *Poet and Peasant*, 158; Idem, *Finding the Lost*, 93.

[12]   Snodgrass, *Stories with Intent*, 114–15.

texts. They miss the Jewish women who served as patrons to Pharisees (Josephus, *War* 1.107–19; *Ant.* 12.398–432; 17.41–43) along with the women in the synagogues and the Temple that the Gospels mention.[13] Rather than hailing Jesus as a progressive amid a negatively and falsely constructed view of Jewish women, we do better to read the parable on its own terms. Alternatively, Ben adds, one could see Jesus as progressive like some others in early Judaism.

Ben agrees that we do not need to paint the Jewish background in noxious colors to highlight the positive light that Jesus shed on women. He nevertheless suggests that Jesus is the first Jewish teacher of that to have women as traveling disciples. In other words, he was a progressive when it comes to women and their roles. Amy-Jill queries the comparison, given that we have no other examples of such traveling teachers but that we do have examples of women patrons of Pharisees. She also wonders if in fact the women did itinerate with Jesus in the Galilee; accompaniment to Jerusalem for the pilgrimage festival of Passover is not the same thing as overnighting between Capernaum and Chorazin.[14] We both conclude that Jesus welcomed women among his followers; we have nuanced differences on the extent to which this welcome indicated something new and what it suggests about gender roles for both Jesus and Luke.

The woman has ten drachmas, which is a fair amount of money. She is therefore financially independent and in control of her own funds, just like the women who, according to 8.2–3, support the Jesus movement, the woman who spent her money on physicians (8.43), the woman who anointed Jesus (7.36), and the widow who put her coins into the Temple treasury (21.2–3). The parable depicts the woman as losing one of her coins; whereas the sheep owner speaks of "my sheep that was lost" (15.6), the woman directly admits, "I have found the coin that I had lost." She takes responsibility for the loss, as she should. The coin did not wander off on its own. Like the sheep owner who searched for his sheep, the woman searches for her coin. Upon finding it, she invites to a celebration her women friends and neighbors (**vs. 9**). They too have freedom of travel and association; they too can party. Suggestions that the first parable is "about a man, who is relatively wealthy and belongs

---

13   Ilan, "Gender."
14   See Amy-Jill Levine, "John Meier, Women, and the Criteria of Authenticity," in Vincent Skemp and Kelley Coblentz Bautch (eds.), *Jesus as a Figure of History and Theology: Essays in Honor of John P. Meier* (Catholic Biblical Quarterly Monograph Series [CBQMS]; Washington, DC: Catholic University of America, forthcoming).

outside," while the second is "about a woman, poor and confined to the house,"[15] overstate.

We do not know whether the woman also had gold and copper coins stashed in the house, owned vineyards and orchards, or ran her own business. The parables are not interested in the contrast between rich and poor; instead, all three of the parables in Luke 15 describe people with more than sufficient funds to host a celebration. Luke has much to say about wealth and poverty, but such topics do not permeate every verse. Ben notes it is possible that this is a story about a woman and her dowry, something quite essential to her ongoing security and well-being. Thus, her celebrating would involve some real sacrifice. Amy-Jill sees no more reason to think the coins have to do with a dowry than that the sheep would be eaten at a wedding banquet.

Luke also has much to say about repenting, and so introduces the theme at the conclusion of the parable. For Luke, the woman who searches for her coin and then celebrates upon finding it indicates that angelic joy "over one sinner who repents" (**vs. 10**). Again, Luke turns the parable into an allegory. This reading does not make Luke "wrong": allegorical interpretations of parables have had a long history in Christian interpretation. Our approach is not to dismiss Luke's reading but to add to it by attempting to recover the parables' import without the allegorical gilding.

Finally, should one conclude that the sheep owner in the first parable symbolizes the divine, and that the father of the two sons in the third parable is also God the Father, then one must conclude that the woman in the second parable, who stands in exactly the same place as the sheep owner and the dad, is also an image for God.[16] Ben thinks this latter interpretation in fact represents Jesus' view of the matter; Amy-Jill thinks that in Jesus' view, none of these figures represents God, but she appreciates Ben's conclusion.

THE LOST SON, AND THE FATHER WHO FORGOT TO COUNT

The third parable introduces "a man who had two sons" (**vs. 11**). The opening does more than suggest an easier task of counting that one hundred sheep or ten coins. It also prompts recognition from the biblically literate listener: Adam, Abraham, Isaac, Joseph, Tamar and Judah, David and Bathsheba – all had two

---

[15]   Lieu, *Gospel According to Luke*, 119.
[16]   Snodgrass, *Stories with Intent*, 114, cites Augustine, *Exposition of the Psalms*, 121–50, on seeing the woman as Wisdom.

sons. The biblically literate reader also knows that the younger son would be the favored one: Abel's sacrifice is accepted, while Cain becomes a fratricide and an exile; Abraham expels Ishmael together with his mother Hagar, while Isaac inherits the patriarchal role; Isaac's elder son Esau barters his birthright to his brother Jacob for a bowl of lentil stew, and then Jacob tricks Isaac into giving him Esau's blessing for the firstborn; Joseph places his older son Manasseh by Jacob's right and his younger son Ephraim by Jacob's left hand, but when the grandfather bestows his blessings, he crosses his hands; Zerah, Tamar's would-be older twin, extends his hand from her womb, and the midwife marks his wrist with a red cord, but the other twin, Perez, pushes himself forward to emerge first (one shudders to think of how Tamar felt); King Solomon is David and Bathsheba's second son, as the child conceived from the adulterous relationship died. Listeners, aware of this long history of second sons, are inclined to identify with the father's second son.

This background coupled with the opening line indicates that the traditional title of the parable, "The Prodigal Son," skews the interpretation. The late fourth-early-fifth-century Church Father St. Jerome offers, "On the prudent and the prodigal sons" (*Lives of Illustrious Men* 135). Today one sometimes hears the parable called "The Prodigal Father," and the designation "The Prodigal God" marks a long-time best seller.[17] The term "prodigal" itself has come to mean "generous"; that is not its original connotation. A "prodigal" is a spendthrift who cares about his own comforts and desires and who focuses on vice rather than virtue. That is a good description of the younger son, less so of God.

The younger son requests his share of the inheritance from his father, to which the father complies by dividing his property between elder and younger brother (**vs. 12**). Contrary, once again, to numerous commentaries, the younger son did not sin against his father or violate the commandment to honor his father.[18] He is not wishing his father dead,[19]

---

[17] Timothy Keller, *The Prodigal God: Recovering the Heart of Christian Faith* (New York: Penguin, 2011). In Keller's view, the parable is about Jesus' desire to show "religious Jews" their "blindness, narrowness, and self-righteousness" (12), and he concludes that this audience would have been "thunderstruck, offended, and infuriated" by the parable (13). Once again, Jesus' Jewish context becomes the narrative foil.

[18] Bernard S. Jackson, *Essays on Halakhah in the New Testament* (Jewish and Christian Perspectives Series 16; Leiden: Brill, 2007), esp. 140–41.

[19] Young, *Parables of Jesus*, proposes that the younger son's words "echo a death wish … tantamount to seeking his father's death … telling his father that he wanted him to die" (138); "drop dead!" (139), and so concludes that "severe punishment or complete rejection would not be out of the question" (144).

dishonoring the household, or acting as a rebellious son who ought to be stoned.[20]

John S. Kloppenborg, after examining how fathers in antiquity distributed their property, observes that such claims seem "more designed to inflate the crime of the younger son, to take it well beyond the boundary of quotidian happenings, and thus to install the son as a foil for the theologized father."[21] Readers familiar with the conventions of Greek comedy would see the young man as conforming to the "stock literary trope of young men (*adulescentes*) who are typically depicted as wasting their patrimony on prostitutes (*meretrices*) in Greco-Roman comedy."[22] Finally, had the younger son sinned, then it would be his father's responsibility to correct him. Instead, the father literally divides his "life" (Greek: *bios*) between his sons. He is generous, perhaps overly so, but neither has he sinned.

Ben adds that it was not the usual practice to give a child an inheritance before the father died and before the elder son got his share; the elder would normally inherit first, and sometimes he would receive a double share. Amy-Jill is not arguing that this was the "usual" practice; we are talking about very rich people here, and most people are not very rich. She is, rather, noting that nothing weird or even unexpected has happened. If it had, then it is the father who bares the major blame for acceding to the younger son's request. Ben takes Amy-Jill's point that the father is the one in control, and could be seen as overly indulgent here, and to blame.

Whether the father is wise is another question. Sirach advises, "When the days of your life reach their end, at the time of your death distribute your property" (33.22–23). The Talmud follows suit in suggesting that the one who "writes a document bequeathing his property to his children in his lifetime, as he becomes financially dependent on them," is responsible for his own misfortune (*b. B. Metz.* 75b). Like the sheep owner who lost his sheep and the woman who lost her coin, the father is about to lose his son. And he is at least partially responsible for this situation. The question of the father's wisdom will resurface toward the end of the parable.

---

[20] Suggested by Snodgrass, *Stories with Intent*, 125.

[21] John S. Kloppenborg, 'The Parable of the Prodigal Son and Deeds of Gift,' in Rieuwerg Buitenwerf, Harm W. Hollander, and Johannes Tromp (eds.), *Jesus, Paul, and Early Christianity: Studies in Honour of Henk Jan de Jonge* (NovTSup 130; Leiden/Boston: Bill, 2008), 169–94 (193).

[22] Callie Callon, "Adulescentes and Meretrices: The Correlation Between Squandered Patrimony and Prostitutes in the Parable of the Prodigal Son," *CBQ* 75.2 (2013): 259–78 (260: Callon provides numerous examples, with connections to Plautus and Terrance).

Gathering up his possessions, the younger son heads to a distant country, where he loses his money (**vs. 13**). The NRSV description of his "squandering his property" misses the nuance of the Greek *diaskorpidzō*, which means "scattering." That the son has moved to a "distant country" and so is in the "diaspora" (the term derives from the same root) provides an elegant emphasis on the young man's displacement. Leaving home, he cuts off his network; neither his family nor his community comes to his aid. He does not affiliate, as far as we know, with the Jewish community in this new setting, where he could have expected to find aid. The same term reappears in Luke's next chapter, which describes the dishonest manager as "scattering" his master's property, save that in his case he was able to count on aid from others.

The son's engagement in "dissolute living" (Greek: *zōn asōtōs*) goes undetailed, and so invites the reader to imagine (but not too long). His squandering is not wise. Ben sees the younger son at the very least as presumptuous, and he concludes that spending one's inheritance on "riotous living" is the classic definition of sinning. For Ben, the son has dishonored his generous and gracious parent and therefore violated the commandment, "Honor your father and mother." Since such honoring would include caring for them in their old age, the son's behavior is the narcissistic opposite of that commandment.

Amy-Jill has her doubts, although she is not condoning riotous living. To spend one's money on wine or beer, to play cards or dice, to attend games in a hippodrome or watch plays in a theater, even to hire prostitutes, could all fall under the category of "dissolute living," but such actions may not be sins from which one needs to repent. Ben asks, "Why in the world not?" Amy-Jill notes that Jesus could have used the term "sin" in the parable; he does not use it here. Nor is the father in need of care: he has plenty of money left, and he still has his older son, upon whom the responsibilities of care must fall. What Ben sees here as "sin," Amy-Jill sees as foolishness.

Now broke, the younger son faces a famine (**vs. 14**). The Scriptures of Israel again provide numerous intertexts, for a famine in the land brings Abraham and Sarah to Egypt; Joseph and his family to Egypt; and the Bethlehemite family of Elimelech, Naomi, and their sons to Moab (of all places). In this case, the play on the convention is that the younger son is already outside the land; the second play is that he does not receive the hospitality that his Jewish forefathers and foremothers received. He hires himself out to a local citizen, a typical thing for those needing funds to do. Contracts for such labor remain from antiquity: the contractor would hire an individual for a set amount of time at a set wage, and then the contractor would set the job. This citizen, perhaps noting the young man's Jewish identity, sends him to the fields to feed his pigs (**vs. 15**). The narrative gives no notice that the son knew his job would involve pigs.[23] Listeners might appreciate the desperation of the son, and even the potential humor of the situation. To the question, "how bad was it?" the answer, "I had to feed pigs," could bring a smile.

Yes, pigs are unclean and so purity is of interest to the parable. But no, the focus of the parable is not primarily on the matter of purity; it is on the matters of hunger and lack of generosity. The young man would have eaten the pods used to feed the pigs, but no one gave him anything to eat (**vs. 16**). Contrary, once again, to standard commentaries, the young man has not violated his Jewish tradition or engaged in apostasy[24] or sin[25] by feeding pigs or by going into "unclean Gentile territory made up of unclean Gentile people."[26] The young man is hungry, no one is giving him anything to eat, and his desire to be filled will be shared by another parabolic figure, Lazarus, starving and dying by the rich man's gates (16.21). In comparison with Lazarus' plight, the young man's situation could be a lot worse.

The next verses are typically read as the young man's repentance and conversion, although that is not exactly what the text says. Rather than use language of "repenting," Jesus describes the young man as having "come to himself"; he has a recognition of both the extremity of his circumstances and the full storehouses of his wealthy father where even the hired hands have a surfeit of food (**vs. 17**). One could regard the son as repentant; Amy-Jill doubts it; Ben is more sanguine.

We hear the son's thoughts, or perhaps he is speaking aloud to himself.[27] He plans. He plots. He says, with an emphasis on relational language, that he will get up and go to his *father* and he will say, "*Father* ..." (**vs. 18**). His very insistence on fatherhood will remind the father that the person seeking his aid is not a stranger but his son. His proposed speech, "I have sinned against heaven

[23] J. Albert Harrill, "The Indentured Labor of the Prodigal Son (Luke 15.15)," Critical Notes, *JBL* 115 (1997): 714–17.

[24] Scott, *Re-Imagine the World*, 73, 76. Ben notes, he has violated purity rules. Amy-Jill disagrees.

[25] Talbert, *Luke-Acts*, 149.

[26] Craig L. Blomberg, *Preaching the Parables: From Responsible Interpretation to Powerful Proclamation* (Grand Rapids: Baker Academic, 2004), 36.

[27] Phillip (Melissa) Sellew compares his comments to the interior monologues of other less-than-ideal parabolic figures: the rich man who contemplates building bigger barns (12.17); the dishonest manager who connives to gain economic advantage (16.3); and the judge bested by a demanding widow (18.4). See "Interior Monologue as a Narrative Device in the Parables of Luke," *JBL* 111 (1992): 239–53.

and before you," sounds sufficiently pious to gain the young man a hearing. The line also echoes Pharaoh's comment to Moses and Aaron, "I have sinned against the Lord your God, and against you" (Exod 10.16).

The final line in the speech, about not being worthy to be called son and to be treated like a hired hand, is both clever and self-serving (**vs. 19**). The young man had already noted that the hired hands had more than enough food, so at the very least he is looking for surfeit. The term "son" serves to reinforce the familial relationship even as the words of his speech seem to deny he deserves it. The younger son knows his father, knows his father's generosity, and can presume that all will be well. Comments such as "A typical Jewish father might have considered this expedient until the son's reformation had been confirmed. It would, moreover, allow the youth to make reparations required by repentance,"[28] find no support. Typical Jewish fathers, at least as far as the Gospels are concerned, would give their sons bread rather than stones, eggs rather than scorpions, display such love for their children that they would beseech Jesus to heal them, teach them trades such as fishing, and otherwise love them. Similarly unsupported are claims that readers expect "the younger son to die of starvation rather than accept the shame of returning to his father" and would have "understood severe punishment from the father who suffered such abuse from his sons."[29]

These various comments on Jewish culture, with an angry and punitive God and angry and punitive fathers, are belied by Jewish texts. To cite one example of many, *Peskita Rabbati* 184b–185a recounts the story of a king who "had a son who had gone astray from his father on a journey of a hundred days. His friends said to him, 'Return to your father.' He said, 'I cannot.' Then his father sent to say, 'Return as far as you can, and I will come the rest of the way to you.' So God says, 'Return to me, and I will return to you.'"[30]

The insistence that the father would beat or otherwise deny his son familial love derives not from Jewish sources but, perhaps, from a concern with an erroneous Christian theology. The notion that Jesus reveals a new and different God from the one worshiped by Jews, a God of compassion and love versus a God of anger and wrath, has been promulgated since the time of Marcion. It was an erroneous view then, and it remains erroneous, although very popular, today. The move to turn the father of the two sons into God, already an allegorical imposition on a text, turns pernicious. The

[28]   Talbert, *Luke-Acts*, 150.
[29]   Young, *Parables of Jesus*, 140.
[30]   For other examples of Rabbinic accounts of fathers (usually representing God) seeking lost sons, see Young, *Parables of Jesus*, 148–50.

portrayal of the father's love for his younger son as unexpected rings false in terms of both family values and theological teaching. Ben notes that what is not false is that this parable is about repenting from sin, as the younger son himself says, whereas it is harder to make a case for that being the case in the sheep parable, and even harder in the coin parable. Amy-Jill is not convinced that the young man repented, but as far as the plot of the parable goes, his repentance does not matter. The father loves him regardless. Yes, says Ben, but the father would never have said 'he was dead, and is alive again' had there not been some personal transformation involved. Amy-Jill doubts this too, although she would be delighted to know that the young man has opted for a life of fidelity rather than foolishness (and she would still be worried if he decided to date her daughter).

False as well is the view that Jesus' audience would have expected the young man to die rather than to return. The young man, son of a wealthy man, and having no shame at dispersing funds for his own benefit, is not about to develop a shame complex now. At the very least, he has nothing to lose. Knowing his father, and his father's generosity shown in his dividing his property, he has every hope to gain acceptance and reintegration into the family.

The young man begins his journey to his father, likely rehearsing his speech on the way. But from a distance, his father sees him. The father's first reaction is one of compassion: the same term used for Jesus' seeing the widow of Nain in her son's funeral procession (7.13); the same term used to describe the Samaritan upon seeing the wounded man (10.33). There is nothing unusual about compassion; the father is not overcoming any sort of legal sense that he should make the son grovel. Running to his son, the father embraces him and kisses him (**vs. 20**). Running to more negative images of Jewish culture, commentators immediately find a distinction between what Jews would normally do and what this father does. We read about "the indignity of a respectable man running to meet his son" with the crowd shocked at the absence of the "expected and deserved rejection or rebuke."[31] We hear that such running would be undignified for an "aged Oriental."[32] We even hear that the father ran out in order to

[31]   Lieu, *Gospel According to Luke*, 121, cf. Talbert, *Luke-Acts*, 150; Snodgrass, *Stories with Intent*, 126; Scott, *Hear Then the Parable*, 70, 75; and his *Re-Imagine the World*, 70, 75, 82; Hultgren, *Parables of Jesus*, 78, following Bailey, *Finding the Lost*, 144–45; and Bruce C. Malina and Richard L. Rohrbaugh, *Social Science Commentary on the Synoptic Gospels* (Minneapolis: Fortress Press, 1992), 372; Buttrick, *Speaking Parables*, 203; Blomberg, *Preaching the Parables*, 39; Reid, *Parables for Preachers, Year C*, 61; and many others.

[32]   Luise Schottroff, *The Parables of Jesus* (Minneapolis: Augsburg Fortress, 2006). 142, citing Joachim Jeremias, *The Parables of Jesus*, 2nd ed. (New York: Scribner's, 1972), 130.

prevent the neighbors from stoning the young man for bringing dishonor on the town.[33]

Nothing in the parable suggests lack of dignity; nothing in any sources suggests a deserved rejection. The younger son, a beloved son, has returned home. The father is thrilled. Philo may have the more perceptive reading: "Parents often lavish kindness on wastrels more than on the well behaved" (Prov 2.2–6).[34] The point holds for today as well. Carol Shersten Lahurd asked Arab Christian women: "What would your husband do if his son returned home after wasting all his money?" The women unanimously agreed that the father would lovingly welcome the son, especially if he were a child of his old age.[35]

The young man launches into his rehearsed speech, beginning with the address "Father." His words of sinning and worth repeat, exactly, what he had planned to say (**vs. 21**). The speech gives the impression of being calculated and rehearsed. The father does not care what the son says; his only concern is that his lost son is now found. He calls to his slaves, the mention of which puts a glitch on the notion that this father is an image for God. God does not have "slaves" in the heavenly Kingdom (unless, for some, we are all "slaves of God" or we take the servants to be the prophets, or the Suffering Servant), and God certainly does not have slaves in contradiction to two sons. The focus here is not on the heavenly Kingdom, but on a quite earthly family. This father orders: give my son the best robe; give him jewelry and sandals (**vs. 22**). That is, restore him to his original state as the scion of a very wealthy household.

The welcome continues with the father's order that the grain-fed (i.e., "fatted") calf be slaughtered for the celebration (**vs. 23**). The calf had been better fed than the younger son, not that it does the calf much good. At this point, readers might wonder how the father enjoys the wealth of the estate. Since he had divided his property (or "life") between elder and younger brothers, he is claiming use of the resources that belong to the older brother. No one seems surprised by this usufruct, although the father's generosity may exacerbate the older brother's resentment.

---

[33]   Bailey, *Finding the Lost*, 143; Malina and Rohrbaugh, *Social Science Commentary*, 372. See also Scott, *Re-Imagine the World*, 75.

[34]   Cited by Snodgrass, *Stories with Intent*, 120.

[35]   Carol Shersten LaHurd, "Re-viewing Luke 15 with Arab Christian Women," in Amy-Jill Levine with Marianne Blickenstaff (eds.), *A Feminist Companion to Luke*, FCNTECW 3 (Sheffield: Sheffield Academic, 2002), 246–68 (259). See also her "Rediscovering the Lost Women in Luke 15," *BTB* 24 (1994): 66–76 (67).

The father's explanation, or celebration, of this generosity receives expression in **vs. 24**: his son who was dead now lives; his son who was lost is now found. Of course, they would celebrate. The verse has both Christological and Eucharistic implications in the context of Luke's Gospel, although whether either would be heard by Jesus Jewish audience is less clear. According to Henri Nouwen, "... Jesus himself became the prodigal son for our sake. He left the house of his heavenly Father, came to a foreign country, gave away all that he had, and returned through his cross to his Father's home."[36] The allegory works, but it breaks with both the first two parables of this chapter and Luke's focus on repentance and forgiveness. This allegorical reading, which can extend to see Jesus as the prostitute, the debauched, and whatever negative connotation one wishes to apply to the younger son, eventually derails. The prodigal did not give generously to the destitute; rather, he spent lavishly for his own dissolute desires.

The first part of the parable ends with the prodigal, newly dressed and accessorized, and likely filling his belly with fatted calf. He was dead and is now alive, lost and now found, as far as his father is concerned. The outline established in the first two parables finds its match in the third: the son was lost, the father ran out to greet him and so fulfilled the convention of the search, and the celebration had begun.

The father had two sons. The older brother, in the field, hears music and dancing (**vs. 25**). Unaware that his younger brother had returned, unaware that this father had arranged a celebration, he calls a slave to inquire about what was happening (**vs. 26**). The parable has trapped us. The parable is about a man who had *two* sons. The lost one is not only the prodigal who returned home; the lost one is also the older brother in the field, as we shall see. The father had failed to count.

The older brother should garner our sympathy. The slave informs him that his brother has returned, that his father slaughtered the grain-fed calf, and that the father celebrated because the younger son returned safely (**vs. 27**). But no one informed the older son. We have just read, in the previous chapter, about a host who sent invitations to guests (14.15–16); no such invitation greets the older brother. He becomes angry, as would anyone so egregiously overlooked by a parent. The celebration is ongoing, but the older brother refuses to join (**vs. 28**). The sheep owner had called his friend

---

[36] Henri J. M. Nouwen, *The Return of the Prodigal Son: A Story of Homecoming* (New York: Doubleday, 1994), 50.

and neighbors, as did the woman who lost her coin. No one called the older brother. With only two sons, the father failed to count.

At some later point – five minutes? an hour? – the father realizes that his older son is missing, and he also recognizes that this son is angry. The NRSV's "began to plead with him" misses the nuances of the Greek term *parakaleō*, which means "to comfort"; the term provides the origins of the Johannine "Paraclete," the advocate or comforter that functions as the Holy Spirit. "Plead" suggests begging; "comfort" suggests sympathy and empathy.

Commentators, rather than having sympathy for or empathy with the overlooked brother, condemn him for his response: he is angry when he should have been joyful; he is resentful when he should have been gracious. Jerome sees the brother as "unrepentant Israel," who "is far from the grace of the Holy Spirit, banished from his father's counsel" (*21st Letter*).[37] In her study of exegetical work and sermons by Presbyterian pastors, Marcia Witten observes that "it is the dutiful, religiously obedient, yet joyless, older brother who tends to serve as the emblem of sin."[38] So much for the younger son's dissolute living or the grace of those pastors. Baptists, on the other hand, connected sin with the younger brother.[39] And Ben notes, Methodists (of which he is one) tend to focus on the forgiving or compassionate father.

The son's next lines then bring fuel to the condemnation, and the NRSV does not help the situation. The NRSV's imperious, "Listen!" translates the simple Greek *idou*, usually translated "behold," and better put in modern English is "see" or "look here" rather than "listen." The son wants his father to see, really to see, him rather than, as he had, overlook him.

He then presents his case. First, he notes that "for all these years I have been working like a slave for you, and I have never disobeyed your command" (**vs. 29a**). Commentators, armed with the view of Judaism as a form of works-righteousness, immediately conclude that this elder brother must represent Pharisees, or the Jewish tradition, that serves a presumed God of wrath as a joyless slave. Jesus' Jewish audience would not recognize that point, that God, or that practice. The issue in play is personal feeling, not theological desperation, as the son's pathetic next line

---

37 See Mikeal C. Parsons, "The Prodigal's Elder Brother: The History and Ethics of Reading Luke 15.25–32," *PRSt* 23 (1996): 147–74; Parsons illustrates the ignoring of the older brother in much of Christian art and literature.

38 Marcia G. Witten, "Preaching About Sin in Contemporary Protestantism," *Theology Today*, 50.2 (1993): 243–53 (245).

39 Ibid.

demonstrates: while the prodigal gets ring, robe, sandals, and barbeque, the father never gave the older brother a goat for him to celebrate with his friends (**vs. 29b**).

Nor, however, had the older brother asked. The father had divided his property between his sons, so that the son could have had that dinner any time. His venting is hyperbolic: to see himself as working "like as slave" would have quite a distinct, and bitter, implication for the slave who, we may imagine, is listening to the father and the son.

The elder brother's next line is one of distancing. Referring to the prodigal as "this son of yours" denies the sibling relationship. Mentioning the prodigal's relationship with prostitutes attempts to besmirch his reputation. Observing that the father provided the dinner implicates the father in rewarding the self-absorbed and ignoring the faithful who has worked for him (**vs. 30**). All three statements are honest, but all also tell only half the story.

The first comment, "this son of yours," could indicate children of different mothers, and there is enough of the Joseph story underlying the parable to support the idea.[40] Joseph, the younger, pampered, favorite son of the favored wife, sold into slavery to a foreign country, rewarded by Pharaoh with new garments, finds some resonance with the prodigal, just as the older brother, like Judah, does the necessary work of preserving the family. And it is through Judah's line that the family's leadership is preserved, as this family will be preserved by the older brother, whose share of the estate is still intact and whose work ethic is not in question.

Although the parable leaves vague the content of the younger son's "dissolute living," the older brother indicates the source of the dissolution was prostitutes. The NRSV's "Devoured your property with prostitutes" is in the Greek more vicious: "the one having eaten up your life with whores." The younger brother is not, contrary to some patristic speculation, an image of Jesus, who left the home of the heavenly father, entered a world full of sin in order to reform it, and then returned to his heavenly home, where he receives his divine status. Luke is not channeling the Christ Hymn of Phil 2.6–11, and the son was not teaching prostitutes the Ten Commandments. The older brother seeks to distance the father from the younger son by enhancing his negative reputation. But the father's love does not diminish because of bad behavior.

---

[40] Suggested by Susan Durber, "The Female Reader of the Parables of the Lost," *JSNT* 45 (1992): 59–78 (73), who comments on mother's absence in the parable.

Finally, the pathos-ridden "you gave him a dinner, the special dinner," indicts the father for rewarding that same bad behavior. The elder brother cannot see the father's joy in the younger son's return. He might also be upset that it is his own property that is being used to fete the prodigal, since by dividing his property, the older brother is technically the owner of that calf.

Attentive readers may at this point recollect Luke's story of Mary and Martha (10.38–42). In this story as well, siblings are separated and they require a mediator to repair their relationship. Martha's anxiety over her ministry and her complaint to Jesus are not matters of whining; her service is rather comparable to that of the older brother. Both perceive themselves to be neglected, whether by Jesus, the father, or their siblings. Both need to learn that there is joy in companionship and that sometimes work takes a second seat to celebration. But Martha is not a symbol of Pharisees or Jews, and neither is the older brother, at least decontextualized from Luke's frame.

It is now the father's turn to explain his actions. Beginning by calling the older brother "son" (Greek: *teknon*), the father reaffirms his intimate relation with his son (**vs. 31**). The same term appears elsewhere in Luke's Gospel, with several of the uses forming helpful intertextual resonances to the father's address. In 1.17, Zechariah proclaims that his son John will act, in the role of Elijah, "to turn the hearts of parents to their children" (Greek: *tekna*); the matter for the parable is whether the father, in comforting his son, can create reconciliation. In 2.48, Mary addresses her son, who had been missing in the Temple for three days, "Child (Greek: *teknon*), why have you treated us like this? Look, your father and I have been searching for you in great anxiety." Her anxiety over losing her son echoes in the father's words. In 11.13, Jesus speaks of parents "who know how to give good gifts to your children"; the father had given splendid gifts to the prodigal, and now he realizes that he has not given to the elder the attention that the elder craves.

The father continues by making both a legal and familial observation: "You are always with me, and all that is mine is yours." Commentators who insist that the older brother represents the Jews, or the Pharisees, rarely note that the intimacy between Father and Jews is never broken. The relationship between this earthly father and his overlooked son is just as intimate although, as Ben notes, the older son doesn't think so. It is also a legal relationship: the elder brother does own all that belonged to the father, given the distribution of the property.

But this intimacy extends to the younger son as well. Speaking of "this brother of yours" and so restoring the sibling relationship, the father concludes by stating that celebration is necessary, for the younger son has returned to the family. He too was lost; he too is found (**vs. 32**). Callon observes that the "restoration of the prodigal to his familial unit, especially his father, via reconciliation – for restoration of the family through a father's forgiveness of a wayward son is the typical ending of Greco-Roman comedy."[41] But this is a parable, not a play. Only the reader can determine if the genre is ultimately comedy or tragedy, for whether the older brother will accept these words of reconciliation and invitation remains with the interpreters.

BRIDGING THE HORIZONS

1. On Repenting, Sin, and the Human Condition

That there were ninety-nine who did not need repentance is a verse usually omitted from church preaching, given the view that everyone needs to repent. We might revisit the audiences of this parable: the sinners and tax collectors on the one hand, and the Pharisees and scribes on the other. It is possible the people in the latter category were among the ninety-nine who are righteous. Paul, a Pharisee, describes himself "as to the Law, blameless" (Phil 3.6); the narrator of the Book of Job says the same about his titular hero (Job 1.1, cf. 1.8; 2.3; 8.20; etc.). The Psalms similarly reflect this more positive view of humanity (Psa 18.23, "I was blameless before him and I kept myself from guilt," cf. Psa 19.13; 37.37; 119.1; and elsewhere), as does Daniel (6.22), Sirach (31.8), and the author of 1 Maccabees (4.42). In Luke's Gospel, Elizabeth and Zechariah were "living blamelessly according to all the commandments and regulations of the Lord."

In many Sunday morning church services today, the focus is on sin and repentance, on the brokenness of humanity, and thus on the need for wholeness and reconciliation that the cross provides. Prayers speak of unworthiness, of confession of sin, of the need for forgiveness. On the Sabbath in the synagogue, in contrast, the focus is on praising God. Judaism does not ignore sin; the tradition takes sin very seriously. However, the tradition also celebrates humanity as in the image and likeness of God and so as celebrating both God and creation.

Recognizing this view of the human condition, in need of final redemption in the messianic age and yet presently glorifying God through obedience to the Torah given by divine love, may help Christian readers overcome

---

[41] Callon, "Adulescentes and Meretrices," 285.

the imposition of a negative image of "the Law" and a sense of Jews as burdened by it. To the contrary, there is joy in the Torah, and those who follow it, in their various ways, celebrate.

2. On Counting

We have made the argument that the three parables play on the theme of counting and so remind us that we all count, in both senses of the term. God counts: "even the hairs on your head are all counted," Jesus teaches (12.7), and so God counts us. In turn, we need to count everyone, that is, to make everyone feel counted, to overlook no one, to take no one for granted.

At Riverbend Maximum Security Prison in Nashville, where Amy-Jill has been teaching for close to two decades, during a course on the parables, she made this argument about the importance of counting. One of the insider students looked up and said, quietly, "Ma'am, we're counted six times a day." And so we learn another lesson. We are not to count people as if they are numbers, with cell block identification, or tattoos on their forearms. Rather we are to make clear that they matter, they all matter.

Similarly, before we turn the father and his two sons into allegorical representations, we might count them as individual characters embedded in a family. When we do, we count ourselves as well. We can all step into their roles, and so we can begin to assess our own attitudes and behaviors. Have we made all our children feel loved? Have we so attended to the prodigal child – the drug addict; the one incapable of holding a job or earning a living; the one who seems to suck all the air out of the room – and consequently ignored the child who does what the parents want, who recognizes their needs but whose own needs go unaddressed? Could we be the older brother, and what are our responsibilities to the problematic, or spoiled, or irresponsible sibling?

The parable may be a story about repenting and forgiving, but it is also much more. It asks about family values, the opportunity for the estranged to meet at the family's table, the need to reassess those family members – Cain, Ishmael, Esau, and such we have left with negative characterizations. In the end, given the history of the parable's interpretation, it also asks Christians to reassess their impressions of their brothers and sisters, the Jews.

3. On the Prodigal Influence of the "Prodigal Son"

Some biblical stories have become *too* familiar, and they have gone through a myriad of adaptations and interpretations over the centuries. One such story is the Parable of the Prodigal Son. Recently, Ben, in working through the classic Methodist sermons of his mentor, C. K. Barrett, observed a not very surprising outcome. Of the some five thousand times Barrett preached over seven decades, the sermon he preached most often, some sixty times between 1932 and 2009, was the Parable of the Prodigal Son.[42] If it is true that familiarity breeds contempt, or at least tone-deafness to the meaning of the original passage, then the Parable of the Prodigal Son, like the Parable of the Good Samaritan, has too often been a victim of overreading and misunderstanding, as the preceding exposition makes very clear. And sometimes it is not merely the preaching but even the artistic representation of the story that has led us astray.

Consider, for example, the famous Rembrandt painting of this parable. In the light, and at the center of the painting, is the forgiving father, with his huge hands on the kneeling younger son. In the shadows stands on the right the elder son looking askance at the whole scene, and the mother with a bit more compassionate look on her face. But the elder son and his "lostness" and his father's neglect of him is just as much a part of this story as the more familiar part.[43]

One of the main keys to giving this story a fair hearing in its original settings (in the ministry of Jesus and in the Gospel of Luke) is ongoing contextual study of the parable. What did it mean in its original Jewish setting, and what has it come to mean for Luke and his audience? The value of detailed knowledge of the original contexts is that it makes clear that certain interpretations can be ruled out rather quickly. For example, this parable is not about critiquing the Pharisees, masquerading as the older brother. Nobody in Jesus' context would have understood it that way. This parable deals with family troubles, not ethnic prejudice. Or, an adventure by a Jewish young man in the Diaspora where he squanders his inheritance on "riotous living" should not be turned into a critique of how immoral his apparently gentile hosts and employers must have been.

Ben sees the parable as indeed about repentance, or turning around, as when the younger son "comes to himself," returns home, and admits his sin and errors of judgment. Amy-Jill agrees that this is what Luke thinks, but she is far less certain that this was the message a Jewish audience, not

---

[42]   See B. Witherington, ed. *Preaching Methodist Theology and Biblical Truth: Classic Sermons of C.K. Barrett* (Nashville: United Methodist General Board of Higher Education, 2017); *Luminescence Volume One. The Sermons of C.K. and Fred Barrett*, ed. B. Witherington (Eugene: Cascade, 2017).

[43]   See Parsons, "The Prodigal's Elder Brother."

swayed by what she sees as Lucan glosses to the first two parables, would have heard.

Too often in the history of Christian interpretation these parables have been wrongly used to bolster anti-Jewish polemics. They have also been spiritualized out of all recognition of their original thrusts, which are not simply spiritual in character. There is a social bite and critique to many of Jesus' parables, and this is one of them. The God of the Bible is gracious and forgiving, and so should human parents be as well. There are many possible valid lessons to be learned from this story. The parable has often been abused and misused to bolster bad, and even antibiblical agendas. However, as the old dictum goes, *abusus non tollit usum* – the abuse of something does not rule out its proper use. Interpreters of this story should not go silent just because it has been misused in the past. But necessary are better contextual study of the parable, familiarity with the range of possibly valid readings, and better teaching and preaching based on that study.

Luke 16 On Serving God and Mammon

THE PARABLE OF THE DISHONEST MANAGER
AND THE TRAPPED MASTER

¹ Then Jesus said to the disciples, "There was a rich man who had a manager, and charges were brought to him that this man was squandering his property. ² So he summoned him and said to him, 'What is this that I hear about you? Give me an accounting of your management, because you cannot be my manager any longer.'

³ Then the manager said to himself, 'What will I do, now that my master is taking the position away from me? I am not strong enough to dig, and I am ashamed to beg. ⁴ I have decided what to do so that, when I am dismissed as manager, people may welcome me into their homes.'

⁵ So, summoning his master's debtors one by one, he asked the first, 'How much do you owe my master?' ⁶ He answered, 'A hundred jugs of olive oil.' He said to him, 'Take your bill, sit down quickly, and make it fifty.' ⁷ Then he asked another, 'And how much do you owe?' He replied, 'A hundred containers of wheat.' He said to him, 'Take your bill and make it eighty.'

⁸ And his master commended the dishonest manager because he had acted shrewdly; for the children of this age are more shrewd in dealing with their own generation than are the children of light.

⁹ And I tell you, make friends for yourselves by means of dishonest wealth so that when it is gone, they may welcome you into the eternal homes.

¹⁰ "Whoever is faithful in a very little is faithful also in much; and whoever is dishonest in a very little is dishonest also in much. ¹¹ If then you have not been faithful with the dishonest wealth, who will entrust to you the true riches? ¹² And if you have not been faithful with what belongs to another, who will give you what is your own?

[13] No slave can serve two masters; for a slave will either hate the one and love the other, or be devoted to the one and despise the other. You cannot serve God and wealth."

INVECTIVES AGAINST PHARISEES

[14] The Pharisees, who were lovers of money, heard all this, and they ridiculed him.

[15] So he said to them, "You are those who justify yourselves in the sight of others; but God knows your hearts; for what is prized by human beings is an abomination in the sight of God.

INSTRUCTION ON TORAH

[16] "The law and the prophets were in effect until John came; since then the good news of the kingdom of God is proclaimed, and everyone tries to enter it by force.

[17] But it is easier for heaven and earth to pass away, than for one stroke of a letter in the law to be dropped.

[18] "Anyone who divorces his wife and marries another commits adultery, and whoever marries a woman divorced from her husband commits adultery.

THE PARABLE OF THE RICH MAN, LAZARUS, AND ABRAHAM

[19] "There was a rich man who was dressed in purple and fine linen and who feasted sumptuously every day. [20] And at his gate lay a poor man named Lazarus, covered with sores, [21] who longed to satisfy his hunger with what fell from the rich man's table; even the dogs would come and lick his sores.

[22] The poor man died and was carried away by the angels to be with Abraham. The rich man also died and was buried.

[23] In Hades, where he was being tormented, he looked up and saw Abraham far away with Lazarus by his side. [24] He called out, 'Father Abraham, have mercy on me, and send Lazarus to dip the tip of his finger in water and cool my tongue; for I am in agony in these flames.'

[25] But Abraham said, 'Child, remember that during your lifetime you received your good things, and Lazarus in like manner evil things; but now he is comforted here, and you are in agony. [26] Besides all this, between you and us a great chasm has been fixed, so that those who might want to pass from here to you cannot do so, and no one can cross from there to us.'

²⁷ He said, 'Then, father, I beg you to send him to my father's house – ²⁸ for I have five brothers – that he may warn them, so that they will not also come into this place of torment.'

²⁹ Abraham replied, 'They have Moses and the prophets; they should listen to them.' ³⁰ He said, 'No, father Abraham; but if someone goes to them from the dead, they will repent.' ³¹ He said to him, 'If they do not listen to Moses and the prophets, neither will they be convinced even if someone rises from the dead.'"

Alan Culpepper suggests that Luke 16 is patterned after Deut 23.15–24.4, which combines teachings on slaves, usury, vows, and restrictions on remarriage.[1] If this is the pattern, then the connection to Deuteronomy tips the meaning of the first parable as having to do with foregoing interest (see Deut 23.19–20). However, Deuteronomy 23 includes teachings on treatment of daughters, prostitution, and eating one's neighbor's crops, and Luke's chapter is a conglomeration of parables, wisdom sayings, insults, and eschatological observations. Thus, the connections to Deuteronomy are at best tenuous. Rather than see Luke's organization as following Torah, it is more likely Luke put the chapter together by theme and then catchword: the material all addresses, albeit in various ways, the dangers as well as the possibilities of financial resources.

THE PARABLE OF THE DISHONEST MANAGER AND THE TRAPPED MASTER

The previous chapter, with its three parables of the lost, depicted an audience combining sinners and tax collectors with Pharisees and scribes. In this chapter, Jesus turns to teaching his disciples (**vs. 1**). It is possible to imagine that the disciples included some of those sinners and Pharisees. Luke will confirm in v. 14 that the Pharisees have been listening to this chapter's teaching as well. What they heard, and understood, at least from the first parable in vss. 1–8a, cannot be securely determined. Even Luke the Evangelist, the only biblical author to preserve this parable, struggles with it.

What is traditionally called the "Parable of the Dishonest Steward" or "Dishonest Manager" (today it might be the "Parable of the Dishonest CFO") or some variant on that, begins not with the manager but with "a rich man."

---

[1]   Culpepper, "The Gospel of Luke," 306.

Luke's parables beginning "there was a rich man who …" often do not end well for the rich man: the rich man who seeks to build bigger barns drops dead (12.16); the rich man encountered later in this chapter not only dies, but suffers in hell (16.19). Given Luke's insistence on the responsibilities of the rich toward the poor, we readers enter the parable with a certain wariness about this fellow. Alan Sherouse observes, "By introducing certain men as 'rich,' Luke indicates something about them he does not wish to connote about the Samaritan, the man who throws a banquet, or the father of two sons … Luke provides an acknowledgment that there is a proper use of wealth that is entirely antithetical to the behavior of his own one percent: Give a banquet, not a private feast; live in community, not separation, and promote human flourishing, not personalized profit."[2]

Complicating this question of the reader's sympathy, the manager will refer to the rich man as his "lord" (Greek: *kyrios*; vs. 3): readers might then see the rich man, in this parable, as a representative of the divine. Yet *kyrios* was commonly used to refer to any "master" of a house, and sometimes of the master of slaves. Not all rich people or kings or mighty men, then or now, are gods.

The rich man "has" an estate manager; the Greek term identifying the manager is *oikonomos*, from the Greek words for "house" and "law"; the term could connote either employment or slavery.[3] To this point, the audience of the parable does not know quite where to enter it: should they identify with the "rich man," especially given the Gospel's complaints about the rich? Should they identify with the manager, a subordinate, charged with dishonesty?

Indeed, how should the reader assess the charge? First, we do not know either who presented these charges or if they are true. What is reported is not necessarily what is accurate. Although vs. 8 will refer to the manager as "dishonest," we do not know if he was originally dishonest, or whether his reaction to the charge led him to engage in financial duplicity. One may start in innocence and end in dishonesty, just as the prodigal descended into dissolute living.

The term "squander" (Greek: *diaskorpidzō*) provides a second opportunity for speculation. It appeared in the previous parable, where the prodigal "scattered" his money (15.13). This association between manager and

---

2   Alan Sherouse, "The One Percent and the Gospel of Luke," *Review and Expositor* 110 (Spring 2013): 285–93 (292).
3   See Fabian E. Udoh, "The Tale of the Unrighteous Slave (Luke 16.1–8 [13])," *JBL* 128.2 (2009): 311–35.

prodigal can be a negative reference to the manager (if one sees the younger son as a conniver) or as a positive signal for the manager (if one sees the younger son as a repentant and reconciled sinner). Ben is inclined to read the connection as a positive: the steward is the sympathetic character who displays preparation for the kingdom. Taking losses on earth may at the same time be storing up treasures in heaven. Amy-Jill reads the connection as negative: the manager is a picaresque figure, or a conniving, deceiving cheat who, like the prodigal, gets what he wants through manipulation. The two readings are not mutually exclusive. A dishonest CFO can become the model of kingdom readiness.

Seeing him as Jesus, however, goes too far for both Ben and Amy-Jill, although we appreciate the effort. Dieter H. Reinstorf argues, "the entrusted property in the parable references first and foremost the *Torah* entrusted to God's people and … the manager mirrors the life of Jesus, who was 'accused' by the religious leaders of being unjust. Despite being threatened, he continued unabatedly to scatter God's mercy, epitomised by the reduction of debt and symbolising the dawning of God's Kingdom."[4]

Reading this parable in light of the previous one also offers new perspectives on the rich man. Alone, the rich man is for Luke a negative figure; in connection to the father of the two sons, then he may be a more positive one. For some readers, that connection coupled with his title as "lord" turns him into a representative of God. Ben sees this representation as more possible than Amy-Jill does, although she grants that Luke may well have this connection in mind.

The rich man does not question the charges, but he appears to think through them as he makes three short statements to his manager (**vs. 2**). First, the rich man asks, "What is this that I hear about you?" The question is a good one, as it gives the accused a chance to explain. But the rich man quickly moves to step 2: "Give an account" of your managing. This step also would give the manager an opportunity to detail his own account of what he had been doing. One can picture him, mouth open and ready to talk. But before he can give an explanation, the rich man issues his verdict: "You are no longer able to manage."

Amy-Jill suspects that our rich man is not a wise one, since rumors should be checked. Her inclination is to read the parable as about people

4   Dieter H. Reinstorf, "The Parable of the Shrewd Manager (Lk 16.1–8): A Biography of Jesus and a Lesson on Mercy," *HTS Teologiese Studies/Theological Studies* 69.1 (2013), Art. #1943. http://dx.doi.org/10.4102/hts.v69i1.1943.

involved in illegal business transactions that all work out for the best. Thus, she finds also problematic the rich man's failure to redress the problem. He asks to see the accounting, but the parable provides no indication that the manager shows him the paperwork. Nor does the rich man engage in any actual management of his own property. Rather, he allows the manager, now dismissed from his position, either to continue to mismanage or to make an initially false accusation true. The rich man appears, at least to Amy-Jill, to be a dope but, eventually, a lucky one. Ben notes that what the rich man says to the manager suggests that he has *already* looked into the matter and has concluded foul play.

Ben sees in the demand to "give an account" one of the parable's many eschatological implications, as in accounting for oneself at the final judgment (see Matt 12.36; Heb 13.17; 1 Pet 4.5).[5] Thus for Ben, the parable is primary about preparation for the Kingdom. It may be that Amy-Jill has captured more of what an initial Jewish audience might hear, while Ben is more in tune to Luke's Christian interpretation. Because the subject is a parable, however, we may both be right. Parables are often multivalent.

The manager does not argue his innocence before his employer (or, possibly, his master). Instead, he engages in an interior monologue (**vs. 3**; cf. 12.17–18). Speaking "to oneself" in biblical texts suggests less thoughtful planning than conniving.[6] While we do not know whether to feel sorry for the manager, or to condemn him, the language of the parable suggests more the latter view.

His worry over his "master's" (Greek: *kyrios*, "lord," here without a Christological or theological connotation[7]) stripping him of his job creates yet another problem. That he regards himself as too weak to dig may well be true, but that he is "ashamed to beg" suggests a pride that runs counter to Jesus' insistence on abrogating personal glory and humbling oneself (14.11; 18.14). The connection to the previous Parable of the Prodigal makes this verse an ironic touch. The manager would be shamed by begging; the earlier parable attributes no sense of shame to the prodigal either for his dissolute living or for his working with pigs, unless, Ben adds that the prodigal is not insincere or disingenuous in saying "I have sinned ..."

---

5   C. F. Evans, *Saint Luke*, 595. Snodgrass, *Stories with Intent*, 416, states, "The parable is about the wise use of possessions *in view of the eschatological crisis*" (emphasis in the original).

6   Dinkler, "Thoughts of Many Hearts."

7   On the possibility that any debt owed is a debt to God, see L. John Topel, "On the Injustice of the Unjust Steward: Lk 16:1–13," *CBQ* 37.2 (1975): 216–27 (224).

Whether plaintive or proud, the manager is certainly desperate. He needs to find a means to secure his future, or as he puts it, "so that people will welcome me into their homes" (**vs. 4**). The verse has the implication of a relationship based not only on economic dealings but on personal hospitality. The manager needs not only to secure a means of earning a living, he also needs to secure friends.

His decision is to cook the books, but even this process is odd. First, he summons his master's debtors (**vs. 5a**). Although dismissed from his position, he still has authority to summon others. The rich man has leveled a charge, but he has done nothing to act on it. Just as the manager was reliant on the rich man for his position, so the debtors rely on the manager for theirs. The system of patrons and clients is firmly in place, and each character plays both roles, for the debtors are the patrons to those who buy their goods. Second, the manager asks debtors how much they owe (**vs. 5b**). The question is peculiar and perhaps manipulative. The manager should know the extent of the debt. Perhaps he is giving the debtors an opportunity to lie about their line of credit (in which case, he is Machiavellian) or he really doesn't know (in which case, he is incompetent). Alternatively, Ben suggests that the master would have kept the books and therefore known the details, whereas the manager did the day-to-day managing of the estate. In any case, the manager and the debtors will collude in dishonesty. The parable thus raises the common question: does the end justify the means?

The first debtor responds that he owes a hundred jugs of olive oil, and the manager advises that he quickly rewrite the bill to decrease the amount by half (**vs. 6**). To the second debtor, admitting to owing a hundred containers of wheat, the manager advises that he shift the account to eighty containers (**vs. 7**). This process, the manager thinks, will prompt the debtors to welcome him into their homes. We may wonder at any business executive who would welcome someone known for deliberately, and illegally, decreasing the company's profit. Is the anticipated welcome to be based on gratitude for the decrease of debt, or is it to be based on manager's knowledge of the debtors' willingness to engage in illegal trading? Much like the Samaritan's promise of return to the inn, we do not know if the innkeeper took the comment as a guarantee or as a threat (10.35).

Commentators frequently note that the original debts were substantial: a hundred "baths" of oil came to about 1,000 denarii or just over three years' wages for a day laborer; a hundred containers of wheat would run to 2,500 to 3,000 denarii, or about eight years' wages.[8] The rich man is engaged in business with other rich men. He resembles the father in the previous parable, such that liquidation of half his estate appears to create no financial hardship.

J. D. M. Derrett proposes that the manager removed the interest on the transactions and so reduced the amount owed to the principle.[9] If this reading is correct, then by being "dishonest" the manager has prevented the rich man from sinning, since Exod 22.24; Lev 23.36–37; and Deut 15.7–8 and 23.20–21 all warn against charging interest. Jesus himself commanded his followers, "lend, expecting nothing in return" (6.35). However, the parable says nothing about interest owed. Nor does it suggest either that the rich man is aware of his sin or that he is grateful that its cause is removed. Were the concern interest, the manager could have appealed to biblical precedent, not personal security. That the manager tells the debtors to act "quickly" reinforces the impression of an underhanded transaction, not a religious conversion. The explication that the manager, by reducing the interest charge, is being righteous is more apologia than exegesis. Readings that tidy up a parable to find a moral message may wind up distorting the parable's challenge. Indeed, because the parable explicitly states that the manager is "dishonest," the justifications run contrary to the punch line.

Fitzmyer, also seeking to put the manager in a good light, suggests that the amounts reduced were the commission on the goods; what remained was the principle.[10] However, a 50 percent commission would be astounding, and nothing in the parable suggests that the manager had such a commission.

Adducing writings of several Roman landowners (Pliny the Younger, Cicero, and Columella) along with leasing contracts from early Roman Egypt, John K. Goodrich seeks to "demonstrate that the instability of land tenancy during the early imperial period quite often required wealthy proprietors to reduce debts (rents and arrears) in order to *enable* and *encourage* their repayment, as well as to secure the longevity of their tenants

---

8 See Marshall, *Gospel of Luke,* 619.
9 See J. D. M. Derrett, *Law in the New Testament* (London: Darton, Longman and Todd, 1970), 48–77. For other approaches and critique, see Dennis J. Ireland, *Stewardship and the Kingdom of God. An Historical, Exegetical, and Contextual Study of the Parable of the Unjust Servant in Luke 16.1–3* (Supplements to *Novum Testamentum* 70; Leiden/ New York/Cologne: E. J. Brill, 1992).
10 Fitzmyer, *Luke X–XXIV,* 1097–98.

and their own long-term profitability."[11] In his reading, the manager's prudence made good economic sense. Yet even this logical approach does not resolve the parable's problems: the manager is still "dishonest." Ryan S. Schellenberg adds that the manager's scheme is "precisely what the agricultural manuals of Cato, Varro, and Columella warn against."[12]

Justo González wryly observes, "It is not uncommon to see on our church windows portrayals of a father receiving a son who has strayed or of a sower spreading seed, or of a Samaritan helping the man by the roadside. But I have never seen a window depicting a man with a sly look, saying to another, 'Falsify the bill, make it less than it really is.'"[13] There's a reason, as we've just seen, for this lack.

The parable proper could end at vs. 7, with the manager having reduced the debts and in expectation that the people with whom he connived would befriend him. It is also possible that the parable initially ended with **vs. 8a**, the master's commendation of the "dishonest" (Greek: *adikia*) manager for having acted prudently, or cleverly. In either case, the manager has secured his position. The ending with the master's praise seems to us the more likely original conclusion.

The master commends the dishonest manager because he "had acted shrewdly" (Greek: *phronimōs*), that is, he has acted in a way a good estate manager should: 12.42 reads, "And the Lord said, 'Who then is the faithful and prudent [*phronimōs*] manager whom his master will put in charge of his slaves, to give them their allowance of food at the proper time?'" Yet there is a difference in connotation between being wise[14] and being shrewd, or cunning. The former has no negative hint; the latter continues the sense that the manager has connived. And that is exactly what he did. He engaged in dishonest business practices, and yet everyone benefits from his machinations. We are hard-pressed to determine whether we should celebrate his cleverness, laugh at his solution to his problem, or feel guilty for enjoying an account of cheating.

---

[11]   John K. Goodrich, "Voluntary Debt Remission and the Parable of the Unjust Steward (Luke 16:1–13)," *JBL* 131.3 (2012): 547–66 (553); emphasis in the original.

[12]   Ryan S. Schellenberg, "Which Master? Whose Steward? Metalepsis and Lordship in the Parable of the Prudent Steward (Lk. 16.1–13)," *JSNT* 30.3 (2008): 263–88 (281), citing Rene Baergen, "Servant, Manager or Slave? Reading the Parable of the Rich Man and His Steward (Luke 16. 1–8a) Through the Lens of Ancient Slavery," *SR* 35 (2006): 25–38, 33, 35.12. Goodrich, "Voluntary Debt Remission," responds with an "admittedly …" on 561 n. 56.

[13]   González, *Luke*, 190–91.

[14]   Johnson, *Gospel of Luke*, 244–45.

David Buttrick summarizes the parable by finding that the manager "quits trying to make money and instead makes friends."[15] Yet the goals are not mutually exclusive. The manager will need to make money; his seeking of friends is predicated on his inability to dig and unwillingness to beg, *and* on his need to gain financial security.

Everyone wins. The rich man has been cheated of his profit, and he can do nothing. He does not have the records to determine the original debts – these remain in the debtors' hands – so he cannot go to his debtors to restore the original amount. Were he to charge the manager with additional mismanagement, then he would look like a fool, and people might ridicule his ineptitude for hiring the manager in the first place. More, the rich man now has the reputation of being generous: his debtors may well sing his praises in the streets.[16] As matters stand, his reputation remains intact if not also improved. Further, his investments are safe; he will still receive funding back from his loans.

That he is owed so much suggests that, like the father of the prodigal, even the loss of half of his estate will cause him no harm. Perhaps he will gain the reputation of being generous, as has the father with his two sons. The connection between the Parable of the Prodigal and our parable here in terms of language ("squandered"), plot (leaving and returning, conniving), and placement in Luke's Gospel commends this economic connection. Like the father of the prodigal and the prudent, the rich man finds his economic capital depleted, and his social capital intact given his generosity. Like the prodigal, the manager has, despite his malfeasance, returned to his house.

The debtors have new documents, supplied by the manager, and they can claim that their reduced rate was fairly brokered. They have no guilt feelings about the change in the credit, since the manager authorized the change. Whether they knew of the charges against him or not, they have plausible deniability; for public view, they have simply done what the rich man, out of his generosity, proposed.

The manager is set as well. He will not dig and he is not reduced to begging. The rich man appears to have restored him to employment, or at least would provide a letter of "commendation." The debtors too will have every reason to befriend him: positively, he lessened their debts; negatively, he could accuse them of participating in fraudulent business practices.

---

[15]   Buttrick, *Speaking Parables*, 211.
[16]   David Landry, "Honor Restored: New Light on the Parable of the Prudent Steward (Luke 16:1–8a)," *JBL* 119.2 (2000): 287–309, speaks of how "The steward's actions make his master appear generous, charitable, and law-abiding" (301).

The manager's dishonesty or unrighteousness (*adikia*) will receive yet one more resonance in Luke's interpretation of Parable of the Widow and the Judge (18.2–5), which describes the judge as *adikia* (18.6).[17] The parable proper does not make clear if the judge has done the right thing for the wrong reason, or the wrong thing for the right reason, but all ends up well for him in the end, just as it does for the manager. The connection raises for the reader even more questions: is the manager, like the judge, one who cares neither about God nor his reputation? How we assess both characters will ultimately say something about our own values, and these values are what the parables interrogate.

What will happen the next day, or with the next contract, can no more be determined than what will happen to the father and his two sons in the previous chapter. We are left again with questions: is the manager a rogue to be condemned or admired? Does the parable suggest that cleverness is more powerful than money? Are we shown how one person's actions necessarily impact the lives of others, for good or ill? What might we learn about lenders and debtors, or the way "the rich" live their lives? Can a dishonest person be honest, or likable, or admirable? Once we make our judgments, we too are trapped by the parable.

Luke is trapped as well, since Luke struggles to make sense of this story. The master's commendation of the manager is the end of the parable proper; the comment about the "children of this age" who are "more shrewd in dealing with their own generation than are the children of light" (**vs. 8b**) has nothing directly to do with manager or debts, save for the catchword "shrewd." In Amy-Jill's view, Luke attempts to tame the parable but flounders. Ben proposes that perhaps Luke realizes that Jesus was not commending the actions of the dishonest steward; rather, this is a cautionary tale warning disciples not to be naïve about the ways of the world.

The "children of light" – a phrase known from the Dead Sea Scrolls – appear to be the followers of Jesus, or the disciples who serve as the primary audience of the parable (vs. 1). The children of this age would then be the people of the world or, given the audience, the Pharisees. What Luke intends by juxtaposing this saying to the parable is less clear. One lesson might be that people who profess faith need to move from belief to action, and to determine the best course of action. Another lesson concerns the importance of shrewd thinking rather than brawn, or polemic, or cajoling. The manager can take his place alongside other biblical shrewd thinkers,

---

[17]   Goodrich, "Voluntary Debt Remission," 563, draws this connection.

or "trickster figures," from Abraham to Jacob to Esther and Ruth. Each achieves personal goals by tricking or at least manipulating others.

With **vs. 9** Luke offers another tangentially connected saying. The manager had sought to be taken into homes and thus to have friends; now Jesus tells his disciples to "make friends for yourself by means of dishonest wealth," so that when the money runs out, an unidentified "they" will welcome them "into the eternal homes" (literally, "eternal tents," an oxymoron, given that tents are portable). The expression "dishonest wealth" is literally "unrighteous mammon."[18] The term *mamon* (Hebrew; Aramaic *mamona*, cf. 1 QS 6.2; CD 14.20; *Pirke Avot* 2.12; *Targum Onqelos* on Gen 37.26 and on Exod 18.21) comes from a Hebrew root meaning "surety" or "trust" (the word "amen" comes from the same root); it came to mean "wealth" or "riches." We know what the verse says; determining what it means requires effort.

Our first problem is whether being "unrighteous" or "dishonest" is a natural trait of money (i.e., all money is dishonest; all mammon is unrighteous), or whether there is such a thing as "righteous mammon" or "honest wealth." It could be argued that Jesus did not think money was inherently evil; he does not tell everyone to sell all they have and give to the poor. Money can be used for building hospitals, stocking food pantries, or providing funding for education. As Johnson states, "although Luke consistently talks about possessions, he does not talk about possessions consistently."[19] On the other hand, "unrighteous mammon" does suggest an alluring quality to money that prompts people to act in unrighteous ways. Therefore, Jesus exhorts, "Sell your possessions, and give alms. Make purses for yourselves that do not wear out, an unfailing treasure in heaven, where no thief comes near and no moth destroys" (12.33). His most intimate followers are those who do precisely that.

Concerning the unknown "they" who welcome those whose dishonest wealth has run out, this welcoming committee could be comprised of angels, or of community members who have already died. The verse can anticipate the following Parable of the Rich Man, Lazarus, and Abraham. The person on earth who gives away all, and thus who has no mammon, is guaranteed a heavenly reward. Compromising this view, however, is that Lazarus did not, as far as we know, give his possessions to the poor.

---

[18]   Culy et al., *Luke*, 523, suggest "unrighteous mammon" refers to mammon associated with an unrighteous world rather than to "ill-gotten gains."

[19]   Luke Timothy Johnson, *Literary Function of Possessions in Luke-Acts* (SBLDS 39; Missoula: Scholars Press, 1977), 130.

Luke enhances the soteriological reading of the parable in the next three verses, which couple the themes of fidelity and true wealth. Jesus begins with the wisdom saying about proportional fidelity: the one faithful with little is faithful with much, and so too with dishonesty (**vs. 10**). Character traits remain consistent: the one willing to commit a minor sin (stealing a pencil) would be more willing to commit a major one (stealing a car).

The next two sayings are both rhetorical questions, although neither has a clear response. First, Jesus asks: "If you have not been faithful with dishonest mammon, who will entrust to you the true riches?" (**vs. 11**). The "true riches" probably refers to the heavenly treasure boxes, in contrast to earthly money. The implied answer is "no one." He continues: "If you have not been faithful with what belongs to another, who will give you what is your own?" (**vs. 12**). This verse suggests that the litmus test of trustworthiness is what one does with another's resources. Again, the implied answer is, "no one." What is "your own," another ambiguous phrase, opens to several interpretations. It may reflect the common Jewish view that all creation belongs to God, and that we are stewards. Thus, the verse has a theological valence. Or it may speak to economic situations: in instances of lending, or borrowing, one's own resources are tied up with the resources of another. If one misuses another's stock, one will not recoup either the initial investment or the profit from it. Fidelity on earth with money, despite its allure to greed, will lead to one's own heavenly treasure being filled. Jesus' sayings can have both a theological and a practical payout; the interpretations are not mutually exclusive but mutually informative.

Connecting these several sayings to the parable remains problematic: we do not know if they were originally spoken by Jesus, or attached to the parable by him, or if they are Luke's attempt to tame the Parable of the Dishonest Manager. Ben opts for the first or second approach; Amy-Jill finds the third compelling, although she grants that the sayings could be authentic.

Without stopping to see if the disciples are grasping any of these teachings, Jesus continues with yet another saying that fits uneasily in its present context. In **vs. 13**, we find the aphorism (cf. Matt 6.24; *Thomas* 47; *2 Clem.* 6.1) about the ability to serve both God and mammon. Jesus uses the imagery of slavery: one is either a slave to money and therefore will hate God, or one is a slave to God and therefore will hate money. The saying locates money, and the power it brings, as a potential master.[20] It also seems to be "built upon a background assumption that fully adequate service requires an exclusive kind of love and attachment to the master (cf. Exod

---

[20]   Nolland, *Luke 9.21–18.34*, 807.

21.5)."[21] Josephus warned about being "enslaved to lucre" (*Ant.* 4.238), and 1 Tim 6.10 famously notes that "love of money is a root of all evil." Luke's audience may have also known the saying of Demophilus: "It is impossible for the same person to be a lover of money and a lover of god."[22]

INVECTIVES AGAINST PHARISEES

Luke uses the reference to the impossibility of serving God and wealth (mammon) to introduce the Pharisees in **vs. 14** as "lovers of money"; the juxtaposition indicates that because they love money, they cannot love and so cannot serve God. Luke's description is belied by Josephus, who records that the Pharisees were known for simple living. Pharisees did not make money on the basis of their religious fidelity; they were generally from the working class and not among the elite in Jerusalem; the elite were affiliated with the High Priest and the Roman government. For Amy-Jill, Luke's comment reflects post-70 polemic, cast in Hellenistic/Roman terms; "love of money" is one of the standard critiques of rival teachers, and it shows up in Christian and Roman sources.[23] For Ben, the statement is an accurate address to "some" but not all Pharisees. In his view, these particular Pharisees thought that wealth was a reward, or a blessing, given in response to their righteous behavior. Furthermore, he observes that wisdom literature tends to deal in generalizations that the audience in the know realized could not be applied to every last member of a group. Much depends on what Luke assumes his audience knows about this kind of literature.

We take the time to address the connection between Pharisees and money because the image of Jews as "money-lovers" remains a major antisemitic trope. The still-read and still-praised biblical scholar Adolf Schlatter expressed the point baldy: "The answer to the question, what caused the Jewish opposition to Jesus, this gospel gives with fresh earnestness: the enmity which separated and separates the Jews from Jesus is Mammon, trade, the lust for possessions and desire for enjoyment kindled through Greek culture."[24] Commenting on this quote, Joseph Tyson concludes, "despite Schlatter's words to the contrary, for him Judaism and materialism are the same thing. The distinction between Mammon and Judaism is

---

21   Ibid.
22   See ibid., 807–8.
23   Cf. 1 Tim 6.10; 2 Tim 3.2; Epictetus *Diss,* 1.9.19–20; Lucian, *Timon,* 56; Juvenal, *Sat.* 14.173–78.
24   Adolf Schlatter, *Das Evangelium des Lukas. Aus seinen Quellen erklärt* (Stuttgart: Calwer, 1960), 149, cited in Tyson, *Luke, Judaism, and the Scholars,* 62.

blurred because, for Schlatter, there really is no distinction."[25] For Christian readers today, the correction to Schlatter's libel must be in place, or the Gospel is not defined, but deformed. For Jesus, and for Luke, avarice and pride are both serious sins. In Jewish sources and pagan ones as well, the same points are consistently sounded. Typical comments include, "In the common view, to possess such wealth [as the rich man in the parable] was an indication of blessing,"[26] and, "At the time of Christ, impoverished beggars were regarded as sinners being punished for their sins."[27] No primary sources are cited; appeals tend to move to select passages in Deuteronomy or Proverbs, and the numerous biblical and postbiblical counterindicators are ignored. Today, the trope of "Jews think that God only loves the rich" are repurposed, so that we read that the ancient "Jewish expectation" is found in today's "Prosperity Gospel."[28] Again, using a reconstruction of Judaism to condemn contemporary Christian theologies is not helpful.

Continuing the anti-Pharisaic polemic, Jesus condemns Pharisees who seek public approval: they "justify" or "make themselves appear right" before others rather than seek divine approval (**vs. 15**). With another hyperbolic comparison, he concludes the invective by insisting that what humans prize – whether the immediate antecedent of public recognition or the general topic of money – is to God an abomination. That final term is a strong one: "abomination" (Greek: *bdelygma*) appears in the New Testament elsewhere only in relation to the sacrilege set up in the Temple (Matt 24.15// Mark 13.14) and in relation to the Whore of Babylon (Rev 17.4, 5; cf. Rev 21.27). The connections could tilt the connotation of the abomination to one of political power: here we might consider Antiochus IV Epiphanes, who set up that original abomination and so attempted to demonstrate his mastery and promote his gods, and also Rome, which insisted on its mastery and its gods.

INSTRUCTIONS ON TORAH

According to Matt 5.17, Jesus did not come to abolish the Law and the Prophets; therefore, when Jesus states in the First Gospel that "all the Prophets

[25] Tyson, *Luke, Judaism and the Scholars*, 65.
[26] Darrell L. Bock, "The Parable of the Rich Man and Lazarus and the Ethics of Jesus," *Southwestern Journal of Theology* 40.1 (1997): 63–72 (66), cf. Snodgrass, *Stories with Intent*, 425.
[27] Buttrick, *Speaking Parables*, 217.
[28] Blomberg, *Preaching the Parables*, 48.

and the Law prophesied until John came" (11.13), readers may conclude that for Matthew the Torah is still in effect. Ben notes that Matthew's saying could be taken to mean that the Law and the Prophets were now complete, since the implication is that the Prophets and the Law no longer "prophesy" after John, but Amy-Jill find this reading to be a stretch. She regards Matthew as continuing to uphold both Torah and the Prophets (this debate could be continued, but not in this volume). Matthew's saying, at least as far as Amy-Jill understands the First Gospel, offers continuity; Luke's version suggests discontinuity. Ben points out that this ignores the normal meaning of the word heōs in Matt 11.13 – it means "until" or "as far as" and indicates a limit, and this is also likely implied by the word "fulfill." When a task is fulfilled, it is complete, finished. In any case, Luke's saying, that the "Law and the Prophets were in effect until John came" (**v. 16a**), can be taken as indicating a break: the term "until" (Greek: *mechri*) in Luke's corpus (see Acts 10.30, 20.7) denotes a delimitation of a period of time. In Luke's soteriology, John is a transitional figure who brings the old age of the Law and the Prophets (see 24.44) to a close and who introduces the Kingdom, the "world to come" (Hebrew: *olam ha-ba*) or the messianic age. For Luke's gentile readers, the time of the Torah and so of Israel's status as the community to bear witness to God has ended; the (primarily gentile) Church, marked not by *halakhic* obedience but by loyalty to Jesus, will be the new witnesses.

The second half of **vs. 16**, "and everyone tries to enter it by force," remains much debated. The problems with the verse began in the early transmission of the Gospel, for the phrase is missing in several manuscripts.[29] Text-critically, both scribal omission and scribal addition can be argued. Substantively, several interpretations are plausible. One commentator suggests that the verse indicates people being persuaded, by forceful preaching, to enter the Kingdom.[30] In 14.23, the master orders his slaves to "compel" people to enter the banquet, which commends that option. Yet the image thus conveyed does not fully fit the point. One should not have to be *forced* into the Kingdom.

The verse could, alternatively, indicate that people are claiming their salvation by insisting on their own righteousness. That image would fit the "goats" of Matt 25 and the ones who knock at the door saying, "Lord, open to us," because "we ate and drank with you" (13.25–26). They can bang at the door all they want, but it will not open.

---

[29]   See for details and discussion see Ilaria L. E. Ramelli, "Luke 16:16: The Good News of God's Kingdom Is Proclaimed and Everyone Is Forced into It," *JBL* 127.4 (2008): 737–59.

[30]   Tannehill, *Luke*, 250.

Conversely, the Kingdom may be suffering violence. Much depends on how we understand the verb *biadzō*. In an active sense, it means "to force" or "to use violence." But in the middle voice it indicates that the subject is facing violence; whereas both active and middle readings are possible, the context commends the middle voice. The Kingdom has faced violent reaction, from the beheading of John the Baptizer to the rejection in Nazareth and the surrounding Galilean towns, to the scoffing of the Pharisees.[31] Ben is more affirmative of this reading than is Amy-Jill, who is concerned that the grammar of the verse, with its final phrase "into it," does not bear this weight of facing violence.

The next verse returns the subject to the Law and the Prophets. Jesus affirms that no single stroke of a letter of Torah will be dropped (**vs. 17**), for "Luke is anxious to avoid leaving the impression that the Law is either irrelevant or, worse yet, broken."[32] The phrase could have an anti-Marcionite valence: Luke needs the Scriptures of Israel to be retained as witness to Jesus; given Luke's knowledge of Paul, this verse can also function to correct the false view of the apostle that he declared these earlier Scriptures defunct. Even though the era of the Law and Prophets, and so the era of Israel as opposed to that of the (gentile) Church, is passing away for Luke, ethics are not dismissed. This new eschatological era is a time of intensified ethical demands. Whether he is talking about money or marriage, Jesus operates from an eschatological viewpoint.

On the subject of marriage, Jesus is stringent: to remarry after divorce, for either a man or a woman, is tantamount to adultery (**vs. 18**). His approach to divorce is neither pastoral not sociological, but theological. This teaching is more limited than what the Torah allows or what most Jews at the time practiced. Deuteronomy permits divorce, and numerous contemporaneous Jewish texts agreed. Their question was not "could one divorce?" but "under what circumstances is divorce permissible?" Some rabbis argued for extreme permissiveness, here not to encourage divorce but to speak to its possibility. Others argued that only adultery (which requires two witnesses) was grounds for separation. Since Jewish women had marriage contracts (Hebrew: *ketubot*), they were financially protected in case of divorce.[33]

---

[31]   See discussion in Witherington, *Matthew*, 233–34. Ramelli, "Luke 16.16," 746, observes, "In the whole of the Bible, *biazomai* has only a passive or an intensive meaning, often with the accusative, but it never bears the sense of 'to go by force.'"

[32]   C. A. Evans, *Luke*, 244.

[33]   See Ilan, "Gender."

Culpepper suggests that Jesus is prohibiting a man from divorcing his wife *in order to marry another woman*. In other words, Jesus seeks to forestall using divorce as a way for a man to get out of a relationship and marry someone else.[34] The point would hold for a gentile audience, but not a Jewish one in Galilee or Judea. In the first century, Jews practiced polygamy, as examples ranging from the multiply married King Herod the Great to Babatha, the co-wife whose personal papyri from the time of the Bar Kochba revolt indicate. In such Jewish contexts, to marry another would not require a man to divorce his wife. Ben sees both these examples as reflecting the social elite, the wealthy. The evidence that ordinary Jews did, or could afford to, practice polygamy seems to be lacking. Amy-Jill questions whether Babatha was among the "social elite," but she acknowledges that Babatha did have access to her own funds.

In either case, Jesus forbids remarriage after divorce. He does not, at least in this context, forbid divorce itself; Luke's focus is on remarriage. Thus, Luke's discussion conforms to Roman values, particular of the *univera*, the wife who married only once. It also conforms to the instructions in 1 Timothy that the bishop be "husband of one wife" (1 Tim 3.2), with "one wife" understood not as the Church (so Christian groups that have celibate clerics) and not as "only one wife" (so Christian groups that permit polygamy), but one wife meaning precisely that, with no remarriage after either divorce or the wife's death.

This teaching about remarriage after divorce is consistent with Jesus' commendation of husbands who leave their wives for the sake of the Kingdom (18.29). His focus is not on continuing the household (Greek: *oikos*) but in disrupting it to create new kinship groups maintained through loyalty to him. In this new group, divorce is not permitted, and marriage is not enjoined.

THE PARABLE OF THE RICH MAN, LAZARUS, AND ABRAHAM

Luke 16 ends with the well-known Parable of the Rich Man and Lazarus. We add "Abraham" to the title, since he has a more active role than does Lazarus and since his contribution points to both the parable's pathos and its puzzles.[35]

---

34   Culpepper, "The Gospel of Luke," 314.
35   For additional discussion, see Levine, *Short Stories*, 247–73.

Reading this parable in its immediate literary context provides two major interpretive options. First is Luke's notice that the Pharisees are "lovers of money" (16.14); for Luke's readers, therefore, the rich man is analogous to the Pharisees. His fate will be their fate. Ben suggests that "some" Pharisees would have fit this description; Amy-Jill finds this to be a likely but unhelpful description. The point that "some people in every group" do not display the group's best ideals is a truism; problems enter when only one group, or some from that group, receive the negative designation. The modern equivalent would be saying that the fellow who announces, "Mexicans are lazy," or, "Black people are stupid," or, "Japanese are treacherous," is not fully in error, since "some" members of those groups do fit the description. In today's ears, we can hear how pernicious such comments are. The idea that the Pharisees were lovers of money who feasted exorbitantly is itself belied even by Luke, who describes a Pharisee who fasts twice a week and who tithes (18.12). Again, Ben notes, this sort of critique of Luke is not quite fair, because this sort of wisdom literature often engages in hyperbole. He agrees that a later person not familiar with such conventions could mistakenly think Luke or Jesus is presenting an accurate picture of a whole group of people, or could mistakenly think that Luke is caricaturing a whole group of people. Furthermore, there are critiques in the NT of gentiles being lovers of money as well, which would only apply to some members of the group (see 1 Tim 6.10).

It is more productive to take a second literary approach and see this parable in light of the two previous parables: the Prodigal and the Prudent, and the Dishonest Manager. The combination of all three parables yields several themes that might not have surfaced clearly had we looked at each parable individually. First, for all three, money is a problem. In the first parable, the younger son squanders his funds and so learns the difficulties of poverty as well as the benefits of benefactors; the older son has not learned to use what he has; the father learns that money does not buy love. The dishonest manager, like the younger son, finds himself in financial peril and makes moves to secure his future – the contrast is with Lazarus, who although placed at the rich man's gates, cannot find security. Lazarus longed to eat (**vs. 21**, Greek: *epithymōn chortasthēnai*), just as did the prodigal (15.16). Lazarus will find himself in the bosom of Abraham, which is the setting of the heavenly banquet, just as the prodigal feasts on fatted calf.

The rich man in our parable is in the same structural position as the father in the first parable and the master in the second. The father is generous, and, in his generosity, he regains one son and perhaps a second. The master in the second parable is tricked into a situation where he is perceived to be generous, and in the end, he likely benefits from this reputation. In the third parable, the rich man refuses to give up his funds, whether through compassion or coercion. Keeping his money, he is damned.

Although the parable gives a short but clear description of the afterlife, most commentators insist that it is not a literal description of heaven and hell; rather, it offers a metaphorical conceit.[36] We see no reason not to take the details literally. To regard Lazarus's rest and the rich man's suffering as metaphoric would deprive the parable of its punch. Further, the details fit contemporary Jewish eschatological descriptions. We wonder if commentators hesitate to take the details literally not because they resist the ideas of heaven or hell, but because the parable suggests both that one can be "saved" (i.e., resting in the bosom of Abraham) apart from the cross and that salvation depends, in part, on works. The rich man laid up treasures on earth and not in heaven; his heavenly account was depleted, and so he landed in hell. The parable makes no mention of Lazarus's piety; given his circumstances, such mention may be irrelevant. The parable reveals that one who suffers in this life will receive whatever the opposite of suffering is in the next. Or conversely, Ben suggests that the piety of the poor person is implied for Luke's Christian audience by his being said to go to heaven, to "the bosom of Abraham."

We first meet a rich man – the designation already establishes him as a negative figure – dressed in the royal purple and expensive linen, who feasts daily (**vs. 19**). His conspicuous consumption contrasts with Luke's emphasis on simplicity and poverty. In 7.25, Jesus contrasts John the Baptizer positively against those who dress "in soft robes ... put on fine clothing and live in luxury." The rich man also contravenes Jesus' advice that one dine with those who are unable to provide reciprocation in kind (14.12–13).

Finally, the rich man's feasting (Greek *euphrainō*, literally, "rejoicing") stands in contrast to Deut 16.11 (LXX), where Moses instructs Israel on the celebration of the pilgrimage festival of *Shavuot* (Greek: *Pentecost*, the "Festival of Weeks"), "Rejoice (*euphrainō*; Hebrew *simcha*) before the LORD your God – you and your sons and your daughters, your male and female slaves, the Levites resident in your towns, as well as the strangers, the orphans, and the widows who are among you ..." The rich man is feasting, but not with the advised table companions. This intertextual connection to Deuteronomy along with the countless other Scriptural admonitions to care

---

[36]   See Bock, *Luke 9.51–24.53*, 1362–64.

for the poor belies Herzog's conclusion that "the Torah and the Prophets are the centerpieces of the rich man's religion. He was Torah-obedient and, whether a Pharisee or a Sadducee, lived accordingly."[37] The rich man never cites his obedience to Torah, so to conclude that he found justification for his lack of action in Scripture does not follow from the text, or from the Torah. Claims that the parable is a critique of Pharisaic views that taught that the rich are good and therefore favored and the poor and sick are sinful and therefore punished both lack supporting sources and mischaracterize the Jewish tradition (see comments on 11.21).

The rich man's contrast with Lazarus (**vs. 20**) is dramatic: the poor man is not covered in purple and linen, but in sores. His placement at the rich man's gate hints that friends placed him there, either because they thought the rich man would be generous, or because they were attempting to shame him into generosity. The ploy fails. Lazarus longed for the scraps from the rich man's feast, but he received nothing. The contrast between the lives of the two men recollects the beatitudes and woes of the Sermon on the Plain: poor and hungry Lazarus will find his place and be filled; the sated rich man has had his consolation; his time to weep has arrived (6.20–25). The verse also hints at the response of the Canaanite woman to Jesus' initial failure to exorcise her daughter from the demons: "Even the dogs eat the crumbs that fall from their masters' table" (Matt 15.27; cf. Mark 7.28; Luke lacks this story).

Lazarus's only companions are dogs, whose licking might have provided him both medicinal benefits and emotional comfort (**vs. 21**). The standard move then to see the dogs as adding a note of "uncleanness" or "impurity" to the parable is unnecessary and erroneous.[38] Lazarus's problem isn't one of ritual purity; it is one of desperation, starvation, and illness. Luke's two verses play on the motifs of food and taste: the filling banquets versus the yearning for crumbs; the dogs who lick contrast the state of rich man, consigned to hell, who seeks cool water for his tongue. Lazarus will recline again, resting on the breast of Abraham and so suggesting dining in symposium setting.

P75, the oldest extant manuscript that contains this parable, names the rich man Neues. The name is otherwise unknown; Jerome's Vulgate calls him Dives, a Latin adjective meaning "rich." Why the rich man is left nameless but

---

[37] William R. Herzog II, *Parables as Subversive Speech: Jesus as Pedagogue of the Oppressed* (Louisville: Westminster John Knox, 1994), 124 cf. 128.

[38] E.g., Bock, "Parable of the Rich Man and Lazarus," 66; and many others.

Lazarus – the only figure in a parable to be named – is called by name remains a debated issue. Amy-Jill finds it plausible that the parable was influenced by, and possibly influenced, John's account of the raising of Lazarus (John 11): both our parable and John 11 describe a man named Lazarus who has died, and whose resurrection or at least discussion thereof prompts a response to whether people will change their lives. For Ben, the connection of the parable to John 11 is incidental: Lazarus (a variant of "Eliezer") was a common name, and the Lazarus of the parable does not return from the dead.[39] Ben also notes that the Johannine Lazarus is not a poor man, whereas the Lazarus of the parable is. Whether John adapted the story of the raising of Lazarus from the parable, the parable developed in light of John's account of Jesus' calling a man from his tomb, or the two stories became mutually informative during the process of oral transmission cannot be determined.

Lazarus dies, and nothing is said about his burial. He finds himself transported by angels to the "bosom of Abraham" (**vs. 22a**), a place of enormous honor (see *b. Kidd.* 72a–b).[40] The rich man's burial is mentioned, laconically (**vs. 22b**), and then the narrative turns to the rich man's post-mortem suffering. He is in "Hades" (**vs. 23**) and tormented by flames and thirst. The Greek term for "tormented," *basanos*, initially referred to the testing of coins by rubbing or scratching to determine their metal content. It came to refer to torture designed to force the truth from the victim.

Commentators continue to refer to the damned fellow as "the rich man," as shall we, although at this point in the narrative, he is anything but. The name sticks, and with it the connection of "riches" to "damnation." To die a "rich man" is not, for this Gospel, an enviable fate. One could claim that the man's problem is not his wealth but that he failed to help Lazarus.[41] Yet given Luke's thoroughgoing critique of money, the idea that being rich in and of itself poses a problem. If we look forward to the time when the hungry are filled with good things and the rich are sent away empty (1.53), then we might be more hesitant in suggesting that the critique is only failure to help. Citing Greco-Roman literature on indulgence, Ronald Hock offers the better conclusion, the rich man "deserved [his fate], not merely because of

---

[39]   Arguing for the authenticity of the last verse and the lack of connection with the John 11 is Bock, *Luke 9.51–24.53*, 1362.

[40]   Fitzmyer, *Luke X–XXIV*, 1132, for other references. This parable provides the earliest example of this phrase.

[41]   See Tannehill, *Luke*, 252. On the poor and rich in Luke's (and Theophilus's) community, see Philip F. Esler, *Community and Gospel in Luke-Acts: The Social and Political Motivations of Lukan Theology* (Cambridge: Cambridge University Press, 1987).

what he failed to do, that is, feed Lazarus, but because of what he habitually did, that is, live hedonistically and immorally."[42]

Our rich man looks up and sees Abraham together with Lazarus.[43] He calls out to "Father Abraham" and then issues two imperatives: have mercy and send Lazarus (**vs. 24**). The verse offers four insights into the rich man's character. First, he knows Lazarus's name. The suffering man at his gate was not an anonymous stranger. The rich man has no plausible deniability. Second, he is still asking for privilege. Despite his being consigned to the fires of hell, it has not occurred to him that Lazarus is not his servant. Lazarus, whom the rich man never directly addresses, remains to him an object, not a person. Third, the rich man addresses Abraham as "father" and so evokes the idea of *Zechut Avot*, the "merits of the fathers" (see comments on 3.8). The fidelity of Abraham is part of the heavenly treasury into which God would reach in order to grant forgiveness to the repentant. John the Baptizer had already warned against claiming privileges based on Abrahamic descent; the rich man missed the message.

Moreover, the rich man is too late with his appeal. Traditionally, Jews invoke the merits of the fathers when they are atoning, which means when they have repented. To attempt to gain access to this treasury postmortem is to have missed the deadline. The rich man failed to act compassionately on earth, and therefore Abraham can do nothing to help him in the afterlife. "Being a child of Abraham, therefore, is no guarantee that one will dwell with Abraham in paradise."[44] Nor is being a follower of Jesus, for those who call "Lord Lord" but do not repent and engage in righteous action.

Fourth, although he claims to be in "agony," the rich man retains a remarkably eloquent and consistent appeal. He is not screaming in torment. His hyperbole resembles that of the older son who speaks of "working like a slave" (15.29) for his father. Had the parable portrayed the rich man's agony with the pathos it granted to Lazarus's suffering, readers may well have more sympathy for him.

Abraham acknowledges the rich man's relationship by calling him "child" (**vs. 25**), the same word, *teknon*, used by the father in 15.31 to address his elder son. This intertextual connection returns us to that earlier parable, now with the question of whether the younger son will learn to care for the poor rather than continue to squander money on himself. Whereas the father in

42 Ronald F. Hock, "Lazarus and Micyllus: Greco-Roman Backgrounds to Luke 16:19–31," *JBL* 106.3 (1987): 447–63 (462).
43 The notion that the saved and damned can see each other appears also in *4 Ezra* 7.36.
44 Culpepper, "The Gospel of Luke," 317.

the first parable can still help both his children, and whereas it is not too late for him to find his family together at the table, Father Abraham cannot help the rich man or welcome him into his bosom. Abraham tells the rich man that he had received good things during his earthly life, whereas Lazarus had not. Their situations are now reversed, a reversal Mary celebrated in her Magnificat (1.52–53). There is no shuttle service from Hades to heaven; a great "chasm" (that is the Greek word) yawns between them (**vs. 26**).

His situation sealed, the rich man then lobbies Abraham again with the address "father…" (**vs. 27**) and so increasingly sounds like the prodigal, who repeats the address and solidifies his filial status even while his words of (seeming) repentance may suggest the relationship is broken (15.18–19). This time, the rich man asks (the NRSV "beg" overreads the Greek; the rich man, still secure of his position, does not "beg") Abraham to send Lazarus to "the house of my father" so that he may warn his brothers lest they suffer a similar fate (**vs. 28**). Abraham refuses this request as well; since the brothers already have "Moses" (i.e., Torah) and the Prophets (**vs. 29**), which consistently mandate care for the poor, the widow, the orphan, and the stranger, they need no other instruction.

Undeterred, the rich man makes one last plea: although his brothers have not listened to Torah or the Prophets, they might repent were someone to return from the dead to provide the impetus (**vs. 30**). Christological readings that see Jesus' resurrection as the prompt to repentance are not inappropriate, but neither are they necessary for the parable to strike at the hearts of listeners. Abraham responds that if the Scriptures were insufficient to persuade the brothers, a supernatural announcement will make no difference (**vs. 31**). Canonical readers will be reminded of John 11, where the raising of Lazarus does not convince the High Priest and his associates of Jesus' authority.

The parable teaches, as did other Jewish accounts did, that life on earth determines postmortem fate. It also suggests that at least for Luke if not also for Jesus, there is no waiting period between death and judgment: Jesus tells the "good thief" also dying on a cross, "Today you will be with me in paradise" (23.43).

BRIDGING THE HORIZONS

1. Capital Gains

A biblical theology of property begins with the recognition that the earth belongs to God (Gen 1; Psa 8) and that humanity is in the role of steward.

A CLOSER LOOK: EARLY JEWISH PERSPECTIVES ON HEAVEN
AND HELL

The Scriptures of Israel have little to say about life after death. Several
texts mention "Sheol," a shadowy place where the dead exist, and most
of the references speak of God rescuing people from the pit of Sheol.
Under Persian rule (538–333) and Greek and subsequently Roman cultural influence, Jewish views of the afterlife developed.

Apocalyptic literature including visionary tours of hell/Hades/
Gehenna began to be composed in the late Persian and early Greek
periods.[45] According to some texts, the righteous and unrighteous
would not have their fate resolved until after the last resurrection and
the final judgment: *1 Enoch* 22 characterizes Hades as a place where one
awaited final judgments, and like heaven it is seen to have several layers
or regions. Other texts, such as the *Apocalypse of Elijah*, taught that
judgment happened at death.

Jewish tradition dating at least to the first century CE (cf. Pseudo-
Philo's *Liber Antiquitatum Biblicarum* 23.6–7; *2 Baruch* 4.4; *4 Ezra* 3.14,
perhaps the *Apocalypse of Abraham*) interpreted Abraham's vision in
Gen 15 as a revelation of the future. The smoking fire pot of Gen 15.17 was
understood to be Gehenna. According to Pseudo-Philo, the torch that
passed between the pieces of Abraham's sacrificial offering was Paradise.
Targum Neofiti proposes that Abraham sees seats and thrones erected,
and immediately thereafter he sees the wicked cast into Gehenna.

By the first century as well, most Jews, as far as we can tell from literary sources, accepted the belief in resurrection. That is why the Gospels
identify the Sadducees as "not believing in the resurrection of the dead"
(Matt 22.23//Mark 12.18//Luke 20.27; Acts 23.8); they are the outliers, or
as we are wont to say, "the Sadducees did not believe in resurrection of
the dead, and that is what made them sad-you-see."

Stories of postmortem judgment were not uncommon in antiquity.
An Egyptian tale describes how Si-Osiris, the son of Setme, returned
from the dead. The two men observe the sumptuous, ornate funeral of a
rich man and the unceremonious funeral of a poor man. Setme declares
that he prefers the lot of the rich man, but his son corrects him by taking

---

[45] See Martha Himmelfarb, *Tours of Hell. An Apocalyptic Form in Jewish and Christian
Literature* (Minneapolis: Fortress Press, 1985).

him on a tour of seven halls of the other world. Setme sees the rich man tormented, while the pauper is elevated to a high rank near Osiris. The son then explains that one's fate is determined by one's deeds on earth; the pauper, unhampered by wealth, merited his eternal reward; the rich man did not.

At least seven Jewish versions of this same story focus on the reversal of fortunes of the rich man and the poor man in the afterlife. The Jerusalem Talmud, in *Sanhedrin* 23c and *Hagigah* 77d, records the story of the rich tax collector and the poor Torah scholar who experience reversals of fortune in the afterlife. Jesus' Jewish followers then would not be surprised that the rich man suffered and Lazarus received the kindness that he had lacked in his life.

The more the Church, in the second century and following, talked about heaven and hell, the more rabbinic sources focused on how best to understand Torah as direction for the present (see "On Hell" in Chapter 12). Thus, the Christian community emphasized salvation in the sense of life after death, while the Jewish community emphasized sanctification in the here-and-now. Yet resurrection is not absent at all from today's Jewish thought. Blessing God, who gives "life to the dead" (Hebrew: *m'chayeh ha-matim*) remains within Orthodox and Conservative Jewish traditions as part of the Amidah prayer. The Reform movement, which initially rejected the idea of resurrection, offers an alternative reading that blesses God, "who gives life to all."

The Scriptures of Israel, and in continuity with them both Jesus and Luke, have very harsh things to say about avarice, and they make it clear that money can be a stumbling block to covenantal fidelity. Both testaments testify that giving to the poor is not optional; it is obligatory. It is what good stewards, and faithful community members, do.

John Wesley, the founder of the Methodist movement, preached during the last decades of his ministry a famous sermon entitled "On the Use of Money." Wesley enunciated three principles that he saw as biblical: make all you can by honest means, save all you can, and then give all you can. One who does the first two but not the third is a living being, but a dead Christian. Wesley got most of his ideas about living simply and giving generously from a close reading of the entire Bible and, and especially, the Gospel of Luke.

Today a rival theology of property, the so-called Prosperity Gospel, is thriving in numerous churches. The Prosperity Gospel proclaims not only that God can bless people with material wealth, but also that if people have such wealth, it *must* be a blessing and a sign that they are in right relationship with God. This view is a distortion of biblical teaching as well as a misreading of how economics functions. Conspicuous consumption, which is what the rich man in the parable epitomizes, is not a sign of blessing, but a sign of failure to serve as God's faithful steward.

The French Christian philosopher Jacques Ellul wisely stated the following:

> When we claim to use money, we make a gross error. We can, if we must, use money, but it is really money that uses us and makes us servants by bringing us under its law and subordinating us to its aims. We are not talking only about our inner life; we are observing our total situation. We are not free to direct the use of money one way or another, for we are in the hands of this controlling power ... That Mammon is a spiritual power is also shown by the way we attribute sacred characteristics to our money [e.g. "the almighty dollar"]. The issue here is not that idols have been built to symbolize money, but simply that for the modern man money is one of his "holy things." ... We understand then why money questions are not considered part of the moral order. They are actually part of the spiritual order.[46]

Or as Jesus said, "where your treasure is, there your heart will be too" (Matt 6.21).

The final word here goes to the Baptist ethicist Tony Campolo: "There is nothing wrong with making a million dollars. I wish you all would make a million dollars. There is nothing wrong with making it, but there is something wrong with keeping it."[47]

2. On Divorce

Jesus forbids divorce, and he also forbids remarriage after a divorce. In an eschatological context, such injunctions are understandable: the status quo is bearable, since we have the assurance that it will end shortly. Perhaps

---

[46] Jacques Ellul, *Money and Power* (Downers Grove: Intervarsity Press, 1984), 76–77.
[47] Tony Campolo, cited in "Campolo to Baptists: 'Rise Up, You Suckers, and Do the Work of Jesus,'" Baptist News Global/ABP News (January 31, 2008), https://baptistnews.com/article/campolo-to-baptists-rise-up-you-suckers-and-do-the-work-of-jesus/#.WYCoFhg7n_Q. See also Amy-Jill Levine and Myrick C. Shinall Jr., "Standard and Poor: The Economic Index of the Parables," in Robert B. Stewart (ed.), *The Message of Jesus. John Dominic Crossan and Ben Witherington III in Dialogue* (Minneapolis: Fortress Press, 2013), 95–116.

Matthew added that divorce is permitted in cases of *porneia* (the Greek term refers to an unacceptable sexual act, but the specifics go undefined; see Matt 5.32; 19.9) to provide a loophole for Church members who were suffering in marriages that had broken down. Or, perhaps Matthew was considering marriages that were legal in Roman contexts but not in Jewish ones, given laws of consanguinity.[48] Paul recognizes that Jesus forbade divorce, but he nevertheless permits couples to separate by mutual agreement, and he does not require people to remain married to "nonbelievers" (see 1 Cor 7.11–13). For Paul, living within an eschatological outlook, it is better to marry than to burn with passion (this is not much encouragement for matrimony), but he would prefer Church members be celibate, as he is (1 Cor 7.7).

In the first century, within elite Roman society, the divorce rate was about 50 percent; it was comparable to that of twenty-first-century America. We do not know what the Jewish divorce rate was, although we have no indication that it was this high. The marriage contract (*ketubah*), the practice of polygamy, and the negative view of divorce found in the tradition (see Mal 2.16) suggest strong social pressures against it.

For those who wish to remain biblically faithful and yet cannot, for good reasons, remain within the marital relationship, options are needed. Celibacy and singleness for the rest of one's life is not in our view a viable option for many. Ben proposes that if one has a good extended family, or a good church or synagogue family, singleness does not have to mean lacking companionship or suffering loneliness. But the value of singleness needs to be taught and affirmed as a good option for those who do not have the gift of marriage. Amy-Jill notes that for some, community is insufficient, especially if that community promotes marriage as both sociologically and theologically desirable.

Deut 24.1 permits divorce. Jesus forbids it. According to Matthew (19.5), Jesus' rationale is neither social engineering nor the protection of women's rights. It is what God intended "from the beginning." Jesus cites Gen 2.4 to bolster his pronouncement against divorce. That same approach can be used today, where many of us live under much different conditions than the first century and where marriage is seen less as a contractual obligation and more as a mutually fulfilling relationship based in love, and where divorce

---

[48]   On Roman marriage and divorce, see Thomas A. J. McGinn, "The Law of Roman Divorce in the Time of Christ," in Amy-Jill Levine, Dale C. Allison Jr., and John Dominic Crossan (eds.), *The Historical Jesus in Context* (Princeton Readings in Religion; Princeton: Princeton University Press, 2006), 309–22.

may be necessary. In Gen 2.18, God says that it is not good for the human being to be alone. If so, then it would be contrary to God's will for people to be forbidden to marry; it would be against the goal of creation to condemn people to lives of celibacy and singleness if they do not have this calling.

3. On Heaven and Hell, Again (cf. "On Hell," Chapter 12)

Claims of a heavenly realm with pearly gates, golden slippers, and yes, resting in the bosom of Abraham have provided countless people with a reason for hope. The claims for the existence of hell are much more problematic. For some, hell is simply part of universal justice: those who abuse others, whether through direct brutality, by ignoring pain, or by being bystanders, should be punished. Amy-Jill has already admitted that she likes the idea of hell, because there are people she'd like to see consigned to it. Yet she does not believe in it, and even the admission that she finds the idea pleasing disturbs her. Belief in eternal torture conflicts with the idea of a merciful God. Nor will physical punishment result in repentance: an apology or a tear prompted by coercion will change nothing. Just as problematic is the view that one can sit in heaven, look down below, and spend eternity in *Schadenfreude*, in taking pleasure at the misery of others.

Ben suggests that since we see through a glass darkly (1 Cor 13.12), it is probably unfair to decide whether the concepts of heaven and hell are compatible or not with the notion of a merciful and compassionate God. Hell could be characterized as the place where God says – "O.K, have it your way if you insist." Some people do not want to live in the presence of God forever. And of course, there is considerable debate as to whether the NT teaches eternal torment or simply extinction at some point, either at death or in the afterlife.

Lazarus is silent throughout the parable that bears his name. What voice should we give him? Would he plead on behalf of the rich man, because he himself understands agony? Or would he gloat? If we were Lazarus, what would we do?

Luke 17 Faith, Fidelity, and Finding the Kingdom

STUMBLING BLOCKS

¹ Jesus said to his disciples, "Occasions for stumbling are bound to come, but woe to anyone by whom they come! ² It would be better for you if a millstone were hung around your neck and you were thrown into the sea than for you to cause one of these little ones to stumble.

³ Be on your guard! If another disciple sins, you must rebuke the offender, and if there is repentance, you must forgive. ⁴ And if the same person sins against you seven times a day, and turns back to you seven times and says, 'I repent,' you must forgive."

⁵ The apostles said to the Lord, "Increase our faith!" ⁶ The Lord replied, "If you had faith the size of a mustard seed, you could say to this mulberry tree, 'Be uprooted and planted in the sea,' and it would obey you.

WORTHLESS SLAVES

⁷ "Who among you would say to your slave who has just come in from plowing or tending sheep in the field, 'Come here at once and take your place at the table'? ⁸ Would you not rather say to him, 'Prepare supper for me, put on your apron and serve me while I eat and drink; later you may eat and drink'? ⁹Do you thank the slave for doing what was commanded? ¹⁰ So you also, when you have done all that you were ordered to do, say, 'We are worthless slaves; we have done only what we ought to have done!'"

TEN HEALED FROM LEPROSY

¹¹ On the way to Jerusalem Jesus was going through the region between Samaria and Galilee. ¹² As he entered a village, ten lepers approached him. Keeping their distance, ¹³ they called out, saying, "Jesus, Master,

have mercy on us!" [14] When he saw them, he said to them, "Go and show yourselves to the priests." And as they went, they were made clean.

[15] Then one of them, when he saw that he was healed, turned back, praising God with a loud voice. [16] He prostrated himself at Jesus' feet and thanked him. And he was a Samaritan. [17] Then Jesus asked, "Were not ten made clean? But the other nine, where are they? [18] Was none of them found to return and give praise to God except this foreigner?" [19] Then he said to him, "Get up and go on your way; your faith has made you well."

SIGNS OF THE KINGDOM

[20] Once Jesus was asked by the Pharisees when the kingdom of God was coming, and he answered, "The kingdom of God is not coming with things that can be observed; [21] nor will they say, 'Look, here it is!' or 'There it is!' For, in fact, the kingdom of God is among you."

SIGNS OF THE END

[22] Then he said to the disciples, "The days are coming when you will long to see one of the days of the Son of Man, and you will not see it.

[23] They will say to you, 'Look there!' or 'Look here!' Do not go, do not set off in pursuit. [24] For as the lightning flashes and lights up the sky from one side to the other, so will the Son of Man be in his day.

[25] But first he must endure much suffering and be rejected by this generation.

[26] Just as it was in the days of Noah, so too it will be in the days of the Son of Man. [27] They were eating and drinking, and marrying and being given in marriage, until the day Noah entered the ark, and the flood came and destroyed all of them.

[28] Likewise, just as it was in the days of Lot: they were eating and drinking, buying and selling, planting and building, [29] but on the day that Lot left Sodom, it rained fire and sulfur from heaven and destroyed all of them [30] – it will be like that on the day that the Son of Man is revealed.

[31] On that day, anyone on the housetop who has belongings in the house must not come down to take them away; and likewise anyone in the field must not turn back. [32] Remember Lot's wife.

[33] Those who try to make their life secure will lose it, but those who lose their life will keep it. [34] I tell you, on that night there will be two in one bed; one will be taken and the other left. [35] There will be two women grinding meal together; one will be taken and the other left."

[37] Then they asked him, "Where, Lord?" He said to them, "Where the corpse is, there the vultures will gather."

Following the Parable of the Rich Man, Lazarus, and Abraham that ends Chapter 16, Jesus' teachings to his disciples about the combined topics of ethics and eschatology continue. Jesus has warned his disciples about the consequences of not attending to the poor at their doorsteps; now he develops those instructions by detailing, often in metaphorical language, the difficulties of discipleship.

STUMBLING BLOCKS

Eusebius of Caesarea in the fourth century had a system of dividing the Gospels into what we would consider chapters, and a ninth-century Latin manuscript (Paris Bibliothèque Nationale ms. Lat. 3) has chapter divisions, but the system of chapter breaks used today was devised by British Archbishop Stephen Langton in the thirteenth century. We suspect that he had far too much time on his hands, for some of his chapter divisions are infelicitous and do not reflect the natural breaks in the books. Luke's early readers would have moved directly from the Parable of the Rich Man, Lazarus, and Abraham to these warnings, also addressed to the disciples. The themes of death, relationship, and the limits of power continue.

Jesus begins by speaking of "occasions for stumbling" (**vs. 1**). The Greek speaks more literally of "stumbling blocks" (the underlying term is *skandala*, whence "scandal"), and the verse could be read with the potentially less threatening meaning, "it is impossible to avoid scandals." To focus on "stumbling blocks" suggests the responsibility lies with the disciples: they are to avoid whatever will cause them to trip in their mission. To focus on "scandal" suggests that whatever they do, someone will take offense. The second part of the verse offers the same ambiguity. Is the "anyone by whom they come" the disciple who stumbles, or is it the one who promotes the scandal?

The second verse offers clarification: the person prompting the stumbling or creating the occasion for scandal is the disciple in the role of teacher: any disciple who prompts a congregational member, "one of these little ones," to stumble, whether in faith or practice, is worthy of a death sentence (**vs. 2**). To have a "millstone hung around your neck" and then to be drowned is more than a terrifying execution. It can also indicate a lynch mob, since such drowning is not part of anyone's legal system. It can also indicate a feminization and so humiliation of an executed man, since millstones were associated with women's work of grinding meal, an image that appears in vs. 35 of this chapter. According to Judg 9.53, a woman killed the false judge Abimelech by dropping a millstone on his head. In a variation of Luke's image, Rev 18.21 describes an angel tossing "a stone like a great millstone" into the sea and proclaiming "with such violence Babylon … will be thrown down."

The connections among the phrase "little ones," the mention of "scandal," and the feminization/sexualization of the millstone image commend themselves to a discussion today concerning child sexual abuse, especially by clergy. As we are writing this chapter, *The New Republic* published a major article on a story that has been breaking over the past several years: "The Silence of the Lambs" speaks of the cover-up of multiple incidents of abuse, over decades, by a pastor employed by the Association of Baptists for World Evangelism.[1] At the same, the Royal Commission into Institutional Responses to Child Sexual Abuse in Australia is preparing its final report regarding abuse in institutions, including the YMCA, the Salvation Army, the Uniting Church, a Chabad yeshivah, an ashram, Scouts Australia, and Catholic churches and schools. The Royal Commission's website lists, as of June 1, 2017, over 23,286 letters and emails received.[2] Responses that erupted over reports of sexual abuse and subsequent cover-ups, which cross religions and denominations, were more than "scandalous" and did more than cause people to "stumble" in their faith. For some victims, the abuse led to suicide, drug addiction, or alcoholism. Other victims lived in pain and silence. The full repercussions of the abuse have yet to be seen, and the full number of victims will remain unknown. Nor, even with new safeguards in place, will the abuse stop.

And yet, are the ones who prompt the stumbling, the ones who abuse children, to be executed? "Better for" or "more advantageous" is the right expression. Jesus is not advocating a lynching. He is expressing the result of what happens when they are caught. Such individuals have violated community standards; more, they have violated people and they should not be allowed to do so again. Yet they too are in the image and likeness of the divine. Luke 17.1–3 gives churches the invitation to address scandals concerning little ones; to fail to do so would be, as Jesus states, tantamount

[1] Kathryn Joyce, 'The Silence of the Lambs,' *New Republic* (June 20, 2017), https://newrepublic.com/article/142999/silence-lambs-protestants-concealing-catholic-size-sexual-abuse-scandal.

[2] http://childabuseroyalcommission.gov.au.

to being cast into the sea with a millstone around one's neck. Hence Jesus insists, "be on your guard" (**vs. 3a**), both for the ones who abuse, and by extension, for the desire for vengeance.

Jesus' next comments speak to the perpetrator's situation. Disciples must rebuke fellow disciples who sin (**vs. 3b**). The mandate follows Lev 19.17: "You shall not hate in your heart anyone of your kin; you shall reprove your neighbor, or you will incur guilt yourself." The verse is the origin of the Jewish practice of *tochekha* (Hebrew for "rebuke"). Because we are all "our brother's [and sister's] keepers" (see Gen 4.9), we are responsible not only for our own acts but for theirs as well. To fail to stop a sin makes us culpable; to fail to seek restitution after we have sinned, if we have the ability to do so, similarly makes us culpable.

The conclusion of the verse can create its own stumbling block. Jesus also mandates forgiveness in the case of repenting (**vs. 3c**). His point is not the standard Christian argument that says "we forgive, because we are already forgiven"; rather, he demands repentance first. How that repentance is manifested, from verbal statement to public confession to restitution if possible, remains unspecified. How one determines sincerity of repentance is also unspecified.

According to Jesus, if a person who sins and repents then sins again and repents over and over – as will many caught in cycles of addiction or abuse – the disciple "must forgive" (**vs. 4**; cf. Matt 18.21–22). His insistence is a possible restating of his prayer, which in its Lucan version reads, "And forgive us our sins, for we ourselves forgive everyone indebted to us" (11.4). To make this connection, we would need to read "indebted" as "having sinned against" rather than "owing money" (see comments on 11.4). Given Luke's focus on repenting and forgiving (e.g., 24.47, "Repentance and forgiveness of sins is to be proclaimed in his name to all nations"), this approach is not incorrect.

Yet the mandate to forgive, especially for victims and their families, is often impossible.[3] John's Gospel recognizes this impossibility by placing forgiveness, as well as nonforgiveness, in the hands of the disciples. After bestowing on them the Holy Spirit, the risen Jesus tells his followers: "If you forgive the sins of any, they are forgiven them; if you retain the sins

---

[3]   See the insightful comments of Maria Anne Mayo, "Chasing the Forgiveness Ideal: Case Studies in Restorative Justice, Post-Apartheid South Africa, and the Pastoral Care of Victims of Domestic Abuse," Ph.D. Dissertation (Nashville: Vanderbilt University, 2013), rev. as *The Limits of Forgiveness: Case Studies in the Distortion of a Biblical Ideal* (Philadelphia: Fortress Press, 2015).

of any, they are retained" (see comments in "Bridging the Horizons," Chapter 6).

The disciples, called "apostles" and so indicating Church leadership, hearing Jesus' mandate to forgive the repentant sinner, repeatedly, address Jesus with the title "Lord" and plea that he increase their faith (**vs. 5**). Such forgiveness requires more than what traditional faith can proffer. Given John's statement about retaining sin, an intertextual reading could see this call for more faith as asking for help in discerning what sins to forgive, and which they do not have the authority to forgive.

Jesus responds with a metaphor – "If you had faith the size of a mustard seed" – and announces that such faith could compel a large tree to uproot and plant itself in the sea (**vs. 6**). The image finds resonance with the earlier comment about the sinner with the millstone. The sinner too was uprooted from the community. In context, Jesus is telling the disciples that their faith can uproot the sinner, even a powerful one, from their midst. Missing in most commentaries is attention to Jesus' phrasing, "you could say ..." To uproot sin requires that the apostles speak out. Once the sin is made known, especially if it has been hidden, knowledge of it does uproot more than trees: it uproots clergy and their churches, television stars and their programs, politicians and their parties.

WORTHLESS SLAVES

From locating his apostles as having the authority to uproot trees, Jesus moves them quickly from the role of master to that of slave. For people having wealth and power, the analogy to slavery can be salutary: it reminds them of their social privilege, of the importance of service, and of the virtue of humility. For people who lack such status, the slave analogy locks them into servitude. For people who have experienced slavery or its legacy, the identification as "worthless slaves" can be toxic. Elizabeth A. Johnson, for example, writes:

> ... the master–slave relationship, now totally abhorrent in human society[, is] no longer suitable as a metaphor for relationship to God, certainly not in feminist theological understanding. African American women who write theology out of a heritage of slavery and subsequent domestic servitude stress this repugnance even more strongly in unmistakable terms. Slavery is an unjust, sinful situation. It makes people into objects owned by others, denigrating their dignity as human persons. In the case of slave women, their masters have the right not only to their labor, but to their bodies, making

them into tools of production and reproduction at the master's wish. In such circumstances the Spirit groans with the cries of the oppressed, prompting persons not to obey but to resist, using all their wiles.[4]

How one hears Jesus' comments in 17.7–10 will depend on one's own subject position.

Jesus begins by casting the apostles as slave owners: "Who among you would say to your slave …" (**vs. 7**). Although the New Testament does not depict Jesus' inner circle as owning slaves, the Gospels presume slavery to be a regular part of society. Among other examples, 7.2 depicts a centurion with a highly valued slave; in 12.43, Jesus compares the slave prepared for the master's arrival to the disciple prepared for the *Parousia*; in 14.17, the host of the unattended banquet sends slaves to the streets to offer invitations; and in 16.13, Jesus speaks of the inability of slaves to serve two masters.

Jesus asks his apostles, and so Luke asks Theophilus and those of his station, three questions about this slave. First: would you welcome this slave into your home and invite him to recline at your table? (**vs. 7**). The implied answer is, "Absolutely not." Jesus confirms this answer by asking a second question: "Would you not tell him to prepare food and serve? Indeed, would you not have him serve you first, until you eat and drink your fill, and only then permit the slave to eat and drink?" (**vs. 8**). The setting suggests a man with a small plot of land; his slave is both agricultural and domestic worker. The NRSV's "apron" translates as Greek for "wrapping something around yourself," so "apron" may be too gentrified. Again, the implied answer is, "Absolutely not." Finally, Jesus asks, "do you thank the slave" for following commandments? (**vs. 9**). The Greek tweaks the question by asking, literally, not "do you have grace to the slave?" There is no grace to be shown in this setting, for again, the implied answer is, "Absolutely not."

To the modern ear, the questions are obscene, and the answers are obscene. In Roman antiquity, the questions and answers are normal, as we see also in the New Testament's household codes (Eph 6.5; Col 3.22–4.1; Tit 2.9; 1 Pet 2.18). Ben notes that those codes stand out noticeably from the Greco-Roman ones in treating wives, slaves, and children as moral agents capable of acting virtuously. He adds that the mutuality of the commands to both husbands and wives, parents and children, masters and slaves places especial emphasis on the responsibilities of the master. He is the only one in the whole household who receives three sets of commands,

4   Elizabeth A. Johnson, *Truly Our Sister: A Theology of Mary in the Communion of Saints* (New York: Continuum, 2003), 255; we thank Barbara Reid for this reference.

and those commands limit his power and authority. Various Greek and Roman household codes simply advise the head of the household on how properly to rule the subordinate members. For Ben, therefore, the NT household codes are attempts to inject Christian values into an existing difficult and fallen social structure, and so *change the structure within the context of the Christian household*. This is hardly just baptizing an existing social structure and calling it good.[5] Amy-Jill agrees with the tempering of the model, but she still finds that it generally conforms to rather than challenges the status quo.

Jesus' hypothetical questions end with the instruction: you apostles are to do what you are ordered to do. More, you may be able to command a mulberry bush to uproot itself and land in the sea, but ultimately you are unprofitable slaves who fulfill your obligations (**vs. 10**).

In 2014, the former CEO of Intervarsity Christian Fellowship, Alec Hill, published in *Christianity Today* an article entitled "The Most Troubling Parable: Why Does Jesus Say We are Like Slaves?"[6] Recognizing the offense people in America often take to this parable, he explains its meaning to him: the parable reminds us that we are not the center of the universe, it teaches that we must cede control to the heavenly master in whose bondage we find our freedom, and it reminds us to do our duty. What works, and it does work well, for this white, male, executive officer may not work for other readers with different histories or different social locations. How we receive the parable is therefore contingent on how we understand our own subject position.

TEN HEALED FROM LEPROSY

Teachings over for the moment, Luke returns to the motif of the itinerary. Since Chapter 9, Jesus and his followers have been traveling from Galilee to Judea. The direct path is through Samaria, although Jesus could have avoided Samaritan territory by taking the longer journey by the coast. The scene begins with no mention of the disciples. Luke depicts Jesus himself as "on the way to Jerusalem" (**vs. 11a.**).

Luke locates this scene in "the region between Samaria and Galilee" (**vs. 11b**). For a number of commentators, the phrase indicates "Luke's

---

5   See Ben Witherington III, *The Letters to Philemon, the Colossians, and the Ephesians* (Grand Rapids: Eerdmans, 2007).

6   Alec Hill, "The Most Troubling Parable: Why Does Jesus Say We Are Like Slaves?" *Christianity Today* 58.6 (2014): 76–79.

geographical ineptitude."[7] Should we wish to rescue Luke from having flunked orienteering, we could see the phrase as indicating, symbolically, a mixture of Galilean and Samaritan concerns. For example, illness does not stop at political borders; neither need healing stop at the borders.

Jesus enters an unnamed village, whether Galilean or Samaritan cannot be determined, although the narrative context suggests that the population is predominantly Jewish. Jesus has already been rejected by one Samaritan village because of his Jerusalem focus (see 9.51–53), and the Samaritan mission is not to begin until Acts 8.

Ten men suffering from leprosy approach (**vs. 12a**). The NRSV's "ten lepers" misses the nuance of the Greek *leproi andres*, "leperous men." Rather than speaking of "lepers," "paralytics," or "demoniacs," Luke speaks of a "man who was paralyzed" (5.18) and a "man who had demons" (8.27). Their humanity is not swallowed up by their diseases.[8]

Nor would it keep them from full human contact, as 5.12 has already indicated. Luke notes that these ten men "stood at a distance from Jesus" (**vs. 12b**). Commentaries, once again, focus on Jewish purity laws,[9] with the standard citation of Lev 13.45–56: "The person who has the leprous disease shall wear torn clothes and let the hair of his head be disheveled; and he shall cover his upper lip and cry out, 'Unclean, unclean.' He shall remain unclean as long as he has the disease; he is unclean. He shall live alone; his dwelling shall be outside the camp." The problem with the association is that the situations are not comparable. Leviticus is speaking of proximity to the wilderness sanctuary, not of living somewhere between Galilee and Samaria. Indeed, should this law be in effect, the men should be calling out "unclean unclean" rather than "Jesus, master, have mercy on us" (**vs. 13**). Their distance does not reflect *halakhic* matters, and it may not even be an indicator of anything other than where they happened to be when they saw Jesus. The NRSV's "keeping their distance" is simply, in Greek, "stood at a distance." They may be raising their voices from that distance, before they had a chance to get close. Finally, their call for mercy repeats the call the rich man raised to "father Abraham" (16.24), where the distance was in fact too great. The call returns us to Lazarus, who, like the ten men with leprosy, is at a distance from what he desires, is in need of healing, and is at the mercy of those around him.

[7] Fitzmyer, *Luke I–IX*, 164; Fitzmyer, *Luke X–XXIV*, 1152.
[8] See Culpepper, "The Gospel of Luke," 326; we thank Rev. Dr. Noel Schoonmaker for his discussion of this pericope, which informs our study.
[9] E.g., Nolland, *Luke 9:51–18:34* (Dallas: Word Books, 1993), 846.

The call for mercy can range from a request for money or food to a healing to human contact. Jesus does not approach them as he did the leprous man in 5.13; to the contrary, he sends them away with the cryptic command, "Go and show yourselves to the priests" (**vs. 14a**). The plural could indicate multiple priests needed for multiple people with leprosy; it could also indicate that priests in number are found in the Temple where the appropriate sacrifice for being healed from leprosy is performed. Jesus' concern here would be in continuity with his command to the man whose leprosy he cleansed in 5.14: "'Go,' he said, 'and show yourself to the priest, and, as Moses commanded, make an offering for your cleansing, for a testimony to them.'" With the implied reference to the Temple, the goal of Jesus' journey to Jerusalem is reinforced. However, if Jesus is speaking about going to the Temple, then he already indicates a separation among the men. Samaritan priests would be in Samaria, not Judea.

In this variation of a healing miracle, the response ("show yourself to the priests") comes before the healing itself. As the ten head to the priests, "they were made clean" (**vs. 14b**). That they were going to the priests indicates their faith: they believed that a cleansing of their leprosy would take place. In going, they were doing what Jesus had commanded them to do. At what point all ten realized that their leprosy had gone remains unknown. Nor does Luke provide medical details. One can tell immediately if one's sight, hearing, or ability to talk has been restored. What would be the evidence that the leprosy is cleansed? Does the skin immediately heal? Do red spots or scales vanish instantly or slowly fade?

One of the ten sees that he is healed, that is, he looks at his body and sees the change. Did the others look? Did they know, or were they still trusting Jesus but afraid to look? This one returns to Jesus, and he glorifies God as he does so (**vs. 15**). The loud voice that first asked for mercy now responds with praise for the mercy shown. This healed man takes his place alongside others who glorify God in response to healing: the man cured from paralysis (5.25) and the women bent over by Satan (13.13); they find fellow travelers in the blind man Jesus will encounter in the next chapter (18.43). Their words will echo in the comment of the centurion at the cross, who glorifies God upon witnessing Jesus' death (23.47).[10]

The healed man gives glory to God; to Jesus, by whose feet he prostrates himself, he gives thanks (**vs. 16a**). From that initial distance, increased by

---

[10] See Dennis Hamm, "What the Samaritan Leper Sees: The Narrative Christology of Luke 17:11–19," *CBQ* 56.2 (1994): 273–87.

his journey to the priests, he has come into direct contact with Jesus. The gratitude expressed sets up an ironic contrast with the immediately preceding parable, in which Jesus speaks of slaves who serve out of a sense of duty and not so that they will receive gratitude or reward (vss. 9–10). Jesus thus reveals himself not to be among these slaves. The Greek term for "giving thanks" is *eucharisteō*, with allusions today if not necessarily to Luke's initial readers, to Eucharistic worship.[11] "Only here in the NT is thanks expressed to Jesus; it is addressed elsewhere to God himself."[12]

Luke then reveals what had previously been hidden from the reader: the one who returned was a Samaritan (**vs. 16b**). Given the Samaritans' earlier rejection of Jesus coupled with the enmity between Jews and Samaritans (see discussion of Luke 10), the story is surprising in several ways. First, despite the ethnic and religious divisions, the ten men with leprosy were united. Illness knows no boundaries. Second, the mercy Jesus shows to the Samaritan reminds us of the compassion the Samaritan, in the parable, showed to the man who fell among the robbers. As illness shows no boundaries, neither should compassion. That all the people in our pericope are on the road, and that Jesus in the next chapters will enter Jericho (18.35; 19.1; cf. 10.30) increases the narrative connections. Finally, Luke winds up reinstantiating the division between Jews and Samaritans.

Noting that all ten were cleansed, Jesus asks after the other nine (**vs. 17**). Specifically, he asks why the other did not "return and give praise to God," and he concludes by distinguishing the others, the insiders, from "this foreigner" (**vs. 18**), who "was found to return."

The healing itself may have separated ten, had the Samaritan gone to Samaria rather than to Judea. The responses to the healing definitely separate the group, and Jesus reinforces the separation by referring to the Samaritan as a "foreigner" (Greek: *allogenēs*). The term appears on an inscription posted in the Jerusalem Temple and found by archaeologists in 1871, warning such "foreigners" not to approach beyond the court of the gentiles. The inscription reads, "No foreigner is to go beyond the balustrade and plaza of the Temple zone. Whoever is caught doing so will have himself to blame for his death which will follow."[13]

Commentators who fault the nine for doing what Jesus had commanded show some lack of sympathy with them; so also does Jesus. Luke has set the

11   Ibid., 284.
12   Fitzmyer, *Luke X–XXIV*, 1155.
13   For convenient discussion, see www.bible-history.com/archaeology/israel/temple-warning.html.

scene up to show that the nine Jews will fail. As Amy-Jill reads the text: if the nine return to Jesus, they are disobeying his command. Alternatively, and more generously, Ben suggests they should have both returned to Jesus to show their gratitude and then located a priest, both of which is what Jesus seems to expect. Although they do not do what Luke's readers would have them do – return, prostrate themselves before Jesus, and express gratitude – they nevertheless receive their healing. All ten were cleansed. But only one is "saved." The language of being found (Greek: *euriskō*, in the passive) echoes the description of the lost sheep, the lost coin, and the prodigal son of Chapter 15, lost and then found, dead and now alive.

The final line of this section ends with Jesus sending the Samaritan away. The NRSV's "go on your way," with a possible implication of the "way" being connected to the way of Jesus (so Acts 9.2), misleads. The Samaritan is sent on his own way; it is not the time yet for Samaritans to join Jesus and his followers. Nevertheless, Jesus indicates that his "faith" (Greek: *pistis*) has "saved" (Greek: *sōzō*) him (**vs. 19**). The reference to faith reminds readers of Jesus' earlier comment regarding faith being sufficiently strong to move trees. It is also capable of healing leprosy. The reference to salvation pushes the story beyond healing into soteriology. The Samaritan has found what is for Luke the correct posture of worship: not in the Jerusalem Temple, but prostrate at Jesus feet.

SIGNS OF THE KINGDOM

Suddenly, apparently still somewhere in the imaginary land between Galilee and Samaria, Jesus is approached by some Pharisees who inquire about the coming of the Kingdom of God (**vs. 20a**). Had they witnessed the healing of the men with leprosy, their question may have been prompted by the miracle. If Jesus can cure leprosy, and if his presence sparks the Samaritan to glorify God, then perhaps the messianic age and the time of the resurrection of the dead are near. The question appears to be legitimate; Luke gives no indication that these Pharisees are setting a trap.[14]

Jesus' response turns the question back to the Pharisees: do not look for external signs or geographical locations; do not look for temporal indicators. The Kingdom is marked neither by place nor by time. Instead, he offers a phrase that can be translated two ways: either the Kingdom is within or inside you, or the Kingdom is among you (**vs. 21**). The first reading makes the

14   See Levine, "Luke and the Jewish Religion"; "Luke's Pharisees."

Kingdom an internal condition, already present if not always accessed; the second locates the Kingdom within community, whether of the Pharisees present, the people Israel, or – reflecting the previous incident with the Samaritan – those who worship (in the presence of) Jesus. Whether these particular Pharisees will realize any of these interpretations goes unsaid. To Ben it seems most unlikely that Jesus would say to the inquiring Pharisees, "the Kingdom is already within each of you," because "Kingdom" means God's saving activity, which Jesus came to give, not merely to state it had happened. Amy-Jill wonders if this Kingdom is present in everyone, but that not all recognize it.

SIGNS OF THE END

The chapter ends with Jesus' return to teaching the disciples, who thus far have been absent. His first comment follows from the eschatological implications of the Pharisees' question in vs. 20. They are looking for indicators, and the disciples will do the same: they seek not the Kingdom but for look its functional equivalent, "to see the days of the Son of Man" (**vs. 22**). The desire is future-oriented: since Jesus has already identified himself with this title (6.5,22; 7.34; 9.22; and so on), the request presumes his absence. More, since Jesus has spoken of the son coming "in his glory and the glory of the Father and of the holy angels" (9.26), the disciples are also anticipating his glory. They are not, however, thinking of the passion predictions (9.44; cf. 13.33–34, the references to their destination, Jerusalem).

Despite their desire, the disciples will not see those days if they seek for them. Although people will tell them to look there or here, Jesus tells them not to pursue these claims (**vs. 23**). The days do not come with their desire, but with God's timing. Seeking signs is the wrong approach. Jesus would find good company with Rabban Yochanan ben Zakkai, who was instrumental in preserving Jewish teaching following the destruction of the Jerusalem Temple. According to *Pirke d'Rabbi Eliezer* (ch. 31), he would say, "If while holding a sapling in your hand you are told that the Messiah is about to arrive, first plant the sapling and then go out to receive the Messiah." The end will come not with mathematical calculations based on passages in Ezekiel, Daniel, or Revelation; it will not come with the birth of a red heifer or the storming of the Temple Mount; it will not come when someone has to make an announcement, put up a billboard, or appear on television. It will come as lights of the sky flashing from one side to another (**vs. 24**), in a way that is evident to the entire world.

Nor is this eschatological expectation where the disciples should be focused. Before the glory comes the cross. Jesus repeats (cf. 9.22) his prediction that the Son of Man is to suffer and to be rejected. Those who reject him are not the "elders, chief priests, and scribes" of 9.22 but the broader "this generation" (**vs. 25**). He thereby indicts not only the residents of Jerusalem and those who refuse the Gospel when it is proclaimed to them in the Book of Acts, he indicts the disciples themselves, who are part of the present generation. These disciples will reject Jesus, as they deny him, betray him, flee from the cross, and refuse to believe the message of his resurrection from the women among them. The indictment also recollects 7.31, where Jesus compares "this generation" to the children in the marketplace who rejected both Jesus and John. It evokes 11.29–32 more closely, since there he described as evil the generation that seeks a sign, as the disciples do here.

Finally, the reference directly refers to 11.50, where "this generation" is the one that kills the prophets. In 11.29–32, Jesus spoke of this "generation" that sought a sign, and he responded with cryptic remarks about Jonah and the Queen of Sheba. Now he cites an earlier biblical antecedent, the "days of Noah" of Gen 6–9. There may be an ironic second connection between Luke 17 and Gen 6, since Gen 6.9 describes Noah as "blameless in his generation." Given that generation, the description is not much of a compliment, either to the time of Noah or to the people of Jesus' own time.

Jesus sets up a parallel. As with the time of Noah, so the time of the coming of the Son of Man in judgment (**vs. 26**). At the time of Noah, people did what people do – eat, drink, marry (the subject is men), and be given in marriage (the subject is women) – until the floods came to wipe out humankind (**vs. 27**), whose "wickedness was great in the earth, and ... every inclination of the thoughts of their hearts was only evil continually" (Gen 6.5). The same quotidian activities mark the "days of Lot" (so Gen 19): eating, drinking, along with buying, selling, planting, building (**vs. 28**), and all the things people do when they do not expect the world to end. The ending came to Sodom as well, not by flood but by fire (**vs. 29**). The coming of the Son of Man fits into these contexts (**vs. 30**). The Rich Fool discovered that planting and building will not stave off death and will not bring salvation (12.18–19). Marrying and being given in marriage can distract from the Gospel message, as the last invited guest of the Parable of the Great Feast made clear (14.20). Commerce can also be a distraction (14.18–19). Life must continue, but the focus for Luke is less on getting married and maintaining a household than it is on joining the kinship group around Jesus and building a church.

At the same time, Luke rejects an imminent eschatology along with any speculation about the timetable. Luke's concern is *that* the *Parousia* with its final judgment will come, not *when* it will come. When it comes, people will know, and people must act. The description of such actions is mundane: if on the roof, don't reenter the house; if in the field, don't return home (**vs. 31**). The call is not a new one; Jesus had already instructed: "No one who puts a hand to the plow and looks back is fit for the kingdom of God" (9.62). What is behind must be left behind (including those apocalyptic novels of the same name); Lot's wife looked back, and she was destroyed (**vs. 32**, alluding to Gen 19.26).

The urgency can be heartbreaking: at this moment, and in anticipation of this moment, nothing must get between the follower of Jesus and the return of the Son of Man; not spouse or child or parent, not house or field or neighborhood. For Mrs. Lot, the destruction of Sodom meant the destruction of her home, her family, her friends. For this, she is turned into a pillar of salt. For Luke, salvific response is an all-or-nothing proposition. Just as one cannot serve God and mammon, so in this apocalyptic scenario, one cannot be fully loyal to God and to earthly matters.

Jesus reinforces these difficult points in the next three verses. First, he insists that any attempt at preservation will lead to loss, but those who are willing to give up everything will gain all (**vs. 33**). There is no point in seeking security by means of earthly matters, as the Rich Fool learned, albeit too late. There is also no means by which we can determine from external factors who will be saved and who will be damned. Pairing gender roles, Jesus speaks of two (men) in one bed, or perhaps at a dining couch; one is taken and one is abandoned (**vs. 34**). Of two women grinding meal together, the same diverse fates await (**vs. 35**). Attempts to depict the two men in the bed as engaged in homosexual relations are no more convincing that attempts to turn grinding into freaking or dirty dancing. Readings that note the unequal gender roles whereby for Luke men eat and women prepare the meals are more on target (contrast Matt 24.40, where the two men are both in the field; some manuscripts include this verse as Luke 17 **v. 36**). Ben stresses that the ones who are taken, are taken away in judgment, whereas the ones left behind are saying, "Whew, thank goodness they didn't come for me." This division is clearer in Matt 24.36–44, where the days of Noah are also drawn into the picture, and clearly the ones taken away by the flood are the judged, whereas Noah and his family are left behind, which is a good thing. Amy-Jill finds neither clarity in terms of who is rewarded and who punished nor comfort in the view that some would rejoice at the misfortune of others.

The final line of the chapter begins with an unspecified group (the NRSV presumes, not without reason, the disciples) asking an odd question, "Where, Lord?" (**vs. 37a**). Jesus had not been speaking of a definite *where*, but of an indefinite but secure *when*. In vs. 23, he explicitly warned them against responding to the question of "where."

Given this unhelpful question, Jesus responds with the ominous comment: "Where the body is, even the eagles gather" (**vs. 37**). The verse has received numerous other translations. For "body" (Greek: *sōma*), the translation "corpse" also fits, given the context of death and destruction. For "eagles," the translation "vultures" fits, given that corpses attract vultures, not eagles. Matt 24.27 offers the same line in Jesus' eschatological discourse, where the connection to the destruction of Jerusalem by the Romans is in play, but Luke does not prompt this allusion. Numerous commentators take the reference to "eagles" as a note to Roman standards and so see the destruction coming not as the universal inbreaking of the Kingdom of God, but as the Roman invasion of Judea. The two readings are not mutually exclusive. For Luke, however, the focus is the end of the ages, not the end of Jerusalem.

The chapter began with a warning against stumbling. That warning continues to the end of the chapter. To lead a follower into apostasy becomes, by the end of the chapter, a warning against leading followers into a false sense of eschatological security, and a false timetable of eschatological surety.

1. On Rebuking

Criticizing others is difficult. We hear remarks that are racist, anti-Semitic, anti-Catholic, anti-Evangelical, homophobic, anti-immigrant, and such and let them go, since ignoring is easier than correcting, and since correcting risks social difficulties. The problem is exacerbated when the comment arises in a public setting, since we don't want to disrupt the politeness that holds together the social fabric. Or, we optimistically think, he didn't really mean what he said; her comment was unintentional; or perhaps that was the alcohol speaking. We may hear an offensive comment in a sermon, and after the service we note the problem. Even if the minister or priest agrees with our comment and apologizes, the damage is still done.

Alternatively, in some settings, rebuke is no longer the process by which correction is made with love and within community. We'd rather shout our views of someone else's bigotry and then attempt to silence the speaker. College campuses become battlegrounds, the Internet and Twitter feeds stoke the judgments, and no one wins.

None of these situations – the saying nothing, the private apology minus the public correction, and the shouting down – is ideal, and all three lack the sense of community that both Lev 19 and Luke 17 require. Rebuke should come from a sense of common humanity (it may be too much to ask for "love") rather than from hate or partisan divide. The goal should be not to humiliate the person seen guilty of transgression, but to correct the problem. For the churchgoer, the problem can surface during the service. As Amy-Jill was drafting this chapter, Ben wrote to her about a hymn that could easily be interpreted as anti-Jewish that was sung by his congregation in church that morning. The question remains: what to do now? Does one speak to the minister? Put an apology in the church bulletin for the following Sunday? Issue a mea culpa from the pulpit? Do we simply say, "I didn't mean it," and move on?

The problem is not just with a hymn having offending lyrics. The problem also surfaces when the singers are oblivious to the implications of what they are singing or, worse, endorse the offensive lyrics. All of us, who have only partial understandings on any given subject, will be guilty of insensitivity. And all of us have inherent preferences that can become prejudices if they prevent us from being compassionate and open to the unfamiliar. Sometimes we take for granted things we have been taught because our teachers cared about us and seemed reliable. But they too may have passed along prejudice, however unintended. Jesus at the beginning of this chapter raised the possibility that his disciples might be so oblivious to the consequences of their beliefs and actions that others would be harmed or destroyed. We all still, and quite regularly, need these kinds of warnings, especially in an age when dialogue has become difficult, and people would prefer to trumpet or tweet their own infallible opinions as if they were the Gospel truth.

Luke 18 Parables and Passion Predictions

PARABLE OF THE WIDOW AND THE JUDGE

¹ Then Jesus told them a parable about their need to pray always and not to lose heart.

² He said, "In a certain city there was a judge who neither feared God nor had respect for people. ³ In that city there was a widow who kept coming to him and saying, 'Grant me justice against my opponent.' ⁴ For a while he refused; but later he said to himself, 'Though I have no fear of God and no respect for anyone, ⁵ yet because this widow keeps bothering me, I will grant her justice, so that she may not wear me out by continually coming.'"

⁶ And the Lord said, "Listen to what the unjust judge says. ⁷ And will not God grant justice to his chosen ones who cry to him day and night? Will he delay long in helping them? ⁸ I tell you, he will quickly grant justice to them. And yet, when the Son of Man comes, will he find faith on earth?"

PARABLE OF THE PHARISEE AND THE TAX COLLECTOR

⁹ He also told this parable to some who trusted in themselves that they were righteous and regarded others with contempt:

¹⁰ "Two men went up to the temple to pray, one a Pharisee and the other a tax collector. ¹¹The Pharisee, standing by himself, was praying thus, 'God, I thank you that I am not like other people: thieves, rogues, adulterers, or even like this tax collector. ¹² I fast twice a week; I give a tenth of all my income.' ¹³ But the tax collector, standing far off, would not even look up to heaven, but was beating his breast and saying, 'God, be merciful to me, a sinner!'

¹⁴ I tell you, this man went down to his home justified rather than the other; for all who exalt themselves will be humbled, but all who humble themselves will be exalted."

AS A LITTLE CHILD

¹⁵ People were bringing even infants to him that he might touch them; and when the disciples saw it, they sternly ordered them not to do it. ¹⁶ But Jesus called for them and said, "Let the little children come to me, and do not stop them; for it is to such as these that the kingdom of God belongs. ¹⁷ Truly I tell you, whoever does not receive the kingdom of God as a little child will never enter it."

THE STUMBLING BLOCK OF POSSESSIONS/INHERITING ETERNAL LIFE

¹⁸ A certain ruler asked him, "Good Teacher, what must I do to inherit eternal life?"

¹⁹Jesus said to him, "Why do you call me good? No one is good but God alone.

²⁰ You know the commandments: 'You shall not commit adultery; You shall not murder; You shall not steal; You shall not bear false witness; Honor your father and mother.'

²¹ He replied, "I have kept all these since my youth." ²² When Jesus heard this, he said to him, "There is still one thing lacking. Sell all that you own and distribute the money to the poor, and you will have treasure in heaven; then come, follow me." ²³ But when he heard this, he became sad; for he was very rich.

²⁴ Jesus looked at him and said, "How hard it is for those who have wealth to enter the kingdom of God! ²⁵ Indeed, it is easier for a camel to go through the eye of a needle than for someone who is rich to enter the kingdom of God."

²⁶ Those who heard it said, "Then who can be saved?" ²⁷ He replied, "What is impossible for mortals is possible for God."

²⁸ Then Peter said, "Look, we have left our homes and followed you." ²⁹ And he said to them, "Truly I tell you, there is no one who has left house or wife or brothers or parents or children, for the sake of the kingdom of God, ³⁰ who will not get back very much more in this age, and in the age to come eternal life."

THE THIRD PASSION PREDICTION

³¹ Then he took the Twelve aside and said to them, "See, we are going up to Jerusalem, and everything that is written about the Son of Man by

the prophets will be accomplished. ³² For he will be handed over to the Gentiles; and he will be mocked and insulted and spat upon. ³³ After they have flogged him, they will kill him, and on the third day he will rise again." ³⁴ But they understood nothing about all these things; in fact, what he said was hidden from them, and they did not grasp what was said.

THE BLIND MAN WHO GAINS SIGHT

³⁵ As he approached Jericho, a blind man was sitting by the roadside begging. ³⁶ When he heard a crowd going by, he asked what was happening. ³⁷ They told him, "Jesus of Nazareth is passing by." ³⁸ Then he shouted, "Jesus, Son of David, have mercy on me!" ³⁹ Those who were in front sternly ordered him to be quiet; but he shouted even more loudly, "Son of David, have mercy on me!" ⁴⁰ Jesus stood still and ordered the man to be brought to him; and when he came near, he asked him, ⁴¹"What do you want me to do for you?" He said, "Lord, let me see again." ⁴² Jesus said to him, "Receive your sight; your faith has saved you." ⁴³ Immediately he regained his sight and followed him, glorifying God; and all the people, when they saw it, praised God.

Chapter 17 ends with eschatological warnings: people doing ordinary things will find themselves separated as one is taken and one not; bodies will rot in the streets. The devastations that will accompany the Son of Man on his return will make Noah's flood and the fire and brimstone that rained on Sodom look temperate in comparison. Chapter 18 changes the tone from dire prediction to an emphasis on one of Luke's favorite themes, prayer. The shift is appropriate, since Chapter 18 approaches the end of the itinerary and prepares for Jesus' passion.

PARABLE OF THE WIDOW AND THE JUDGE

For both parables that begin Chapter 19,¹ Luke provides unusually explicit introductions focusing on prayer (vss. 1, 7, 10). Ben finds the interpretations consistent with Jesus himself; Amy-Jill sees the consistency, but she proposes that they are Lucan redaction, both because they turn the parables into allegories and because Luke emphasizes Jesus as continually praying

---

¹ For a fuller discussion of the Parable of the Widow and the Judge, see Levine, *Short Stories*, 221–46.

(3.21; 6.12; 9.18, 28–29; 11.1).[2] Almost all parables have allegorical elements in them; the question then becomes one of the *extent* of the allegory along with determining the correct allegorical equivalents, if allegory is necessary for understanding.

In view of the warnings in the last chapter, Jesus now provides the disciples comfort. The opening line of the chapter, concerning the need to pray always and not lose heart (**vs. 1**), which echoes in vs. 8, establishes for Luke's readers the meaning of the parable sandwiched between the verses. The subject of judging also comes forward from the previous chapter, where Jesus speaks of the Son of Man's bringing about the final judgment (17.22–30). Ben proposes that vss. 1 and 8, with their concern for the delay of the Son of Man's return, are original to the parable and that the parable was eschatological *from the outset*. Amy-Jill suggests both vss. 1 and 8 are Luke's redaction since neither is necessary to the parable proper, since vindication is a Lucan concern, and since Luke similarly emphasizes prayer. Readers can choose to read the parable as a commendation of prayer and hope, or they may choose to see more than prayer and hope. They may choose to see the commendation of action in the public sphere. We do agree that these parables have more than one message to convey.

The parable first introduces a judge (Greek: *kritēs*, a local magistrate), in an unnamed city, who was neither God-fearing nor concerned about others (**vs. 2**). Given his narrative context, readers might immediately judge the judge negatively; in 12.14, Jesus denies the role of judge, and in Acts 18.15, Paul rejects the same role. The parable's concern for this judge is less his judicial role than his attitude. This judge is governed by self-interest and self-preservation; in a culture where honor is of import, the judge eschews social regard. Whereas he could also be seen as fiercely independent and so exactly the person one would want involved in adjudication, contemporaneous authors regard his disposition as uncommendable.[3] Josephus (*Ant.* 10.5.2) uses similar terms to describe King Jehoiakim: "He was of an unrighteous (Greek: *adikos*) disposition, and ready to do evil; he was neither pious (Greek: *housios*) towards God, nor forbearing (Greek: *epieikes*) towards people"; Dionysius of Halicarnassus (10.10.7) speaks of those who "neither fear divine wrath nor respect human fate."[4]

---

2   France, *Luke*, 284.
3   Cited by Fitzmyer, *Luke X–XXIV*, 1178.
4   C. F. Evans, *Saint Luke*, 637.

Commentators generally exacerbate these negative traits by locating the judge within a corrupt judiciary system. Several propose that the widow's adversary bribed the judge to obtain the outcome he desired.[5] Although possible, negative views of both the court system and the widow's opponent read into the parable information that is not present. The parable says nothing about bribes. Because we have no details about the widow's opponent, we cannot determine whose case – hers or his – is just. Ben sees the parable as evoking empathy for the widow, and her need to be vindicated; Amy-Jill agrees that the widow, on first appearance, could be a sympathetic character, but she also offers alternative readings.

The phrase "in the city" is easily overlooked, but it recurs in the opening of vs. 3 to introduce the widow as well, and so it requires attention. The urban setting reminds readers of the "women *from the city*" who was a sinner (7.36); reading the parable's widow in light of the anointing woman emphasizes such topics as women's entering traditionally male space, their economic resources, their tenacity, and their problems with men (mis)judging them. The anointing woman in the city was a sinner, but she loved much; we do not know if the parable's widow is a sinner – the connection to Chapter 7 raises the possibility – but she certainly does not epitomize love. The Pharisee in Chapter 7 does not want to see the woman, but Jesus forces him to look. The judge is forced, by the widow herself, to attend.

So far, we have a morally ambiguous and likely negatively categorized judge, an absent third party, and now, the widow. Amy-Jill finds her morally ambiguous; Ben sees no ambiguity at all.

Once Luke tells us that the judge's antagonist is a widow who, persistently coming to him, demands *ekdikēson* (Greek for both "justice" and "vengeance") against her adversary (**vs. 3**), biblical tropes flood the text. For most readers, whether familiar with these tropes or not, this widow is both righteous and oppressed. Cross-culturally, we generally recognize widows as sympathetic if not pitiable. The widow, *along* with the poor, the orphan, and the stranger, represents society's vulnerable, who are under divine protection and who, Torah insists, must be treated generously and respectfully (cf. Deut 10.18; 14.29; 16.11,14; 24.19–21; 26.12–13). Deut 27.19 even pronounces a curse on the one who prevents justice being done to a widow. Providing widows justice becomes, in the prophets, almost a

---

[5]   See J. D. M. Derrett, "The Parable of the Unjust Judge," in Idem, *Studies in the New Testament Vol. 1* (Leiden: Brill, 1977), 32–47.

shorthand for covenant faithfulness (Mal 3.5; Isa 1.17, 23; 10.2; Ezek 22.7; cf. Psa 93.6).[6]

Sirach (34.12–18) speaks of God as the impartial judge who aids the pathetic widow: God "will not ignore the supplication of the orphan, or the widow when she pours out her complaint. Do not the tears of the widow run down her cheek …" Ben sees underlying the parable Sirach's proclamation in the next chapter: "The prayer of the humble pierces the clouds, and it will not rest until it reaches its goal; it will not desist until the Most High responds and does justice for the righteous and executes judgment. Indeed, the Lord will not delay …" (Sir 35.21). Thus, Ben follows Ben Sira (we did enjoy this little pun; by the way, "Ben" in Hebrew means "son of"). Ben (Witherington, not Sirach) also reads the parable as having eschatological implications. The day the Most High responds is the day when the Son of Man returns.

Ben sees the widow as helpless, marginalized, disenfranchised, and a moral exemplar; Amy-Jill sees her not as necessarily helpful, marginal, or disenfranchised. Instead, recognizing that what the widow wants (*ekdisen*) can mean either "justice" or "vengeance," Amy-Jill finds the widow to be morally ambiguous. Further, she finds the widow in the parable as prompting readers to determine the difference between "wanting justice" and "wanting vengeance": at times, the outcomes can look alike.

Reading with different biblical intertexts, she finds the Bible to be replete with widows who are active, subversive, sometimes rich and powerful, and sometimes dangerous. Tamar (Gen 38) is a trickster, as are Ruth and Naomi (see Ruth 3), Abigail (2 Sam 3.3), the Wise woman of Tekoa (2 Sam 14.5), Bathsheba, and Judith. Even the widow of Zarepath is demanding (1 Kings 17). Judith, a widow, is rich and beautiful; she is also an assassin. The New Testament knows of rich widows and young widows with their own income, as well as poor widows dependent on the church (1 Tim 5).

For Luke's literary context, the widow in the parable finds herself in good company: Anna, the widow in the Temple (2.37); the evocation of the widow of Zarepath (4.25–26); the widow of Nain (7.12); the poor widow in the Temple (21.2–3); and the various widows, both needy and not, in Acts (6.1; 9.39–41). From these depictions, we may conclude that Luke wants to circumscribe the roles of widows and of women in general: their job is to support the Church financially, but otherwise to remain silent. By turning

---

[6]   Johnson, *Gospel of Luke*, 269.

the feisty widow in the parable into a model of prayer, Luke eliminates her courage to enter the public sphere and make her case. Ben does not see how presenting her as an image of persistent prayer rules out her also being an image of courageous confrontation of an injustice in the public sphere. Our disagreement may stem from a matter of emphasis: Ben sees the prayer as not mutually exclusive to public confrontation and so reads Luke as offering a both/and moral exemplar; Amy-Jill sees Luke as constraining the woman by redefining public confrontation as private prayer and sees more of an either [in court]/or [at prayer] illustration.

Some feminist readers see the woman as a figure for God, who continually pleads with us to do justice; Amy-Jill does not go this far,[7] but she appreciates the attempt to locate the widow as an image of the divine, and she finds this a potentially helpful reading "in front of the text." Ben notes that there are no parallels for a morally ambiguous widow elsewhere in Luke-Acts. Always they are presented sympathetically. Amy-Jill grants Ben's general point; she also notes that Sapphira of Acts 5.1–11 is not entirely sympathetic; then again, she is not a widow for long.

Whether rich or poor, our widow persists. She "kept coming" to the judge; the imperfect verb signals continuous action. What she wants is less certain. Ben finds she demands justice or vindication (Greek: *ekdikēson*); he supports this view by regarding the parable as something of a twin to the Parable of the Pushy Pal (11.5–8). He sees the widow as crying either for protection from the one trying to disenfranchise her, or as seeking validation of her claim to her own belongings. He concludes that her opponent (Greek: *antidikos*) is the person who beat her to court making a claim for her property.

Amy-Jill sees nothing in the parable about the opponent coming first, and nothing about the case as involving property. The Greek *ekdikēson* can be translated "grant me justice"; it can also be translated "avenge me"; the first reading suggests the widow has a just cause and seeks restoration; the second sees her as vindictive and retributive. We do not know the details of the widow's case; we do not know anything about the opponent. Thus Amy-Jill wonders, if we sympathize with the widow *because she is a widow*, are we already engaging in stereotype and perhaps in injustice? Lev 19.15 mandates: "You shall not render an unjust judgment; you shall not be partial to the poor or defer to the great: with justice you shall judge your neighbor."

---

[7]   Barbara E. Reid, "A Godly Widow Persistently Pursuing Justice: Luke 18:1–8," *Biblical Research* 45 (2000): 25–33 (31).

Ben also suggests the widow's characterization invokes the negative stereotype of the nagging woman, which Jesus then reverses by presenting the widow as a positive exemplar. For this stereotype, Ben cites Prov 19.13, "a wife's quarreling is a continual dripping of rain." Amy-Jill does not find the intertext convincing: the widow is no longer a wife, and she is not quarreling (the term suggests an argument) with the judge; she is nagging, or to use the Yiddish, nudzhing. Prov 19 is the only place in Scripture where quarreling is predicated of a woman, so Amy-Jill finds no biblical stereotype of quarrelsome women. Scripture's only nagging women are not Israelites: they are Samson's first wife (Judg 14.17) and then his paramour, Delilah (Judg 16.16). If there is no stereotype of a nagging wife, or if the evidence for the stereotype is weak, then Jesus has not reversed it. Nor is Amy-Jill convinced that the widow is a role model in terms of displaying righteousness, no matter how much Ben and Luke the evangelist want to make her one.

Ben notes that the demand for vindication is a cry for justice. One only needs vindication if one has been wronged. The Greek seems clear enough to Ben. And again, the other person in the parable is called by Jesus "the adversary," a phrase that reminds one of "the Satan." Amy-Jill observes that the dominant uses of the term *ekdikēson* in the New Testament suggest "avenging"; the connotations are violent. Febbie Dickerson neatly sums up the canonical uses:

> Paul advises the Roman congregation, "never avenge yourself, for vengeance (*ekdikesis*) is mine, I will repay, says the Lord" (Rom 12.19 NRSV cf. Deut 32.35); "it is the servant of God to execute wrath (*ekdikos*) on the wrongdoer" (Rom. 13.4 NRSV). The violent desires increase in Revelation, as the martyrs ask: "Sovereign Lord, how long will it be before you judge and avenge (*ekdikeis*) our blood on the inhabitants of the earth?" (Rev 6.10). The seer assures them, "he has avenged (*ekdikesen*) on her [the great whore] the blood of his servants" (Rev 19.2). Moreover, the term is also understood as retributive. Paul says, "We are ready to punish (*ekdikesai*) every disobedience" (2 Cor 10.6), and the Petrine writer says, "For the Lord's sake accept the authority of every human institution … as sent by him to punish (*ekdikesin*) those who do wrong" (2 Pet 2.14). Given that *ekdikesis* is most often understood as vengeance, it is plausible that the widow is seeking vengeance rather than justice. Rather than regard widows as weak, we may want to see widows as capable of acting in unpleasant, if perhaps necessary, ways.[8]

---

[8]   Febbie C. Dickerson, "The Parable of the Widow and Judge (Luke 18:2–5): Talking Back to African American Stereotypes," Ph.D. Dissertation (Nashville: Vanderbilt University, 2017). Dickerson adds Paul's comments: "No one should wrong or exploit a [sister or]

Ben notes that one person's justice is viewed by another person as vengeance and the word in question means both. But one doesn't generally go to a representative of the judicial system for proxy revenge; one goes for vindication after being been wronged. The *lex talionis* speaks of personal revenge and the attempts to limit it, but this story is about something else. Since Jesus speaks of an adversary, there is every reason to think this widow has been wronged, and her only recourse is to keep petitioning the judge for redress. Amy-Jill concludes that Ben has a more positive view of human nature than she does: she has no doubt that people use the justice system for revenge. She would also like Ben to be right here.

For some time, the judge resists the woman's pleas (**vs. 4a**). Resistance, however, is futile. To show his resistance, the judge repeats, verbatim, the narrator's description of him: he neither fears God nor respects people (**vs. 4b**). That he is speaking to himself shows his own isolation; it also shows that he is likely conniving, as we have seen elsewhere with interior monologue.

The repetition of his lack of fear makes ironic and possibly humorous his next comment: he has no fear of human or divine, but he fears this widow. He will grant her what she wants, so that she will not give him a black eye (**vs. 5**; the Greek *hypōpiadzō*, often translated "wear out," is a boxing term). Ben suggests that the judge fears shame: were the woman to shame him, he might lose his authority; his embarrassment would be especially potent given that it would come at the hands of a marginal woman.[9] Amy-Jill again disagrees. Because the judge does not care about what others think, he does not fear shaming. Were shaming the issue, the judge already would have been shamed by the widow's persistent demands. The judge, fearing a blow to the eye, is boxed in. By ignoring the woman, he faces physical threat and so public humiliation by a widow, which is indeed an honor and shame issue; by acceding to her demands, he shows she has defeated him.

---

brother, because the Lord is the avenger (*ekdikos*) in all these things" (1 Thess 4.6); "for it is indeed just of God to repay with affliction those who afflict you … in flaming fire, inflicting vengeance (*ekdikesen*) on those who do not know God" (2 Thess 1.6–8); and lists several Church fathers and medieval commentators who read the term as indicating "vengeance." See also Levine, *Short Stories by Jesus*, 243.

9   See C. Spicq, "La parabole de la veuve obstinée et du juge inerte, aux decisions impromptues (Lc. Xviii,1–8)," *Revue Biblique* 68.1 (1961): 68–90 (76), on a papyrus describing a frustrated woman who hits someone in public, disgracing him, in order to obtain what she wants. Derrett, "Unjust Judge," 43–46, suggests that the phrase is metaphorical: to "blacken the face" (i.e., reputation) and so to disgrace.

For Amy-Jill, the parable proper ends here in vs. 5 with the judge's acqui-
sition to the widow's demand, and it resists closure. Meeting the widow's
demands, the judge may have been coerced into justice; alternatively, he
may have become complicit in an act of injustice, just as are the debtors
who help the dishonest manager change the account books. As Evans notes,
"The parable shares with 16.1–8 a certain racy humor, and the choice of a
knavish character as the central figure, about whom the audience has to be
reassured."[10]

Ben sees continuity between vss. 2–5 and the following verses: Jesus himself (Luke refers to him as "Lord" to indicate an authoritative interpretation) states that we attend to what the unjust judge says (**vs. 6**). The verse,
although short, is beset with multiple problems. First, the judge is speaking
in interior monologue, so "listening" to him is difficult. Second, only here,
in the narrative voice, are we actually told that the judge is unjust. We do
not know if he deserved the label from the opening of the story, or whether
his lack of justice is coeval with his positive decision for the widow. He has
a certain connection with the "unjust manager": was he unjust from the
start, or does he become so in order to secure his position? Third, what the
judge said concerned making a decision not out of justice, but out of fear.
Motivation by fear might be a good way of getting what one wants, but it is
not a good way of proclaiming a gracious God.

Either Jesus (so Ben) or Luke (so Amy-Jill) turns the judge's words into
a *qal v'homer* argument: if an unjust judge will vindicate a disenfranchised
person in perpetual petition, *how much more* will the one true God hear
the cries of his people? If the unjust judge delays, how much sooner will
the true God provide help? (**vs. 7**). The concern for perpetual crying out
evokes the Lucan theme of prayer (6.28; 11.1–2; 18.1–14; 22.40, 46; Acts 1.14;
2.42; 3.1; 6.4, 6; 10.4, 9, 30–31; 12.5, 12; 16.13, 16, 25; 20.36; 21.5; 22.17; 28.8).
Thus, in Luke's hands if not originally in Jesus' telling, the parable becomes
an allegory,[11] as we saw with the Lost Sheep and Lost Coin (see comments
on Luke 15). Nothing in the parable proper requires a connection between
the widow and prayer, let alone between the judge and God. Then again,
nothing precludes this connection.

In **vs. 8a**, the questions receive answers: yes, God will avenge the elect;
no, God will not delay long. But the real question for Luke is not whether
God will be faithful, but whether his followers will be. The section ends

---

[10]   C. F. Evans, *Saint Luke*, 636.
[11]   See Stephen Curkpatrick, "Dissonance in Luke 18:1–8," *JBL* 121.1 (2002): 107–21 (110).

with another rhetorical question: will the Son of Man find "the" faith on earth when he comes? (**vs. 8b**). The definite article before "faith" indicates not just any kind of faith or trust, but rather "the" faith that the Son of Man seeks at his return. "The faith" for Luke is faith in Jesus as Lord. "The early churches believed that faithfulness and endurance were required now because at any time the returning Lord could break into their lives and demand an accounting."[12]

At the end of the parable encased in its narrative frame, readers have a model of a woman who prays always and does not lose heart. We do not have the model of an independent woman who may be demanding vengeance, who has not reconciled with her opponent, who has entrenched herself in the judicial process against which Jesus had warned (12.58), and who gets the verdict she wants by threatening violence. Were the widow to be a gang-banger, or a Fortune 500 CEO, or a movie star, we would read the parable differently, and so the parable also interrogates our stereotypes, if we could read it without the Lucan frame. The point is not that Luke's frame is incorrect; it is rather that, at least as far as Amy-Jill is concerned, it boxes in the parable.

Luke reassures us that the widow is a model of prayer; Amy-Jill sees Luke as attempting to tame the widow and so tamping down all the issues of stereotype and justice the parable addresses. For example, by applauding the widow's success, we readers may be condoning threats of violence, and we are surely ignoring the widow's lack of attempts at reconciliation with the opponent. We find ourselves in the position of "judging," which is something Jesus seeks to preclude rather than praise. For Amy-Jill, the parable interrogates our sense of justice and of the court system; it questions stereotypes of widows and judges; it forces us to ask whether we are interested in justice or vengeance; it shows our inevitable entanglements with others. The parable also shows and perhaps commends women's tenacity, public appearance, and self-interest. Ben does not disagree that this could be part of the message of the parable, but at the end, he concludes that the parable is primarily about persistent prayer.

PARABLE OF THE PHARISEE AND THE TAX COLLECTOR

Ben, reading the chapter's first parable in light of its traditional title, "The Importuning Widow and the Unjust Judge," sees the widow as marginalized

---

[12]   Tannehill, *Luke*, 265.

and oppressed and therefore discovers a connection between the widow and the marginalized and outcast tax collector.[13] Amy-Jill sees nothing necessarily marginalized about either figure. Nor does she see the tax collector as an "outcast"; not only is he in the Temple, he was not thrown out of anything. To the contrary, working for the Roman occupation makes one not an outcast, but a traitor to those who seek political independence. Despised, yes; shunned, perhaps; "outcast" is the wrong word. Ben thinks, on further review, "despised" is a better word.

The Parable of the Widow and the Judge is, in its narrative context, a demonstration of the power of persistent prayer; we then move to the Parable of the Pharisee and the Tax Collector,[14] which can be seen as about the perils of presumptuous prayer.[15] The title is clever; it is also misleading. Commentators typically extol the simple prayer of the tax collector and excoriate the Pharisee's prayer as hypocritical, sanctimonious, or otherwise terrible. *Both* prayers have problems. Just as both characters in the previous parable can be seen as problematic (Amy-Jill is more inclined to go in this direction than is Ben), so both characters in the second account leave questions.

The connections between the parables run even more deeply: both parables are about our sense of justice, our stereotypes, and our mutually implicated lives, since in both cases, we find ourselves to be our brother's (and sister's) keepers. What one person does necessarily impacts the lives of others. We have seen similar motifs surface in the Good Samaritan with the innkeeper, the Pushy Pal at Midnight, and the Unjust Manager: in each, one person whose motives may be suspect draws another into relationship. Both parables brilliantly interrogate our own moral centers. The widow raises questions of justice versus vengeance, of stereotype versus actuality, and of our views of violence and the threats of violence. The judge asks questions about complicity, wisdom, and the meaning of justice. The Pharisee will raise matters of self-understanding as well as relationality; the tax collector raises questions about how repentance functions personally as well as theologically. And once again, at least as Amy-Jill reads the text, Luke has framed the parable and so limited its message.

In **vs. 9,** Luke shifts the narrative audience from "the disciples" (17.22) to those who are persuaded that they are righteous and others are not. Judith

---

[13]   Witherington, *Women in the Ministry of Jesus*, 35–38.
[14]   For a fuller discussion of this parable, see Levine, *Short Stories*, 169–96.
[15]   See Culpepper, "The Gospel of Luke," 340.

Lieu correctly notes, "It is natural to think that the Pharisees were in mind. Yet Luke does not say this, and his more general phrasing suggests that he knew that such could be found elsewhere, perhaps even within his church."[16]

The setting of the second parable is the Jerusalem Temple, the location where the Gospel began. Two men have gone for public prayer (9:00 A.M. and 3:00 P.M.), though they could have gone at any time to pray privately[17] (**vs. 10**). The two, one a Pharisee and the other a tax collector, are in states of ritual purity; commentators who insist that the tax collector is ritually impure misunderstand the purity system. Ritual purity concerns the body's coming into contact with elements representing life or death (birth, a corpse, menstruation, leprosy, etc.), not a matter of sin and not a matter of acquisitions.

For Jesus' Jewish audience, the Pharisee would epitomize righteousness; tax collectors represent sinfulness. Pharisees were public, lay leaders who not only taught righteousness, but also were known for practicing it. Tax collectors sold out their own people in the interest of pleasing the Romans and making a profit. For Luke, the roles are reversed. Luke has already presented venal Pharisees (e.g., 16.14) who refuse John's baptism (7.30), represent greed and elitism (11.38–44; 16.15), love money (16.14), ask Jesus potentially hostile questions (17.20), complain about his dining companions (5.30; 7.39; 15.2), dispute his claim to forgive sins (5.17–26), fuss at his disciples (6.6–11), and so on. Conversely, the next chapter will present a darling tax collector (19.1–10), and we have already seen admirable tax collectors who come to John for baptism (3.12; 7.29); listen to Jesus (15.1); dine with him (5.29–30 cf. 7.34); and join his band (5.27).[18] How we assess the parable depends on whether we take it within Luke's literary context or whether we hear it through Jesus' own setting.

According to the NRSV, the Pharisee is "standing by himself" (Greek: *statheis pros heauton*, **vs. 11a**). He may be praying by himself; he may be praying to himself; he may be praying about himself, or he may be praying in opposition to the tax collector. The simplest reading, "standing by himself," makes the most sense: the prayer is directed to God; it is a personal prayer rather than a communal one. And it begins, appropriately, addressing God and offering thanksgiving.

---

[16] Lieu, *Gospel According to Luke*, 141.

[17] Fitzmyer, *Luke X–XXIV*, 1186.

[18] See F. Gerald Downing, "The Ambiguity of 'The Pharisee and the Toll-collector' Luke (18:9–14) in the Greco-Roman World of Late Antiquity," *CBQ* 54.1 (1992): 80–99 (81).

The specifics of the prayer bother a number of commentators, who take the Pharisee's giving thanks that he is not like thieves, the unrighteous, adulterers, or even the tax collector (**vs. 11b**) as indicating legalism and self-righteousness. While Luke would likely find such a reading congenial, whether Jesus' audience or Luke's reader should is another matter. The Pharisee is not hypocritical – he really *is* thankful he has not lived like the tax collector (cf. similarly 1QH 7.34; *B.T. Ber.* 28b). His prayer might be seen as a variant on the saying, "There but for the grace of God go I." Jesus himself offers prayers that distinguish among people; for example, in 10.21 he prays, "I thank you, Father, Lord of heaven and earth, because you have hidden these things from the wise and the intelligent and have revealed them to infants ..." Rarely do commentators condemn him for offering the same type of prayer.

Jesus, and his Jewish audience, may have regarded this Pharisee as a caricature[19]; he is not a figure to despise, but one to amuse, for he does so much more than the Torah requires. No one was expected to fast twice weekly as a form of spiritual discipline; no one was required to tithe everything.

Continuing their negative impression of the Pharisee, commentators often remark on the number of times "I" appears in his prayer and conclude that the Pharisee "has no real sense of his own sinfulness and unworthiness before God, and therefore he has an inadequate appreciation of God's grace."[20] Or, "He has not seen that he cannot justify himself, but can only receive such a status as a gift from God, as the tax collector does."[21] Such comments may run counter to Luke's own point that one can be "blameless" (1.6; cf. Phil 3.6). Luke is not Luther, and the point of the parable is not an *apologia* for justification by faith.

More often than not, commentators also cite what they perceive to be Jewish parallels to the Pharisee's prayer, and so they attempt to make it normative rather than the caricature that it is. The frequently cited prayers that thank God for not making the individual a gentile, a woman, or a slave[22] are not comparable. These prayers speak to the obligation to fulfill the commandments, not to the glorification of the one

---

[19]   Frederick C. Holmgren, "The Pharisee and the Tax Collector: Luke 18.9–14 and Deuteronomy 26.1–15," *Interpretation* 48 (1994): 252–61 (254); Robert Doran, "The Pharisee and the Tax Collector: An Agonistic Story," *CBQ* 69.2 (2007): 259–70 (269). Snodgrass, *Stories with Intent*, 472, disagrees.

[20]   C. A. Evans, *Luke*, 268.

[21]   Ben Witherington III, *New Testament Theology and Ethics*, Vol. 1 (Downers Grove: Intervarsity Press, 2009), 711.

[22]   E.g., *t. Ber.* 6.18, and *b. Ber.* 28b.

praying.[23] The popular claim that the Pharisee asked for nothing and so received nothing falters on its failure to recognize a prayer of thanksgiving. It is also an ungenerous reading. Such commentaries presume that the Pharisee should begin from one stereotypical Christian perspective and see himself as unworthy and sinful, rather than begin from one traditional Jewish perspective, thankful to God and able to celebrate his gratitude. The Pharisee has done more than any Pharisee was expected to do, and he is grateful that he has the ability to do so.

One could conclude that the Pharisee is at fault because he judges the tax collector harshly when he does not know what is in the tax collector's heart. Here a comparison of this Pharisee with Simon, the Pharisee at whose home the woman anointed Jesus, is apt. Conversely, readers do not know all that is in the heart of the Pharisee, but that has by no means prevented them from seeing the Pharisee as epitomizing everything wrong with (the Jewish) religion.

The tax collector, also at a distance (**vs. 12**), has nothing to celebrate and no reason to be thankful. He beats his breast, a sign of grief and atonement, and asks for propitiation (**vs. 13**). He is comparable to the fallen angels who "did not raise their eyes to heaven out of shame for their sins" (*1 Enoch* 13.5). However, Gentile readers, such as Luke' ideal audience, may have regarded him as unable to stand before his God. F. Gerald Downing captures their tone: "What kind of deity would insist on being placated thus? So nervous a response, so lacking in trust that the speaker dared not even look up ... [is] nothing short of an insult."[24]

The tax collector's prayer translates literally as, "God may you be propitiated (Greek: *hilaskomai*) for me, a sinner."[25] He is asking that divine anger at his sin be turned away. One could read the tax collector as manifesting a palpable sense of remorse and repentance. He offers no list of virtues, nor a list of excuses, but rather a frank recognition that he has sinned and a simple appeal for propitiation.[26] On the other hand, he makes

---

[23] See discussion in Doran, "The Pharisee and the Tax Collector," 267; see a similar critique of such analogies in Downing, "Ambiguity," 94–95; Timothy A. Friedrichsen, "The Temple, a Pharisee, a Tax Collector, and the Kingdom of God: Rereading a Jesus Parable (Luke 18:10–14a)," *JBL* 124.1 (2005): 89–119 (94). For the typical discussion, see, e.g., Snodgrass, *Stories with Intent*, 465.

[24] Downing, "Ambiguity," 83.

[25] The translation "Lord have mercy on me" goes back to Wycliffe some six hundred years ago. See Culy et al., *Luke*, 570. On "propitiate," see Psa 24.11; 64.3; 77.38; 78.9; all in the LXX, and compare Rom 3.25; Heb 2.17; 1 John 2.2,4,10. See Johnson, *Gospel of Luke*, 272; and Bock, *Luke 9.51–24.53*, 1464.

[26] See C. A. Evans, *Luke*, 271.

no comment about repenting, he shows no interest in changing his job, he demonstrates no concern in reconciling himself to the people he may have wronged. While the Pharisee may have said too much in expressing his own piety, the tax collector may say too little, and his words are not supported by his action.

Jesus ends the parable with the pointed remark usually translated, "this man went away justified/set right rather than the other" (**vs. 14a**). The second half of the verse justifies this translation; Luke adds the floating line, "all those who exalt themselves will be humbled," and its converse (**vs. 14b**). Again, Luke presents the theme of reversal (cf. 1.52–53; 6.20–26; 10.29–42; 11.37–41; 12.21; 14.11).[27] Several commentators, knowing this theme, then conclude, "The Pharisee who trusted that he was righteous is replaced by the tax collector who is declared to be righteous because of his earnest prayer for forgiveness."[28]

The parable could have a much more profound meaning, but to find it requires first distinguishing Jesus material from Luke's redaction and second retranslating vs. 14. Amy-Jill argues that the final line of the parable proper is 18.14a, the comment about justification. The line regarding eschatological reversal is not necessary to the parable's narrative flow, and that Luke appended it here is suggested by its appearance elsewhere in the tradition (cf. 14.11; Matt 23.12).

Along with bracketing 14b, Amy-Jill suggests translating the preposition in 14a, usually rendered as "rather than," as "alongside." The Greek *para*, as in "parable" or "parallel," can have this meaning. She finds that the tax collector "went down to his home justified alongside" the Pharisee.[29] As Robert Doran has noted, "the only factor in the context that has led interpreters to choose an exclusive meaning is a disinclination to say that a Pharisee is upright/justified (*dedikaiomenos*)."[30] Ben argues that while *para* can mean "beside," it can also mean "contrary to" and "instead of" as well. Therefore, he finds that is it not mere prejudice that leads to such a translation. Amy-Jill concludes that Jesus offers no zero-sum game; he presents a picture of divine mercy that his Jewish audience would have understood. In reading the restrictive translation "contrary to" or "instead of," the zero-sum model is in place and the Pharisee is damned.

27 Green, *Luke*, 649.
28 Tannehill, *Luke*, 267.
29 See Friedrichsen, "The Temple, a Pharisee, a Tax Collector," 117–18.
30 Doran, "The Pharisee and the Tax Collector," 262.

Jews, who emphasize the communal more than the individual, recognized that just as one person's sin negatively impacts the entire community, so one person's righteousness, or faith, can have a positive impact. We have seen this concern with the *Zechut Avot*, the merits of the fathers, a concern that underlies the Parable of the Rich Man and Lazarus. In our parable, the Pharisee has more merit, more righteousness, than a single person needs. Given this surplus, the tax collector may have tapped into the Pharisee's treasury. The pinch of the parable becomes evident. To read the parable as damning the Pharisee and justifying the tax collector is to leave the reader feeling self-satisfied, and to produce a theology of limited goods. To read the parable as showing that the deeds of one person impact another, and thus to prompt us to care for those who benefit from our works, is a greater challenge. Ben notes that nothing in the parable itself, even leaving aside Lukan redaction, suggests that something the Pharisee had done somehow now benefited the tax collector. He adds that, more to the point, vs. 14's "this man" coupled with Luke's comment about self-exaltation strongly suggests that only one person is being commended here, not two, and so Luke has rightly interpreted Jesus' intent. Amy-Jill notes that the Pharisee's surplus of good deeds provides the benefit. Amicably disagreeing, we move on, side by side to the next section.

AS A LITTLE CHILD

In vss. 15–17, Luke returns to Markan source material (cf. Mark 10.17–22; Matt 19.16–22), last encountered in 9.49. Here, Luke frames the journey narrative with Jesus' teaching on children (cf. 10.46–50).[31] Commentators frequently insist that by having children serve as a positive exemplar, Jesus is creating a Kingdom of "nobodies," since children were seen as having little value. The opposite is the case.[32] Children were highly valued in Jewish culture, as the very act of people bringing infants (Greek: *brephē*) to Jesus (**vs. 15a**) demonstrates. The parents and caregivers likely thought that Jesus' touch had beneficial, even healing effects (cf. 6.19). Given the high infant mortality (estimates are that 30 percent or more of children died in infancy, and about 60 percent would not survive to adulthood[33]), no wonder so many people wanted this miracle worker to touch their children.

---

[31]   Nolland, *Luke 9.21–18.34*, 880–81.
[32]   On this issue, see Witherington, *Women in the Ministry of Jesus*, 13–16.
[33]   Culpepper, "The Gospel of Luke," 344.

The disciples rebuke those bringing their children to Jesus (**vs. 15b**). To read the disciples as indicating a normative Jewish view that discounted children or saw them as marginal and then to see Jesus as reversing cultural values here mischaracterizes Judaism. By affirming children, Jesus is confirming what the parents and caregivers are already doing. Here as elsewhere, the disciples are perhaps portrayed as not understanding Jesus' ministry to one and all, even to infants.

His teaching that the Kingdom belongs to children (**vs. 16**) is not a romanticizing of childhood innocence, not an encouragement to behave in a childish manner, and not an announcement that the Kingdom means giving up social status.[34] Had that last idea been the case, Jesus would have used the example of a slave, not an infant. The children of royalty have status. In their families, if the family is not dysfunctional, children and especially babies are the focus of attention, not the problem.

Vs. 17 (cf. Matt 18.3) – the third of six sayings prefaced by "Amen" in this Gospel (4.24; 12.37; 18.29; 21.32; 23.43; cf. Matt 18.13; John 3.3, 5) – concludes this vignette with the insistence that the child is an exemplar: unless adults receives the Kingdom as children receive it, they will never enter it.[35] The analogy does not mean that one receive the Kingdom by becoming a nobody or by being humble (anyone who has spent time with a toddler knows that humility is not the dominant trait). Rather, children are distinguished by their dependence on others. They cannot secure what they want, or need, on their own. Little children must be in relationship. The Kingdom cannot be separated from community.

THE STUMBLING BLOCK OF POSSESSIONS/INHERITING ETERNAL LIFE

Ben and Amy-Jill came to different titles for 19.18–30. Ben notes that Luke is developing the theme of "eternal life," which surfaced already in 10.25, when a lawyer introduced the question. Here the question has a different valence, for the "certain ruler" (Greek *archōn tis*) is not seeking to test Jesus. He is asking this "good teacher" about what he should do, because he feels that something is lacking in his life or his religious practice (**vs. 18**). Amy-Jill agrees with Ben, but she tips the discussion away from soteriology to

---

34   E.g., Tannehill, *Luke*, 269, proposes that Jesus is telling the audience they must "welcome the kingdom that now appears without status and power" like an infant.

35   See Nolland, *Luke 9.21–18.34*, 882. Culy et al., *Luke*, 573 correctly argue that the reading "as you receive a child" is less likely, but see Green, *Luke*, 551.

ethics; she finds the emphasis to be less on inheriting eternal life than on the problems in this life, and in particular our attachment to our stuff. Ben agrees that this is part of the subject matter.

The opening account, typically called "the rich young ruler," is better read in its distinct presentations. For Mark 10.17–31, the questioner is a "rich man," and in Matt 19.16–22, he is "young." For Matthew, the burden of the story is "youth" and with it, perhaps a lack of accomplishment. For Mark and also for Luke, the concern is that riches do not satisfy or, more provocatively, wealth itself is the problem. For Luke, the problem is exacerbated by the fact that the questioner is a "ruler" and therefore has power or, in modern terms, social capital. Luke knows about people in authoritative positions: emperors, governors, police captains, magistrates, and so on (12.58; 23.13, 35; 24.20; Acts 4.5, 8; etc.; see also John 4.46's "royal official"). There is no reason to make this figure a "synagogue ruler" or a religious authority figure; Luke knows the term "synagogue ruler" (13.14; cf. 8.41) but does not use it here. Luke's account is about how concern for authority and status ultimately proves incomplete.

Jesus responds, "why do you call me good?" and then insists that only God is good (**vs. 19**; cf. Mark 10.18). The verse has yielded no end of exegetical wrestling, especially among those who hold both strong Trinitarian views (Jesus is God) and the view that Jesus was sinless (following Heb 4.15, which describes Jesus as a high priest "without sin"). Theologically, Jesus is saying that the ruler's focus ought not to be on him but on God (cf. 1 Chron 16.34; 2 Chron 5.13; Psa 25.8; 34.8; 106.1; 118. 1,29; 136.1; Nah 1.7), just as he advises his followers to pray "Our Father" and not "Dear Jesus."

He continues by citing what God has commanded, including the prohibitions against adultery, murder, stealing, bearing false witness, and the mandate to honor parents (**vs. 20**). Ben finds significant the omission of the command to honor the Sabbath, since Jesus viewed the Sabbath differently than his contemporaries. Amy-Jill finds this conclusion unlikely, as she does not see Jesus as abrogating the Sabbath. However, neither Jesus nor his fellow Jews, in general, expected gentiles – Luke's ideal readers – to honor the Sabbath. To include the Sabbath here would have been irrelevant to Luke's gentile readers. Ben adds that we do not know either that Luke has no Jewish persons in the audience, nor do we know that Theophilus is not a God-fearer. The audience seems to be expected to know a good deal of the LXX. Amy-Jill sees knowledge of the LXX irrelevant to the question of the audience: for Jesus' gentile followers, the LXX was their Scripture. Further and more important, Amy-Jill sees the list as focusing on *interpersonal relations*, which is a secondary issue regarding honoring the Sabbath but a primary one regarding honoring one's parents. The commands Jesus lists are all related to the human community. It is the ruler's status and wealth that block him from community: the status makes him ruler rather than brother; the wealth becomes his identity marker, not family or friends.

The ruler replies that he has kept these commandments (**vs. 21**). That is, he has done what was required, with most of the commandments listed as negatives: do not murder, do not steal. Jesus did not mention those commandments that would have brought the ruler greater fulfillment, such as "love the neighbor" or "love the stranger."

Luke also omits Mark's note that Jesus, looking at the man, loved him. Instead, Jesus responds that there is still something missing (**vs. 22a**), a point made clear by the ruler's initial question. Continuing the concern for interpersonal relations, Jesus advises him to distribute all he has to the poor in order to have treasure in heaven (**vs. 22b**). González observes that for Luke's Gospel, the "one thing still lacking" is "precisely to come to the point where things are actually lacking!"[36] This rigorous demand can be compared to what Elijah asks of Elisha (1 Kings 19.19–21): Elisha divested himself of all his possessions and then followed Elijah.

This command to total divestment applies to only some of Jesus' followers, as we have seen. He does not ask Martha to sell her home; to the Pharisees, he commands inclusive table fellowship, not itineracy. Some people are called to the life of being like infants, completely dependent on others and sharing the good news of the Kingdom in return; others are like the parents and caregivers, mothers and brothers and sisters, providing support.

Jesus' suggestion is more than the ruler is willing to pay; he is unable to part from his wealth, even though his decision saddens him (**vs. 23**). While Mark 10.22 indicates that Jesus' interlocutor did not follow Jesus, Luke leaves the ruler's fate open.

Luke replaces Mark's reference to the man's departure with Jesus' famous aphorism: "How hard it is for those who have possessions/property/money (Greek: *chrēmata*) to enter the Kingdom of God (**vs. 24**), for it is easier for a camel to go through the eye of a needle than for a rich person to enter the Kingdom of God" (**vs. 25**). The hyperbole suggests not difficulty, but impossibility. Attempts to make the saying more palatable to those who hold earthly treasures – for example, early manuscripts that replaced "camel"

---

36   González, *Luke*, p. 217.

(Greek: *kamēlon*) with "rope" (Greek: *kamilon*)[37]; claims that Jerusalem had a gate that was so low that, to enter, camels had to bend down in a form of dromedary gymnastics – are bankrupt. C. S. Lewis humorously remarked: "All things are possible, it's true, /But picture how the camel feels, squeezed out /In one long, bloody thread from tail to snout."[38]

Omitting also Mark's reference to the disciples' astonishment at Jesus' saying, Luke goes immediately to their question "who then can be saved?" (**vs. 26**). Lest they despair, Jesus replies that what is impossible for human beings is possible for God (**vs. 27**). God is able to compensate for human weakness; for those unable fully to store up treasure in heaven, God will add to their account. The verse may provide some comfort for Luke's rich readers: they learn that they do not have to divest fully, but they must use their funding to support those in need.

Peter, recognizing that Jesus commended divesting, affirms his commitment: unlike the ruler, he has left his home and chosen to follow Jesus (**vs. 28**). He sounds a bit like the Pharisee in the parable: "Look at us," he says; "we've done more than most." Commentators generally commend Peter's boast. Whether Peter's wife and mother-in-law had the same view is another matter.

Jesus affirms Peter's statement with his comment "amen" (the English "truly" strips out the liturgically formal nuance) and adds a comment about divesting not only from *everything*, but also from *everyone*: "wife or brothers or parents or children" (**vs. 29**). Attempts to mitigate the shock of this pronouncement are no more successful than attempts to turn camels into ropes in order to thread the needle. Leaving home, and leaving families, is precisely what the inner circle of disciples has done. Although the language is androcentric, for the verse says nothing about leaving husbands, Luke may have intended that women, too, should leave husbands and children: Joanna, the wife of Herod's steward (8.2), could be an example. She follows Jesus to Jerusalem; her husband, apparently, remained in Herod Antipas's service.

To those who give up everyone and everything for the Kingdom, Jesus gives the assurance that they will be compensated "very much more in this age" and will then receive eternal life (**vs. 30**). The point is not that men get more wives. Disciples will receive membership in the new

---

[37] See Metzger, *Textual Commentary*, 169. Only S, 13, 59, and a few other later manuscripts have this reading.

[38] C. S. Lewis, *Poems* (New York: Harper One, 2017), 203.

family of faith based on loyalty to Jesus rather than on marital relations or consanguinity.

THE THIRD PASSION PREDICTION

Following the theme of giving up everything and everyone for the Kingdom, Luke presents the third Passion prediction (cf. 9.45; 12.50; 13.33–35; 17.25) to the Twelve alone. They who have given up all are included in his passion: "we" are going up to Jerusalem (**vs. 31a**). Then, shifting to the third person, he speaks of the fate written by the prophets about the Son of Man (**vs. 31b**). The notice of such prophetic prediction will repeat in Jesus' Bible study with the two on the road to Emmaus (24.26–27, 32, 45). Jews at the time were not expecting a Messiah who would suffer and die on their behalf. Jesus' followers, and perhaps Jesus himself, saw in passages such as Isa 53 a suffering Messiah and so understood their lives in light of this paradigm.

In this passion prediction, the focus is on the "gentiles" (**vs. 32a**). Nearing Jerusalem, Jesus and his followers will have their first direct meetings with the Roman government. That gentle gentile centurion who built the synagogue and loved the Jewish people (7.1–10) will be replaced by Pilate and his soldiers, who have no love for the Jewish people. Those who mock, insult, spit upon, flog, and kill Jesus (**vss. 32b–33a**) go unidentified. The proximity of the reference to "gentiles" suggests that gentiles are responsible for these actions, although the passive voice leaves open the roles that others, such as the High Priest and the Sanhedrin, will play (see already 9.22). Outside of a brief reference in 19.39, set during Jesus' entry into Jerusalem, Pharisees drop out of Luke's Passion Narrative. By omitting direct references to Jerusalem's leadership, Luke also avoids the impression that the "ruler" unable to follow Jesus was among his persecutors. Ben notes that had Luke really an ax to grind against Pharisees, it is hard to explain their disappearance at the crucial climax of his ministry and in his trials.

No matter the severity of the torture, no matter the death, Jesus assures his disciples that the Son of Man will rise again on the third day (**vs. 33b**). The disciples do not understand (**vs. 34**). Luke reformulates 9.45: "But they did not understand this saying; its meaning was concealed from them, so that they could not perceive it. And they were afraid to ask him about this saying" (partially based on Mark 9.32). This reformulation is meant to emphasize the disciples' lack of understanding. By suggesting the meaning of Jesus' words is "hidden" but by avoiding the question of who prompted the hiding, the verse opens to two possibilities. More likely, Luke is reserving full understanding for a post-resurrection revelation, when Jesus will explain to his disciples everything that happened according to the Scriptures (18.31; cf. 24.26–28, 44–46), and when the disciples will come to understanding in acts of hospitality and, especially, the breaking of bread (cf. 24.30–31). Less likely is the claim that Satan is responsible for their failure of insight (cf. 8.12).[39]

Such lack of comprehension comports with the mystery of Jesus' death. The disciples did not think he was going to die; a suffering and dying Messiah was not part of their soteriological understanding. Nor did it make sense to them that a man who could walk on water and raise the dead would himself be overcome by political force. Some Christians today speak of "born again experiences" wherein the truth claims of the Gospel are not determined by logic or study but by grace and revelation; others speak of the role of grace in showing them the truth of something that cannot be grasped by human reasoning. Such claims fit with Luke's description of the disciples. Such experiences should also be helpful guides for missionaries who think they can *prove* Jesus' messianic status by proof-texting.

THE BLIND MAN WHO GAINS SIGHT

Notice of the disciples' inability to grasp Jesus' statement segues neatly into Luke's account, taken from Mark, of the blind beggar on Jericho Road (vss. 35–43). The previous passage had focused on the disciple's spiritual inability to see; now Luke turns to physical blindness. The healing of the blind evokes the verses from Isaiah quoted in the inaugural sermon in Nazareth (4.18); the setting in Jericho will remind readers of the Parable of the Man Who Fell Among the Robbers, but who received nursing care first from the Samaritan and then in Jericho, the City of Palms. Reinforcing the connection to the parable, Jesus – like the Samaritan – attends a man "by the roadside" (**vs. 35**). By omitting Mark's mention of the name "bar Timaeus" (Mark 10.48), Luke also avoids any speculation about the limits of philosophy, given that Plato's *Timeaus* was a well-known text.

The blind man had asked the crowd what was happening (**vs. 36**), and they told him that "Jesus of Nazareth is passing by" (**vs. 37**). No messianic title appears; no mention of why the crowd had gathered. By the end of Chapter 18, Luke can presume readers understand the draw: Jesus can heal; Jesus can

---

[39] See Nolland, *Luke 9.21–18.34*, 514.

raise the dead; Jesus has wisdom from which anyone might learn. The blind man knows that Jesus can heal, so he shouts, "Jesus, Son of David, have mercy on me!" (**vs. 38**). Here Luke reintroduces the theme of Jesus as David's son (cf.1.27, 32; 2.4, 11, 32; Acts 2.29–32; 13.22–23), which, as Jesus nears Jerusalem, reopens the discussion to politics. For Luke, the true king is one who mercifully heals the blind, not one who mercilessly conquers by the sword. In 16.24, the rich man of the parable had called out to Father Abraham for mercy; the patriarch could not provide it. For the blind man on the Jericho road as for the victim saved by the Samaritan in the parable, the call can be answered.

In a structural comparison to vs. 15, where the disciples sought to prevent parents and caregivers from bringing infants to Jesus, now "those who were in front sternly ordered [the blind man] to be quiet" (**vs. 39**). Once again, Jesus cuts through attempts to protect him by limiting his contact with others. He orders the man brought forward (**vs. 40**). Whereas the infants cannot speak for themselves, the blind man can. Jesus asks him what he wishes (**vs. 41**), which might seem an odd question. Perhaps readers are to see irony: the man does not wish for world peace, the end to disease, or a pot of gold. He says simply, "Lord (Greek: *Kyrios*), let me receive sight." (The English "see again" suggests that the man had been sighted at one point; the Greek *anablepō* is less clear about his previous condition. He may have been blind from birth, as was the blind man in John 9.)

Despite the common view today that the man, and everyone else, would have regarded his blindness as the result of sin, Jewish sources do not support this reading. The only hint of this view, noted in John 9.2, is dismissed by Jesus. Isaac was blind, as was Eli the priest; nothing is suggested that their blindness was caused by sin. Were sin the cause for blindness or any disability, then Lev 19.14 – "You shall not revile the deaf or put a stumbling block before the blind; you shall fear your God: I am the Lord" – would make no sense.

Nor would people be likely to provide alms to a blind beggar if they thought he somehow deserved his disability. Sin is not mentioned in this narrative, and there is no reason to import it into the interpretation.

Jesus not only grants the man his sight, but diagnoses its prompt: his faith (**vs. 42**). The term "save" (Greek: *sōzō*) here, as elsewhere in Luke's Gospel (see 7.50), has the primary connotation of "healing" rather than spiritual salvation or eternal life,[40] although the man's "following" Jesus shows not only

---

[40]   On Luke's use of "salvation" language in a Greco-Roman way in many places in Luke-Acts, see Witherington, *Acts*, 821–43. It often has the sense of helped, cured, or rescued, rather than the later Christian spiritual sense of saved.

that he becomes a disciple, but also that he can do what the rich ruler could not. The contrast between the ruler and the beggar allows Luke to demonstrate both the entrapment of money and the possibility of becoming a disciple. The account ends with the characteristic notice (**vs. 43**) of the people glorifying God (e.g., 7.16).[41]

1. On Prayer

Luke sets up the parables in Chapter 18 to address prayer. We first hear the evangelist's approval of the ones who "pray always" and do not "lose heart" (vs. 1), who "cry to [God] day and night" (vs. 7). The tax collector does neither: his prayer is a single verse (13b), and the parable in which he appears gives no indication of perpetual prayer, or perpetual repentance. Thus, the chapter poses the question of prayer: is the focus quantity or quality?

The widow in vss. 3–5 raises another question of prayer: should we pray for justice or revenge, and how do we distinguish between the two? When our opponents are defeated, do we rejoice, or are we able to recognize that our opponents are also in the image and likeness of the Divine? A well-known midrash from the Babylonian Talmud, *Megillah* 10b, comments on Exod 15, the Song of the Sea. When the Egyptians were drowning, "the ministering angels wished to sing God's praises," but God said to them: "My own creatures are drowning in the sea, and yet you would sing?" God is talking about the Egyptians. Do we rejoice when our enemies are defeated, or do we seek their execution or their imprisonment ("Lock her up" vs. "love your enemy")? Do we celebrate a capital punishment, or do we mourn? When our opponents suffer, are our reactions sympathy or *schadenfreude*?

A third question about prayer surfaces with our understanding of the Pharisee's comments. Most readers dismiss as inappropriate, or sanctimonious, prayers of self-congratulation. And yet, how do we distinguish between a prayer of self-congratulation and a genuine expression of thanksgiving? Daniel prays: "To you, O God of my ancestors, I give thanks and praise, for you have given me wisdom and power …" (Dan 2.23). Jesus states, "I thank you, Father, Lord of heaven and earth, because you have hidden these things from the wise and the intelligent and have revealed

---

[41] See Marshall, *Luke*, 691–92.

them to infants" (10.21). Could there be pride in his prayer? Do we distinguish prayers that express our appreciation for the gifts we have been given, and prayers that (may) exult that others are denied what we have received? Sanctification and sanctimoniousness may be closer than we think. What then distinguishes the two: Language? Attitude? Action?

It would be hypocritical for us to respond to the Pharisee's prayer by echoing his words, "God, I thank you that I am not like other people ... even like this Pharisee." Most of us do not fast twice a week and give the money we would have spent on food to the local food bank; most of us do not support the poor with a tenth of our income. Once we start comparing ourselves to others, the parable traps us

Exalting oneself at another's expense is inappropriate. Using spiritual disciplines in order to offer a public demonstration of one's righteousness is inappropriate. But the disciplines themselves can be helpful. To practice the disciplines – fasting, tithing, praying – in Jewish thought necessarily puts one into communal relations, because the disciplines benefit not only the individual, but the entire community. When we do things for ourselves, we may well benefit others. Once we remember this, we are in a better position to become less self-centered, and less judgmental.

2. On Prayer and Grace

Alan Culpepper offers this reflection on the Pharisee and the Tax Collector:

> The nature of grace is paradoxical: It can be received only by those who have learned empathy for others. In that regard, grace partakes of the nature of mercy and forgiveness. Only the merciful can receive mercy, and only those who forgive will be forgiven (6.36–38). The Pharisee had enough religion to be virtuous, but not enough to be humble. As a result, his religion drove him away from the tax collector rather than toward him.[42]

This reading of grace as a zero-sum game and of the Pharisee's "religion" as the problem opens helpful areas for discussion. If "only the merciful can receive mercy, and only those who forgive will be forgiven," then we have a paradox: the tax collector has done nothing to display either mercy or forgiveness, yet he receives both. The cross teaches that forgiveness comes not as the response to repenting, but as the prompt to encourage it. The Pharisee, by tithing, is showing mercy, and yet for most Christian readers

---

[42]   Culpepper, "The Gospel of Luke," 343.

of the parable, he receives none. Finally, the problem with the Pharisee is not his "religion"; to the contrary, his religion – Judaism – insists on communal involvement: in extending one's hand to the poor, the widow, the orphan and the stranger. The problem enters when judgment of others enters, whether that judgment is made by the Pharisee or by the readers who condemn him.

3. On Humility

Jesus' welcoming of the children and his promoting them as examples of life lived toward, or in, the Kingdom are often read as an exhortation to humility. Given the plausibility that the Pharisee's prayer could be understood as a manifestation of his pride, the comparison of Pharisee and infant is not inappropriate. Yet children are not good examples of humility, and infants even less so: they are demanding, they cry when they do not get what they want, and they perceive the world as limited to their own needs. Tithing is not on their radar, nor voluntary fasting, nor even prayer. Indeed, some Christians would even say that infants are proof of original sin, as they are the most self-centered creatures on earth – "feed me, clothe me, hold me," and so on.

Instead of taking the usual move of comparing the prideful Pharisee to the humble child, we might compare these children to the widow: she, like they, demands what she wants, does not care what sort of public shame she might create or endure, and displays the type of tenacity that prompts a response that may well have a sense of reluctance, or even defeat ("yes, I'll feed you at 2:00 A.M. despite how tired I am; yes, I'll change your diaper, even though I changed it only five minutes ago; yes, I'll walk with you in the snuggly for another half-hour …"). We attend to children because they need our attention: can we recognize that others need our attention as well? How do we balance our own concern for self-preservation with God's demands that we attend to others?

These concerns lead us to the final account in our chapter: the blind man who, despite pressure from the crowd to remain quiet, shouted out his concern. He, like the widow and like the children, did not care about convention, and he was certainly not at the moment interested in the needs of others. He knew what he wanted, and he obtained it. Perhaps the widow, the children, and the blind man are lessons less in humility than in recognizing our own needs, and the importance of shouting out to make sure they are addressed. Humility can be a virtue, but the type of humility that trumps a sense of self-worth, that suppresses our own needs, that prevents us from achieving our full status as children of God – in such cases, humility becomes not a virtue but a vise (the spelling here is not incorrect).

Finally, in Phil 2.5–11, Jesus epitomizes humility. Ben suggests that if there was one person on earth who did not likely suffer from feelings of inferiority or low self-worth, it was Jesus. Humility according to Phil 2.5–11 is not about feelings about oneself; rather, it is the posture of a strong and self-confident person stepping down and serving others. The model of Jesus' humility, humbling one's self and serving others, has to do with actions on behalf of others. There is such a thing as false pride, but there is also such a thing as false humility, and we sometimes seem to be guilty of both or either one. By focusing on the example of Jesus, as well as on his teaching, such false postures can be avoided.

Luke 19 From Jericho to Jerusalem: Tax Collector, Triumphal Entry, Temple Teaching

ZACCHAEUS, "MR. RIGHTEOUS"

¹ He entered Jericho and was passing through it. ² A man was there named Zacchaeus; he was a chief tax collector and was rich. ³ He was trying to see who Jesus was, but on account of the crowd he could not, because he was short in stature. ⁴ So he ran ahead and climbed a sycamore tree to see him, because he was going to pass that way.

⁵ When Jesus came to the place, he looked up and said to him, "Zacchaeus, hurry and come down; for I must stay at your house today." ⁶ So he hurried down and was happy to welcome him.

⁷ All who saw it began to grumble and said, "He has gone to be the guest of one who is a sinner." ⁸ Zacchaeus stood there and said to the Lord, "Look, half of my possessions, Lord, I will give to the poor; and if I have defrauded anyone of anything, I will pay back four times as much."

⁹ Then Jesus said to him, "Today salvation has come to this house, because he too is a son of Abraham. ¹⁰ For the Son of Man came to seek out and to save the lost."

PARABLE OF THE POUNDS/PARABLE OF COMPETENCE AND COMPENSATION

¹¹ As they were listening to this, he went on to tell a parable, because he was near Jerusalem, and because they supposed that the kingdom of God was to appear immediately.

¹² So he said, "A nobleman went to a distant country to get royal power for himself and then return. ¹³ He summoned ten of his slaves, and gave them ten pounds, and said to them, 'Do business with these until I come back.'

¹⁴ But the citizens of his country hated him and sent a delegation after him, saying, 'We do not want this man to rule over us.' ¹⁵ When he returned,

having received royal power, he ordered these slaves, to whom he had given the money, to be summoned so that he might find out what they had gained by trading.

[16] The first came forward and said, 'Lord, your pound has made ten more pounds.' [17] He said to him, 'Well done, good slave! Because you have been trustworthy in a very small thing, take charge of ten cities.'

[18] Then the second came, saying, 'Lord, your pound has made five pounds.' [19] He said to him, 'And you, rule over five cities.'

[20] Then the other came, saying, 'Lord, here is your pound. I wrapped it up in a piece of cloth, [21] for I was afraid of you, because you are a harsh man; you take what you did not deposit, and reap what you did not sow.'

[22] He said to him, 'I will judge you by your own words, you wicked slave! You knew, did you, that I was a harsh man, taking what I did not deposit and reaping what I did not sow? [23] Why then did you not put my money into the bank? Then when I returned, I could have collected it with interest.' [24] He said to the bystanders, 'Take the pound from him and give it to the one who has ten pounds.' [25] (And they said to him, 'Lord, he has ten pounds!')

[26] 'I tell you, to all those who have, more will be given; but from those who have nothing, even what they have will be taken away. [27] But as for these enemies of mine who did not want me to be king over them – bring them here and slaughter them in my presence.'"

TRIUMPHAL ENTRY

[28] After he had said this, he went on ahead, going up to Jerusalem. [29] When he had come near Bethphage and Bethany, at the place called the Mount of Olives, he sent two of the disciples, [30] saying, "Go into the village ahead of you, and as you enter it you will find tied there a colt that has never been ridden. Untie it and bring it here. [31] If anyone asks you, 'Why are you untying it?' just say this, 'The Lord needs it.'" [32] So those who were sent departed and found it as he had told them.

[33] As they were untying the colt, its owners asked them, "Why are you untying the colt?" [34] They said, "The Lord needs it."

[35] Then they brought it to Jesus; and after throwing their cloaks on the colt, they set Jesus on it. [36] As he rode along, people kept spreading their cloaks on the road. [37] As he was now approaching the path down from the Mount of Olives, the whole multitude of the disciples began to praise God joyfully with a loud voice for all the deeds of power that they had seen,

³⁸ saying,

> "Blessed is the king
>> who comes in the name of the Lord!
> Peace in heaven,
>> and glory in the highest heaven!"

³⁹ Some of the Pharisees in the crowd said to him, "Teacher, order your disciples to stop." ⁴⁰ He answered, "I tell you, if these were silent, the stones would shout out."

SECOND LAMENT FOR JERUSALEM

⁴¹ As he came near and saw the city, he wept over it, ⁴² saying, "If you, even you, had only recognized on this day the things that make for peace! But now they are hidden from your eyes. ⁴³ Indeed, the days will come upon you, when your enemies will set up ramparts around you and surround you, and hem you in on every side. ⁴⁴ They will crush you to the ground, you and your children within you, and they will not leave within you one stone upon another; because you did not recognize the time of your visitation from God."

TEMPLE INCIDENT

⁴⁵ Then he entered the temple and began to drive out those who were selling things there;
⁴⁶ and he said, "It is written,

> 'My house shall be a house of prayer';
>> but you have made it a den of robbers."

TEMPLE TEACHING

⁴⁷ Every day he was teaching in the temple. The chief priests, the scribes, and the leaders of the people kept looking for a way to kill him; ⁴⁸ but they did not find anything they could do, for all the people were spellbound by what they heard.

From Jericho to Jerusalem, Chapter 19 continues not only to repeat the themes sounded earlier in the Gospel but also to show their implications in practice. A rich tax collector turns out to be the model of community care and so shows the potential of the tax collector in Chapter 18's parable. In the Parable of the Pounds, Jesus indicates the importance of moving from having good gifts to sharing them; faith needs to be actualized. Then Jesus actualizes his own role by entering Jerusalem, where he will, as he repeatedly announced, suffer and die. From the Triumphal Entry to the Temple incident to his daily teaching in the Temple, he brings his various messianic roles together: king and prophet, teacher and healer, fulfilling Scripture and announcing future blessings and woes.

ZACCHAEUS, "MR. RIGHTEOUS"

The travel narrative draws near its end as Jesus enters Jericho (**vs. 1**). The city, which has already been mentioned in the Parable of the Good Samaritan as the site of the inn where the wounded man received additional care (10.30), is mentioned close to seventy times in the full Bible (i.e., including the Deuterocanonical materials). Looking at the reference intertextually, we can draw numerous observations. For example, we can see Jesus' coming to Jericho as anticipating a conquest, as Joshua with his troops took the city (Josh 6). We can see a connection to Jesus in the mysterious "commander of the army of the Lord" (Josh 5.14) who, in two verses, appears to morph into "The Lord" (Josh 6.2). We can cite the one non-Gospel reference to Jericho in the New Testament, Heb 11.30, "By faith the walls of Jericho fell after they had been encircled for seven days," as anticipating the fall of Jerusalem. The simplest way of explaining why Jesus came to Jericho was that he was passing through on his way to Jerusalem. Events may have symbolic value; it is also possible that the text records simply what happened.

Jesus was passing through the city on his way to Jerusalem, but the narrative, and Jesus, stop to engage a fellow named Zacchaeus. Although his name derives from the Hebrew term for "fidelity" or "righteousness," this fellow has all the marks of someone who is neither: he was both a chief tax collector and rich (**vs. 2**). Given these markers, readers have three models for assessing his character. First, the positive presentations of tax collectors, ending with the Parable of the Pharisee and the Tax Collector in the previous chapter (18.10–14a), suggest that Zacchaeus too will turn out to be righteous and faithful. Second, since Jesus has a tax collector among his apostles (5.27–30), Zacchaeus may become a disciple. Third, his economic designation puts him in the same category as the rich man who built barns he will never use (12.16–20), the rich man whose fate contrasts that of Lazarus (16.19–31), and the rich ruler choked by his possessions (18.22).

We meet Zacchaeus neither in the toll booth nor in the Temple, but on the road. The Greek of **vs. 3** can be read in two ways: either Zacchaeus, because he short, is unable to see Jesus over the heads of the crowd, or

Jesus himself is short and therefore Zacchaeus could not see him. Although Amy-Jill notes that Jesus eats a great deal, especially in the Gospel of Luke, and therefore suspects he was on the husky side, the solution to the grammatical problem is that the short person is Zacchaeus, not Jesus. To be short was, for Roman antiquity, a marker of being a lesser person. Mikael Parsons offers the following visual description: "a traitorous, small-minded, greedy, physically deformed tax collector sprinting in an ungainly manner ahead of the crowd...."[1] It may be overreading to see this short person as modeling what being "like a little child" is (being small is one marker of children). Zacchaeus also resembles children in climbing trees, although that activity is not limited to the under-ten set.

Undeterred, Zacchaeus runs ahead of the crowd and climbs a sycamore tree on the route Jesus is taking (**vs. 4**). The scene is designed to be humorous. The humor continues as Jesus, stopping by the tree, looks up. Zacchaeus sought to see him, but he is the one to see Zacchaeus. More than notice him, Jesus calls to him, by name. Even more, just as the tax collector hurried to find a good vantage point, so Jesus insists that he now hurry and come down. Finally, Jesus demands that Zacchaeus be his host for the day (**vs. 5**). Zacchaeus immediately, and happily, obeys these commands (**vs. 6**).

Jesus' comments can be taken as miraculous: he knows both Zacchaeus's identity and his economic ability to play host. Alternatively, the chief tax collector may be a well-known figure. He may even be notorious. That suggestion follows from the next verse, which indicates that the crowd following Jesus also knew Zacchaeus, and also knew his sinful reputation; they are not pleased that Jesus determines to stay with the tax collector. They grumble, since Jesus has determined to eat with a "sinner" (**vs. 7**). This identification does not indicate that the tax collector was loathed because he associated with gentiles and therefore violated purity laws. The crowd's concern is not ritual purity but political loyalty: the people presume Zacchaeus to be a sinner because he takes goods from the Jewish people and gives them to Rome.

Although he speaks to Jesus, whom he addresses as "lord," Zacchaeus is also heard by the crowd. The chief tax collector affirms that he gives half of his possessions to the poor, and if he happens to have misused his position (e.g., taken a kickback, shaken down –compare John the Baptizer's teaching

---

[1]   Mikeal C. Parsons, *Body and Character in Luke and Acts: The Subversion of Physiognomy in Early Christianity* (Waco: Baylor University Press, 2011), 107; see also his "Short in Stature: Luke's Physical Description of Zacchaeus," *New Testament Studies* 47.1 (2001): 50–57.

to the tax collectors in 3.14), he makes restitution of four times the amount (**vs. 8**). Although usually seen as the tax collector's moment of repentance, the verbs are all in the present tense ("I give" in contrast to the NRSV's "I will give"). Here he follows Exod 21.37a, "When someone steals an ox or a sheep, and slaughters it or sells it, the thief shall pay five oxen for an ox, and four sheep for a sheep." For Amy-Jill, Zacchaeus is not repenting of a sin since the text never mentions "repenting"; the tax collector is explaining that he has been judged, incorrectly, as sinful. Amy-Jill sees the salvation as the restitution of the man to the community, which occurs when he states what he actually does, rather than what the crowd thinks he has been doing. Jesus has provided him the public forum to state what he has always done and thereby to reinstate his positive reputation with the crowds. Lieu keenly observes, Zacchaeus is "protesting against the summary dismissal of his character by the crowd by affirming how he already behaves."[2]

Ben reads the Greek as suggesting that Zacchaeus is *prepared* to rear-range his finances, presumably due to the presence and welcoming influence of Jesus. Thus, Ben also takes the present-tense verbs as indicating, "I am *now* prepared to give ..." Ben sees the proof of this reading in Jesus' comment that salvation has showed up in that house *today*, not previously. Something happened on that day that changed him.

Jesus affirms his comment. By labeling Zacchaeus a "son of Abraham," Jesus reinforces the tax collector's membership in the covenant community. By speaking of his "salvation," Jesus focuses not on eternal life but on restitution with others in that same community (**vs. 9**). Zacchaeus himself keeps his day job; he remains a chief tax collector. Whether he should or not remains a matter for discussion: can one who works for the occupation government be a "good" person?[3] Is the Roman government necessarily evil? Can empire bring the good as well as the bad?

The scene closes with the general assertion that Jesus, called "Son of Man," comes to seek and save the lost (**vs. 10**). The statement recalls the lost figures of Luke 15, with the focus on saving both the prodigal son and his equally lost brother. Zacchaeus recalls all the other tax collectors, whether followers of John the Baptizer, or among the Twelve, or Jesus' table companions, or figures in parables; these tax collectors either leave their toll booths or, remaining, recognize their membership in the covenant community.

---

[2]   Lieu, *Gospel According to Luke*, 148.
[3]   See discussion of this issue in Wyndy Corbin-Reuschling, "Zacchaeus's Conversion: To Be or Not to Be a Tax Collector (Luke 19:1–10)," *Ex Auditu* 25 (2009): 67–88.

Although identified as a "rich man," Zacchaeus is not condemned. Because he uses his funds not only to host Jesus but also to help the poor, he shows that the rich, through divine grace and appropriate income distribution, can enter the Kingdom.

PARABLE OF THE POUNDS/PARABLE OF COMPETENCE AND COMPENSATION

Luke does not provide details concerning Jesus' table fellowship with the chief tax collector.[4] Instead, Jesus sets the Parable of the Pounds in the context of the chief tax collector's affirmation of his actions. Luke presents Zacchaeus as using his resources honestly and generously and thus as an appropriate steward. The parable extends the question of resource usage and contextualizes it in terms of both economics and eschaton.

The parable also speaks to the question of long-term investment, in funding and in faith. Jesus and his followers are nearing Jerusalem, and the followers are expecting the eschaton at their arrival (**vs. 11**). Since Luke has already allowed that the Kingdom was in their midst, what the disciples are seeking is the consummation of the Kingdom. Luke, however, focuses not on the Kingdom but on Jesus as king. For Luke, the eschaton is far off, coming only after the world has been evangelized. The disciples are the stewards who must do what Zacchaeus does: use their talents wisely in growing the mission.

Jesus begins by describing how a "nobleman" (Greek: *eugenēs*, i.e., a man of good or noble birth; Matt 25.14–30 offers the related "Parable of the Talents," which refers to a man who takes a journey) travels to a foreign land to gain a kingdom (**vs. 12**). Since the only mechanism in Jesus' or Luke's context for gaining such a kingdom was the Roman system, the parable invokes images of Roman colonialism. Jesus' listeners, or Luke's readers, might have thought immediately of Herod the Great's trip to Rome to gain his rule in Judea, Samaria, and Galilee. Other readers might have thought of the prodigal son, who also journeys to a distant country: such journeys, in Luke's Gospel, do not end well. The Book of Acts will tell a different story. Still others, recalling the Jericho setting, may have thought of Herod Archelaus, who engaged in urban construction near the city (Josephus, *Ant.* 17.340). Finally, the nobleman might be Jesus himself, who will leave the earth, be rewarded by the divine for his fidelity, and then return. Not every

---

4   See Snodgrass, *Stories with Intent*, 519–43.

king or ruler or father in a parable must be a cipher for the divine, but nor should this view be ruled out.

Before he leaves, he entrusts ten of his slaves each with ten pounds (Greek: *mna*, the equivalent of 60 talents; the mina was worth about 100 denarii,[5] a very nice chunk of change) and commands them to engage in trade with it in order to earn more money (**vs. 13**). The notice that the citizens of that kingdom hated the nobleman and sent envoys rejecting his claim (**vs. 14**) goes frustratingly underdeveloped in the parable. It serves no narrative need other than to confirm the ruler's negative reputation. It does, however, help ancient readers locate the parable in their own contexts. Delegations of Judeans and Samaritans opposed Herod (Josephus, *Ant.* 17.299–314; *War* 2.80–92); a delegation of Judeans opposed the rule of Herod Archelaus in 4 BCE; Rome deposed him in 6 CE (see Josephus, *Ant.* 17.300)[6]; still others, after the time of Jesus, might have been reminded of Herod Antipas's attempt to gain his father's rule, which Rome gave to Herod Agrippa I (Herodias's brother).

The verse also opens up two possible readings of the parable. On the one hand, we can see the nobleman as representing foreign leaders who colonize, exploit, and demean their subjects. Thus, we readers are placed in the position of resisting him. On the other, we can see the nobleman as representing Jesus, who entrusts his good(s) to his followers and expects those followers to multiply his household by both people and the material goods they bring with them. If we take the first option, then we are left with a nobleman who wins in the end by slaughtering his opponents. This is not new, and it is not good news. If we take the second option, then Jesus is cast in the role of a ruler who damns his opponents to torture and death. That reading does conform to several of the New Testament's eschatological pronouncements, but it is not entirely consistent with a Gospel that proclaims love and peace. Since parables are not exact replicas of the real world, and since the characters go undefined, we are left with problems and paradox, which is what parables often do.[7]

5 Hultgren, *Parables*, 285.
6 For detailed treatment of this connection, see Brian Schultz, "Jesus as Archelaus in the Parable of the Pounds (Lk. 19:11–27)," *Novum Testamentum* 49 (2007): 105–27.
7 See Francis D. Weinert, "The Parable of the Throne Claimant (Luke 19:12, 14–15a, 27) Reconsidered," *CBQ* 39.4 (1977): 505–14, who states, "The story raises the issue of wicked *vs.* just behavior by setting two parties in irrevocable opposition, ascribing action to each that can be justified only if that party is right" (510).

Having obtained his kingship despite the protests, the nobleman summons those ten slaves to see what profit they obtained (**vs. 15**). The first slave produces ten more minas (**vs. 16**), and the nobleman, calling him "good slave," rewards his trustworthiness by giving him authority over ten cities (**vs. 17**). The slave is now also a ruler; the two roles are not incompatible, especially if seen in an ecclesial context where the follower of Jesus, running a church, is to engage in servant leadership. On the other hand, the parable supports the truism that good work is rewarded by *more work*. It does not, as far as we can tell, suggest that the slave made friends by "unrighteous mammon" (cf. 16.9); the text does not speak of making friends, and although the nobleman may have gained the money by exploitation or misappropriation, Luke does not here, as far as we can tell from the parable, consider the slave's action inappropriate.

The same process occurs with the second slave. Having turned the single mina into five (**vs. 18**), he receives rule over five cities (**vs. 19**). According to Elizabeth Dowling, "the first two slaves make outrageous profits of 1000% and 500% ... This would seem to bear out the notion that these slaves have engaged in exploitation so that some of the Earth community will be impoverished by their actions."[8] Adam Braun cites a similar reading from the Gospel of Solentiname: it is a "lousy parable" because it is about "giving the money to others so they can work and work with it and hand over the profits to the owner of the real money."[9] These readings offer astute, modern perspectives. For Luke's own context, or for that of Jesus, the issue is no more suggestive of exploitative practice than is Jesus' promise that those who leave their homes will "get back very much more in this age" (18.30).

Skipping the rest of the slaves, Jesus now focuses on "the other." This final slave, calling the nobleman "Lord" (Greek: *kyrios*), and so enhancing a Christological reading, returns the mina (**vs. 20**). He explains that he had wrapped it in a *soudarion*; normally translated "handkerchief," the term carries the connotation of a "cloth used for perspiration."[10] His excuse is that he feared the nobleman, who is severe (the Greek *austēros*, whence "austere") and who takes money and goods that others obtained for him (**vs. 21**). Otherwise put, the nobleman can be seen as exploiting his slaves, and others under his authority; he can also be seen as patron as well as

---

8   Elizabeth V. Dowling, "Hearing the Voice of Earth in the Lukan Parable of the Pounds," *Colloquium* 48.1 (May 2016): 35–46 (41).

9   Adam F. Braun, "Reframing the Parable of the Pounds in Lukan Narrative and Economic Context: Luke 19:11–28," *Currents in Theology and Mission* 39.6 (2012): 442–48 (442).

10   Fitzmyer, *Luke X–XXIV*, 1236.

imperial retainer. We now have some understanding of why the citizens of the kingdom he received resisted his rule.

And yet, the description of the nobleman can also fit Jesus. In 4.38, Jesus states, "I sent you to reap that for which you did not labor. Others have labored, and you have entered into their labor." If we read the parable Christologically, then the first two slaves have increased the number of people who follow Jesus and so receive ecclesial responsibility for their good work; the one who fears is condemned. Were Jesus to have told the parable to his Jewish contemporaries, they would not get this message. Luke's readers might. All depends on our assessment of the nobleman. If we see parables as allowing for morally problematic characters, and if we see the nobleman as a negative exemplar, we will assess the parable differently than if we are looking for an exemplar or even a positive figure. Jesus often used morally ambiguous characters that had some particular trait to draw an analogy with God's behavior or Kingdom behavior. As Ben notes, granting that Jesus only had flawed human beings with whom to draw analogies, they would never be entirely analogous with God or even with Jesus himself.

How we understand this third slave also will vary depending on our political and religious views. For some, the slave did exactly the right thing: he kept the nobleman from making more money and thus, in a zero-sum economic picture, prevented him from taking funds out of the hands of the poor. He is, as Dowling puts it, "taking his stand against exploitation,"[11] and he has "deliberately chosen ... to take an active stance of resistance against exploitation and unethical practice."[12] William Herzog's reading in favor of the third slave is even stronger: "The servant has unmasked the 'joy of the master' for what it is, the profits of exploitation squandered in wasteful excess, and he has demystified 'good' and 'trustworthy' by exposing the merciless oppression they define."[13] Conversely, the act of counter-exploitation would have been not to return the money to the nobleman, but to use it to fund insurgent activities, or at the least give it to the poor. Had the slave wanted to destroy the nobleman's capital, he could have done a whole lot more than bury a coin. The dishonest steward (16.1–8) proves an apt foil here: books can be cooked, and everyone can win. In contrast, this "other slave" does nothing.

[11]   Dowling, "Hearing the Voice of the Earth," 42.
[12]   Ibid., 44.
[13]   Herzog, *Parables as Subversive Speech*, 165.

The nobleman condemns the "wicked slave" who failed both to follow instructions and to learn from the ruler's own well-known reputation (**vs. 22**). The presentation of the ruler follows that of the judge in the previous parable (18.2,4): first the narrator describes him, and then the characters confirm the description. The man is also practical. He reminds the slave that he had other options aside from burying the mina and using it for trade: he could have put it "on the table" or, in the NRSV's translation, put it "into the bank" so that it could have collected interest (**vs. 23**). A Jewish audience would have recognized that while Torah mandated against taking interest from fellow Jews (cf. Exod 22.25, "If you lend money to my people, to the poor among you, you shall not deal with them as a creditor; you shall not exact interest from them"; and cf. Lev 25.36–37), Deut 23.20 states, "On loans to a foreigner you may charge interest, but on loans to another Israelite you may not charge interest." The nobleman's international travels support the interpretation that charging interest to gentiles is in view.

Concluding the parable, Jesus describes the nobleman as instructing the bystanders to give the buried mina to the slave who already has ten (**vs. 24**), with the bystanders noting that the fellow already has numerous additional funds as well as responsibilities (**vs. 25**). Asserting that the haves will have more, and that the ones who have nothing will have less than nothing (**vs. 26**; the saying echoes 8.18, where Jesus tells his disciples, "pay attention to how you listen; for to those who have, more will be given; and from those who do not have, even what they seem to have will be taken away"), the nobleman concludes his comments by ordering that the people who opposed his rules should be slaughtered before him (**vs. 27**). In contrast to those citizens (and in contrast to Matt 25.30, where the wicked slave is thrown "into the outer darkness"), the "wicked slave" got off easy.

Like the morally ambiguous widow and judge, and the similarly morally ambiguous dishonest manager and his collaborators, neither the slaves nor the noblemen seem unambiguously good. The nobleman is hated by his citizens, but we do not know what specifically he had done to create their dislike. He reaps where he does not sow, but so do most patrons and retainers, for that is how the world works. And, as we have seen, so does Jesus. The slaves follow the orders their master gives them, which is a position Luke commends, several times. Yet if the orders they are following lead to exploitation, should they be praised? On the other hand, we do not know if their extraordinary gains are the result of exploitation. Every new money-maker does not automatically mean that laborers are exploited or the earth is stripped of resources. For many today, the third slave is a hero; we do not share this view. The slave has done nothing to improve anyone else's lot, and he has not revealed anything that was not previously known.

The end of the parable also fails to satisfy. No slaughter is acceptable, and thus the nobleman's action must be condemned. Had the third slave invested the money in rebel activities, would that have helped? We also wonder why the bystanders were concerned with the first slave receiving more, but no one spoke up about the slaughter. We wonder if other readers have the same concern.

TRIUMPHAL ENTRY

A parable containing a ruler whose people do not want him, greater responsibilities given to those who serve, and a mass slaughter sets the context for Jesus' journey to Jerusalem. In the city that "kills the prophets" (13.24), Jesus will face rejection and then death. From that city, the Church will begin its mission to the world. And in that city, the Romans will, a few decades later, destroy the Temple and sell much of the population into slavery.

Instead of going immediately to Jerusalem (**vs. 28**), Jesus "goes up" toward two smaller towns, Bethany (the home of Mary and Martha according to John 11.1, 18) and the otherwise unknown Bethphage (**vs. 29**). The "going up" is the standard idiom for approaching Jerusalem (one could be on the moon and still "go up" to Jerusalem), but, in light of the Gospel of John, readers might hear a resonance of his ascending to the cross and then to heaven. Bethphage, mentioned also in Mark 11.1//Matt 21.9, could be the origin of the mysterious scene that Mark 11.12–25 and Matt 21.18–22 note but that Luke omits, the "cursing of the fig tree." The name Bethphage may derive from the Aramaic "house of unripe figs."

The scene changes to the Mount of Olives, where Zech 14.4 locates the beginnings of redemption, with "the Lord" preparing for the eschatological battle; here the messianic figure known as the Egyptian prepared his attack on Jerusalem (Josephus, *War* 2.262). From this location, Jesus sends two disciples in either one of those towns or another and tells them to search for and bring to him an unridden colt (**vs. 30**). How they would tell that the colt had not been ridden remains unclear. Matthew mentions a "donkey" in order to turn this event into a fulfillment quotation: "Look, your king is coming to you, humble, and mounted on a donkey, and on a colt, the foal of a donkey" (Matt 21.5, citing Zech 9.9; see also John 12.14–15). Luke omits this material, perhaps because it suggests an eschatological focus: Jesus is entering Jerusalem to die, not to bring about the messianic reign just yet.

Jesus tells his disciples that if they are questioned, they only need say "The Lord needs it" (**vs. 31**). The scene can be seen as indicative of Jesus' telepathy. It is also plausible that Jesus has contacts in the city, and they know what he wants. The colt might have come from Bethany, and one of the servants of Mary and Martha could have known who "the Master" was.

A third option is that Jesus' reputation had already reached the city. For a comparable incident, we might imagine two fellows walking into a car dealership, finding a Prius that has never been driven, and opening the door in order to drive the car off the lot. When the sales director queries, "Where are you going with that car?" the fellows respond, "The Lord needs it." Either the sales director has been in touch previously with this "lord" or he has heard enough about him that he does not want to cross him. This "Lord," especially given the immediately preceding parable, may carry the reputation of having his enemies slaughtered.

The plan worked, exactly as Jesus had described (vs. **32**). The colt's owners query the disciples; the disciples give the password, "The Lord needs it" (**vs. 34**); and leading the colt away, they park it before Jesus. As Jesus had stated, "Ask, and it will be given to you" (11.9).

The two disciples put their cloaks on the colt and then place Jesus atop (**vs. 35**). Others on the road produce the ancient version of the "red carpet" by spreading their cloaks before the colt's feet (**vs. 36**). Whether these others are people from the towns or the disciples traveling with Jesus remains unclear. Luke mentions only the disciples who "praise God" for the miracles they had seen (**vs. 37**), although their words are more a praise of Jesus. Alluding to Psa 118.26 ("Blessed is *the one* who comes in the name of the Lord"), one of the Hallel Psalms, they shout, "blessed is *the king* who comes in the name of the Lord" (cf. **38a**). The kingship term functions not only to grant Jesus royal status, but also to evoke the nobleman of the parable, who entered into a city that did not recognize him as its ruler (19.14). At the same time, the focus is on the "king" Jesus, not on the Kingdom, which will not be fully realized until the king's return. Yet the Psalm also speaks of peace (**vs. 38b**), a chorus already heard in the infancy accounts, when the angels praised God for people who find divine favor (2.14).

Readers recognizing this scene as "Palm Sunday" and therefore looking for the palms will have to go to John 12.13. Readers expecting to hear "Hosanna" should turn to Matt 21.9, Mark 11.9–10, or the same verse in John. Luke tends to omit Aramaic and Hebrew terms. Despite the lack of palms, hosannas, and donkeys, Luke's pageant is political, as any witnessing it would have realized. Brent Kinman observes, "For Luke the kingship of

Jesus is revealed at his entry by: (1) his acceptance of the label 'son of David' (18.35–43); (2) his implied identification with the nobleman in the parable of 19.11–27; (3) his commandeering of the animal in accordance with *aggareia* [unpaid labor] conventions; (4) the special animal he rides; (5) the garments from the onlookers used to saddle the animal and pave the path beneath Jesus; and (6) the acclamation of the disciples and, in particular, their address to him as 'king.'"[14]

Some Pharisees (Luke is fairly consistent in noting that not all Pharisees are in opposition to Jesus), addressing Jesus not as "Lord" but as "teacher," ask him to silence his disciples (**vs. 39**). They find their literary counterparts in the parable's description of the citizens who rejected the nobleman's rule. Historically speaking, their concern is warranted. The season, as Luke will soon tell us, is Passover, when Jewish pilgrims come to Jerusalem. It is also the time when Pontius Pilate, the governor, brings his troops from Caesarea Maritima into the city. Luke had already noted that Pilate had mingled the blood of Galileans with their sacrifices (13.1); there is no reason to think that this Passover will be any different.

Jesus rejects the Pharisees' plea. To the contrary, he insists that the message would be shouted by the stones (**vs. 40**). His comment echoes the words of John the Baptist: "God is able from these stones to raise up children to Abraham" (3.8). This scene also silences the Pharisees; this is their last Gospel appearance.

SECOND LAMENT FOR JERUSALEM

Seeing the city, Jesus weeps (**vs. 41**). His reaction is an antithesis to the acclamations of his followers. They are seeing glory; he is predicting destruction. Jesus recognizes what the residents of Jerusalem do not: his is a message of peace, as the acclamation of vs. 38 insisted, but the residents of the "city of peace" are prevented from seeing it. The passive "are hidden" (**vs. 42**) can suggest both divine action and personal ability, as we see also with the two on the road to Emmaus from whom Jesus' identity is hidden (24.16). Predicting the destruction of the city in some detail (**vs. 43**), Jesus laments the deaths of the people alive now and of their children. With some exaggeration, he predicts that no stone will be left on another, that no building will survive. With a theological verdict, he claims that Rome will destroy

---

14   Brent Kinman, "Parousia, Jesus' 'A-Triumphal' Entry, and the Fate of Jerusalem (Luke 19:28–44)," *JBL* 118.2 (1999): 279–94 (288–89).

Jerusalem because the people did not recognize "the time of your visitation from God," that is, the time of his arrival as divine messenger (**vs. 44**).

Jesus' statement can be seen as *ex eventu* prophecy, a prediction after the fact. Luke knew of the destruction of Jerusalem. On the other hand, the city and Temple had already been destroyed once, by the Babylonians in 587 BCE, and Jeremiah's prophecies about this destruction remained part of the Jewish people's collective memory (see also Hab 2.8). Jesus may well have predicted Jerusalem's destruction; he would not have been the first person to do so, nor the last. According to 4QpHab 9.5–7, the city would fall to the army of the "Kittim" (Greeks); Josephus records that one Jesus son of Ananias, in ca. 62 CE, announced at Sukkot (the fall pilgrimage festival of Booths, or Tabernacles), "A voice from the east, a voice from the west, a voice from the four winds, a voice against Jerusalem and the sanctuary, a voice against the bridegroom and the bride, a voice against all the people" (see *War* 6.300–9). Despite being roughed up by the Roman guards, he continued his lament until, during the Roman siege, a stone struck and killed him.

Jesus' weeping over the city provides an alternative to the glories of battle. Wikipedia has a site that records a "List of Battles Since 2001."[15] When we hear the news of the victor and the conquered, do we celebrate or do we weep? Do we claim that cities fall because the people worshiped "the wrong God" or practiced "the wrong religion"? Do we hail the destruction as part of a divine plan? Is Holy War really just wholly war? Nowhere is the mixture of politics and religion more dangerous than when war is thought to be the divine directive.

TEMPLE INCIDENT

Luke does not describe Jesus' entry into the city, and there is no "withering of the fig tree" familiar from Mark and Matthew. Instead, moving directly from lament to Temple, Luke describes Jesus as "driving out those who were selling things" (**vs. 45**). The entry into the Temple fits contemporaneous scenes of the victor's entry into a conquered city[16]; the technical term for this is *Parousia*, the word used in New Testament studies to describe the second coming of Jesus in victory and eschatological judgment (cf. Matt 24.3, 27; 1 Cor 15.23). Luke avoids the term.

---

[15] https://en.wikipedia.org/wiki/List_of_battles_since_2001.
[16] Kinman, "Parousia," 283.

The familiar scene of overturning tables and expelling the moneychangers, which half the readership today think are moneylenders (thereby both confusing the Gospels with the *Merchant of Venice* and reinforcing the idea of Jews as the poster children for late global capitalism), appears in Matt 21.12, Mark 11.15, and John 2.14. The well-known commentary by William Barclay displays the common view of its rationale: "Jesus cleansed the Temple with such violence because its traffic was being used to exploit helpless men and women … It was the passion for social justice which burned in Jesus' heart when he took this drastic step."[17] The problem is that there is no historical evidence for this claim.

The people selling things would be, in historical context, vendors needed to provide the sacrificial offerings for the pilgrims. One does not bring on the journey a sheep or a dove; vendors are needed. Readers are inclined to take these sellers, along with their moneychanging associates, as overcharging and/or selling damaged goods. Nothing in the text, or the history of the Temple, suggests this reasoning. Had the problem been overcharging, Jesus could have said something about the inappropriate use of money; he had hardly been silent about such concerns in the past. Had the problem been damaged goods, again, he could have mentioned this. Even the authors of the Dead Sea Scrolls, which speak against the Jerusalem Temple and posit their own version of this institution (11QTemple) are not concerned with corruption in terms of buying and selling, or moneychanging. They were concerned that the high priests were illegitimate.

The Temple incident fits the Gospel narrative in that it, along with the Triumphal Entry, provides the explanation for how Jesus came to the attention of the High Priest and, eventually, of Pilate. But this explanation creates several problems. First, the claim that Jesus had engaged in such a cleansing two times, once at the beginning of his activities (so John 2) and once the week he died (so the Synoptics), strains credulity. As Ben states, all four Gospels mention only one such action in the Temple, not two. The problem is that *if* this event happened, when did it happen – at the beginning of his public appearances, or in the week he died? Second, had Jesus stopped Temple operations, there is no reason the Temple authorities would allow him to continue to teach there. Third, had Jesus wished the Temple to close, there is no reason for his followers to continue to worship there, as the Book of Acts

¹⁷   William Barclay, *The Gospel of Luke. The New Daily Study Bible* (Louisville: Westminster/ John Knox, 2001; originally published 1953), 287. Barclay's (outdated) commentaries are staples in most Protestant church libraries and many a minister's study.

makes clear. Nor would Paul list Jewish "worship," meaning the Temple service, as among the blessings of the Jewish community (see Rom 9.4).

Determining what prompted Jesus' anger remains a matter of speculation. It is possible, Ben suggests, that selling the animals within the Temple precincts was a new action on the part of the Temple authorities, designed to gain more revenues for the running of the Temple or for the completion of its construction. Jesus would then be objecting to using the holy space, in this case, the court of the gentiles, for such activities.[18] Alternatively, since Amy-Jill sees no reason for the move of the vendors from the Mount of Olives to the Temple precincts to have led to increased Temple revenue, perhaps Jesus wanted to keep trade out of the Temple in line with Zech 14.21, "And there shall no longer be traders in the house of the Lord of hosts on that day."

Alternatively, the entire incident may have developed "as Mark's invention"[19] based either on charges leveled against Jesus that he spoke against the Temple or that he spoke of the Temple as his body that would be destroyed. Amy-Jill finds this an intriguing possibility, and one that explains both how Jesus was able to continue teaching in the Temple and why his followers continued to worship there. Ben thinks the idea is ridiculous.

Complicating the question of historicity is the comment that Luke attributes to Jesus on this occasion. Jesus first quotes Isa 56.7 on the Temple being a "house of prayer" (**vs. 46a**). Mark 11.17 includes the phrase "for all nations," but both Luke and Matthew (21.13) lack the phrase, either because they already knew the Temple was a house of prayer for all nations, or because they knew that the Temple would be destroyed and thus would not be a haven for the nations, or anyone else, or both.

Luke also knows that the Temple already is a house of prayer. In the Parable of the Pharisee and the Tax Collector, both Pharisee and tax collector pray, efficaciously. The Temple is also where Mary and Joseph, Anna and Simeon, and Zechariah, the Father of John the Baptist, participated in liturgical activities. It is also possible that Mark added in the phrase, missing in some earlier accounts. When Herod the Great rebuilt the Temple, he built it as such an international center, with the outer court being the "Court of the Gentiles."

The second comment, about the "den of robbers" or "cave of thieves" (**vs. 46b**), is a direct quote from Jer 7.11. Jeremiah is speaking about those who see the Temple as a place where thieves feel comfortable. A den of thieves is not where robbers rob; it is a place where robbers go after their

---

[18]   See Witherington, *Christology of Jesus*, for extended discussion.

[19]   Paula Fredriksen, *Jesus of Nazareth, King of the Jews* (New York: Vintage, 1999), 210.

crimes to count and stash their loot. The modern analogy would be a thief who enters church on a Sunday morning, puts stolen money into the collection plate, and feels reconciled to God and community. Attempts to read the word for "thief" (Greek: *lēstēs*) as synonymous with "freedom fighter" or "social bandit" do not work for Luke's context.

In Luke, thieves (*lēstēs*) beat, strip, and rob the fellow on the road to Jericho (10.30, 36); they are not, for the purposes of the parable, freedom fighters or dispossessed peasants, and they would not have the reader's sympathy. The term reappears in 22.52, at Jesus' arrest, when he asks if the arresting party seek him as they would a robber. The robbers are involved with criminal activity, not nationalism. They would be among the "sinners" whom Jesus calls. It was not, finally, the case that Rome reserved crucifixion only for sedition. This torturous death was meted out to slaves who proved disobedient, and so served as a warning to other slaves; it was applied to brigands as a similar warning. David Chapman summarizes: not only did slaves, especially "if they participated in rebellion or sought to significantly harm their masters," face crucifixion, but also "crucifixion was repeatedly employed as a punishment against robbers. These were not usually mere thieves, but often they were violent criminals working in gangs. 'Brigands' is perhaps the best term … Perhaps it was the (particularly Roman) concern with peaceful commerce that led to the regular implementation of such a gruesome penalty against those who would disrupt the peace of the empire through banditry and rebellion."[20] Ben notes that while it is true that "majestas" or high treason was not the only grounds for crucifixion – slave revolt was another – "majestas" is the only charge that Jesus could be charged with that would have even been remotely plausible. Ben concludes that Roman law did not exact the death penalty for ordinary theft. Bandits or revolutionaries are one thing, petty thieves or robbers another. Amy-Jill sees Roman "justice" as much more arbitrary, especially in the colonies.

Luke's view of the Temple is, like the historical question of what if anything exactly happened, fraught. The Third Gospel has presented the Temple as the place where prayers are answered; as Gabriel says to Zechariah in 1.13–14, "Your prayer has been heard." Mary and Joseph take Jesus to the Temple for purification offerings, and it is in the Temple that Anna and Simeon bless him. Chapter 3 finds Jesus in the Temple and amazing all by his teaching – a scene that is about to replay in 19.47–48. The Parable of the Pharisee and the Tax Collector shows the Temple as a

---

[20]   David W. Chapman, *Ancient Jewish and Christian Perceptions of Crucifixion,*" WUNT 2.244 (Tübingen: Mohr Siebeck, 2008), 44.

site for reconciliation. Luke ends the Gospel with the reference to Jesus' followers being "continually in the Temple blessing God" (24.54). The Book of Acts continues to feature the followers of Jesus, including Paul, in the Temple. But the Temple is also a "den of robbers" that will be destroyed.

TEMPLE TEACHING

Despite the previous episode, Jesus continues to teach in the Temple. It is possible that the Temple incident, if it happened, was relatively minor. The outer court wall surrounding the Temple enclosed approximately 169,900 square feet. Had Jesus "begun to drive out people," this episode would be comparable to knocking over a stand or two at the football game and then imagining the stadium to be hosting twelve games at the same time. As Luke portrays it, Jesus' action was a prophetic sign act, not an attempt to eradicate selling and money changing from the Temple.

Luke notes that the entire political infrastructure – chief priests, scribes, and leaders – were attempting to kill Jesus (**vs. 47**). The description comes without explication. Why were they attempting to kill him? Was it because he spoke against the Temple? That action would not have been completely anomalous, as we see with the case of Jesus, son of Ananias. Was their ire promoted by the content of his teaching? That would be odd as well, for if the teaching were a problem, getting him off the scene immediately would have been the logical move. Jesus was by no means always in the Temple or holding overnight study sessions; he had taken up lodgings elsewhere in the city, where he could have been arrested.

The final verse of the chapter poses its own set of historical problems. Luke states that the people were "spellbound" by his teaching or, better, "hung upon him" (**vs. 48**). Were this the case, their willingness to see him killed within a week makes little sense. Or, perhaps the crowds were different. Ben notes that there is a clear distinction made between the crowds' reactions to Jesus and those of the Temple leadership.

BRIDGING THE HORIZONS

1. Short People

Randy Newman's parody song, "Short People," could have been based on what the people of Jericho thought of Zacchaeus:

> They got little baby legs
> That stand so low

You got to pick 'em up
Just to say hello
They got little cars
That go beep, beep, beep
They got little voices
Goin' peep, peep, peep
They got grubby little fingers
And dirty little minds
They're gonna get you every time
Well, I don't want no Short People
Don't want no Short People
Don't want no Short People
'Round here

Luke plays on the stereotype of the short person for comedic effect,[21] and Luke should be challenged. Jokes concerning physiognomy, like jokes concerning race or ethnicity, risk harm.

Randy Newman intended that "short" be understood as poking "fun at people who are short-tempered and small-minded, which is quite the opposite of the literal meaning. A lot of people didn't get the joke and thought of Newman as a bigot."[22] One need only substitute "short people" with any other group – the French, Methodists, Hindus, Mormons, whoever – to see the damage that can be done. Given the Gospel's view of disability as connected with demon possession or something that makes an individual incomplete, the difficulty of Luke's presentation of Zacchaeus remains all the more problematic.

2. Welcoming the King

When the disciples then, or today, welcome Jesus, what exactly are they welcoming? Luke says nothing here about eternal life, immortality of the soul, or resurrection of the dead. For Luke, the coming of Jesus is empty unless there is a focus on "peace on earth to people of goodwill."

The scene provokes questions of contemporary politics. When the president or the prime minister comes to town, amid all the hoopla that accompanies such visits, what do we expect to see? What message do we want? Are we beguiled by the show – the limousine, the advance team, the bands – or are we attentive to the message? The Gospel has social implications

---

[21]   See discussion in Richard Vinson, "The Minas Touch: Anti-Kingship Rhetoric in the Gospel of Luke," *Perspectives in Religious Studies* 35.1 (2008): 69–86.

[22]   Randy Newman, "Short People," Live in London (Nonesuch Records, 2011); commentary from www.songfacts.com/detail.php?id=6188.

in terms of loving even one's enemies and praying even for persecutors. Jesus' prayer from the cross for the forgiveness of his executioners reminds that we must not separate the spiritual substance of the narrative from its clear social implications.

3. Not One Stone …

Jesus' predicted the complete destruction of the Temple. The *Kotel* or *Kotel ha-Ma'aravi* (Hebrew: "wall" or "western wall") that partly surrounded the Temple Mount stands as a pilgrimage site for Jews and others. The expression "wailing wall," which is not used in Hebrew, refers to the perception of gentiles watching Jews praying there. Although a place of prayer, and of peace, for many, the site has also been a place of controversy. Christians, in control of the area following Constantine's conversion, treated the site as a garbage dump. In 638 the Muslim ruler, Caliph Omar ibn al-Khattab, restored the site and set up a prayer house. Fifty years late, Caliph Abd al-Malik built the Dome of the Rock, and shortly thereafter the al-Aqsa Mosque was constructed. Crusaders baptized the Dome of the Rock into a church; Saladin returned it to Muslim hands in 1187.

When Jordan gained control of the site in 1948 (the time of the partition of the State of Israel), it barred Jews entry to the Temple Mount. The site came under Israeli control in 1967 (the Six Day War). While Jews then, and to this day, continue to go to the Kotel, the Temple Mount itself has always remained in Muslim control; Israel has barred Jews from praying on the Mount in order to keep the peace. The peace is a fragile one.

4. The Empire

Commentators working from a post-colonial or empire-critical perspective correctly note the abusive powers of empire as well as the allure of hybridity. For teaching about Judea under Roman control, the Monty Python movie *Life of Brian* offers the following helpful dialogue:

REG: They've bled us white, the bastards. They've taken everything we had, and not just from us, from our fathers, and from our fathers' fathers.
LORETTA: And from our fathers' fathers' fathers.
REG: Yeah.
LORETTA: And from our fathers' fathers' fathers' fathers.
REG: Yeah. All right, Stan. Don't labour the point. And what have they ever given us in return?!
XERXES: The aqueduct?

REG: What?

XERXES: The aqueduct.

REG: Oh. Yeah, yeah. They did give us that. Uh, that's true. Yeah.

COMMANDO #3: And the sanitation.

LORETTA: Oh, yeah, the sanitation, Reg. Remember what the city used to be like?

REG: Yeah. All right. I'll grant you the aqueduct and the sanitation are two things that the Romans have done.

MATTHIAS: And the roads.

REG: Well, yeah. Obviously the roads. I mean, the roads go without saying, don't they? But apart from the sanitation, the aqueduct, and the roads –

COMMANDO: Irrigation.

XERXES: Medicine.

COMMANDOS: Huh? Heh? Huh …

COMMANDO #2: Education.

COMMANDOS: Ohh…

REG: Yeah, yeah. All right. Fair enough.

COMMANDO #1: And the wine.

COMMANDOS: Oh, yes. Yeah …

FRANCIS: Yeah. Yeah, that's something we'd really miss, Reg, if the Romans left. Huh.

COMMANDO: Public baths.

LORETTA: And it's safe to walk in the streets at night now, Reg.

FRANCIS: Yeah, they certainly know how to keep order. Let's face it. They're the only ones who could in a place like this.

COMMANDOS: Hehh, heh. Heh heh heh heh heh heh heh.

REG: All right, but apart from the sanitation, the medicine, education, wine, public order, irrigation, roads, a fresh water system, and public health, what have the Romans ever done for us?

XERXES: Brought peace.

REG: Oh. Peace? Shut up![23]

23 Monty Python, *Life of Brian*. Scene 10: "Before the Romans Things Were Smelly" (http://montypython.50webs.com/scripts/Life_of_Brian/10.htm). For something (more) serious, see Steve Mason, "'What Have the Romans Ever Done for Us?' *Brian* and Josephus on Anti-Roman Sentiment," in Joan E. Taylor (ed.), *Jesus and Brian: Exploring the Historical Jesus and His Times via Monty Python's Life of Brian* (London: Bloomsbury T&T Clark, 2015), 185–206.

Luke 20 Questions in the Temple

¹ One day, as he was teaching the people in the Temple and telling the good news, the chief priests and the scribes came with the elders ² and said to him, "Tell us, by what authority are you doing these things? Who is it who gave you this authority?"

³ He answered them, "I will also ask you a question, and you tell me: ⁴ Did the baptism of John come from heaven, or was it of human origin?"

⁵ They discussed it with one another, saying, "If we say, 'From heaven,' he will say, 'Why did you not believe him?' ⁶ But if we say, 'Of human origin,' all the people will stone us; for they are convinced that John was a prophet." ⁷ So they answered that they did not know where it came from.

⁸ Then Jesus said to them, "Neither will I tell you by what authority I am doing these things."

PARABLE OF THE MURDEROUS TENANTS

⁹ He began to tell the people this parable: "A man planted a vineyard, and leased it to tenants, and went to another country for a long time. ¹⁰ When the season came, he sent a slave to the tenants in order that they might give him his share of the produce of the vineyard; but the tenants beat him and sent him away empty-handed. ¹¹ Next he sent another slave; that one also they beat and insulted and sent away empty-handed. ¹² And he sent still a third; this one also they wounded and threw out.

¹³ Then the owner of the vineyard said, 'What shall I do? I will send my beloved son; perhaps they will respect him.' ¹⁴ But when the tenants saw him, they discussed it among themselves and said, 'This is the heir; let us kill him so that the inheritance may be ours.' ¹⁵ So they threw him out of the vineyard and killed him.

What then will the owner of the vineyard do to them? ¹⁶ He will come and destroy those tenants and give the vineyard to others." When they heard this, they said, "Heaven forbid!"

¹⁷ But he looked at them and said, "What then does this text mean: 'The stone that the builders rejected has become the cornerstone'? ¹⁸ Everyone who falls on that stone will be broken to pieces; and it will crush anyone on whom it falls."

¹⁹ When the scribes and chief priests realized that he had told this parable against them, they wanted to lay hands on him at that very hour, but they feared the people.

PAYING TAXES TO CAESAR

²⁰ So they watched him and sent spies who pretended to be honest, in order to trap him by what he said, so as to hand him over to the jurisdiction and authority of the governor.

²¹ So they asked him, "Teacher, we know that you are right in what you say and teach, and you show deference to no one, but teach the way of God in accordance with truth. ²² Is it lawful for us to pay taxes to the emperor, or not?"

²³ But he perceived their craftiness and said to them, ²⁴ "Show me a denarius. Whose head and whose title does it bear?" They said, "The emperor's." ²⁵ He said to them, "Then give to the emperor the things that are the emperor's, and to God the things that are God's."

²⁶ And they were not able in the presence of the people to trap him by what he said; and being amazed by his answer, they became silent.

QUESTIONS ABOUT RESURRECTION

²⁷ Some Sadducees, those who say there is no resurrection, came to him ²⁸ and asked him a question, "Teacher, Moses wrote for us that if a man's brother dies, leaving a wife but no children, the man shall marry the widow and raise up children for his brother. ²⁹ Now there were seven brothers; the first married, and died childless; ³⁰ then the second, ³¹ and the third married her, and so in the same way all seven died childless. ³² Finally the woman also died. ³³ In the resurrection, therefore, whose wife will the woman be? For the seven had married her."

³⁴ Jesus said to them, "Those who belong to this age marry and are given in marriage; ³⁵ but those who are considered worthy of a place in that age

and in the resurrection from the dead neither marry nor are given in marriage. [36] Indeed they cannot die anymore, because they are like angels and are children of God, being children of the resurrection. [37] And the fact that the dead are raised Moses himself showed, in the story about the bush, where he speaks of the Lord as the God of Abraham, the God of Isaac, and the God of Jacob. [38] Now he is God not of the dead, but of the living; for to him all of them are alive."

[39] Then some of the scribes answered, "Teacher, you have spoken well." [40] For they no longer dared to ask him another question.

JESUS' FINAL QUESTION

[41] Then he said to them, "How can they say that the Messiah is David's son? [42] For David himself says in the book of Psalms, "The Lord said to my Lord, "Sit at my right hand, [43] until I make your enemies your footstool." ' [44] David thus calls him Lord; so how can he be his son?"

WARNINGS AGAINST SCRIBES

[45] In the hearing of all the people he said to the disciples, [46] "Beware of the scribes, who like to walk around in long robes, and love to be greeted with respect in the marketplaces, and to have the best seats in the synagogues and places of honor at banquets. [47] They devour widows' houses and for the sake of appearance say long prayers. They will receive the greater condemnation."

Luke 20, containing five controversy narratives and a concluding warning about the scribes, follows Mark's Gospel closely; the major omission is the question about the greatest commandment, which Luke reframed in the run-up to the Parable of the Good Samaritan (10.25–28; cf. Mark 12.28–34). Together with the account of the widow who puts her coins into the Temple treasury (21.1–4) and the eschatological warnings and woes that conclude in 21.38, Chapters 20 and 21 present Jesus as teaching daily in the Temple (cf. 19.47). Theophilus, Luke's ideal reader, might have associated these teachings, including debates with those who doubt Jesus' authority, with the public philosophical discussions common in the Roman world (cf. Acts 17.18–34; Lucian of Samosata, *Zeus Rants* 4; *Alexander the False Prophet*, 44–46). Luke carefully portrays Jesus as rhetorically clever, critical, and competent. At the same time, Luke portrays the various groups of opponents as at best inept and ultimately as venal.

THE SOURCE OF AUTHORITY

In the Temple (**vs. 1**), Jesus teaches the Gospel (Greek: *euangelizō*, whence "evangelical"). The setting jars, given the incident in the previous chapter where Jesus sought to expel people from that same setting. Ben says it was not *people in general* whom he was previously expelling, in particular not people who were not vendors, and in any case, Jesus was performing a prophetic sign act, not an actual cleansing of the Temple. One could see Jesus as having taken possession of the Temple, at least temporarily, after expelling its previous inhabitants; it is better, however, to see both Jesus and the Temple as working together here. That the Temple can be a place of reconciliation has already been demonstrated both by the infancy materials and, in Amy-Jill's view, by the Parable of the Pharisee and the Tax Collector (18.10–14). The leadership of "chief priests, scribes," and "elders" – Jerusalem's political infrastructure – will attempt to do to Jesus, unsuccessfully, what he had done to those who were selling things (19.45). What Jesus has to "sell," he gives away for free, even as he will ultimately pay for his activities with his life.

The leadership, who ostensibly have authority in the Temple setting, begin their attack by questioning Jesus about the source of his authority (**vs. 2**). The chief priests had gained their authority courtesy of Pontius Pilate, who controls the priestly vestments and, as governor, would be concerned that the Temple run smoothly. They had earlier gained their authority when the legitimate heirs of the priesthood were first replaced by the Hasmonean (Maccabean) rulers, and then by Herod the Great, who put into the Temple men from priestly families he could control. Rome simply took up the system. The scribes derive authority from their ability to read, write, and interpret Scripture. The elders gain authority through their age and, perhaps, long service to the Temple and so to the people. In their case, authority is earned rather than simply ascribed. Yet as with most political systems, wealth and networking serve to keep particular people in control and particular views in place.

Their questioning Jesus, "by what authority are you doing these things?" is not on the surface illegitimate: even Satan can quote Scripture (so 4.3–12), and the distinction between benevolent miracle and demonic sign is not always clear. Already in 11.15–16, unnamed people from the crowd had questioned whether Jesus' exorcisms were performed on behalf of the devil. However, because Jesus had predicted that the "elders, chief priests, and scribes" would reject him (9.22), and because Luke had stated, without explanation, that the "chief priests, the scribes, and the leaders of the people kept looking for a way to kill him" (19.47) – these are the only previous references to the three groups – their questioning should be taken as hostile.

The double question, which concerns both the source of Jesus' authority and the "things" that he is doing (Greek: *poieis*), addresses not only his teaching. That verb "doing" adverts to the leaders' own inability to "do anything" (19.48) to him, because "all the people" were hanging on his every word. What Jesus is *doing* is influencing the crowds, not with miracles but with teaching. This distance between the leadership and the people will be confirmed as the discussion continues.

Jesus responds with a question of his own (**vs. 3**); he had earlier used this technique, the so-called Socratic method of answering a question with a question, on the lawyer who had asked him about eternal life (10.26). His question produces an honor challenge along the same lines as the questions to be put to him in this chapter about taxation and resurrection of the dead: each is designed both to show the cleverness of the questioner and to shame the interlocutor. These questions cannot be answered with a simple "yes" or "no"; either of those responses will create problems. Jesus' question, "Did the baptism of John come from heaven, or was it of human origin?" (**vs. 4**) traps his questioners. It also engages the readers, who last encountered the Baptizer in 16.16, when Jesus had spoken of the "good news of the Kingdom." Recollection of that verse in turn echoes the first verse of Chapter 20, where Jesus himself teaches the "good news."

The leaders are aware that Jesus has trapped them. Were they to say that John's authority came from heaven (and how would they know?), the crowd would accuse them of hypocrisy for not supporting him (**vs. 5**). Were they to state that John's authority was of human origin (and again, how would they know?), the crowd, taken to be John's supporters, would not only reject them but seek to kill them (**vs. 6**). Their reaction, hyperbolic, ironically reverses what they had planned to do to Jesus.

The scene develops the role of the people in the Passion Narrative. Luke presents the people as supporters of John and therefore on the side of Jesus. It also distinguishes the political authorities both from "all the people" (and from Luke's audience, who know about John's commission; cf. 1.76; 3.2–20; 7.26–30; 16.16). The audience knows the earlier stories; the priests and elders do not. The audience will also recognize the irony of the leaders' fear of being stoned, both because Jesus himself, the popular leader, is the one who will be put to death without a violent response from the crowd, and because

Jesus' follower, Stephen, will be stoned by a contingent of Temple leadership (Acts 7.57–58).

By asking about John's authority, Jesus compares his work to that of John, and he sees the general validation of John's ministry as validating of his own.[1] The source of authority in both cases – John's baptism and Jesus' teachings – is a theological one, and such a source cannot be proved or disproved. There is no empirical evidence to which Jesus could point that would convince people about the source of John's baptism, or his own ministry. Nor could any argument talk the followers of John and Jesus out of their belief. That is why professional apologists and professional atheists speak only to their own choirs. Belief in Jesus, or John, does not arise simply from logical argument; it comes to the believer as a gift. For Luke, it comes also by narrative confirmation: if one believes the earlier chapters of Luke to be accurate reporting, one must believe what Jesus states.

Stymied, the leaders admit their inability to answer Jesus' question (**vs. 7**). Jesus responds in kind: if they cannot answer his question, he will not answer theirs (**vs. 8**). Readers, however, can easily supply the answer, since Luke has been depicting the heavenly source of Jesus' authority since the first chapter.

PARABLE OF THE MURDEROUS TENANTS

As if ignoring the leaders, Jesus now begins to speak with "the people," and he tells them a parable about a man who planted a vineyard, leased it to tenants, and went to another country (**vs. 9**). Luke likely derived the Parable of the Wicked Tenants from Mark 12.1–12 (with allusion to Isa 5.1–7; truncated versions appear in Matt 21.33–46 and *Thomas* 65). For most readers, the parable has both earthly and allegorical functions. The story of a person who plants a vineyard, rents it to tenant farmers, and goes away for an extended period (**vs. 9**) would be a familiar tale to anyone living in the Roman Empire. However, the parable also has allegorical connections: the man on the journey is either God or Jesus (or both), the slaves are the prophets (Isaiah, Jeremiah, etc.), the son is Jesus, and the wicked tenants are Israel's leaders if not all Jews who refuse to join Jesus and his followers.[2]

The mention of the "vineyard" would have had particularly strong associations for anyone familiar with Israel's Scriptures. Along with Isaiah's

---

[1]   See Witherington, *Christology of Jesus*, 38–55.
[2]   See details in Snodgrass, *Stories with Intent*, 292.

famous Parable of the Vineyard, which begins, "Let me sing for my beloved my love-song concerning his vineyard: My beloved had a vineyard on a very fertile hill ... For the vineyard of the LORD of hosts is the house of Israel, and the people of Judah are his pleasant planting" (Isa 5.1–7 cf. 27.2–5), Jeremiah (2.21) and the Psalmist (80.8–9) also depict Israel as a vineyard planted by God. While parables are not allegories in that not every element has a connection in the world outside the parable, some images retain strong associative values. Both Jesus' and Luke's audience would have understood the vineyard to be related both to the land of Israel and to the people Israel.

Luke's readers have another association: Jesus had just told a parable about a man who entrusts his property to slaves while he journeys to a distant region to gain political control (19.12–27). At the end of the parable, the noble commands that the people who resisted his reign be slaughtered. The same motifs recycle here: a man with property given to others, the man's temporary absence, the question of whether the slaves/tenants will make good use of the property, how much of the investment the man will gain, the fate of the slaves/tenants, a slaughter. The recycling also includes moral questions, including that of whether the citizens should be slaughtered. Is any killing justified? What should be the fate of those who kill?

The note that the man was away "for a long time" intimates another allegorical association: the delay of the *Parousia*. Importing this concern into the parable creates another possible interpretation: if Jesus is the one who leased the land, then the tenants would be the people to whom he entrusted his authority, the disciples. Luke resists this interpretation by noting at the end of the parable that the "scribes and chief priests realized that he had told this parable against them" (vs. 19). Christian readers today, if they listen closely, should hear not only an indictment against Jerusalem's political leadership in the first century, but also an indictment against those political and ecclesial authorities in the twenty-first century who put their self-interests above the concerns of the people.

At the appropriate "season" (Greek: *kairos*, the appropriate "time"), the man sends a slave (Greek: *doulos*) to collect his share of the produce, but the tenants beat him and send him off without the funds (**vs. 10**). The parable passes over any concern for the slave. Readers tend to sympathize with the traveler who is beaten by robbers in the Parable of the Good Samaritan; rarer is empathy for the beaten slave. It would have been rare among Luke's audience as well: beating of slaves was normative practice, just as in some times and cultures across the globe the beating of children and the beating of wives are common practices. Careful readers should take the time to hear, and react, to such beating. But the reader who understands that the slaves are actually the revered prophets should have sympathy with them and their plight.

The man, undeterred by this result, sends another slave. At this point, the parable begins to leave the real world and enter the world of imagination. There is no reason for the man to think that a different slave would create a different result. One wonders also what the second slave was thinking. He had no choice in the matter of assignment despite the violence he knew would meet him. He is comparable to the slaves of the previous parable: they faced the threat of their harsh master, and now this slave faces the threat from the tenants. Here the allegory breaks down, for as in all parables, a full connection between elements inside and out is not maintained. We do not need to claim that God, or Jesus, forces people into slavery or torture.

The second slave experiences the same result, although the violence is exacerbated (**vs. 11**). He is not only beaten and sent away, he is "insulted" or, better, "dishonored" (Greek: *atimadzō*). Luke's readers would not think of the slave himself as having honor, for "honor" belongs only to the free. The slave himself has no honor to lose, but again prophets do, hence the reference to honor. The slave is the representative of his master, so what is done to the slave is symbolically done to the one who sent him. To dishonor the slave is to dishonor his master. Allegorically, the beating of the slave/prophet is the dishonoring of God.

The slaveowner sends another slave. The violence increases: the tenants beat the first slave and dishonor and beat the second. The third they wound (**vs. 12**). Mark 12.4 states that the third slave is killed, but Luke reserves the maximum horror for the owner's son.

After three attempts, the slaveowner finally realizes that he has a problem. Applicable here is the old line, sometimes attributed to Albert Einstein but tracked earlier to a 1981 statement by Narcotics Anonymous: "Insanity is repeating the same mistakes and expecting different result."[3] Luke helps to mitigate the sense that the slaveowner has acted foolishly by emphasizing the parable's allegorical import. The NRSV's "owner of the vineyard" (**vs. 13a**) mistranslates the Greek *kyrios,* "lord" and so masks the allusion to the "lord of the vineyard" (Isa 5.7). The allegory continues with the lord's voice-over. He first asks what he should do (**vs. 13b**). His question recollects Isa 5.4: "What more was there to do for my vineyard, that I have not done in it?"

---

[3]   http://quoteinvestigator.com/2017/03/23/same/.

In Isaiah, the vineyard is the problem; in Luke, the problem shifts to the evil tenants. Note that the critique here is not against the vineyard itself, that is, Israel, but against the tenants or tenders of it.

The narrative audience of the question goes unmentioned, so the reader has the responsibility for providing the answer. What would *we* do were we in the lord's sandals? Sending another slave would only result in more violence. Contacting local political authorities might have been a smart move; even hiring soldiers might have helped. Given the language of dishonor, perhaps using social capital to shame the tenants might have had some import. And what do we want the result to be? Gaining the produce, yes, but also punishing the tenants? If punishing, then what punishment?

The Lord of the Vineyard opts for what looks like the most insane decision: he will send his "beloved son." The allegory is heavy-handed. "Beloved son" is the title bestowed upon Jesus at this baptism (3.22) and Transfiguration (9.35). The lord will send his son in the expectation that the tenants will "respect" him (**vs. 13c**). C. F. Evans notes, "The story is so artificial and implausible as not to be intelligible with reference to actual conditions of life, or any likely course of events, but only as an allegory of God's dealings with Israel's leaders ..."[4] Yet even with this allegory in place, the questions still remain. For example, do prophets have any choice in their calling? What would we, as readers, have God do with these wicked tenants? If the tenants believe they can do violence in the absence of their "lord," should we conclude that the only thing keeping us moral is the "fear of God" or the fear of hell? If we do reach this conclusion, then we have also determined that fear is more potent than love, and that divinity is not benevolent but coercive. How far we extend the allegory is our choice.

When the son arrives, the tenants recognize him as the heir and plot to kill him (**14a**). There is no messianic secret, and the tenants have no excuse. Whereas Jesus will ask for divine forgiveness for those "who do not know what they are doing" (23.34), no such plea is appropriate here. The tenants know exactly what they are doing. And whereas the violence shown toward the slaves could have been spontaneous, the violence done to the son is premeditated. The notion that the tenants could then acquire the vineyard, the "inheritance," fits within ancient legal theory. With no one left to claim the property, the ownership becomes a matter of finders-keepers or better said, "squatter's rights."

---

4   C. F. Evans, *Luke*, 698.

By describing the tenants as first casting the heir out of the vineyard and then killing him (**vs. 15a**) – a reversal of the order in Mark 12.8 – Luke may be hinting at the location of the crucifixion outside Jerusalem (cf. Heb 13.12–13). We hear nothing of what the son said, if he said anything at all. His role is solely to represent his father and to be the victim. Given not only the parable itself but also Jesus' predictions of his death, no other result would be expected.

As the "lord of the vineyard" had rhetorically questioned what he should do concerning the mistreatment of his slaves, so Jesus the narrator now asks what the "lord of the vineyard" should do to the tenants who had killed his beloved son (**vs. 15b**). Perhaps the early reciters of Luke's Gospel paused here to see how the audience would respond. Would they call for more violence? Would they say something about forgiving seventy-seven times? Would a few be thankful that they do not have to answer the question, since like the questions regarding John the Baptizer that began this chapter, there are no unproblematic responses?

Jesus then provides the answers: the lord will destroy the tenants and lease the vineyard to others (**vs. 16a**). The sentence moves the parable away from Isa 5, where the vineyard's failure to yield crops results in its destruction; here the vineyard – the people and the land – are protected, but the caretakers are not.

Only Luke has the people respond, "may it not be so" (**vs. 16b**, the only NT use of *mē genoito* outside of Paul's Epistles; the NRSV's "heaven forbid" unnecessarily injects a religious connotation). Why the people react in this way remains unclear. It is unlikely they regarded the tenants as oppressed peasants appropriately revolting against a stratified social system.[5] Murder is still murder, and the allegorical elements of the parable – the lord, the vineyard, the delay – all suggest a theological rather than economic or sociological import. It is possible that the narrative audience listening to this parable, the people listening to Jesus in the Temple setting, recognized Jesus as the son/Son, and so rejected the entire scenario, from the death of the son to the destruction of the tenants.

Jesus then looks at the people as he poses another question (**vs. 17**), this one about the meaning of Psa 117.22 (LXX): "the stone that the builders rejected has become the cornerstone." Whereas Mark (12.11) and Matthew (21.42) record Psalm's next verse, which speaks of the amazing acts of God, the Third Gospel keeps the focus on the rejection. Not waiting for the answer,

[5]   *Contra*, e.g., Buttrick, *Parables*, 80; Herzog, *Parables as Subversive Speech*, 98–113.

Jesus in Luke adds the notice that this rejected stone will destroy any who comes up against it (**vs. 18**). The allusion may be to Isa 8.14, which speaks of a stone of stumbling that would ensnare the inhabitants of Jerusalem. The empire-destroying stone of Dan 2.34, 44–45 may also underlie Luke's reference.[6] The verse shifts the emphasis from the parable's foreshadowing of Jesus' own death to the destruction of the people Luke takes as responsible for both killing Jesus and dooming themselves. Luke leaves Jesus' question about the two quotations, "what then does this text mean?" (vs. 17) unanswered in the narrative: readers will need to determine what those verses mean in full.

The "scribes and chief priests" realize that the parable targeted them (**vs. 19a**). Although spoken to the people, the parable serves primarily to indict those same chief priests, scribes, and elders who are seeking to undermine Jesus' authority. By describing the local leaders as recognizing Jesus' condemnation, Luke not only condemns them but also exculpates the Romans.

Wanting to arrest Jesus, they fulfill Jesus' prediction about their plotting as well as their rejection. Fear of the people prevents these leaders from arresting Jesus (**vs. 19b**), and fear of the people adds nuance to the parables. The people are not without agency: the people can choose their loyalties; the people can revolt or comply. How the people will react as the Passion Narrative continues will help to determine Jesus' fate, and for narrative purposes, their own. Luke has already depicted Jesus as weeping not over the Temple or its authorities, but over the city of Jerusalem. We can therefore anticipate that the popular acclaim the people give him here will dissipate. If we take the parable as speaking not only about false leaders in Jerusalem in the 30s but also about any false leaders who abuse and execute rather than serve as good tenants, then the message about the power of the people continues to speak to readers. The people have some control, always. Saying "too bad" or "heaven forbid" but not acting is not a good response.

Rather than arrest Jesus and so risk popular revolt, the local authorities plan to catch him in a political trap and have the Roman governor condemn him. Their conclusion adds another layer of interpretation to the parable. If the vineyard stands for the land of Israel and the people Israel,

---

[6]   Luke seems to know the same catena of stone texts the author of 1 Pet 2.4–8 knew and perhaps that Paul knew as well (Rom 9.32–33). See Ben Witherington III, *Isaiah Old and New: Exegesis, Intertextuality, and Hermeneutics* (Minneapolis: Fortress Press, 2017) and Ben Witherington III, *Psalms Old and New: Exegesis, Intertextuality, and Hermeneutics* (Minneapolis: Fortress Press, 2017).

and if the other tenants are the Romans, then these other tenants are also under threat. What the "lord" did to the first set of tenants he can do to the second, or the third. Thus, the parable may see not only an end to the local Jerusalem authority, but also to Roman authority, and to those who then will replace Imperial Rome.

PAYING TAXES TO CAESAR

The chapter began with a question of Jesus' authority (Greek: *exousia*). The subject of authority now resurfaces as the chief priests and scribes send proxies to Jesus in order to trap him and bring him under the authority (*exousia*) of Rome. Jesus' parable becomes a self-fulfilling prophecy, as the plans to kill him are set in motion.

Questions designed to trap continue. The first question, about the authority of John, Jesus leaves unanswered. The second series of questions, from the lord of the vineyard's "What shall I do?" to Jesus' question of what should be done to the tenants, receive their answers in the parable. Jesus' question about the meaning of Psa 117.22 will receive a partial answer in the rest of the Gospel and Acts since for Luke, the damage created by the stone will be fulfilled in Jerusalem's destruction.

Under the pretense of righteousness, the "spies" sent by the Temple leaders – both details are Lucan additions to Mark's account – begin with sycophantic compliments, *captatio benevolentiae*, that, ironically, speak truth. They address Jesus as "teacher" and so locate themselves in the same category as the Pharisee who questioned in interior monologue Jesus' recognition of the woman anointing his feet (7.40), the lawyer who attempted to trap Jesus with his own question about defining neighbors (10.25, 29), and the ruler unwilling to give up his wealth (18.18). Yet the title "teacher" is a correct title (**vs. 20**). The spies state that Jesus is "right" (Greek: *orthōs*, whence "ortho-doxy") in his words and teachings, and that he shows deference (Greek: *lambaneis prosōpon*, literally, "receives face") to no one (**vs. 21**). Conversely, the spies' pretense (Greek: *hypokrinomai*, a cognate with *hypokrisis*, whence "hypocrisy") shows that they are trying to manipulate him with compliments. Enhancing the irony is the fact that their hypocrisy would not be known to the narrative audience, the people in the Temple who were listening to Jesus, but readers cannot miss its mark.

In **vs. 22**, Luke adds "for us" to the Markan question – "is it permitted *for us* to pay a tax to Caesar or not?" The addition makes the question specific for Jews: does the Torah allow the paying of a poll or head tax

(Greek: *phoros*, the proper term; see 23.2)? The Torah does not speak to the question, but it suggests, as does Rabbinic Judaism, that the law of the land is the law; one abides by the dictates of the state unless those dictates force the breaking of the commandments. Luke portrays Joseph as willing to register for the census, which meant compliance with Roman taxation (2.2). According to Josephus, King Herod Agrippa II advised the people to pay the Roman tribute in order to prevent the occasion for revolt, and the people at first gladly heeded him (*War* 2.403–406). On the other hand, Josephus is writing in Rome and with Roman imperial sponsorship; the "glad" payment may be more apologetic than accurate, for people rarely pay taxes with joy. Conversely, Judas the Galilean, who led the tax revolt in 6 CE, regarded the payment of taxes to Rome as a betrayal of Israel's status as God's people (cf. Josephus, *Ant.* 18.1–25; 20.102; *War* 2.117–118; 7.253–258). Luke knows about Judas the Galilean (see Acts 5.37) and rejects any connection between him and Jesus.

The spies' question is not simply a matter of the Torah interpretation. Were Jesus to advise against payment, Rome would see his response as treason. Were he to advise payment, he would lose support from some among the people. Given the Passover setting in Jerusalem, with Rome's presence made paramount and resentment of the Empire heightened, the question is loaded.

Jesus recognizes the trap (**vs. 23**). Luke states that he sees their "craftiness" (Greek: *panourgia*, a rhetorical term indicating cleverness of speech; Mark reads "hypocrisy"). In response, he traps the spies. First, he tells them to display a denarius (**vs. 24**): that they are carrying this coin, and he by implication is not, shows that they are the ones who participate in the Roman system. Then he asks them – another question – about the image (the NRSV's "head" is an inaccurate translation of the Greek *eikon* [whence "icon"] meaning "image") and inscription. The reference to "image" evokes Deut 4.16 (LXX): "do not act corruptly by making an idol for yourselves, in the form of any figure (*eikon*) – the likeness of male or female." The coin smacks of idolatry. The spies respond that the image is that of Caesar; the inscription on a denarius reads, "Tiberius Caesar, son of the divine Augustus, Augustus." The connection to idolatry is secured: either Jesus is the son of the divine, or Caesar is. Here the options are mutually exclusive, and the political challenge is in play.

Jesus responds, "pay back to Caesar the things which are Caesar's, and to God the things that are God's" (**vs. 25**).[7] This saying does not, contrary to some popular readings, endorse the separation of church and state. Nor

[7] See also *Gospel of Thomas* 100, *Egerton Papyrus* 2; and Justin Martyr, *Apol.* 1.17.2.

is it necessarily a recognition of Caesar's authority, even in a limited way. Nor is it even an answer to the question, since it poses a question of its own: what do *you* think belongs to Caesar, and what do *you* think belongs to God? Jesus may be suggesting that Caesar be given back his unrighteous mammon; since "the things of/from Caesar" do exist, and can be returned to him.[8] Or, Jesus' view might be that nothing is owed to Caesar, since all is owed to God. Jesus returns the responsibility for determining the answer to the spies, and so Luke returns the responsibility to the readers. For Luke, given the narrative context, the followers of Jesus are to obey Rome's laws, including payment of taxes, as the Nativity story indicates. For the historical Jesus himself, the response is less clear. For the reader today, the response is also less clear: are there some governments one cannot support? The question of the power of the people, which the local leaders surfaced in vs. 19b, lingers in the background.

Like the local leaders, the spies are stunned into silence (**vs. 26**). They will speak about the matter later to Pilate, when they accuse Jesus of "forbidding us to pay taxes to the emperor" (23.2), a Lucan addition to the charges presented in Mark, and something Jesus manifestly did not do.

QUESTIONS ABOUT RESURRECTION

The traps continue in vss. 27–40, the chapter's third controversy account. Here the inquisitors are the Sadducees (**vs. 27a**), who make their first appearance in the Gospel (cf. Acts 4.1; 5.17; 23.6–8), and here the question turns from orthopraxy to orthodoxy. Like the spies, the Sadducees have no interest in obtaining information: because they did not accept the concept of bodily resurrection (**vs. 27b**; see Josephus, *Ant.* 18.16), the question they pose to Jesus has to serve a purpose other than that of obtaining information. Thus, although Luke does not make the point explicit, the Sadducees also are trying to trap Jesus.

Their question concerns another legal issue. In speaking about what "Moses wrote" (**vs. 28**) – the Sadducees are expressing the standard view that Moses was the author of the Torah – they inquire about the practice described Deut 25.5–6: "When brothers reside together, and one of them dies and has no son, the wife of the deceased shall not be married outside the family to a stranger. Her husband's brother shall go in to her, taking her in marriage, and performing the duty of a husband's brother to her, and the

---

[8]   See Witherington, *Matthew*, 410–13.

firstborn whom she bears shall succeed to the name of the deceased brother, so that his name may not be blotted out of Israel." Although by the first century, levirate marriage (*levir* is Latin for "husband's brother") was no longer being practiced, the tradition was known (see also Gen 38.8; Deut 25.5; Ruth 4.1–12; cf. Tobit 6.9–12; 7.12–15; Josephus, *Ant.* 4.254–56).

In the Sadducees' hypothetical case, a woman is married to the oldest of seven brothers, who then dies childless (**vs. 29**). She then marries the second brother (**vs. 30**), and the third, and then the rest (**vs. 31**). Finally, she dies (**vs. 32**). The Sadducees then pose their *reductio ad absurdum* question: whose wife will she be in the resurrection (**vs. 33**)? Their question is designed both to trap Jesus and to demonstrate why, in their view, the concept of physical resurrection is ludicrous.

For Jesus' reply, Luke generally follows Mark 12.18–27 but omits the rebuke about the Sadducees not knowing the power of God. Jesus' response begins with several allusions to earlier sayings. His mention of the "children of this age" echoes 16.8b, the comment about how the children of this age are more shrewd than the "children of light." Thereby Luke signals to readers that Jesus recognizes the shrewdness, and the illegitimacy, of the questioners. Jesus' comment about the children belonging to this age, who marry and are given in marriage (gender roles apply here; he speaks of men who actively marry and women who passively "are given") (**vs. 34**) alludes to his earlier mention of the generation of Noah, those who ate and drank and who were married and given in marriage, and so did not anticipate the flood (17.27).

Jesus then distinguishes between the (unworthy) children of the present age and the worthy ones both in the present age and in the resurrection age to come: these children do not marry (**vs. 35**). That the Sadducees do not believe in angels or resurrection is irrelevant to Jesus: they asked him a question premised on a belief they do not hold; Jesus responded with a belief they also do not hold.

Amy-Jill sees Luke here as foregrounding the celibate life, if not on earth then certainly in the resurrection. In Luke's Gospel and Acts, procreation is not enjoined; to the contrary, husbands and wives separate in the new fictive kinship group of mothers and brothers and sisters (cf. 14.26; 18.29). Thus, Jesus corrects the Sadducees' mistaken understanding about the resurrected life: this new age is not a time of marriage, for the resurrected bodies are like the bodies of angels (**vs. 36**), and angels have no desire for sexual activities or need for procreation. Reference to "children of the resurrection" suggests that the resurrected beings take their roles *as* children rather than procreators. The Sadducees, who also do not believe in angels (Acts 23.8), would be sputtering at this point.

The notion of the desexualized resurrected or angelic body appears elsewhere in contemporaneous Jewish literature. In his treatise on *Abel* (5), Philo describes Abraham as having become "equal to the angels," who are incorporeal (Greek: *asōmaoi*, lit. "without bodies"). A late first-century Jewish apocalyptic book, *2 Baruch* 51.5, 10, similarly says the risen righteous will be turned into the splendor of angels. The Babylonian Talmud, *Berakot* 17a, states, "The World to Come has no eating, drinking, reproduction, commerce, jealousy, hatred, or rivalry. Rather, the righteous sit with their crowns on their heads, enjoying the shine of the Divine Presence, as it says, 'And they saw the Lord and they ate and drank'" (the citation is to Exod 24.11). On the other hand, that same tractate states that three things provide a foretaste of this blessed life: the Sabbath, a sunny day, and sexual intercourse (*b. Ber.* 57b). Rabbinic views of the afterlife vary, and nothing other than resurrection receives extensive commentary. Indeed, the more Christian authors talked about issues of salvation, heaven and hell, and final judgment, the more the Rabbinic writers talked about sanctification in this world.

Ben offers an alternative reading that finds Luke approving of sexuality on earth. He notes that angels could be seen as sexually active beings. There was a fascination with Gen 6.1–4 in both parts of early Judaism and among NT authors as shown in 1 Pet 3, Jude, and 2 Pet 2. Some believed that Gen 6.2, "the sons of God saw that they were fair; and they took wives for themselves of all that they chose" was a reference to angels who mated with human women and thereby produce a race of giants, the so-called Nephilim (Gen 6.4), literally from the Hebrew, "fallen ones." If this was also Jesus' view of angels, then more likely Jesus is not talking about being sexually inactive in the resurrection, but rather being deathless, having a permanent body. The whole drift of the argument about Levirate marriage assumes the reality of death. But in the resurrection, death is no more, and so questions about Levirate marriage are irrelevant. Presumably, Jesus could then have said, *obviously the woman will be married to the first husband*, because the other marriages were not contracted on the same basis as the first one, but because of the duty of the Levir. Hence the Sadducees know neither the Scriptures nor the power of a God who can raise the dead.

Jesus next alludes to Exod 3.1–4.17, "the story about the bush" (**vs. 37**); here he operates by the Sadducees' own system, since they accepted as Scripture the Torah but not the more fulsome canons, including the Prophets and the Psalms, held by other Jewish groups at the time. Jesus mounts the following argument: "God will not have continued to advertise himself as God of the Patriarchs if he had finished with them and abandoned them to the grave."[9] Similar attempts to find resurrection attested in the Pentateuch appear in rabbinic literature (see *b. Sanhedrin* 90b, 91b). The rationale is as follows: God promised the patriarchs land and descendants. Therefore, the patriarchs must be alive to see the promise come to fruition. Jon Levenson explains how the rabbis view resurrection "as a normative and defining doctrine, not simply as one option among many that a Jew may or may not elect without destroying the central claims of Judaism."[10] The view was inevitable: one is a Jew *in the body*, and therefore for Jews to exist in the resurrection, they must have a corporeal as well as a corporate presence. Levenson states, "The Jewish expectation of resurrection of the dead is always and inextricably associated with the restoration of the people Israel; it is not, in the first instance, focused on individual destiny. The question it answers is not, 'Will I have life after death?' but rather, 'Has God given up on his promises to his people?' "[11]

In line with some current Jewish thought, Jesus proposes that the patriarchs and thus other deceased people are alive now (**vs. 38**), as they await their resurrection (cf. Acts 17.28; 4 Macc 7.19; 16.25).[12] In light of 16.22–23, the Parable of the Rich Man and Lazarus, it would appear that Jesus believed that God preserves the righteous dead in a place of glory, where they await the resurrection.

Some of the scribes offer a positive assessment of Jesus' teaching on resurrection (**vs. 39**) and so distinguish themselves both from the scribes who appeared at the start of the chapter and from the Sadducees. The united effort against Jesus thereby begins to show cracks. At this point, all the questioners have been silenced (**vs. 40**).

Now Jesus, once again, will pose another of his own trick questions.

---

[9]   Nolland, *Luke 9:51–18.34*, 967.
[10]   Jon Douglas Levenson, *Resurrection and the Restoration of Israel: The Ultimate Victory of the God of Life* (New Haven and London: Yale University Press, 2006), 10.
[11]   Ibid., 165.
[12]   Craddock, *Luke*, p. 238, observes: "Notice how far this is from the notion of the immortality of the soul, an idea which has intruded itself into Christian doctrine. Immortality is based on a doctrine of human nature that denies death; resurrection is based on a doctrine of God which says that even though we die, God gives life to the dead."

JESUS' FINAL QUESTION

Citing Psa 110.1, Jesus asks, "How can the messiah be David's son" (**vs. 41**) when David calls him "Lord" (**vs. 42**)?[13] For Jesus and for other Jews of the time and in subsequent tradition, David is the author of Psa 110. The assignment of authorship then creates the problem of identifying the characters: who is "the Lord" and who is "my Lord"? For the Psalm, "the Lord" is God and "my Lord" is David. But if David is seen as the author, "my Lord" has to be someone else. Jesus implies that "the Lord" is God and "my Lord" is the Messiah. These identifications thus create a quandary: David, the ancestor, would not be expected to yield status to his descendant.

To make his point about his own status, Jesus did not have to include the next verse of the Psalm, which concerns the defeat of this "lord"'s enemies (**vs. 43**). In Luke's context, the "enemies" are those who oppose Jesus; here they are the chief priests, some scribes, and some Sadducees. As for the answer to the riddle about who is "Lord," Jesus provides no resolution. Luke, however, has already provided the answer. Readers will fill in that detail for themselves.

WARNINGS AGAINST SCRIBES

The chapter concludes, as Luke still follows Mark (12.38–39), with Jesus turning explicitly to his disciples, but with the people still listening (**vs. 45**). This is the second displacement: earlier, he had taught the people, but the political establishment was listening. With these last two verses of the chapter, Jesus shows that the leaders had good reason to fear him and to fear his influence with the crowd.

No longer speaking in parables or riddles, Jesus is fiercely critical. He warns the disciples, and so the people, about the "scribes" who flaunt their status and who value honor (**vs. 46**). By focusing on three public settings – marketplaces, the front seats in the synagogues, and the first seats at banquets – he associates them with public acclaim. Conversely, he does not associate them with the Temple. Thus, he is extending his critique beyond

---

[13]   The phrase "son of David" carried no eschatological or messianic connotations at the time the Psalm was written; only with *Ps. Sol.* 17.23 (ca. 63 BCE; see also 4QFlor. 1.11–13; CD 7.16 and the much later *b. Sanhedrin* 97a; 98a) does "son of David" begin to have a technical messianic sense. The phrase "son of David" in sapiential contexts referred to Solomon, the assumed originator of Jewish wisdom literature (see also Matthew's genealogy 1.6). For example, the cry of the blind man in 18.38–39 for healing mercies to the Solomon-like "son of David," namely Jesus, refers to the belief that Solomon could both cure sickness and exorcise demons.

Temple leadership. At the same time, he is implicitly connecting these scribes with the Pharisees, who have appeared several times in this Gospel in banquet settings and against whom Jesus had previously warned his disciples (12.1). His polemic should be taken as selective. The critique is against the particular scribes who seek honor, not against those who find his teaching congenial, such as the scribes who had just affirmed his teaching (vs. 39).

Then, Jesus heightens his polemic by criticizing not simply the attitude of the scribes, but also their actions: they take advantage of wealthy widows (**vs. 47a**). "To devour a house" is a technical phrase in extrabiblical Greek sources for bilking individuals of funds or property.[14] Again, implicitly the verse also indicts the Pharisees, whom Luke had described as "lovers of money" (16.14).

One could claim that Luke finds widows to be particularly vulnerable (cf. 4.25–26; 7.12; 21.1–4),[15] although Luke also mentions Anna, a widow who does not appear in need of economic protection (cf. 2.37). Luke's concern may be women's patronage of scribes, just as women served as patrons of Pharisees, or of Jesus' own movement (see 8.1–3). This concern for poor widows will return at the beginning of the next chapter: readers may see the impoverished widow who puts her two remaining coins in the Temple treasury to be a victim of these rapacious scribes. On the other hand, the one place Jesus does not locate the rapacious scribes is in the Temple.

Jesus' condemnation of the scribes ends not with claims of economic exploitation but of reciting long prayers for the sake of pomposity rather than piety. Claims that the scribes offered long prayers in the Temple for a fee, an interpretation both Ben and Amy-Jill have heard, finds no purchase in the sources.[16] The point is not that the scribes are paid for prayer; the point is that they pray "for the sake of appearance." The condemnation they will receive is eschatological judgment, although we might hear a condemnation already in Jesus' words and the reaction to them (**vs. 47c**). The people are listening.

BRIDGING THE HORIZONS

1. On Listening, or Eavesdropping

In Luke 20, Jesus speaks to diverse audiences: his teaching the people receives a response from the Jerusalem elite; the instruction he gives

---

[14]   J. D. M. Derrett, "'Eating Up the Houses of the Widows': Jesus' Comment on Lawyers?" in Idem, *Studies in the New Testament*, 118–27.

[15]   See Johnson, *Gospel of Luke*, 315.

[16]   See Fitzmyer, *Luke*, for various speculations on what the scribes did.

disciples is heard by the people; the Gospel is heard by its readers. What we overhear or intuit can be just as meaningful, or problematic, as information directly conveyed to us. While Jesus had occasions for teaching the disciples in private, the Gospels indicate that he also taught in public places; he anticipated that those outside the inner circle would be party to his words.

The distinction between direct and indirect audiences reminds Ben of modern church discussions about target audiences and "seeker" services. This pedagogical dynamic, akin to having seekers in the church or auditors in a course, calls for reflection: how specific should an address be to a mixed audience? Would it be wise always to see a congregation, or a class, as a mixed audience – with some seekers, some disciples, some just curious onlookers, and the inevitable curmudgeon? Amy-Jill has frequently found herself in a Christian worship service where she wondered, "if the pastor knew that a Jew is in the back pew, would the sermon have gone in a different direction? Would comments about 'the Jews' be rephrased?"

What would we want to say to a "mixed" crowd? We could target our words to a specific subset, but if we make that a regular practice, how will seekers become finders, and how will strangers find a language in which they can be at home? Will students shopping for a course find enough interest to spark enrollment, or will they be alienated by technical terminology or unexplained presuppositions?

We can also instruct disciples, or students, indirectly by addressing another part of the congregation or class, as Jesus does with the Parable of the Vineyard. Sometimes it is easier for people to accept a correction if they, or we, are not the direct targets of the critique. On the other hand, the task of the clergy is not to confess the sins of some third party; a critique of the local authorities should be focused on those who have authority today, so that the Church confesses its own sins, not the sins of others.

For this chapter, the concern should be to interrogate present leadership and not confess the sins of "the Jews," which is how the Parable of the Wicked Tenants is frequently preached. Clark Williamson, speaking of Matthew's version of the Parable of the Wicked Tenants, which concludes, "Therefore, I tell you, the kingdom will be taken away from you and given to a people that produces the fruits of the kingdom" (Matt 21.43), offers the standard summary: "Jesus, Christians said, used this parable to lay bare the murderous extremes to which Jews were able to go in resisting God; finally, they murdered God's beloved son. Consequently, God abandoned Israel and transferred the covenant to the church."[17] Is this what Christians believe, and is this what they want outsiders to hear?

2. On Marriage in Heaven

To speak of God as a living God, the Bible means not merely that God is real or alive, but that God, as the beginning of Genesis makes clear, is the very source of life. Therefore, God is just as capable of raising people from the dead as of giving life. However, as God's aliveness is different from that of human life, so also for Jesus the resurrected life is different from the lives we spend between birth and death. Attempts to draw detailed analogies between life now and life in the Kingdom, or human relationships now, including marriage, and human relationships in the Kingdom fail to do justice to the eschatological state as Jesus and some other Jews at the time imagined.

According to Jesus, marriage is an earthly institution for the earthly good of human beings; it is neither necessary nor in some cases desirable. Luke 14.26 states, "Whoever comes to me and does not hate father and mother, wife and children, brothers and sisters, yes, and even life itself, cannot be my disciple," and 18:29–30 repeats the point: "Truly I tell you, there is no one who has left house or wife or brothers or parents or children, for the sake of the kingdom of God, who will not get back very much more in this age, and in the age to come eternal life." The man who leaves his wife does not receive "very much more" wives. The disciples in Luke's Gospel have no spousal accompaniment as far as we know; the women who follow Jesus are also not accompanied by their husbands, unless Cleopas's companion on the road to Emmaus is his spouse. These disciples, who already have one foot in the Kingdom of Heaven, are the model for the heavenly state, when people become like the angels, who are neither married (men) nor given in marriage (women).

In a world where there is no suffering, sin or sorrow, no disease, decay, or death, and all are caught up in love of God and neighbor, such earthly institutions as marriage will no longer be necessary. The idea of a universal love, in which the deep love we have for a spouse becomes the same sort of deep love we have for everyone, can be comforting. And yet, for those of us – especially those of us whose life partner has died – the idea

---

[17]		Clark M. Williamson, *A Guest in the House of Israel: Post-Holocaust Church Theology* (Louisville: Westminster John Knox, 1993), 72.

that the love we shared on earth, that special, intimate, and *physical* love, would not be present in the Kingdom, can make the picture of heaven seem more like hell. Jesus likely was celibate, and Luke appears to prefer, as did Paul and the author of Revelation, a celibate lifestyle. Such people do not know the unique relationship that people in love, and who share that love physically, know.

Perhaps we might take comfort in the warm embrace of universal love. Perhaps physical desire might fold itself completely into religious ecstasy. Or perhaps this physical embodiment that is resurrection offers both the joys that can be found on earth and more. A few years ago, Amy-Jill was asked by *Moment Magazine* to comment on the Jewish idea of heaven. Here's what she wrote:

> Jewish beliefs in the afterlife are as diverse as Judaism itself, from the traditional view expecting the unity of flesh and spirit in a resurrected body, to the idea that we live on in our children and grandchildren, to a sense of heaven (perhaps with lox and bagels rather than harps and haloes). Belief in an afterlife typically correlates with our theology. If we believe in a just and compassionate living God, faithful to the promises made to Israel, we may well also believe in resurrection in the Messianic age, when justice and compassion will prevail over sin, evil and death.
>
> Perhaps what sparks belief today is less traditional teaching than personal experience. I was by my mother's bedside in the local hospital; she was 80, and her body was failing. Late in the evening she woke from her sleep, opened her eyes, and asked me, "What will happen to me when I die?"
>
> I immediately answered, "You'll see Daddy." My father had died decades earlier.
>
> She replied, "I look like hell."
>
> "Well, Mom, you've looked better, but when you see Daddy, you'll look as beautiful as you looked the day you got married."
>
> "How do you know this?"
>
> "Mom, I've got a Ph.D. in religion; I know these things."
>
> She smiled. I began to cry; my husband took my place by my mother's bedside and held her hand as she died. Afterward, my husband looked at me and said something to the effect of, "I've never heard you say anything like that before. You don't believe in an afterlife." But when I was talking to my mom, I believed every word.[18]

Ben notes that when a loved one dies, one finds out what one really believes or hopes, deep down. This was his experience when his oldest child

---

[18]   www.momentmag.com/is-there-life-after-death/.

Christy, suddenly died of an embolism at thirty-two in 2012. All of a sudden, he looked at some texts differently, for instance the story of the raising of Jairus' daughter. What he then looked forward to was the day Jesus would say to Christy "Talitha cumi" and she was embodied again, and Ben could give her a hug and welcome her back to some kind of normal life. Meeting in heaven as spirits suddenly seemed less real or preferable to Ben, though he still believed in that as well.[19]

3. On Paying Taxes to Caesar

Jesus does not answer the question of whether one should pay taxes or not. The decision is left in the hands of his interlocutors, and therefore in our hands as well. In his Epistle to the Romans, Paul exhorts both: "Let every person be subject to the governing authorities; for there is no authority except from God, and those authorities that exist have been instituted by God" (13.1), and, "Pay to all what is due them – taxes to whom taxes are due, revenue to whom revenue is due, respect to whom respect is due, honor to whom honor is due" (13.7). Most interpreters propose that Paul has in mind the Roman authorities, although it is possible these taxes and revenue are in reference to Jews who would pay the Temple tax and whatever support was needed for synagogue upkeep.

The First Epistle of Peter is more explicit about state taxes: "For the Lord's sake accept the authority of every human institution, whether of the emperor as supreme, or of governors, as sent by him to punish those who do wrong and to praise those who do right. For it is God's will that by doing right you should silence the ignorance of the foolish. As servants of God, live as free people, yet do not use your freedom as a pretext for evil. Honor everyone. Love the family of believers. Fear God. Honor the emperor" (2.13–17). In other words, do what the government requires of you, regardless of whether these requirements might appear to compromise your moral or theological views. For the author of 1 Peter, outwardly supporting the state, and so keeping oneself and one's fellow believers in Jesus safe, was permitted, for God knows what is in our hearts.

Conversely, the Book of Revelation advises withdrawal from Roman society, even to the point of refusing coinage, which is probably what Rev 13.17 – "so that no one can buy or sell who does not have the mark, that is,

---

[19]   See Ben Witherington III, *When a Daughter Dies* (Christianity Today e-Book Publications, 2012).

the name of the beast or the number of its name" – references. For the apocalypse of John, the Roman government is a great whore, and to do business
with her is to violate one's purity.

Christians, as well as adherents to other religions, throughout the ages
have had to negotiate their relationship with governments. Some, in their
refusals, became martyrs, as we see already with the Jewish men and women
tortured to death for refusing to eat pork and so compromise their Torah
obedience (2, 4 Maccabees). Others do what the state requires, whether out
of fear or out of recognition that God knows what is in their hearts.

Jesus leaves the issue of taxation in our hands: do we support the government, even if we think it is perpetrating evil, or do we become consci-
entious objectors to government policies that we regard as violating biblical
teachings? Jesus does not answer the question for us, but he demands that
we answer it for ourselves.

4. On Trick Questions and Political Discourse

Luke 20 offers a number of rhetorically clever moves on the parts of both
Jesus' interlocutors and Jesus himself. In posing questions that cannot
simply, or perhaps ever, be answered, both Jesus and his opponents reveal
the dangers of political discourse and of our all-too-frequent desire for the
soundbyte over substance.

The chapter should alert us to how such questions, and their responses,
impact us today. To ask the politician, "Will you raise taxes?" simplifies a
complicated subject. Were the politician to say, "no," then the community
may become at risk for a financial shortfall, as schools and roads, needing
governmental support, go underfunded. Were the politician to say, "yes,"
then the candidacy is likely doomed, as the voters think with their wallets
rather than with their brains or their hearts. The same problems fit with
questions such as, "will you declare war?" or, "do you support health care?"
or, "would you restrict people's ability to marry or to use the bathroom
appropriate to their gendered identity?" The art, or poison, of political
debate is to score points at the expense of the opponent. Surely, we can do
better.

We return to the questions in Luke 20. Jesus' interlocutors want to
know about the source of his authority. Only those who already accept his
authority will see the question as misguided. For those on the outside, however, the question is a good one, and it is well put to anyone. The best way
of determining whether to accept an individual's authority is to see how

that individual acts; the best position from which to raise the question is to ensure that one's own actions are above reproach.

Jesus' interlocutors inquire about paying taxes, and Jesus shifts the question to the matter of coinage. Do we know who is on our coins, or what inscriptions they bear? Do we find ourselves worshiping the idol that money can become? Do we hail the people on our coins and our bills? Do we even know who they are?

A third set of questioners, who have no investment in the answer to their question, query Jesus about resurrection. The question itself is not a bad one – none of the questions posed in the chapter is illegitimate – the problem is not the question but the motive behind it. At the least, we might interrogate the questions asked today, whether by us or by others, to see its point: is it designed to elicit information, or is it designed to score points? (Underneath this question, our question, lurk classroom experiences both Ben and Amy-Jill have had.)

Finally, Jesus asks his own question, and yet again he refuses to provide an answer. His question is one of biblical exegesis. Perhaps divinity and seminary students might take a special lesson here: you may know more than members of your congregation, but you are not Jesus. Do not use your knowledge to obscure, and do not seek to engage in proof-texting, as if your understandings of texts will convert the guest in your church, or the person next to you. Belief comes not from clever exegesis – it obviously did not work for Jesus' interlocutors here – it comes from grace.

Luke 21 Dedication and Destruction

THE WOMAN'S DONATION

[1] He looked up and saw rich people putting their gifts into the treasury; [2] he also saw a poor widow put in two small copper coins. [3] He said, "Truly I tell you, this poor widow has put in more than all of them; [4] for all of them have contributed out of their abundance, but she out of her poverty has put in all she had to live on."

APOCALYPTIC WARNINGS

[5] When some were speaking about the temple, how it was adorned with beautiful stones and gifts dedicated to God, he said, [6] "As for these things that you see, the days will come when not one stone will be left upon another; all will be thrown down."
[7] They asked him, "Teacher, when will this be, and what will be the sign that this is about to take place?" [8] And he said, "Beware that you are not led astray; for many will come in my name and say, 'I am he!' and, 'The time is near!' Do not go after them. [9] "When you hear of wars and insurrections, do not be terrified; for these things must take place first, but the end will not follow immediately."
[10] Then he said to them, "Nation will rise against nation, and kingdom against kingdom; [11] there will be great earthquakes, and in various places famines and plagues; and there will be dreadful portents and great signs from heaven.
[12] "But before all this occurs, they will arrest you and persecute you; they will hand you over to synagogues and prisons, and you will be brought before kings and governors because of my name. [13] This will give you an opportunity to testify. [14] So make up your minds not to prepare your

defense in advance; ¹⁵ for I will give you words and a wisdom that none of your opponents will be able to withstand or contradict.

¹⁶ You will be betrayed even by parents and brothers, by relatives and friends; and they will put some of you to death. ¹⁷ You will be hated by all because of my name. ¹⁸ But not a hair of your head will perish. ¹⁹ By your endurance you will gain your souls.

THE DESTRUCTION OF JERUSALEM

²⁰ "When you see Jerusalem surrounded by armies, then know that its desolation has come near. ²¹ Then those in Judea must flee to the mountains, and those inside the city must leave it, and those out in the country must not enter it; ²² for these are days of vengeance, as a fulfillment of all that is written.

²³ Woe to those who are pregnant and to those who are nursing infants in those days! For there will be great distress on the earth and wrath against this people; ²⁴ they will fall by the edge of the sword and be taken away as captives among all nations; and Jerusalem will be trampled on by the Gentiles, until the times of the Gentiles are fulfilled.

THE RETURN OF THE SON OF MAN

²⁵ "There will be signs in the sun, the moon, and the stars, and on the earth distress among nations confused by the roaring of the sea and the waves. ²⁶ People will faint from fear and foreboding of what is coming upon the world, for the powers of the heavens will be shaken.

²⁷ Then they will see 'the Son of Man coming in a cloud' with power and great glory. ²⁸ Now when these things begin to take place, stand up and raise your heads, because your redemption is drawing near."

PARABLE OF THE FIG TREE

²⁹ Then he told them a parable: "Look at the fig tree and all the trees; ³⁰ as soon as they sprout leaves you can see for yourselves and know that summer is already near. ³¹ So also, when you see these things taking place, you know that the kingdom of God is near. ³² Truly I tell you, this generation will not pass away until all things have taken place.

³³ Heaven and earth will pass away, but my words will not pass away.

³⁴ "Be on guard so that your hearts are not weighed down with dissipation and drunkenness and the worries of this life, and that day catch you

unexpectedly, [35] like a trap. For it will come upon all who live on the face of the whole earth. [36] Be alert at all times, praying that you may have the strength to escape all these things that will take place, and to stand before the Son of Man."

TEMPLE TEACHING

[37] Every day he was teaching in the temple, and at night he would go out and spend the night on the Mount of Olives, as it was called. [38] And all the people would get up early in the morning to listen to him in the temple.

THE WIDOW AND HER DONATION

Luke's chapter divisions distinguish the excoriation of rapacious scribes who devour widows' houses, found ending Chapter 20, from the widow whom we meet in 21.1. A distinction is not improbable; Luke (following Mark) locates the scribes in the marketplaces, the synagogues, and at banquets; our widow appears in the Temple. Perhaps had those scribes spent more time in the Temple and less time at banquets, they would be less venal.[1] However, given Luke's penchant for pairing stories by gender, the two accounts can be read as depicting contrasting modes of attitudes toward money. The (male) scribes take everything they can; the poor widow, who has two coins, does not hold back even one.

The scene begins with Jesus still speaking to the disciples but in the hearing of the people (20.45). Looking up, he sees wealthy people putting funds into the Temple treasury (**vs. 1**). Contrary to popular views, there were no trumpets sounded when a donation was made, and no one announced either the names of the contributors or the amounts. The idea may have come from the Mishnah's notice that there were thirteen "shofar chests" (a shofar is a ram's horn; the translation "trumpet" is viable), or receptacles with fluted openings for coins, in the Temple court. The Mishnah (*m. Sheq.* 6.5) reads: "Thirteen shofar chests were in the sanctuary. Written on them were the following [in Aramaic]: 'New shekels' and 'old shekels,' 'bird offerings,' and 'young birds for a burnt offering'; 'wood' and 'frankincense'; 'gold for the Mercy seat,' and on six, 'for freewill offerings …'" We might think of offerings today that are targeted for specific goals, from support for the poor to maintenance of the building to memorials and honoraria.

---

[1]   See discussion of the "widow's mite" with a focus on Mark 12.40–44 in Levine, "This Poor Widow."

Amid the people, Jesus notices a poor widow who puts in two small coins (**vs. 2**), and he draws the contrast between her contribution and that of the others. In his estimation, her donation was greater than theirs (**vs. 3**), since they gave a percentage of what they had, but she gave "all she had to live on" (**vs. 4**). The Greek, *panta ton bion*, literally means that she gave up her "whole life."

Numerous contemporary readings of Luke's account as well as the longer version in Mark 12.41–44 regard the widow as the victim either of the scribes who devour widows' houses (20.47) or of the Temple establishment, or both, and therefore read her story as a condemnation of the Temple and a lament for the victimized widow.[2] Neither Ben nor Amy-Jill sees the widow, in either Jesus' eyes or Luke's presentation, as a victim; neither of us sees Luke here as condemning the Temple.

Had Jesus regarded the Temple system as exploitative, he could have said something to the widow or prevented her from making her donation; he does not. Had Luke thought the offering was a waste of funds, then the numerous scenes the Book of Acts sets in the Temple would be counterproductive. Luke even portrays Paul as willingly making an offering in the Temple (Acts 21.4). Had Luke included the discussion of Qorban funds dedicated to the Temple rather than used to support parents (Mark 7.10–13), then we could make the claim that Luke saw the Temple system as open to exploitative purposes; Luke lacks this discussion. Moreover, Luke ends the Gospel as it began, in a scene of piety in the Temple. The widow is in continuity with the disciples, who at the end of the volume are found "continually in the Temple blessing God" (24.53). The woman's generosity, in both Jesus' historical context and Luke's narrative, is therefore praiseworthy. The widow models Jesus' advice to the ruler, "sell all you have and give to the poor" (18.22). She can also be helpfully compared to Anna, the Gospel's first widow, also located in the Temple.

Readings that use this passage to condemn the Temple system remove the widow from both the broader teaching of Jesus and Luke's narrative context. They also remove from the widow any agency; instead, they draw her as victim. Conversely, we can view this widow as the ideal disciple, who gives all she has, without hesitation, who epitomizes appropriately placed generosity, and who models for the rich that the amount of the donation is of less value than the percentage of income it represents. The same teaching

---

[2]   Addison G. Wright, "The Widow's Mites: Praise or Lament? – a Matter of Context," *CBQ* 44 (1982): 256–65.

appears in the much later rabbinic text *Leviticus Rabbah* 3.5. The story
goes, "A woman once brought a handful of meal as an offering. The priest
despised it. He said, 'What sort of offering is that? What is there in it for
eating or for a sacrifice?' But in a dream, it was said to the priest, 'Despise
her not; but reckon it as if she had offered *herself* as a sacrifice.'"[3] What is
being praised here is truly self-sacrificial giving.

APOCALYPTIC WARNINGS

The subject changes from charity to catastrophe as Luke turns to an
unnamed "some," likely the disciples, remarking on the Temple's beautiful stones and votive gifts (**vs. 5**). Although Luke may have never seen the
Temple, the description fits what Josephus records, for example, "Now the
Temple was built of stones that were white and strong, and each of their
length was twenty-five cubits, their height was eight, and their breadth
about twelve … the Temple had doors also at the entrance, and lintels over
them, of the same height with the Temple itself. They were adorned with
embroidered veils, with their flowers of purple, and pillars interwoven: and
over these, but under the crown-work, was spread out a golden vine, with
its branches hanging down from a great height, the largeness and fine workmanship of which was a surprising sight to the spectators, to see what vast
materials there were, and with what great skill the workmanship was done"
(*Ant.* 15.392, 394–95).

Jesus' interests in aesthetics, at least as far as the Gospels record, focuses
on the natural world rather than what people construct: "Consider the
lilies, how they grow; they neither toil nor spin, yet I tell you, even Solomon
in all his glory was not clothed like one of these" (12.27). The decades-
long labor that went into the construction of the Temple offers a brilliant
intertext: both Temple and lilies are beautiful, and both will not survive the
season. Regarding the Temple, Jesus predicts that none of those beautiful
stones will remain in place (**vs. 6a**). The passive voice at the end of this
sentence, "all will be thrown down" (**vs. 6b**), does not state the cause of the
destruction. Historically, the Roman general Titus and his troops destroyed
the Temple in 70 CE. Theologically, Luke attributes the destruction of
Jerusalem to the city's failure to acknowledge Jesus as its savior. Narratively,
readers may recall the last use of "stone" imagery: Jesus had just described
how the rejected cornerstone would cause destruction: "Everyone who falls

3   See Levine, "This Poor Widow," for discussion.

on that stone will be broken to pieces; and it will crush anyone on whom it falls" (20.18); with this reading, the agents of the Temple's destruction become those who reject Jesus' claims.

Jesus' interlocutors, addressing him as "teacher," then ask for the time-table and the sign (**vs. 7**). Earlier, Jesus had rejected the demands for a sign, and he had explained that only the "sign of Jonah" would be provided (see commentary on 11.29). The signs he provides his disciples here concern what will happen following his death; whether these are *ex eventu* prophecies retrojected back onto the lips of Jesus by the evangelists and other early disciples, designed to warn followers about false teachers and comfort disciples in case of persecution, or whether Jesus himself anticipated these issues cannot be determined. Ben sees every reason to attribute the following verses to Jesus, in substance if not in terms of actual wording, and he notes that the language is traditional Jewish apocalyptic phrasing. Amy-Jill, who sees Jesus as believing that his death would be instrumental in ushering in the Kingdom of Heaven/the World to Come, sees the predictions as a combination of traditional apocalyptic teachings about universal destruction, which Jesus may well have made, coupled with compositions by the early Church designed to provide guidance and comfort.

In effect, we are basically in agreement on the quality of the historicity of these predictions, if not on the quantity of the details. Attempts to attribute all apocalyptic materials to later sources and see Jesus as only interested in ethics strike us as denying material that runs across the spectrum of Gospel sources, denying Jesus' connections to both John the Baptizer and Paul, and sometimes smacking of liberal apologetic designed to keep Jesus from sounding either misguided, promoting images of violence, or wrong on the timetable. We are not saying that all Jews were apocalyptically oriented; an eschatological focus is not a litmus test for determining what Jesus the Jew did or did not say. Rather, we are saying that we find Jesus to have had an eschatological, apocalyptic orientation. Many people today find apocalyptic materials alien; they would not have been to either Jesus or to many of the people around him.

Jesus' discourse begins with a warning about being led astray; the concern for apostasy is not about the doctrinal or Christological issues that beset the Johannine literature, ethical issues regarding wealth and poverty such as Paul addresses to the Corinthian Church and the Epistle of James addresses to its readers, or domestic matters explored in the household codes of 1 Peter and Ephesians. The concern here is for rival teachers who claim to speak in Jesus' name. Some of these teachers are even saying, "I am" (Greek: *egō eimi*), the title Jesus uses for himself in the Gospel of John (e.g., "I am the true vine" [John 15.1]). The NRSV's "I am he" misses the allusion to Moses' encounter with God at the burning bush (Exod 3.14) as well as the connection to the messianic identification in John's Gospel.

Still other false teachers are predicting an imminent eschatology with the call "the time is near" (**vs. 8**), and Luke more so than Matthew and Mark downplays the type of urgency that sees an end to time as we know it. Luke's Gospel and the companion volume Acts promote not the end of the world, but the growth of the Way. Separating Jerusalem's destruction from the eschaton, Jesus states clearly that wars and rebellions must come "first"; the end is not yet (**vs. 9**). From Luke's perspective, it should not be wars that terrify, but the return of Jesus and the final judgment. As Jesus had stated, "... do not fear those who kill the body, and after that can do nothing more. But I will warn you whom to fear: fear him who, after he has killed, has authority to cast into hell. Yes, I tell you, fear him!" (12.4–5). The rest of the eschatological scenario is traditional. Predictions of nations rising against nations (**vs. 10**) appear in 2 Chron 15.6. Earthquakes, famines, plagues, and heavenly portents are part of the stock apocalyptic repertoire, although readers of Acts may specifically think of the famine that occurred sometime between 41 and 54 during the reign of the Emperor Claudius (Acts 11.28; see also Josephus, *Ant.* 20.49–53, 101) or the earthquake in Philippi mentioned in Acts 16.26. To make these specific connections, however, thwarts the point of apocalyptic literature: the signs cannot be located in real time; they have not yet happened. When they do occur, according to the apocalyptic scenario, the signs will not be local but universal; there will be no question, anywhere, about their import (**vs. 10**). Even Mark 13, the earlier version of Jesus' apocalyptic teaching, draws a distinction between the events leading to the destruction of the Temple and the cosmic events occurring at some unspecified "after those days" when the Son of Man returns. In Mark 13.32, Jesus emphasizes that in regard to the events "after those days," no one, including himself, knows the timing. Luke omits this disclaimer.

Instead of focusing on signs of the end, the Lucan Jesus attends to what will happen to his disciples in the near future: arrests, persecutions, imprisonment, and trials before rulers (**vs. 12**). The verse sounds like the outline for the Book of Acts, with its depictions of the trials of Peter and then Paul. Stoically, Jesus states that such persecutions are opportunities to bear witness (**vs. 13**). Paul, who counts his imprisonment as an opportunity to evangelize the Praetorian Guard, makes similar comments. As he explains to his friends in Philippi, "... what has happened to me has actually helped to spread the gospel, so that it has become known throughout the whole imperial guard and to everyone else that my imprisonment is for Christ; and most of the brothers [and sisters], having been made confident in the Lord by my imprisonment, dare to speak the word with greater boldness and without fear" (Phil 1.12–14).

Under such circumstances, Jesus' followers are not to dwell on what they would say (**vs. 14**), although had they read Acts, they would find several speeches that could serve as templates. Rather, Jesus promises to inspire them such that their words will have potency (**vs. 15**). His demonstration, in the previous chapter, that none of his opponents could withstand his verbal arguments lends credence to this claim. Reinforcing his promise is also his earlier assurance that the Holy Spirit would provide his followers, in times of trial, the necessary words (12.12).

Jesus' predictions continue with the notice that those who reject his followers will not be stationed only in the synagogue (i.e., local Jewish communities) or among Roman governmental officers; families, too, will become opponents. Parents and siblings and friends will turn against the disciples; some of these family members will be responsible for their deaths (**vs. 16**). Earlier, Jesus stated "Whoever comes to me and does not hate father and mother, wife and children, brothers and sisters, yes, and even life itself, cannot be my disciple" (14.26); now it appears that the hatred may be mutual. Indeed, according to Jesus, "all" will hate his followers, and they will hate his followers because of "my name" (**vs. 7**; see Mark 13.13). The text finds some resonance with 1 Pet 4.16, "Yet if any of you suffers as a Christian, do not consider it a disgrace, but glorify God because you bear this name."

The final words of this section provide comfort, which is needed after predictions of apocalyptic demise and personal suffering. After telling his disciples that their friends and family will put them to death, Jesus assures them that not one of their hairs will perish (**vs. 18**). The comment echoes his earlier observation that God counts even the hairs of their heads, so that they need not fear (12.7). In context, this counting suggests less the preservation of the body from torture or death and more the sense of everlasting life, such as the angels and the patriarchs have. This soteriological implication receives support from the conclusion of this section, the promise that by enduring, by persevering despite the trials, the disciples with gain their souls or lives (Greek: *psychē*) (**vs. 19**).

THE DESTRUCTION OF JERUSALEM

The chapter began with the notice of the beautiful stones being turned to rubble. Jesus returns to this subject by describing Jerusalem's fate. The details partially match the records found in Josephus's writing; the related instructions Jesus offers complement the Gospel's concerns for gentiles, for familial disruption, and for divine judgment.

Roman troops who surround Jerusalem are the first sign of the city's "desolation" (**vs. 20**). For this "desolation," Luke uses the Greek term *erēmōsis*, whereas both Mark (13.14) and Matthew (24.15) speak of "desolating *sacrilege*" or the "*abomination* of desolation" (Greek: *bdelygma tēs erēmōseōs*). Luke knows the term "abomination" (see 16.15), but chooses not to use it here. With the full expression, the other two Gospels allude to 1 Macc 1.54a, the outrages of Antiochus IV Epiphanes and his followers: "Now on the fifteenth day of Chislev, in the one hundred forty-fifth year, they erected a desolating sacrilege on the altar of burnt offering"; Dan 7 stands behind this allusion as well. By changing the term, Luke strips out allusions to the Maccabean revolt and refocuses attention away from the Temple and toward the city.

The instructions form, for Luke's audience, a description of what had happened to the city rather than what would happen, for Luke is writing well after the First Revolt of 66–70. Exhortations to flee the city as well as to avoid entering (**vs. 21**) may have led in part to the story that Jesus' followers left Jerusalem at the outbreak of the war and relocated to the city of Pella in the Decapolis.[4] However, excavations of Pella yield scant remains of a first-century city, and the narrative of the flight first surfaces in the writings of the fourth-century Church historian Eusebius (*Ecc. Hist.* 3.5,3).[5] Eusebius states, "The people of the church in Jerusalem, in accordance with a certain oracle that was given through revelation to those who were worthy in the place, were commanded to migrate from the city before the war and to settle in … Pella … to which those who believed in Christ migrated from Jerusalem, so that when holy men had completely abandoned the royal

[4] See Craig Koester, "The Origin and Significance of the Flight to Pella Tradition," *CBQ* 51.1 (1989): 90–106 (esp. 104–5).
[5] On the Pella tradition as an invention of second-century followers of Jesus who claimed themselves heirs of the Jerusalem church, see Gerd Lüdemann, "The Successors of Pre-70 Jerusalem Christianity: A Critical Evaluation of the Pella Tradition," in E. P. Sanders (ed.), *Jewish and Christian Self-Definition*, Vol. 1 (Philadelphia: Fortress Press, 1980), 161–73. Koester, "Origin and Significance," finds some supporting evidence for the Pella tradition in several early Christian texts.

capital of the Jews and the whole land of Judea, the judgment of God might at last overtake them for all their crimes against the Christ and his apostles, utterly blotting out that very generation of the wicked from among human-kind."[6] The connections to Luke 21.21 are not strong, although Eusebius's apologetic interests are on full display.

The "days of vengeance" of which Jesus speaks (**vs. 22a**) and that find an echo in Eusebius's view of Jerusalem are themselves echoes of materials from Israel's Scriptures. In Deut 32.35 (cf. Hos 9.7), God states: "Vengeance is mine, and recompense ... because the day of their calamity is at hand, their doom comes swiftly." Paul similarly speaks of vengeance as something God, not humanity, accomplishes (Rom 12.19). The term translated here as "vengeance" (Greek: *ekdikēsis*) is what the widow in the Parable of the Widow and the Judge (18.17,18) seeks. The NRSV has the widow asking not for "vengeance" but for "justice." Readers may want to ask themselves, once again, about how to determine the difference between the two. Do we want to see cities destroyed? Do we want to see populations "utterly blotted out," as Eusebius endorsed?

In speaking of fulfilling what was written (**vs. 22b**), Luke alludes to sixth- and early fifth-century BCE predictions of Jerusalem's destruction made by Jeremiah and others. Yet Luke's narrative also situates figures in the Gospel itself as prophets. Luke had already depicted Simeon announcing that Jesus would be the cause of the "fall" of many in Israel (2.34), and Jesus earlier described Jerusalem as the city that murders its prophets (13.34). Consequently, "what is written" is not only the Scriptures of Israel, in what-ever canonical form Luke had them; "what is written" includes Luke's own narrative of Jesus' life and death. These earlier comments about Jesus' role in relation to other Jews and in relation to the city, in turn, explain why God wreaks "vengeance" on Jerusalem.

The destruction of a city means more than the toppling of stones or the razing of buildings. It means attacks on human bodies: mutilations, rapes, killing. In describing the siege of Jerusalem, Josephus does not hes-itate to foreground the suffering of the people. Luke, instead, keeps focus on instructions. Amy-Jill finds that the woe to the pregnant and nursing mothers as especially vulnerable during this time of great distress (**vs. 23**) comports well with the several earlier comments about familial disrup-tion. Women who are pregnant or who have given birth, that is, women who marry, engage in sexual intercourse, and have children will have the

---

[6] Translation by Koester, "Origin and Significance," 91.

harder burdens. Luke, for whom this verse is unique, may be continuing the promotion of celibate insiders. Alternatively, Ben proposes that Luke is simply making graphic who will bear the hardest burdens when such things happen, without suggesting anything, one way or another, about the marriage and pregnancy under normal circumstances.

The final verse depicts what happened when Titus and his troops entered Jerusalem in the summer of 70 CE. The Roman army killed thousands and brought thousands of others, "taken away as captives," to the slave markets throughout the Empire (**vs. 24a**). Josephus describes the initial invasion by Roman troops:

> ... when they went in numbers into the lanes of the city, with their swords drawn, they slew those whom they overtook, without mercy, and set fire to the houses wither the Jews were fled, and burnt every soul in them, and laid waste a great many of the rest; and when they were come to the houses to plunder them, they found in them entire families of dead men, and the upper rooms full of dead corpses, that is of such as died by the famine; they then stood in a horror at this sight, and went out without touching anything. But although they had this commiseration for such as were destroyed in that manner, yet had they not the same for those that were still alive, but they ran every one through whom they met with, and obstructed the very lanes with their dead bodies, and made the whole city run down with blood, to such a degree indeed that the fire of many of the houses was quenched with these men's blood (*War* 6.404–6).

The siege concludes in a description that could easily find its way into an apocalyptic text:

> Now the number of those that were carried captive during this whole war was collected to be ninety-seven thousand, as was the number of those that perished during the whole siege eleven hundred thousand, the greater part of whom were indeed of the same nation [with the citizens of Jerusalem], but not belonging to the city itself; for they were come up from all the country to the feast of unleavened bread, and were on a sudden shut up by an army, which, at the very first ... came a pestilential destruction upon them, and soon afterward such a famine, as destroyed them more suddenly (*War* 6.420–21).

Jesus ends his discussion by the first explicit mention of those who created the catastrophe: the gentiles. The name "Roman" is not invoked. The "times of the Gentiles" (**vs. 24**) means, in context, the time of Roman rule. As far as Luke is concerned, that rule will remain for quite a while. The time of the gentiles is also what the Book of Acts ushers in, as the movement in Jesus' name goes beyond its Jewish borders into Samaria and then the Diaspora, and as more and more gentiles join the Church.

Luke closes the two-volume work with Paul's distress that the Jews in Rome are not accepting his message; Paul states, "Let it be known to you then that this salvation of God has been sent to the Gentiles; they will listen" (Acts 28.28). The time of the gentiles is the time of the Church. Paul himself explains that the general Jewish rejection of his Gospel is part of the divine plan, but at the end-time and following the completion of the gentile mission, "all Israel will be saved" (Rom 11.26). Ben sees Luke-Acts as agreeing with this program, for what Paul says in Acts 28.28 reflects the same procedure followed throughout Luke's second volume, namely, offering the Gospel to the Jews first, and then to the gentiles, particularly if it is largely rejected by the Jews. Luke is probably also indicating that he expects that pattern of largely Jewish rejection and considerable gentile acceptance to continue, and likely he had observed it continuing in his own day. Nothing is said in Luke-Acts, including in Acts 28, about a final or definitive cessation of the offering of the Gospel to Jews. Amy-Jill finds that openness to Jewish acceptance to be a generous reading of Luke's two volumes. Paul retains an opening for Israel "according to the flesh"; she does not find Luke to have such an optimistic view.

THE RETURN OF THE SON OF MAN

From the destruction of Jerusalem, predicted as a future event but described by Luke, writing from hindsight, the text turns to the end of time. The wars and rumors of wars, which for Luke are local affairs, do not predict the end. Instead, when the eschaton arrives, everyone will know. Using traditional apocalyptic imagery (e.g., Isa 13.10; 24.23), Jesus depicts a cosmic upheaval (**vs. 25**), with humanity in distress because at this point, there is no question about what these portents mean. The shaking of the "powers in heaven" (**vs. 26**) reveals that the distress is experienced not only by human beings, but also by the angelic retinue, the "heavenly host."

This dire material is designed not to frighten but to give confidence. It shows, in its predictive quality, that the cosmic upheaval is part of the divine plan and not some accident. Joel (2.30–32) had stated: "I will show portents in the heavens and on the earth, blood and fire and columns of smoke. The sun shall be turned to darkness, and the moon to blood, before the great and terrible day of the Lord comes. Then everyone who calls on the name of the Lord shall be saved; for in Mount Zion and in Jerusalem there shall be those who escape, as the Lord has said, and among the survivors shall be those whom the Lord calls." This is the passage Luke depicts Peter as paraphrasing in Acts 2.19–21.

At that eschatological moment, according to Luke, the Son of Man arrives (**vs. 27**). The figure of the Son of Man had already found his way into apocalyptic texts such as Dan 7.13 and *1 En.* 31. Daniel predicted the arrival of a figure called "the Son of Man" in a cloud; the "Ancient of Days," a metaphor for God, then invests this figure with power and glory. Jesus had already predicted his return after his death in the context of final judgment (12.8–9); here he develops the theme in a manner designed both to encourage his followers and to accentuate his authority.

The juxtaposition of the shaking of the "powers in heaven" to the coming of the Son of Man suggests both the Son's power and his divine status. Today we tend to think in binary terms: there is humanity and there is divinity; for Christians, the one being who transcends or, better, combines both is Jesus. In antiquity, there was a ladder of divine beings: angels, principalities, and powers (see Col 1.16 for another use of the term "powers" to refer to divine beings). According to the Epistle to the Colossians, which Ben believes Paul wrote and which Amy-Jill finds generally consistent with Paul's thought but likely written by a follower during "a period when church leaders turned away from Judaism, even while some church members continued to find Jewish practice meaningful,"[7] as well as for Luke's Gospel, Jesus is superior to all of these divine beings, and so it would be incorrect to understand him as a super-angel or otherwise subordinate entity. With Jesus as superior to all these powers, his followers can be assured that in the eschatological moment, he will protect them. The imagery is consistent with Phil 2.6–11, where Paul had already indicated Jesus' divine role.

With this knowledge of their Lord's authority, the disciples need not fear. They can stand proudly, because they have remained steadfast (cf. vs 19) through endurance, and because they have listened to Jesus (or the Spirit) during any time of trial (**vs. 28a**). Unlike Jerusalem, the disciples will be redeemed (**vs. 28b**). This redemption (Greek: *apolytrōsis*) – the term is unique to Luke – suggests a loosing or releasing (Greek verb *luō*) from anything that is constraining them. The Greek verb is connected to the term for "ransom" (see, e.g., Matt 20.26; Mark 10.45; 1 Tim 2.6), which conveys the

7   Peter Zaas, "The Letter of Paul to the Colossians," in Amy-Jill Levine and Marc Z. Brettler (eds.), *The Jewish Annotated New Testament*, 2nd ed. (New York: Oxford University Press, 2017), 407–18 (408).

idea that Jesus paid the "ransom" or the penalty that was keeping humanity, from the time of Adam and Eve, bound to the power of Satan. Although Luke does not describe Jesus as dying as a ransom, this verse hints at a similar understanding; Acts 20.28, where Paul speaks to the Ephesian elders about "the church of God that he obtained with the blood of his own Son," can be read as supporting this idea.[8]

PARABLE OF THE FIG TREE

Interpreting an apocalyptic and eschatological text by means of a parable could increase the frustration of the reader rather than lead to clarity of the material. Parables tend to use mundane imagery whereas an apocalyptic text addresses the cosmic and the supernatural. Yet the two genres share much in common: elements in each find some connection to the experiences and expectations of the target audience, and both speak in metaphorical terms.

The "parable" (that is the Greek term appearing here) Jesus offers is less a parable in the generic sense of a short story meant to challenge or indict than it is a sign. Jesus tells his followers to look not only at the fig tree but all trees (**vs. 29**). Had he simply mentioned the fig tree, readers would have a basketful of associative connections: the fig tree under which one sits in the peaceful age of good politics (1 Kings 4.25; cf. 2 Kings 18.31; Isa 36.16), to the future age of security (Micah 4.4) to Jesus' cursing of the fig tree in relation to his activities in the Temple (Mark 11.13–20). Luke's readers will remember other references to fig trees in the Gospel. In 6.44, speaking of how trees are known by their fruit and so people are known by their actions, Jesus observed, "figs are not gathered from thorns, nor are grapes picked from a bramble." In 13.6–8, Jesus offered another parable concerning a fig tree that failed to yield fruit. If even after fertilizing it fails to produce, it will be cut down. That image of the cut-down tree applies directly to the chapter's descriptions of both Jerusalem's destruction and the eschatological judgment.

This parable begins with a truism: trees in leaf indicate the arrival of summer (**vs. 30**). The point is not that one should watch for the trees to bloom; it is that once the trees bloom – or the stars fall out of the heavens – the Kingdom of God is about to arrive (**vs. 31**). The signs will be as obvious

---

[8] For helpful development of the concept of ransom with particular application to Matthew's Gospel, see Nathan Eubank, *Wages of Cross-Bearing and Debt of Sin: The Economy of Heaven in Matthew's Gospel* (Berlin/Boston: De Gruyter, 2013).

as that of trees growing leaves; one does not need special biblical knowledge, a computer or calculator, or divinely granted revelation to determine the timing of the end.

Nevertheless, biblical knowledge does help with understanding the richness of the images. Not only do biblically literate readers import into this saying other references to fig trees, the parable reminds these readers of another reference to summer bloom. According to Amos 8.1–2, God shows the prophet a basket of summer fruit (Hebrew: *kayitz*), which signals through a wordplay that "the end (Hebrew: *kaytz*) has come upon my people Israel; I will never again pass them by." The section in Amos ends with the woeful prediction that applies directly to Luke's chapter, "'The songs of the temple shall become wailings in that day,' says the Lord God; 'the dead bodies shall be many, cast out in every place. Be silent!'" (Amos 8.3). Jesus thus assures his followers that the end-times will bring both divine vengeance against their enemies and divine protection of those who remain steadfast.

The followers also have his guarantee, which begins with the Hebrew "amen," meaning "so be it" (the NRSV's "truly" is banal) of the truth of the predictions (**vs. 32a**). This section concludes with the floating saying in which Jesus assures the disciples that his predictions will come to pass *in their own generation* (**vs. 32b**), their own time. Yet immediately he restricts the literal meaning of the saying by adding the eschatological points that even if heaven and earth pass away, his teachings – literally, his "words" (Greek: *logia*) – will prevail (**vs. 33**). Jesus had made a similar statement in 9.27, just prior to his Transfiguration, "Amen, I say to you, there are some standing here who will not taste death before they see the kingdom of God." Amy-Jill proposes that Jesus did make such a statement about the inbreaking of the Kingdom of God; since the inbreaking has not come in any universally acknowledged way, Jesus was in error in this prediction regarding "this generation." This view does not invalidate his concern for justice; it rather notes that the timing is off. She finds compelling Dale Allison's statement, "Jesus the millenarian prophet, like all millenarian prophets, was wrong: reality has taken no notice of his imagination,"[9] but "despite everything, for those who have ears to hear, Jesus, the millenarian herald of judgment and salvation, says the only things worth saying, for his dream is the only

9   Dale C. Allison Jr., *Jesus of Nazareth: Millenarian Prophet* (Minneapolis: Augsburg Fortress, 1998), 219.

one worth dreaming …," that is, a dream that included good news to the poor and the raising of the dead.[10]

Ben sees the statement as also from Jesus, but as viable for all the generations of humanity and therefore not in error in any sense. One could associate these eschatological statements with those moments, few but precious and memorable, when one realizes, in the mundane world, the presence of the Kingdom. Further, Ben thinks the coming of the Kingdom is one thing, the return of the Son is another: Jesus was referring to the former in 9.27 and perhaps here.

As with many apocalyptic sayings, the teachings resist logical application. The point of most apocalyptic texts is not to give signs of the end, as if one could check off details on the calendar or predict the coming of the late great planet earth or the entry of Armageddon. The details speak to surety, not chronology. It is the certainty of the return of the Son of Man, not the timing, that is being taught here. The disciples to whom Jesus, according to Luke's Gospel, spoke these words, are long dead. Nevertheless, according to Jesus, God is not the God of the dead but of the living (20.38). Therefore, the disciples, although deceased in the body, are still within the divine purview. Like the patriarchs of Genesis, they will live again, in the age of the resurrection, to see the coming of the Son of Man.

Regardless of whether the end comes during their earthly lives or after, the disciples must live in the state of preparation. Evoking the imagery of the Parable of the Prudent Manager (or the Parable of the Slovenly Slaves) from 12.35 through 12.48, Jesus offers practical advice to the disciples: be alert, don't get drunk, do not be bogged down by quotidian anxieties (**vs. 34**). Be assured that the Son of Man will return, but do not either attempt to calculate the date or to prepare what to say in case of persecution. Do not think that local signs, no matter how traumatic, from war to earthquake to martyrdom, will tell you that the end is coming. To the contrary, personal suffering in testimony to Jesus is not a sign of the end, but of endurance. When the end comes, no one will be expecting it but everyone will know (**vs. 35**).

The discourse concludes with a warning that the disciples not take their salvation for granted (**vs. 34**). Jesus encourages them to be alert and to pray, and here evokes the run-up to the Parable of the Widow and the Judge: pray always and do not lose heart (18.1). Be concerned not about the body but about the spirit (12.4–5). Ending with the messianic title "Son of Man," Jesus

---

[10] Ibid., 219.

claims the authority to speak about apocalyptic matters. At the end of this teaching, no one questions him.

TEMPLE TEACHING

From recording this astounding apocalyptic teaching, Luke now laconically notes that Jesus was teaching daily in the Temple. Jesus does not live there in his Father's house (see 2.49), as apparently did Anna the prophet. In the evenings, he retires to the Mount of Olives (**vs. 37**), previously mentioned in 19.29 as the place from which he sent his disciples to prepare for his entering the city (19.37). The geographic reference immediately signals messianic implications, based on the prophecy from Zechariah.

In a few early manuscripts,[11] all from what is known as "family 13" in the manuscript traditions, the story of the "woman taken in adultery" (John 7.53–8.2; the same text floats in other places in John's Gospel) appears here, and it does fit the narrative context. It introduces opposition to Jesus, which continues the themes of Chapter 20, including public questions designed to score points; it fits Luke's interest in depicting women, and especially women dependent on men to save them. How we read a Gospel passage, how we read most texts, depends on the context in which we read them.

Continuing on with Luke's Gospel as it appears today, we find in the chapter's last line that each day the people rose early to listen to Jesus' teachings in the Temple (**vs. 38**). The last mention of an explicit audience was back in 20.45, where Luke notes that Jesus is speaking to his disciples, but in the hearing of all the people. How the disciples heard the apocalyptic warnings and how the others heard them may have differed. The context suggests that the people were enthralled by the eschatological and apocalyptic material. They will find their companions in churches today that speak primarily about the violent end of the earth and the salvation of the few who are faithful. But if this is all that they heard, they cannot be counted among the disciples: Jesus' teaching includes, but is by no means limited to, eschatological persecution and final judgment.

Throughout this chapter, Luke has not mentioned Jesus' opposition, which includes the chief priests. The eschatological teachings are given within their earshot as well, but they offer no question or response. Their silence speaks to his authority, just as does the attention of the people. At

---

[11] See Bruce M. Metzger, *A Textual Commentary on the Greek New Testament,* 2d ed. (Stuttgart: German Bible Society, 1998), 147.

the same time, Luke sets up a profound irony: the very location where Jesus describes the end of the world will itself be destroyed. The burning of the Jerusalem Temple and the devastation of the city thus serve not as signs of the end, but as templates by which that final ending can be understood.

Josephus, whom we have cited, describes the destruction of a city. Jerusalem was not the first city, or the last, to face such devastation. Nanking, Dresden, Hiroshima and Nagasaki, Mosul ... the list continues. These are not signs of the end-times, but they are warnings. Each destruction should send the followers of Jesus back to this chapter, to remind them of the devastations their brothers and sisters face. But too often these followers are silent. They do not remain awake; they do not work to help their brothers and sisters endure.

BRIDGING THE HORIZONS

1. The Poor Widow and Her Offering

In his insightful article on the story traditionally called "The Widow's Mite," Addison G. Wright asks, "Apart from the text, if any one of us were actually to see in real life a poor widow giving the very last of her money to religion, would we not judge the act to be repulsive and to be based on misguided piety because she would be neglecting her own needs?"[12] The answer to this rhetorical question, posed in a way not dissimilar to the difficult questions Jesus had faced in the previous chapter, might be "Yes, *but* ..." There is no doubt that a televangelist, encouraging people on limited incomes to contribute their social security check in order to be a prayer partner and so allow that televangelist to have a private jet, several homes, and the lifestyle that Lazarus's counterpart enjoyed, is abusive. And yet, those televangelists may be the only people who appear to give personal care; they give love and hope, and they speak of the Christ in a way that touches the lonely heart. The line between giving hope and creating abuse can be a fine one.

No one is encouraging the widow to contribute *her whole life*. We do well to set this story in the context of the Church today. A widow of limited income sits in one of the back pews. When the collection plate is passed, she puts in all that she has in her wallet, two dollars. In making this contribution, she feels that she is giving to Jesus what Jesus wants from her. At the same time, she knows that the church will provide her lunch after the

---

[12] Wright, "Widow's Mites," 256.

service, and that its food bank will sustain her for the rest of the week. To tell this widow to withhold her cash would be an insult to her; to suggest that she keep her meager offering would also suggest that the poor have nothing to contribute.

How then should we speak to the people in churches who are on limited income? If we – that is, "we" the ones in the pulpit or on the finance committee – tell them to hold on to their money, we rob them of the satisfaction of making a contribution to the good work of the church even as we deny them agency. If we encourage them to give, then we may be taking funds that would be better saved for the electric bill, groceries, or health care. At the very least, churches might provide envelopes for when the collection plate is passed, so that great sums given by rich members are not celebrated and smaller sums do not serve as sources of embarrassment.

Ben remembers a story his father told him about the every-member canvas at their home church, Myers Park Methodist, in Charlotte, North Carolina. The every-member canvas involved going to each member's home to collect the pledge for the following year. On Ben's father's team was a well-to-do lawyer whose visitation list included a widow on a fixed income and living in a trailer. Basically, she was a shut-in. When the lawyer saw her circumstances, he resolved not to ask her for her pledge, but simply to visit with her, and resolve to give more himself. After sweet tea and cookies and good conversation about their church, the lawyer rose to go and told the woman not to worry about the pledge: he would give more on her behalf. She became upset, even indignant. She then came up to the lawyer and got right in his face. With tears in her eyes, she said, "Don't you take away from me the privilege of giving to the ministry of Jesus. You wait right here while I get my pledge card off the refrigerator." The lawyer, who meant well, felt badly after this exchange, but her comment speaks to the kind of person this widow was, very much like the self-sacrificial and generous widow in Luke 21.

2. The Eschatological Timetable

Judith Lieu writes, "we cannot be sure whether [Luke] thought the end would come within the lifetime of his own readers."[13] Both Ben and Amy-Jill have had students, met individuals in churches, and, especially, receive emails and phone calls from people beguiled by preachers announcing

---

[13]   Lieu, *Gospel According to Luke*, 172.

the end of the world. Signs sprout up in Nashville and Lexington, and no doubt elsewhere, advertising talks on how to prepare for the apocalypse. We also have met people who, as children, were traumatized by the idea that everyone they loved would be raptured into heaven, and they would be left alone on earth. Books such as the *Left Behind* series exacerbate the problem.

In the same way that it is difficult to pin down exactly what Luke the evangelist thinks about eschatological matters, so biblical scholars debate Jesus' view on the subject. Some propose that all the eschatological and apocalyptic material, especially the material marked by violence, could not possibly come from Jesus. Instead, they propose that Jesus' followers, distressed not only that the end did not come but also by the refusal of the majority of Jews to flock to their master and message, imported traditional apocalyptic language and placed it on the lips of Jesus. Others, including Ben and Amy-Jill, have no doubt that Jesus used such apocalyptic imagery.

Our remaining question is not an historical Jesus issue but a Christological one. If Jesus did predict the end of the world, complete with a general resurrection of the dead and a final judgment, to come during the lifetimes of his immediate followers, then he misjudged the date. And if he got the date wrong, then does this glitch compromise his divine nature?

For the sake of argument, and for the sake of those in churches who have wondered the same thing but who have been afraid to ask their question for fear of being labeled a heretic or a nonbeliever, let's say that Jesus was too optimistic about the nearness of the end. Such a miss on the date should compromise neither the value of his other statements nor claims of his divine status. One hanging thread need not unravel the entire sweater. The hoops through which some readers jump in order to bring these apocalyptic statements into line with history are signs not of fidelity, but of desperation. Apocalyptic is not history; records of the past are not the same thing as fantastic texts designed to give us hope in the future.[14]

Ben finds it hard to doubt that Jesus said what Mark 13.32 records: "But about that day or hour no one knows, neither the angels in heaven, nor the Son, but only the Father." He finds it preposterous to think that the Church would place *ignorance* of the timing about Jesus' return from heaven on his lips, given that they regarded him as Lord. Amy-Jill agrees that Jesus may well have indicated that he could not predict the exact date, although she has some doubts about Jesus' using what sounds like the beginnings

---

[14] See Dale C. Allison Jr., *The Historical Christ and the Theological Jesus* (Grand Rapids: Eerdmans, 2009), esp. 90–100, on eschatology.

of Trinitarian language. We agree that apocalyptic language is inherently hyperbolic; in Luke, as in the rest of the New Testament, it serves to increase the seriousness about watching and waiting for Jesus' return. It is not, however, meant to be taken literally. The most one can determine from the Synoptic Gospels' apocalyptic material, including Luke 21, is the notion of "possible imminence" of the return of the Son of Man. He might come soon, he might come later. It will be at an unexpected time, like a thief in the night.

3. Be Prepared

Jesus assures his followers that they need not prepare their defense in advance, for he will provide them with "words and a wisdom" that none of their "opponents will be able to withstand or contradict" (21.14–15). He similarly assures them that the Holy Spirit will teach them what they ought to say (12.12). Both Amy-Jill and Ben have encountered the occasional student who does not study, and the occasional minister who gets into the pulpit unprepared, because they have the assurance that their testimonies, or their exams, will be Spirit-inspired. To such individuals, we advise: give the Spirit something to work with. To do otherwise is to put God to the test (see 4.2, Jesus' conversation with Satan).

Luke 22 Last Supper, Arrest, and Sanhedrin Trial

THE PLOT AGAINST JESUS

¹ Now the festival of Unleavened Bread, which is called the Passover, was near.

² The chief priests and the scribes were looking for a way to put Jesus to death, for they were afraid of the people.

³ Then Satan entered into Judas called Iscariot, who was one of the twelve; ⁴ he went away and conferred with the chief priests and officers of the temple police about how he might betray him to them. ⁵ They were greatly pleased and agreed to give him money. ⁶ So he consented and began to look for an opportunity to betray him to them when no crowd was present.

PREPARATIONS FOR THE PASSOVER

⁷ Then came the day of Unleavened Bread, on which the Passover lamb had to be sacrificed. ⁸ So Jesus sent Peter and John, saying, "Go and prepare the Passover meal for us that we may eat it." ⁹ They asked him, "Where do you want us to make preparations for it?" ¹⁰ "Listen," he said to them, "when you have entered the city, a man carrying a jar of water will meet you; follow him into the house he enters ¹¹ and say to the owner of the house, 'The teacher asks you, "Where is the guest room, where I may eat the Passover with my disciples?"' ¹² He will show you a large room upstairs, already furnished. Make preparations for us there." ¹³ So they went and found everything as he had told them; and they prepared the Passover meal.

THE LAST SUPPER

¹⁴ When the hour came, he took his place at the table, and the apostles with him.

¹⁵ He said to them, "I have eagerly desired to eat this Passover with you before I suffer;

¹⁶ for I tell you, I will not eat it until it is fulfilled in the kingdom of God."

¹⁷ Then he took a cup, and after giving thanks he said, "Take this and divide it among yourselves; ¹⁸ for I tell you that from now on I will not drink of the fruit of the vine until the kingdom of God comes."

¹⁹ Then he took a loaf of bread, and when he had given thanks, he broke it and gave it to them, saying, "This is my body, which is given for you. Do this in remembrance of me." ²⁰ And he did the same with the cup after supper, saying, "This cup that is poured out for you is the new covenant in my blood.

²¹ But see, the one who betrays me is with me, and his hand is on the table. ²² For the Son of Man is going as it has been determined, but woe to that one by whom he is betrayed!" ²³ Then they began to ask one another, which one of them it could be who would do this.

²⁴ A dispute also arose among them as to which one of them was to be regarded as the greatest. ²⁵ But he said to them, "The kings of the Gentiles lord it over them; and those in authority over them are called benefactors. ²⁶ But not so with you; rather the greatest among you must become like the youngest, and the leader like one who serves. ²⁷ For who is greater, the one who is at the table or the one who serves? Is it not the one at the table? But I am among you as one who serves.

²⁸ "You are those who have stood by me in my trials; ²⁹ and I confer on you, just as my Father has conferred on me, a kingdom, ³⁰ so that you may eat and drink at my table in my kingdom, and you will sit on thrones judging the twelve tribes of Israel.

³¹ "Simon, Simon, listen! Satan has demanded to sift all of you like wheat, ³² but I have prayed for you that your own faith may not fail; and you, when once you have turned back, strengthen your brothers." ³³ And he said to him, "Lord, I am ready to go with you to prison and to death!" ³⁴ Jesus said, "I tell you, Peter, the cock will not crow this day, until you have denied three times that you know me."

³⁵ He said to them, "When I sent you out without a purse, bag, or sandals, did you lack anything?" They said, "No, not a thing." ³⁶ He said to them, "But now, the one who has a purse must take it, and likewise a bag. And the one who has no sword must sell his cloak and buy one. ³⁷ For I tell you, this scripture must be fulfilled in me, 'And he was counted among the lawless'; and indeed, what is written about me is being fulfilled." ³⁸ They said, "Lord, look, here are two swords." He replied, "It is enough."

THE ARREST ON THE MOUNT OF OLIVES

³⁹ He came out and went, as was his custom, to the Mount of Olives; and the disciples followed him. ⁴⁰ When he reached the place, he said to them, "Pray that you may not come into the time of trial."

⁴¹ Then he withdrew from them about a stone's throw, knelt down, and prayed, ⁴² "Father, if you are willing, remove this cup from me; yet, not my will but yours be done." ⁴³ Then an angel from heaven appeared to him and gave him strength.

⁴⁴ In his anguish he prayed more earnestly, and his sweat became like great drops of blood falling down on the ground.

⁴⁵ When he got up from prayer, he came to the disciples and found them sleeping because of grief, ⁴⁶ and he said to them, "Why are you sleeping? Get up and pray that you may not come into the time of trial."

⁴⁷ While he was still speaking, suddenly a crowd came, and the one called Judas, one of the twelve, was leading them. He approached Jesus to kiss him; ⁴⁸ but Jesus said to him, "Judas, is it with a kiss that you are betraying the Son of Man?"

⁴⁹ When those who were around him saw what was coming, they asked, "Lord, should we strike with the sword?" ⁵⁰ Then one of them struck the slave of the high priest and cut off his right ear. ⁵¹ But Jesus said, "No more of this!" And he touched his ear and healed him.

⁵² Then Jesus said to the chief priests, the officers of the temple police, and the elders who had come for him, "Have you come out with swords and clubs as if I were a bandit? ⁵³ When I was with you day after day in the temple, you did not lay hands on me. But this is your hour, and the power of darkness!"

PETER'S DENIALS

⁵⁴ Then they seized him and led him away, bringing him into the high priest's house. But Peter was following at a distance.

⁵⁵ When they had kindled a fire in the middle of the courtyard and sat down together, Peter sat among them. ⁵⁶ Then a servant-girl, seeing him in the firelight, stared at him and said, "This man also was with him." ⁵⁷ But he denied it, saying, "Woman, I do not know him."

⁵⁸ A little later someone else, on seeing him, said, "You also are one of them." But Peter said, "Man, I am not!" ⁵⁹ Then about an hour later still another kept insisting, "Surely this man also was with him; for he is a Galilean." ⁶⁰ But Peter said, "Man, I do not know what you are talking about!" At

that moment, while he was still speaking, the cock crowed. [61] The Lord turned and looked at Peter. Then Peter remembered the word of the Lord, how he had said to him, "Before the cock crows today, you will deny me three times." [62] And he went out and wept bitterly.

[63] Now the men who were holding Jesus began to mock him and beat him; [64] they also blindfolded him and kept asking him, "Prophesy! Who is it that struck you?"

[65] They kept heaping many other insults on him.

CONDEMNATION BY THE COUNCIL

[66] When day came, the assembly of the elders of the people, both chief priests and scribes, gathered together, and they brought him to their council. [67] They said, "If you are the Messiah, tell us." He replied, "If I tell you, you will not believe; [68] and if I question you, you will not answer. [69] But from now on the Son of Man will be seated at the right hand of the power of God." [70] All of them asked, "Are you, then, the Son of God?" He said to them, "You say that I am." [71] Then they said, "What further testimony do we need? We have heard it ourselves from his own lips!"

Framing the Last Supper with the plot to betray Jesus, Luke 22 begins the Passion Narrative. The chapter concludes with Peter's denial, predicted at the Last Supper and confirmed while Jesus is interrogated by the Jerusalem authorities. The narrative time now slows, day by day and then hour by hour. In this chapter and the next, all forces human and supernatural converge against Jesus: the chief priests, Temple officers, and elders conspire to kill him; Satan enters into Judas Iscariot and prompts his betrayal; Jesus predicts that his followers will desert him; Herod Antipas and Pilate collude in his execution. The journey to the cross is inexorable, driven by forces both cosmic and earthly.

THE PLOT AGAINST JESUS

Vs. 1 sets the time as the "Festival of Unleavened Bread, which is called the Passover" (following Mark 14.1). At least by the time of the Babylonian exile (sixth century BCE), the Feast of the Unleavened Bread was conjoined with the Feast of the Passover. By the time of the Mishnah (early third century CE), the expression "Feast of Unleavened Bread" drops out, and the double holiday simply becomes "Passover," or, in Hebrew, "Pesach." *The Festival* refers to the eight-day celebration in commemoration of the

Exodus from Egypt (see Exod 12.6–15; Lev 23.5–8); the Passover itself is the first night of the holiday, when Jewish families eat the Passover offering. While the Temple was still standing, Jews would come to the Jerusalem on pilgrimage, obtain a lamb sacrificed in the Temple as a paschal offering, and eat this offering with family and friends within the city. Today, Jewish families continue to celebrate Passover, in their own homes in Israel and in the Diaspora, but with many traditions developed after the destruction of the Temple.

The opening of the Passion Narrative with this calendrical notice is more than a temporal marker. The Gospel throughout has emphasized references to bread and to meals; readers therefore bring to the Last Supper all the dishes previously tasted: open table fellowship with sinners and tax collectors as well as with Pharisees and lawyers; the multiplication of the loaves and so the affirmation of divine generosity; the prayer for "daily bread"; the role of the meal as a place for the reconciliation of sinners, from the woman who anoints Jesus to Zacchaeus the tax collector; the image of heavenly or eschatological banquets; and so on. These themes continue past the Last Supper into the resurrection accounts, where Jesus will again meet his followers at table, and it is in the context of a meal that they recognize him. The Passover is a meal that celebrates freedom from slavery in Egypt; the Gospel takes this idea and develops it in terms of freedom from sin and death.

References to Passover evoke not only freedom from slavery but also the horrors of slavery itself: "they [the Egyptians under Pharoah's rule] set task-masters over them to oppress them with forced labor ... [they] became ruthless in imposing tasks on the Israelites, and made their lives bitter with hard service in mortar and brick and in every kind of field labor. They were ruthless in the tasks that they imposed on them." Pharoah next demands that the midwives kill all newborn boys and when the midwives use a ruse to protect the women and their babies, he "commanded all his people, 'Every boy that is born to the Hebrews you shall throw into the Nile'"[1] (Exod 1.11, 13–14, 16, 22). In the place of Pharaoh, Luke locates the chief priests and scribes, who were seeking to kill Jesus (**vs. 2**; cf. Mark 14.2). Evocative connections to the opening of the Book of Exodus continue as Luke notes that the local leaders feared the people, for Exod 1.12 states: "the Egyptians

---

[1]   "To the Hebrews" appears in the LXX but not the Hebrew version (MT). The LXX makes more logical sense, but the Hebrew is more prescient: in his hastily issued command, Pharoah ironically foreshadows the deaths of Egypt's firstborn sons.

came to dread the Israelites" because their numbers were growing. The verse confirms what Jesus had already predicted: at the beginning of the travel narrative, he alerted his followers that the "elders, chief priests, and scribes" would reject him; by 20.19, Luke announces their intent to kill him.

Amy-Jill suggests that, by continuing accusations against the chief priests, along with Temple officials, elders, and scribes, Luke keeps the responsibility for Jesus' death primarily in their hands and not that of the Romans. By continuing to note that this cabal would have acted themselves were they not fearful of the reaction of the Jerusalem crowds (cf. 20.19), Luke further exculpates Pilate and so Rome even as the Gospel holds out hope that the people Israel will reject the local authorities and follow Jesus instead.

Ben disagrees. He notes that Jesus from the cross forgives his Roman executioners and perhaps also the Jewish critics who watch him die, because they acted in "ignorance," that is, they did not realize the implications of their actions. The penitent bandit speaks for some Jews when he speaks to Jesus' innocence. Peter in Acts 3.17 says directly *to his fellow Jews* that they acted in ignorance in regard to their part in Jesus' demise. This theme of ignorance, which ties together the death of Jesus with the early preaching of how the responsibility for that death was to be viewed, means that Luke is not likely simply exonerating the Romans. To the contrary, according to Chapter 23, it is Romans soldiers who lead Jesus to the place of execution, nail him to the cross, and one of them, a Roman centurion, is the one who remarks about Jesus being a righteous person.

Ben therefore regards Luke as presenting both some of the Jewish leaders and the Romans as playing a part in Jesus' death. Luke is not interested in exonerating Pilate here, any more than when noting the time that Pilate mingled the blood of Jews and Samaritans with their sacrifices (13.1). In short, the picture is much more complex than the notion that Romans are exonerated and Jews are blamed by Luke. Luke's portrait is one of some Jewish officials and some Romans being involved in the demise of Jesus.

Finally, Amy-Jill would nuance these comments. She is not saying that Rome has no part in the execution of Jesus. She is saying that the impression Luke leaves the reader, or at least herself as reader, is one in which responsibility is consistently shifted to the Jewish authorities: it is they who have planned the death, as Luke repeatedly mentions; it is they who work with Judas; it is they, the "chief priests," possibly the "Temple police" (this identification is discussed later in this section) and "the elders" who arrest him; they who abuse him in the home of the High Priest; they as a whole who bring him to Pilate and make false accusations against him;

they who pressure Pilate to execute Jesus even though Pilate finds him innocent of wrongdoing; they who taunt Jesus as he dies. The focus on the authorities continues on the road to Emmaus, when the travelers note "how our chief priests and leaders handed him over to be condemned to death and crucified him" (24.20). No wonder Peter tells the Jews in Jerusalem: "you killed the Author of life" (Acts 3.15). Rome is always in the background, but in the foreground of the Gospel is the guilt of the Jewish leaders, and in Acts that guilt becomes the guilt of all the people in Jerusalem.

Given Luke's several references to the local authorities' fear of the people, combined with the previous two chapters where the people flock to Jesus in the Temple, Luke's narrative requires some mechanism for the chief priests to implement their plan. For Luke, as for John (13.27), but not according to Matthew or Mark, the mechanism is Satan's possession of Judas Iscariot (**vs. 3a**). Although Jesus declared that he had seen Satan fall from heaven (10.18), Satan remains active through demonic possession as well as earlier prediction: in 4.13, at the conclusion of the Temptation Narrative, Luke mentions that Satan departed until an "opportune time" (Greek: *kairos*). The time has come. The last of the three temptations took place in Jerusalem (4.9); given Luke's comments about the city, one gets the impression that Satan had never left.

Coupled with the notice of Satanic involvement, Luke reiterates that Judas was "one of the Twelve" (**vs. 3b**). Judas thereby serves as a warning: one's enemies may be members of one's own household. He also provides Luke's narrative another connection: just as the Temptation hinted that Satan would return, so Luke's only earlier explicit mention of Judas, in the enumeration of the Twelve, is that he "became a traitor" (6.16 NRSV) or, literally, "became the one handing over" (*paradidōmi*).

At this point in Luke's story, we do not know if Judas is possessed in the sense of lacking free will or if Satan's presence is triggering an evil impulse he already had. Only in vs. 31, when Jesus speaks of Satan's sifting of Peter and the others, do we realize that Satan can be resisted, as Jesus had resisted him according to the Temptation Narrative. In Acts 26.28, Paul similarly announces to King Agrippa II that Jesus provides the means by which people "may turn from darkness to light and from the power of Satan to God." One implication of this comment is that those who do *not* turn to Jesus are therefore under the power of Satan. Such demonization of groups, including Jews who will be connected to Judas, does not bode well for Jewish–Christian relations. Fred Craddock helpfully writes, "The church is at its best when it stops asking, 'Why did Judas do it?' and instead examines its own record of discipleship."[2]

A CLOSER LOOK: JUDAS ISCARIOT

Judas Iscariot remains historically unrecoverable, with the Gospel writers attempting to fill in gaps in the tradition. Mark gives him no motive; Judas simply decides to provide the authorities information on where Jesus can be found. Matthew (26.15) attributes Judas's motive to greed, and John 12.6 reinforces this view by describing Judas as a thief. In postbiblical treatments, Judas is a political revolutionary seeking to force Jesus' hand (*Jesus Christ Superstar*); the only brave one among the Twelve who can help Jesus implement his plan to die (from the *Gospel of Judas* to *The Last Temptation of Christ*); or the incarnation of the perfidious, eternal Jew. Dietrich Bonhoeffer, a central figure in the Confessing Church's struggle against Nazism, suggested that Judas stood for the "deeply divided people from whom Jesus came, the chosen people, who had received the promise of the Messiah and nevertheless rejected him … Christianity has again and again seen in Judas the dark secret of the rejection of God and eternal damnation."[3] Similarly, the great Protestant theologian Karl Barth taught that Judas, "in his concentrated attack upon Israel's messiah, does only what the elect people of Israel had always done toward its God, thus finally showing itself in its totality to be the nation rejected by God … This Judas must die, as he did die; and this Jerusalem must be destroyed, as it was destroyed."[4] Paul Chung helps us contextualize a remark like this. He says: "However, Barth's view of the synagogue can arouse suspicion of an anti-Jewish residue, remaining a stumbling block to Barth's contribution to Jewish–Christian relations. In the section entitled 'The Determination of the Rejected', Barth tends to fall into a gray area, seeming to dispute Israel's right to exist: 'Israel's right to existence is extinguished, and therefore its existence can only be extinguished.'"[5]

---

2   Craddock, *Luke*, 253.
3   Dietrich Bonhoeffer, "Predigt am Sonntag Judika über Judas"[Sermon on Judas. March 14, 1937], in *Gesammelte Schriften*, Vol. 4, ed. Eberhard Bethge (Munich: Chr. Kaiser, 1965), 406–13 (412), cited in Susan Gubar, *Judas: A Biography* (New York: W. W. Norton, 2009), 276.
4   Karl Barth, *The Doctrine of God. Vol. 2 Part 2 of Church Dogmatics*. Trans. G. W. Bromiley et al. (Edinburgh: T&T Clark, 1957), 505, cited in Gubar, *Judas: A Biography*, 276.
5   Paul S. Chung, *Hermeneutical Theology and the Imperative of Public Ethics: Confessing Christ in Post-Colonial World Christianity* (Missional Church, Public Theology, World Christianity 2; Eugene: Pickwick, 2013), p. 138.

That Judas' name means "Jewish man" or "man of Judea" adds to this reception history. We mention Bonhoeffer among the myriad of people who associated Judas with Jews because he is recognized as a Protestant saint, a man of integrity, and because he knew what the Nazis were doing to Jews. We mention Barth since he is often regarded as the twentieth century's most important Protestant theologian. Both authors are required reading in most Protestant seminary curricula. And we mention these two great men to show that the connection of Jews and Judas was so intimate in the Christian imagination that even Bonhoeffer and Barth could not see its perniciousness.

That *Luke* associated Judas and "the Jews" is, however, not likely. The name Judah (Hebrew) or Judas (Greek) was common at the time of both Jesus and Luke, as the unfortunately titled disciple "Judas, not Iscariot" (John 14.22), the better-identified disciple "Judas son of James" (Luke 6.16), Saul/Paul's host Judas (Acts 9.11), the evangelist Judas Barsabbas (Acts 15.22), Jacob's son Judah (Matt 1.2–3), the famous Maccabean hero Judas Maccabaeus, Jesus' brother Judas (Matt 13.55//Mark 6.3), and even the "Jude" of the Epistle indicate. With Judas, we have an instance where the text itself does not equate Judas with Jews and therefore all Jews with betrayal; that is an issue of reception history.

In Matt 27.4, Judas confesses to the chief priests, "I have sinned by betraying innocent blood," and so, apparently, repents. Matthew also depicts Judas as a new Ahitophel who betrays the son of David and, realizing that Absalom will not follow his advice, puts his affairs in order and hangs himself (2 Sam 15–17, and see Matt 17.23). Luke has none of this. For Luke, Judas purchases a field "with the reward for his wickedness" (the implication is that Judas received money for handing Jesus over to the authorities), and he dies, ignominiously: "he burst open in the middle and all his bowels gushed out" (Acts 1.18).

By the time of the Passion Narrative, Jesus had been predicting his own death for many chapters, and he had spoken of Jerusalem as the city that kills its prophets. He did not require anyone to "betray him." He could have easily made himself available to any of the local authorities, at any time. The betrayal by Judas, mentioned by Mark and then developed over the centuries, makes for a better story, but it does not necessarily make for better history.

In Paul's own narrative of Jesus' Last Supper, there is no Judas and there is no betrayal. Paul simply mentions "the night when [Jesus] was handed over …" (1 Cor 11.23). The NRSV's "on the night when he was betrayed" is an overreading of the Greek verb *paradidōmi*, which can mean "betray" but literally means "handed over." Context determines connotation. Paul does not think Jesus was "betrayed"; if he were, then his fidelity to his own mission would be compromised. A willing martyr does not require a betrayal. Rather, Paul sees *God* as "handing over" Jesus. The apostle explains how God "did not withhold his own son, but handed him over [*paradidōmi*; the NRSV reads "gave him up"] for all of us" (Rom 8.32).

Ben regards Judas as an historical figure, one of the Twelve, who betrayed Jesus. Amy-Jill admits that this is a plausible reconstruction of events, but she emphasizes that much of the story of Judas, like much of the Synoptic Passion Narrative, including the full trial by the Council, rings more like Christian apologetic than details of what actually happened. She sees the story of Judas as developing from Mark to John and on through apocryphal texts, and she sees the Gospels as interdependent rather than as independent witnesses. We know the story of Judas developed; at what point the story begins is more difficult to determine. Was there a Judas? Amy-Jill thinks there may have been, but she also sees how Mark could have invented his role, and so instead of having God "hand over" (*paradidōmi*) Jesus has one of the inner circle "betray" him. The story of the friend who betrays is well grounded in classical literature, with Brutus's betrayal of Julius Caesar in 44 BCE being the most well known.[6]

Ben replies that Amy-Jill's reconstruction ignores the fact that in all four Gospels and in Acts, the portrayal is negative of Judas from start to finish, even in the listing of the Twelve. There has to have been some deep betrayal by a member of the inner circle of Jesus for this consistent portrait to be affirmed by four different evangelists. And as for Paul, he is citing the tradition that was handed down to him from his encounters with Peter and James the brother of Jesus (see 1 Cor 11.23); indeed, he says the tradition goes back to Jesus the Lord himself! And that tradition includes not only Jesus' prediction of his being betrayed by a member of his inner circle, but the report of this perfidy after the fact by his disciples. The issue is not whether Jesus *needed* someone to betray him to produce his march to the cross. Obviously, it could have happened some other way. The issue is that one of Jesus' inner circle, who had traveled, eaten,

---

6   See Hyam Maccoby, *Judas Iscariot and the Myth of Jewish Evil* (New York: Free Press, 1992), for an imaginative development of this idea.

and ministered with him for years, had in the end handed him over to the Jewish authorities for whatever inscrutable reasons. It is the deep shock and pain that this betrayal caused Jesus himself and his earliest followers that led to this consistent portrait of the man in the Gospels and Acts. In an honor and shame culture, Judas's betrayal was one of the most shameful acts one could imagine. Christian apologetics would not make up this story, not least because it would reflect badly on Jesus' ability to keep the loyalty of his disciples to the end of his life.

As Luke presents the story, the betrayal is efficiently accomplished. Judas confers with the "chief priests and officers," the same group who will arrest Jesus (22.52; see also Acts 4.1; 5.24), about how he might facilitate the betrayal (**vs. 4**). This move signals that the chief priests are doing Satan's bidding; they are not possessed by Satan, but they are in league with him and therefore, potentially, more culpable. The officers (Greek: *stratēgoi*, whence "strategy") are generally troop leaders (cf. Josephus, *War* 6.5.3; *Ant.* 20.6.2), but the term can indicate a more general office and thus "official"; the NRSV's "Temple police" offers one possible reading, and one that reinforces the guilt of the Jewish authorities rather than that of the Romans. The people who control Jerusalem politically, with influence and arms, are united in their opposition to Jesus and in their solidarity with Satan.

The officials, delighted with this opportunity, decide to pay Judas for the deed (**vs. 5**); Luke lacks the reference to the thirty denarii (Matt 26.15). Judas accepts the money (**vs. 6**), and so a contract has been made. When Jesus will soon speak of the covenant in his blood (vs. 20), readers might recall this earlier contract: one leads to death; the other to life. As Judas looks for the opportunity to find Jesus apart from the crowd (**vs. 6**), Jesus begins to plan for celebrating the Passover. The union of the Jerusalem establishment, Judas, and Satan provides the backdrop to the Last Supper.

PREPARATIONS FOR THE PASSOVER

Returning to the temporal setting mentioned in 22.1, Luke notes the arrival of the "day of Unleavened Bread," when the Passover lambs are sacrificed in the Temple (**vs. 7**). Peter and John, who will emerge in the beginning of Acts (3.1–4; 4.13, 19; 8.14) as the leaders of the Jerusalem assembly, step forward for the first time as a pair, as Jesus tells them to "prepare the Passover meal" (**vs. 8**); James (Jacob) the brother of John, who had been the third member of the Twelve's inner circle (8.51; 9.28), drops out; his absence, unexplained here, in retrospect anticipates his early execution (Acts 12.2). Judas represents one of the Twelve who defects; Peter and John are two of the remainder who will, despite trials and failures, prove ultimately faithful. Herod Agrippa I kills James, after which the full complement of the Twelve is not restored, at least according to Acts. The stories of the other apostles are left to extracanonical legend.

James and John, by asking about the location for the Passover meal (**vs. 9**), indicate that Jesus is not planning on dining with any friends or family; his disciples, as his new family, will be the ones present. Their question of finding a room for rent is a good one: Jerusalem at pilgrimage festivals hosted thousands of pilgrims, and tradition held that pilgrims celebrating the Passover were to eat the Paschal lamb in Jerusalem. Passover preparations included, along with the lamb sacrificed in the Temple, *matzo* (unleavened bread) and bitter herbs. None of the Gospels mentions any of these foods at the Last Supper. The "bread" Jesus takes according to the Synoptics could have been matzo, but the Gospels do not make this point specific. The Gospel narrative mentions wine, and the Mishnah, *Pes.* 10.1–7, states that participants were to drink four cups of wine. The meal itself, as Luke presents it, does not fully resemble the *Seder* (Hebrew for "order," and here the details of the meal) as described in rabbinic literature, although what exactly that meal would have looked like in the late Second Temple period, when the sacrificial system was still operative, remains a matter of scholarly debate. The Mishnah also says that along with eating unleavened bread, the lamb, and bitter herbs, the story of the redemption from Egypt should be told. For Luke, the story is one of Jesus' redemption of his followers from sin and death.

Given the lack of details of the Supper combined with discrepancies between the Synoptic and Johannine accounts, questions arise as to the date of this final meal. Here Ben and Amy-Jill have disagreements. Amy-Jill observes that in John's Gospel, the Last Supper is not a Passover meal. John depicts Jesus as crucified at the time the lambs are sacrificed, and so Jesus becomes, symbolically, the Passover offering. Paul describes Jesus in Paschal terms – "Clean out the old leaven so that you may be a new batch, as you really are unleavened. For our paschal lamb, Christ, has been sacrificed" (1 Cor 5.7) – but does not set the date for the Last Supper at Passover. Chronologically, John's Gospel makes more historical sense: the Fourth Gospel depicts no Passover Seder, and Jesus is not killed on the first day of the holiday. He is, both symbolically and probably historically, killed at the time the lambs are being sacrificed in the Temple. John also depicts no Sanhedrin trial.

Conversely, Ben notes that the presentation in John 13, for the most part, is of a meal earlier in the week rather than the "Last Supper" meal portrayed in the Synoptics. This means that Judas was involved and left both the meal early in the week to plan Jesus' demise, and then later in the week, to lead the officials to where Jesus could be found. The meal in John 13 has footwashing and no words of institution ("This is my body ..."), the meal in the Synoptics has "this is my body," "this is my blood," and no footwashing. In order to associate the meal in John 13 with the later betrayal of Jesus, John imports some elements of the betrayal story from Synopic Thursday evening Last Supper and thereby conflates the two meals. John inserts a long block of Jesus' teaching and final prayer in John 14–17 rather than depict another meal from later in the week.[7] Yet Ben also agrees with Amy-Jill that the Johannine chronology makes the better sense of timing, so if the Last Supper in the Synoptics was a Passover meal, it had to be a proleptic one, celebrated in advance of the normal day, on Thursday evening.

Jesus had instructed two unnamed disciples to find a colt in the local village and to bring it to him in preparation for the Triumphal Entry (19.30–31), and he now instructs Peter and John to follow through on plans already made. There is no reason to attribute Jesus' instructions in either case to supernatural knowledge, and Matt 26.18 suggests that Jesus had prearranged this meeting. Jesus tells the two apostles that in Jerusalem, a man carrying a water jar will meet them; they are to follow him to a house (**vs. 11**). Commentators typically suggest that carrying water jars was women's work and therefore the man would be notable. The claim overstates; men also carried water jars, and Peter and John are not looking for any oddity in behavior. The man will find them.

The two apostles are to tell the homeowner that "the teacher" (Greek: *didaskalos*) seeks the guest room where he will eat the Passover with his disciples (**vs. 11**). The guest room is, in Greek, a *katalyma*; this is the same term Luke uses in 2.7, where there was no space in the "guest room" for Mary to give birth. The baby in the manger, born in the back of the house where there was the feeding trough for the family animals, is about to become "bread" for his followers.

---

[7] For a detailed discussion of the tradition history of these two stories and two meals, see Ben Witherington III, *John's Wisdom: A Commentary on the Fourth Gospel* (Louisville: Westminster John Knox, 1995), and especially the Excursus at John 13.

Jesus tells Peter and John they will find a large, furnished, "room upstairs" (**vs.12**). The Greek phrase *anagaion mega estrōmenon* refers to a large "strewn" or "spread" room; Luke is not here alluding directly to the famous "upper room" (Greek: *hyperōon*) of Acts 1.13 where the apostles would gather in Jerusalem after Jesus' death. The disciples follow the instructions and prepare the Passover (**vs. 13**). For Luke's narrative, that preparation would have included the Paschal lamb, which again indicates that the Temple is not an illegitimate institution. It also indicates that someone, perhaps the women patrons of 8.3, provided the funds for the dinner. Whether these women or others were present at the final meal Jesus had with his followers, however, goes unmentioned. Absence of evidence is not the same thing as evidence of absence, but given Luke's tendency to restrict women's roles and to focus on the Twelve, Amy-Jill finds it unlikely that Luke envisioned the women at the meal. She further observes that Luke's use of the term "apostles" rather than the broader term "disciples" for those reclining with Jesus (vs. 14) precludes the argument that women were present. Mark has the similarly limited "the twelve" (14.17). Ben thinks, on the contrary, that Luke is not trying to restrict women's roles, especially since in the Gospel's concluding chapter it is the women who remembered Jesus' teaching about his death and res- urrection (see also 23.55–56), and faithfully reported what they found and heard at the empty tomb to the male disciples, who react to the report with male prejudice.

THE LAST SUPPER

Luke's notice that "when the hour had come" (**vs. 14a**) is, in canonical con- text, more than simply a temporal marker. Readers of the Gospel of John will recall Jesus' frequent mention of his hour (2.4; 4.21–23 [in relation to the Temple]; 5.25, 28; and so on). For Luke, the "hour" would be sundown on the fourteenth day of Nisan, the date that the angel of death passed over the Israelites who had marked their doors with the blood of lambs but killed all of Egypt's firstborn sons. The timing is not just chronological, it is Christological.

The meal begins in **vs. 14** with Jesus, together with the apostles, reclining at table (the NRSV's "taking their place" hides the Passover implications, where one reclines at the table to symbolize the dining of free people). In Luke's Gospel, the Supper (vss. 7–38) resembles a Roman symposium, with a meal followed by an after-dinner speaker (vss. 24–38); Johnson suggests

Luke presents Jesus as a philosopher, comparable to Socrates.[8] That Jesus will reflect in his talk on gentile rulers and benefactors commends this association. The same symposium ideal underlies how John 13–17 depicts the meal and the after-dinner discourses. The Passover tradition itself as it is presented in rabbinic literature also took shape as a type of symposium, a formal meal featuring teaching and discussion.

Luke's meal begins not with eating or a story, but with lament. Jesus speaks of his longing to eat "the Passover" (i.e., not just the lamb, but the *Seder* meal) prior to his suffering (**vs. 15**). The Greek term for Passover, *pascha*, sounds like the Greek verb *paschō*, which means "to suffer, endure." The connection between the Jewish festival and Jesus' suffering and death is thus secured linguistically. Then, unexpectedly, he announces that he will not eat it until "it is fulfilled in the kingdom of God" (**vs. 16**). The "it" appears to be his death and resurrection. He may also be alluding to the messianic banquet, the final Passover, when liberation is complete.

Ben, along with the majority of the interpreters, thinks Jesus means that he will consume the wine traditionally enjoyed at the Passover; Amy-Jill wonders if Luke is portraying Jesus as fasting, as he did in the wilderness before Satan tempted him. Luke does not make explicit that Jesus takes sour wine offered to him as he hangs on the cross (23.36). Nor does Jesus eat with the two travelers he met on the road to Emmaus (24.30). Only back in Jerusalem, after his followers had come to believe in his resurrection, as foretold, does he ask for something to eat (24.42–43). And only here do the followers provide him food; in all these other cases, he feeds them.

Jesus then takes the cup, gives thanks (to God), and instructs the Twelve to share it among themselves (**vs. 17**). "On occasion the host [at a symposium] might send his own cup to a particular guest as a special mark of honor and as a means of bestowing a blessing, but each of the guests would drink from his own cup for the sequence of cups of wine that marked the course of the meal."[9] Jesus does not explicitly drink from the cup himself; rather, he repeats that he will not drink wine until the Kingdom comes (**vs. 18**).

Next, taking the bread and again giving thanks (to God), he breaks it and distributes it to the Twelve. The distribution parallels the giving of the cup. Jesus then provides what have come to be called the "words of institution": "This is my body, which is given for you. Do this in remembrance

8   Johnson, *Gospel of Luke*, 348–49.
9   Nolland, *Luke 18.35–24.53*, 1048.

of me" (**vs. 19**).[10] After the supper, he makes a parallel claim regarding the cup: "This cup that is poured out for you is the new covenant in my blood" (**vs. 20**). What we have here is not a traditional Passover meal, or a traditional meal at all. Something new is being created. The focus is changing from the Passover liberation of Israel from slavery to the liberation Jesus offers in his ministry and, we shall soon see, in his resurrection.

Jesus' language is shocking, provocative, and ultimately obscure. To suggest, even if metaphorically, that the bread and wine were his body and blood, would connote cannibalism, something the Jewish tradition abhors. The commandment given to Noah and his family to avoid consuming blood is, according to Gen 9.4 ("You shall not eat flesh with its life, that is, its blood"), incumbent not simply on Abraham's descendants, but on the entire world. The shock of the language is made explicit in John 6.53, where Jesus states, "unless you eat the flesh of the Son of Man and drink his blood, you have no life in you," and the many of the disciples, not inappropriately, respond, "This teaching is difficult; who can accept it?" (John 6.60).

From that time until the present, the followers of Jesus have continued to debate the meaning of Jesus' instructions: transubstantiation (the bread and wine served in the Church is literally Jesus' body and blood), consubstantiation (the elements are literally Jesus' body and blood, but they do not lose their actual substance as bread and wine), a symbolic but not mystical meal wherein Jesus is remembered, the tradition that Christ is spiritually present with the Eucharist, and so on.[11] The connection to Passover and to blood suggests an apotropaic function: just as the ancient Israelites put lambs' blood on their doorposts to ward off the angel of death, so Jesus' blood keeps death away.

The expression "new covenant" derives from Jer 31.31–34:

> The days are surely coming, says the LORD, when I will make a new covenant with the house of Israel and the house of Judah. It will not be like the covenant that I made with their ancestors when I took them by the hand to bring them out of the land of Egypt – a covenant that they broke, though

---

[10]   A few early manuscripts omit half of vs. 19 and all of vs. 20, but this omission appears to be a correction to limit the references to the cup in light of later Christian practice. See Metzger, *Textual Criticism*, 173–77. See also D. C. Parker, *Codex Bezae: An Early Christian Manuscript and Its Text* (Cambridge, UK: Cambridge University Press, 1992); Bradley S. Billings, "The Disputed Words in the Lukan Institution Narrative (Luke 22.19b–20): A Sociological Answer to a Textual Problem," *JBL* 125.3 (2006): 507–26.

[11]   On this, see Ben Witherington III, *Making a Meal of It* (Waco: Baylor University Press, 2008).

I was their husband, says the LORD. But this is the covenant that I will make with the house of Israel after those days, says the LORD: I will put my law within them, and I will write it on their hearts; and I will be their God, and they shall be my people. No longer shall they teach one another, or say to each other, "Know the LORD," for they shall all know me, from the least of them to the greatest, says the LORD; for I will forgive their iniquity, and remember their sin no more.

The language of "new covenant" appears in Luke, but not the other Gospels, although it appears as well in 1 Cor 11.25; 2 Cor 3.6; and several times in the Epistle to the Hebrews (8.8, 13; 9.15; 12.24).

Luke is not replacing the "old covenant" made at Sinai, any more than the Sinaitic covenant replaces the one made with Noah, or the covenant with David replaces the covenant with Moses. The Law and the Temple are still in effect. Luke is not a Marcionite who rejects the "Old Testament," as the infancy materials in particular attest. Just as Jesus' followers needed to determine how to understand the crucifixion (a sacrifice, a ransom, a martyrdom …), they also needed to understand what this new covenant meant, especially since Jeremiah's new covenant is with the "house of Israel" and not with the gentile nations and since missionaries, two thousand years later, are still instructing, "know the Lord."

Luke's version of this ritual seems to have come from the same stream of tradition that Paul cites in 1 Cor 11.23–26 (cf. also the *Didache*). The words, the private setting, and the specific references to the apostles indicate that this memorial was not a meal for just anyone, such as was the feeding of the five thousand, but rather for insiders. They will be part of this new covenant. Given the Passover connections, Jesus is placing himself in the role of Moses, who led his people out from slavery and mediated the covenant at Sinai. As Moses had stated regarding the Passover celebration: "That you may remember the day of your departure from the land of Egypt all the days of your life" (Deut 16:3), so Jesus is instituting a new memory, this one regarding his death and its implications.

Because Luke omits the "first supper" where an unnamed woman anointed Jesus' head and where Mark and Matthew both proclaim that the story of her actions will be told "in remembrance of her" (Matt 26.13; Mark 14.9; John's version of this account, which also draws on Luke 7.36–50, names Mary the sister of Martha and Lazarus as the one who anointed Jesus' feet), Luke secures the idea that Jesus' followers will celebrate only his memory, not that of the unnamed woman.

Without explaining the words about the covenant, Jesus changes the subject to his betrayal. In **vs. 21**, he reveals that the one who will hand him over reclines at the table with him. The traitor has shared the bread and the cup. Participation in the ritual without repentance and love in the heart is possible, but it makes a travesty of Jesus' memory. What the ritual will mean necessarily depends in part on the person who participates in it. For the other apostles, sitting at Jesus' "table" will result in sitting on thrones and judging the twelve tribes of Israel (vs. 30); for Judas, it will result in ignominy.

And this ignominy is, in Luke's view, deserved. Although Jesus willingly goes to his death, and although that death is preordained, the one who betrays him bears responsibility (**vs. 22**; Luke omits the grim statement found in Mark 14.21b that "it would be better for [the betrayer] had he never been born"). Judas is not a puppet manipulated by Satan, nor is he simply a cog in the divine soteriological plan. He did what he was fated to do, *and* what he did was his own fault. This apparent paradox that combines fate and free will – philosophers call the approach "compatibilism" – plays out by Luke's placing the emphasis on choice and so free will. Jesus has already shown that Satan can be resisted, and he will go on, in this chapter, to speak of praying that Peter have the faith to resist (vs. 32). The same approach to human responsibility appears throughout much of Christian history, where those who do not accept the Gospel are seen both as cursed by God in a predestinarian way and also as responsible for their own damnation. While there have been many Christians who thought this, there have also been millions of Christians through the last two thousand years who do not believe God predestined anyone to be cursed or damned, and Ben is one of them.

Whereas readers know that Judas will betray Jesus, the other apostles do not know the informant's identity (**vs. 23**). Their befuddlement indicates that to this point, Judas had done nothing to draw their suspicion. In Mark 14.19, they question Jesus about his identity; here, they (oddly) question each other. They do not have self-doubts, but rather doubts about some of the others![12] Despite the solemnity of the immediate context, in which Jesus speaks of his death and betrayal, the apostles completely miss the point. One could picture this verse acted out, with Andrew saying to James, "So, are you the traitor?" and with Judas smiling into his wine cup.

---

[12]   Craddock, *Luke*, 257–58.

This questioning moves the disciples to argue about which of them would have the greatest reputation (**vs. 24**). Ironically, with the possible exception of Peter, Judas Iscariot will be the best known of the Twelve. The segue, unspoken, would be their protestations about the extent of their fidelity: how much they had given up in order to follow Jesus; how many hours they had dedicated to his mission. Luke places this dispute here (contrast Mark 10.42–45; Matt 20.25–28; cf. Luke 9.46) to heighten the pathos of the scene. The disciples' inability to engage either Jesus' provocative teaching about the bread and wine or to speak comforting words about his betrayal shows the very self-centeredness that Jesus told them to eschew. Jesus has spoken about a meal in his memory, since he is going to die on their behalf. They are worried about their own reputation, about how they will be remembered. Luke, in a mastery of irony, thus ensures that the apostles will be remembered as bickering at the Last Supper.

The master now has to instruct his disciples. Drawing on the convention of the farewell discourse known in Jewish, Greek, and Latin sources,[13] Luke constructs Jesus' speech in vss. 25–38. Consistent with the genre, Jesus "the leader takes leave of his followers, warning, exhorting, and encouraging them for the days ahead."[14]

Jesus first responds to the disciples' quarreling by teaching that the subject of comparative greatness is inappropriate. In the gentile world, kings "lord it over" (Greek: *kyrieyō*, from *kyrios*) others (**vs. 25a**). In Jesus' world, people are not to be lords but to be slaves. Moving from the reified topic of royalty to the more general topic of economic inequity, he observes people with authority are called benefactors (Greek: *euergetēs*, literally, "good doers"; **vs. 25b**). The phrasing could equally be put: benefactors – people with money to spare – are people in authority. In other words, money talks; the issue is what it says.

Emperors in numerous inscriptions called themselves "benefactors"; Josephus accords the title to both Vespasian (*War* 3.459) and Titus (*War* 4.113),[15] but the term is accorded to anyone, man or woman, in the system of patron/client relations that permeated the Empire. The rich and powerful (the patrons, i.e., the benefactors) would dole out favors to those with

---

[13] Cf. 1 Kings 2.1–10; 1 Macc 2.49–70; Diogenes Laertius, *Epicurus* 10.16–18; Plato, *Phaedo*; W. S. Kurz, "Luke 22.14–38 and Greco-Roman and Biblical Farewell Addresses," *JBL* 104 (1985): 251–68; and Tannehill, *Luke* I, 316–23.

[14] Craddock, *Luke*, 257.

[15] See Frederick W. Danker, *Benefactor: Epigraphic Study of a Graeco-Roman and New Testament Semantic Field* (St. Louis: Clayton, 1982).

less power and fewer resources (the clients). Clients were expected to offer public praise to those who supported them. This is the system in which the master cheated out of his funds by the dishonest manager found himself (see 16.1–8): he has, at least as far as the public is concerned, provided a benefaction to his client-debtors, and they in turn will laud his generosity. To be a benefactor was an expected role of the social elite, and the non-elites did benefit from the system. Yet the system was both premised upon and reinforced unequal social roles.

It is this lack of equality that Jesus decries. Disciples are not to involve themselves in honor challenges meant to determine social rank. They are not to give gifts in order to make people dependent on them, and they are not to become clients of anyone and so forced into a patronage system. Paul had already spoken of the allure of the patronage system as well as his refusal to participate in it (2 Cor 11.7–15); although Luke locates women in patronage capacities (e.g., 8.2–3), these women have no (apparent) say on how the mission functions. For Jesus, and so for his followers, God is the only lord and patron.

Disciples are not simply to opt out of the system of social stratification; they are to reverse how it functions. The ones with greater skills and resources and the respect that comes with age should act as slaves to the rest; the leader (Greek: *hēgeomai*, whence "hegemonic") is the one who serves (Greek: *diakoneō*) rather than is served (**vs. 26**, cf. 9.48). Luke is not eliminating hierarchy: there are still apostles and there are still leaders; the issue is how they inhabit their roles. Jesus is their model. He reminds his apostles of his earlier teaching regarding the correct attitude of slaves: the slaves are to serve the master, and both slave and master recognize the inequality of the system (see, e.g., 17.7–9). Jesus locates himself as the master who reclines at table; that they are at a table where he is host reinforces this identification. Yet he is also their servant (again, *diakoneō* language). Here the setting of the teaching is pedagogical: they are all reclining at the same table. The Greek is definitive – he is "in your midst as *the* one who serves" (**vs. 27**). Jesus is not running an egalitarian movement; he is reversing the understanding of how the powerful, including himself, function.

From locating himself as the one reclining at the table and the apostles as those who serve, Jesus continues the metaphor by describing these same apostles as those who did not recline with him, but "stood by" him in his trials (**vs. 28**). The saying drips with irony, as these same apostles will fail to stand by him. Judas is about to divulge his whereabouts to the chief priests; Peter is about to deny him three times; the other disciples flee from the arresting party. The term "trial" (Greek: *peirasmos*) reminds readers of the "trial" or "temptation" by Satan, whose presence at this meal, incarnated in Judas and intoned in Jesus' teaching, is palpable. It also recollects the prayer Jesus taught, "do not bring us to the time of trial" (11.4; the more familiar translation is "lead us not into temptation") perfectly fits what the apostles now should be seeking. Twice more Jesus will use this term in this chapter (vss. 40, 46), and in each case the apostles at their trials are convicted.

Once the apostles recognize their role as servants rather than as lords, they are ready to receive Jesus' benefaction, which he had received from his Father. What Jesus institutes is a variant on the patron/client relationship, for "King" Jesus confers upon the disciples who had remained faithful a "Kingdom" of their own (**vs. 29**). The disciples become comparable to the faithful slaves who increased their initial investments and so were rewarded by the nobleman with control over cities (see 19.17, 19). Whereas Jesus has throughout the Gospel spoken of the Kingdom of God, this is the first time he indicates that the Kingdom belongs to him. This elevation in the disciples' rank, from slave to king, is confirmed by their invitation not to serve Jesus but to eat and drink with him at his table (**vs. 30a**, cf. the eschatological banquets suggested in 13.29 and 14.16–24). The setting of this teaching, still at the Passover meal and still in the context of the "Words of Institution," show both the solemnity and the magnitude of this benefaction.

Finally, Jesus tells the disciples that they will sit on thrones and judge the twelve tribes of Israel (**vs. 30b**). For Matthew (19.28), the saying is the reward for the disciples who "have left everything" and followed Jesus, and who wonder "What then will we have?" (Matt 19.27). For Luke, the prediction suits the farewell discourse with the bequest of gifts and promises to the ones left behind. Jesus' saying promises the apostles more than an eschatological bounty. It suggests that Israel still has a role to play in salvation history, even as it anchors the apostles to Israel, the Jewish people.[16] It alludes to the regathering of the twelve tribes, and so to the continuing mission to the Jews, despite the fact that most rejected the Gospel message. If it finds its background in Psa 122.4–5 – "To [Jerusalem] the tribes go up, the tribes of the Lord, as was decreed for Israel, to give thanks to the name of the Lord. For there the thrones for judgment were set up, the thrones of the house of David" – then it also evokes both Jesus' lament over the city

---

[16] David L. Tiede, "Glory to Thy People Israel: Luke-Acts and the Jews," in Joseph B. Tyson (ed.), *Luke-Acts and the Jewish People* (Minneapolis: Augsburg, 1988), 21–34.

Last Supper, Arrest, and Sanhedrin Trial

and the city's destruction. The next verse in the psalm is the famous line, "Pray for the peace of Jerusalem" (Psa 122.6a).

Whatever questions the disciples may have had, Luke does not record them. Instead, the subject shifts again, from promises of rewards for fidelity to warnings about earthly trials and failures. Having been promised the benefactions of King Jesus, the disciples have the assurance that they can pass the tests their association with him will create. Ironically, through this entire discussion of eschatological rewards and earthly assurances, Judas is still reclining with Jesus and the other apostles at the table.

In Mark's version of the Last Supper (Mark 14.27), Jesus tells the disciples that they will desert him and then paraphrases Zech 13.7, "I will strike the shepherd, and the sheep will be scattered." Omitting this verse, Luke offers Jesus' warnings directly to Peter. Although the narrative had referred to Simon as "Peter" since his call in 6.14, Jesus returns to the apostle's given name (4.38), and he repeats it: "Simon, Simon" (**vs. 31a**). Earlier, Jesus addressed Martha with the same duplication of names (10.41). Martha had been "worried and distracted"; Peter too will be distracted from his apostolic duties. Culpepper suggests that the repetition of Simon's given name means that he needs to be reevangelized and restored,[17] although this is not quite what happens. Peter is not reevangelized, at least in the sense of being excommunicated and reconverted to Jesus' mission; he rather repents and returns. It is in John 21 that we have a narrative of the restoration of Peter where Jesus once again calls Peter by his given name, but this story is not found in Luke.

Jesus warns Peter that Satan has demanded to "sift *all of you* like wheat" (**vs. 31b**). The sifting image, perhaps an echo of Amos 9.9 ("I will command, and shake the house of Israel among all the nations as one shakes with a sieve, but no pebble shall fall to the ground"),[18] is one of testing: the impurities will drop out, and fidelity will remain. Since Jesus has not revealed to the apostles that Judas is the one to betray him, the question of the betrayer's identity, earlier debated, takes on a heightened sense. We know that Satan has entered into Judas; now we learn that Satan has set his sights more broadly.

Despite the threat, the apostles find themselves protected: Jesus has already prayed on Peter's behalf (the "you" in **vs. 32** is singular) that his faith will endure. The verse puts Jesus in the role of advocate; he is pleading Peter's

---

[17] See Culpepper, "The Gospel of Luke," 427.
[18] See Nolland, *Luke 18.35–24.53*, 1072.

cause in the heavenly court (the verb *deomai* here suggests petitionary prayer; see 21.36). Luke had already emphasized the power of prayer (cf. 18.1), and Jesus had instructed, "pray for those who abuse you" (6.28). Here, Jesus practices what he preaches. The focus on Peter, however, means that Jesus has not prayed that all the apostles, including Judas, be strengthened in their faith. Jesus does not here pray for Judas.

This "faith" (Greek: *pistis*) does not suggest confessional purity; Peter is not to be tested regarding the details of the Apostles' Creed. "Faith" here means fidelity to Jesus' mission and, in particular, the servant leadership discussed and displayed at this Last Supper. Yet Jesus also knows that his apostle will both fail and recover, as his comment about Peter's "turning back" (*epistrephō*) indicates. The verb *epistrephō* can signal simply a change in direction as well as a conversion, but its underlying import here is one of repenting, of turning away from the bad and back to the good.[19] Comparable is Deut 30.2, "return (LXX: *epistrephō* MT: *shuv*) to the Lord your God, and you and your children obey him with all your heart and with all your soul, just as I am." When Peter does turn around – colloquially, when he "gets back on track" – he is to focus on strengthening his "brothers" (Greek: *adelphoi*). These brothers include not only Peter's fellow apostles, but all the followers of Jesus who may be tested (cf. Acts 1.15; 9.30; 15.23). The verse anticipates not only Peter's denial and then reconciliation with Jesus in the Gospel, it anticipates the trials he and others will face in the Book of Acts as well.

Vs. 33 returns to Marcan material, which Luke softens. In Mark 14.29 (cf. Matt 26.33), Peter insists, "Even though all become deserters, I will not." In Mark's telling, Peter fails to understand the message of solidarity rather than the point about internal competition. His phrasing is part of the "who is the greatest" debate. Luke eliminates the competition by having Peter respond, "Lord, I am ready to go with you to prison and to death!" (**vs. 33**). The verse projects Peter's fate: he will follow Jesus by being imprisoned (Acts 4.3–22; 5.18–21; 12.3–12,17; cf. John 21.18–19) and, as noncanonical sources state, being put to death as well (cf. John 13.37; 21.18–19). Peter's enthusiasm is commendable, and given that Jesus had just stated that he has prayed for Peter personally, the apostle justifiably can feel secure. Nevertheless, even Jesus' prayer does not prevent apostasy. Peter, like Judas, makes choices, and those choices have consequences.

---

[19] Cf. Neh 1.9; Hos 3.5; 5.4; 6.1; Amos 4.6; Joel 2.12; Isa 6.10; 9.13; Jer 3.10 cf. Luke 1.16–17; 17.4; and especially in Acts 3.19; 9.35; 11.21; 14.15; 19; see Johnson, *Gospel of Luke*, 346. The Hebrew *shuv* has the same connotation.

Peter will choose to deny knowing Jesus, three times, before morning (**vs. 34**; cf. Mark 14.30; Matt 26.34; John 13.38). Here, Jesus returns to Peter's nickname: the one named "rock" will prove himself shakable, or to mix the metaphor, sifted. Luke may be softening Mark's "deny me"; there is a slight difference between denying Jesus himself, including his messianic identity, and denying knowledge of him. In either case, Peter has gone over to the Satanic side. Jesus had wanted, like a mother hen, to gather Jerusalem's children under his wings (13.34); now the rooster will show Peter's failure in Jerusalem to proclaim Jesus Lord (cf. 13.35). The apostle offers no rebuttal. There is nothing at this point he can say. Since Jesus has yet to name the betrayer, Peter may be wondering if he is the one.

Jesus has spoken of Peter strengthening his brothers. He next describes the mission they are about to take. Again, the apostles are reassured that they will remain faithful. What Judas, still present, is thinking cannot be determined. Jesus asks the Twelve about their accessories carried on their earlier missions (**vs. 35a**). The details he lists – purse, bag, and sandals – were not included in their earlier instructions (9.1–6), but they were part of the commission of the 70/72 (10.4). This allusion to the second mission fits neatly into the Last Supper conversation, since it is the 70/72 who report that "even the demons submitted to us"; this is the comment that prompted Jesus notice of Satan's fall (10.17–18).

Responding to Jesus' question about resources, the Twelve indicate that they lacked for nothing on their journey (**vs. 35b**). Jesus now anticipates that the apostles will face increasing hardships in this mission: proclaiming the Kingdom, healing and teaching, were greeted with joy. No one had yet persecuted the messengers. But persecution will come. Exorcism and healings are welcome; exorcisms and healings in the name of a crucified man and thus an enemy of the state anticipate a more difficult reception. Given this negative response, the followers need more than faith to accompany them on the road. Jesus tells them to take a purse and a backpack. More, he advises that those without swords (the phrasing implies some already own swords) must obtain them by selling their outer garment (**vs. 36**).

In the exhortation that the disciples sell their coats and purchase swords, Ben hears dramatic hyperbole. He does not think Jesus was encouraging the Twelve either to sell their cloaks or to purchase swords. They should not be expected go around in their underclothes all the time, especially not in winter. Further, two swords would hardly be enough to protect eleven or twelve men on the road. And Jesus' ironic or sarcastic response to "we have two swords" is "enough of that," not "that is enough." Jesus just called them to be servants and to emulate his own example, which means being prepared to lay down their lives, not harm other people's lives. Therefore, Ben sees Jesus' imagery as indicating only that his followers need to be prepared for dangerous times ahead.[20] Amy-Jill sees no reason not to take Jesus at his word. She does not think it necessary to read the purse and backpack literally but the sword as metaphorical. The mission will require money and arms, and the disciples, soon to be without Jesus' earthly presence, need material resources. What one has, such as a weapon, does not immediately mean that one must deploy it. Prior to the cross, they have not needed the sword; after it, when they are on the road, they will, if only for defensive purposes. There is no reason they should be easy targets.

Yet both Ben and Amy-Jill agree that Jesus is not speaking about the Second Amendment; the issue is not the "right to bear arms"; the motto is not "welcome to church, lock and load." The disciples are to act as servants, not as thugs. The possession of a weapon does not, for the Gospel, give the wielder carte blanche to use it, and Jesus will tell his disciples not to use the sword to fight for his release from the Temple authorities (22.40–51). If they are not to use their swords to defend Jesus, then they might think twice about using the swords to defend themselves.

Anticipating the use of swords in his arrest, Jesus now moves to what must happen: his fate as he finds prophesied in Israel's Scripture. In citing the phrase "he was counted among the lawless" (**vs. 37**), Jesus alludes to Isa 53.12 (LXX). This "suffering servant" passage is an important text for Lukan Christological reflection; Acts 8.32–35 cites Isa 53 extensively. Jesus had already alluded to Isaiah in 4.21, where he cites Isa 61.1 and 58.6 in his comments in Nazareth's synagogue. From Luke's viewpoint, all Scripture points toward the suffering and glory of the Messiah (see 24.27, 44; Acts 1.16). The citation of Isaiah not only interprets Jesus' death as part of God's plan, it also suggests this death will be a vicarious suffering for and with the lawless (Greek: *anomoi*, which indicates criminals; Isaiah's Hebrew reads "with the transgressors"). Jesus himself will be reckoned with the lawless by those in authority.[21] The reference to the "lawless" is not to social banditry; Isaiah is describing people who engage in personal criminal activity for their own benefit; he is not speaking of freedom fighters.

[20] See the discussion in Johnson, *Gospel of Luke*, 347; Fitzmyer, *Luke X–XXIV*, 1432–34.
[21] Culy et al., *Luke*, 681–82, find a cumulative force to the passion predictions, with increasing specificity (cf. 9.22, 44; 18.31).

Jesus is arrested as a brigand (22.52) and is crucified between two criminals (23.32). The Gospel's only other reference to brigands is to the people who attacked the traveler on the road to Jericho in the famous parable (10.30, 36). Attempts to read these passages as indicative of Jewish anti-Roman political activists and so depict Jesus as a Zealot invested in Israel's autonomy display more modern wishful thinking than ancient historical understanding. Nothing in our sources suggests an alliance between the followers of Jesus and the Zealot movement. To the contrary, the one "Zealot" among the Twelve, Simeon (6.15; cf. Acts 1.13) is not seen as engaged in political Zealot activities. Nor was the term "Zealot" used as a code for revolutionaries during Jesus' time. This Simeon may have been equally zealous about the Temple (Psa 119.139; for God (Jdt 9.4; Bar 4.28; Rom 10.2); for Torah (1 Macc 2.26; 2.50, 58) or for his mission (cf. 2 Cor 9.2).

In response to Jesus' citation of Isaiah, the apostles ironically fulfill the instruction by announcing that they already have two swords (**vs. 38a**). Short daggers were the regular part of travelers' gear in Roman times, and they were designed for protection, not for offensive purposes. Yet the disciples are more likely not talking about short daggers but about actual swords. They can be seen as depicting themselves as lawless, that is, armed brigands, and Jesus is counted among them.[22] To their announcement, Jesus responds, likely with bitter irony, "it is enough" (**vs. 38b**). He does not say "they are enough" or "they will suffice"; therefore, the antecedent of "it" would not be "two swords" but the violence the swords can bring.[23] Yet, "it" can refer to the collective. Perhaps what we have here is an idiomatic expression used to close off a discussion.[24] No evidence from Church history supports the view that Jesus encouraged people to buy weapons. Interpreters of Luke's Gospel, with few exceptions, never understood vs. 36 either to be a command to buy weapons or to serve as an excuse to own them. Fred Craddock says: "In the battles facing the Twelve, swords will be useless [against the Devil]: a sword would not help Judas, a sword would not help Simon, a sword would not help frightened and fleeing disciples. But they thought so. Jesus knew they did not understand, and so he said, 'Enough of this talk: drop this subject.'"[25]

---

[22] Nolland, *Luke 18.35–24.53*, 1077.
[23] C. A. Evans, *Luke*, 322.
[24] Marshall, *Luke*, 827; Culy et al., *Luke*, 684. See also Culpepper, "The Gospel of Luke," 430.
[25] Craddock, *Luke*, 260.

THE ARREST ON THE MOUNT OF OLIVES

Leaving the supper, Jesus follows his regular practice (see 21.37) of going to the Mount of Olives (**vs. 39**). Matthew (26.36) and Mark (14.32) set the scene in a place called Gethsemane; John (18.1) calls it a "garden." Luke, who generally avoids Hebrew and Aramaic terms, speaks instead of the arrest on the Mount of Olives. The disciples, still without indication that Judas is the traitor, follow him. Given Jesus' several predictions, including his recent comments about Satan's involvement with Peter, his road to the cross and the disciples' failures are both inevitable.

At this setting, redolent with messianic implications, Jesus advises his followers that they pray that they not come to the time of trial, or "lead us not into temptation" (**vs. 40**). He then will model this prayer, when he prays that the cup pass from him (see vs. 42). Whether or not the apostles follow his advice, Luke does not record. Nor does Luke follow Mark and Matthew in having Jesus take with him only Peter, James, and John. For the Third Gospel, all the apostles are indicted in the failure of faith. They who argued about who was greatest will prove themselves least and lost.

Vs. 41 says that Jesus withdrew about a stone's throw away and knelt down to pray. He is already separating himself from the disciples; they will not be together until after his resurrection. The separation begins in prayer, and it will end in prayer (24.50–51, 53). His prayer, a Lucan theme (3.21; 5.16; 6.12; 9.18, 28), shows his continual contact with God. Kneeling suggests intense worship (cf. Acts 7.60; 9.40; 20.36; 21.5). His prayer begins with his address to God as "father," and thus he prays as he taught his disciples to pray (11.2). There is no Aramaic "*abba*, father" here; for that the reader must see Mark 14.36. Jesus then offers his petition that his death sentence be rescinded (**vs. 42**). At the same time, he recognizes the inevitability of his trial; the "cup" he seeks to avoid is the cup that has been poured since the mission began and before, with the predictions from Isaiah.

A number of commentators remark that the cup is a regular image of God's wrath being poured out on someone or a group of people (cf. Psa 75.8; Isa 51.17, 22; Jer 25.15; 49.12; Lam 4.21), but here the issue is not divine wrath. Luke says nothing about an "Old Testament God of wrath" who demands satisfaction for sin by requiring his son to die. The "cup" is better understood as an image showing the manifestation of divine will in its fulsome nature. Thus, the Psalmist can praise God by explaining, in the King James Version translation, "My cup runneth over" (Psa 23.5; cf. Psa 16.5). Psalm 116.13 provides a better intertext than images of wrath: "I will lift up the cup of salvation and call on the name of the Lord." To lift the cup, at this moment in Jesus' life, is a heavy responsibility, but it is God's that the cup poured out "is the new covenant in [Jesus'] blood" (22.20).

Jesus' prayer serves to fortify him; he has spoken openly of his feelings; he does not withhold his reluctance, and in his honesty, he models prayer for anyone seeking to avoid the divine call. Jesus also taught his followers to pray, "your kingdom come" (11.2), and he had announced at the Last Supper that he would not taste the Passover until he tasted it in the Kingdom. The meal, the arrest, the death, and the Kingdom are interrelated.

What happens next depends on the biblical translation one is using. According to the New English Bible (NEB), the English Standard Version (ESV), and the Contemporary English Version (CEV), as well as in the works of the second-century Church Fathers Justin, Irenaeus, and Hippolytus,[26] an angel from heaven comes to strengthen Jesus (**vs. 43**), and Jesus, being anguished, prayed so earnestly that his sweat became like great drops of blood falling onto the ground (**vs. 44**). The 1971 edition of the Revised Standard Version (RSV) puts these verses in a footnote. The NRSV puts them in brackets. Many important early manuscripts do not have vss. 43–44 (p69, 75, Aleph, B, T, W, Clement, Origen), and others mark them with the obelisk, which is a sign indicating a doubtful reading (Delta, Pi, 1079, 1195, et al.). These verses follow Matt 26.39 in one textual family and in several lectionaries, which suggests that they, like the story of the woman accused of adultery, are verses looking for a home rather than originally at home in any text.

Ben and Amy-Jill, following the majority of commentators, see the verses as having been added into the text by pious scribes.[27] The verses appear to be an early addition to Luke's Gospel probably from the Western textual tradition (D et al.). The ministering angel (see Dan 3:25, 28) recalls Jesus' temptation as Mark presents it; Mark 1.13, also set at the "time of trial," reads, "He was in the wilderness forty days, tempted by Satan; and he was with the wild beasts; and the angels waited on him." For Luke, Satan is about to reappear to the person of Judas; the arresting party replaces the wild beasts, and the angels provide the support for what is about to happen.

In evident anguish, with or without the angels and the bloody sweat, Jesus returns to his disciples to find them asleep "because of grief" (**vs. 45**).

26 See Metzger, *Textual Commentary*, 177.
27 See Bart D. Ehrman and Mark A. Plunkett, "The Angel and the Agony: The Textual Problem of Luke 22:43–44," *CBQ* 45.3 (1983): 401–16.

Nolland suggests that "the impending tragedy has brought them to emotional exhaustion."[28] Amy-Jill finds it more likely that Luke is trying to control the story of the disciples' failure to remain awake and perhaps control as well the rumor that they were drunk with new (i.e., cheap) wine (see Acts 2.13). At the Passover *Seder*, the tradition is to consume four cups of wine; we do not know if this practice was known to either Jesus or Luke, but the idea of the disciples being drunk and not simply tired would explain why all slept.

Jesus berates them for falling asleep and again repeats his command that they pray not to come to the time of trial (**vs. 46**). For Jesus, that time has already arrived, as his anguished plea had shown. Jesus is on his knees in prayer; the disciples are lying down in sleep. This same juxtaposition of the faithful and the faithless will reappear in the courtyard of the High Priest, when Jesus remains faithful to his mission and Peter denies knowing him.

Omitting the third time that Jesus prays and then accusing his sleeping disciples of infidelity (see Mark 14.41), Luke moves efficiently to the arrest. A crowd, led by Judas, appears; Luke reiterates that Judas was "one of the Twelve" (**vs. 47a**). Ben sees this identification as indicative of an underlying oral tradition, in that it appears to introduce Judas as a new character. Amy-Jill sees the hand of Luke the redactor, who has several times already noted that Judas is part of the inner circle. The repetition does not suggest to her an early story awkwardly spliced in, but a literary trope designed to highlight Judas' perfidy as well as warn people in the Church that insiders might betray them. And Ben thinks she might be right about this!

Luke's narrative also suggests that Judas initially may have been with Jesus and the others on the Mount of Olives; Luke does not say Judas reconnoitered with the arrest party in Jerusalem following the Last Supper. Just as Jesus had planned through his connections in local areas to obtain first a colt and then an upper room for celebrating the Passover, so Judas draws on his connections to arrest Jesus along with the local authorities.

Judas approaches Jesus to give him the traditional kiss of greeting (**vs. 47b**), but Jesus stops him and asks, "Judas, are you betraying the Son of Man by means of a kiss?" (**vs. 48**). This query, which has no Marcan counterpart, heightens the scene's irony as well as Judas' perversion. Judas does not answer in this account, nor does he greet Jesus or call him rabbi. Nor do we ever see him actually kiss Jesus. The only other place in the Gospel

[28] Nolland, *Luke 18.35–24.53*, 1084.

the term "kiss" appears is in the account of the anointing woman (7.45). The kiss is the sign of hospitality, of love, and now of betrayal. Like other rituals, including baptism and Eucharist, its meaning depends substantially on who is performing it.

In **vs. 49**, the disciples finally do something active, but the question they ask – "Lord, should we strike with the sword?" – is the wrong question. Yet, given Jesus' earlier instruction about swords, the question is also understandable. Without waiting for an answer, one of these followers cuts off the right ear of the High Priest's slave (John 18.10 names the slave Malchus and the sword-wielder as Peter). Jesus responds quickly by stating *heōs toutou*, which the NRSV translates "no more of this," and so, by implication, depicts Jesus as a pacifist. However, the expression, particularly when placed together with *eate*, "permit, pass over," is better translated as "permit this," that is, permit this arrest to happen.[29] Jesus is not speaking of pacifism; he is speaking of the necessity of his arrest.

In a final vignette unique to Luke, Jesus heals the servant's ear (**vs. 51**). This is Jesus' last act of healing in the Gospels, done in service of someone who came as part of the arresting party. Whether this slave was party to the violence, or whether he, like the slaves in the Parable of the Vineyard (20.10–12), was pressed into service by his master, cannot be determined. The verse can be taken as an indication of "love of enemies."

Jesus now addresses his opponents, the familiar litany of "chief priests, the officers … and the elders" (**vs. 52a**), and the familiar historical problem of why these officials, on the first night of Passover, would be running around on the Mount of Olives for a stealth arrest. Their presence at the arrest is not needed and it finds no historical warrant, but it does serve the Gospel's apologetic purpose of casting guilt on the local officials. Mark (14.43), more logically, simply notes that the authorities sent people to arrest Jesus. Although these authorities are arresting Jesus, Jesus himself has the upper hand as he controls what is said. His question, "Have you come out with swords and clubs as if I were a bandit?" (**vs. 52b**), fulfills, as will his crucifixion, his earlier comment that he would be counted among violent criminals.

He continues to speak as if he is having a civilized conversation about a political disagreement rather than being about to be arrested, charged, condemned, and crucified – again, Amy-Jill sees the conversation as having

---

[29]   David Lertis Matson, "Pacifist Jesus? The (Mis)translation of *eate eos toutou* in Luke 22:51," *JBL* 134.1 (2015): 157–75.

literary but not historical merit; Ben sees no reason this conversation could not have happened. Jesus reminds the arresting officials that he had been teaching daily in the Temple, and they could have arrested him then (**vs. 53a**). Were the officials to respond, "No, we could not, for the people would have protected you," they would appear even more pathetic than they do here. Jesus then adds only in Luke's account, "but this is your hour – and the authority (Greek: *exousia*) of darkness" (**vs. 53**). The point confirms the allegiance of the officials not to the reign of God, but to the Kingdom of Satan. The night that began with the celebration of the Passover meal is descending into darkness.

PETER'S DENIAL

Seizing Jesus, "they" (the entire arresting party?) lead him to the house of the high priest (**vs. 54a**).[30] Luke says nothing of the fleeing of the disciples (cf. Mark 14.50; Matt 26.56); they will not reappear until after Jesus' death. Peter follows at a distance, but readers already know what he will do (**vs. 54b**). We do not, however, know the circumstances by which he will come to deny knowing Jesus. Is he to be tortured into confession? Will he be summoned before a clever lawyer? Or will his denial be simply craven? Nor, ironically, do we know if the High Priest himself was present for the questioning.

The scene begins with a fire being kindled in the middle of the High Priest's courtyard, and with Peter sitting down with those who made the fire (**vs. 55**). The "they" among whom Peter sits go unidentified; the nearest antecedent would be some of the people involved in Jesus' arrest. Were this identification correct, then Peter's fear over admitting he was a colleague of Jesus is more easily understood. Yet Luke does not designate any of the people around the fire as soldiers or guards. To the contrary, the first person to speak is a servant girl (Greek: *paidiskē*). Seeing Peter seated by the fire (we are reminded of the rich man, burning in the fire of hell), she announces, "this man was with him" (**vs. 56**). The "him," which has no antecedent in the narrative, has to be "Jesus." Without making the point explicit, Luke lets the readers know that Jesus is the topic of conversation not only in the High Priest's house but also outside, "among the people." The girl's comment implies she had seen Peter

---

[30]   On the numerous differences in the four accounts of Peter's denials, see the lists and the discussion in C. A. Evans, *Luke*, 325–29; cf. Nolland, *Luke 18.35–24.53*, 1092–94.

and Jesus together in the Temple precincts earlier in the week. Perhaps she was one of Jesus' admirers.

Peter's denial is personal: "I do not know him, woman" (**vs. 57**). In no case is Peter examined by some authority figure, and yet shamefully he wilts under the pressure of a young girl's question.

Peter has a second chance, when a fellow recognizes him and states, "You also are one of them." Peter again denies the charge, this time with the address "man" in parallel to his earlier address "woman" (**vs. 58**). For all the officials' concerns about the crowd, these non-elites in the courtyard, who represent the people of Jerusalem, could be Jesus' supporters. Peter kills any hope for this support, even were it initially preset: if Jesus' immediate followers will not speak up for him, why should the rest of Jerusalem's non-elite population?

The minutes go by, an hour passes. Peter has had time to think about his two denials. Then a third figure approaches with the same accusation, but now with evidence: "for he is a Galilean" (**vs. 59**). Peter's accent betrays him (cf. Matt 26.73). Peter denies any knowledge of Jesus. He has progressed or, better, regressed from denying knowing Jesus, to denying he is one of his circle, to denying, most feebly, anything about the subject at hand, the man arrested by the Temple authorities and now being questioned in the home of the High Priest.

At this juncture, as the rooster crows, Jesus turns and looks intently at Peter (**vs. 61**). With this stare, only in the Third Gospel, the evangelist refers to Jesus as "Lord" and reiterates the title in describing Peter's recollection of Jesus' prediction. Peter has denied not only his friend, but his savior. Worse, we readers did not know, from the beginning of the scene, that Jesus was physically present. That Jesus can see Peter, and so the possibility that Peter can see Jesus, makes the apostle's denials more tragic, and more pathetic. Whether Jesus' intently looking at Peter signaled condemnation, resignation, or compassion, Luke does not state.

Peter leaves the courtyard, and so the presence of Jesus. All he can do is weep (**vs. 62**), but whether of shame, repentance, relief that he has escaped charges against him for collaboration, fear for Jesus' fate … Luke also leaves this detail to the reader's imagination. Peter will not reappear in the story until 24.12, 34 and he will not resume his prominent role until the early chapters of Acts, where, finally, he will "turn and strengthen his brothers" (see 22.32). The good news about this story is that if even Peter can be restored and go on to do meaningful ministry, then restoration is possible for others who display infidelity.

The scene ends by adding injury to insult. From Peter's denial, Luke turns to the reaction of the men "holding Jesus"; they were also present to hear Peter's denials. Luke has told us that Jesus had the support of the people; Peter had every opportunity to speak to these very people about his Lord. He does not. He denies any involvement.

The men holding Jesus not only mock him (contrast Mark 14.65/Matt 26.67, which set this mocking after the hearing) but also beat him, a mention that underscores Peter's cowardice, since he was under no physical threat (**vs. 63**). The men blindfold Jesus, and so prevent him from staring at Peter, or anyone. They demand that he prophesy, which is exactly what he had just done regarding Peter's denials; that they will turn him over to Pilate confirms his prophecy about being handed over to gentiles (18.32). They ask him, "Who struck you?" (**vs. 64**). This is not how prophecy functions; the men do not know the difference between revelation designed to prompt repentance, and torture. Finally, they insult him (**vs. 65**), and in so doing deny his identity even as, unknowingly, they confirm his prophecies to be accurate.

CONDEMNATION BY THE COUNCIL

The scene shifts from Peter's nighttime trial, at the end of which he stands judged guilty of failing the test, to Jesus' morning trial before the Council (Greek: *Sanhedrin*) (**vs. 66**). The hearing begins with the assembled political leaders questioning Jesus: Are you the Messiah? (**vs. 67a**). Luke lacks all reference to the false witnesses who spoke of Jesus' words about the Temple,[31] so the Temple is not an issue, despite the Temple affiliation of the questioners.

Ben finds this messianic question an appropriate way to begin the trial of Jesus, since Jesus' activities – from healings to the Triumphal Entry to the Temple incident to the teaching in the Temple – would have suggested a messianic agenda. For Amy-Jill, the question makes no sense in historical terms. To claim to be the Messiah is not an actionable charge. No prior text describes the Messiah as a healer, as involved with the Temple, or primarily as a teacher. Nor according to Luke's narrative had there been charges against Jesus concerning his messianic status. Had the Council needed the excuse to charge him with something of relevance to Rome, they could have asked him about his view of the Temple (in which Rome also had an investment),

---

[31] See James Bradley Chance, *Jerusalem, the Temple, and the New Age in Luke-Acts* (Macon: Mercer University Press, 1988), who argues that Luke distinguishes between leaders who abuse their Temple connections and the Temple itself.

of taxation, or of the Empire. The question does, however, make narrative sense, since Luke's agenda is to proclaim Jesus the Christ.

Jesus refuses to answer (**vs. 67b**), as he had earlier refused to tell the similarly assembled group about the source of his authority (20.8). In contrast, in the same setting, the Marcan Jesus explicitly answers, "I am" (14.62). Then, once more taking control as he did at his arrest in Luke's account, he tells the Council that they would not respond to his questions either (**vs. 68**). Instead of participating in a question and answer session that would lead nowhere, since the Council has already determined its verdict, Jesus shifts the conversation to eschatology. He speaks, cryptically, of the "Son of Man seated at the right hand of the power of God" (**vs. 69**). The reference combines the "Son of Man" figure from Dan 7.13 LXX and Psa 110.1, which Jesus had earlier cited in his question to the chief priests (21.27). The reference also foreshadows the vision of Stephen (Acts 7.55). Gospel readers, aware that Jesus has referred to himself several times as the "Son of Man," will see in his comment the answer to the Council's question. In narrative context, the Council may not know that Jesus has applied this title to himself, and they may conclude that he is speaking about someone else. On the other hand, they may have heard reports about Jesus' teaching, which included regularly referring to himself as the Son of Man.

Ben finds that claiming to be the human yet divine Son of Man of Dan 7.13–14 could be taken as blasphemy, especially if the assertion were associated with the claim that the Son of Man would come and judge the very people who were now attempting to judge Jesus. Amy-Jill sees nothing blasphemous in claiming to be the Danielic Son of Man. Jesus is not invoking the name of God, he is not stating that he is God or the equal of God; to the contrary, by speaking of being "seated at the right hand," Jesus is stating, explicitly, that this Son of Man is not God. Finally, to claim to be the Messiah was not considered blasphemous. Ben counters that the Son of Man figure in Dan 7 is also worshiped and given a forever Kingdom. And only an eternal king can rule forever. This contrasts with the promise of dynastic succession of human kings in 2 Sam 7.12–14. Thus, in Ben's view, Jesus is making a divine claim.

The question the Council should have asked (thereby making happy biblical scholars, who have debated the nuances of "Son of Man" for centuries) is, "What do you mean by this title?" Instead, they ask, "Are you the Son of God?" (**vs. 70a**). In the space of just a few verses, the narrative uses three titles: Messiah, Son of Man, and Son of God. In this context, although not in all ancient texts, they appear to function as synonyms. Jesus gives a partial answer; rather than state his identity, he accuses his accusers of according to him the titles: "You say I am" (**vs. 70b**). On this half-answer, the Council declares its verdict. The "testimony" that the Council members cite is their own (**vs. 71**). What they attribute to hearing from Jesus' own mouth is the repetition of their charge, not his admission of messianic identity. Omitted is the rending of the High Priest's garments, the reference to Jesus blaspheming, and the judgment that he is worthy of death (Mark 14.65). Luke keeps the focus on Christology.

A CLOSER LOOK: WAS THERE A SANHEDRIN TRIAL?

Ben believes that the Sanhedrin trial, recorded although with differing details in each of the Synoptics, captures what happened to Jesus the early morning of his crucifixion. He also notes that some scholars even argue for two trials, both a preliminary hearing and then a morning trial.[32] In his view, there was a hastily convened meeting meant to lead to some kind of judicial decision that would in turn lead to the handing over of Jesus to someone who had the power of capital punishment (either Herod Antipas or Pilate).[33] Ben's approach requires acceptance of the claim, found only in John 18.31, that the Jewish authorities "are not permitted to put anyone to death."

Amy-Jill finds the Sanhedrin trial to be a pre-Marcan or Marcan invention that the other Synoptics adapted. That the same story appears in all three Gospels does not indicate a triple confirmation, but the use of one source (likely Mark) by two other writers. Ben notes, however, that the later Gospel writers are not mindlessly following Mark. They accept his tradition because they think it is correct. Amy-Jill finds the Johannine Passion, which records no Sanhedrin trial but only a hearing by Annas, the former High Priest and Caiaphas' father-in-law (John 18.13, 19–24), to be more historically credible. Claims that there were two trials she finds to be apologetic and designed to bring John into harmony with the Synoptic accounts. There was no necessary reason for the Sanhedrin to try Jesus; Caiaphas had the authority to arrest Jesus and the political connections to bring him to Pilate. The full Sanhedrin trial only serves

---

[32]   Bock, *Luke 9.51–24.53*, 1779–81.
[33]   Ben Witherington III, *New Testament History* (Grand Rapids: Baker, 2001), 148–50.

to implicate the entire political infrastructure in condemning Jesus, and so to condemn that infrastructure.

Regarding local political authority, Amy-Jill sees no law found in either Roman or Jewish sources preventing local authorities from carrying out capital punishment related to religious concerns. Such authority is not on the same level as having a standing army; it poses no threat to the Empire. An example of this local authority in Judea would be the Temple inscription that threatens death to gentiles who go beyond the outer court. Josephus confirms this observation. In *War* 6.126, he quotes Titus as asking, "Have not we [Rome] given you [Jews] leave to kill such as go beyond it, though he were a Roman?" Had Caiaphas wished to execute Jesus, he could have made a case that Jesus endangered the Temple. He did not, although the "cleansing" episode (if historical) would have given him good cause.

Ben disagrees. He finds that the Romans, in all their directly ruled provinces, including Judaea, reserved capital punishment to themselves. The situation with client kings, such as Herod Antipas, is different and fell under different Roman rules and laws. This provincial reservation of any deadly force into the hands of the provincial governor is also the very reason why the governor would have considerable troops in the province, to quell riots, rebellions, and the like.

In Ben's view, the Jewish authorities had no authority to execute Jesus, and if they did it they would be guilty of both vigilante justice (see the case of Stephen) and violating Roman law. He supports his claim by referring to the martyrdom of James the brother of Jesus in the 60s at the hands of another high priest. When the governor arrived in the province, he deposed the priest precisely because he had usurped the authority of the governor in regard to capital punishment. Amy-Jill here notes that this is not how she understands the report of James's death. Josephus records in *Ant.* 20.200–2:

> … Festus was now dead, and Albinus was but upon the road; so he [the high priest] assembled the sanhedrin of judges, and brought before them the brother of Jesus, who was called Christ, whose name was James, and some others, [or, some of his companions]; and when he had formed an accusation against them as breakers of the law, he delivered them to be stoned; but as for those who seemed the most equitable of the citizens, and such as were the most uneasy at the breach of the laws, they disliked what was done; they also sent to the king [Agrippa II], desiring him to send to Ananus that he should act so no more, for that what he had already done

was not to be justified; nay, some of them went also to meet Albinus, as he was upon his journey from Alexandria, and informed him that it was not lawful for Ananus to assemble a sanhedrin without his consent.

The issue is not the execution; it is the assembling of the Council. But Ben notes that if they did not have the authority to have a trial without permission of the Roman governor, they did not have the authority to execute James either.

Debates over the historicity of the Sanhedrin trial frequently take the form of evaluating legal procedure, and regarding that question, the Sanhedrin trial is a violation of numerous procedures known from rabbinic sources, from the timing (at night, on a holiday, without public notice for supporting or exculpatory evidence, etc.) to the lack of defense witnesses to the problems of whether the charges are legal. Such debates immediately face three intractable problems. First, we do not know exactly what procedures were in place in the 30s; rabbinic texts, written at least a century afterward, cannot be a secure basis for procedure. Indeed, rabbinic commentary about the composition of the Sanhedrin may be post-Temple reconstruction based on the rabbis' own sense of history, rather than what actually happened. The Sadducees might offer a different version, and Josephus is vague. Second, any legal system can be manipulated: "what is illegal" is not the same thing as "what could not have happened." Third, the Gospel writers may realize that the story they are telling is one of illegal practices: this conflict between legality and actuality makes for good storytelling. None of these uncertainties decides the issue.

BRIDGING THE HORIZONS

1. On Ambition

In a poignant discussion of the meaning of Luke's Last Supper account for the church, Fred Craddock addresses the dispute about greatness:

> Luke has spoken two very strong words to the church. First, betrayal of Christ has occurred and can again occur among those who partake of the Lord's Supper. The finger of indictment points at that first table, to be sure, but, for Luke, betrayal lies not prior to the covenant meal, hence becoming an item of history, but within the circle of the covenant, and hence a continuing warning. Second, by placing the dispute about greatness at the Lord's table, Luke again changes an ugly moment in the history of the Twelve into a very real and

present exhortation to those who share the table. Love of place and power was a problem for the first followers of Jesus, to be sure, but it continues to be so. The remainder of the New Testament, church history, and today's ecclesiastical journals concur in their witness to this infectious disease among so many who lead Christ's church. Luke will not allow us simply to scold the ambitious apostles; every time we sit at the Lord's table, these words (vv. 24–27) on humility and service return as a reminder and a warning.[34]

2. On Prayer

From the Jordan to the Mount of Olives to his crucifixion, Jesus relies on prayer. Luke depicts him as a model of how a lifetime of prayer can be a source of strength and guidance. Henri Nouwen has many wonderful reflections on Jesus and on prayer, and we consider a few of his words at this juncture. Asking what prayer accomplishes, Nouwen finds that it can shape our character and approach to life:

> Dealing with burning issues without being rooted in a deep personal relationship with God easily leads to divisiveness because, before we know it, our sense of self is caught up in our opinion about a given subject. But when we are securely rooted in personal intimacy with the source of life, it will be possible to remain flexible without being relativistic, convinced without being rigid, willing to confront without being offensive, gentle and forgiving without being soft, and true witnesses without being manipulative.[35]

I (Ben) find that in my own life, when I do not spend enough time in prayer I have trouble discerning what God's will is for my life, trouble facing the *crise de jour*, trouble avoiding being manipulative and trying to control situations that I should leave in the hands of God. Jesus' time with Abba prepared him to face what he was called to do, even though he had no death wish or personal desire to encounter the judgment or wrath of God. Getting in touch with the Source is certainly a major key to facing life in general, never mind a major life crisis.

I (Amy-Jill) do not think that lack of prayer makes a person psychologically unhealthy or emotionally arrested. Prayer can be the source of life; it can also be irrelevant. Not all people have the same spiritual makeup, and I am wary of negative judgments placed on people because of a

34 Craddock, *Luke*, 257.
35 Henri Nouwen, *In the Name of Jesus* (New York: Crossroad, 1989), 31–32.

lack of a prayer life. Personally, I find participation in prayer, especially in the communal prayers of my synagogue, sustaining and enriching. I appreciate reciting the prayers that I remember hearing my parents and my grandmother recite. I value how the ancient words still speak to present contexts. I cherish the aesthetics of the Hebrew and Aramaic, the cadences of the terms and the medieval chants. But I do not find myself deep in prayer in personal moments. At those times, I am more inclined to seek the wisdom of friends and family and then to trust in my own decision-making. My friends tell me that when it comes to major decisions, they are inclined to "pray about it." I'm more inclined to do a cost-benefit analysis.

3. On Violence

In his reflections on the violence done to Jesus, González reflects on the power of violence to repeat:

> On the one hand, violence often creates a violent reaction, as in the case of the disciple who cut off the ear of one who came to arrest Jesus. On the other, violence also reproduces by contagion. The men who mocked and beat Jesus may well have been respectable folk who would never do such a thing like that on their own. But now, in the heat of the moment, each inspired the rest, they became a mocking and cruel mob. These two ways in which violence exerts and extends its power require two different but parallel responses. The only way to prevent violence from begetting more violence is by reacting to it in ways that disarm and destroy it. This is what is often called "non-violence"; but one could also say that it is "doing violence to violence." Violence can only be destroyed by peace … Practicing peace, one undoes the power of violence – one "does violence to violence." … The other response, the way to undo the contagion of violence, is to create a community in which love and forgiveness take the place of hatred and violence.[36]

4. On Judas

Reflecting on Judas in the context of teaching at Riverbend Maximum Security Prison, I (Amy-Jill) developed four questions. The reference to "four questions" follows from the Passover *Seder*, when the youngest child at the table asks, with reference to four practices, "why is this night different

[36] González, *Luke*, 254–55.

from all other nights?" These four questions about Judas ask, in effect, "how is this person different from all other people?"

1. Do we need scapegoats? Do we need to make sure that someone is worse than us?
2. Is it our nature to condemn without knowing the whole story? Do we fill in the gaps with the most lurid details possible, so as time passes the presumed guilt becomes worse and worse, extending from individuals to groups. Does the sin of one person become the stain that curses the many?
3. Do we think of the murderer, the betrayer, the rapist, in terms of the crime, rather than as an individual, a person with his own story, her own family, their own hurts? I don't want to think of my Riverbend students as "the murderer" or "the child molester" or "the rapist." I want to think of them as individuals. I do not dismiss the hurt and the harm they have done. But I do not want to deny that they, too, are individuals, in the image and likeness of God. I would not want to be judged by the worst thing I have ever done.
4. Can we find compassion for Judas? Should we?

Luke 23 Pilate and the Cross

FIRST HEARING BEFORE PILATE

[1] Then the assembly rose as a body and brought Jesus before Pilate. [2] They began to accuse him, saying, "We found this man perverting our nation, forbidding us to pay taxes to the emperor, and saying that he himself is the Messiah, a king." [3] Then Pilate asked him, "Are you the king of the Jews?" He answered, "You say so." [4] Then Pilate said to the chief priests and the crowds, "I find no basis for an accusation against this man." [5] But they were insistent and said, "He stirs up the people by teaching throughout all Judea, from Galilee where he began even to this place."

HEARING BEFORE HEROD ANTIPAS

[6] When Pilate heard this, he asked whether the man was a Galilean. [7] And when he learned that he was under Herod's jurisdiction, he sent him off to Herod, who was himself in Jerusalem at that time. [8] When Herod saw Jesus, he was very glad, for he had been wanting to see him for a long time, because he had heard about him and was hoping to see him perform some sign.

[9] He questioned him at some length, but Jesus gave him no answer. [10] The chief priests and the scribes stood by, vehemently accusing him. [11] Even Herod with his soldiers treated him with contempt and mocked him; then he put an elegant robe on him, and sent him back to Pilate. [12] That same day Herod and Pilate became friends with each other; before this they had been enemies.

SECOND HEARING BEFORE PILATE

[13] Pilate then called together the chief priests, the leaders, and the people, [14] and said to them, "You brought me this man as one who was perverting

the people; and here I have examined him in your presence and have not found this man guilty of any of your charges against him. ¹⁵ Neither has Herod, for he sent him back to us. Indeed, he has done nothing to deserve death. ¹⁶ I will therefore have him flogged and release him." [¹⁷ He had to release someone to them on (the) feast.]

¹⁸ Then they all shouted out together, "Away with this fellow! Release Barabbas for us!" ¹⁹ (This was a man who had been put in prison for an insurrection that had taken place in the city, and for murder.)

²⁰ Pilate, wanting to release Jesus, addressed them again; ²¹ but they kept shouting, "Crucify, crucify him!" ²² A third time he said to them, "Why, what evil has he done? I have found in him no ground for the sentence of death; I will therefore have him flogged and then release him."

²³ But they kept urgently demanding with loud shouts that he should be crucified; and their voices prevailed. ²⁴ So Pilate gave his verdict that their demand should be granted. ²⁵ He released the man they asked for, the one who had been put in prison for insurrection and murder, and he handed Jesus over as they wished.

VIA DOLOROSA

²⁶ As they led him away, they seized a man, Simon of Cyrene, who was coming from the country, and they laid the cross on him, and made him carry it behind Jesus.

²⁷ A great number of the people followed him, and among them were women who were beating their breasts and wailing for him. ²⁸ But Jesus turned to them and said, "Daughters of Jerusalem, do not weep for me, but weep for yourselves and for your children. ²⁹ For the days are surely coming when they will say, 'Blessed are the barren, and the wombs that never bore, and the breasts that never nursed.' ³⁰ Then they will begin to say to the mountains, 'Fall on us'; and to the hills, 'Cover us.' ³¹ For if they do this when the wood is green, what will happen when it is dry?"

CRUCIFIXIONS

³² Two others also, who were criminals, were led away to be put to death with him. ³³ When they came to the place that is called The Skull, they crucified Jesus there with the criminals, one on his right and one on his left.

³⁴ Then Jesus said, "Father, forgive them; for they do not know what they are doing." And they cast lots to divide his clothing.

35 And the people stood by, watching; but the leaders scoffed at him, saying, "He saved others; let him save himself if he is the Messiah of God, his chosen one!" 36 The soldiers also mocked him, coming up and offering him sour wine, 37 and saying, "If you are the King of the Jews, save yourself!" 38 There was also an inscription over him, "This is the King of the Jews."

39 One of the criminals who were hanged there kept deriding him and saying, "Are you not the Messiah? Save yourself and us!" 40 But the other rebuked him, saying, "Do you not fear God, since you are under the same sentence of condemnation? 41 And we indeed have been condemned justly, for we are getting what we deserve for our deeds, but this man has done nothing wrong."

42 Then he said, "Jesus, remember me when you come into your kingdom." 43 He replied, "Truly I tell you, today you will be with me in Paradise."

44 It was now about noon, and darkness came over the whole land until three in the afternoon, 45 while the sun's light failed; and the curtain of the temple was torn in two.

46 Then Jesus, crying with a loud voice, said, "Father, into your hands I commend my spirit." Having said this, he breathed his last. 47 When the centurion saw what had taken place, he praised God and said, "Certainly this man was innocent."

48 And when all the crowds who had gathered there for this spectacle saw what had taken place, they returned home, beating their breasts. 49 But all his acquaintances, including the women who had followed him from Galilee, stood at a distance, watching these things.

ENTOMBMENT

50 Now there was a good and righteous man named Joseph, who, though a member of the council, 51 had not agreed to their plan and action. He came from the Jewish town of Arimathea, and he was waiting expectantly for the kingdom of God. 52 This man went to Pilate and asked for the body of Jesus. 53 Then he took it down, wrapped it in a linen cloth, and laid it in a rock-hewn tomb where no one had ever been laid.

54 It was the day of Preparation, and the sabbath was beginning. 55 The women who had come with him from Galilee followed, and they saw the tomb and how his body was laid. 56 Then they returned, and prepared spices and ointments.

On the sabbath they rested according to the commandment.

All four Gospels recount the death of Jesus, and all four provide different perspectives. Luke's distinctive contributions include the hearing before Herod Antipas, the presence of the "daughters of Jerusalem" on the road to the cross, the comments by and about the two men crucified alongside Jesus, and the centurion's proclamation of Jesus' innocence or righteousness instead of his being the (or a) "Son of God" (so Matthew and Mark). Although apparently following Mark's outline, Luke lacks any explanation of the demand for the release of Barabbas, omits the "cry of dereliction" ("my God, my God, why have you forsaken me," the first line of Psa 22; see Matt 27.46//Mark 15.34), and the tossing of dice for Jesus' robe.

How we assess these distinctive elements will depend on our choices of methods and emphases. If we begin with the view that Luke sought to replace other Gospels, including those of Mark and Matthew, because they were not accurate and in order (cf. 1.1), we will come to different conclusions than if we see Luke as supplementing these other texts. If we regard Luke as recording "what happened" (so Ben), we will have a different starting point than if we regard Luke as providing information that is primarily designed to express theological points (so Amy-Jill). Ben begins with the presupposition that Luke faithfully records the events before Pilate, on the road, and at the cross, in the sense that one could capture these events based on the testimonies of faithful eyewitnesses and servants of the word (i.e., the male and female disciples, to whom Luke appeals in 1.1–4); Amy-Jill finds much of the account to be embellished, so that the narrative tells what the death of Jesus meant to his followers. The two points are not mutually exclusive when it comes to ecclesial teaching. Historical or not, the accounts have meaning for the Church. Ben thinks that when it comes to important matters written up as an historical or biographical account, what is historically false cannot be theologically true. Amy-Jill finds that stories can convey truth, as can parables and myths, even if the events are inventions rather than eyewitness reports.

FIRST HEARING BEFORE PILATE

The Sanhedrin, unanimous in its verdict, brings Jesus to Pilate (**vs. 1**). The NRSV's "rose as a body" masks the potential contradiction in the Greek, which literally reads "rose all their number," i.e., everyone. We will learn later that Joseph of Arimathea, a Council member, "had not agreed to their plan and action" (see 22.50–51). Ben suggests that Joseph along with Nicodemus simply abstained from voting; Amy-Jill, who tends to take political abstentions as tacit approval (influenced by the quote attributed to Eldredge Cleaver, "You either have to be part of the solution, or you're going to be part of the problem"; cf. Matt 12.30), finds that view apologetic.

To Pilate, the Council levels against Jesus three politically charged accusations (**vs. 2**). "Perverting our nation" (Greek: *ethnos*), a generic charge, offers in the context of a trial before the Roman authority and in the company of two more specific political charges, a whiff of insurrection. "Perverting" (Greek: *diastrephō*) can signal leading the nation away from loyalty to Rome. Elsewhere, the verb appears in Luke's Gospel only in 9.41, where Jesus accuses the people of being a "perverse generation." The charge he laid against the people is now laid against him. The Book of Acts (16.19–21; 17.6–7; 21.28, etc.) depicts both gentiles and Jews charging Paul with similar offenses. In Exod 5.4, Pharaoh charges Moses and Aaron with social disruption (LXX: *diastrephō*) by taking the Israelite slaves away from their work; in 1 Kings 18.17, Ahab charges Elijah with troubling (LXX: *diastrephō*) Israel. Given these antecedents combined with Jesus' public criticisms of the chief priests and scribes, the first charge is not entirely illegitimate.

The second charge, "forbidding the paying of taxes," relates to 20.20–25, the conversation in which Jesus responded to the question of the legality for Jews to participate in Rome's tax system: "Then give to the emperor the things that are the emperor's, and to God the things that are God's." Jesus did not forbid the paying of taxes, although one could have interpreted his comment as moving in that direction: if everything belongs to God, one could claim that Caesar deserves nothing. Again, the charge, although false, has just enough connection to what Jesus said to make it sound credible. The Sanhedrin offers no evidence for this claim, and nor would evidence be found. Neither does Luke address the charge again.

The third charge, that Jesus claimed to the Messiah (Greek: *christos*), glossed with the title "king," explains to Pilate what a "Christ" is; that term, as well as the Hebrew *meshiach* (whence the English "messiah") had no meaning for Roman gentiles. At the time of Jesus, not all messianic figures were associated either broadly with royalty or specifically with King David. Jesus did not claim explicitly to be "the Messiah, a king." In the previous chapter, to the High Priest's question, "If you are the Messiah, tell us," Jesus responded, "If I tell you, you will not believe" (22.67). The High Priest imputes the claim to Jesus. Again, the charge has a subtle credibility. It is this accusation, of royal pretentions, that Pilate finds the most pressing.

Pilate asks Jesus, "Are you the king of the Jews?" (**vs. 3**), the same title that will appear on the *titulus* (23.38). Because the ancient manuscripts lack punctuation, Pilate's comment could be read as a declarative statement: "You are king of the Jews"; the Roman authority thus (ironically, and sarcastically) names Jesus' authority. Jesus, once again coyly, responds, *"you* say" (cf. the similar nonanswer in 22.67). *Why* he refuses to answer the question goes unexplained. In speaking of the trials his followers will face, Jesus encourages them to proclaim their beliefs boldly. It is difficult to imagine his suggesting to a disciple, "If you are brought before governors and kings, and they ask you, 'Are you a disciple of Jesus?' just reply, 'You say.'" Perhaps for Luke, who here follows Mark 15.2, the concern is less Jesus' self-proclamation than the need for Pilate to come to this conclusion himself. Perhaps it relates to Jesus' rejection of the role of "king" as the gentiles understand it (22.25).

Pilate's response is to tell not the Sanhedrin but the "chief priests and the crowd" that he finds no basis for accusing Jesus (**vs. 4**). The Sanhedrin had taken Jesus' enigmatic responses to their questions of kingship, messianic status, and divine sonship as affirmations; the governor takes the same statement, "you say" (cf. 22.69), as a denial. One hears what one wants to hear.

The shift in audience from Sanhedrin to chief priests and crowd creates a few interpretive possibilities. Luke earlier mentioned several times that the local authorities did not arrest Jesus for fear of the people. Could that fear be abated as long as Pilate is in charge? Or, did the nonpriestly members of the Sanhedrin depart, lest the people realize their involvement in Jesus' arrest? Conversely, could Luke have omitted them because Luke knew a Roman governor was not likely to disagree with seventy or seventy-two united members of the local political infrastructure?

The governor's verdict also raises questions: is Pilate so nonchalant that he can dismiss, on the basis of one coy response, major political accusations of disloyalty to Rome? Ben, regarding Pilate as generally uncaring, sees nothing odd here; Amy-Jill finds the response difficult to believe. We both agree, however, that Pilate reveals the lack of Roman justice.

Desperate to have Pilate condemn Jesus, "they" (the antecedent would be "chief priests and crowds" and so Luke, subtly, begins to distribute the responsibility for Jesus' death to the people as a whole) pursue the matter of rebellion. They have a point, given that Jesus has challenged the Jerusalem political infrastructure as well as disrupted Temple activities. The reference to Galilee along with Judea (**vs. 5**) might have suggested to Pilate, and it does suggest to Luke's careful readers, the association of Galilee with tax revolts and rebellions, as we saw in the discussion of the census (2.1) and of Judas the Galilean (Acts 5.37). The notice might also remind readers of the absent Peter, identified just a few verses back as a "Galilean" (22.59).

HEARING BEFORE HEROD ANTIPAS

The regional notice prompts Pilate's question of Jesus' Galilean identity (**vs. 6**). According to Luke, Jesus was born in Bethlehem of Judea, but this technicality goes ignored: Jesus is known for being from Nazareth, where he grew up.

Learning that Jesus was from Galilee, literally, "under Herod's authority" (Greek: *exousia*), Pilate sends him to Antipas, who was in Jerusalem at the time (**vs. 7**). Again, questions appear. Luke does not explain Herod's presence in Jerusalem, although his coming to the city for Passover would not be unexpected.

Herod is delighted to see Jesus (**vs. 8**), and so Luke brings to closure the foreshadowing of this meeting in 9.9: "Herod said: 'John I beheaded, but who is this about whom I hear such things?' And he tried to see him." Luke's presentation allows Jesus to occupy the role John the Baptizer plays in Mark 6.20: Mark depicts Antipas as recognizing John to be righteous and holy as well as enjoying his teaching; Luke omits the scene of the banquet, the dancing daughter, and the Baptizer's head on a platter. In Luke's account, Antipas is not interested in Jesus' teaching but in his performing a sign. The *desideratum* locates Herod among the "evil generation" that seeks a sign (cf. 11.16, 29–30).

Jesus gives Herod neither sign nor teaching. He is even more nonresponsive here than he was before the Sanhedrin and Pilate. Despite Herod's questioning, Jesus offers no answer (**vs. 9**). Fitzmyer states, "His serene assurance before his tormentor only heightens the mockery that is to follow."[1] Yet the questioning need not be seen as torment. Later tradition understood Jesus as fulfilling the prophecy of Isa 53.7: "He was oppressed, and he was afflicted, yet he did not open his mouth; like a lamb that is led to the slaughter, and like a sheep that before its shearers is silent, so he did not open his mouth." Luke quotes this verse in Acts 8.32.

Suddenly, the "chief priests," now accompanied by "scribes," show up to play the same accusatory role they along with the crowds just played before Pilate (vs. 3). They accuse Jesus (**vs. 10**), but of what, Luke does not say. Antipas, who sought his father's kingdom, had every reason both to garner the priesthood's support and to execute a person who would speak against Rome or Roman taxation. Yet Antipas does not execute Jesus as he did John; he likely lacked the authority to do so in Judaea. Instead, he and his soldiers mock Jesus (**vs. 11**). This scene replaces the mocking by

---

[1] Fitzmyer, *Luke X–XXIV*, 1481.

Pilate and his soldiers even as it makes for better irony. Herod Antipas had pretentions of royalty; Rome deposed him in 39 for seeking, in opposition to his brother-in-law Agrippa I, the kingdom accorded his father Herod the Great. Thus, the would-be king mocks the real king. Dressing Jesus in "bright breast-band" (Greek: *esthēs lampros*; the NRSV's "elegant robe"; the same expression describes the "man in dazzling clothes" who greets Cornelius in Acts 10.30; see also Jas 2.2 in describing rich people), Antipas sends Jesus back to Pilate.

The vignette concludes with Luke's observation that the exchange of Jesus turns Pilate and Herod, former enemies, into friends (**vs. 12**). Josephus, our major historical source for this period, says nothing about either enmity or friendship between the tetrarch and the governor. Nor does either Pilate's sending Jesus to Herod or Herod's sending Jesus back to Pilate explain what would prompt the friendship. Were Pilate interested in seeing Jesus executed, then he failed in sending Jesus to Herod. Were Pilate interested in having Jesus set free, he failed. Were Herod interested in gaining support from both the Temple officials and the Roman governor, he would have had Jesus executed. Yet Herod also fails in this process, but then, as Ben notes, Herod had no authority to execute anyone in the Roman province of Judaea.

For Ben, Luke has recorded an event missing from the other Gospel accounts; for Amy-Jill, Luke has invented a scene designed to show increasing culpability for Jesus' death, to highlight Jesus at the expense of John the Baptizer, and to anticipate the roles other Herodians will play in the Book of Acts, so that Peter and especially Paul can be seen in Jesus' role. Ben does not dispute that some of these factors may explain why Luke included this scene, which resolved nothing directly, but it does not explain why Luke would go to the trouble of inventing such a scene. Perhaps, we both speculate, Pilate and Herod were passing the buck, and they did not want the responsibility for executing a popular Jew at Passover season.

SECOND HEARING BEFORE PILATE

Pilate now summons everyone: chief priests, leaders (Greek: *archōns*, literally, "first ones"), and the people (**vs. 13**). The procedure makes little legal sense. Pilate had already determined that Jesus was not guilty (vs. 4), so there is no need for another trial. Luke may be suggesting that Pilate, seeking to release Jesus, anticipated popular support against the chief priests. The move is not wise politically, as Pilate and the chief priests needed to work together as overlords and local elites usually do to maintain the peace.

The governor begins by summarizing events to this point (**vs. 13**): "You brought me this man," he states, with the "you" being the all-encompassing plural: the people as well as the chief priests (**vs. 14a**). Pilate mentions the general charge of perverting the people, but he ignores what a Roman official would find of greater interest: the issues of taxation and kingship. Pilate states that he examined Jesus: he had asked one question, to which he received a non-answer. He concludes, again, that Jesus is guilty of nothing (**vs. 14b**). That he repeats his verdict hints at his lack of authority: Jesus' accusers are not accepting his judgment. Pilate then reinforces this second proclamation of Jesus' innocence by adding that Herod also found Jesus to have done nothing warranting capital punishment (**vs. 15**). Given that datum, Herod's sending Jesus back rather than releasing him or advising Pilate to release him again shows the injustice of the entire proceedings.

Pilate concludes his speech to the assembled Jews by stating that he will release Jesus after "instructing" him (**vs.16**). The Greek *paideuō* (whence "pedagogy") can also mean "discipline," which the NRSV chooses to translate "torture." The best English cognate would be "teach him a lesson." In Luke's Gospel, Jesus' body is not (explicitly) attacked either by the Sanhedrin (contrast Mark 14.65) or by Herod Antipas (contrast the beheading of John) or, perhaps, by Pilate.

The next verse reveals a text-critical problem, an historical problem, and another point of disagreement between Ben and Amy-Jill. Some ancient manuscripts read, "He had a need to release someone to them on (the) feast" (**vs. 17**); many, however, do not. The NRSV does not include the verse in its main text. The verse could be a scribal addition designed to explain why suddenly the case of Barabbas appears, to bring Luke's Gospel into harmony with the other Gospels, which record that Rome had a tradition of releasing a prisoner to the crowds at Passover (see John 18.39; cf. Matt 27.15; Mark 15.7–8).

Pilate has stated his plans to release Jesus. "They all" – leaders, chief priests, and people – reject his judgment. The crowds have turned against Jesus. Luke reiterates this corporate responsibility for Jesus' death in Peter's speech in Acts 3.13, when the apostle charges people with having "handed over and rejected [Jesus] in the presence of Pilate, though he had decided to release him." Peter goes on to say they acted *in ignorance,* so the condemnation is neither final nor as severe as it might have been were this pure apologetics.

At the same time, by rejecting Pilate's decision, "they all" have turned against him as well. They demand that the governor do away with Jesus

A CLOSER LOOK: THE PASSOVER AMNESTY

Ben sees Luke as recording an historical incident that has profound theological implications. He also states there is evidence from Egypt under Roman rule of such a tradition.[2]

Amy-Jill suggests that Luke, likely familiar with the claims made in Mark, omitted the verse regarding the custom of a Passover amnesty as being unhistorical. Outside the Gospels, she finds evidence of no such tradition. In her view, the several apologetic attempts to document such a practice do not offer compelling evidence.[3] These attempts usually take four forms. First is the citation of Josephus, *Ant.* 20.215: "But when Albinus heard that Gessius Florus was coming to succeed him, he was desirous to appear to do something that might ingratiate the people of Jerusalem; so he brought out all those prisoners who seemed to him to be the most plainly worthy of death, and ordered them to be put to death accordingly. But as to those who had been put into prison on some trifling occasion, he took money from them, and dismissed them; by which means the prisons were indeed emptied, but the country was filled with robbers."[4] This example has nothing to do with amnesty at a feast, the motivation for the release of the prisoners is not custom but political capital, and according to the Gospels, Barabbas was hardly charged with "trifling" miscreancy.

Second is the claim that Mishnah records, "that they may slaughter the Passover lamb for one ... whom they have promised to bring out of prison," and so indicates prisoners being released at Passover.[5] The quote appears to be drawing on *m. Pes.* 8.6, which reads, "In behalf of one who suffers a bereavement of a close relative on that same day, one who has the task of clearing away a ruin [and may, in fact, thereby suffer corpse uncleanness], and so too: one whom they have promised to free from prison; a sick person, and a senile person [both of whom] can eat an olive's bulk of the meat of a Passover offering – they slaughter [a Passover offering] ..." The connection to an amnesty must be inferred. The

---

[2]   See Witherington, *John's Wisdom,* and his *Acts of the Apostles,* on Roman protocols in regard to releasing a prisoner during a festival season.

[3]   See, for example, UK Apologetics, "Would Pontius Pilate Have Released a Prisoner at Passover" (Saturday, April 7, 2012), at http://apologeticsuk.blogspot.com/2012/04/would-pontius-pilate-have-released.html.

[4]   Ibid.; the Site's listing of *Ant.* 20.9.3 is incorrect; the alternative versification is 20.9.5.

[5]   Ibid. The Site misdates the Mishnah to ca. 300 rather than 200 and gives no specific Mishnaic citation.

context concerns those who may not have a family or group of people with whom to share the meal.

Third is the adducing of a papyrus (p. Flor. 61), dated ca. 85 CE, which records the Roman governor of Egypt saying, "You were worthy of scourging but I gave you to the crowds."[6] The governor in question is G. Septimius Vegetus, and the context of the quote is, apparently, a debt pardon of a fellow named Phibion. Again, there is no tradition of amnesty, no connection to Passover, and no release of insurrectionists.

Fourth is an early second-century citation from the letters of Pliny the Younger: "It was asserted, however, that these people were released upon their petition to the proconsuls, or their lieutenants; which seems likely enough, as it is improbable any person should have dared to set them at liberty without authority" (*Epistles* 10.31)."[7] Again, the citation has nothing to do with festival amnesties.

A century ago, Richard Wellington Husband observed, "there is absolutely no evidence that the pardoning or release of a prisoner had ever occurred, even once, before the time of Pilate ... There seems to be no instance on record, either from Rome or from the provinces, in which a Roman officer pardoned any person who had been convicted of a crime."[8] The evidence has not changed. Amy-Jill adds it makes little sense that Rome would release anyone whom the crowd wanted: the Empire would have worked against its interests by releasing either a murderer or, worse, an insurrectionist. Nor is the release "for the feast" logical in the Synoptic accounts, for the "feast" (eating the Paschal lamb) would have been the night before. Nor again is Pilate, recorded by both Josephus and Philo as by no means a lover of the Jewish people, one to engage in or even invent such a practice.

Yes, a Roman official could release a debtor from prison; yes, a Roman official could reduce the prison population by freeing people guilty of minor crimes, but the scenario depicted in the Gospels is, at least for Amy-Jill, a theological parable of sorts in which the (very) guilty human being, the "son of a father," which is what *bar* plus *abbas* means,

---

[6] Ibid., and see here and for the previous notes the comments on the website, esp. by Richard Colledge.
[7] Ibid.
[8] Richard Wellington Husband, "The Pardoning of Prisoners by Pilate," *American Journal of Theology* 21.1 (1917): 110–16 (112, 114). Husband sees the Gospel accounts as recording Pilate's releasing Barabbas as likely achieved by having the prosecutor withdraw the suit.

is released, while the (very) innocent Son of the Father dies in his place. Regardless of the historical credibility of the verse, the theology of the account is profound. Ben points out that while Amy-Jill is right about some of the alleged historical evidence for a Roman releasing a prisoner at a festival time, Livy (*History* 5.13.7–8) says that there was indeed a Roman custom, going all the way back to 339 BCE, to release prisoners. His particular comment is about the Roman feast of Lectisternia, but there is no reason, with that sort of long-standing precedent, that a procurator might not use the precedent to release a prisoner at a Jewish festival.

Ben adds one more key point to consider. Roman officials from the emperor on down knew that one of the chief and long-standing virtues of a Roman ruler was "clementia," the offering of mercy on a conquered foe or a condemned person. There are numerous stories in Caesar's *Gallic Wars*, and in Tacitus, Suetonius, Cicero, Seneca, and elsewhere, about "clementia" being one of the chiefest virtues of Roman rulers. In an honor and shame culture, this is one of the ways an official could gain honor with the people and be seen to be not merely just but merciful. Pilate's attempt to avoid condemning Jesus and to release a prisoner would just be one more example of such a Roman practice. Amy-Jill finds that the Gospel depictions of the choice between Jesus and Barabbas have nothing to do with "clementia."

and instead release Barabbas (**vs. 18**). If vs. 17 were not in the earliest manuscripts, then the demand comes as a non sequitur, given that without vs. 17, Luke says nothing about any tradition of releasing a prisoner. Not only does the crowd want Jesus killed, they now also want Barabbas released. Symbolically, not only do they want to execute the model of righteousness, they also embrace violence.

The mysterious Barabbas, hitherto unmentioned, also has a mysterious name, which is otherwise unattested. *Bar* is Aramaic for "son of"; *abba* is Aramaic for "father." Thus, Barabbas is also "son of [a] father"; he is the perfect countertype to Jesus (in Matthew's Gospel, 27.16, Barabbas's first name is also "Jesus"). Luke, who lacks Aramaic terms present in Matthew and Mark, may not have recognized the symbolic implications of the name. Luke only notes that Barabbas was imprisoned on charges of rioting (Greek: *stasis*, "riot" or "revolt"; for Rome, there would be no difference) and murder (**vs. 19**); the NRSV offers "insurrection," a plausible reading which puts an anti-Roman spin on the charge. Why the crowd would want him, or how his case is related to Jesus, goes unexplained. Again, Ben sees history as well as profound theology, and Amy-Jill finds profound theology only.

Becoming desperate, and wanting to release Jesus, Pilate tries again (**vs. 20**). He earlier had no problem in executing other Galileans although as Ben notes, there weren't several hundred thousand festival attending Jews on his doorstep then (13.1), but in the case of Jesus, he appears to be speaking on behalf of justice; having twice proclaimed Jesus innocent, Pilate needs to regain his authority despite the crowd's demands. Earlier the chief priests had been afraid to arrest Jesus because of the crowds; now Pilate is fearing the crowds if he fails to execute Jesus. Luke does not explain why the people have deserted Jesus. Nothing is said of the chief priests stirring them up. They all simply continue to shout, "Crucify him, crucify him" (**vs. 21**). This is the Gospel's first reference to the type of death Jesus will face, and it comes from his own people.

Ben notes that Pilate's vacillations are attested not just in Luke but also independently in the Fourth Gospel. He finds that this affirmation of Pilate's situation strongly suggests that it goes back to an historical datum. And in view of Pilate's anti-Jewish tendencies, he may well have not wanted to give the authorities what they wanted in regard to Jesus, if he could avoid doing so. He did not want to appear to be acting on their say so. Amy-Jill increasingly doubts that John is writing independently of the Synoptics, so she does not find John as offering independent testimony. However, the thesis that Pilate does not want to acquiesce to the authorities makes abundant sense to her. Pilate's actions here are explicable in light of what else we know about his character, and particularly his anti-Jewish attitudes.

For a third time, Pilate proclaims Jesus' innocence and announces his decision to release Jesus after *educating* him (**vs. 22**). And for a third time, the assemblage demands Jesus' death. The crowds prevail (**vs. 23**). Pilate has lost charge of the populace, and he is defeated in his own desires. He proclaims a formal decision that the crowds should receive what they demand (**vs. 24**), although he never explicitly states that Jesus should be crucified. Pilate releases the one guilty of riot and murder, and he hands Jesus over (**vs. 25**); by withholding from his verdict the details of the death sentence, Luke hints that the crowds, i.e., the Jews, are responsible for the cross. At the same time, Luke shows that Roman authority embodied by Pilate is bankrupt. The governor has released Barabbas, who violated the peace of the city and so the peace of Rome; he is permitting an innocent man to be executed.

How much responsibility Pilate should bear in the death of Jesus depends on how we read not only Luke but also the other earlier sources. Matthew depicts Pilate as protesting his innocence in Jesus' death sentence by washing his hands; John has Caiaphas manipulating Pilate by questioning his political loyalties. Postcanonical documents increasingly vilify the Jews and exculpate Pilate, and the Greek Orthodox and Coptic churches proclaimed Pilate a saint.[9] Luke depicts the governor as increasingly power-less and as corrupting Roman justice. Ironically, Pilate resembles the Judge in Jesus' parable (18.2–5): he cares neither about public opinion nor about God, but because of the increasing demands of those less powerful than he, he capitulates. There is no "justice granted" (18.3) here.

VIA DOLOROSA

In the previous verse, Pilate handed Jesus over to "them"; the antecedent, those to whom Pilate gave Jesus, are the people, the chief priests, and the leaders. Luke depicts no scourging of Jesus by the Romans. Therefore, the "they" who led Jesus away (**vs. 26a**) are, at least in terms of the narrative, the Jewish population of Jerusalem, the city that kills its prophets. However, in what follows, that "them" becomes the Roman soldiers who crucify Jesus and gamble for his clothes. "They" who carry out the execution are Pilate's soldiers (so 23.36, 47).

On the way, "they" seize a fellow named Simon of Cyrene and compel him to carry Jesus' cross (**vs. 26b**). Cyrene, which on the northwest coast of Africa, is today's Libya. Simon was likely a Jew, although no Gospel text specifies his ethnicity. Luke notes in Acts 6.9 a synagogue of Cyrenians, so associating Simon with that community would not be unwarranted. That he was "coming in from the field" is an odd but not impossible notice for a Jew celebrating the first full day of Passover. For Luke's Gospel, Simon's role is also odd, since Luke gives no indication of why Jesus was unable to carry his own cross. To this point, he has suffered verbal insult, but no physical torture. Again, Amy-Jill suspects theology rather than history, whereas Ben presumes that Jesus, like other victims of crucifixion, was tortured prior to

---

9   Robin Jensen, "How Pilate Became a Saint," *Bible Review* 19.06 (December 2003) www
      .basarchive.org/sample/bswbBrowse.asp?PubID=BSBR&Volume=19&Issue=6&Articl
      eID=2.

his being nailed to the cross. In John's Gospel, Jesus carries his own cross, as victims of crucifixion were expected to do. Following Jesus and carrying his cross, Simon symbolizes the perfect disciple.

Along the road, Jesus encounters not hostile crowds but mournful sympathizers. Luke specifies that among the people were "women who were beating their breasts and wailing for him" (**vs. 27**). The verse has resonances of Zech 12.10, "And I will pour out a spirit of compassion and supplication on the house of David and the inhabitants of Jerusalem, so that, when they look on the one whom they have pierced, they shall mourn for him, as one mourns for an only child, and weep bitterly over him, as one weeps over a firstborn." For the Gospel narrative itself, the verse recollects the other references to breasts (something most [male] commentators ignore). In the Parable of the Pharisee and the Tax Collector, the tax collector also "beats his breast" while confessing his sin (18.13; the word for "breast" [Greek: *stethos*, whence "stethoscope"] is different from the term used in this verse. The closer reference to 23.27 is 11.27, where the woman from the crowd (the same structural position as the women on the Via Dolorosa) calls out to Jesus blessings upon the breasts that nursed him (11.27). The mention of women's breasts thus may also allude to Mary, her Magnificat, and the prediction by Simeon that a "sword will pierce her own soul" (2.35).

As he does with the woman in Chapter 11, so too with the women who weep for him on the road, Jesus deflects their focus from him and back to his followers. He addresses them as "daughters of Jerusalem" and tells them to weep rather for their children (**vs. 28**). The focus here is on the city and its residents. Jesus had predicted Jerusalem's destruction: the children of these women would live during the horrific events of 66–70, ending in the destruction of the Temple. Behind his comment here is his warning about those who are "pregnant and nursing" in those days (21.23), which receives emphasis in his next comment to the weeping women: the days are coming when the infertile will be considered the blessed ones (**vs. 29**). The time of Elizabeth, who faced reproach for her infertility, has passed away (1.25).

Additional biblical references to "daughters of Jerusalem" increase the pathos of this scene. The phrase appears multiple times in the Song of Songs (also called Song of Solomon and Canticles), where the female lover repeatedly tells the "daughters of Jerusalem" of her love for her beloved (Song 2.7; 3.5, 10; 5.8,16; 8.4; cf. 1.5). Isa 4.4 speaks of the Lord as having "washed away the filth of the daughters of Zion and cleansed the bloodstains of Jerusalem." Luke has not mentioned *how* the cross atones, but this intertext hints at its redemptive import.

Continuing to speak of Jerusalem's destruction, Jesus suggests that natural disaster would be better than Roman destruction. Earlier he had told his disciples that their faith could move trees (17.6); now he speaks of people exhorting mountains and hills to cover them (**vs. 30**). Hos 10.8 employs a similar expression: "The high places of Aven, the sin of Israel, shall be destroyed. Thorn and thistle shall grow up on their altars. They shall say to the mountains, 'Cover us, and to the hills, Fall on us.'" Destruction, for Hosea, comes from apostasy. Luke, similarly, blames the destruction of Jerusalem on the city's failure to recognize Jesus as Lord. In a detailed study of the rhetoric of Luke's Passion Narrative, Peter Rice concludes: "By amplifying the guilt of the Jerusalem leaders, especially the Temple authorities, Luke guides the reader toward implicit acknowledgement of God's righteous judgment against Jerusalem and its cultus, while simultaneously undermining any charges that Israel's God is after all weak, all by framing the cause of Jerusalem's destruction in terms of human faithlessness rather than divine failure."[10]

The scene ends with his enigmatic saying about the turning of damp (Greek: *hydros*) wood into dry wood (**vs. 31**). No explanation of this saying is fully satisfactory, but the most likely meaning is the *qal v'homer* formulation (from the lighter to the weightier) that if the innocent Jesus (the damp or green wood that does not kindle easily) can be killed, how much easier it will be for the guilty Jerusalem to go up in flames.

CRUCIFIXIONS

The daughters of Jerusalem weep for Jesus; we are not told if anyone wept for the two men also being led to their deaths (**vs. 32**). Luke identifies these men as "evil doers" (Greek: *kakourgoi*). The verse also fulfills the prophecy about Jesus being counted among the criminals (22.37). Yet these are men, with their own stories and perhaps their own families; they should be regarded as more than props needed to check off a verse that Luke reads as prophetic. The disciples have deserted Jesus. Are the men who die as he will die also deserted, in both their historical setting and in the imaginations of Luke's readers?

The executions occur "at the place of the skull," a name translating the Aramaic *Golgotha* (**vs. 33a**; see Mark 15.22; the Latin is "Calvary"). The

---

[10]   Peter Rice, "The Rhetoric of Luke's Passion: Luke's Use of Common-Place to Amplify the Guilt of the Jerusalem Leaders in Jesus' Death," *Bib. Int.* 21.3 (2013): 355–76 (376).

designation also goes unexplained: suggestions vary from the shape of the area to the place where bones are tossed. Artistic representations of Jesus' crucifixion in the Middle Ages came to locate a skull at the foot of the cross. The skull belonged to Adam. Visually the blood of Jesus descends from the crown of thorns on his head and the wound in his side onto Adam's skull; theologically, the artistic message is that Jesus' blood redeems humanity from the sin of Adam.

"They," with the antecedent still being the Jewish assemblage although the historical setting necessarily indicates the Roman soldiers, crucify Jesus between the two evildoers (**vs. 33b**). Jesus now utters his famous comment, unique to Luke, "Father, forgive them," because they act in ignorance (**vs. 34**). The comment lacks a clear reference: Jesus could be speaking about the two men between whom he hangs, the Jewish assemblage, or the Roman soldiers, who, although not yet explicitly mentioned, are also at the cross. Nathan Eubank concludes, "After examining early interpretations of Luke 23:34a, I have discovered no evidence suggesting that anyone ever understood Jesus' prayer to be on behalf of the soldiers. Occasionally commentators universalized the sin of the crucifixion, claiming that Jesus was killed by the human race, but, if a specific culprit is mentioned, it is invariably the Jews."[11] Yet in that same reception history, Christian readers have heard the prayer as unanswered. Acts 3.17–18, which implicates the people as well as the rulers in Jesus' death, states that they acted in ignorance and in order that predictions of the Messiah's suffering would be fulfilled. That the people did not recognize Jesus' identity may have something to do with Jesus' own refusal to announce it: he does not reveal it to the Sanhedrin, to Pilate and the crowds, or to Herod Antipas. That the majority of the Jews do not then convert led to the conclusion that, following Jesus' resurrection and Peter's preaching, they should not be forgiven. They now know what they did, and yet they still refused to accept Jesus as Lord. Christian readers must decide for themselves what they will do with this possible interpretation.

The prayer for forgiveness has served over the centuries as a means of distinguishing Christianity from Judaism: numerous Christians have seen their tradition, epitomized by Jesus, as merciful and interested in restorative justice; they have in turn seen Judaism as vengeful and interested in "an eye for an eye." This configuration, which is a variant of the "Old Testament

---

[11]   Nathan Eubank, "A Disconcerting Prayer: On the Originality of Luke 23:34a," *JBL* 129.3 (2010): 521–36 (527).

God of Wrath" versus the "New Testament God of Love" idea is another tragic example of anti-Judaism born in ignorance and apologetic. Shelly Matthews observes concerning the reception history of Jesus' invocation, "As an expression of self-mastery and the ability to refrain from retaliating in the face of undeserved violence, it is an assertion of the ethical superiority of Christianity over Judaism ... The dying declaration indelibly inscribes followers of the Way as radically forgiving, in stark contrast with the barbarous *Ioudaioi* who are radically unforgivable."[12]

While acknowledging the accuracy of this summary of the verse's reception, Ben entirely disagrees with its conclusion. He finds this dichotomy, and its terms, to ignore that the Jew named Jesus represented the gracious side of the Jewish tradition. He stresses that Luke, in uniquely presenting Jesus as forgiving and in emphasizing both here and in Acts 3 the "ignorance" motif, does not seek to blame Jews or Judaism. Jesus' followers, like Jesus himself, offer forgiveness even in extreme situations where blame might be expected. Ben also emphasizes that Jesus and his followers are, at this juncture in history, all Jews themselves! Amy-Jill also notes the error behind the reception history that Matthews correctly depicts. It is a deformed reading of the God of the Tanakh and of the Jewish tradition. However, she understands how certain seeds planted in the Gospel of Luke and the Acts of the Apostles could produce such weeds.

As we have seen throughout, forgiveness is a difficult topic. The prayer from the cross conforms to Jesus' earlier teachings about love of enemies (6.35), and it impinges on his emphasis on forgiveness (17.4). However, Jesus does not forgive the people who are in the process of torturing him to death. He asks his Father to forgive. As Maria Mayo suggests, perhaps he does so because he is not prepared to issue the forgiveness himself. There is no repentance on the part of those killing him, and he is, to repeat, being tortured to death.[13]

Jesus' prayer not only lacks a clear designation of the *they* who are to be forgiven, it also lacks details on *what* they are doing. People involved in an execution – injecting the drug, pulling the switch, aiming the gun – know exactly what they are doing. They are killing. The bystanders also know what they are doing. They are allowing a human life to be taken. Finally,

---

[12] Shelly Matthews, "Clemency as Cruelty: Forgiveness and Force in the Dying Prayers of Jesus and Stephen," *Bib. Int.* 17.1 (2009): 118–46 (120, 134).
[13] Mayo, *Limits of Forgiveness*.

Luke may be hinting at one more element of ignorance: they are unaware of *whom* they are killing.

Another identified "they" at the cross – Luke's readers would recognize to be Roman soldiers – shoot dice to see who would win Jesus' clothes (**vs. 34b**). The verse serves as a fulfillment citation: the tradition reads Psa 22.18 as a prediction rather than the description of present circumstances of the psalmist: "They divide my clothes among themselves, and for my clothing they cast lots."

Continuing to evoke the psalm (Psa 22.7), Luke next mentions the mockery by the bystanders at the cross. Although earlier united, the people who watch are separated from the leaders who scoff. These leaders (Greek: *archōns*) adduce Jesus' correct title and function, "the Messiah of God, his Chosen One," who has the ability to "save," but they are ignorant of the full meaning of their words (**vs. 35**). Structurally, these leaders are in the same place as Satan (4.2–13): they are tempting Jesus, in a very weakened state, to perform a miracle for his own benefit. Jesus refused the temptations then, and he will do so here. Historically, Amy-Jill finds it unlikely that among these "rulers" are the "chief priests"; in the interests of avoiding corpse impurity, they would not likely come to a place of execution. Ben notes that corpse impurity was not transmitted through the air, it required touching a corpse or being in contact with a grave. The narrative does not indicate either here.

At last, Luke mentions the soldiers. They too, like Herod's soldiers, engage in mockery. They offer Jesus sour wine (**vs. 36**) and tempt him to save himself (**vs. 37**). The sour wine functions as another fulfillment citation to another present-tense Psalm now understood to be a prediction: "in my thirst they gave me vinegar to drink" (Psa 69.21). In Mark's version of this account (Mark 15.23), the sour wine is mixed with myrrh, which serves as a narcotic. Wine vinegar was the Gatoraide of its day, used for thirst-quenching in an arid climate, so it is possible that the offer was not an act of cruelty but of kindness, that is, assuming that this tradition reflects some historical datum. Jesus had stated at his Last Supper that he would not drink wine again until he could drink it in the Kingdom (22.18). Luke offers no confirmation that Jesus drank the sour wine. Thus, it too serves as a temptation to which Jesus will not succumb.

The leaders mocked Jesus by calling him "God's Messiah" and the "chosen one," and the soldiers mock him with the title "king of the Jews" (**vs. 37**). The title serves as a mockery not only of Jesus, but also of the Jewish people: crucifixion is what Rome did to anyone who claimed the title "king" apart from imperial sanction. That mocking is the point of the titulus, "King of the Jews" (**vs. 38**): it serves not only to warn potential rebels that crucifixion will be their fate, it also shows the Jewish population that this "king of the Jews" is one who represents abject humiliation and suffering, not power and glory. If Pilate did insist on this *titulus* over the cross, designating Jesus' crime, then he was mocking not just Jesus, but Jews as well; given what we know of Pilate's temperament, such mocking would be entirely in character.

Following the script of the rulers and the soldiers, one of the men hanging next to Jesus both mocks and tempts. This dying man has enough energy to deride (Greek: *blasphēmeō*, whence "blaspheme") Jesus as well as to challenge his messianic credentials. Instead of saying only "save yourself," the man adds "and us" (**vs. 39**). This is the harder temptation for Jesus to refuse: he has come to "save the lost" (19.10).

Before Jesus can respond – and other than the disputed line about forgiveness, he has said nothing to his opponents and nothing to anyone save the daughters of Jerusalem – the other victim responds with a rebuke. He begins by asking, "do you not fear God," given that you too are about to die? (**vs. 40**). The time has come to stop reviling others and to begin repenting. Although Luke does not state that this second condemned man has repented, the implication is present in this initial reference to the fear of God. The man continues by affirming that he and the man who mocked them deserve their sentence, but that "this man," Jesus, has committed no evil deed (**vs. 41**). Thus, he joins the chorus of Pilate (three times) and Herod Antipas in proclaiming Jesus innocent. Ben notes again that this indicates that Luke believes some Jews thought Jesus innocent. The narrative is not a general polemic against the Jews of that day.

The "good thief," as he has come to be called, even though Luke does not explicitly name his "evil deed," serves to make the correct confessions. But we should ask, is crucifixion, is being tortured to death by being stripped naked and hung from a cross, to die finally and agonizingly of asphyxiation as air can no longer get into one's lungs, a death "justly deserved"? Not only does this scene inform us that justice can miscarry and that the state does put the innocent to death, it also raises the question of what constitutes a "just" punishment.

Having silenced his opponent, this unnamed criminal acknowledges Jesus' kinship, although without the title. He implores Jesus, by name, "remember me when you come into your kingdom" (**vs. 42**). This "kingdom" could be, in the man's imagination, a heavenly realm, or it could be the Jerusalem over which he expects the Messiah to reign. He does not ask explicitly for either forgiveness or for salvation, but for being remembered.

Jesus grants him more than he asks. "Amen," Jesus states (the NRSV offers "truly"), and he promises him a place in Paradise before the sun sets (**vs. 43**). Like Lazarus, another sufferer in a tortured body, he will find himself at rest. The man had spoken about a "kingdom," as had Jesus earlier; now the conversation turns to paradise, to a free garden. Jesus' comment is more than assurance to the man dying beside him; it is an assurance to his followers that he understands and embraces not only his destiny, but theirs as well. Thus, in his dying, he saves the lost.[14]

With the reference to paradise, another term for heaven, or a particular part of heaven, nature receives its cue. Darkness covers the land for three hours (**vs. 44**). Attempts to date a solar eclipse or explanations of a sandstorm mistake symbolism for history. As Jesus dies, so for his followers the world plunges into darkness. Jesus had stated about his death: "But this is your hour, and the power of darkness" (22.53). Ben notes that this may well be correct, but many famous events in history have been presaged or accompanied by portents in heaven or on earth. For example, he cites the story of Constantine, and his seeing a cross in the sky before his final victory. The Bible is replete with such tales, for example in connection with the Exodus. They need not all be literary symbols added to a story after the fact. The fact that something has symbolic significance does not mean it could not have happened. Many actual historical events do have such significance.

The symbolism continues in the note that the Temple curtain "was torn" in half. Although commonly argued, the point is not that now gentiles, once restricted from the Temple, now have access to the God of Israel; they had always had that access, and they had always been welcomed in this Temple. It rather serves other functions. First, it joins several other verses in foreshadowing the destruction of the Temple in 70. Second, at least for Mark and Matthew, who set the tearing after Jesus' death, it signals the mourning of the Father for the Son, since tearing a garment is a Jewish mourning ritual. By backdating the tearing, Luke has lost this symbolism. Third, the Temple veil depicted the universe, and the death of Jesus thus

---

14   Ben notes that the Greek of vs. 43 could be read to mean, "Amen I say to you today – you will be with me in Paradise." It depends on how one punctuates a sentence without original punctuation. If this rendering is correct, then Jesus is making a promise on the day he dies, and not suggesting he and the bandit will both be entering Paradise immediately upon death. Amy-Jill finds the standard scholarly punctuation to be correct; otherwise, the "today" has no force, since the day on which Jesus speaks is evident.

creates a tear in the universe, a time of cosmic change. Josephus, whose works might have been familiar to Luke, writes, "but before these doors there was a veil of equal largeness with the doors. It was a Babylonian curtain, embroidered with blue, and fine linen, and scarlet, and purple, and of a texture that was truly wonderful. Nor was this mixture of colors without its mystical interpretation, but was a kind of image of the universe..." (*War* 5.212, 214).

The cosmos opened and the darkness encircling, Jesus speaks his last words from the cross. Luke makes no mention of suffering or despair; rather, Jesus calmly commends his spirit to his Father (**vs. 46**). His comment evokes Psa 31.5: "Into your hand I commit my spirit; you have redeemed me, O Lord, faithful God." Luke does not state, "Jesus died." None of the Gospels does. By stating instead that Jesus "breathed his last," Luke suggests that Jesus was in full control of his body until he chose to stop breathing.

There is no crying from any disciples at the cross. There is only silence, broken by the voice of a centurion, whose presence had to this point gone unremarked. This Roman army officer, having seen what had taken place, including the three-hour period of darkness and the stoic death of this kingly figure, praises God (**vs. 47a**). The praise, unexpected on the lips of a pagan, may hint at his Jewish sensibilities. He will remind readers of the centurion who built the synagogue (7.1–10), and he anticipates the conversation of the God-fearing Cornelius (Acts 10). His verdict corresponds to those of Herod, Pilate, and the crucified man: Jesus was innocent or, more literally, he was "righteous" (Greek: *dikaios*), here in the sense of being in a right relationship both with the legal system (he committed no crime) and with God.

As Luke introduces the centurion abruptly, so now Luke abruptly mentions that there were "crowds" at the cross. The crowds may be that original "they" comprised of the chief priests, the leaders, and the people, but given the distinction Luke has just drawn between the leaders and the people (23.35), the people who had gathered "for the spectacle," the "thing to see" (Greek: *theōria*), are not likely the leaders. They had come not because they were disciples, and not because they wanted to "see justice done"; they came to watch the show. Public executions throughout history have functioned as forms of popular entertainment. Rome gathered crowds, and public support, through gladiatorial contests, often fights to the death and through the colorful killings of a variety of peoples deemed enemies of the state. Today, in parts of the world, beheadings are filmed and then distributed on the Internet. No wonder some returned home in mourning, "beating their breasts" (**vs. 48**). Symbolically, they bang on their hearts, and in this action, recall viscerally what life means, and how easily it can be snuffed out. Symbolically, the action reminds us of the tax collector in the Temple and so indicates both guilt and repentance. When "the state" kills someone, every citizen bears some responsibility.

The people who return to their homes are not the same as Jesus' acquaintances, whose presence had also gone unmentioned. It is not clear if these "acquaintances" (literally "all who knew him") are the disciples, since Luke does not use the term here. We see no reason why the disciples are not included among the group; the lack of technical terminology may indicate that they have not recently been acting as disciples should. The last appearance of the term "disciples" was in 22.45, the notice that Jesus found the disciples asleep on the Mount of Olives. Included among those who knew him are the Galilean women (**vs. 49**), Mary Magdalene, Joanna, and Susanna as well as many others (8.2–3). They have not deserted Jesus, but nor do they come close to the cross. They may have feared arrest, although Rome has shown no interest in arresting anyone other than Jesus. Positively, we can read their role as one of "watching"; while others turned out for the spectacle, the ones who knew Jesus came to bear witness. Negatively, we could see in this verse an allusion to Psa 38.11: "My friends and companions stand apart from my affliction, and my neighbors stand far off." Luke once again offers readers choices: what we see depends on our Christology as well as, here, on how we assess Luke's depiction of women. Ben notes, that in light of what follows in Luke 24, this is surely an example of the women bearing positive witness to the end of Jesus' life. They were last at the cross, first at the tomb, and first to see the angels at the tomb and then the risen Jesus. Amy-Jill also acknowledges, as does Luke, the women's fidelity to Jesus; she simply does not see them taking leadership roles in the narrative and so, likely, in Luke's vision of the assemblies held in Jesus' name.

A CLOSER LOOK: THE CRUCIFIXION OF JESUS

People in Roman antiquity often believed that how an individual faced death revealed character: a noble death demonstrated admirable conviction; a cowardly death suggested a craven personality. Crucifixion presented a particular problem: this form of execution, combining both pain and shame, was antithetical to the heroic or the admirable. Thus, the death of Jesus required explanation. More, it required apologetics, for as Paul correctly observed, a crucified Messiah was a stumbling block (*skandalon*, whence "scandal") to Jews and foolishness (*mōros*, whence "moron") to gentiles (1 Cor 1.23). Yet for many of Jesus' followers, his death atoned for the sins of the world, and this too required explanation.

The Passion Narrative was probably the first part of the Gospel story to reach a relatively fixed form. Teachings, accounts of miracles, and controversy stories could be depicted in various orders, but the Passion required a plot: betrayal, arrest, judgment, crucifixion. "Most impressively there is the highest degree of agreement between the Gospels at this point in the story … This part of the story is both too well known and too important for excessive literary license."[15] For Ben, this greater connection among the four canonical Gospels speaks to the historicity of the events recorded. Amy-Jill is less sanguine, given that the Synoptics derive much of their material from the same Marcan account; John may have been familiar with the Synoptic narrative, and multiple attestation among related sources is not necessarily the same thing as historical fact, even as countless studies of so-called eyewitness testimony demonstrate. Yet for us both, each event needs to be understood not only in terms of historical likelihood (where Ben is more likely to accept Luke's claims as factually "what happened" and where Amy-Jill remains doubtful), but in terms of theological message, where we two are in substantial agreement. The crucifixion of Jesus required explanation; it still does.

For Matthew (28.20) and Mark (10.45), the cross is Jesus' ransom for many.[16] Jesus pays the ransom, but to whom remains unclear. The Gospel writers may have understood Jesus as paying the ransom to God: humanity has emptied the heavenly treasures, and Jesus, by his supererogatory righteousness, refills the account. Or, they may have seen the ransom as paid to Satan, to whom humanity has been in bondage since Adam and Eve disobeyed the divine command. As Satan stated in the Temptation Narrative, "To you I will give their glory and all this authority; for it has been given over to me, and I give it to anyone I please" (4.6). For Paul (Rom 3.5, 24–25) and for the author of the Epistle to the Hebrews (e.g., Heb 9.26), Jesus' death is a sacrifice of atonement, modeled on the Levitical sacrificial system (see Exod 29–30, Lev 23, 25).

[15]   Johnson, *Gospel of Luke*, 334.
[16]   Eubank, *Wages of Cross-bearing and Debt of Sin*.

Soteriologies of Jesus as ransom or Jesus as sacrifice create the idea of "substitutionary atonement," that is, Jesus gave up his life on behalf of the world. The cross saves humanity from a sin too great to bear and/or from Satan's bondage.

Luke uses neither the language of ransom nor the language of sacrifice to explain Jesus' death. "Rather than expiatory or substitutionary sacrifice, the dominant way of speaking about soteriology in Luke-Acts is in terms of liberation."[17] Yet questions remain: liberation from what?

For Luke's Gospel, the question of soteriology and so the meaning of the cross remains open. From what does the Gospel save: death, sin, Satan, alienation from God, economic and political oppression? Should Jesus' death *in Luke's Gospel* be seen as a martyrdom, a sacrifice, a ransom? Is the cross meant to recall Isaiah's suffering servant (cf. Pss 22; 31; 69; Wisdom 2)? Is it a mechanism for salvation, a model of righteousness, or both? All of these things are possible, but in the Lukan account, Jesus' own word from the cross associates forgiveness with the dying Jesus, a message already highlighted earlier in the Gospel. And if persons can be forgiven for crucifying someone like Jesus, then God's grace must really be considerable, to say the least.

ENTOMBMENT

The Gospel's second Joseph appears in **vs. 50**: a "good and righteous man" as well as a member of the Sanhedrin. Given the Gospel's portrayal of the Council in the previous chapter, the presence of such a fellow among the members is unexpected. Luke notes, however, that Joseph did not agree with their actions against Jesus, an apparent contradiction to those earlier comments about how "all of them" questioned him (22.70) and how "all the number of them" brought Jesus to Pilate (23.1). That Joseph did not agree with the majority may have something to do with his hometown; he is *not* from Jerusalem but from the Judean town of Arimathea.

Joseph awaits the Kingdom of God, although Luke does not indicate whether Joseph was a disciple of Jesus. Luke also does not detail Joseph's economic status, but he would have had to have both a comfortable amount of funds as well as political clout, since he has no trouble gaining access

---

[17]   Timothy Reardon, "Recent Trajectories and Themes in Lukan Soteriology," *Currents in Biblical Research* 12.1 (2012): 77–95 (90). This, however, neglects Luke's use of the phrase "release from sins." See pp. 104, 668.

to Pilate and asking for Jesus' body (**vs. 52**). The request makes sense
from a Jewish perspective: being a righteous Jew, Joseph would have been
concerned about corpses being left on crosses on the Sabbath. His righteousness would be comparable to that of Tobit, also known for caring for
the bodies of strangers. From a Roman perspective, Pilate's agreeing to this
request is more problematic. Pilate might have wondered, as should we
readers, why Joseph only asks for the body of Jesus and not for the corpses
alongside his. If Pilate knew that Jesus had a popular following, he might
also have been concerned that his tomb would be a site for revolutionaries
to gather. Luke does not bother to depict Pilate's granting of permission.

Joseph himself takes the body down from the cross, wraps it in a fine
cloth, and deposits it in an unused rock-cut tomb (**vs. 53**). These actions
should have been taken by Jesus' brothers and, if not by them, by his
disciples. By noting that there had been no other corpses interred in the
tomb, Luke (and the other evangelists) avoid the possibility that a corpse
found in the tomb was that of Jesus. Commentators typically take the burial
in a "new" tomb as indicating the honoring of the corpse, although archae-
ologist Byron McCane argues that being placed in a new tomb is less than
ideal. He notes that Jesus is not buried in the family tomb and that no one
participated in rituals of mourning for him.[18] The corpse is not said to have
been anointed, and Luke lacks the account of the unnamed woman who
anointed him for his burial (Mark 14.8). Preferable to being cast in a lime
pit, the burial of Jesus suggests loss of family and lack of appropriate rituals.

Luke ends Joseph's role with the temporal notice that the time of interment was "the day of Preparation," that is, Friday, "and the sabbath was
beginning," that is, sundown on Friday evening (**vs. 54**). The Sabbath is not
only a day of rest, it is also a day of joy. Therefore, mourning rituals on the
Sabbath are discouraged. The point is not to force mourners into revelry; it
is to recognize the goodness of the divine and the sanctity of the Sabbath in
all circumstances.

The Sabbath provides the verbal link between Joseph, the stranger, and
the women who had accompanied Jesus from Galilee (**vs. 55**). Luke notes
how the women had followed Joseph and, as they did at the cross, served
as witnesses to the location of the tomb and the position of the corpse
(**vs. 55**). Thus, the women provide Luke eyewitness testimony that *Jesus'*

[18] For the popular version of this detailed thesis, see Byron R. McCane, 'The Scandal of
the Grave,' *Christian History* 59, *Christianity Today* (1998) at www.christianitytoday.com/
history/issues/issue-59/scandal-of-grave.html. See also his *Roll Back the Stone: Death
and Burial in the World of Jesus* (Harrisburg: Trinity Press International, 2003).

tomb was empty. There could be no mistake about the location of the tomb or the details of its contents.

Their preparation of spices follows Mark but not Matthew, who suggests only that the woman came to watch the tomb (**vs. 56a**). And as with Mark's narrative, the women here are too late. Bodies are to be treated with spices prior to the burial, not afterward. For Mark, the women who prepare spices and go the tomb on Sunday morning are, in Amy-Jill's view, failed disciples; they do what the woman who anointed Jesus in Mark 14.3–9 had already done: anointed him for his burial. Ben notes this is probably incorrect. Since mourning went on for up to a week, the body would need to be reanointed and more spices applied, especially with a body that had suffered such severe trauma as crucifixion. Amy-Jill sees no reason for a body to be "reanointed," especially after it is entombed.

Matthew, recognizing this possible glitch, simply notes that the women came to "see" the tomb (Matt 28.1). That the women prepare spices (in Matthew and Luke), let alone that in John's account, Joseph of Arimathea and Nicodemus entomb Jesus with one hundred pounds of myrrh (John 19.39), indicates that no one involved expected Jesus to rise from the dead. The myrrh and spices function to keep the corpse from putrefying. At this point in the Gospel, no one is expecting a resurrection, despite Jesus' teachings to the contrary. Jesus taught, "The Son of Man must undergo great suffering, and be rejected by the elders, chief priests, and scribes, and be killed, and on the third day be raised" (9.22). Since the first part of the prediction has come to pass, readers can be confident in the second.

Luke concludes this chapter on a note of piety: the women, faithful Jews, put the spices down and rest, because it was the Sabbath (**vs. 56b**). There is no violation of Torah among Jesus' followers. They have prepared what they need, but they do not go to the tomb to anoint the body with the spices, because the anointing would constitute work.

BRIDGING THE HORIZONS

On History and Theology

All four Gospels present the Passion Narrative with different elements and emphases. Such distinctions are to be expected: even eyewitness testimony to events differs, as we see today in watching coverage of the same event by members of opposing political parties. For some readers, everything the

Gospels report is "historically true"; for others, much of the story is based on templates provided by the Scriptures of Israel combined with theological reflection on the meaning of Jesus' death.

We cannot definitively get behind the evangelists to the actual events. About half a century ago, New Testament scholars began to develop so-called "criteria of authenticity" that could help us penetrate back behind the texts of the Gospels, back behind the oral tradition, and to Jesus himself. The impulse was a good one. The criterion of multiple attestation suggested that a datum found in two or more independent sources has a greater chance at historical authenticity. However, today we are not certain about independence of sources, or indeed about source-critical conclusions. We do not know if there was a "Q," that hypothetical document seen as comprised of material common to Matthew and Luke but not Mark. Luke may have had access to both Matthew and Mark, and if so, there is no need to posit a Q. We do not know if John wrote independently of the Synoptics. The criterion of dissimilarity or embarrassment suggested that material running counter to the interests of the evangelists or of the early Church is more likely to be historical. Here, too, the idea was better than the application: we cannot clearly determine that the material is antithetical; had it been that problematic, the evangelists were not constrained to mention it.

At the start of this historical-critical enterprise, scholars with more conservative Christian views found the criteria unhelpful as well as potentially blasphemous, especially when the yield from the application limited what could be considered historical. For example, in his *Who Killed Jesus?* biblical scholar John Dominic Crossan concluded that about 80 percent of the Passion Narrative is "prophecy historicized" rather than "history remembered."[19] Today, more conservative Christians are applying these criteria along with other methodological approaches, such as memory theory and sociology of religion. They have not found anything falsifiable. For Ben, this nonfalsifiability indicates the historical truths of the Gospel record; for Amy-Jill, this nonfalsifiability shows that the approach does not work. After fifty years of application, the criteria have failed to yield any consensus.

Ben finds the historical methodology to be of *some* usefulness, as it can provide *some* confirmation of what is historically likely and what may not be. But methodology is not a neutral net; it catches what it is intended to catch, and often the results say more about the limits of the method than

---

19   John Dominic Crossan, *Who Killed Jesus? Exposing the Roots of Anti-Semitism in the Gospel Story of the Death of Jesus* (New York: HarperSanFrancisco, 1995), 6.

about the limited historical substance in the data. Ben agrees with Amy-Jill, however, that what we have are portraits in the Gospels, even in the Passion Narratives, not snapshots. This means that the authors had some flexibility to edit, arrange, and amplify their material to highlight and bring out its theological, ethical, and even historical significance. They should not be faulted for following ancient canons in regard to history and biography rather than the more strict (and more secular) modern ones.

Ben and Amy-Jill do not agree on the details of what happened. We do, however, substantially agree on the import of the story. Faith is not something to be "proved"; if it were, then it would not be "faith." As we have seen several times in our study of Luke, texts can be interpreted in different and even mutually exclusive ways. In the end, the more important question is not, "Did it happen the way Luke describes?" but, "What are we to do with the story Luke tells us?"

On Capital Punishment

What happens to the bodies of the men crucified with Jesus goes unrecounted. They may have had friends and family who also mourned them, but for their wives and children, there would be no Easter Sunday. Jesus is restored to his friends; the corpses of these men, likely tossed into a lime pit, would decay, were they not eaten by dogs.

In Luke's Gospel, Jesus does not die alone. Luke's narrative reminds us that other people are put to death, across time and across the globe. We need to attend to them while they are alive rather than warehouse them in prisons; we need to attend to their bodies when they die. All people want to be remembered. If we take seriously Jesus' claim to have come for the "lost," then we might begin with our own prison system in the United States. What are we doing to acknowledge that the "evildoers" are also human beings and might also, as does the proverbial "good thief," have the correct Christology? Furthermore, it is passing strange that the very people who seem to most believe that human character can be changed and redeemed are often the very ones most vocal about the need for capital punishment. This was not Jesus' view.

More, what is our relation to be to the bad thief, the one who blasphemes Jesus even as he asked to be saved? He is the one found today who blasphemes the Church, since no one from his congregation comes to visit him, since no one at the local cathedral takes the time to visit. He also wants salvation, but those who claim to speak in the name of Jesus vote into office people who support his dehumanization. From Pilate to Judas, from the Sanhedrin members to the "bad thief," from the mocking soldiers of Herod Antipas to the mocking Roman soldiers at the cross, the Passion Narrative introduces a number of unsympathetic characters. Do we wish them to be tortured to death for their crimes? Do we wish them to suffer for eternity? Or, can we love our enemies and pray for those who persecute us?

Luke 24 Resurrection and Responses

THE WOMEN AT THE TOMB

¹ But on the first day of the week, at early dawn, they went to the tomb, taking the spices which they had prepared. ² And they found the stone rolled away from the tomb, ³ but when they went in they did not find the body. ⁴ While they were perplexed about this, behold, two men stood by them in dazzling apparel; ⁵ and as they were frightened and bowed their faces to the ground, the men said to them, "Why do you seek the living among the dead? ⁶ Remember how he told you, while he was still in Galilee, ⁷ that the Son of man must be delivered into the hands of sinful men, and be crucified, and on the third day rise." ⁸ And they remembered his words, ⁹ and returning from the tomb they told all this to the eleven and to all the rest. ¹⁰ Now it was Mary Magdalene and Joanna and Mary the mother of James and the other women with them who told this to the apostles; ¹¹ but these words seemed to them an idle tale, and they did not believe them.

THE ROAD TO EMMAUS

¹³ That very day two of them were going to a village named Emmaus, about seven miles from Jerusalem, ¹⁴ and talking with each other about all these things that had happened. ¹⁵ While they were talking and discussing together, Jesus himself drew near and went with them. ¹⁶ But their eyes were kept from recognizing him. ¹⁷ And he said to them, "What is this conversation which you are holding with each other as you walk?" And they stood still, looking sad. ¹⁸ Then one of them, named Cleopas, answered him, "Are you the only visitor to Jerusalem who does not know the things that have happened there in these days?" ¹⁹ And he said to them, "What things?" And they said to him, "Concerning Jesus of Nazareth, who was

a Prophet mighty in deed and word before God and all the people, [20] and how our chief priests and rulers delivered him up to be condemned to death, and crucified him. [21] But we had hoped that he was the one to redeem Israel. Yes, and besides all this, it is now the third day since this happened.

[22] Moreover, some women of our company amazed us. They were at the tomb early in the morning [23] and did not find his body; and they came back saying that they had even seen a vision of angels, who said that he was alive. [24] Some of those who were with us went to the tomb, and found it just as the women had said; but him they did not see."

[25] And he said to them, "O foolish men, and slow of heart to believe all that the prophets have spoken! [26] Was it not necessary that the Christ should suffer these things and enter into his glory?" [27] And beginning with Moses and all the prophets, he interpreted to them in all the scriptures the things concerning himself.

RECOGNITION

[28] So they drew near to the village to which they were going. He appeared to be going further, [29] but they constrained him, saying, "Stay with us, for it is toward evening and the day is now far spent." So he went in to stay with them. [30] When he was at table with them, he took the bread and blessed, and broke it, and gave it to them. [31] And their eyes were opened and they recognized him; and he vanished out of their sight. [32] They said to each other, "Did not our hearts burn within us while he talked to us on the road, while he opened to us the scriptures?"

[33] And they rose that same hour and returned to Jerusalem; and they found the eleven gathered together and those who were with them, [34] who said, "The Lord has risen indeed, and has appeared to Simon!" [35] Then they told what had happened on the road, and how he was known to them in the breaking of the bread.

THE FINAL RESURRECTION APPEARANCE

[36] As they were saying this, Jesus himself stood among them. [37] But they were startled and frightened, and supposed that they saw a spirit. [38] And he said to them, "Why are you troubled, and why do questionings rise in your hearts? [39] See my hands and my feet, that it is I myself; handle me, and see; for a spirit has not flesh and bones as you see that I have." [41] And while they still disbelieved for joy, and wondered, he said to them, "Have

you anything here to eat?" [42] They gave him a piece of broiled fish, [43] and he took it and ate before them.

[44] Then he said to them, "These are my words which I spoke to you, while I was still with you, that everything written about me in the law of Moses and the prophets and the psalms must be fulfilled." [45] Then he opened their minds to understand the scriptures, [46] and said to them, "Thus it is written, that the Christ should suffer and on the third day rise from the dead, [47] and that repentance and forgiveness of sins should be preached in his name to all nations, beginning from Jerusalem. [48] You are witnesses of these things. [49] And behold, I send the promise of my Father upon you; but stay in the city, until you are clothed with power from on high."

THE ASCENSION

[50] Then he led them out as far as Bethany, and lifting up his hands he blessed them. [51] While he blessed them, he parted from them, and was carried up into heaven. [52] And they returned to Jerusalem with great joy, [53] and were continually in the temple blessing God.

The Gospel ends where it started, in the area around Jerusalem and in the Temple. After the first twelve verses, Luke departs from the Marcan account and offers several unique scenes, including the male disciples' disbelief at the women's proclamation of Jesus' resurrection; the two followers who encounter Jesus on the road to Emmaus, who learn from him how to interpret Israel's Scriptures in the light of a suffering, dying, and rising Messiah, and who recognize him only in the breaking of bread; Jesus' appearance in Jerusalem in the context of a meal; and Jesus' ascension. Luke will offer an expanded version of this same material as a beginning for the Book of Acts, where the journey will move outward from Jerusalem, and where scenes of recognition, bread, and teaching will repeat.

The accounts are distinct from those in the other Gospels as well as in Paul's letters. Mark (16.8) presents three named women who flee from the tomb and say nothing to anyone (materials following 16.8 are additions to the earliest versions of the Gospel), and John (chapter 20) offers Peter and the Beloved Disciple at the tomb, but only Mary Magdalene has an initial resurrection appearance; it is Thomas, in John's Gospel (20.24–27), who does not believe that Jesus had appeared to his fellow *male* disciples. Matthew (28.2–7, 9–10) depicts an appearance first of an angel and then of Jesus himself to "Mary Magdalene and the other Mary." Paul mentions resurrection appearances to numerous disciples, but he offers no reference either to the women or to an empty tomb (1 Cor 15.3–7). Finally, Luke describes how "Mary Magdalene, Joanna, Mary the mother of James, and the other women" (24.10) see two men, dressed in dazzling clothes, who proclaim the resurrection (24.4); later we learn the men were angels (24.23). Luke's account itself is insecure, as the manuscript tradition offers numerous variant readings for vss. 5, 12, 36, 40, 51, and 52.

History has its limits on the questions of what happened, to whom, how, where, and when. One reading of the empty tomb story argues that the entire episode of the women at the tomb, in any version, is an early Church construction designed to secure the teaching that Jesus was raised "in the flesh," that the risen body was also the body that died, although it was also a body transformed. The empty tomb story was needed, so this version goes, in order to counter readings of Paul's comment, "Flesh and blood cannot inherit the kingdom of God," and so the belief that Jesus was basically a "friendly ghost" rather than a resurrected body. Thus, the scene, in their view, is a later, apologetic construction. Supporting this argument is the absence of both the women and the empty tomb from Paul's early catechism: "that he was buried, and that he was raised on the third day in accordance with the scriptures, and that he appeared to Cephas, then to the twelve" (1 Cor 15.4–5). Neither Ben nor Amy-Jill finds this argument convincing. Given Paul limiting of women's roles in Corinth (e.g., 14.33b–36, which both Amy-Jill and Ben see as an original part of the letter and not an interpolation by a later scribe), his promoting women's role here would be counterproductive.

A second approach is the popular claim, arguing the opposite point: no one would invent such a story, for no one would believe the witness of women. The Gospel of John belies that point: no one questions Mary Magdalene's pronouncement. Claims that "the Jews" did not accept women as witnesses are, simply, incorrect. The reason the men in Luke do not believe the women is not because they are Jews following a particular legal system: the reason they did not believe is because the idea of a dead person rising was incredible, unbelievable, to them.

A third approach concludes that Mary Magdalene, formerly demon-possessed (8.1) and therefore prone to visionary experiences, saw Jesus in the same way that others through the centuries and across cultures experience the return of the dead, and her story developed in the various ways now present in the Gospels. A variant of this approach has the empty tomb story developed in circles of women as a countertext to the male-dominated Pauline account.

Ben finds the general account, including the empty tomb and the physical resurrection of Jesus, historical. He does not find the discrepancies in the accounts damaging to the claim of the resurrection; to the contrary, the discrepancies, in his view, reinforce the factuality of the basic proclamation. Since Jesus appeared to various people in various places, sometimes to individuals, sometimes to groups, in both Judaea and Galilee over a period of forty days or so, it is not surprising that there are diverse accounts. After the crucifixion, the disciples, by all accounts, were not looking for a risen Jesus. More important is the telling information that Jesus did not just appear to his own disciples – according to our earliest witness (the list in 1 Cor 15), Jesus appeared to his brother James, who, according to John 7.5, had not believed in him or been his disciple. Further, the last person to whom Jesus appeared, "out of due season" (1 Cor 15.8), was Paul, an ardent opponent of the Jesus movement. For Ben, these data scotch the idea that the resurrection accounts were cooked up by male or female disciples after the crucifixion to salvage something of their faith. It is only the appearance of the resurrected Christ that, in Ben's view, explains the continuation of Jesus' followers and the growth of the Church.

Amy-Jill finds credible the claim that Mary Magdalene, with or without other women with her, believed she saw Jesus. Similarly, she finds credible claims by Paul, Peter, and others that they saw Jesus. People have visions, and sometimes these visions change their lives. This phenomenon is cross-cultural, as we see with the extraordinary experiences claimed by Mohammed, Joseph Smith, the Emperor Constantine and numerous Roman Catholic saints, and the mystics and visionaries of today, across the globe. Whether their experience could be caught, by a third person, on a camera is another question.

Finally, Amy-Jill finds the various debates about the historicity of Jesus' resurrection to be, generally, unhelpful. Trying to talk someone into or out of belief is like trying to talk someone into or out of love. What the heart says is not logical, but for the person in whose chest that heart is beating, what the heart says is indelibly true. Since *Luke* believed the historical truth of the Resurrection Narrative, she is interested in why Luke tells the story in such a distinct manner; she is also interested in how people who proclaim Jesus' resurrection manifest this proclamation in their lives. In the following discussion, our concern is less the "did it or did it not happen" question, since history cannot provide a resolution. Our principle concern for this commentary is on what meaning the story might have for Luke's readers, then and now.

THE WOMEN AT THE TOMB

The opening verse of Chapter 24 is a continuation of the last verse of the previous chapter. Luke 23 ends with the notice that the women who had journeyed with Jesus from Galilee to "the Skull" (23.33) saw Joseph of Arimathea entomb Jesus, and then they went to prepare the spices and ointments; their plan, although Luke does not specify it, is to anoint the corpse. Since the entombment took place late on Friday afternoon, the women wait until Sunday morning to attend to the corpse. As Jews, they faithfully follow the Torah's commandment to rest on the Sabbath (23.55–56; see Exod 20.10; Deut 5.12–15). On the first day of the week, Sunday, at "deep dawn" (Greek: *orthrou batheōs*), they come to the tomb (**vs. 1**).

The first day of the week will become the first day of their new understanding of Jesus. Therefore, translating "the first day of the week" as "day one" (Greek: *mia tōn sabbatōn*) is apt. Immediately, they discover the stone rolled away from the tomb (**vs. 2**). Luke does not record their thoughts, but people in Luke's audience, unfamiliar with the story and disbelieving Jesus' several predictions of his resurrection, may have drawn the logical conclusion that the tomb was robbed. Nails used to fix victims to crosses were considered to have magical powers; tombs, as opposed to common graves, sometimes contained valuable objects. The position of the stone is not necessarily good news.

Next, they discover that the body "of the Lord Jesus" is not in the tomb (**vs. 3**). Luke includes the messianic title to indicate that although the women at this point believe that Jesus is dead, he is still "the Lord." The readers therefore know more than the women do. Luke also plays on the idea of finding: the women found (Greek: *euriskō*, whence "eureka") the stone rolled away, but the body of Jesus is not found (*euriskō*). Finding Jesus recurs as a motif throughout the Gospel: the shepherds are told they will "find" the baby in the manger (2.12); Mary and Joseph are unable to find Jesus and therefore search until they find him in the Temple (2.45–46); Jesus' opponents seek to find an opportunity to trap him (6.7); healed individuals are found in good health (7.10), a sheep owner finds his lost sheep (15.5–6), a woman finds her lost coin (15.8–9), a father finds two lost sons (15.24), and so on. Of the numerous uses of this common term, two have particular resonances in this scene at the tomb. Jesus had stated, "search and you will find … for everyone who searches finds" (11.9–10), and he had asked, "When the Son of Man comes, will he find faith on earth?" (18.8). The women seek the body of Jesus, and they will find him as their resurrected Lord. The women then will have the faith and the courage (contrast Mark 16.8) needed to carry out their apostolic mission of proclaiming his resurrection.

As they were puzzling over the empty tomb, two "men" appeared in dazzling apparel (**vs. 4**). When the male disciples later recount what the women saw, they describe these "men" as "a vision of angels" (24.23), which is what their apparel signifies. The Greek underlying the NRSV's "dazzling" is *astraptō* (from *astra*, meaning "star," whence "astronomy"), which really means "flashy." At this appearance, the women behave as people traditionally do in the presence of a supernatural being: they become fearful, and they prostrate themselves (**vs. 5a**). The gesture may indicate profound reverence, fear, supplication, or a combination. The "men" then ask them – whether sympathetically or as berating – why they seek the living among the dead. Then they proclaim that Jesus has been raised (**vs. 6**; the NRSV's "risen" mistakes the Greek passive; Jesus does not raise himself; he *is raised*). As far as the men are concerned, the women should have known that Jesus would be raised; therefore, their bringing of spices to anoint the corpse is not an indication of reverence, but evidence of their lack of belief.

The men next remind the women, and so Luke's readers, of Jesus' teachings in Galilee (**vs. 6**).[1] The geographical reference serves several functions. First, it highlights both the consistency of Jesus' teaching, from the earliest stages of the mission until this moment at the tomb. Second, it reinforces the presence of the women throughout the mission; they had been with him from the start. Third, it replaces the Galilean postresurrection mission hinted at in Mark 14.28 and made explicit in the resurrected Jesus' commandment to the women in Matt 28.10: "Do not be afraid; go and tell my brothers to go to Galilee; there they will see me." The men's comment in vs. 6 is Luke's last reference to Galilee, but it assures readers that Galilee has heard the message.

As the women listen, the men remind them of the details: the Son of Man must be handed over to sinners, he must be crucified, he will rise on the third day (**vs. 7**). Jesus did not, however, predict his death by crucifixion (9.22; 18.32–33). The first reference to crucifixion per se as the means of his death is in 23.21, where the chief priest, leaders, and the Jerusalem crowds demand that Jesus be crucified. Part of the shock of what happened

---

[1]   See Witherington, *Women in the Ministry of Jesus*, 9–10 and the notes there.

to Jesus is the unforetold *manner* of his death.[2] Nor had Jesus mentioned the role of the "sinners" in his death. The men do not identify these "sinners," although the narrative suggests that they are, primarily, the Jewish people of Jerusalem, the ones who pressed for crucifixion.

These men at the tomb have created what today is called "social memory." When the followers of Jesus now remember his passion, they will remember it not simply according to his own prediction of death, but in relation both to sinners and to the cross. The men are thus the first developers of a post-resurrection Christology. *What* we remember depends not only on what we have witnessed, but on how we over time tell the story, and how others tell the same story with different words and different emphases.

The women "remember his words" (**vs. 8**), although their memory is now shaped by the retelling of events just spoken to them. It is not that they had forgotten what Jesus said. To remember is not only to call to mind something gone from consciousness, it is to reinforce what had been heard but not believed. Had Jesus been explicit on the details of his death, the crucifixion would have been less of a shock. Had Jesus been explicit on the details of his resurrection, or spent more time preparing his followers for the resurrection moment, the women would not have prepared the spices. Thus, despite the men's chiding, the women have done nothing wrong. If they are to be berated for having forgotten the passion predictions, then the male disciples bear the greater burden, for not only have they also failed to remember, they will also disbelieve the women. Finally, this verb "remembered" signals once more that these women were indeed disciples of Jesus, not just the traveling hospitality and patronage brigade. They were more than groupies. They heard and remembered his teaching, and so they count among those "eyewitnesses and servants" (1.2) whose testimony underlies the Gospel.

Returning from the tomb, the women report what they have seen and heard "to the eleven and to all the rest" (**vs. 9**). The men they met at the tomb did not commission them, as did the young man in Mark 16.7, the angels in Matt 28.7 and Jesus himself in Matt 28.10. The women in Luke receive no instruction about proclaiming the resurrection, as does Mary Magdalene, from Jesus himself, in John 20.17. Nor do they receive an appearance from the risen Jesus, as do the women in Matthew and John.

Amy-Jill finds this lack of both direct commission and of resurrection appearance to be consistent with Luke's overall treatment of women: their

---

[2]   See Culpepper, "The Gospel of Luke," 469.

task is to support the male disciples, but they are not the primary bearers of the teaching or preaching roles. Therefore, although they may have the same qualifications as other disciples to fill the sandals that Judas vacated – they may have "accompanied us during all the time that the Lord Jesus went in and out among us, beginning from the baptism of John until the day when he was taken up from us – one of these must become a witness with us to his resurrection" (Acts 1.21–22) – they are not in the running.

Ben offers an alternative view of the Lukan portrait. He refers first to the male disciples' rejection of the women's witness, although these women have reported faithfully what they found at the tomb and what the angels said. To disbelieve the women is tantamount to disbelieving Jesus, because he himself had predicted his death and his resurrection. While Luke does not depict Jesus as commissioning the women, nevertheless, the women remain the first to bear witness to the resurrection. Indeed, the note of reversal – the women go to the tomb, see "men" and hear the Easter message; the men go and see and hear nothing extraordinary – shows Luke's true evaluation of these women. They are more perceptive disciples than the Eleven!

Luke now identifies the women who saw the empty tomb. Mary Magdalene and Joanna appeared in 8.2–3, where Luke presents them both as individuals whom Jesus healed and as patrons of the movement. Luke includes the otherwise unknown "Mary of James" (whether James's mother, wife, sister, or daughter) and a catch-all "the other women." Thus, at least five women made the report to the apostles (**vs. 10**). The indication of the number of women shows that the report is not the invention of an individual. This multiple witnessing is consistent across the canonical Gospels, although the names of the women differ. Even John's account, which explicitly features only Mary Magdalene, offers a hint of other women: "So she [Mary Magdalene] ran and went to Simon Peter and the other disciple, the one whom Jesus loved, and said to them, 'They have taken the Lord out of the tomb, and *we* do not know where they have laid him'" (John 20.2). That "we" can suggest the presence of other women.

These women did not simply mention what they had seen and heard once. The NRSV's "told this" is a bland rendition of the Greek imperfect verb, which is better translated "kept on saying." This persistence is needed, for the apostles, in receiving this message, are not at their apostolic best.

Assessing the women to be speaking nonsense, they did not believe them (**vs. 11**). The Greek for "believe" is *pisteuō*, so the verse can be read as saying "they did not have faith in them" or "they did not trust them" (i.e., the women). Commentators race at this point to explain the lack of belief in terms of Jewish practice. The argument goes as follows: since Jews did not recognize the testimony of women as legally valid, they claim, the apostles' reaction is appropriately both Jewish and, for these Christian commentators, wrong. Carolyn Osiek calls this approach "an unexamined scholarly commonplace in Christian exegesis."[3]

When any Jewish text is cited, the most popular citation is to Josephus, *Ant.* 4.219. The text reads, "… let not the testimony of women be admitted, on account of the levity and boldness of their sex, nor let servants be admitted to give testimony on account of the ignobility of their soul; since it is probable that they may not speak truth, either out of hope of gain, or fear of punishment." The statement is the personal view of one man, who is himself attempting to fit in with the conservative elite of Roman society; it is not general Jewish practice. No Torah statement and no rabbinic majority policy forbids women witnesses or the witnesses of servants in general.

The reason the apostles do not believe the women is *not* because the witnesses are women. The reason the apostles do not believe the women is *not* because they are living with a repressive misogynist Jewish mindset. The reason the apostles do not believe is because the message is, simply, unbelievable. Nor, to quote from the two men at the tomb, did the apostles "remember" Jesus' predictions. In the apostles' view, no one rises after dying on a cross and being entombed for three days. Had women's witness been the problem, then Peter and the beloved disciple would never have listened to Mary Magdalene (so John 20), and no woman prophet would have been accepted (from Anna in 2.36 to the daughters of Phillip in Acts 21.9).

Not believing is not the same thing as not questioning. One can have doubts, but still act to confirm or deny them. Although not believing the women – or perhaps even questioning his lack of belief, for the women to this point had not demonstrated anything other than faithful service – Peter runs to the tomb. He sees the grave clothes and then, marveling, he returns to where he had been staying (**vs. 12**). The NRSV again misleads with its reference to Peter's returning "home"; his "home" is in Galilee, and Jesus' followers are in Jerusalem. Luke makes no reference to his returning to speak to the other apostles and followers. The scene of Peter's going to the tomb repeats in John's Gospel, although there he is accompanied by the Beloved Disciple, and it is this unnamed disciple who sees and believes (John 20.8).

[3]   Carolyn Osiek, "The Women at the Tomb: What Are They Doing There?" in Levine with Blickenstaff (eds.), *A Feminist Companion to Matthew*, 204–20 (215).

Vs. 12 is a problem both textually and narratively. Codex D and some other Western manuscripts omit it, but a variety of early and good witnesses (p76, Aleph, A, B, K, L, W, X) include it.[4] Ben finds it unlikely that this verse was invented by later scribes since it puts Peter in a subordinate position to the women: the women see angels while Peter only sees clothes. He also regards the verse as a natural antecedent to vs. 24, the notice that some of the men also went to the tomb. Amy-Jill sees some merit in the argument that the verse is a secondary addition. It conforms Luke's Gospel to John's account, and it allows Peter to be a witness to the tomb. Had Peter seen the women's comments as nonsense, there is little reason for him to go to the tomb, unless we readers invent (as we in fact do in the previous paragraph) a motivation. She also sees vs. 12 less as a transition than as an interruption in the smooth flow of the narrative. The next account, the story of the two on the road to Emmaus, follows neatly from the report that the men doubted the women. The Emmaus story explains in part *why* they doubted: until they first relearn their own Scriptural tradition from the lenses of the resurrection and until they participate in the breaking of bread, they cannot fully remember Jesus or experience him as alive.

For Luke, the last appearance of the women as a distinct group appears here. Mary Magdalene does not appear in Acts; nor do Joanna, Susanna, or any of the others named in the Gospel's final chapter.[5] Acts 1.14 records that "women" – likely including these women – were present and praying in the upper room when the decision is made about Judas's replacement, and as they await the Holy Spirit.

THE ROAD TO EMMAUS

The heart of the Gospel's final chapter, vss. 13–35, is the uniquely Lukan story of the appearance of Jesus on the road to Emmaus to two otherwise unknown followers. The story is typically Lukan, including the journey motif, allusion to Israel's Scriptures, particularly the story of Abraham and Sarah at Mamre (Gen 18.1–15), and there are also evocations of a number of

---

[4]   The Western text of Acts has a bias against women playing prominent roles in the Jesus movement. See Witherington, "The Anti-Feminist Tendencies of the Western Text in Acts," 82–84.

[5]   Ben suggests that the mother of John Mark (Acts 12.12), whose name is Mary, may have been one of these women. Mary of Clopas is referenced at John 19.25. Even more speculative is the notion that the young man who fled naked in Mark 14.51–52 was John Mark (making a cameo appearance in his own Gospel, like the famous producer in a Hitchcock thriller), which might also suggest his mother's association with, or discipleship to, Jesus.

classical motifs. Questions of history cannot be resolved, so we focus on the literary and theological impact of the narrative.

The story begins as two "from them" (i.e., two out of the number of Jesus' followers designated as "the rest" in 24.9) were going to Emmaus, a village some sixty stadia or six to seven miles from Jerusalem on "the same day," that is, Sunday or "day one" (**vs. 13**). Josephus records a city called Emmaus some thirty stadia outside of Jerusalem (*War* 7.217; cf. 1 Macc 9.50), so perhaps Luke meant a sixty-stadia round trip from Jerusalem. The distance serves less to mark space than to indicate the time it took for the conversations to take place.

As the two are discussing what had transpired (**vs. 14**), that is, the events involving Jesus' death, suddenly "Jesus himself" (the Greek *autos*, "he," is emphatic) walks up to them (**vs. 15**). As far as the two disciples are concerned, the setting is simply the chance encounter on the road. The two may have thought that Jesus was another pilgrim leaving Jerusalem after the Passover celebration.

Using the passive voice, Luke states that "their eyes were held back" or even "seized" (**vs. 16**). The construction could be understood as a divine passive and so an indication that God had prevented them from recognizing Jesus. The expression could also reflect the more common experience of not believing what one sees. The two are convinced that Jesus is dead; therefore, the man walking next to them cannot be Jesus. These two explanations are not mutually exclusive. Luke has twice before noted the inability of the disciples to understand Jesus, and both in cases where his instruction was, simply, unbelievable to them. Following the first passion prediction, Luke records: "But they did not understand this saying; its meaning was concealed from them, so that they could not perceive it" (9.45a). The same thing occurs following the passion prediction in 18.33. Into this category of the unbelievable fits the women's proclamation of the empty tomb and the information they received from the two "men." As the disciples are unable to understand the predictions of Jesus' death and unable to believe the women's testimony, so they are unable to understand, to this point, that Jesus is walking alongside them.

The chapter begins with the two "men," at the empty tomb, chiding the women for not remembering Jesus' prediction of his resurrection. By including the motif of the travelers' eyes being held from seeing fully, Luke also reminds readers of the details of those earlier reports. The flashback functions to reframe readers' memories: when they read the Gospel again or hear it read to them and they come to the passion predictions, they will recall the story of the two on the road to Emmaus. The texts speak to each other, sharpen the memory about Jesus, and help assuage doubt as well as correct misunderstanding.

Along with connections to the other passion predictions and the psychological effect of not being able to believe what one sees, a third element is in play in this lack of recognition. In the Greek and Roman worlds, gods suddenly appear and disappear, often after brief conversations with humans.[6] Luke knows such scenes, as the Book of Acts demonstrates. During their mission to Lystra, Paul with Barnabas heals a paralyzed man. "When the crowds saw what Paul had done, they shouted in the Lycaonian language, 'The gods have come down to us in human form.' Barnabas they called Zeus, and Paul they called Hermes, because he was the chief speaker" (Acts 14.11–12). The story resonates with accounts of the appearance of Zeus and Hermes to Philemon and Baucis. Similar stories of gods, angels, saints, and other holy beings are told across the globe. Luke's early readers would have recognized the convention, and smiled: as readers, they are more informed than the two on the road, who will soon present themselves as the informed speakers.

The unrecognized Jesus, schmoozing, asks his new traveling companions about their conversation. The two men stop walking. This is not a topic for a casual chat with the stranger. Before beginning their answer, Luke mentions how they look (**vs. 17**). The adjective *skythrōpos* means "sad" or "angry"; Ben finds that the meaning of "sad" is assured, but Amy-Jill wonders about a hint of anger as well. The soon-to-be-heard comments can be heard as sarcastic, even irate. The two on the road are devastated by Jesus' death, and devastation, especially regarding an event that in their view should not have happened and could have been prevented, can lead to anger. "Sad," for Amy-Jill, does not capture the emotional turmoil these men are facing.

Luke now identifies one of the two as "Cleopas" (**vs. 18a**). The other traveler could be Cleopas's wife, son or daughter, slave or friend; the masculine plural form of the verbs would mask the presence of a woman. Eusebius reports that various Church fathers thought that Cleopas was Clopas (*Ecc.l Hist.* 3.32). His reasoning is not without support: the name "Clopas" appears in John 19.25, the notice that "standing near the cross of Jesus were

---

[6] Ovid reports that "Romulus was seen, standing in the middle of the road ... he gave the order and he vanished into the upper world from Julius' eyes" (*Fasti* 2.489; cf. Philostratus, *Life of Appollonius* 8.5; Livy, *Roman History* 1.16). See Georgia Petridou, *Divine Epiphany in Greek Literature and Culture* (Oxford: Oxford University Press, 2015).

his mother, and his mother's sister, Mary the wife of Clopas, and Mary Magdalene."

The connection between the two names, Cleopas and Clopas, cannot be secured. Cleopas is a shortened version of the Greek name Cleopatris; the feminine is the more famous name Cleopatra. The origin and even meaning of "Clopas" is unknown; it may have Aramaic roots. Nevertheless, that the names are not connected etymologically would not prevent Luke, who tends to drop Aramaic words, from turning the Semitic Clopas into the Greek Cleopas. One could extend Eusebius's comment and so see the second traveler as Mrs. Clopas. Yet Luke does tend to list husbands and wives together by name: Ananias and Sapphira (Acts 5.1–11), Priscilla and Aquilla (Acts 18), Festus and Druscilla (Acts 24.24), as well as the siblings Berenice and Herod Agrippa II (Acts 25). If the second traveler is Cle[o]pas' wife, she lets her husband do the talking (Amy-Jill is not surprised, given her sense of the limited leadership role for women in Luke's Gospel).

Speaking for himself and his companion, Cleopas asks whether this stranger from Jerusalem is the only person unaware of the local events (**vs. 18b**). What is major and meaningful to one person may be irrelevant or unknown to another, so the question reflects more what the two experienced than what "all of Jerusalem" knew. Even today, the execution of an individual will be known, and either mourned or celebrated, by the people invested in the case; the rest of the population will not know, and will not care. One might ask the family and friends of the two other men crucified alongside Jesus what they were thinking about events in Jerusalem. Cleopas cannot fathom how the traveler would not have known about what to him is earth-shattering.

Jesus responds, "What things?" (**vs. 19a**), which in Greek is a single word (*poia*). With Jesus' prompt, Luke utilizes another literary convention: the reader knows more than the characters in the story; indeed, the readers could answer Jesus' question. We readers understand that the questioner is Jesus; the two others on the road do not. More, we readers know that underneath the "sadness" or "anger" of the two on the road is comedy, in both senses of the term: the scene becomes amusing to readers who know the questioner's secret identity; and the scene has, as classical comedy does, a very happy ending. One could even see how this verse connects Cleopas with the stock comedic character of the *alazon*, the pompous fool who perceives himself to be more important and more informed than he actually is, and Jesus with the *eiron*, the powerful one who engages in self-deprecation.[7] Cleopas is not

---

7   Culpepper, "The Gospel of Luke," 477.

necessarily a bloviator, and the recitation he is about to give regarding Jesus is, although limited by his own partial insight, accurate. Yet in performance, a skilled narrator could easily depict him as this stock comedic figure. And while Jesus does not engage in self-deprecation, he does withhold his own identity and so both his knowledge and his power.

Cleopas begins by naming "Jesus of Nazareth" (or "Nazarene"; the manuscript evidence offers both titles), identifying him as a prophet powerful in both actions and words, and as present to both God and the people (**vs. 19b**). Each phrase opens up to multiple implications. By identifying Jesus as "of Nazareth" the two miss by silence the titles readers by now expect: "Lord" Jesus, or "Jesus the messiah." By this title, the travelers may be indicating that they have lost the belief that Jesus was more than an interesting teacher and a talented miracle worker. At the same time, the title recollects the two other times "Jesus of Nazareth" appears in the Gospel. The first is in 4.34, when the demons call out: "What have you to do with us, Jesus of Nazareth? Have you come to destroy us? I know who you are, the Holy One of God." The second is in 18.37, when the blind man on the road to Jericho asks about the commotion he hears, and the crowd tells him, "Jesus of Nazareth is passing by." The blind man then shouts: "Jesus, Son of David, have mercy on me" (18.38). By speaking of "Jesus of Nazareth," Cleopas evokes for the reader demonic destruction, the "Holy One of God" and "Son of David," and healing. It also evokes what can happen on the road.

Speaking of Jesus as a prophet mighty in word and deed, Cleopas uses the same terms Stephen will use to describe Moses (Acts 7.22), and so other intertextual allusions blossom. Moses too appears in disguise: Stephen notes that Moses, an Israelite, is raised by Pharaoh's daughter as an Egyptian (Acts 7.21). Reference to Moses the prophet also anticipates Acts 3.22, where Peter quotes Moses as saying, "The Lord your God will raise up for you from your own people a Prophet like me. You must listen to whatever he tells you." The citation is to Deut 18.15, 18; whereas in the context of Deuteronomy, the statement simply means that a prophet will stand up among the people, in light of the proclamation of Jesus' resurrection, the expression "raise up" (Greek: *anistēmi*) takes on heightened connotations. Jesus had prophesied that he would return, but his followers, although hailing him as a prophet, cannot yet see the fulfillment of his words. Further, Luke emphasized Jesus' ability to heal and to raise the dead, yet his followers cannot yet see the miraculous presence of the resurrected Jesus.

Cleopas continues by stating that "our" chief priests and leaders handed him over (cf. 9.22, 44; 18.32; 24.7) to be sentenced to death and that they crucified him (cf. 24.7; Acts 2.36; 4.10) (**vs. 20**). The Romans, unmentioned, are exculpated; so is the Jerusalem population in general. Responsibility for Jesus' death, in Cleopas's estimation, rests on the political infrastructure. The two travelers do not express personal responsibility for Jesus' death; they do not explain where they were as the events were unfolding. Luke will later extend the blame for the cross on the entire Jewish people. Peter announces in Acts 3.12–16, "You Israelites ... you handed over and rejected [Jesus] in the presence of Pilate, though he had decided to release him; you rejected the Holy and Righteous One and asked to have a murderer given to you, and you killed the Author of life." Rome, on the road to Emmaus and in Solomon's portico, is exculpated both implicitly for Luke 24 and explicitly for Acts 3. On the other hand, Cleopas could just be a Jew who holds his own leaders largely responsible for Jesus' demise.

Cleopas continues by changing the subject from what happened to Jesus to what happened to him and his companion: "we," he says, "had *hoped* that he was the one who was going to redeem Israel" (**vs. 21a**). This redemption or liberation is typically read as militaristic: Cleopas (and his fellow Jews) had hoped that Jesus would drive the Romans out of the country. This conclusion is only partially correct. Several biblical passages on redemption do concern politics: redemption from Babylonian exile (Isa 41.14; 43.14; 44.22–24) and deliverance from the persecutions of the Syrian-Greeks under Antiochus IV Epiphanes (1 Macc 4.11). In the Second Revolt against Rome, Bar Cochba minted coins in 132–135 with such inscriptions as "Year One of the Redemption of Israel" and "Year Two of the Freedom of Israel." Cleopas, perhaps knowing of the triumphal entry, perhaps knowing that Jesus advised his followers to obtain swords, might have been hoping for an end to Roman rule.

To limit messianic interests to politics would be to reify the messianic concept. Some Jews were looking for the end of Roman rule; others were looking for the return of the exiles to the homeland, a general resurrection of the dead along with final judgment, and end to war, etc. There is no reason to limit Cleopas's comment to the material and political. In her Magnificat, Mary praises the "Lord God of Israel" who "has looked favorably on his people and redeemed them" (1.68, cf. Anna's concerns in 2.38). The Greek term underlying "redeem" is *lutroō*, which means "ransom." The verb appears only here in Luke's Gospel, and only in two other places in the New Testament (the other uses are nouns). In neither of the others does it carry political import. In Titus 2.14, Jesus redeems "from all iniquity"; in 1 Pet 1.18, Jesus ransoms "from futile ways." Because the end-times

have not come, manifested either in the practical sense of national liberation or the eschatological sense of the final judgment by the Son of Man,
the Church will need to find new answers to the question: "liberation
from what?"

Cleopas then notes that three days have passed (**vs. 21b**). He and his companion have given up whatever expectations they had, and they are leaving
town. In the same breath, however, he reveals a hint of hope, or as Paul
would put it, hope against hope (Rom 4.18, also in the context of belief in
the impossible). He recounts how some women among the followers (i.e.,
the male followers and perhaps some other women with them) astounded
them that very morning (**vs. 22**). "Some women" can sound dismissive: the
names are gone. Once names are erased, the witness is more easily erased.
What created the astonishment Cleopas leaves unmentioned: that they did
not find the body? that they "had a vision of angels" (**vs. 23a**)? That the
angels said Jesus was alive? (**vs. 23b**). All of these?

His summary both downgrades and upgrades what the women reported.
On the one hand, the women do not speak of having had a "vision"; their
experience, as Luke records, is neither dream nor hallucination but a real
encounter. On the other hand, Luke's description speaks of two "men,"
but Cleopas speaks of a "vision of angels." Did the women realize that the
men were angels and so promoted this version of the story to the fellow
disciples? Or is Cleopas, in his recounting, dismissing the women's testimony as some kind of emotive, subjective experience (cf. v. 11). The irony
of his making this comment to the disguised Jesus is delicious. Cleopas will
not later announce to Jesus' other followers that what he experienced on the
road to Emmaus was simply an emotive, subjective experience.

Yet Cleopas also mentions that "some of those with us" went to the tomb
and that they confirmed the women's testimony about the lack of a body
(**vs. 24**). The men would have to see Jesus to believe he was alive; they would
not take the women's word.[8] The women, conversely, believed the men at
the tomb. Cleopas's comment also hints at another possible upgrade by
announcing that "some of those who were with us" went to the tomb: the
disputed vs. 12 only mentions Peter's visit. Finally, the logic of their report
completely breaks down: finding the empty tomb should not have sent
these two travelers away from Jerusalem. Was no one concerned about
what happened to the body? The disciples have not only failed to remember
Jesus' words, they have failed to attend to his corpse. What was the women's

---

[8]   See Witherington, *Women in the Earliest Churches*, 132–33.

report: about men, or about angels? Which men went to the tomb? How did they react?

Jesus has had enough. His words, like those of the men to the women at the tomb, take the form of a rebuke: you are foolish; you are dull of heart; you do not believe what the prophets have declared (**vs. 25**). Included among these "prophets" is Jesus himself, whom Cleopas had described as a prophet (v. 19) and who had predicted his death and resurrection. While Jesus' reference to "all the prophets" as culminating in him is necessarily a retrospective reading, his point that there had been multiple predictions of what would happen to him, from commentary in Israel's Scripture to his own teachings, logically fits into Luke's narrative.

Jesus then begins to unpack the text; that the two on the road as well as the disciples had been prevented from understanding either the prophecies or their fulfillment in him offers the opportunity for this Bible study. Luke's concern with this Bible study is twofold: first, believing in Jesus is connected with the proper understanding of the Scriptures; second, all of Israel's Scripture is to be seen as a prophetic corpus with messianic significance.[9]

The Bible study begins with Jesus upbraiding Cleopas and his companion by asking the rhetorical question: "Was it not necessary that the messiah suffer these things and then enter his glory?" (**vs. 26**). The verb of necessity (Greek: *dei*) refers to God's divine plan of salvation. Apart from Jesus' instruction, the disciples would have likely responded: "We did not know this." The idea of an incarnate suffering or dying Messiah is not found outside of Christian literature; Jesus, however, had mentioned his suffering in 17.25. The disciples would also have been confused by the reference to "glory." In relation to the plot of the Gospel, the term has to involve something other than Jesus entering into heaven or serving as judge at the final judgment. For Luke, this "glory" more likely refers to the resurrected state Jesus entered after death, a state the two travelers do not yet recognize but Luke's readers do. This change in the body was previewed in the Transfiguration (9.32) and it will be more evident as the Gospel draws to its end.

The Bible study proper then begins as Jesus draws upon the Torah ("Moses") and the prophetic corpus as well as the Psalms (cf. v. 44) to demonstrate his fulfillment of the divine plan (**vs. 27**). Although Jesus mentioned no texts explicitly here, Luke has already listed a number of fulfillment citations (e.g., 20.17 cites Psa 118.22; 20.42–43 quotes Psa 110.1; 22.37 cites

---

9   Johnson, *Gospel of Luke*, 395.

Isa 53.12; 23.34b–35 suggests Psa 22.7,18). None of these texts serves, in its own literary context, as a messianic prediction. The predictive aspects are seen as such only in retrospect. Read through Christian eyes, the entire Old Testament reflects Jesus' presence; read through non-Christian eyes, it does not. On this matter, the Pontifical Biblical Commission's 2002 document, "The Jewish People and Their Sacred Scriptures in the Christian Bible," states: "Although the Christian reader is aware that the internal dynamism of the Old Testament finds its goal in Jesus, this is a retrospective perception whose point of departure is not in the text as such, but in the events of the New Testament proclaimed by the apostolic preaching. It cannot be said, therefore, that Jews do not see what has been proclaimed in the text, but that the Christian, in the light of Christ and in the Spirit, discovers in the text an additional meaning that was hidden there."[10]

RECOGNITION

The impression left by **vs. 28** is that this Bible study went on while Jesus and the two men walked to Emmaus. That is, it lasted for hours. As they approach the village, Jesus seems to indicate he is going farther, but the two prevail upon him to stay with them in the village as evening was beginning (**vs. 29**). The two travelers thus model hospitality. They may also have wanted the study to continue; as they will state later, they were moved by the stranger's teachings.

What occurs next is what rhetorical handbooks and Greek drama call a recognition scene (*anagnorisis* –see Aristotle, *Poetics* 1452a,1454b–55a). The identity of the stranger in disguise must be revealed. Luke's original readers, familiar with the convention and anticipating it from the earlier reference to the unrecognized visitor, have been waiting for this moment. That it would come is not in doubt; Luke's artistry appears in the description of how the unknown is made known.

Luke allows the actions to carry the story along, as Aristotle recommended: there are no further words from Jesus in this vital scene. The three recline at table and Jesus breaks bread and distributes it; although the two travelers are technically the hosts, as they extended the invitation, Jesus takes that role. And only then, in the blessing, breaking, and distributing of the bread, do Cleopas and his companion realize that the one walking

---

[10]   www.vatican.va/roman_curia/congregations/cfaith/pcb_documents/rc_con_cfaith_doc_20020212_popolo-ebraico_en.html (6).

with them and instructing them is Jesus himself (**vs. 30**). The scene evokes the Last Supper (22.19), where Jesus "took a loaf of bread, and when he had given thanks, he broke it and gave it to" the apostles. At that earlier meal, Jesus then said, "This is my body." At this meal, the two followers are able, finally, to see the body as that of Jesus. They recognize him, and so the inability to recognize mentioned in vs. 16 is rectified (**vs. 31a**). For his followers then and subsequently, his presence will be recognized, and remembered, in the breaking of bread.

Immediately, without speaking a word or tasting the bread, Jesus disappears from their sight (**vs. 31b**), as gods in disguise and angels are wont to do (e.g., 2 Macc 3.34). The body the two recognize is a transformed body; the "glory" is present in its disappearance.

Now the two understand. *Now* they can refashion their memory and fill in the details. *Now* they realize why their hearts were burning during the extensive Bible study (**vs. 32**).[11] "The connection between the two phases of the Emmaus story is strengthened by reuse of the word 'open' [Greek: *dianoigo*]. Before their eyes 'were opened' Jesus was 'opening' the Scriptures to them."[12] Rather than spending the night in Emmaus, they get up at once and return to Jerusalem to report what they have seen and learned. The day has ended, but the next phase in their journey is just beginning.

When they arrive in Jerusalem, they find assembled "the Eleven and those with them" (the NRSV's "companions" is generous; **vs. 33**). Luke does not mention the women explicitly, but there is no reason to discount them. The two travelers report what the Jerusalem contingent already knows. The Eleven and the others report that "the Lord" has risen. This is the first use of the messianic title since its emphatic repetition in 22.61, "The Lord turned and looked at Peter. Then Peter remembered the word of the Lord, who he had said to him: 'Before the cock crows today, you will deny me three times.'" Now we learn that the risen Jesus, "the Lord," had appeared to Simon, that is, to Peter (**vs. 34**). Without making the point explicit, Luke demonstrates that Peter has been reconciled to Jesus. However, Luke withholds any description of this appearance to Peter. We could conclude that Luke did not have the details; alternatively, the absence of the details both keeps the focus on the community as a whole and allows readers to

---

[11]   Ben remarks that this text is the origin of John Wesley's much later language about a heart strangely warmed, when he had his Aldersgate experience.

[12]   Tannehill, *Luke*, 358.

draw the connection between what Jesus said at the Last Supper and what will happen at future meals. Less generously, we could also see Luke slipping in a reference to the appearance to Peter in order to make this apostle the first person to see the resurrected Jesus.

The scene concludes with the travelers' recounting of their experiences both on the road and at table (**vs. 35**). Their focus, which comes at the end, is in the meal setting. Jesus will continue to be known, and remembered, at table. The two travelers become the first witnesses to the experience of seeing Jesus even as they become the ones to connect biblical prophecy with resurrection fulfillment. Luke is telling a story in which failure is followed by fulfillment, remorse by resurrection appearances, and absence followed by presence.[13]

THE FINAL RESURRECTION APPEARANCE

As with the account of the travelers on the road to Emmaus, so with the account of Jesus' departure from his friends, Luke sets a similar scene: Jesus appears to his disciples while they are having a discussion about him, the disciples do not quite recognize him, Jesus rebukes them for doubting, food is shared, and they respond in wonder and joy. A Scripture lesson is found in both stories as well, though here it is delayed until the commissioning.[14] Luke thus indicates by the repetition that seeing Jesus is not enough; one must also understand God's divine plan as outlined in Scripture insofar as it involves Jesus' life, death, and resurrection.

There is still something missing. The disciples have seen the risen Jesus, but they still have not yet received the Holy Spirit. Luke 24 ends by pointing forward to the Book of Acts, where Jesus is mostly absent and the Spirit takes his place among his followers.

The anticipation of Acts begins when the conversation about Jesus is interrupted by an appearance of Jesus himself (**vs. 36**). As he does in John 20.19, he offers the traditional greeting, "Peace be to you" (the Hebrew would be *shalom aleichem*). The reaction of the assembly is not joy but terror (**vs. 37**). Their reaction is not "this is Jesus" but "this is a spirit" (Greek: *pneuma*). Despite Jesus' unnarrated appearance to Peter and his breaking bread with the two in Emmaus, his followers are unprepared. One can never be prepared for a christophany.

---

[13] Suggested by Bock, *Luke 9.51–24.53*, 1923.
[14] Craddock, *Luke*, 289.

Whatever they thought of the details of his appearance, their reaction is not to be seen as a failure. They may be expecting him to bring about that final judgment now, and no one's salvation is secure. They may be fearful that he will remind them of their failures, particularly during his Passion. The return of Jesus, whether at the end of Luke 24 or at the end of the age, is not necessarily only a time of great joy, even for his followers. It can also be a time of judgment.

Jesus then asks them, chidingly and rhetorically, why they are afraid; more, he asks them why they doubt (**vs. 38**). The question is posed not only to the Jerusalem followers but also to all of Luke's readers. The followers were not, at least as far as the Gospels are concerned, without doubts. Matt 28.17 states that the Eleven saw the resurrected Jesus and even worshiped him, "but some doubted"; "Doubting Thomas" has become a proverbial image, though the Greek of John 20:25 has Thomas announcing, "Unless I see the mark of the nails in his hands, and put my finger in the mark of the nails and my hand in his side, I will not believe." Thus, his more accurate designation is "unbelieving Thomas." To doubt, especially to doubt something that comes by revelation rather than by logic, is not a sign of bad faith; it is a sign of human nature. Even saints have doubts. The famous Mother Teresa of Calcutta (Saint Teresa of the Roman Catholic Church) faced doubts daily; these did not stop her from living the Gospel as she understood it.[15]

We mention this concern for doubt especially with regard to readers who may feel that they are "bad Christians" because they doubt. We mention it in particular for those who conclude that the reason their prayer is not answered – prayers for healing, for economic security, for love – is because their faith is insufficient. The people who encountered Jesus that night in Jerusalem were not excommunicated because of their doubts. John Calvin wrote: "Surely, while we teach that faith ought to be certain and assured, we cannot imagine any certainty that is not tinged with doubt, or any assurance that is not assailed by some anxiety" (*Institutes* 3.2.17). He was right. To persevere despite the doubt is the best that many can do.

Encouraging his disciples as well as providing an instruction in Christology, Jesus invites them to examine his hands and feet, to touch him, and thus to feel his corporeality (**vs. 39**). He even holds out his hands and feet to them (**vs. 40**). He has bones and flesh; his body is not that of a ghost,

[15]   Mother Teresa, *Come Be My Light. The Private Writings of the Saint of Calcutta*, ed. Brian Kolodiejchuk (New York: Doubleday/Random House, 2007).

but it is not a normal human body either. He is something new. The body that died on the cross and the body that rested in the tomb is the body that stands before them now. One cannot blame the disciples for their fear and confusion. Luke does not, by the way, report that any of the disciples actually accepted the invitation; no curious hands touch Jesus' wounds.

The doubting continues, although now the followers are doubting due to joy and amazement (**vs. 41a**). In a startling non sequitur, as if everything were as it had been, Jesus then asks if they have anything to eat (**vs. 41**). Given the images of food, feeding, and table that permeate the Gospel, the request is more than just a wish for a late-night snack. Nor does Jesus state that he is hungry. The food he requires is not for his own sustenance, but for the disciples' instruction. Ghosts do not eat. Neither do angels (cf. Tob 12.19; Philo, *On Abr.* 118). Resurrected bodies do. His request sets up a foretaste of the messianic banquet even as his eating will confirm that he has a resurrected body.

The followers provide him a piece of broiled fish (**vs. 42**), which he eats while they watch (**vs. 43**).[16] The scene resembles John 21, and one could wonder if in an earlier version, the story were set in Galilee (where broiled fish is more likely to be on the menu). Luke is not interested in these details. Luke is interested in assuring readers that Jesus exists in a real body, and that resurrected bodies, like their mortal counterparts, will eat together.

The subject turns from Jesus' body back to the Scriptures. As he did with the two on the road to Emmaus, so now he does with the Eleven and the others. He begins with the focus on memory, although that term is not used. He reminds them of what he said "while I was still with you," i.e., in his mortal body (**vs. 44a**). Luke is ensuring a consistency from what Jesus said, back to the Scriptures of Israel and forward to the life of the Church. Reasserting that everything that the Torah and prophets, and now also Psalms, spoke about him must be fulfilled (**vs. 44b**), Jesus insinuates that the primary purpose of the Scriptures of Israel is to point to him. At the same time, he assures that these Scriptures are themselves of ongoing value to the Church. The sense of eschatological moment is also present in this fulfillment theme. The age of fulfillment is, for Jesus' followers, also the age of understanding more profoundly what the Scriptures say and mean, especially about the Son of Man.

---

[16] Augustine, unable to resist finding something symbolic in the piece of fish, says, "Grilled fish means martyrdom, faith proved by fire." *Sermon 229j.3*, in A. Just (ed.), *Ancient Christian Commentary on the NT Vol. III, Luke* (Downer's Grove, IL: Intervarsity Press, 2003), 386.

Then, Jesus opens their minds so they could understand the Scriptures
(**vs. 45**), in particular so they could understand that the Messiah would
suffer and then rise from the dead on the third day (**vs. 46**). This is the third
time Luke hammers this creedal point. Judith Lieu correctly notes, "the
term *messiah* is not used technically for this hoped-for figure and nowhere
are his *sufferings* or *rising* foretold."[17] The confession of a crucified and risen
Messiah, not evident in the Scriptures except when they are read through
the eyes of those who already recognize Jesus as Lord, would remain both
a scandal and an indication of foolishness, as Paul stated (1 Cor 1.23). This
concern for revelation is also why contemporary evangelists, who insist on
"proving" that Jesus is Lord on the basis of Old Testament texts, get little
traction from Jews conversants with their own tradition, for whom the
same texts have different meanings. For the Jew who does accept the fulfillment claims, Luke indicates that this acceptance is a matter of revelation,
not logic.

The subject turns from *how* one is to understand Jesus to *what* that understanding means. Jesus teaches his followers that there is a direct connection
from the suffering, dying, and rising of the Messiah to repentance and
forgiveness of sins (**vs. 47a**). The exact mechanism that determines the
connection goes unexpressed. Luke does not state, as do Matthew (20.45)
and Mark (10.45; cf. 1 Tim 2.6), that Jesus dies "as a ransom." Luke does not,
as does John, reconfigure the Paschal sacrifice as a sin offering and so present Jesus as the "lamb of God who takes away the sin of the world" (John
1.29). John the Baptizer had already preached repentance and forgiveness of
sins, so the change in Luke's narrative is not in the action but in the mechanism. Something about Jesus' life and death creates a new opportunity for
repenting and forgiving. Ben notes that Acts 2.38 and elsewhere use the
phrase "release from sins," which suggests being freed from bondage. The
particulars of that "something" will be worked out by theologians over
the next two millennia.

Jesus now moves from *how* and *what* to *where*: the proclamation, starting
in Jerusalem, will go to all the nations (**vs. 47b**). The verse anticipates the
Acts of the Apostles. By emphasizing the role of Israel's Scriptures and of
Jerusalem, Luke anchors this new proclamation in Jewish history and geography, and this anchor could be taken as a very positive move. Conversely,
one could claim that Luke colonizes both text and land: Jewish history
and Jewish geography, in Luke's hands, become not only connected to but

---

[17]   Lieu, *Gospel According to Luke*, 207; emphasis in the original.

fulfilled in and by the Christ: their only legitimate heirs are those who follow Jesus. Whether Jews and Christians today can share this history and this attachment for Jerusalem and Israel depends on the people involved in the conversation.

Finally, the *who*: it will be the Eleven, and those unnamed others, who will serve to give testimony to Jesus (**vs. 48**). This frightened and doubting bunch of disciples will be Jesus' witnesses. The term in Greek for "witness" is *martys*, whence "martyr." In retrospect, readers realize that not only will these followers and others take the message of the crucified and risen Messiah to all nations, some will die for this witness. Some are dying for this witness today.

To comfort and guide them, Jesus enigmatically states that he is "sending upon you what my Father promised" (**vs. 49a**; cf. Acts 1.4, which uses the same expression), that is, being "clothed with power from on high." The disciples, were they inclined to question Jesus, might have asked, "what promise?" Luke's readers, already having received some instruction, will know the reference is to the Holy Spirit. By leaving the reference unspecified, Luke encourages readers to continue. At the same time, Luke sets up a promise-to-fulfillment model for the Gospel. Just as Jesus fulfills what was said about him by Moses and the Prophets and the Psalms, so the Book of Acts will fulfill what is promised in the Gospel. The role of the Spirit throughout the Gospel, but especially in the infancy materials, provides a lovely segue to the second volume: just as the Spirit is present at the conceptions of Jesus and John, so it will be present at the birth of the Church. The apostles and their companions, who are to be the witnesses to the nations, need all the power they can get. Their task, at present, is to wait in Jerusalem until this next phase of the mission begins.

THE ASCENSION

As if anticipating their movement out of Jerusalem, Jesus leads his followers to Bethany (**vs. 50a**). The setting may be connected to the Mount of Olives, as the only other reference to Bethany in the Gospel is 19.29: "When he had come near Bethphage and Bethany, at the place called the Mount of Olives." However, geography of the land of Israel is not Luke's strong suit. Acts 1.9, in Luke's second description of this event, notes that after watching Jesus depart, (only) the Eleven, the "men of Galilee" (Acts 1.1) "returned to Jerusalem from the mount called Olivet, which is near Jerusalem, a Sabbath's day's journey away."

Jesus lifts his hands to bless the assembled (**vs. 50b**), and we might recall his inviting them to touch those very hands that he had displayed to them. Luke is not depicting Jesus as a priest: fathers could lift their hands to bless their children; Moses, who is not a priest, lifts his hands to bless Israel. As he is blessing his followers, he is carried into heaven (**vs. 51b**). The ascension functions to bring closure to Jesus' earthly, embodied work. When he appears again in Acts 9.3–4 (cf. 22.6–10; 26.13–18) in commissioning Paul, he does not appear in the body.

It is at this juncture, and only at this juncture in Luke (cf. Matt 28.17) that the disciples are said to worship Jesus (**vs. 52b**). He has made the transition from mortal body to resurrected body, and from earth to heaven; his followers make the transition from disciples to devotees. If Jesus is to be worshiped, then Jesus must be divine.

Having turned from sadness to joy, from not recognizing to full recognition, from fearful to empowered, the Eleven return to Jerusalem (**vs. 52**). Luke concludes with the notice that they stayed continually in the Temple, where they were praising God (**vs. 53**). The Gospel ends where it began, in the Temple. There are no references to high priests or scribes; as with the start of Luke's narrative, everything is in the Temple as it should be. And yet we readers anticipate something more will happen, as it happened to Zechariah. The joy and praising and blessing that punctuated the beginning of the story in 2.10,20, 28,37 also punctuate its ending. And there is more joy awaiting the reader, for Power is coming from on high.

BRIDGING THE HORIZONS

1. Jewish-Christian Dialogue

In the late 1970s, my wife and I (Ben) were living in Durham, England, and I was preaching on the local Methodist circuit. Easter Sunday rolled around and I was scheduled to preach at a tiny chapel in an outlying village, just on the edge of Durham. I got off the bus and was trundling up the hill to the little chapel when a man in his overcoat came barreling down the hill to meet me. He was nervous and jittery. He looked at me and said, "Are you Reverend Witherington?" and I replied, "yes." Then he said, "I must ask you something." I told him to go ahead. Mustering up his courage, he said, "You do believe in the resurrection, don't you?" And when I told him I certainly did, I could see the relief written all over his face. He replied, "Excellent. I am ever so relieved, because the chap we had last Easter didn't and preached some nonsense about the return of spring and the cycle of the seasons."

I could see why he was worried. It's bad enough jumbling up eggs with Easter, but when you jumble up the return of the flowers with the rising of Jesus, that's going too far. Jesus' resurrection was not something that happened every spring by natural processes; it was something that happened once in a lifetime, indeed, once in all of human history.

The resurrection of Jesus is, according to Paul, "the first fruits," an inaugural eschatological event. And Paul believes as well that Christ's history is the believer's destiny, for "we shall all change … and be made like him." The Pharisees, whom we have seen in this commentary so often debated or dialogued with Jesus, also believed in a future resurrection, indeed believed in it far more than in the notion of a crucified messiah (if any of them expected that at all). And so perhaps here is a place for Jews and Christians today, the spiritual descendants of the Pharisees and of Jesus' first disciples, to begin a conversation on a subject concerning which their ancestors had strong beliefs.

Years ago, when I was attending the University of North Carolina–Chapel Hill, my Bible professor, Dr. Bernard Boyd, had a conversation with a local rabbi. The two had been talking about Isa 53, and Dr. Boyd had gingerly asked whom the rabbi thought that text was about. The rabbi smiled at Dr. Boyd and with a twinkle in his eyes said, "If when messiah comes, he has the face of Jesus, we will accept it. After all, he was a Jew." Indeed, he was, and Luke would not have us forget it.

2. On What We See, and When

In academic year 2004–2005, my (Amy-Jill's) student, the poet Lisa Dordal, wrote a paper that won Vanderbilt Divinity School's Luke-Acts Prize. That work, "On the Way to Emmaus: Deception as a Vehicle for Illumination," recounted her experience in teaching an Introduction to New Testament class at another campus. During the semester, these undergraduates made numerous derogatory remarks about gay men and lesbians, which she gently corrected. Only at the end of the semester, when the grades were in, did she tell them that she herself is a lesbian. Had she come out at the beginning of the semester, she might have lost the job. Nor would she have been able to gain the students' respect. Her silence allowed the students, when their eyes were finally opened, to realize not only the truth about their teacher, but the truth about their own homophobia. What would we say if we knew the stranger who had come near was Jesus?

In the fall of 2009, Lisa published a poem about this experience in the *Journal of Feminist Studies in Religion*. It includes the following lines:

It's easy to see Jesus.
We can't *not* see him, with his thick carpenter arms,
hair the color of Galilee night, eyes vexed with knowing.

Jesus himself came near.
But you, *you*, we do not see:
the woman, the wife, the one with Cleopas.
You, the stranger, we do not see, still.

I know something of what it's like not to be seen;
what it's like to be smoothed over by Discourse;
flattened into something tasteless and sterile.
To have the bumpy parts gone, your own rich texture of being
dulled into round slivers of yearning –
a dark, holy heaviness lost.

I know something of what it's like to be draped and cloaked
by someone else's idea of who you should be:
the year I taught New Testament –
Paul, the Gospels, Revelation –
and everyone thought I was straight....

I know something of what it's like but, still,
my eyes faltered and all I saw was two men walking,
one of whom, true stranger in the text, was you.[18]

3. On Respect

Ben takes the Gospel narratives as true both historically and theologically. For me (Amy-Jill), the claims that Jesus returned from the dead and that he ascended into heaven find no home either in my heart or my head. This distinction between Ben's stance and mine should not turn into a debate, where I say something like, "so, Jesus went up – has he gotten past Jupiter yet?" and Ben responds, "You completely miss the point." As we have noted throughout, and as Luke emphasizes, faith in Jesus comes from the outside, from revelation. And as we have stated, faith is not like Sudoku, where it follows logically; faith is like love.

[18]   Lisa Dordal, "On the Way to Emmaus," *JFSR* 25.2 (2009): 88.

Rather than engage in a debate over Jesus' resurrection, I'd (Amy-Jill) prefer to talk about its implications. If we begin with the premise both that Jesus is the incarnation of the divine and that he returned from the dead in a real body, then we must conclude that bodies are important. The story could have been told differently: Jesus was a divine presence inhabiting a human body temporarily; Jesus came back as a disembodied spirit; etc. No, the message is that bodies are important. We already should have realized that point from Gen 1.26, which states that all bodies are in the image and likeness of God.

Once we conclude that bodies are important, then the mandate from that conclusion is that we need to care for bodies. That means concern for clean water, for health care, for food and shelter. To insist on a literal resurrection but to have no concern for bodies seems to me a strange way of proclaiming Jesus as risen. Further, to insist on resurrection and not to realize that this is but a part of the new creation the Scriptures say is coming, and so ignore the call to do ecotheology, and care not merely about bodies, but about the earth, about our environment that we are supposed to tend, is to fail to see the implication of a faith in resurrection. That sometimes philosophical musician Sting once sang words to the effect of: "what good would a resurrection body be in an old, worn out, polluted earth?"[19] Exactly. All God's creation is to be not only respected, but cared for, as a harbinger of good things yet to come.

4. A Concluding Word and Wish

We have attempted, in this commentary, to tease your minds into active thought. We have written as colleagues and friends who not infrequently disagree, without becoming disagreeable, but also find many things to agree on. If there is truth in the saying that we should "speak the truth in love," or at least speak what we think is the truth about Jesus and the Gospels in love, we have done so. We hope and trust you have or will read this commentary with that in mind. We all have more things to learn from Luke's rich Gospel, and we all may be wrong about some of things we think we know. We see in part, but a good dialogue can help us see more clearly. We believe we have both learned a good deal in the process of writing this commentary. May it be for a blessing to all of you, as the process of writing has been for us.

---

[19]   See "All This Time" in *Lyrics by Sting* (New York: Dial Press, 2007). He is reflecting on the "meek shall inherit the earth."

Select Bibliography

(This is a selective bibliography indicating sources we found especially useful in preparing this commentary.)

Aichele, George and Richard Walsh, "Metamorphosis, Transfiguration, and the Body," *Biblical Interpretation* 19.3 (2011): 253–75.

Alexander, Loveday, *The Preface to Luke's Gospel*. Cambridge: Cambridge University Press, 1993.

Allison, Dale C. Jr., *The Historical Christ and the Theological Jesus*. Grand Rapids: Eerdmans, 2009.

  Jesus of Nazareth: Millenarian Prophet. Minneapolis: Augsburg Fortress, 1998.

  "Rejecting Violent Judgment: Luke 9:52–56 and Its Relatives," *Journal of Biblical Literature* 121.2 (2002): 459–78.

Ancient Christian Commentary on the NT. Vol. III, *Luke*. A. Just ed. Downers Grove: InterVarsity Press, 2003.

Anderson, Gary, *Sin: A History*. New Haven: Yale University Press, 2010.

Baergen, Rene, "Servant, Manager or Slave? Reading the Parable of the Rich Man and His Steward (Luke 16. 1–8a) Through the Lens of Ancient Slavery," *Studies in Religion/Sciences Religieuses* 35 (2006): 25–38.

Bagnall, Roger S., "Jesus Reads a Book," *Journal of Theological Studies* 51.2 (2000): 577–88.

Bailey, Kenneth E., *Finding the Lost: Cultural Keys to Luke 15*. Concordia Scholarship Today; St. Louis: Concordia Publishing, 1992.

  Poet and Peasant/Through Peasant Eyes: A Literary-Cultural Approach to the Parables in Luke. Grand Rapids: Eerdmans, 1983.

Bar-Ilan, Meir, "Literacy Among the Jews in Antiquity," *Hebrew Studies* 44 (2003): 217–22.

Barclay, William, *The Gospel of Luke. The New Daily Study Bible*. Louisville: Westminster/John Knox, 2001 [original publication 1953].

Barr, James, "*Abba* Isn't Daddy," *Journal of Theological Studies* 39 (1988): 28–47.

Barth, Karl, *The Doctrine of God. Vol. 2 Part 2 of Church Dogmatics*. Trans. G. W. Bromiley et al. Edinburgh: T&T Clark, 1957.

Bauckham, Richard, *The Fate of the Dead*. Leiden: Brill, 1998.

Baur, F. C., *Kritische Untersuchungen über die kanonischen Evangelien, ihr Verhältniß zu einander, ihren Charakter und Ursprung*. Tübingen: Fues, 1847.

Baynes, Leslie, *The Heavenly Book Motif in Judeo-Christian Apocalypses*, Supplements to the *Journal for the Study of Judaism* 152; Leiden and Boston: Brill, 2012.

Billings, Bradley S., "The Disputed Words in the Lukan Institution Narrative (Luke 22.19b–20): A Sociological Answer to a Textual Problem," *Journal of Biblical Literature* 125.3 (2006): 507–26.

Binder, Donald, "The Synagogue and the Gentiles," pp. 109–25 in David C. Sim and James S. McLaren (eds.), *Attitudes to Gentiles in Ancient Judaism and Early Christianity*, Library of New Testament Studies; London: Bloomsbury, 2013.

Blinzler, J., "The Jewish Punishment of Stoning in the New Testament Period," pp. 147–61 in E. Bammel (ed.), *The Trial of Jesus*. London: SCM Press, 1970.

Blomberg, Craig L., *Preaching the Parables: From Responsible Interpretation to Powerful Proclamation*. Grand Rapids: Baker Academic, 2004.

Bock, Darrell L., *Luke 1:1–9:50*. Baker Exegetical Commentary on the New Testament; Grand Rapids: Baker Academic, 1994.

Luke 9:51–24:53. Baker Exegetical Commentary on the New Testament; Grand Rapids: Baker Academic, 1996.

"The Parable of the Rich Man and Lazarus and the Ethics of Jesus," *Southwestern Journal of Theology* 40.1 (1997): 63–72.

Bonhoeffer, Dietrich, "Predigt am Sonntag Judika über Judas" [Sermon on Judas. March 14, 1937], pp. 406–13 in *Gesammelte Schriften*. Vol. 4, ed. Eberhard Bethge. Munich: Chr. Kaiser, 1965.

Bovon, François, *A Commentary on the Gospel of Luke 1:1–9:50*. Hermeneia; Minneapolis: Fortress Press, 2002.

Bradshaw, Paul, *Early Christian Worship: A Basic Introduction to Ideas and Practice*, 2d ed. Collegeville: Liturgical Press, 2010.

Braun, Adam F., "Reframing the Parable of the Pounds in Lukan Narrative and Economic Context: Luke 19:11–28," *Currents in Theology and Mission* 39.6 (2012): 442–8.

Brooten, Bernadette J., "Female Leadership in the Ancient Synagogue," pp. 215–23 in Lee I. Levine and Zeʿev Weiss (eds.), *From Dura to Sepphoris: Studies in Jewish Art and Society in Late Antiquity.* Portsmouth: Journal of Roman Archaeology, 2000.

  Women Leaders in the Ancient Synagogue: Inscriptional Evidence and Background Issues. BJS 36; Chico: Scholars Press, 1982.

Brown, Raymond E., *The Birth of the Messiah: A Commentary on the Infancy Narratives in the Gospels of Matthew and Luke,* new updated ed. ABRL; Garden City: Doubleday, 1993.

Bryan, C. *Render to Caesar: Jesus, the Early Church and the Roman Superpower.* Oxford: Oxford University Press, 2005.

Buttrick, David, *Speaking Parables: A Homiletic Guide.* Louisville: Westminster John Knox, 2000.

Buxbaum, Yitzhak, *The Life and Teachings of Hillel.* Lanham: Rowman and Littlefield, 1994.

Cadbury, H. J., *Style and Literary Method of Luke,* Part I. Cambridge: Harvard University Press, 1920.

Callon, Callie, "Adulescentes and Meretrices: The Correlation Between Squandered Patrimony and Prostitutes in the Parable of the Prodigal Son," *Catholic Biblical Quarterly* 75.2 (2013): 259–78.

Campolo, Tony, cited in "Campolo to Baptists: 'Rise Up, You Suckers, and Do the Work of Jesus,'" Baptist News Global/ABP News (January 31, 2008), https://baptistnews.com/article/campolo-to-baptists-rise-up-you-suckers-and-do-the-work-of-jesus/#.WYCoFhg7n_Q.

Carman, Jon, "The Falling Star and the Rising Son: Luke 10:17–24 and Second Temple 'Satan' Traditions," *Stone-Campbell Journal* 17.2 (2014): 221–31.

Carroll, John T., *Luke: A Commentary.* New Testament Library; Louisville: Westminster John Knox, 2012.

Carter, Warren, "Getting Martha Out of the Kitchen: Luke 10:38–42 Again," *CBQ* 58.2 (1996): 264–80; reprinted pp. 214–31 in Amy-Jill Levine with Marianne Blickenstaff (eds.), *A Feminist Companion to the Gospel of Luke,* FCNTECW 3; Sheffield: Sheffield University Press/ New York: Continuum, 2002.

Chance, James Bradley, *Jerusalem, the Temple, and the New Age in Luke-Acts.* Macon: Mercer University Press, 1988.

Chapman, Cynthia R., *The House of the Mother: The Social Roles of Maternal Kin in Biblical Hebrew Narrative and Poetry*. ABRL; New Haven and London: Yale University Press, 2016.

Chapman, David W., *Ancient Jewish and Christian Perceptions of Crucifixion*, WUNT 2.244. Tübingen: Mohr Siebeck, 2008.

Chesterton, G. K., *The Quotable Chesterton*, eds. G. J. Marlin et al., San Francisco: Ignatius Press, 1986.

Chung, Paul S., *Hermeneutical Theology and the Imperative of Public Ethics: Confessing Christ in Post-Colonial World Christianity*. Missional Church, Public Theology, World Christianity 2; Eugene: Pickwick, 2013.

Clark, Melinda, "Magdalene and Thistle Farms Offer Prostitutes a Chance for Regrowth," impact April 26, 2011, updated December 23, 2012; *Huffington Post*, www.huffingtonpost.com/2011/04/26/ magdalene-and-thistle-farms_n_854130.html.

Clarke, H., *The Gospel of Matthew and Its Readers*. Bloomington: Indiana University Press, 2003.

Clarke, Sathianathan, "Global Cultural Traffic, Christian Mission, and Biblical Interpretation: Rereading Luke 10:1–12 Through the Eyes of an Indian Mission Recipient," *Ex Auditu* 23 (2007): 162–78.

Cohick, Lynn, *Women in the World of the Earliest Christians: Illuminating Ancient Ways of Life*. Grand Rapids: Baker Academic, 2009.

Conzelmann, Hans, *The Theology of Saint Luke*. London: Faber and Faber, 1960.

Corbin-Reuschling, Wyndy, "Zacchaeus's Conversion: To Be or Not to Be a Tax Collector (Luke 19:1–10)," *Ex Auditu* 25 (2009): 67–88.

Cosgrove, Charles H., "A Woman's Unbound Hair in the Greco-Roman World, with Special Reference to the Story of the 'Sinful Woman' in Luke 7:36–50," *JBL* 124.4 (2005): 675–92.

Craddock, Fred B., *Luke*. Louisville: Westminster/John Knox, 1990.

Crossan, John Dominic, *The Greatest Prayer: Rediscovering the Revolutionary Message of the Lord's Prayer*. New York: HarperOne, 2010.

The Historical Jesus. San Francisco: HarperSanFrancisco, 1991.

Croy, Clayton N., "Mantic Mary? The Virgin Mother as Prophet in Luke 1.26–56 and the Early Church," *Journal for the Study of the New Testament* 34.3 (2012): 354–76.

Culpepper, Alan, "The Gospel of Luke," pp. 3–490 in Leander E. Keck (ed.), *The New Interpreter's Bible*. Vol. 9, *Luke-John* (Nashville: Abingdon, 1995); excerpted in R. Alan Culpepper, "Nazareth: Final Thought,"

friarmusings; posted January 29, 2016, https://friarmusings.wordpress
.com/2016/01/29/nazareth-final-thought/.

Culy, M. M. and M. Parsons, *Luke. A Handbook on the Greek Text.*
Waco: Baylor University Press, 2010.

Curkpatrick, Stephen, "Dissonance in Luke 18:1–8," *Journal of Biblical
Literature* 121.1 (2002): 107–21.

D'Angelo, Mary Rose, *"Abba and Father: Imperial Theology in the Contexts
of Jesus and the Gospels,"* pp. 65–78 in Amy-Jill Levine, Dale C. Allison,
Jr., and John Dominic Crossan (eds.), *The Historical Jesus in Context.*
Princeton: Princeton University Press, 2006.

Danker, Frederick W., *Benefactor: Epigraphic Study of a Graeco-Roman and
New Testament Semantic Field.* St. Louis: Clayton, 1982.

Jesus and the New Age: A Commentary on St. Luke's Gospel. Philadelphia:
Fortress Press, 1988.

De Boer, Esther, "The Lukan Mary Magdalene and the Other Women
Following Jesus," pp. 140–60 in Amy-Jill Levine with Marianne
Blickenstaff (eds.), *A Feminist Companion To Luke*, FCNTECW 3;
Sheffield: Sheffield University Press/New York: Continuum, 2002.

Derrett, J. D. M., " 'Eating Up the Houses of the Widows': Jesus' comment
on Lawyers?" pp. 18–27 in Idem, *Studies in the New Testament.* Vol. 1.
Leiden: Brill, 1977.

Law in the New Testament. London: Darton: Longman and Todd, 1970.

"The Parable of the Unjust Judge," pp. 32–47 in Idem., *Studies in the New
Testament.* Vol. 1. Leiden: Brill, 1977.

Destro, Adriana and Mauro Pesce, "Fathers and Householders in the
Jesus Movement: The Perspective of the Gospel of Luke," *Biblical
Interpretation* 11.2 (2003): 211–38.

Dickerson, Febbie C., "The Parable of the Widow and Judge (Luke 18:2–
5): Talking Back to African American Stereotypes," Ph.D. Dissertation.
Nashville: Vanderbilt University, 2017.

Dillon, Richard J., "The Benedictus in Micro- and Macrocontext," *Catholic
Biblical Quarterly* 68.3 (2006): 457–80.

Dinkler, Michal Beth, "The Thoughts of Many Hearts Shall Be Revealed:
Listening in on Lukan Interior Monologues," *Journal of Biblical
Literature* 134.2 (2015): 373–99.

Dodd, C. H., *The Interpretation of the Fourth Gospel.* Cambridge: Cambridge
University Press, 1953.

The Parables of the Kingdom. New York: Charles Scribner's Sons, 1961.

Doran, Robert, "The Pharisee and the Tax Collector: An Agonistic Story," *Catholic Biblical Quarterly* 69.2 (2007): 259–70.

Dowling, Elizabeth V., "Hearing the Voice of Earth in the Lukan Parable of the Pounds," *Colloquium* 48.1 (May 2016): 35–46.

Downing, F. Gerald, "The Ambiguity of 'The Pharisee and the Toll-collector' Luke (18:9–14) in the Greco-Roman World of Late Antiquity," *Catholic Biblical Quarterly* 54.1 (1992): 80–99.

Duncan, Carrie, "Inscribing Authority: Female Title Bearers in Jewish Inscriptions," *Religions* 3 (2012): 37–49.

Durber, Susan, "The Female Reader of the Parables of the Lost," *Journal for the Study of the New Testament* 45 (1992): 59–78.

Ehrman, Bart D. and Mark A. Plunkett, "The Angel and the Agony: The Textual Problem of Luke 22:43–44," *Catholic Biblical Quarterly* 45.3 (1983): 401–16.

Ellul, Jacques, *Money and Power*. Downers Grove: InterVarsity Press, 1984.

Epp, E. J., *Junia: The First Woman Apostle*. Minneapolis; Augsburg Fortress, 2005.

Esler, Philip F., *Community and Gospel in Luke–Acts: The Social and Political Motivations of Lukan Theology*. Cambridge: Cambridge University Press, 1987.

Esler, Philip F. and Ronald Piper, *Lazarus, Mary and Martha: Social-Scientific Approaches to the Gospel of John*. Minneapolis: Fortress Press, 2006.

Eubank, Nathan, "A Disconcerting Prayer: On the Originality of Luke 23:34a," *Journal of Biblical Literature* 129.3 (2010): 521–36.

Wages of Cross-Bearing and Debt of Sin: The Economy of Heaven in Matthew's Gospel. Berlin/Boston: De Gruyter, 2013.

Evans, Craig A., *Luke*. NIBCNT 3; Peabody: Hendrickson, 1990.

Evans, C. F., *Saint Luke*. London: SCM, 1990.

Fagenblat, Michael, "The Concept of Neighbor in Jewish and Christian Ethics," pp. 645–50 in Amy-Jill Levine and Marc Z. Brettler (eds.), *The Jewish Annotated New Testament*, 2d. rev. ed. New York: Oxford University Press, 2017.

Fehribach, Adeline, *Women in the Life of the Bridegroom*. Collegeville: Michael Glazier, 1998.

Fiensy, David A., *Christian Origins and the Ancient Economy*. Eugene: Cascade, 2014.

Fischer, Irmtraud, "Déjà-vu for Proving Soteriological Pertinence: Gender-Relevant Reception of the Hebrew Bible in the Narrative Texts of the New Testament," pp. 69–96 in Mercedes Navarro Puerto and

Marinella Perroni (eds.) and Amy-Jill Levine (ed. English transla-
tion), *Gospels: Narrative and History.* The Bible and Women: An
Encyclopedia of Exegesis and Cultural History; Atlanta: Scholars
Press, 2015.

"Die Rede weiser Menschen ist höflich: Über die Umgangsformen von
Weisen in den Davidserzählungen und dem multikausalen Bias in der
Exegese derselben," pp. 21–38 in Andreas Vonach and Georg Fischer
(eds.), *Horizonte biblischer Texte: Festschrift für Josef M. Oesch zum 60.
Geburtstag.* Studies on Ancient Near Eastern Artefacts and the Bible
(OBO) 196; Freiburg/Schweiz: Academic Press Fribourg, 2003.

Fitzmyer, Joseph A., *The Gospel According to Luke I–IX: A New Translation
with Introduction and Commentary.* AB; New York: Doubleday,
1970.

*The Gospel According to Luke X–XXIV: A New Translation with
Introduction and Commentary.* AB; New York: Doubleday, 1985.

Fornara, Charles W., *The Nature of History in Ancient Greece and Rome.*
Berkeley: University of California Press, 1983.

France, R. T., *Luke.* Teach the Commentary Series; Grand Rapids: Baker, 2013.

Fredriksen, Paula, "Did Jesus Oppose the Purity Laws?" *Bible Review* 11.3
(1995): 20–25, 42–47.

Jesus of Nazareth, King of the Jews. New York: Vintage, 1999.

"Mandatory Retirement: Ideas in the Study of Christian Origins Whose
Time Has Come to Go," *Studies in Religion/Sciences Religieusses* 35.2
(2006): 231–46.

"Review of N.T. Wright, 'The Faithfulness of God,'" *Catholic Biblical
Quarterly* 77 (2015): 387–91.

Friedrichsen, Timothy A., "The Temple, A Pharisee, A Tax Collector, and
the Kingdom of God: Rereading a Jesus Parable (Luke 18:10-14a),"
Journal of Biblical Literature 124.1 (2005): 89–119.

Funk, Robert W., "The Looking Glass Tree Is for the Birds," *Interpretation*
27.01 (1973): 3–9.

Furnish, Victor P., *The Love Commandment in the New Testament.* Nashville:
Abingdon, 1972.

Garcia Serrano, Andrés, "Anna's Characterization in Luke 2:36–38: A Case of
Conceptual Allusion?" *Catholic Biblical Quarterly* 76.3 (2014): 464–80.

Garrett, Susan R., "Exodus from Bondage: Luke 9:31 and Acts 12:1–24,"
Catholic Biblical Quarterly 52.4 (1990): 656–80.

Gaventa, Beverly Roberts and Cynthia L. Rigby (eds.), *Blessed One: Protestant
Perspectives on Mary.* Louisville: Westminster John Knox, 2002.

Gilbert, Gary, "The Gospel of Luke," pp. 219–80 in Amy-Jill Levine and Marc Z. Brettler, *The Jewish Annotated New Testament* 2d rev. ed. New York: Oxford University Press, 2017.

González, Justo L., *Luke (Belief: A Theological Commentary on the Bible)*. Louisville: Westminster John Knox, 2010.

Goodrich, John K., "Voluntary Debt Remission and the Parable of the Unjust Steward (Luke 16:1–13)," *Journal of Biblical Literature* 131.3 (2012): 547–66.

Gray, Rebecca, *Prophetic Figure in Late Second Temple Jewish Palestine: The Evidence from Josephus*. New York: Oxford University Press, 1993.

Green, Joel B., "Internal Repetition in Luke–Acts, Contemporary Narratology and Lukan Historiography," pp. 283–99 in Ben Witherington (ed.), *History, Literature, and Society*. Cambridge: Cambridge University Press, 2007.

———, "Jesus and a Daughter of Abraham (Luke 13:10–17): Test Case for a Lucan Perspective on Jesus' Miracles," *Catholic Biblical Quarterly* 51.4 (1989): 643–54.

———, *The Gospel of Luke*. NICNT; Grand Rapids: Eerdmans, 1997.

Gubar, Susan, *Judas: A Biography*. New York: W. W. Norton, 2009.

Hallig, Jason Valeriano, "The Eating Motif and Luke's Characterization of Jesus as the Son of Man," *Bibliotheca Sacra* 173.690 (April–June 2016): 203–18.

Hamm, Dennis, "What the Samaritan Leper Sees: The Narrative Christology of Luke 17:11–19," *Catholic Biblical Quarterly* 56.2 (1994): 273–87.

Harrill, J. Albert, "The Indentured Labor of the Prodigal Son (Luke 15:15)," *Critical Notes; Journal of Biblical Literature* 115 (1997): 714–17.

Harris, Sarah, "Why Are There Shepherds in the Lukan Birth Narrative?" *Colloquium* 44.1 (2012): 17–30.

Hartsock, Chad, "The Healing of the Man with Dropsy (Luke 14:1–6) and the Lukan Landscape," *Biblical Interpretation* 21.3 (2013): 341–54.

Heiser, Michael S., *The Unseen Realm: Recovering the Supernatural Worldview of the Bible*. Bellingham: Lexham Press, 2015.

Herzog, William R. II, *Parables as Subversive Speech: Jesus as Pedagogue of the Oppressed*. Louisville: Westminster John Knox, 1994.

Hesemann, Michael, *Mary of Nazareth: History, Archaeology, Legends*. San Francisco: Ignatius Press, 2016.

Hezser, Catherine, *Jewish Literacy in Roman Palestine*, TSAJ 81; Tübingen: Mohr Siebeck, 2001.

Himmelfarb, Martha, *Tours of Hell: An Apocalyptic Form in Jewish and Christian Literature*. Minneapolis: Fortress Press, 1985.

Hobart, W. K., *The Medical Language of St. Luke*. London: Longmans Green, 1882.

Hock, Ronald F., "Lazarus and Micyllus: Greco-Roman Backgrounds to Luke 16:19–31," *Journal of Biblical Literature* 106.3 (1987): 447–63.

Holmgren, Frederick C., "The Pharisee and the Tax Collector: Luke 18.9–14 and Deuteronomy 26.1–15," *Interpretation* 48 (1994): 252–61.

Hornsby, Teresa, "The Woman Is a Sinner/The Sinner Is a Woman," pp. 121–32 in Amy-Jill Levine with Marianne Blickenstaff (eds.), *A Feminist Companion To Luke*, FCNTECW 3; Sheffield: Sheffield University Press/New York: Continuum, 2002.

Hultgren, Arland J., *The Parables of Jesus: A Commentary*. Grand Rapids: Eerdmans, 2000.

Hultgren, Stephen, *Narrative Elements in the Double Tradition: A Study of Their Place Within the Framework of the Gospel Narrative*. BZNW 113; Berlin/New York: De Gruyter, 2002.

Husband, Richard Wellington, "The Pardoning of Prisoners by Pilate," *American Journal of Theology* 21.1 (1917): 110–16.

Ilan, Tal, "Gender," pp. 611–14 in Amy-Jill Levine and Marc Z. Brettler (eds.), *The Jewish Annotated New Testament*, 2nd rev. ed. New York: Oxford University Press, 2017.

Ireland, Dennis J., *Stewardship and the Kingdom of God: An Historical, Exegetical, and Contextual Study of the Parable of the Unjust Servant in Luke 16.1–3*. Supplements to *Novum Testamentum* 70; Leiden/New York/Cologne: E. J. Brill, 1992.

Jackson, Bernard S., *Essays on Halakhah in the New Testament*. Jewish and Christian Perspectives Series 16; Leiden: Brill, 2007.

Jennings, Theodore W., Jr. and Tat-Siong Benny Liew, "Mistaken Identities but Model Faith: Rereading the Centurion, the Chap and the Christ in Matthew 8:5–13," *Journal of Biblical Literature* 123.3 (2004): 467–94.

Jensen, Robin, "How Pilate Became a Saint," *Bible Review* 19.06 (December 2003), www.basarchive.org/sample/bswbBrowse.asp?PubID=BSBR&Volume=19&Issue=6&ArticleID=2.

Jeremias, Joachim, *Jerusalem in the Time of Jesus*. London: SCM, 1969.

Jesus' Promise to the Nations. London: SCM, 1958.

New Testament Theology. London: SCM Press, 2012.

"ποιμήν," *TDNT* 6 (1974):488–89.

The Parables of Jesus, 2d ed. New York: Scribner's, 1972.

The Prayers of Jesus, Studies in Biblical Theology 2d Series 6. London: SCM Press, 1967.

Jervell, Jakob, *Luke and the People of God*. Eugene: Wipf and Stock, 2002.

Johnson, Alan F., "Assurance for Man: The Fallacy of Translating *Anaideia* by 'Persistence,'" *Journal of Evangelical Theology* 22.2 (1979): 123–31.

Johnson, Elizabeth A., *Truly Our Sister: A Theology of Mary in the Communion of Saints*. New York: Continuum, 2003.

Johnson, Luke Timothy, *Literary Function of Possessions in Luke-Acts*. SBLDS 39; Missoula: Scholars Press, 1977.

The Gospel of Luke. Sacra Pagina. Collegeville: Liturgical Press, 1991.

Joyce, Kathryn, "The Silence of the Lambs," *New Republic* (June 20, 2017) https://newrepublic.com/article/142999/silence-lambs-protestants-concealing-catholic-size-sexual-abuse-scandal.

Kahl, Brigitte, "Reading Luke Against Luke: Non-Uniformity of Text, Hermeneutics of Conspiracy and the 'Scriptural Principle' in Luke 1," pp. 70–88 in Amy-Jill Levine with Marianne Blickenstaff (eds.), *A Feminist Companion To Luke*, FCNTECW 3; Sheffield: Sheffield University Press/New York: Continuum, 2002.

Keener, Craig, *The Gospel of John: A Commentary*. Vol. 1. Peabody: Hendrickson, 2003.

Miracles: The Credibility of the New Testament Accounts, 2 volumes. Grand Rapids: Baker, 2011.

Keith, Chris, *Jesus Against the Scribal Elite: The Origins of the Conflict*. Grand Rapids: Baker Academic, 2014.

Jesus' Literacy: Scribal Culture and the Teacher from Galilee. Library of Historical Jesus Studies 413; London: T&T Clark, 2011.

Keller, Timothy, *The Prodigal God: Recovering the Heart of Christian Faith*. New York: Penguin, 2011.

Kinman, Brent, "Parousia, Jesus' 'A-Triumphal' Entry, and the Fate of Jerusalem (Luke 19:28–44)," *Journal of Biblical Literature* 118.2 (1999): 279–94.

Kirk, Alan, " 'Love Your Enemies,' the Golden Rule, and Ancient Reciprocity (Luke 6:27–35)," *Journal of Biblical Literature* 122.4 (2003): 667–86.

Kittel, Gerhard, "Abba," pp. 5–6 in Idem (ed.) *Theological Dictionary of the New Testament*. Vol. 1. Grand Rapids, MI: Eerdmans, 1964; English translation of the German original (1933).

Klawans, Jonathan, "Josephus on Fate, Free Will, and Ancient Jewish Types of Compatibilism," *Numen* 56 (2009): 44–90.

Klinghardt, Matthias, *Gesetz und Volk Gottes: Das lukanische Verständnis des Gesetzes nach Herkunft, Funktion und seinem Ort in der Geschichte des Urchristentums.* Tübingen: J. C. B. Mohr [Paul Siebeck], 1988.

Kloppenborg, John S., "The Parable of the Prodigal Son and Deeds of Gift," pp. 169–94 in Rieuwerg Buitenwerf, Harm W. Hollander, and Johannes Tromp (eds.), *Jesus, Paul, and Early Christianity: Studies in Honour of Henk Jan de Jonge*, Supplements to *Novum Testamentum* 130; Leiden/ Boston: Brill, 2008.

Kodel, Jerome, "Luke and the Children: The Beginning and End of the Great Interpolation (Luke 9:46–56; 18:9–23)," *Catholic Biblical Quarterly* 49.3 (1987): 415–30.

Koester, Craig, "The Origin and Significance of the Flight to Pella Tradition," *Catholic Biblical Quarterly* 51.1 (1989): 90–106.

Kraemer, Ross S., "A New Inscription from Malta and the Question of Women Elders in the Diaspora Jewish Communities," *Harvard Theological Review* 78.3/4 (1985): 431–38.

Unreliable Witnesses: Religion, Gender, and History in the Greco-Roman Mediterranean. New York: Oxford University Press, 2012.

Kuhn, Karl A., "Deaf or Defiant? The Literary, Cultural, and Affective-Rhetorical Keys to the Naming of John (Luke 1:57–80)," *Catholic Biblical Quarterly* 75.3 (2013): 486–503.

Kurz, William S., "Luke 22.14–38 and Greco-Roman and Biblical Farewell Addresses," *Journal of Biblical Literature* 104 (1985): 251–68.

LaHurd, Carol Shersten, "Rediscovering the Lost Women in Luke 15," *Biblical Theology Bulletin* 24 (1994): 66–76.

"Re-viewing Luke 15 with Arab Christian Women," pp. 246–68 in Amy-Jill Levine with Marianne Blickenstaff (eds.), *A Feminist Companion to Luke*, FCNTECW 3. Sheffield: Sheffield Academic, 2002.

Landry, David T., "Honor Restored: New Light on the Parable of the Prudent Steward (Luke 16:1–8a)," *Journal of Biblical Literature* 119.2 (2000): 287–309.

"Narrative Logic in the Annunciation to Mary (Luke 1:26–38)," *Journal of Biblical Literature* 114 (1995): 65–79.

Lee, Dorothy, "On the Holy Mountain: The Transfiguration in Scripture and Theology," *Colloquium* 36.2 (2004): 143–59.

Levenson, Jon Douglas, *Resurrection and the Restoration of Israel: The Ultimate Victory of the God of Life.* New Haven and London: Yale University Press, 2006.

Levine, Amy-Jill, "Discharging Responsibility: Matthean Jesus, Biblical Law, and Hemorrhaging Woman," pp. 379–97 in D. R. Bauer and M. A. Powell (eds.), *Treasures Old and New: Recent Contributions to Matthean Studies*. Symposium Series 1. Atlanta: Scholars Press, 1996; reprinted pp. 70–87 in Amy-Jill Levine with Marianne Blickenstaff (eds.), *Feminist Companion to Matthew*, FCNTECW 1; Sheffield: Sheffield University Press, 2000.

"Is There Life After Death?" *Moment Magazine,* July 27, 2011, www .momentmag.com/is-there-life-after-death/.

"John Meier, Women, and the Criteria of Authenticity," in Vincent Skemp and Kelley Coblentz Bautch (eds.), *Jesus as a Figure of History and Theology: Essays in Honor of John P. Meier.* Catholic Biblical Quarterly Monograph Series (CBQMS); Washington, DC: Catholic University of America, forthcoming.

"Luke and the Jewish Religion," *Interpretation* 68.4 (2014): 389–402.

"Luke's Pharisees," pp. 113–130 in Jacob Neusner and Bruce Chilton (eds.), *In Quest of the Historical Pharisees.* Waco: Baylor University Press, 2007.

Short Stories by Jesus: The Enigmatic Parables of a Controversial Rabbi. New York: HarperOne, 2014.

"Tabitha/Dorcas, Spinning Off Cultural Criticism," pp. 41–65 in Harold W. Attridge, Dennis R. MacDonald, and Clare K. Rothschild (eds.), *Delightful Acts: New Essays on Canonical and Non-canonical Acts.* WUNT 391; Tübingen: Mohr Siebeck, 2017.

"The Gospel According to Luke," pp. 219–79 in Amy-Jill Levine and Marc Z. Brettler (eds.), *The Jewish Annotated New Testament,* 2nd rev. ed. New York: Oxford University Press, 2017.

The Misunderstood Jew: The Church and the Scandal of the Jewish Jesus. New York: HarperOne, 2007.

"'This Poor Widow …' (Mark 12:43): From Donation to Diatribe," pp. 183–94 in Susan Ashbrook Harvey and N. Desrosiers (eds.), *A Most Reliable Witness: Essays in Honor of Ross Shephard Kraemer.* BJS 358; Providence: Brown University Press, 2015.

Levine, Amy-Jill and Sandy E. Sasso, *The Marvelous Mustard Seed.* Louisville: Westminster John Knox, 2018.

Who Counts? 100 Sheep, 10 Coins, and 2 Sons. Louisville: Westminster John Knox, 2017.

Levine, Amy-Jill and Myrick C. Shinall Jr. "Standard and Poor: The Economic Index of the Parables," pp. 95–116 in Robert B. Stewart (ed.),

The Message of Jesus: John Dominic Crossan and Ben Witherington III in Dialogue. Minneapolis: Fortress Press, 2013.

Levine, Amy-Jill with Marianne Blickenstaff (eds.), *A Feminist Companion to Luke*. FCNTECW 3; Sheffield: Sheffield University Press/New York: Continuum, 2002.

Lewis, C. S., *Poems*. New York: Harper One, 2017.

Lieu, Judith, *The Gospel According to Luke*. London: Epworth Press, 1997; reprinted, Eugene: Wipf and Stock, 2012.

Lincoln, Andrew T., "Luke and Jesus' Conception: A Case of Double Paternity?" *Journal of Biblial Literature* 132.3 (2013): 639–58.

Longenecker, Bruce W., "A Humorous Jesus? Orality, Structure and Characterisation in Luke 14:15–24, and Beyond," *Biblical Interpretation* 16 (2008): 179–204.

Longstaff, Thomas M. R., "What Are Those Women Doing at the Tomb of Jesus? Perspectives on Matthew 28.1," pp. 196–224 in Amy-Jill Levine with Marianne Blickenstaff (eds.), *A Feminist Companion to Matthew*, FCNTECW 1; Sheffield: Sheffield Academic Press, 2001.

Lüdemann, Gerd, "The Successors of Pre-70 Jerusalem Christianity: A Critical Evaluation of the Pella Tradition," pp. 161–73 in E. P. Sanders (ed.), *Jewish and Christian Self-Definition*, Vol. 1. Philadelphia: Fortress Press, 1980.

Maccoby, Hyam, *Judas Iscariot and the Myth of Jewish Evil*. New York: Free Press, 1992.

Malina, Bruce C. and Richard L. Rohrbaugh, *Social Science Commentary on the Synoptic Gospels*. Minneapolis: Fortress Press, 1992.

Mandel, Paul, "Scriptural Exegesis and the Pharisees in Josephus," *Journal of Jewish Studies* 58.1 (2007): 19–32.

Marshall, I. Howard, *The Gospel of Luke*. New International Greek Testament Commentary; Grand Rapids: Eerdmans, 1978.

Mason, Steve, " 'What Have the Romans Ever Done for Us?' Brian and Josephus on Anti-Roman Sentiment," pp. 185–206 in Joan E. Taylor (ed.), *Jesus and Brian: Exploring the Historical Jesus and His Times Via Monty Python's Life of Brian*. London: Bloomsbury T&T Clark, 2015.

Massaquoi, Momolu Armstrong, "Jesus' Healing Miracles in Luke 13.10–17 and Their Significance for Physical Health," *Ogbomoso Journal of Theology* 18.1 (2013): 98–123.

Matson, David Lertis, "Pacifist Jesus? The (Mis)translation of *eate eos toutou* in Luke 22:51," *Journal of Biblical Literture* 134.1 (2015): 157–75.

Matthews, Shelly, "Clemency as Cruelty: Forgiveness and Force in the Dying Prayers of Jesus and Stephen," *Biblical Interpretation* 17.1 (2009): 118–46.

Perfect Martyr: The Stoning of Stephen and the Construction of Christian Identity. New York: Oxford University Press, 2010.

Mayo, Maria Anne, "Chasing the Forgiveness Ideal: Case Studies in Restorative Justice, Post-Apartheid South Africa, and the Pastoral Care of Victims of Domestic Abuse," Ph.D. Dissertation. Nashville: Vanderbilt University, 2013.

The Limits of Forgiveness: Case Studies in the Distortion of a Biblical Ideal. Philadelphia: Fortress Press, 2015.

Mbiti, John. S., "Theology in Context," pp. 7–8 in G. H. Anderson and T. F. Stransky (eds.), *Mission Trends No. 3: Third World Theologies*. Grand Rapids: Eerdmans, 1976.

McColl, Mary Ann and Richard Ascough, "Jesus and People with Disabilities: Old Stories, New Approaches," *Journal of Pastoral Care and Counseling* 63.3 (2009), www.academia.edu/5608299/Jesus_and_the_Disabled_Old_Stories_New_Approaches_2009_with_Mary_Ann_McColl.

McGinn, Thomas A. J., "The Law of Roman Divorce in the Time of Christ," pp. 309–22 in Amy-Jill Levine, Dale C. Allison Jr., and John Dominic Crossan (eds.), *The Historical Jesus in Context*. Princeton Readings in Religion; Princeton: Princeton University Press, 2006.

McGowan, Andrew, "The Hungry Jesus," *Bible History Daily*, March 18, 2015, www.biblicalarchaeology.org/daily/biblical-topics/bible-inter pretation/the-hungry-jesus/.

McKnight, Scot, *The Real Mary: Why Evangelical Christians Can Embrace the Mother of Jesus*. Brewster: Paraclete Press, 2006.

McKnight, S. and J. Modica (eds.), *Jesus Is Lord. Caesar Is Not*. Downers Grove: IVP Academic, 2013.

Meier, John P., *A Marginal Jew: Rethinking the Historical Jesus. Volume 5, Probing the Authenticity of the Parables*. ABRL; New Haven: Yale University Press, 2016.

Metzger, B. M. "The Nazareth Inscription Once Again," pp. 75–92 in *New Testament Studies: Philological, Versional, and Patristic*. NTTS 10; Leiden: Brill, 1980.

Metzger, Bruce, *A Textual Commentary on the Greek New Testament (Ancient Greek Edition)*. New York: United Bible Societies, 1971; 2d ed. Stuttgart: German Bible Society, 1998.

Miller, Amanda, "Bridge Work and Seating Charts: A Study of Luke's Ethics of Wealth, Poverty, and Reversal," *Interpretation* 68.4 (2014): 416–27.

Moss, Candida, "The Man with the Flow of Power: Porous Bodies in Mark 5:25–34," *Journal of Biblical Literature* 130.4 (2011): 643–62.

Moss, Candida and Joel S. Baden, *Reconceiving Infertility: Biblical Perspectives on Procreation and Childlessness*. Princeton: Princeton University Press, 2015.

Nanos, Mark, "Romans," pp. 285–320 in Amy-Jill Levine and Marc Z. Brettler (eds.), *The Jewish Annotated New Testament*, 2nd rev. ed. New York: Oxford University Press, 2017.

Nolland, John L., *Luke 1–9.20*. WBC 35a; Nashville; Thomas Nelson, 2000.
Luke 9:51–18:34. WBC 35b. Nashville: Thomas Nelson, 1993.
Luke's Readers: A Study of Luke 4.22–28; Acts 13.46; 18.6; 28.28 and Luke 21.5–36. Cambridge: Cambridge University Press, 1977.

Nouwen, Henri J. M., *In the Name of Jesus*. New York: Crossroad, 1989.
The Return of the Prodigal Son: A Story of Homecoming. New York: Doubleday, 1994.

Oakman, Douglas E., *Jesus and the Economic Question of His Day*. Lewiston and Queenston: Edwin Mellen, 1986.

Oliphant, Rachel, and Paul Babie, "Can the Gospel of Luke Speak to a Contemporary Understanding of Private Property? The Parable of the Rich Fool," *Colloquium* 28.1 (2006): 3–26.

Otieno, Pauline A., "Biblical and Theological Perspectives on Disability: Implications of the Rights of Persons with Disabilities in Kenya," *Disability Studies Quarterly* 29.4 (2009), www.dsq-sds.org/article/view/988/1164.

O'Toole, Robert F., "Luke's Message in Luke 9:1–50," *Catholic Biblical Quarterly* 49.1 (1987): 74–89.

Oyemomi, Emmanuel, "The Challenges of the Concept of Medicine and Healing in the Gospel of Luke for the Church in Africa," *Ogbomoso Journal of Theology* 18.3 (2013): 113–27.

Parker, D. C., *Codex Bezae: An Early Christian Manuscript and Its Text*. Cambridge: Cambridge University Press, 1992.

Parsons, Mikeal C., *Body and Character in Luke and Acts: The Subversion of Physiognomy in Early Christianity*. Waco: Baylor University Press, 2011.
"The Prodigal's Elder Brother: The History and Ethics of Reading Luke 15.25–32," *Perspectives in Religious Studies* 23 (1996): 147–74.

"Short in Stature: Luke's Physical Description of Zacchaeus," *New Testament Studies* 47.1 (2001): 50–57.

Patterson, Stephen and Marvin Meyer, "The Gnostic Society Library" in Robert J. Miller (ed.), *The Complete Gospels: Annotated Scholars Version*. Sonoma: Polebridge Press, 1992, 1994, www.gnosis.org/naghamm/gosthom.html.

Pearson, Brook W. R., "The Lucan Census, Revisited," *Catholic Biblical Quarterly* 61.2 (1999): 262–82.

Peppard, Michael, *The Son of God in the Roman World: Divine Sonship in Its Social and Political Context*. New York: Oxford University Press, 2011.

Peterson, David, "The Motif of Fulfilment and the Purpose of Luke–Acts," pp. 83–104 in Bruce W. Winter and Andrew D. Clarke (eds.), *The Book of Acts in Its First Century Setting*. Vol. 1, *The Book of Acts in Its Ancient Literary Setting*. Grand Rapids, Eerdmans/Carlisle: Paternoster, 1993.

Pilch, John J., *Visions and Healing in the Acts of the Apostles: How the Early Believers Experienced God*. Collegeville: Liturgical Press, 2004.

Poirier, John C., "Jesus as an Elijianic Figure in Luke 4.16–30," *Catholic Biblical Quarterly* 71.2 (2009): 349–63.

Quesnell, Quentin, "The Women at Luke's Supper," pp. 59–79 in Richard J. Cassidy and Philip J. Scharper (eds.), *Political Issues in Luke-Acts*. Maryknoll: Orbis, 1983.

Ramelli, Ilaria L. E., "Luke 16:16: The Good News of God's Kingdom Is Proclaimed and Everyone Is Forced into It," *Journal of Biblical Literature* 127.4 (2008): 737–59.

Reid, Barbara E., " 'Do you See This Woman?' A Liberative Look at Luke 7.36–50 and Strategies for Reading Other Lucan Stories Against the Grain," pp. 106–20 in Amy-Jill Levine with Marianne Blickenstaff (eds.), *A Feminist Companion to Luke*. FCNTECW 3; Sheffield: Sheffield University Press/New York: Continuum, 2002.

"A Godly Widow Persistently Pursuing Justice: Luke 18:1–8," *Biblical Research* 45 (2000): 25–33.

Parables for Preachers, Year A. Collegeville: Liturgical Press, 2001.

Parables for Preachers, Year C. Collegeville: Liturgical Press, 2000.

Reilly, Frank, "Jane Schaberg, Raymond E. Brown, and the Problem of the Illegitimacy of Jesus," *Journal of Feminist Studies in Religion* 21.1 (2005): 57–80.

Reinstorf, Dieter H., "The Parable of the Shrewd Manager (Lk 16.1–8): A Biography of Jesus and a Lesson on Mercy," *HTS Teologiese Studies/Theological Studies* 69.1 (2013), Art. #1943. dx.doi.org/10.4102/hts.v69i1.1943.

Rice, Peter, "The Rhetoric of Luke's Passion: Luke's Use of Common-Place to Amplify the Guilt of the Jerusalem Leaders in Jesus' Death," *Biblical Interpretation* 21.3 (2013): 355–76.

Robbins, Vernon K., "The Social Location of the Implied Author of Luke-Acts," pp. 305–32 in J. H. Neyrey (ed.), *The Social World of Luke-Acts*. Peabody: Hendrickson, 1991.

Saddington, D. B., "The Centurion in Matthew 8:5–13: Consideration of the Proposal of Theodore W. Jennings, Jr., and Tat-Siong Benny Liew," *Journal of Biblical Literature* 125.1 (2006): 140–42.

Sanders, Ed P., *Jesus and Judaism*. Philadelphia: Fortress Press, 1985.

    Paul. The Apostle's Life, Letters, and Thought. Minneapolis: Fortress Press, 2015.

Satlow, Michael L., *Jewish Marriage in Antiquity*. Princeton: Princeton University Press, 2001.

Schaberg, Jane, *The Illegitimacy of Jesus: A Feminist Theological Interpretation of the Infancy Narratives, Expanded Twentieth Anniversary*. Sheffield: Sheffield Phoenix, 2006; original 1987.

Schaberg, Jane with Melanie Johnson-Debaufre, *Mary Magdalene Understood*. New York and London: Continuum, 2006.

Schellenberg, Ryan S., "Kingdom as Contaminant? The Role of Repertoire in the Parables of the Mustard Seed and the Leaven," *Catholic Biblical Quarterly* 71.3 (2009): 527–43.

    "Which Master? Whose Steward? Metalepsis and Lordship in the Parable of the Prudent Steward (Lk. 16.1–13)," *Journal for the Study of the New Testament* 30.3 (2008): 263–88.

Schlatter, Adolf, *Das Evangelium des Lukas. Aus seinen Quellen erklärt*. Stuttgart: Calwer, 1960.

Schottroff, Luise, *The Parables of Jesus*. Minneapolis: Augsburg Fortress, 2006.

Schultz, Brian, "Jesus as Archelaus in the Parable of the Pounds (Lk. 19:11–27)," *Novum Testamentum* 49 (2007): 105–27.

Schweizer, Eduard, *Jesus*. London: SCM, 1971.

Scott, Bernard B., *Re-Imagine the World: An Introduction to the Parables of Jesus*. Santa Rosa: Polebridge Press, 2001.

    Hear Then the Parable: A Commentary on the Parables of Jesus. Minneapolis: Augsburg Fortress.

Segal, Alan, *Life After Death: A History of the Afterlife in Western Religion*. New York: Doubleday, 2004.

Seim, Turid Karlsen, *The Double Message: Patterns of Gender in Luke-Acts*. London: Bloomsbury T&T Clark, 2004.

Sellew, Philip (Melissa), "Interior Monologue as a Narrative Device in the Parables of Luke," *Journal of Biblical Literature* 111 (1992): 239–53.

Shanks, Herschel and Ben Witherington III, *The Brother of Jesus*. New York: HarperOne, 2003; rev. updated ed. 2005.

Sherouse, Alan, "The One Percent and the Gospel of Luke," *Review and Expositor* 110 (Spring 2013): 285–93.

Simons, R., doctoral dissertation on Lukan rhetoric submitted at Bristol in 2008, summarized in *Tyndale Bulletin* 60.1 (May 2009).

Smith, Mark D., "Of Jesus and Quirinius," *Catholic Biblical Quarterly* 62.2 (2000): 278–93.

Snodgrass, Klyne, "*Anaideia* and the Friend at Midnight (Luke 11:8)," *Journal of Biblical Literature* 116.3 (1997): 505–13.
  Stories with Intent: A Comprehensive Guide to the Parables of Jesus. Grand Rapids: Eerdmans, 2008.

Spencer, Scott F., "To Fear or Not to Fear the Creator God: A Theological and Therapeutic Interpretation of Luke 12:4–34," *Journal of Theological Interpretation* 8.2 (2014): 229–49.

Spicq, Ceslaus, *Agape in the New Testament*, 3 volumes. Eugene: Wipf and Stock, 2006; 1966 original.
  "La parabole de la veuve obstinee et du juge inerte, aux decisions impromptues (Lc. Xviii,1–8)," *Revue Biblique* 68.1 (1961): 68–90.

Squires, J. T., *The Plan of God in Luke–Acts*. Cambridge: Cambridge University Press, 1993.

Stein, R. H., *The Method and Message of Jesus' Teaching*. Philadelphia: Westminster, 1978.

Talbert, Charles H., *Literary Patterns, Theological Themes, and the Genre of Luke–Acts*. Missoula: Scholar's Press, 1974.

Tannehill, Robert C., *Luke, Abingdon New Testament Commentaries*. Nashville: Abingdon, 1996.

Ten Boom, Corrie, "I'm Still Learning to Forgive," *Guideposts* (1972), www.guideposts.org/better-living/positive-living/guideposts-classics-corrie-ten-boom-on-forgiveness.

Thompson, Marianne Meye, *The Promise of the Father: Jesus and God in the New Testament*. Louisville: Westminster John Knox, 2000.

Tiede, David L., "Glory to Thy People Israel: Luke–Acts and the Jews," pp. 21–34 in Joseph B. Tyson (ed.), *Luke–Acts and the Jewish People*. Minneapolis: Augsburg Fortress, 1988.

Topel, L. John, "On the Injustice of the Unjust Steward: Lk 16:1–13," *Catholic Biblical Quarterly* 37.2 (1975): 216–27.

Twelftree, Graham, *Jesus the Exorcist*. Tübingen: Mohr, 1993.

Tyson, Joseph B., *Luke, Judaism, and the Scholars: Critical Approaches to Luke–Acts*. Columbia: University of South Carolina Press, 1999.

Udoh, Fabian E., "The Tale of the Unrighteous Slave (Luke 16.1–8 [13])," *Journal of Biblical Literature* 128.2 (2009): 311–35.

UK Apologetics, "Would Pontius Pilate Have Released a Prisoner at Passover" (April 7, 2012), http://apologeticsuk.blogspot.com/2012/04/would-pontius-pilate-have-released.html.

Vinson, Richard, "The God of Luke–Acts," *Interpretation* 68.4 (2014): 376–88.

———. "The Minas Touch: Anti-Kingship Rhetoric in the Gospel of Luke," *Perspectives in Religious Studies* 35.1 (2008): 69–86

Voros, G., "A Palace-Fortress with Multiple Mikva'ot," *Bibical Archaeology Review* 43.4 (2017): 30–39, 60.

Waetjen, Herman C., "The Subversion of the 'World' by the Parable of the Friend at Midnight," *Journal of Biblical Literature* 120.4 (2001): 703–21.

Weinert, Francis D., "Luke, the Temple, and Jesus' Saying About Jerusalem's Abandoned House (Luke 13:34–35)," *Catholic Biblical Quarterly* 44.1 (1982): 77–90.

———. "The Parable of the Throne Claimant (Luke 19:12, 14–15a, 27) Reconsidered," *Catholic Biblical Quarterly* 39.4 (1977): 505–14.

Wiesenthal, Simon, *The Sunflower: On the Possibilities and Limits of Forgiveness* (newly expanded paperback ed.). New York: Schocken Press, 1998.

Williamson, Clark M., *A Guest in the House of Israel: Post-Holocaust Church Theology*. Louisville: Westminster John Knox, 1993.

Wilson, Brittany E., "Pugnacious Precursors and the Bearer of Peace: Jael, Judith, and Mary in Luke 1:42," *Catholic Biblical Quarterly* 68.3 (2006): 436–56.

Witherington III, Ben, *The Acts of the Apostles: A Socio-Rhetorical Commentary*. Grand Rapids: Eerdmans, 1997.

———. "The Anti-Feminist Tendencies of the Western Text of Acts," *JBL* 103 (1984): 82–84.

———. *The Christology of Jesus*. Minneapolis: Fortress Press, 1990.

———. *The Gospel of Matthew*. Macon: Smyth and Helwys, 2005.

———. *Isaiah Old and New: Exegesis, Intertextuality, and Hermeneutics*. Minneapolis: Fortress Press, 2017.

———. *Jesus and Money: A Guide for Times of Financial Crisis*. Grand Rapids: Brazos Press, 2010.

Jesus, Paul, and the End of the World, Downers Grove: InterVarsity Press, 1992.

Jesus the Sage: The Pilgrimage of Wisdom. Minneapolis: Fortress Press, 2000.

Jesus the Seer. Minneapolis: Fortress Press, 2014.

John's Wisdom: A Commentary on the Fourth Gospel. Louisville: Westminster John Knox, 1995.

Letters and Homilies for Jewish Christians. Downers Grove: InterVarsity Press, 2007.

Making a Meal of It. Waco: Baylor University Press, 2008.

New Testament History. Grand Rapids: Baker, 2001.

New Testament Theology and Ethics, Vol. 1. Downers Grove: InterVarsity Press, 2009.

"On the Road with Mary Magdalene, Joanna, Susanna, and other Disciples: Luke 8.1–3," *Zeitschrift für die neutestamentlich Wissenschaft* 70.3–4 (1979): 242–48; reprinted pp. 133–39 in Amy-Jill Levine with Marianne Blickenstaff, eds., *A Feminist Companion to Luke,* FCNTECW 3; Sheffield: Sheffield University Press/New York: Continuum, 2002.

Psalms Old and New: Exegesis, Intertextuality, and Hermeneutics. Minneapolis: Fortress Press, 2017.

When a Daughter Dies. Carol Stream: Christianity Today e-Book Publications, 2012.

Women and the Genesis of Christianity. Cambridge: Cambridge University Press, 1990.

Women in the Earliest Churches. SNTSMS 59; Cambridge: Cambridge University Press. 1988.

Women in the Ministry of Jesus, SNTSMS 51; Cambridge: Cambridge University Press, 1984.

Witherington III, Ben and L. Ice, *The Shadow of the Almighty.* Grand Rapids: Eerdmans, 2002.

Witten, Marcia G., "Preaching About Sin in Contemporary Protestantism," *Theology Today,* 50.2 (1993): 243–53.

Wright, Addison G., "The Widow's Mites: Praise or Lament? A Matter of Context," *Catholic Biblical Quarterly* 44 (1982): 256–65.

Young, Brad H., *The Parables: Jewish Tradition and Christian Interpretation.* Grand Rapids: Baker, 2008.

Zaas, Peter, "The Letter of Paul to the Colossians," pp. 407–18 in Amy-Jill Levine and Marc Z. Brettler (eds.), *The Jewish Annotated New Testament,* 2nd rev. ed. New York: Oxford University Press, 2017.

Zapata-Meza, Marcela, "Magdala 2016: Excavating the Hometown of Mary Magdalene," *Bible History Daily* (July 7, 2016), www.biblicalarchaeology .org/daily/archaeology-today/magdala-2016-excavating-the-home-town-of-mary-magdalene/.

Zimmermann, Reuben in cooperation with D. Dormeyer, G. Kern, A. Merz, C. Münch, and E. E. Popkes (eds.), *Kompendium der Gleichnisse Jesu*, Gütersloh: Gütersloher Verlagshaus 2007.

Scriptural Index

Note: Excludes references to Luke.

Author Index